Russia and Europe
The Emerging Security Agenda

sipri

Stockholm International Peace Research Institute
Frösunda, S-171 53 Solna, Sweden
Cable: SIPRI
Telephone: 46 8/655 97 00
Telefax: 46 8/655 97 33
E-mail: sipri@sipri.se
Internet URL: http://www.sipri.se

Russia and Europe
The Emerging Security Agenda

Edited by
Vladimir Baranovsky

OXFORD UNIVERSITY PRESS

OXFORD
UNIVERSITY PRESS

Great Clarendon Street, Oxford OX2 6DP

Oxford University Press is a department of the University of Oxford.
It furthers the University's objective of excellence in research, scholarship,
and education by publishing worldwide in

Oxford New York

Athens Auckland Bangkok Bogotá Buenos Aires Cape Town
Chennai Dar es Salaam Delhi Florence Hong Kong Istanbul Karachi
Kolkata Kuala Lumpur Madrid Melbourne Mexico City Mumbai Nairobi
Paris São Paulo Shanghai Singapore Taipei Tokyo Toronto Warsaw

with associated companies in Berlin Ibadan

Oxford is a registered trade mark of Oxford University Press
in the UK and in certain other countries

Published in the United States
by Oxford University Press Inc., New York

British Library Cataloguing in Publication Data
Data available

Library of Congress Cataloging in Publication Data
Data available

ISBN 0–19–829201–5

3 5 7 9 10 8 6 4 2

Typeset and originated by Stockholm International Peace Research Institute
Printed in Great Britain on acid-free paper by
Biddles Ltd., Guildford and King's Lynn

Contents

Part VI. The Slav triangle: challenges and opportunities

Part VII. The Baltic dilemma and relations with Nordic Europe

Part VIII. Russia and East–Central Europe after the Warsaw Pact

Part IX. The Balkan connection

Part X. Challenges from the south

Part XI. Economic factors: implications for relations with Europe

Part XII. The emerging international order in Europe: what place for Russia?

Preface

Russia's security agenda is in the process of taking shape. Internal developments rather than, as in the past, external threats will be decisive for its definition. Both Russia's domestic situation and the international security environment deserve thorough attention and analysis.

The main tasks of this study are to highlight the major conflict-generating issues in Russia's interaction with Europe and the ways in which they could be addressed; to assess the most important trends in Russia's security thinking and policy-making *vis-à-vis* Europe; to speculate on Russia's role in the post-cold war European setting; and to consider the implications of developments in Russia and Russia's policy for preserving stability on the continent of Europe. Many of the questions which arise in this context suggest no obvious and clear-cut answers. Within the Russian policy-making and academic communities there are intense and highly controversial debates on the country's European perspectives. For Europeans, uncertainties both about Russia's domestic developments and about its international role are also a source of serious confusion. Thus, it is hoped that the findings of this project and its overall conclusions will be of interest for academics, politicians, government officials and opinion leaders—both inside Russia and in other countries.

This book is the result of a three-year research project which was launched by SIPRI immediately after the demise of the USSR to assess the security relationship between post-Soviet Russia and Europe. Russia's evolving foreign and security policy agenda is analysed against the background of the political, social and economic transformations that are taking place in the new states of the former Soviet Union. The main geopolitical dimensions of Russia's relations with Europe are explored, focusing on the Slav 'core area' of the former USSR, the Nordic and Baltic states, East–Central Europe, the Balkans and the Caucasus. The impact of economic factors on Russia's relations with Europe, its interaction with other major actors on the continent, and its attitude towards and eventual role in the evolving pan-European security architecture are also examined.

Adam Daniel Rotfeld
Director of SIPRI
December 1996

Russia and Europe:
The Emerging Security Agenda

Advisory Committee

Acknowledgements

The Advisory Committee held intensive discussions on the overall concept of the project, its research subjects and structure, and the principal findings. Some meetings of the Advisory Committee were attended by Oleg Grinevskiy, Ambassador of Russia to Sweden; Lena Jonson (Swedish Institute of International Affairs, Stockholm); Lothar Rühl (Forschungsinstitut für Politische Wissenschaft, Cologne) and Alexander Tsipko (Gorbachev Foundation, Moscow). I am grateful to all the participants at these exciting brain-storming meetings, and particularly to those who contributed to the present volume.

Over 20 other experts engaged both in the academic debate and in the policy-making process were involved in the project as commissioned authors. Each particular area within the study, with few exceptions, has been addressed by a Russian specialist on the one hand and a non-Russian specialist on the other; their informal 'dialogue' offers a more comprehensive analysis from both the 'inside' and the 'outside' perspectives, making it possible to define alternative perceptions of and options for Russia's foreign and security policy in Europe.

Early versions of the papers were the subject of in-depth discussion along the whole spectrum of Russia's foreign policy at a conference in Moscow with the participation of experts from 10 countries. An appreciable role in the organization of the conference and in arranging meetings with high-ranking officials from Russia's Security Council and the President's staff was played by the Moscow-based Institute of Europe (Sergei Karaganov and Andrei Stepanov). Valuable comments on the draft volume were received from Alex Pravda (St Anthony's College, Oxford) and Nikolai Kosolapov (Institute of World Economy and International Relations, Moscow). Some preliminary results of the project, as well as a detailed report from the conference in Moscow, were published in the monthly journal *Mirovaya Ekonomika i Mezhdunarodnye Otnosheniya* by Sergei Chugrov and Sergei Chebanov.

Throughout the work on this book I have been particularly indebted to Shannon Kile, Research Assistant on the SIPRI Project on Russia's Security Agenda, who has given invaluable help in organizing expert meetings and reviewing drafts and has done extensive work on data collection. Eve Johansson accomplished the formidable job of editing the volume—a challenging task both in terms of substance and not least because few of the contributors are native English-speakers.

A significant contribution was made by my other SIPRI colleagues. Christina Barkstedt, Cathy Walsh Söderquist and Janice Auberg worked as project secretaries; Mark Salter was the editor of the early drafts; Billie Bielckus prepared the maps; Sten Wiksten and Gerd Hagmeyer-Gaverus provided computer support; Anna Helleday dealt with administrative issues and Ingvor Wallin ensured communications. SIPRI interns Martin Klatt (Germany), Georgi Otyrba

(Abkhazia/Georgia) and Magnus Hedenstierna (Sweden) participated in the data collection. I am grateful to all of them.

I am particularly thankful to Natalia Lebedeva for unvarying support and personal commitment as well as for professional assistance in organizing the project archive at SIPRI.

Finally, a scope as broad as that of this research project would have been impossible without the generous support of the John D. and Catherine T. MacArthur Foundation, which is most gratefully acknowledged.

Vladimir Baranovsky
SIPRI
December 1996

Acronyms and abbreviations

ABM	Anti-ballistic missile
ALCM	Air-launched cruise missile
ASW	Anti-submarine warfare
C^3I	Command, control, communications and intelligence
CBM	Confidence-building measure
CCMP	Confederation of Caucasian Mountain Peoples
CFE	Conventional Armed Forces in Europe
CIS	Commonwealth of Independent States
CMEA	Council for Mutual Economic Assistance
CPC	Caucasian Peoples' Confederation
CPSU	Communist Party of the Soviet Union
CSCE	Conference on Security and Co-operation in Europe
EBRD	European Bank for Reconstruction and Development
EC	European Community
ECE	East–Central Europe
EU	European Union
FYROM	Former Yugoslav Republic of Macedonia
G7	Group of Seven (industrialized countries)
GATT	General Agreement on Tariffs and Trade
GNP	Gross national product
ICBM	Intercontinental ballistic missile
IFOR	Intervention Force (in Bosnia and Herzegovina)
IMF	International Monetary Fund
INF	Intermediate-range nuclear force
IPP	Individual Partnership Programme (Partnership for Peace)
KGB	Committee of State Security (USSR)
LMD	Leningrad Military District
LDPR	Liberal Democratic Party of Russia
MD	Military District (Russian)
MTCR	Missile Technology Control Regime
NACC	North Atlantic Cooperation Council
NATO	North Atlantic Treaty Organization
NKVD	People's Commissariat for Internal Affairs (USSR)
NNWFZ	Nordic Nuclear Weapon-Free Zone
NPT	1968 Non-Proliferation Treaty
OECD	Organisation for Economic Cooperation and Development
OSCE	Organization for Security and Co-operation in Europe (formerly CSCE)
PFP	Partnership for Peace

R&D	Research and development
RSFSR	Russian Soviet Federative Socialist Republic
SDI	Strategic Defense Initiative (USA)
SLCM	Sea-launched cruise missile
SSBN	Nuclear-powered, ballistic-missile submarine
START	Strategic Arms Reduction Talks
TLE	Treaty-limited equipment
TVD	Theatre of military action
UNPROFOR	UN Protection Force
WEU	Western European Union
WTO	Warsaw Treaty Organization

I. Introduction

Alexei Arbatov, Vladimir Baranovsky, Pierre Hassner, Robert Legvold,
John Roper and Adam Daniel Rotfeld

This book addresses the interaction of Russia with Europe as it is emerging in a post-cold war setting. It is a formidable task for historical, political and analytical reasons. Indeed, even the definition of the problem—Russia *and* Europe—might be questioned, since half of Europe *is* Russia. However, politics, in contrast to geography, does not necessarily take this as axiomatic. What seems nevertheless indisputable is the extremely complicated and contradictory pattern of relations between the two entities—both inherited from the past and generated by new circumstances.

I. The enduring connection

Over the past 1000 years, Russia and Europe have developed a peculiar pattern of relations, with variable combinations of centrifugal and centripetal trends and intermingling elements of mutual attraction and repulsion.

For Europe, Russia was a remote and almost exotic peripheral land—a significantly different civilization alienating and at the same time fascinating the Europeans. Its vast territorial space put Russia in a unique position in Europe and generated fears about its expansionism. Its huge demographic potential inspired respect and consideration—as well as the feeling that the value of human life was treated as being significantly less in Russia than in Europe. Russia was regarded as possessing enormous resources which might eventually make it extremely rich and powerful were it not for its anachronistic economic system. The impressive military might of Russia has been traditionally perceived as threatening Europe (although, eventually, redirecting other threats from Europe and absorbing them).

For Russia, Europe was both alluring and frightening, tantalizing and disturbing, radiating light and incarnating darkness. Russia was anxious to absorb Europe's vitality—and to ward off its contaminating effects; to become a fully-fledged member of the European family of nations—and to remain removed from it; to enjoy its courtesies and even its devotion but at the same time to inspire fear and trepidation. Indeed, the whole history of Russia is cast in this contradictory feeling: its own centuries-long territorial expansion towards Europe—and memories of invasions from Europe; all the tormented searching of Russian sociological thought with its European-oriented 'Westernism'—and anti-European zeal of Orthodox and communal identity; and the 300-year long record of social experiment from Peter the Great to this day, when models imported from Europe evolved into such grotesque forms in Russia that even wider rifts opened between Russia and Western Europe.

Not only this contradictory legacy of the past, but also the intrinsic 'commonness' of Russia's and Europe's destinies endure. There is no doubt that the future of Europe will be fundamentally affected by the future role of Russia on the continent. Whatever the depth of its current crisis, the economic, political and military potential of the country will without question remain a substantial factor influencing the situation in Europe. At the same time, domestic developments in Russia and its place in the overall international system are to a considerable degree contingent upon the depth and the character of its European connection.

In Europe, the overcoming of the cold war division and the emergence of new state actors have transformed many basic parameters of the international system on the continent. These changes are multidimensional; they have occurred in all the major fields of interaction between states and societies, deeply affecting economics, politics, military security and ideology, and have given rise to a whole set of new challenges with the potential for turning the continent into a region of explosive conflicts.

Thus, the legitimacy of frontiers inherited from the post-World War II period is called into question; there are no rules for handling the disintegration of the state, nor criteria for the responses of other states; and the very notion of 'sovereignty' has become a matter for serious reassessment. Moreover, many of the existing patterns of behaviour which gradually came to be consolidated during the *détente* era in order to preserve stability in Europe have become dysfunctional with respect to new developments on the continent. Most importantly, the old balance of forces in Europe has been dramatically upset, pushing the states to search for a new status and thereby generating the uncertainties of a transitional period. The new international system on the continent is still in the making, and Russia is undoubtedly one of the major players in the European arena.

In Russia the 'European predicament' is also a matter of special importance. Domestically, notwithstanding all the arguments that support the view of Russia as a specific civilization, its further ascent (or decline) will depend on its ability (or failure) to develop such generically European values as democracy and human rights, freedom and social responsibility, the rule of law and a market economy. Internationally, Russia's role as great power emerged in Europe in the 18th century and since then has continued to be associated above all with Europe. While Europe is by no means the only foreign policy priority for Russia, it is in many respects the most important one.

Last but not least, both Europe and Russia may have similar concerns and common, interrelated or complementary interests regarding certain trends in the international system, such as the growing role of China and threats emanating from Islamic fundamentalism. Even the USA, in its capacity as the only remaining superpower, may create direct or indirect incentives for a *rapprochement* between Europe and Russia.

Thus, the question whether Russia and Europe can operate independently is only theoretical—in fact irrelevant. Each of them will certainly have other options, but they both are doomed to share the same continent, to co-exist within adjacent geopolitical areas, to influence and be influenced by each other, and eventually to respond to common challenges.

II. A new agenda

The collapse of the post-World War II international order in Europe and the disintegration of the USSR have brought about tectonic shifts in Eurasian geopolitics. This has inevitably put the problem of Russian–European relations into a fundamentally new context in at least three ways.

First, today's Russia represents a peculiar mixture of continuity and discontinuity with regard to the former Soviet Union and the pre-1917 tsarist empire. The country has certainly inherited much of their legacies, and its operation in the international arena has an undeniable solid historical background. At the same time, Russia has never existed in such a territorial configuration and within such a geopolitical environment as now, which creates considerable confusion with respect to its self-identification in the international arena and, thus, unpredictability and uncertainty about its foreign and security policies.

The very fact that debates continue, even if less intensely, in the political and academic communities of the country on the foreign and security policy options available with respect to Europe means that a 'window of opportunity' is open for Russia's strategy in the international arena to be responsive to new realities and to be cooperatively oriented. At the same time, these positive expectations seem to be significantly qualified by two factors. On the one hand, replacing the political terminology of the communist period with a superficial pseudo-democratic credo is certainly not sufficient for creating a solid conceptual basis on which to build an effective foreign and security policy. On the other hand, a substantial inertia exists both on the level of perceptions, norms and values and in terms of military and political 'hardware': the legacy of the empire/superpower mentality endures, the military–industrial complex looks for self-justification and seeks to reproduce itself, and powerful interest groups profess a clear sympathy for isolationist protectionism or even confrontational assertiveness rather than for openness, adaptation and cooperation.

Second, today's Russia is gradually (albeit not always successfully) getting rid of the old obsessions, suspicions and fears with regard to the West, thereby it would seem clearing the way for a pan-European pattern which could include Russia among the international actors operating on the continent. However, although the collapse of the old regime may have made Russia ideologically closer to Europe, it is not necessarily making the two more compatible. Ironically, even the contrary may prove true: it was sufficient for the former Soviet Union simply to proclaim its 'Europeanism' to gain a sympathetic reaction from Europe, but this is no longer the case for post-Soviet Russia. Since it pretends to operate as a 'normal' member of the international community, the quality of the factors certifying its participation in the family of 'civilized' countries (democracy, human rights, market economy and so on) becomes a critical test. It is quite obvious that the country is having serious difficulties in passing this test, which may lead to the paradoxical conclusion that Russia would have better chances of interacting with Europe as an 'outsider' rather than as an 'insider'.

Third, with the end of the bipolar division of Europe, Russia has unexpectedly found itself pushed to the periphery of European political development. What used to be the immediate neighbourhood for the state which controlled half of Europe is now separated from Russia by two territorial belts comprising the former socialist countries and the former western republics of the USSR. Having suddenly become the most remote territory of Europe, Russia has lost some of the options that were available to the former Soviet Union and its ability to affect developments in Europe has significantly decreased. Does this mean that assertiveness with respect to the 'lost' territories might give Russia greater weight in Europe? After all, playing on the reluctance of the latter to re-establish the old confrontational pattern may seem—or may prove—to be a better strategy than looking for painful accommodation with the external environment and laboriously developing 'conventional' means of gaining influence and prestige.

This logic seems to be inscribed in the five-year record of post-Soviet Russia's foreign policy. The excessive euphoria, enthusiasm, hopes, illusions and misperceptions of the initial post-cold war period have given way to calculations, statements and actions aimed at promoting Russia as an influential international actor. Deliberations on Russia's 'great powerness', 'special responsibilities' and 'sphere of national interest' have become a new obsession— sometimes evolving into arrogance, assertiveness and what is clearly perceived as neo-imperial inclinations. In respect of Russia's relations with Europe, this tendency has been most clearly manifested by Russia's attitude towards the issue of the enlargement of NATO membership and, to some extent, by its policy within the Commonwealth of Independent States (CIS) area.

There are two alternative readings of this phenomenon. It could certainly be ascribed to legitimate—or at least understandable—attempts to overcome post-imperial frustration, to compensate for the mistakes committed in the initial period of the new Russian statehood and to develop an adequate understanding of the country's national interests in the international arena. Alternatively there could be a more worrying, even alarmist, interpretation—that Russia has opted to aim to re-establish the legacy of the past associated with the USSR or the tsarist empire or with both and to consolidate its international status as an expansionist, militaristic and confrontational power.

Both these interpretations may be simplistic; both are most probably elements in the more complex reality of the emerging Russian policy thinking and policy making. It is thus important properly to assess the actual combination of these elements, their relative weights and mutual influence, their sources and the resulting output in terms of practical policy. Russia's relations with Europe will first of all depend on these general parameters.

III. The domestic framework

Identification and evaluation of the relative impact of key domestic factors on Russia's evolving relations with Europe are probably the most logical starting-point of the analysis. Indeed, the policy debates in Russia with respect to Europe have developed across a broad spectrum. The perceptions and approaches of the main political forces in the country are determined by their ideological preferences, but even more so by basic domestic constraints which are a function of the painful process of transition from the old system of organizing society to a new one, with dramatic political, economic and social implications. How the perceived interests of domestic actors are associated with *rapprochement* with, or alienation from, Europe is a critical question.

Foreign and security policy is also affected by the confrontational pattern of interaction between new actors operating in the absence of established rules and traditions of political dialogue. Moreover, since the 'great debate' over the future course of Russia is developing at a time of great domestic flux, the very notion of 'national interest' often becomes a matter of political gamesmanship and a stake in the power struggle among competing political groups. Under such conditions, external policy easily becomes a hostage to domestic political conflicts, while consensus on the issues of relations with the outside world either is not looked for or, if exceptionally achieved, remains superficial, fragile and temporary. As for Russia's partners in the international arena, they have good reason to worry about discontinuity in the event of domestic changes, even if those changes result from democratic elections.

Russia's recent experience points also to other foreign policy implications of an immature political culture and the questionable viability of the political system. The profound dislocations and turmoil accompanying its emergence out of the Soviet Union have undermined dramatically the coherence of the country's foreign and security policy. The rapid rise of new élites resulted in insufficient professionalism in addressing foreign policy issues—a shortcoming which, in principle, will be corrected by time but which may be especially harmful in the formative period when basic choices are made and priorities defined. The weakness of the political regime was impressively manifested by attempts to compensate for domestic failures by outward-oriented assertiveness; the latter also had to serve as a sign of the government's responsiveness to the success of its political opponents.

The chaotic distribution of competence and power between the state's central authorities is even more disturbing. Different official bodies and personalities, although operating on behalf of the state in the international arena, have not only lacked coordination but in some cases actually conducted mutually exclusive foreign policies. The dramatic interpretation of this phenomenon suggests that Russia is in the thrall of an ungoverned bureaucracy, one free of control by a state above it and by a well-represented public below it. Indeed, the issue is not merely the warped and rudimentary relationship between state and society, but also the simple weakness of the state—which is in contrast to many of the popular fears in the outside world that assume a strong and potentially authoritarian Russian state.

Significant implications for Russia's relations with Europe may be produced by centrifugal trends in Russia calling into question its ability to survive as a single entity. Even more important is Moscow's performance in addressing these trends. Viewed from this angle, the war in Chechnya has become a litmus test in two respects. On the one hand, there are no doubts that the indiscriminate bombing and shelling have destroyed not only numerous villages in Chechnya and its capital, Grozny (with tens of thousands of civilian casualties), but also most of the residual image of Russia's 'Europeanness'. On the other hand, the Chechnyan crisis has also clarified the character and the limits of external pressure on Russia in connection with what is recognized as being basically a domestic affair and Moscow's policy of preserving its territorial integrity. The risk of alienating and antagonizing Russia seems to have been judged to be an unacceptable price for demanding in the strongest terms that Russia be internationally accountable.

The war in Chechnya has also revealed a new phenomenon in the Russian political process—the emergence of independent public opinion which might overwhelmingly confront the official policy line. Indeed, most of mass media strongly condemned the methods used by the central authorities to 'pacify' the secessionist republic, with criticism sometimes reaching the level of a broad public outcry. It is true that the government's immediate reaction to this pressure was characterized by defiant indifference; but the very prospect of having to pass the ultimate test in the general election by and large contributed to making the authorities more publicly accountable in their policy. The general public, however, has proved less sensitive towards the problems of relations with the external world—which in principle might allow the government more manoeuvrability.

Among domestic factors affecting Russia's foreign policy in general and its relations with Europe, economic reforms have undoubtedly a prominent place. Their basic orientation towards the establishment of a free market is certainly making Russia more open and cooperative towards the West. At the same time, the vulnerability and poor competitiveness of the new business élites in terms of world market requirements are pushing them to lobby for highly protectionist policies. The political and intellectual weakness of the central administration makes it highly receptive to pressures emanating from powerful domestic interest groups; considerations of controlling oil resources and pipelines seem increasingly to be substituting for a coherent long-term strategy on the international arena. Formidable economic constraints will, however, inevitably create serious obstacles to any would-be expansionist policy.

IV. Military security

Military aspects were fundamental to the bipolar confrontation, providing a certain framework for relations between Europe and the Soviet Union. The collapse of the latter, preceded by the loss of its 'outer empire' and accompanied by the defeat of the communist regime, has substantially altered traditional assumptions, both in Russia and in Europe, about the role of military factors in their relations.

In Europe, concerns about the 'threat from the East' have practically evaporated. Russia's withdrawal of its armed forces 1500 km away from the centre of the continent has resulted in a new strategic situation. Russia continues to possess the largest armed forces in Europe, although their possible use, whether for military or for political purposes, is problematic to say the least. The re-emergence of a military threat from Russia cannot be excluded, but the warning time will be more than sufficient for responding to such an eventuality.

In Russia, the changes in security thinking generated by the controversial reassessment of the country's overall *raison d'être* are considerably more painful and ambivalent. Official doctrinal statements declaring that 'Russia no longer has enemies' are certainly very important both from the point of view of 'high politics' and in terms of ideological reorientation. At the same time they can be either misinterpreted or misleading on the level of practical security policy. The latter, even if the intention is to make a new start, cannot be elaborated without a relatively clear-cut understanding of its rationale.

Here again, a telling example is Russia's attitude towards NATO's eastward enlargement: the argument that it will undermine the country's military security is in flagrant contradiction with the professed recognition of this alliance as non-threatening and even stability-promoting. It is to be noted, however, that NATO, for its part, might (indeed, should) have found significantly more weighty arguments to convince Russia that radical changes are under way in NATO, that it is no longer a cold-war military bloc oriented against an external enemy, and that, in any case, Russia is not viewed as that enemy—although the enlarged alliance will approach its frontiers without considering it as a potential participant.

Among Russian statesmen, soldiers and academics there is a wide range of opinion as to what now constitute the principal military threats to Russia's security and what the role of the armed forces should be in meeting these threats. Two additional factors contribute to making these debates even more controversial: on the one hand, the financial burden of preserving a huge military potential is broadly recognized as being prohibitive for a country experiencing enormous economic hardships; on the other hand, a large military establishment is being presented as Russia's only claim to significant international status, since no other means of achieving it, such as ideological attractiveness, economic resources or the existence of a network of clients, is available. Ironically, this was precisely the theme of great criticism of the state into which the Soviet Union had fallen by its last years.

Not surprisingly, highly contentious debates rage over proposed doctrinal and organizational reforms of the Russian armed forces. Military reform, which is running into many serious obstacles (or, more accurately, was never started either in Gorbachev's period or afterwards, having been openly and covertly sabotaged by the top military establishment), remains a sensitive issue on the Russian security policy agenda—not least in view of its potentially explosive implications for the political role of the armed forces. It should be noted, however, that developments in Russia have not showed much evidence of the widely shared stereotype of the military as an increasingly influential and independent policy and decision maker.

In a broader sense, threat assessments and visions of available security options are to a significant extent a function of the country's self-identification in the international arena. Here again, divergent and sometimes incompatible views are a source of considerable confusion: post-imperial syndrome coexists with emerging ambitions for great-power status; nostalgia for the past goes in parallel with alarmism about the future; Russia's perception of itself as pre-eminently a European power does not exclude appeals to mobilize its 'Asian-ness' or to operate as some kind of bridge between North and South; and so on. Against this background, the sporadic ups and downs in Russia's relations with Europe are by no means surprising.

V. Russia's post-Soviet identity

Apart from domestic factors, another crucial 'independent variable' affecting Russia's interaction with Europe is the overall developments within the post-Soviet space. Indeed, the emergence of Russia as a sovereign state and international actor was inseparably linked with the breakup of the USSR. The new political élites which came to power in Russia at that time played the decisive role in destroying the Soviet Union or, more accurately, in finalizing its self-destruction. However, even if in the immediate post-USSR period they considered the option of getting rid of the burdensome, less developed 'fraternal republics' on the basis of a 'divorce and forget' principle (as in the former Czechoslovakia), that logic did not have chance to prevail. The links between the constituent parts of what was for several decades a single economic and political entity are so significant that to disregard them would be fraught with catastrophic consequences even for Russia, although it is by far the largest and most powerful of the former Soviet republics. Russia's sensitivity with respect to numerous problems emerging in the so-called 'near abroad' is also self-explanatory. It seems only logical that relations with the other post-Soviet states have moved into the focus of Russia's foreign policy agenda.

There are, however, three aspects of this development which may significantly disturb Russia's relations with Europe.

First, the means which Russia considers necessary and legitimate for protecting and promoting its interests in the post-Soviet space could be viewed in

Europe as inappropriate or unacceptable. In this respect, it is worth noting the difference between a natural, uncoerced process of reintegration and one that is dictated or manipulated. Many in the West, however, have great difficulty distinguishing between the two—particularly when distracted by the rhetoric that surrounds the issue.

Second, the forms, mechanisms and ultimate outcome of centripetal trends within the post-Soviet space could be assessed in quite different, if not completely opposite, ways. This may become an especially contentious issue to the extent that the building up of a Russia-dominated 'velvet empire' could be viewed as effectively the same thing as the re-establishment of the USSR, even if in a reduced format—a scenario which seems to be feared in the West as the most disturbing one.

Third, Russia's reluctance to let other international actors operate within its 'sphere of vital interests' may also have a discouraging effect on relations between Russia and Europe. In this respect, the worst-case scenario may be represented by a transformation of the CIS into a new military alliance operating as a counterweight to an expanded NATO-based Europe—a situation which could not only evolve into a 'cold peace' pattern but result in a new edition of the cold war.

On Europe's part, the development of positive relations with Russia may require a better understanding of Russian concerns and difficulties in forging satisfactory new patterns with the other former Soviet republics. To some extent these difficulties are psychological in nature, as Russian public opinion still has to adapt itself to the country's radically changed geopolitical situation—a phenomenon not unfamiliar to some former European colonial empires. In Russia, however, the 'tragedy of the collapse of a thousand-year state' is broadly perceived as being unique and unprecedented; similar historical patterns (like those of the Ottoman or Austro-Hungarian empires) are considered to be irrelevant. Not surprisingly, even in the most liberal-oriented circles the loss of superpower status and the sudden emergence of new foreign neighbours are sources of considerable unease and confusion, which are often exploited by conservatives, nationalists, proponents of the restoration scenarios, those who believe that Russia is in an 'imperial predicament', and so on.

The problems confronting Russia are certainly not only of a psychological character. Of equal, if not greater, importance is the fact that a number of traditional parameters affecting the security status of the country, such as access to the open ocean, availability of critical resources and so on, have been significantly altered by the disintegration of the USSR. Furthermore, new problems of the utmost sensitivity have emerged—like that of the plight of tens of millions of ethnic Russians who have suddenly found themselves living outside 'their' country. Assisting Russia in looking for civilized and responsible ways of addressing such issues is of paramount importance.

In terms of international stability, Russia's increasing role in the post-Soviet space might be rationalized by its potential to marginalize or minimize the scope of conflicts on the territory of the former USSR. Indeed, many of these conflicts seem either to be frozen or to have developed in less dramatic forms as compared with the recent past. On the other hand, Russia's 'peacemaking' efforts have promoted, directly or indirectly, its predominance in the CIS area and contributed to suspicions about its actual intentions.

However, such suspicions—whether justified or not—are irrelevant in the light of the reluctance or inability of the international community to become effectively involved, which actually makes Russia the only instrumental force for containing conflicts on the territory of the former USSR. At the same time, mandating Russia to operate as the Eurasian pacifier would entail much more than its military capabilities, and even these are limited in view of the formidable task of conflict management in numerous areas of instability.

In any case, the conflicts emerging in the post-Soviet space (including those in Russia's relations with the other former Soviet republics) have already absorbed much of the foreign policy energy of Moscow, and the situation will hardly change in the foreseeable future. The ability of Russia to find convincing arguments and effective means for reorganizing the former Soviet geopolitical space will be vital for Russia's security and may well constitute the most serious test of its maturity. For Europe, promoting such a reorganization together with, and not against, Russia will be crucial for preventing the emergence of new dividing lines on the continent.

VI. Russia's European vicinity

Russian–European relations are developing within a multidimensional geopolitical context; problems emerging in different areas are far from being structurally the same and may generate dissimilar patterns of relations. In particular, there is a need to focus on the principal geopolitical regions which are of primary importance for Russia's relations with Europe: the Slav 'core area' of the former USSR; the North-West European (Baltic/Nordic) neighbours; the former Warsaw Treaty Organization members from East–Central Europe; the Balkans and surrounding areas; and the Caucasus.

1. Russia's relations with its two Slav neighbours, Belarus and Ukraine, will be of paramount importance in determining what the future of the European part of the post-Soviet geopolitical space will look like. A number of questions arise in this regard. Will this 'Slav triangle' emerge as a regional entity playing a dominant role in the CIS and infusing the latter with dynamism and cohesion? Or, on the contrary, will the centrifugal forces preclude any kind of alliance between the three, generating instead acrimony and conflict? Are there grounds for a Russian 'dual-track' strategy here—a confrontational course *vis-à-vis* Ukraine as a natural rival but *rapprochement* with Belarus as a potential client? More generally, how will Russia's policy towards its two Slav neighbours be incorporated into its global foreign and security policy priorities? Finally, what will be the role of Western attitudes and sensitivities, especially towards Ukraine? Similar questions are appropriate with respect to Belarus and Ukraine

themselves; as in Russia, their foreign and security policy choices are also the subjects of domestic debates and controversies on the one hand and external pressures on the other.

2. In the Baltic region, foremost on Russia's new security agenda are the practical problems that emerged with the collapse of the Soviet Union, such as the withdrawal of Russia's residual armed forces and military infrastructure, the status of the Russian-speaking populations and the resolution or marginalization of conflicting territorial claims. A special challenge is posed by the issue of the future status of the Kaliningrad region. In a broader sense, the north-western vicinity of Russia has ceased, with the end of the cold war, to be a strategically meaningful area of East–West confrontation, as in the recent past. However, the area remains one of considerable relevance for Russia's relations with Europe in two respects: first, because of its role in terms of Russia's strategic interests (the increasing importance of the Kola peninsula in the light of the 1993 Russian–US Treaty on Further Reduction and Limitation of Strategic Offensive Arms, the START II Treaty, access to the open ocean and so on); and second, because of security concerns that the Baltic/Nordic countries might have about Russia.

3. Relations with the former allies in East–Central Europe represent one of the most significant failures of post-Soviet Russia in the international arena, reflecting above all the deficiency in strategic thinking in Moscow. Whether the latter would have been able to launch 'a new start' here by disassociating itself from the Soviet-style 'big brother' model and cultivating the cooperative links inherited from the socialist past is now a purely theoretical question: this option does not seem even to have been considered seriously. Instead, Moscow has focused on assessing the area through the prism of Russia's broader strategic considerations; in particular, concerns about the possibility of Russia being isolated from Europe by the much faster Westernization of the former allies became almost hysterical when their joining NATO was put on the agenda. Paradoxically, even if slowing down NATO enlargement eastward may be quite legitimate from the point of view of Russia's pan-European rationales, this will most probably have to be paid for in terms of Russia's future relations with East–Central Europe. The area where Moscow could realistically count on quite good prospects might be alienated by the over-reaction of the 'new Russia' even more than by the practice of the 'old USSR'.

4. Further to the south, Russia is facing an increasingly complex set of challenges in the Balkans and surrounding areas. Here, two problems seem especially salient for its foreign and security policy agenda.

The phenomenon of the Trans-Dniester area of Moldova is basically the heritage of the Soviet past facing Russia with a traditional set of questions: how to deal with secessionism in the successor states (especially when there is a great temptation to use it as leverage against them), how to protect the rights of Russians living outside the Russian Federation (or to respond to their irredentist demands), how to channel the withdrawal of residual troops into the 'reorganization' of Russia's military presence, and so on. What makes these problems specific is the fact that Russia has found itself deeply involved in a region with which it does not even have a common frontier. In addition, the prospects for Moldova's unification with Romania, although admittedly often exaggerated, are by no means insignificant for Russia's assessment of the geopolitical balance in South-Eastern Europe—which may only increase Moscow's interest in turning this country into a client state.

The developments in the former Yugoslavia became the first serious test for Russia's 'out-of-area' post-Soviet foreign policy. Although its performance was not much more effective than that of other external 'pacifiers', Russia was basically successful in establishing itself as an actor in the area—even if in a less prominent role than expected. In terms of Russia's gaining involvement in European politics it was a major breakthrough. However, a number of key questions have yet to be clarified. What are the implications of the 'Dayton logic' for Russian geopolitical interests in the area? How might domestic changes in Russia affect its policy in the former Yugoslavia? And to what extent would Russia be ready and able to take part in the power game in the Balkans?

5. The tumultuous situation in the Caucasus poses some of the most serious challenges confronting Russian foreign and security policy-makers. The high level of domestic political instability prevailing in all three new states in the area, Armenia, Azerbaijan and Georgia (although to a lesser degree in Armenia), the divisive role of religion, the trans-border links of numerous ethnic groups and a host of other factors have contributed to making the Caucasus a volatile and conflict-prone region—one which holds grave perils for Russian foreign and security policy. Moscow considers its stakes in the region to be extremely high. They are linked both to the question of political influence in this strategically important area and at the same time to the fact that Russia is more vulnerable domestically with respect to its policy choices in the Caucasus than perhaps in any other region, given the serious disintegrative trends in the contiguous areas of the Russian Federation. The dilemmas arising here are directly related to the broader issues emerging on Russia's post-Soviet foreign and security policy agenda ('challenges from the south', the choice between European and Asian priorities, the balance between a regional and a more global focus, the viability of the CIS, and so on) and to the changes taking place in the international system as a whole (the role of the Islamic factor, containment of local instabilities, interventionism for peacemaking, territorial integrity and the right to self-determination, and so on).

VII. Searching for a role in Europe

The volatility and unpredictability of Russia's self-identification, its relations with other post-Soviet states and its domestic political developments represent a formidable challenge to European security. The latter is unthinkable without including the 'Russia plus' factor. The expansion and proliferation of local conflicts have an intrinsic potential to involve one or more major powers; their strategic concerns may be strained by eventual post-communist 'security vacuums'; the well-being of the wealthier part of Europe could be threatened by socio-economic and political developments if they are mishandled in the coun-tries in a state of transition—refugee movements, criminality, drugs, illegal transfers of arms and fissile materials and environmental degradation. Europe is thus by no means in a position to build up a Chinese wall which would separate it from developments in Russia and Russia's immediate environment, as well as from Russia's activities within the post-Soviet geopolitical space.

Europe, for its part, is by no means irrelevant to Russia's security and to the security of the post-Soviet area at large. Its cooperative engagement is essential for preventing Russia from choosing self-isolation, alienation and the 'do-it-alone' option.

Against this background, Russia's relations with the other major international actors in Europe are developing as a combination of variable patterns, some-times offering an image of poorly coordinated policies, but more often inscribed into a broader strategy of promoting the country's role on the conti-nent and re-establishing its international status. The West European countries are perceived as providers of economic assistance and partners for addressing issues of common interest, but also as potential rivals who could impede future attempts by Russia to reassert its waning influence on the continent. There are also symptoms of Russia's re-emerging interest in *realpolitik* within Europe. In particular, it seems quite possible that playing on the disagreements and contra-dictions between Western Europe and the USA will be attractive and tempting—especially since transatlantic solidarity is now exposed to signifi-cantly stronger stresses than in the recent past, when 'threats from the East' were a predominant consolidating factor.

In fact, this is an impressive example of the remarkable continuity of some problems, challenges and options inherited from the period of bipolar con-frontation. In this context it is to be noted that the 'conspiracy mentality' blam-ing the West for all the failures in Russia (and, retrospectively, for the collapse of the Soviet Union) has become a more prominent feature of political thinking in the country. One challenging question is the extent to which such a return of cold-war patterns of thought could affect Russia's future foreign and security policy.

Finally, Russia's involvement in Europe has to be considered from the per-spective of its possible role in an evolving pan-European security architecture. This requires above all clarifying Russian attitudes towards the multilateral security policy-relevant institutions operating in Europe—NATO, the North Atlantic Cooperation Council (NACC), the Organization for Security and Co-operation in Europe (OSCE), the European Union (EU) and the Western European Union (WEU). This task is complicated by the welter of opinions and policy pronouncements coming from Russian research analysts and government officials. Another side of the problem is linked with these institutions' search for new roles and specific functions in the post-cold war world, which is a painful and controversial process

More generally, the problem consists in identifying means and forms of bilateral and multilateral security interactions in Europe which would respond to a number of conditions. To sum up only the most important of them, the question is how:

– to alleviate the security concerns of the post-cold war international actors—without, however, exacerbating the 'security dilemmas' of others;

– to take into account the balance of forces in Europe that is actually emerging—without resorting to traditional power politics in the international arena;

– to avoid antagonizing Russia—without, however, providing it with a right of veto over the security choices of other former socialist states;

– to respect the intrinsic centripetal trends and Russia's legitimate interests within the post-Soviet geopolitical space—without accepting its becoming a 'closed area' under Russia's control; and

– to preserve the viability of the existing institutions—without denying an eventual option of developing new institutional structures.

In a sense, these may be considered as conflicting requirements, but they are commensurate with the challenging task of elaborating and implementing a cooperative strategy aimed at strengthening international stability. The fact that the major geopolitical equations have significantly changed for both Russia and Europe creates new challenges and opens new prospects for their interaction in the security field. The vector of this interaction (cooperative or confrontational) will be of paramount importance for both Russia and Europe; joint efforts by the two are a fundamental condition for organizing a safer post-Soviet and post-cold war international order.

Part I
The security context

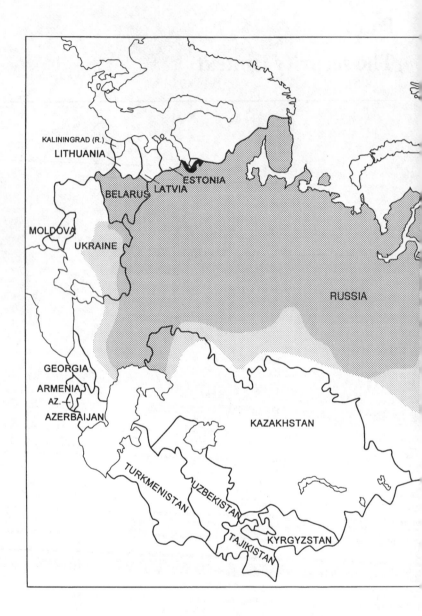

The territory of Russia by 1600 and 1700

Source: Based on Shaw, D. J. B., *The Post-Soviet Republics: A Systematic Geography* (Longman Scientific and Technical: Harlow, 1995), figure 1.3., p. 5, reproduced by permission of Addison Wesley Longman Ltd. In addition, the following sources were consulted: Gilbert, M., *Imperial Russian History Atlas* (Routledge and Kegan Paul: London, 1978), pp. 26, 29, 30, 36, 37, 47; and *New Encyclopædia Britannica*, 15th. edn, 1985, vol. 8, p 983.

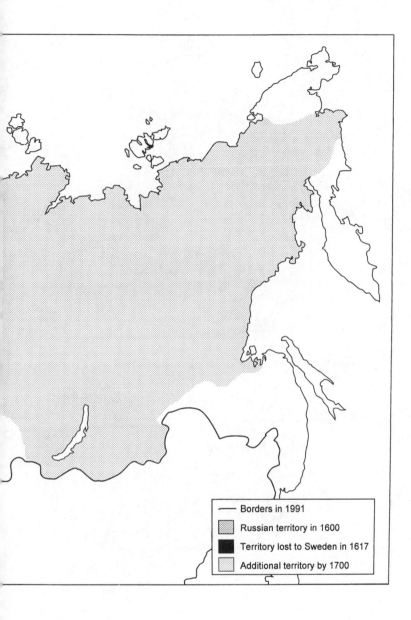

Note:

At the beginning of the 17th century, the population of Russia was *c.* 6 million.
At the beginning of the 18th century, the population of Russia was *c.* 14 million.

The Russian Empire by 1800 and 1900

Source: Based on Shaw, D. J. B., *The Post-Soviet Republics: A Systematic Geography* (Longman Scientific and Technical: Harlow, 1995), figure 1.3, p. 5, reproduced by permission of Addison Wesley Longman Ltd. In addition, the following sources were consulted: Gilbert, M., *Imperial Russian History Atlas* (Routledge and Kegan Paul: London, 1978), pp. 43, 48, 50; and Baev, P. K., *The Russian Army in a Time of Troubles* (Sage Publications: London, 1996), p. 8.

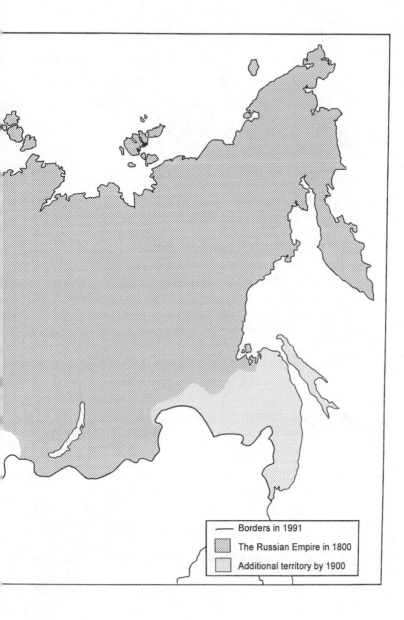

Note:

By 1917 the Russian Empire had a territory covering *c.* 22.6 km^2 and a population of 163 million. Before its dissolution in 1991, the USSR covered 22.4 million km^2 and had a population of 280 million. The post-Soviet Russian Federation has a territory of 17.1 million km^2 and a population of 148 million.

2. The historical background of Russian security concepts and requirements

Lothar Rühl

I. Introduction

The subject of this chapter is essentially the legacy of Imperial and Soviet Russia. What, if any, is its relevance to the security of the Russian Federation now?

Russia today can be considered either as the present form of what remains of the empire or as the re-creation of the Russian state without the empire. In the second case, a large allowance must be made at least for the multi-ethnic if not multinational composition of Russia with its associated ethnic or ethno-territorial units and territories of mixed population, such as Tatarstan, Bashkortostan and Kalmykia and, of course, the northern Caucasus. The Chechnyan attempt at secession points to the reality of the latent conflicts over the meaning of autonomy and of the legal status of what the new Russian Constitution of 1993 calls the 'subjects of the Federation'.

In reality, what is at issue is no less than the unity of Russia and its territorial integrity. There is no doubt that the common cause of these problems lies in the past of the Russian Empire, in the centralist structure of the Russian state before 1917 and in the results of the solutions chosen by the USSR under the heading of 'Soviet federalism' with regional autonomy under strict political control and economic domination by 'the centre'. Lessons from this past should therefore be relevant to explaining the linkage between 'internal' and 'external' security and to both the definition and the defence of Russia's borders.

The territory of today's Russian Federation is identical with the territory of the former Russian Soviet Federative Socialist Republic (RSFSR) as a part of the Soviet Union. This is less than the hard core of historic Russia, which was enlarged by conquests from the middle of the 16th century (in the south and east) to the last third of the 19th century (in Central Asia) but now reduced in the west since the dissolution of the USSR in 1991 by the loss of Belarus and Ukraine. Other lands which were incorporated in Russia in the past lie within its 'outer borders' but do not belong to Russia proper. Their populations have kept their original culture and identity although they have certainly developed strong links with the population of Russia proper.

There are other 'border cases' such as Ossetia, North Ossetia being part of the Russian Federation and South Ossetia part of independent Georgia. Inside Russia itself, in the areas inhabited by some of the non-Russian peoples of Mongol-Turkic origin (such as the Tatars, Bashkirs, Kalmyks and north

Caucasian peoples), there has been a significant trend to claim sovereignty and even independence from Russia.[1] The complex relationship between these territories and peoples or ethnic groups inside the frontiers of the Russian Federation is part of the structure of Russian history. Its effect is a continuing tension between national and imperial elements—a tension that could not be overcome either in the tsars' empire or in the Soviet Union and that may well harm the Russian Federation.

What then is the 'national' substance in the national interest, the national security and the national defence of the Russian Federation? Is it more properly Russian or multinational, or perhaps something between the two? The question was relevant even in the time of the Soviet Union, in spite of all the efforts by Moscow to promote the notion of the Soviet people at the expense of national identities: it has only become more prominent in the light of the obvious unrest of the non-Russian ethnic groups within Russia and the separatist movements in the northern Caucasus.

The new Russian military doctrine of November 1993 clearly reflects these problems since it defines, as one of eight different 'factors which facilitate the escalation of military danger into a direct military threat to the Russian Federation', the specific contingency of 'illegal activities of nationalist, secessionist and other organizations designed to destabilize the internal situation of the Russian Federation or to violate its territorial integrity and carried out with the use of armed force'.[2]

This was precisely the case of Chechnya in 1994–96. The Chechnyan war recalls the turbulent past of Imperial Russia over more than three centuries, beginning with Ivan IV's active interest in expanding his dominance southwards and local princes' desire for protection from their powerful northern neighbour.[3] It is also undeniable that there is a contemporary significance in the Russian conquest of the Caucasus in the 19th century with its military experiences and its political consequences for relations between the peoples of the Caucasus and Russia after almost half a century of war, rebellion and repression. This becomes clear in the links between the 19th-century conflicts, the revolution of 1905, the Russian Civil War with the reconstruction of the empire in the guise of the Soviet Union, the reorganization of the Caucasus and Trans-

---

[1] *Rußland: Risikofaktor Tschetschenien* [Russia's Chechnyan risk factor], Deutsche Bank Research no. 117 (Frankfurt-am-Main: Oct. 1994); Bischof, H., *Sturm über Tschetschenien: Rußlands Krieg im Kaukasus* [Storm over Chechnya: Russia's war in the Caucasus], Studien zur Außenpolitik no. 65 (Friedrich-Ebert-Stiftung: Bonn, Jan. 1995); Rahr, A., *Rußlands Krieg in Tschetschenien* [Russia's war in Chechnya], Aktuelle Kurzanalyse no. 11 (Forschungsinstitut der DGAP: Bonn, Feb. 1995); and Halbach, U., Bundesinstitut für ostwissenschaftliche und internationale studien, *Krieg im Kaukasus* [War in the Caucasus], Aktuelle Kurzanalyse 1/1995, 2/1995 (BIOSt: Cologne, 1995).

[2] Presidential decree no. 1833, 2 Nov. 1993, accompanying the military doctrine. *Izvestiya* published extensive excerpts in 'Osnovnye polozheniya voennoy doktriny Rossiyskoy Federatsii' [The basic provisions of the military doctrine of the Russian Federation] on 18 Nov. 1993; and *Krasnaya Zvezda* published a slightly longer excerpt on 19 Nov. 1993. A translation into English was published by *Jane's Intelligence Review*, Special Report, Jan. 1994. For a full discussion, see chapters 8 and 9 in this volume.

[3] In 1557 Kabardinian Prince Temryuk, seeking protection from the Crimean Tatar Khanate, offered to become a vassal of the Tsar; in 1566 the first Russian fortress was built on the Terek River on Kabardinian territory at Temryuk's request. It had to be abandoned later because of Turkish pressure.

caucasian regions by Stalin with repressive force in the 1920s, and the action of a small part of the population in siding with the Germans in 1942, when the *Wehrmacht* recruited about 60 000 volunteers for 53 battalions formed in Poland to fight the Red Army.[4]

This in turn provoked renewed repression and mass deportation. All in all, Soviet Russia had to fight for the Caucasian and Central Asian conquests of Imperial Russia, even if it could rely, as the tsars had been able to do, on the collaboration or at least the passivity of a large part of these populations. The essential fact is the constant need for Russia to protect its borders with the Orient from the inside at least as much as against the outside. Security in such situations cuts both ways; defence and repression form a double-edged sword. Security becomes ambivalent: defence is almost impossible without conquest and punitive war against peoples either astride the borders of the empire or pressed inside these borders by force. There always was some kind of 'near abroad' around the imperial frontiers, where Russian armies sought to secure the safety of the empire or to impose imperial authority. Were Stalin's attempts to establish small Soviet republics across the border with Iran in 1945–47 or the Soviet penetration of Afghanistan since the late 1960s, leading to the Afghan War in 1979, essentially different in nature, as far as Soviet interest went?

These particular cases show the relevance of the question whether historical lessons can be identified for contemporary Russian thinking on national defence and security, especially in 'border cases'. Are there criteria from the past, still valid for the definition of Russia's national interest and for the concept of security? Can defence requirements for the future be found in the historical experience, and can a fundamental geopolitical continuity in Russia's situation be recognized in spite of the considerable territorial changes since 1991? Can it be said that a historical trend of disintegration of the surviving imperial structures around the national core of Russia continues and that the entire Russian Federation is at actual risk, as former Soviet Foreign Minister Eduard Shevardnadze, now President of Georgia, has argued?[5]

What would the significance of such lessons and criteria be for policy, for the setting of national priorities in resource allocation, for the defence posture, the size and structure of the armed forces, the military budget, the development of military technology and the national armaments industries? Can deterrence with nuclear arms or the meaning and usefulness of military power be essentially the same as before 1991? Are there differences between military strategy and the possible use of the armed forces as the instrument of national policy today and the same things in the time of the Soviet Union or of the tsars' empire? And can a case be made either for maintaining essentially the same concepts with a measure of adaptation or for changing them?

---

[4] Sarkisyanz, E., *Geschichte der orientalischen Völker Rußlands bis 1917* [History of the Asiatic peoples of Russia up to 1917] (Oldenbourg: Munich, 1961).

[5] He did so in 1992–93 on several occasions during talks with Western official visitors.

II. Lessons of Russian history

The patterns of Russian policy making on relations with its neighbours, on expanding its borders, on building the Russian Army and creating a navy can be placed in historical perspective for a comprehensive review of national attitudes on the significance of territory to be protected or territory simply to be used for the protection of Russia; on domination of foreign countries; on foreign alliances; on the value of international treaties for Russia's security; and not least on military and naval power as an instrument of national policy. The basic issues under discussion are continuity and discontinuity in Russian perceptions and the weight of traditional thinking.

Continuity of concepts, trends and traditions over long periods of time is always questionable: like beauty, it can be in the eye of the beholder rather than in reality. Could the Byzantine empire have had a strategy over more than seven centuries, as has been suggested? Was there a 'Roman imperial strategy' or at least in practical terms a political–military tradition of Roman rule over the Mediterranean and the adjacent lands over some 700 or 800 years, complete with a colonizing and organizing presence north of the Alps for almost 500 years? Was there more than just *divide et impera*? Were the Spanish, Portuguese, British or French colonial empires built and managed by continuous policies, based on time-honoured concepts and on national behaviour, and did they produce a lasting attitude? Did Palmerston and Disraeli, so different in character, conduct their imperial policies in the 19th century according to a continuing tradition of authoritative thinking on the balance of power and British rule of the seas? Similar questions can be asked about France and Austria as well as about Russia since Peter the Great.

Any reasonable view of the history and national attitudes or the traditional policies of a country has to link its historical background and geography to the other long-standing physical features of the theatre of events where the policies are produced—population, natural resources, access to the wider environment such as the high seas and basic long-term economic activities. Russia's dependence in the 19th century on the export of grain for the accumulation of capital, on foreign imports of industrial goods, on foreign investment and foreign credits for modernization, industrialization and the building of railways through Siberia and Central Asia—that is, for strategic control of its own land mass as well as for economic development to lay a solid foundation for Russian colonization, military power and international competition—shows the importance of these factors for the equation of power and security.

Such features, however, do not necessarily remain unchanged over time. Discontinuity is as permanent a feature of history as continuity. Russia itself changed considerably during the 18th and again during the 19th century in economic, social, cultural and political terms.

Russian military forces and thinking changed greatly between the days of Tsar Alexis in the middle of the 17th century and the reign of Peter the Great, who rebuilt Russian military strength, created the Russian Navy with the maritime tradition, conquered the Baltic coast and made Russia the 'Power of the North' after his victory over Sweden. In doing all this he ruined his empire's finances and exhausted the energies of his people for decades to come, and Russia remained in internal disorder and weakness. During Elizabeth I's reign the empire rose to a prominent role in Europe again and contributed greatly to the balance of power on the continent. Territorial expansion towards the west was pursued in peace and war, but at the same time the victorious empire was run down. The fleet rotted in sanded-up ports and the army in Prussia had neither been paid nor supplied for three years in the Seven Years' War. Under Catherine the Great the renewal of the administration, the finances and economy, the army and the navy transformed Russia into a truly great power in Europe, enlarging the Russian Baltic coast, winning most of Poland and Crimea, and ending the Turkish domination of the Black Sea.

Could there have been continuity in foreign policy and strategy, security and defence thinking in Russia from the end of Tsar Alexis' reign in 1676 to the beginning of Catherine the Great's in 1762, or from the start of Alexander I's rule in 1801 to the end of Nicholas II's in 1917? The answer is complex and difficult. There are obvious repetitions and recurring patterns, even between the late Muscovite tsardom and the Petrine empire in St Petersburg, as well as obvious differences. These patterns stand out particularly in the military and naval forces, in Russia's alliances and foreign wars, and in its vulnerabilities to invasion and its resilience in national defence once energies were galvanized. Changes have been so extreme over short periods, however, that they seem to exclude any meaningful notion of continuity in concepts of security and defence, even allowing for irrational behaviour on the part of rulers or illogical decisions.

There are examples of policies directly detrimental to Russian national and imperial interests. The most telling example was Peter III's decision to take Russia out of the war against Prussia in 1762 because of his admiration of Frederick the Great, thus giving away the gains already secured and frustrating the Russian war aims of winning eastern Prussia and establishing Russia firmly as a power equal to Austria and France, with Saxony as its vassal and Poland under its control.

There are also more frequent instances of inadequacy in pursuance of an ambitious foreign policy with far-reaching war aims. The first and most spectacular instance in modern times is offered by the dramatic developments in the last quarter of the 17th century—the new standing army which Tsar Alexis had created in the first effort of modernization was actually lost during peacetime and by the ensuing ill-fated campaigns against Crimea and Narva.[6] The defi-

---

[6] The Russian historian Klyuchevsky has made this point about the situation Peter I found in 1695, when he launched his war to conquer Azov and later turned against Charles XII of Sweden. According to Klyuchevsky the regular army, left by Alexis to his successors in 1676 at a strength of about 90 000 soldiers in the European fashion, had dwindled by about 60 000 men in 20 years and Peter I was able to muster barely 15 000 professional soldiers for his first campaign. Klyuchevsky, V., *Peter the Great* (Random House/A. A. Knopf: New York, 1958).

cient state of the army did not permit a successful war, let alone an offensive one. Russia had neither the means nor the strategy for the anti-Turkish alliance with Austria and Venice in the Holy League. There was no coherent policy in Moscow nor the money for a war and there were no warships to attack the Turks at sea before Azov or to use a breakthrough to Crimea in the south or to the Baltic in the north. There was certainly no concept for either defence or offensive employment of the army to serve the chosen foreign policy. Peter later had the greatest difficulties in overcoming this weakness and forging Russian military power.

Hence it cannot be said that there was any continuity in military affairs or even a concept for a coherent use of military force before Peter the Great. It has already been noted that neither the army and navy he had created nor a concept for their effective use as instruments of foreign policy survived the first Emperor of Russia.[7]

His successors did not develop what could be called a national strategy or a lasting concept of security for their empire. Catherine the Great, however, progressively acquired territorial and strategic policy aims: Crimea with Kerch as her 'Gibraltar' in order to gain access to the Black Sea and establish Russian sea power in what had been a Turkish lake at the beginning of her reign; control of the entire Baltic coast between Prussia and Finland; dominance over Poland; the conquest and incorporation of Moldavia and Wallachia; and the general defeat and definitive expulsion from Europe of the Ottoman Empire. She achieved most of her objectives, even if she was frustrated after victory on the Lower Danube by Austria and Turkey remaining out of her reach. While any vision on Catherine's part of conquering Constantinople and establishing a Russian emperor on a renewed Byzantine throne can be discounted,[8] she reaffirmed Peter the Great's ambitious designs for expansion of the empire to the Danube and into the Balkans as well as via Crimea towards the Caucasus. In the Baltic and in Poland she completed Peter's initial success.

Since Catherine II the expansion of Russian power, Russia's *Drang nach Westen*, as Karl Marx described it in the 19th century,[9] has been a continuous effort to the very end of the tsars' empire and beyond the Russian Revolution, the Soviet Union having become the last form of the empire, reassembled between 1919 and 1945 minus Finland and Poland. Catherine created the permanent system of reference (she even called her foreign policy a 'system' in the fashion of her time): control of Poland and the Lower Danube, destruction of Turkish rule over the Balkans and dominance of the Baltic and Black seas,

[7] Klyuchevsky (note 6).

[8] Catherine II thought of her grandson Constantine becoming Greek Emperor of Constantinople after the annexation of Crimea in 1783, following her first great victory over the Ottoman Empire in the Turkish War of 1768–74. She visited Crimea in 1787 and formed her 'Greek Project' which was the direct reason for the Sultan renewing the war with Russia. Stökl, G., *Russische Geschichte* [Russian history] (Kröner: Stuttgart, 1973), p. 422. The Empress did not follow up on her idea after her successful war of 1787–92.

[9] Marx, K. and Engels, F., *Rußlands Drang nach Westen: der Krimkrieg und die europäische Geheimdiplomatie im 19 Jahrhundert* [Russia's westward expansion: the Crimean War and European secret diplomacy in the 19th century] (Manesse-Verlag: Zurich, 1991), p. 21.

aiming at control of the Turkish Straits. Her successors added an opening into the Mediterranean with permanent naval bases in the Aegean and Adriatic seas to these permanent objectives of Russian expansion far beyond the boundaries of Russia. This trend was apparent during the entire 19th century and the expansion was almost achieved between 1939 and 1949, when Stalin succeeded where the tsars had been held in check by the Western powers.[10] Even Egypt and Syria came within the sights of Russian outward-looking strategy, for the first time in the 19th century, and later in the penetration of Soviet power into the Near East during the 1960s up to 1972–73, Stalin having failed in his attempt in 1945–47.

Russia has been active in the European power game ever since the beginning of the 18th century. This legacy from Peter the Great was maintained by Elizabeth I and renewed by Catherine the Great, by Paul I, who sought the sovereign possession of Malta and a permanent naval presence for Russia in the Mediterranean, and by Alexander I, who advanced Russian influence in Europe after 1812, and about whose achievements the British historian Hugh Seton-Watson wrote: 'in 1815 Russia appeared the strongest single power on the Continent'.[11] It exercised a determining influence on the tsars' foreign policy until the very end in 1917. Emperor Nicholas I, who ordered the conquest of the Caucasus, the submission of Poland by force and the military intervention of 1849 in Hungary to save the legitimate monarchical order of Europe against rebellion, followed the old line of expansion. He tried to create a European coalition with Britain and Austria for a war against Turkey, the 'sick man of Europe', in order to gain control of the Turkish Straits, expand the Russian Empire from the Caucasus far into Anatolia and establish a Russian predominance in the Balkans. The legacy was maintained by the last three tsars with the weakest of them, Nicholas II, almost winning the supreme prize of Constantinople, the Turkish Straits and the whole of Poland, where he celebrated the reunion of Galicia with the 'Russian motherland' after the initial victories of 1914–15 against the Austrians. Acquisition of territory has thus often been described as a vital necessity for security on the vast Eurasian plain, where no natural obstacles offer barriers to an intruder and bulwarks for defence. Klyuchevsky and Vernadsky, a century and a half apart, have made this case, as other historians did.[12]

Only Lenin broke the pattern after October 1917, when he took Soviet Russia out of World War I in order to save the embattled and still shaky Bolshevik power in Petrograd. The traditional quest for expansion and control of the country's neighbours in order to obtain increased security and political domination of a sphere of interests remained relevant to Soviet policy after Lenin

[10] Rühl, L., *Aufstieg und Niedergang des russischen Reiches* [The rise and fall of the Russian Empire] (DVA: Stuttgart, 1992), p. 503, with quotation from Laloy, J., *Yalta, Hier, Aujourd'hui, Demain* [Yalta, yesterday, today, tomorrow] (Éditions Robert Laffont: Paris, 1988).

[11] Seton-Watson, H., *The Russian Empire 1801–1917* (Oxford University Press: Oxford, 1967), p. 331.

[12] Klyuchevsky (note 6); and Vernadsky, G., *A History of Russia*, 9th edn (Yale University Press: New Haven, Conn., 1994).

with Stalin as the great revivalist of Russian imperialism. Stalin added hegemony to empire after the victory over Germany in 1945. His policy was about security by conquest and a firm hold on the conquered lands, either inside the Soviet Union (Finnish Karelia, the Baltic republics, the northern part of East Prussia, eastern Poland and eastern Romania) or outside in a 'Socialist commonwealth', as the outer empire was later called in General Secretary Leonid Brezhnev's day.

This begs the question whether Russia was pursuing security through expansion or imperialist ambition. Simple equations such as 'expansion and forward projection of power equals security of the empire' or 'spheres of strategic interest equal advanced forward defence and broader margins of safety' are inadequate to the case.

It can be said, however, that there is historical continuity in certain geographical features, trends and concepts of Russian policy, for expansion and for security, for offensive and defensive purposes, based on the acquisition of territory and of military power to make use of gains for further advantage. What seems essential for present Russian thinking and acting in dealing with issues of security is a large margin of safety for reaction to crisis, reliance on superior numbers after a build-up of forces over time, and the direct and prolonged use of massive force.

All these characteristics are determined by the combination of Russia's vast space, which offers a 'cushion' in the sense of time in which to react, its large reserves of forces, and its capabilities and stocks in excess of requirements, which permit the country to absorb initial defeat, replace losses, correct mistakes and use the experience in new approaches to the solution of a problem, as happened in the Winter War against Finland in 1939–40. This goes back directly to Peter the Great's first military experiences in war and the sieges of Azov and Narva. Stalin in 1941 before the German invasion thought that the *Wehrmacht* had nothing much to offer in modern warfare and that the German soldiers were disheartened.[13] After the lessons of defeat, the Red Army recovered and fought back until victory in Berlin, repeating the feats of the Russian Army in 1812 and 1813–14.

In all these cases the time–space factor offered the margin of safety. The resources of Russia made the reversal of the tides of war possible. Above all the possession of vast territory and of large forces combined to Russia's advantage in strategic defence against invasion. The arithmetic of advance into the enemy's country, the greater part of which would remain out of reach, made each mile forward eat up the strength of the invader. This is true for other large countries, like China, as well, but it has had a specific significance in Russia since the Polish invasion at the beginning of the 17th century, and, so far, it has not been disproved by events. The result is a proven capacity to endure tactical

---

[13] Rühl (note 10), pp. 482–83, quoting Lev Bezymenskiy on Stalin's address to officers in the Kremlin on 5 May 1941.

set-backs and repeated political failures without suffering decisive defeat, as in 1812 or in 1941–42.

III. Enduring security: patterns of thought

The most important single difference between today's Russia and the 'old' one in terms of security policy lies in the availability of nuclear arms and options. Security against nuclear threats, however, does not seem to be the most vital current preoccupation in Moscow. This can be explained by reliance on the Russian–US special relationship now that the START (Strategic Arms Reduction) treaties have been concluded and all nuclear warheads eliminated from Ukraine.[14] However, Russia must still reckon with nuclear arms, air power and missiles in the event of conflict.

In this respect the value of territory has shrunk since 1945, as has the advantage of numerically superior forces and a large industrial war potential. Security can no longer be based on control of territory by large forces and a central authority imposing its rule. The quality of forces and command structures, central authority, organization and planning, immediate availability of reserves and war stocks and the efficiency of rapid mobilization and reinforcement are more important than ever before. This new reality was shown in the 1991 Persian Gulf War. While territory also offers forward air defence and echeloned anti-air barriers, added reconnaissance and hence reaction time to attack, the enhanced options of offensive air power and missiles limit the usefulness of a territorial strategic glacis for national defence.

For the first time in history, Russia is exposed to air and especially to missile attack with no strategic sanctuary. This has been the case for most parts of the USSR since the 1970s. The combination of nuclear warheads, missiles and bombers armed with missiles has created the ultimate and omnipresent threat, which cannot be avoided and against which there is no defence, which could not be saturated and finally overcome. The strategy of nuclear deterrence was the only possible solution to the problem and has remained so. While the new military doctrine takes this strategic factor into account and deals with nuclear options in response to an attack, it nevertheless counts on the possibility 'to avert the threat of a nuclear war by precluding an aggression against the Russian Federation and its allies'. In particular, it refers to the possible first use of Russian nuclear arms against a state 'which has allied relations with a nuclear state [and] attacks the Russian Federation, its territory, armed forces . . . or its allies' or a state which 'collaborates with a nuclear power in carrying out or supporting an invasion or an armed aggression against the Russian Federation . . . or its allies'.[15]

---

[14] Kile, S. and Arnett, E., 'Nuclear arms control', *SIPRI Yearbook 1996: Arms Control, Disarmament and International Security* (Oxford University Press: Oxford, 1996), pp. 628–29.

[15] See note 2.

In 1993–94 high-ranking Russian General Staff officers, who had participated in the formulation of the new military doctrine, simply admitted to Western experts that the question when nuclear arms had to be used in a critical military situation in order not to put Russia at risk in a conventional war would have to be resolved by setting lines of defence not to be breached by the attacking enemy since the Russian Army could no longer retreat as had formerly been possible on a geographical glacis outside Russian territory before bringing the superior forces to bear which would allow Russian arms to win.

This remark sums up quite well the historical experience and the traditional Russian military thinking for an initial defensive posture of limited forward strength at the beginning of a conflict. However, the military policy of Russia, as far as it can be identified and evaluated by means of the military doctrine and public statements by Russian officials, seems to be squarely based on conventional forces and contingencies in conflict short of general war, nuclear power or military aggression backed up by nuclear arms being held in reserve. In the past, the Soviet Union's preference for land-based strategic missiles (which had its operational and logistic reasons and suited the political demand for central control) largely froze the strategic posture into immobility, even after submarines were available for strategic missiles. This lack of flexibility gave way to flexible options with mobile intercontinental ballistic missile (ICBM) launchers, intermediate-range nuclear force (INF) systems and improved submarines in the late 1970s. However, the START II Treaty (the 1993 US–Russian Treaty on the Further Reduction and Limitation of Strategic Offensive Arms) reduces flexibility as it eliminates multiple warheads on land-based ICBMs. The nuclear posture will further revert to a limited retaliatory capability for a minimum deterrence.

Hence non-nuclear forces will remain as the main forces for armed conflict in Europe, and probably in Asia as well. This will have consequences for Russia's alliance and security policies. Russia would have to back up its allies with its conventional forces. The argument made by Russian military officers, that the independence of Central Asia brought with it 6000 km of borders to be guarded around Russia if the outer borders of the Commonwealth of Independent States (CIS) cannot be kept secure by a common defence and surveillance, emphasizes the value of territorial control and of territory as a shield against aggression. With this argument, Russian military thinking on security has come full circle on the pattern of Russian history. Security is equated with entrenchment in territorial defences and the radius of the perimeter must be as long as possible. Indeed, the Russian military doctrine, whatever it may be worth, like Soviet operational strategy for war until 1986–88, is still based on a resolute forward defence using all available territory beyond the Russian borders (then the USSR's borders), striking at the enemy on his own ground and pushing him back as fast and as far as possible without risk of overstretching, then delivering the decisive blows, with nuclear as well as conventional arms, at a safe distance from Russia if at all possible. Swift conflict termination 'to the advantage' of the Russian Federation remains the general aim.

IV. Extended security space

The military doctrine contains a brief comment on the situation and physical conditions of Russia: the development of the armed forces will take into account 'the geopolitical and geo-strategic situation of the country'.[16] This means, of course, the geographical, physical, economic, and therefore the strategic conditions for the defence and security of the Russian Federation as well as for its long-term strategies and policies.

In the context of the geopolitical and geo-strategic situation which the military doctrine takes into account, there are several constants: (a) the sheer physical size of Russia relative to all other European countries, comparable only with Canada and the USA, which remains a dominant feature even without the Western border lands or the Caucasus; (b) the related essential quality of Russia as a Eurasian country with most of its still valuable natural resources in Siberia; and (c) outside the Russian Federation but partly inside the CIS, the geographical area of transition and contest between Russia and the West with the Baltic states, Poland, Belarus, Ukraine, Hungary, Romania, Bulgaria and the Caucasus forming the historical theatre of conflicts with Sweden, Turkey, Austria, France and later Germany.

Throughout history, the most significant factors have been time and space— the result of territorial depth and long distances for lines of communication. They have determined the outcome of many conflicts and to a great degree the Russian infrastructure, with Moscow in the centre of European Russia and St Petersburg in the far north-west, each with a specific historical value and national significance for the political evolution and territorial expansion of Russia. Russian economic development has been conditioned by them and has been governed by security and defence considerations as much as by the location of necessary natural resources: attempts were made to synthesize political– economic choices and military considerations in the building of industries as long as this was possible. However, the distances to the exposed western or southern borders and the distances between the resources and the markets have often combined to create conflicts between objectives and decisions.[17]

Time and space remain a formidable challenge to Russia's security thinking: (a) the changing relevance of the concepts of defensible borders, a strategic glacis, territorial depth and the 'central position' for Russia's defence; (b) the meaning and usefulness of territorial expansion for increased security in case of conflict; (c) the significance of numerically superior forces, redundancy of operational capabilities and available reserves; (d) the value of war potential and mobilization capacity related to the lead time needed to bring these reserves

---

[16] See note 2.
[17] Stalin's decision to transfer large parts of industry from western Russia and Ukraine to far away in the east in order to create a protected war production base out of reach of an invader from the west carried the liability of compounding the logistic support problems of national defence on a western front once the remaining close production base was lost. It was, however, the right decision to make before 1941.

into play; and (e) the relationship between offensive and defensive options and force structures for Russian military strategy and external policy.

Political rationales for thinking in terms of 'extended security' are even more indicative. They are expressed in frequent references to a Russian 'sphere of special responsibilities and interests', which stretches over the post-Soviet space around the Russian Federation, to 'Russia's special role and responsibility within the former Soviet Union', since it is 'a stabilizing factor', and to Russia's great-power status which it is 'predestined' to retain, even in 'a period of transitional difficulties'.[18]

These references anchor present concepts of the security and defence requirements of the Russian Federation firmly in the imperial past, whatever the political intentions of the Russian Government of the day. What could be the influence of Russia's centuries of experience as a great power? Does the conviction that Russia is predestined to remain a great power have an impact on its foreign policy and security concepts beyond national defence (whatever 'national' may mean in the case of the Russian Federation)? There is not necessarily an imperialist temptation in Moscow, nor an 'imperial consciousness as a national trait of the Russian people' at work behind contemporary developments. On the contrary, the peaceful reintegration of the former Soviet republics into a common framework such as an organized CIS, centred around Russia for mainly economic reasons, can be a legitimate objective of Russian policy within the post-Soviet geopolitical space.

The CIS could also organize common security and defence so long as they were based on the mutual consent of the partners. The 1993 military doctrine envisages this option, since it considers the CIS as the 'priority' framework of international cooperation for the common purpose of 'solving collective defence and security problems and coordinating issues relating to military policy and defence building'.[19]

It follows that Moscow seems to have an understanding of greatness related to power as defined by technological and military capabilities, based on important national resources, hence on valuable territory, protected by a geopolitical–geo-strategic space under Russian control and structures of economic integration, centred around Russia. Is should be noted that Russia's active campaign against an expansion of NATO to the east is based on classic geopolitical–strategic arguments: that to extend NATO to East–Central Europe would mean undermining the existing strategic balance created by the 1990 Treaty on Conventional Armed Forces in Europe (the CFE Treaty) between the North Atlantic alliance and the then existent Warsaw Treaty Organization; that it would destroy the status quo in Europe as defined in 1990 between Gorbachev

---

[18] Kozyrev, A., 'The lagging partnership', *Foreign Affairs*, May/June 1994, pp. 59–71.

[19] The founders of the CIS had this purpose in mind when in 1991–92 they concluded agreements on strategic forces and other aspects of common defence. A 'defence community' did not materialize after 1991, but it remains a possibility based on common interests and 'space'.

for the USSR and the four NATO powers in the agreement on the unification of Germany;[20] and so on.

A virtual geopolitical reality emerges from these arguments—the former Soviet Union, that is, the last form and configuration of the Russian Empire. Whether this now non-existent entity is considered in formal terms as the collection of all former Soviet republics or only as those which have become members of the CIS, that is, whether the three Baltic states are excluded, is another matter. It is, however, quite clear that Moscow entertains a notion of historical and geopolitical continuity to which the expression 'near abroad' is obviously related (even if it is no longer used in official parlance).

Acquisition of territory alone cannot shield a country, even if it does provide a strategic glacis to fight a defensive war and buy time with terrain in order to reinforce and redeploy for a counter-offensive. This has been the historical case of Russia *vis-à-vis* the West. The 1993 military doctrine seems to rely on this historical experience, since it envisages forward deployment of Russian troops as 'stationed forces in allied countries' and Russian military installations outside the Russian Federation.

The military doctrine names several 'main existing and potential sources of military threat outside the Russian Federation',[21] of which four are relevant to Russian security in classical geopolitical terms, concerning territory beyond the national borders: (*a*) 'existing and potential seats of local wars and armed conflicts, above all in direct proximity to the Russian borders'; (*b*) 'the suppression of rights, freedoms and legitimate interests of citizens of the Russian Federation in foreign states'; (*c*) 'attacks on military facilities of the armed forces of the Russian Federation situated on the territory of foreign states';[22] and (*d*) 'expansion of military blocs and alliances to the detriment of the interests of military security of the Russian Federation'.

A number of further contingencies are envisaged and evaluated as 'factors which facilitate the escalation of military danger into a direct military threat to the Russian Federation', all of which are relevant to the territorial notion of security: (*a*) 'the build-up of troops on the borders of the Russian Federation to limits which upset the existing balance of forces'; (*b*) 'attacks on the facilities and structures on the state border of the Russian Federation and the borders of its allies, border conflicts and armed provocations'; (*c*) 'the training of armed formations and groups on the territory of other states for dispatch to the territory of the Russian Federation and its allies'; (*d*) 'actions of other countries which hinder the operation of the logistics systems of the Russian strategic

---

[20] President Yeltsin's messages of Sep. 1993 to the 4 principal NATO allies in Europe were significant. Reuter, 30 Sep. 1993; and Rühl (note 10), pp. 344–45. The letter to US President Clinton is reproduced in *SIPRI Yearbook 1994* (Oxford University Press: Oxford, 1994), pp. 249–50; For further detail on this implicit bargain, see an interview given by Col-Gen. Boris Gromov in *Die Welt*, 12 June 1995, p. 5. Discussion continues. Gorbachev, M., *Erinnerungen* [Memoirs] (Siedler: Berlin, 1995), p. 1109; and Zelikov, P., 'NATO expansion wasn't ruled out', *International Herald Tribune* (Paris edn), 10 Aug. 1995.

[21] See note 2.

[22] While Russian forces may be stationed far away from the Russian Federation, since their complete withdrawal in 1994 from Germany and Poland the situation envisaged here can only apply to members of the CIS, including Georgia and Moldova.

nuclear forces . . . above all their space-borne elements'; and (*e*) 'the deployment of foreign troops on the territory of states adjacent to the Russian Federation', unless this is done to restore or maintain peace, in accordance with a decision of the UN Security Council or a regional agency of collective security, and by agreement with the Russian Federation.

The formulation 'no foreign forces are to be deployed to countries bordering on the Russian Federation without Russian consent' means a *droit de regard* for Russia on the relations of all these neighbours with other countries and 'military blocs and alliances', and in fact amounts to a claim of a veto power for Russia. Taken literally, it means that in joining NATO or allowing Western forces on their territory, Azerbaijan, Belarus, Estonia, Finland, Georgia, Latvia, Poland or Ukraine would facilitate the emergence of 'a direct military threat' to Russia. The old Soviet notion of encirclement and the isolation of Russia by the West or by the outside world as a whole reappears in the logic of this formulation. Stalin's phrase of 1943, a 'Polish corridor' for the invasion of Russia,[23] rings in these phrases as well as in warnings against a cordon sanitaire policy designed to isolate Russia, following the example of the allied powers in 1917–20 and of containment after 1946.

Generally speaking, this part of the military doctrine corresponds exactly to the old geopolitical view of a buffer zone around Russia where no foreign forces and no foreign alliances or military blocs (such as the Western European Union, the WEU, which Stalin called a military 'bloc' in 1948) are supposed to operate. This is essentially an 'exclusion zone', but it amounts to a Russian claim of a sphere of special relations and privileged interests with a Russian *droit de regard* on the foreign and security policy of such countries in East–Central Europe and Central Asia. (It may be assumed that China and Japan are exempt from this rule.)

The positive notion in this concept, drawn from the historical pattern of territorial thinking in Russia on security and applied to the present strategic situation of the Russian Federation, lies in the virtual description of a Russian area of at least indirect political dominance, based upon common borders and the former shared status as Soviet republics in the USSR. Taken together with reintegration within the CIS and the possible creation of a defence community, official Russian security thinking shows the historical pattern for the reconstruction of a geopolitical–geo-strategic unity in the area of the former Soviet Union.

This, however, implies the challenging task of operating partly across borders which are politically unsafe and even contested.

The case of Crimea is probably the most critical one, since Sevastopol is an original Russian creation as a naval base and there are no alternatives for support of a larger fleet in the Russian part of the Black Sea. Here the importance of territory for security and defence is obvious. The quarrel between Russia and Ukraine about both the former Soviet Black Sea Fleet and Crimea is truly

[23] Laloy (note 10).

strategic beyond the political issue of territorial control and borders. Without the secure use of the Crimean ports and supply bases in conflict, Russia cannot maintain an operational fleet of international importance in the Black Sea. Here the historical reason for extending Russian sovereignty to Crimea, which determined Russian policy from the late 17th to the 19th century and prompted the Western–Turkish assault on Sevastopol in the Crimean War, is still valid. Even if international relations are no longer a priori conflictual, the possession of Crimea or at least the use of its naval ports is still of value to Russia. The same applies to Russian maritime trade and civil navigation. The entire strategic situation in the Black Sea area revolves around the central position of Crimea.

The Baltic states present a similar, equally important problem. The Baltic ports west of St Petersburg and Kronshtadt were of great value to Russia in the 18th and 19th centuries. Possession of this coast was a strategic objective for Peter I and Catherine II as it had been in the 16th century for Ivan IV. However, the geopolitical significance of the Baltic Sea changed fundamentally in the 20th century even before the two world wars and the demise of both German and Russian power. At the end of this stormy century, Northern Europe has no 'northern power', as both Sweden and Russia were once called; it has become entirely dependent on Western Europe, of which it will become an integral part if the process of integration in the European Union (EU) continues.

The demise of the Soviet Union has almost completely undone Russia's historical achievements. The basis of Russian naval power has been reduced to a sub-strategic level, and a large Russian Baltic Fleet is neither useful nor possible under the changed conditions. It is true that, since the western border of Russia has fallen back between 600 and 700 km in the northern and 1300 km in the southern part, the territorial glacis is gone in any case. The loss of most of the Baltic coast is marginal compared to the loss of Ukraine with Crimea. On the other hand, Russia is at peace in Europe and can consolidate itself as a European power without the command of the Baltic and Black seas. The strategic air and anti-missile defences are no longer needed against NATO.

However, even in a peaceful international environment, control of outer territories beyond the Russian border can offer a lasting advantage for the security and even more for the European importance and influence of Russia. It can be argued that in the Baltic area Russian military thinking has to deal with a transitory situation, not with long-term strategic forward deployments of Russian forces. The Russian forces have been withdrawn and the strategic radar installation in Latvia belongs more to the Soviet past than to the Russian future. However, there remains the exclave of Kaliningrad between Lithuania and Poland, which could become the cause of new tensions.

More important is the political relevance of the Baltic situation to Russia's relations with the EU and the West generally. Will it be political cooperation or isolation? Will the Western policy be that of the outstretched hand or containment of Russia? Here, the political meaning of security is more important than the military meaning. In such situations, any concept of military security in territorial terms of control and forward deployment of armed forces on a strategic glacis risks being self-defeating in as much as it may antagonize the neighbouring countries and create a politically hostile environment. This would be the political price to be paid by Russia for dominance over a Baltic 'near abroad'. Such dominance is not possible without aggression and permanent conflict.

The Russian geopolitical–strategic notion of territory, deeply embedded in Russian history and thinking and enhanced above all by Stalin's annexation in 1940 and again in 1944–45, tends to alarm the newly independent Baltic states and also Finland, Poland and Sweden. If there is a 'cold peace' to be had for Russia, to use Russian President Boris Yeltsin's term at the December 1994 Budapest summit meeting of the Conference on Security and Co-operation in Europe (CSCE), then it will be in the north if Russia puts pressure again on the Baltic states. EU and NATO enlargement could thus take on a confrontational character *vis-à-vis* Russia, in order to shield this part of Europe from reintegration by force into a Russian 'near abroad' or 'sphere of strategic interests'.

V. The problem of allies

The decisive question about security with allies for common defence in conflict is about shared objectives and central control by mutual agreement. There are examples in Russian history of failed alliances as there are of useful ones.

The Holy League alliance with Austria and Venice against the Ottoman Empire, which Peter the Great found in place at the time of his accession to power in 1694 as a left-over from Golitsyn's unsuccessful attack on Crimea during Sophia's regency and tried to use to his advantage, was an example of an alliance which did not bring Russia results, even though it was renewed in Vienna in February 1697. The Austrian victory in the battle of Zenta in early September 1697 changed the Emperor's perspective in view of the approaching end of the Spanish dynasty and the inevitable conflict with France over the succession. The Peace of Carlovitz of 1699 was negotiated with Turkey at Russian expense. Peter's claim to win Kerch in Crimea was abandoned by the Austrians when Turkey simply refused it.

This is a case in point for the complexities and political risks of coalition warfare. Peter had entered the European scene as a junior actor of secondary importance to the play on the stage. Russia's interests were neglected by the Tsar's Western allies since Russia was remote and Russian military contributions to the war against the Turks had been marginal. Larger interests were at stake in the West. The envisaged Spanish succession would almost coincide with the succession to the vacant Polish throne, for which Austria and France were vying, and Turkish concessions were needed by the Emperor in Vienna to buy the election of his candidate, Augustus II of Saxony, with the return of Turkish-held Podolia to the Polish Crown.

In the West the other coalition war against France was swiftly brought to an end after the victory at Rijswijk by large French concessions to Austria, Britain and Holland in the same month. The Tsar's voyage through Europe with his visits in the Western capitals had no influence on the decisions of the old powers. Russia was disregarded as an ally without further use and out-manoeuvred.

The case of the Franco-Russian alliance of the 1890s and the common war against the Central Powers in 1914–17 was different in purpose and importance as it occurred in an entirely different European setting. Again it turned out to be a failed alliance, this time with catastrophic consequences for Imperial Russia as well as for the Russian nation and the whole of East–Central Europe. This time Russia was a vital ally for Britain and France. Russia was engaged by France to make a massive military contribution at a high price in Russian blood from the start in order to divide the German Army in a war on two fronts and reduce the German forces on the Western theatre at the beginning as during the entire duration of the war. The Russian commitment was essential for France's defence and capability to win against Germany. The military conventions between the French and the Russian general staffs before the war required the Russian Army to deliver a forceful offensive against East Prussia and the Vistula in the first weeks after mobilization in order to penetrate into the Prussian heartland and pose a direct threat to Berlin. It was, however, obvious from the correlation of forces that the Russian Army was incapable of such an offensive à l'outrance which the Russian railways could not support against Germany and Austria. Any large-scale offensive in the European theatre was therefore handicapped by lack of support and supply on the rails, while auto-mobile transport was limited and not available for large loads, and the roads could not carry much.

The war supply situation on the import side was almost as bad. The new Murmansk railway would be usable only in 1916 and the Trans-Siberian Rail-way did not reach Vladivostok until 1917. Hence goods imported from the West and Far East to the open-sea ports not blockaded by the Central Powers could not be transported by rail to sustain the Russian war production and to arm the Russian forces in time.

Every single technical, economic and logistic consideration pleaded for a Russian defence on the Western borders to hold a German–Austrian offensive and simply immobilize the enemy until a more favourable balance of forces could be achieved. This meant a longer war, and Russia was unable to sustain a long war because of its still limited industrial capabilities for arming the large army which was called up and put to the front; mobilization had critically reduced agricultural manpower and hence grain production. Social tensions were the consequence of reduced supplies to the cities because of the growing demand by the army. The war with the distant allies of the West against the German neighbours pushed Russia against the limits of endurance from the very first day. Only a swift victory could have saved the Russian Empire from ultimate defeat, but its forces were insufficient against the combined German and Austrian armies, given the national Russian war aims in Galicia and against

Turkey in eastern Anatolia. The contradictions and discrepancies of Russia's strategic situation could not be surmounted.

In consequence, Russia could not enter the war with the time-honoured optimal national military strategy—initial defence in depth, which would have been difficult and risky for the Russian war economy in any case, because of the location of a large part of the production base in the west of the country. This economic asset was duly lost to the Germans after the initial Russian successes against Austria in the south-west in 1917–18, and with it, and the exorbitant losses of the Russian Army which helped to save France and even Italy until the critical terminal phase in 1918, the empire of the Tsar.

Stalin seems to have had these lessons in mind and to have acted on them between 1938 and 1945. His policy was to enter a war only once the Western powers were definitely and actively engaged against Germany and the war could be fought with limited risk and a permanent Soviet option to withdraw with the initial gains safe.[24] The same strategy was pursued *vis-à-vis* Japan and China in the Far East.

Stalin's war strategy still needs elucidation and critical analysis. With this qualification, however, it can be said that the USSR pursued a successful war effort in a strategic as well as in an operational sense from late 1941 under extremely difficult and risky conditions after having lost again, as in 1915–17, about 25 per cent of the production base.[25] This effort would not have been successful or even sustainable had it not been for considerable Western help from 1942 onwards.

This time, coalition war with the Western powers proved to be to the USSR's advantage. The Great Alliance, as Winston Churchill called it, did not fail. Stalin's Red Army won the greatest military victory in Russian history, comparable only to that of 1812–15 under Alexander I against Napoleonic France.[26] Most of Stalin's war goals in Europe were, at least for one historic moment, reached in as much as an historical pattern re-emerged from the Baltic to Poland and Germany via the Danube and the Balkans to the Middle East.

Stalin's political strategy of forward power projection in war had used the Western Alliance in a two-front effort to make the most of the opportunities offered by coalition warfare from two opposing directions. In this situation no really coordinated war effort was necessary and disagreements on the post-war order of Europe could be left open for a time after the common victory. The

---

[24] Stalin's instructions to the Soviet Ambassador in London, Mayskiy, in the summer of 1939 made this abundantly clear. In view of this it is immaterial whether Stalin did or did not prepare an option of offensive war against Germany from early 1941 onwards. Soviet forces were not launched against the Germans.

[25] The losses after the successful German offensive in the initial stages of the war amounted to about 30 000 factories, 50% of steel production, 65 000 km of railway track, 15 800 locomotives, 428 000 railway flat cars, 4200 river boats, 137 000 tractors and the whole of Ukrainian and west Russian agriculture.

[26] It is interesting that in Potsdam in 1945 Stalin made the comparison with Alexandrine Russia in 1814–15: he answered a compliment to the effect that it had been a great achievement to take the Red Army to Berlin with the recorded remark that the Tsar had taken the Russian Army to Paris. Even short of the French border, the expansion of Soviet power was epochal.

separate war operations in Europe against Germany permitted separate, even opposing political strategies with military means. In this sense, the Great Alliance was incomplete and politically even inconclusive beyond the occupation of Germany by the Allies from both directions—and of all of East–Central Europe by the Red Army. In the Soviet Russian interest it did not need to be complete or lasting since Soviet communism and Western liberal democracy shared no common goals beyond defeating Germany. The anti-fascist alliance was only a loose coalition of temporary if vital interests.

The common purpose was consummated almost before the war ended, when Poland was submitted to communist rule and Soviet conditions for an alliance with the USSR, as were Romania, Bulgaria, later Hungary and still later Czechoslovakia, Yugoslavia in a somewhat different but still pro-Soviet communist political setting, and Albania. Stalin made precautionary concessions to the Western Allies in Finland and Austria, while the fate of Greece remained unsettled. However, he had effectively opposed Turkish participation in the terminal war effort and prevented a Western Balkans campaign which would have competed with the advance of the Red Army and frustrated Soviet post-war political strategy in South-Eastern Europe.

In all, the war alliance served the Soviet Union well from Europe to the Far East, even if not all Stalin's objectives in China were achieved and Japan remained out of reach as a US conquest. However, the experience could hardly be repeated and it cannot serve as an example for future Russian policy, since the unique historical situation cannot be re-created.

The post-Soviet setting confirms that a defensive strategy can be bolstered by strong and willing allies. Their territory, if adjacent to Russia proper, can form a military glacis playing an important role for the defence of Russia. However, the geopolitical configuration of East–Central Europe has fundamentally changed, to Russia's disadvantage in a conflict. The western frontiers of Russia have fallen back roughly to the borders of Muscovy towards the end of the 16th century after Ivan IV lost the First Nordic War and all the territorial gains in the north-west. The entire military infrastructure for wartime deployment of Russian armies to the west has been lost with the independence of the Baltic states, Belarus and Ukraine, including the historical garrison areas held since the early 18th century.

Can Russia and Ukraine agree on common defence and security, and under what conditions? Without a common interest *vis-à-vis* other countries or Western Europe as a whole, there can be no agreement. The case of Belarus is ambiguous, and in any case not closed. Defence cooperation between Russia and Belarus seems possible and useful for Russia. With Ukraine, however, a *rapprochement* would have to go much farther towards Moscow than even the pro-Russian politicians in Kiev envisage as being compatible with Ukrainian independence inside the CIS, in order to recreate a common defence organization of substance and efficiency.

The case of the Baltic states is similarly critical in naval military terms and even more critical in political ones. Russia needs cooperation with the EU on a long-term basis for economic and political reasons. Territorial and naval criteria of Russian security will have to be brought into line with long-term peacetime political objectives. For this reason alone, the withdrawal from the Baltic states was necessary in Russia's own higher interest as a European country. At the same time there is no foundation left for any kind of common security and defence between Russia and the three Baltic states, especially bearing in mind their wish to join NATO in order to be protected against Russia.

Thus, on both western flanks Russia has to cut back military defences because of loss of territory. The Caucasian border is in doubt. The only option for allies lies within the CIS and within borders which appear to be politically unsafe on the Russian side and even contested. Contested, unsafe, mobile borders to the west and south were part of the features of Muscovy's situation *vis-à-vis* the immediate neighbours.

Where the solution to this problem lies is uncertain. Classical military solutions are no longer applicable and would not be tolerated politically by Europe. The price to be paid would be Russia's isolation and a renewal of former Western containment policies. Hence the historical notion of the all-important possession and military control of territory, the former policy of security by expansion, or in this case by recovery of lost lands around the Russian heartland, can no longer be the solution to Russia's security and defence equation in the changed geopolitical environment.

Nor is such a solution necessary, since Russia no longer confronts a hostile Europe and since the perspective of cooperative rather than confrontational security with the West was opened in 1990. There is room for Russia to be secure within the Organization for Security and Co-operation in Europe (OSCE)[27] and in partnership with NATO. How far this opportunity is perceived in Russia and how it can be used are other matters. It is noteworthy, however, that there are numerous signs of an adequate assessment of this new situation—both in the Russian military doctrine of 1993, notwithstanding all its conventional wisdom and traditional thinking, and in the official statements by members of the Russian Government on foreign policy and international security.

VI. Conclusions

The fundamental change in the significance of defence and security has not only reduced and largely neutralized the protective value of territory and sea room beyond the coast against missiles and aircraft carrying weapons of mass destruction or with precision-guided stand-off weapons against defended and protected targets. There is no sanctuary any more and defence of the heartland has become irrelevant as a concept unless an impenetrable as well as resilient anti-missile/anti-air defence can be organized and reliably maintained operational at all times and under all physical conditions.

---

[27] On 1 Jan. 1995 the CSCE became the OSCE.

The demographic, economic and environmental dimensions of international security have added challenges to national and regional security, which cannot be dealt with successfully either by one country, even one as large as Russia, or predominantly with military means even if such means were abundant. Nuclear, chemical and biological warfare could cancel out the advantage offered in former times by numerically larger forces, space and distance to the enemy. Under these circumstances, Russia as all other countries with values to protect must rely less on military capabilities and classical space–time/force ratios for the calculation of its security in conflict, and rather more on cooperative arrangements and arms control.

This even applies to deterrence and to counter-proliferation against the spread of nuclear, chemical and biological means of destruction, including terrorism. Such proliferation and its possible consequences have become the most dangerous security risk for Russia as for most other European, Middle Eastern and Asian countries. In this perspective, special forces, rapid-deployment forces for long-range airborne operations, a high-performance air force and air defence with an anti-missile capability in selected directions of threat to Russia and, last but not least, high-quality nuclear forces over all ranges for minimal deterrence with flexible options against selected relevant targets seem to be indispensable.

Russia would probably have to reassess the value of all these tools in the light of its own historical experience. History also provides Russia with various patterns of alliance relationship. They have not always served Russia well in the past. They did not during World War I, when Russia had to fight in strategic isolation and Russian forces were overtaxed by the demands of the Western allies, but did serve Russia well in 1813–15 and the USSR in 1941–45. A defensive strategy can be bolstered by close allies. For Russia such allies may be valuable again. In a broader sense, a formidable challenge would be a common security pattern under agreed political conditions. This might seem to be the essence of a strategic partnership with the USA and NATO. There is no 'splendid isolation' any more and no great power has the forces and the remoteness to war and global insecurity necessary to hold a balance of power to its own advantage. The answer to the problems lies in general policy and mental attitude. Here the lessons from the past and historical traditions can only serve a useful purpose, provided they are reviewed critically.

3. The 'Russian Question'

Robert Legvold

I. Introduction

Some nations are 'more equal than others', not simply because they may be richer, larger or more powerful but because their quest to find themselves affects the fortunes of nearly every other state. For almost 150 years, Germany was one such country: from the time of German unification in 1870 under Chancellor Otto von Bismarck until the unification of the country under Chancellor Helmut Kohl in 1990, Germany's struggle to sort out both its national identity and its international role had a pivotal influence on world politics. Whatever the regime or historical era, the 'German Question' cast its long shadow over the character and course of international events. What Germany was becoming or might become always greatly distracted the other major international powers. Germany always represented a challenge for them, either because it was disproportionately powerful or because it was disruptively weak. In particular, Germany's uncertain, sometimes threatening, sometimes stabilizing, but always substantial impact on its immediate neighbours created turbulence in the existing international order.

Russia has the potential to become our era's counterpart to Germany. Its unfinished search for identity, its unresolved relationship with neighbouring states and its unpredictable political future already agitate European politics. The agitation, however, could be much greater. Thus, when the topic turns to Russian foreign policy and European security, too much is at stake not to push matters, not to take from history as much as one can.

Vast differences, of course, distinguish the German and Russian cases, and to suggest a parallel is not to imply the possibility of guessing what comes next for Russia and Europe on the basis of earlier experience. Not even the comparison that seems to many observers to be the closest—between the ill-fated Weimar Republic (1919–33) and contemporary Russia—offers enough to justify predictions. The comparison is not offered on the mistaken assumption that a precise analogy exists between the histories of these two countries or between any particular German era and the present moment in Russia, but it is not intended as merely a literary device. There are lessons and insights to be gathered from the earlier experience. Perspectives on the present can be enlarged by reflecting on these antecedents, lessons and insights—by considering, in particular, the way the international environment, fundamental domestic realities and human agency shaped outcomes in the German instance.

Despite the contrasts between Bismarck's and Hitler's Germany or even between Wilhelmine (before World War I) and Weimar Germany, the German Question endured for three reasons. First, at every stage Germany remained a country struggling to establish its place among other nations as a power on the rise, as a pariah, as, in its own eyes, a victim, as a victimizer, and ultimately as a state torn asunder. Second, Germany's relations with neighbouring states never escaped the effects of ethnic Germans residing beyond its borders or, alternatively, of a single German state fractured into two, or many, parts. Third, over the decades, a stunted or distorted relationship between state and society complicated German behaviour abroad, usually for the worse. Russia, too, struggles today with its place among other nations; it, too, brings to relations with neighbours the frustrations of a truncated state, one with great numbers of ethnic Russians living beyond its borders; and its foreign policy suffers the burdens and passions of a half-formed political order encompassing a weakly integrated citizenry.

Out of this come the two fundamental concerns of this chapter. First, to have judged the German Question in its day or to judge the 'Russian Question' today merely by the policies emanating from these states misses much. If uncertainty hangs over the future course of Russian policy, ultimately the reasons are profound. They involve not simply who, what, when and how, but the biography of Russia itself. They are imponderables at a deep structural level, involving stages of development and the potential consequences of building democracy (as opposed to having built it). Second, in this situation, the actions of others and, even more so, the understandings guiding their actions are more fateful than at less dramatic moments. More is at stake than the normal intercourse of states—more even than the challenge of coping with a particular state's ambitions and frustrations. The condition of international politics itself is at issue.

II. Russia and the problem of European security

If Europe faces a future Russian Question, it is likely to share with its German predecessor two elemental qualities. First, with the clear exception of the Nazi period and to a degree Kaiser Wilhelm II's reign, the challenge raised by Germany for Europe stemmed from circumstance rather than from German malevolence. The challenge arose not because German leaders (except Hitler) rejected the existing international order and meant to overthrow it, but because the pursuit of national interest unloosed or promised to unloose a chain of reactions ending in great, even fatal instability. In 1906 an Englishman, J. L. Garvin, wrote: 'Suspicious of all sentimentalities in foreign affairs, we have always acknowledged that from the German point of view the aims of German foreign policy are entirely justified. The only objection to them is that in no point of the world can they be realized without threatening the security and independence of existing states or destroying their present order. That is not the fault of the German nation, it is its misfortune'.[1]

From this followed Europe's historic dilemma: 'Germany', again, borrowing from Pierre Hassner, 'has always been either too weak or too strong for Europe'.[2] It has also, he added, been a country whose 'division . . . was no more natural than her unity'.[3] So, at least, it seemed in the mid-1960s when Hassner wrote, and the essence of the East–West order was a divided Germany at the core of a divided Europe. Eventually German unity was restored, but for this to happen the collapse of Soviet power was needed, an event which only brought unification about; it did not in itself make the process 'natural'. For German unity to become 'natural', that is, for both a unified Germany and a viable European order to exist, something else was needed. (This 'something else' is discussed below, since it has a bearing on the issue of Russia and Europe.) In the face of this dilemma, Hassner argued, throughout the ages European nations acted more wisely when making Germany's neighbours strong than when plotting ways to render Germany weak.

This leads directly to a second quality at the heart of Europe's historical relationship with Germany and, now, with Russia: neither country's security could or can be separated from that of the rest of Europe. To have thought that the peace and tranquillity of Europe might be distinguished from the agonies, anxieties and ambitions of Germany would have been utterly pointless. To have believed that Germany could pursue its own national interests, security and destiny without complicating the fate of Europe would have been no less deceptive. Russian fortunes and European stability, in all likelihood, are inextricably related to one another. It would be foolish to assume that Europe can insulate itself from what happens to Russia or within the space of the former Soviet Union. Equally so, a Russia that imagines itself free or even obliged to counter threats on its own will corrupt far more than its immediate surroundings.

General propositions like these, basic as they may be, are helpful only up to a point. European and Russian security may indeed be intertwined, but with what precise effect? How is Russian behaviour or the relations between Russia and its neighbours likely to alter the well-being and safety of the rest of Europe? Conversely, how might different approaches to European security affect Russian behaviour and the course of events in the eastern part of Europe?

The place to begin is with what could go wrong; not with specific scenarios, whose numbers may be infinite, but with general categories of calamity. Viewed in this way, the potential dangers seem to be fourfold, beginning with the grandest and most straightforward threat.

Historically Europe's gravest moments arrive when the agenda and behaviour of a major European state or combination of states threaten the international

---

[1] Quoted in Hassner, P., International Institute for Strategic Studies, *Change and Security in Europe,* Part II, Adelphi Paper no. 49 (IISS: London, July 1968), p. 9.

[2] Hassner (note 1), p. 10.

[3] Hassner (note 1), p. 10, citing A. J. P. Taylor.

equilibrium of the area. In turn, however, this requires two things, neither of which is present today: (*a*) basic competition, mistrust and even antagonism between the great powers; and (*b*) a special momentum, dynamism or growing power in the state or states seen as threatening the equilibrium. By some stretch of the imagination Russia—and only Russia among Europe's great powers—might be thought of as a potential rebel against the status quo. Its discontents could eventually swell to something on this scale and its domestic politics could yet succumb to pathological twists. None the less, if this is to be Russia's fate, Europe's underlying equilibrium need not be endangered so long as Russia remains comparatively weak and relations among the other great powers are marked by what Soviet writers once liked to call 'non-antagonistic contradictions'. Since both conditions appear certain to endure for some time, the first of the four threats to European security considered here seems a remote one.[4]

General stability in Europe, however, need not be menaced directly by great collisions between the region's major powers. It could also be slowly undone by the creeping expansion of local conflicts, whether civil wars or regional conflicts. The threat will be greatest if the civil war or regional conflict occurs within or directly involves a major power. Long before Europe's other leading powers throw themselves into a fracas, the mere possibility that the outcome might affect their strategic interests—thereby creating the prospect of escalation—would shake the confidence on which European stability rests. In the case of the war in the former Yugoslavia, for instance, were the conflict to spread to Kosovo or Macedonia, drawing in even secondary players like Greece and Turkey, the anxiety level in Europe would rise instantly. The only plausible instances of turmoil where, from the start, a major power would be engaged and the strategic interests of other major West European powers might soon appear to be at stake involve Russia and its important neighbours—Belarus, Kazakhstan and Ukraine.

To consider a third category of trouble, even if in peacetime the insecurity of states in crucial parts of Europe were to mount significantly, the uncertainty and unpredictability introduced into the European system might be considerable. Security vacuums or 'grey zones' in key regions of Europe—even without the presence of clear-cut aggression by any major power, simply owing to the growth of local anxieties—might well raise doubts radiating far beyond the subregion itself. At a minimum, the importuning or, worse, the casting about by insecure states would add an unhappy ambiguity to European politics. If any part of Europe risks becoming a grey zone, it is East–Central Europe and the Baltic states. At the moment only Russia—whether deservedly or not—casts a shadow over this region, stirring uncertainties of this sort.

[4] The factors which at least at present militate against a return to the raw great-power competitions of the European past are being discussed and debated in many places, but one particularly clear statement of the case is in Jervis, R., 'The future of world politics: will it resemble the past?', *International Security*, vol. 17, no. 3 (winter 1991–92), pp. 39–73.

Finally, European security, to the degree that it derives from the welfare of societies, could be damaged or diminished by whatever threatens the social and economic well-being of the European powers and their common enterprises, such as the European Union (EU). The West European states themselves are the most serious source of threat in this case. If these states mishandle their domestic agendas, fall short in making the deep structural adjustments required by current socio-economic developments or fail to harmonize their actions and strategies as a group of states, European security will be compromised by them alone.[5] Other influences from outside could do damage, but for the very well-being of European countries to be touched, they would have to be almost grotesquely grand in scale. Once more, the only part of Europe capable of generating this degree of mayhem is the former Soviet Union. Only from the successor states of the USSR, and Russia most of all, could the numbers of refugees, the activities of organized crime, the volume of drugs, the flow of arms and fissile materials, or the effects of Chernobyl-scale nuclear disasters reach levels affecting even the healthiest European societies.

In the end, whether any or all of these dangers come to pass depends on the combined effect of powerful historical processes and human choice. Where Russia is concerned, these choices begin with what is by now a frequently noted reordering of preoccupations. Russia's first-order concern is with its nearest neighbours, the other successor states of the former Soviet Union. The key to its foreign policy orientation, the passionate focus of its attention and ultimately the well-spring of whatever challenge it poses to European security centre on the 'near abroad'. Russia's relationship with the larger world, including its relations with the great powers and the West, is now a function of Russia's relations with the new post-Soviet states—not the other way around.

The other half of Russia's security preoccupation represents a still greater reshuffling of priorities since the Soviet era. It focuses even closer to home, in fact, on the domestic situation itself. Russians, in the current period of uncertain passage, worry about the stability of their society and think about the possibility of large-scale civil disorder, inter-regional violence and ethnic conflict paralleling the searing example of the former Yugoslavia. Even before the war in Chechnya, they worried enough to make this one of the two primary dimensions of national security and to insist that a reluctant military prepare to deal with it.[6] After Chechnya, theory has been turned into battle-hardened reality.

---

[5] For 2 European sources that make the same point, see Carlos Alonso Zaldivar's prologue to the Spanish-language version of the Carnegie Endowment's report *Changing Our Ways: The United States and the New World* (Estudios de Política Exterior: Madrid, 1994); and the report of the Netherlands Central Planning Office, *Scanning the Future*, cited in Alonso, p. 6. (Alonso was a policy planning adviser to then Spanish Prime Minister Felipe González.)

[6] The formal definition of Russia's national security requirements is most explicit in the new military doctrine adopted in Nov. 1993. *Izvestiya* published extensive excerpts from the military doctrine in 'Osnovnye polozheniya voennoy doktriny Rossiyskoy Federatsii' [The basic provisions of the military doctrine of the Russian Federation] on 18 Nov. 1993 and *Krasnaya Zvezda* published a slightly longer excerpt on 19 Nov. 1993. A translation into English was published by *Jane's Intelligence Review*, Special Report, Jan. 1994. For a full discussion, see chapters 8 and 9 in this volume.

On the other hand, Russia, according to the pronouncements of its leaders, no longer faces an explicit threat from any particular state or group of states, including any of the great powers. That has been the formal position, despite the angry clamour over NATO enlargement, and it is constructive to the extent that it helps people to think in these terms if they repeat the formula often enough. It should not, however, be seen as closing the matter. Even before second thoughts were stirred by plans to expand NATO into Central Europe, there was what might be called latent threat perception when it comes to the USA, NATO and, for that matter, China and Japan. For many Russians, the tendency to detect evil intent lurking behind objectionable Western initiatives remains strong. When the issue of NATO enlargement arises, or the West's stake in the security of the Baltic states, or the scope and direction of Russian arms sales abroad, an uncomfortably large percentage of politicians, significant portions of the media, and even some parts of the policy-making community instinctively view Western policies as not merely ill-advised or insensitive to Russian concerns but as aimed at diminishing or endangering Russia. During the uproar in the autumn of 1994 over the alleged smuggling of weapon-grade fissile materials from Russia, half a dozen Russian officials reacted indignantly, dismissing the accusations as more than a mistake—as a plot to sabotage Russia's domestic nuclear programme, to compromise Russia in the eyes of the outside world or to cloud Russian–German relations.[7] National leaders may be confident that NATO and the USA no longer belong on Russia's security agenda, but other political forces are less sure.[8]

Moreover, these long-nurtured instincts parallel the natural inclination of the Russian military to design forces and their missions with the aim of defeating any NATO move in the region of the former Soviet Union.[9] Perhaps in the normal course of events all major militaries measure themselves against the most formidable agglomerations of military power, wherever they may be and whatever the nature of the political atmosphere between nations. Perhaps the Russian military is doing no more than establishing an abstract benchmark against which to judge the adequacy of its forces, not responding to a perceived threat. Nevertheless, the precision with which various Russian military services imagine scenarios involving the large-scale use of NATO forces in the former Soviet Union, and the still greater precision with which they describe the

---

[7] For instance, Alexander Mikhailov, the spokesman for the Russian Federal Counter-Intelligence Service, called the charges 'part of a Western propaganda campaign' intended to bring 'Russian nuclear installations under Western control'. ITAR-TASS report, 17 Aug. 1994.

[8] Even clearer and more well-developed is the tendency to envisage China, with its size and dynamism, as an increasing strategic concern. Only a minority among élites (it is difficult to judge the proportion among the public) currently regard China as a threat to Russian security. Given the uneasiness that most feel when they contemplate the dynamism of the Chinese economy, however, it would not take much to convert this concern to an active fear.

[9] As an autumn 1994 report of the Russian Foreign Intelligence Service shows, the tendency to see US, NATO, Chinese and Japanese military power as part of the security challenge facing Russia is not confined to the Russian military. *Rossiyskaya Gazeta*, 22 Sep. 1994, pp. 1, 6.

capabilities the Russian Air Force or Army must have in order to prevail, seems to blur the line between planning yardsticks and genuine threat analysis.[10]

How short a step it is from abstract planning to a live fear of NATO has become evident in the debate over NATO enlargement. Not only have Russian politicians, including the president, delivered grim warnings of a renewed cold war and a divided continent, but leading military figures have threatened all manner of military retaliation, including the targeting of the prospective new members with nuclear weapons and the renewed forward deployment of tactical nuclear weapons. There has even appeared a military study, under auspices which are shadowy but suspiciously close to the Defence Ministry, suggesting that Russia should plan for a pre-emptive occupation of the Baltic states in the event of NATO moving to bring them into the alliance and emphasizing that the USA was once again the primary threat to Russian security.[11] Putting it mildly, thinking of this sort suggests that Russia's national security concept remains a work in progress.

III. The domestic setting: praetorianism and other deep structural factors

How these various dimensions of Russia's security agenda develop will depend heavily on the course of events within the country. That is to say, the extent to which Russia's behaviour and outlook influence the kind of threat that emerges in the surrounding region or within the country itself—or, for that matter, the likelihood of other great powers again being seen as a threat—will, in turn, be greatly affected by the evolution of the domestic political setting.

For some time, Russia's historic, ongoing internal transition has left a strong imprint on the country's foreign policy. Russia continues on its way from one political and economic system to another, and the consequences for foreign policy are more fundamental than those deriving from the normal course of domestic politics in a settled environment. Again, as with the German parallel, Russia's eventual relationship with neighbouring states and the larger European community of states remains a matter of deep trends within the society, not simply, as in any country, a question of which political personalities or parties control the helm of state.

The connection between democracy and international peace is again, as 75 years ago, being asserted (and contested) among Western social scientists and by the current US President.[12] The problem is that Russia is not a democracy

---

[10] For an excellent and revealing example of how this is being done in the Russian Air Force, see Arbatov, A., 'Russian air strategy in combat aircraft production: a Russian Air Force view', ed. R. Forsberg, *The Arms Production Dilemma: Contraction and Restraint in World Combat Aircraft Industry* (MIT Press: Cambridge, Mass., 1994), pp. 17–60.

[11] The report was issued by an organization called the Defence Research Institute. It was reported both by *Segodnya*, 20 Oct. 1995, and by Associated Press, 22 Oct. 1995.

[12] The standard literature cited includes: Doyle, M., 'Kant, liberal legacies and foreign affairs', *Philosophy and Public Affairs*, vol. 12, nos 3, 4 (1983), pp. 205–35, 323–33; and Russett, B. M., *Grasping*

and neither are most of the other post-Soviet states, including Ukraine. The most advanced among them—and Russia is among the most advanced—are what some would call pre- or proto-democracies.[13] Proto-democracy also has an impact on international politics and on issues of war and peace, but here concepts, let alone theory, are not nearly so well developed.[14]

Proto-democracies have democratic aspirations and some of the institutions essential to a fully functioning democracy, including, as Timothy Colton stresses, experience in 'the filling of key policy-setting offices through honest, competitive elections'.[15] In general, however, they are marked by weak political institutions and thus lack the means to mediate among powerful social forces and key political groupings. Similarly, they lack the means to mobilize, refine and moderate mass participation in the state. At the same time, unlike well-institutionalized political orders, political actors do not 'agree on the procedures to be used for the resolution of political disputes, that is, for the allocation of office and determination of policy'.[16] As a result, politics can jump the tracks, can explode beyond anything recognizable as falling within the rules of the game, much as they did in Russia in early October 1993, when President Boris Yeltsin's opponents incited their followers to violence and he answered by blowing up the parliament building.

Samuel Huntington, the source of these ideas, developed them to characterize a somewhat different political phenomenon dubbed the 'praetorian society', a setting where 'community and effective political institutions' are missing and, therefore, one prone to intervention on the part of the military.[17] Neither Russia, Ukraine nor most of the other post-Soviet states match any of the three types of Huntington's model, although they come closest to what he calls 'mass praetorianism'.[18] In mass praetorianism political participation by the populace—already considerable—is unstructured and inconstant, in contrast to what

the Democratic Peace: Priming for a Post-Cold War World (Princeton University Press: Princeton, N.J., 1993).

[13] Timothy Colton, borrowing from Joseph Schumpeter and others, invented the term for the post-Soviet states. Colton, T., 'Politics', eds T. Colton and R. Legvold, After the Soviet Union: From Empire to Nations (Norton: New York, 1992), pp. 22–38.

[14] A recent exception is Mansfield, E. D. and Snyder, J., 'Democratization and the danger of war', International Security, vol. 20, no. 1 (summer 1995), pp. 5–38.

[15] Colton and Legvold (note 13), p. 22.

[16] Huntington, S. P., Political Order in Changing Societies (Yale University Press: New Haven, Conn., 1968), p. 196.

[17] Huntington took the notion of praetorian society from the dissertation of David C. Rapoport, who describes it as a state where 'private ambitions are rarely restrained by a sense of public authority; [and] the role of power (i.e. wealth and force) is maximized'—a not inappropriate description of contemporary Russia, Ukraine and the other new post-Soviet states. Huntington (note 16), p. 81.

[18] Why they do not need not be explained here, but, in a nutshell, in Russia: (a) social forces are not so politicized as Huntington's model requires; (b) the challenge of incorporating new social forces into the polity is not so acute; (c) the clash across the urban–rural divide is not so great; and (d) the capacity and will of the military to dictate the course of the country are not so clear-cut. On the other hand, it is probably worth mentioning that when Russians define domestic disorder as a threat to national security and assign responsibility to the military for thwarting it, they are, in effect, creating an institutional basis for praetorianism.

Huntington calls a 'participant polity', where a 'high level of popular involvement is organized and structured through political institutions'.[19]

Russia may not qualify as a praetorian society but it and its neighbours could be praetorian societies in the making. Such was Germany under Kaiser Wilhelm II and during the Weimar Republic. Jack Snyder, whose argument is borrowed here, was the first to draw a parallel between Wilhelmine Germany, with its 'truncated democracy', special interests, weak voters and reform-ravaged masses, and the post-socialist societies of Eastern Europe and the Soviet Union.[20] In late 19th-century Germany, praetorian features, such as a parliament with authority but not responsibility, an executive controlled only by the Kaiser and dominated by 'the uneasy coalition of "iron and rye", including aristocratic Junker landowners, Ruhr heavy industrialists, Prussian bureaucrats, the army and the navy', and a manipulated rather than a represented public, had profound foreign-policy consequences.[21] For it is in such environments that the advantage goes to cohesive, parochial interests, often the more militaristic, protectionist and nationalistic elements in society, not to the broader public with its more diffuse and moderate inclinations.

To the extent that a critical aspect of the German Question originated in the distorted character of German politics, Wilhelmine Germany was hardly the only case in point. Weimar Germany suffered comparably. 'The extremists' sudden rise after 1930', Alfred Grosser notes, 'should not blind us to the fact that at any time after 1920 it was very hard to draw a dividing line between those who accepted the rules of the game and those who hoped to transform the regime into something of a more authoritarian stamp'.[22]

Lacking strong institutions, particularly those most able to draw citizens into the state constructively, dull the clash of social forces and transcend the natural advantages of special interests—such institutions as real political parties and a respected constitution with roots—Russia, like Germany in the latter half of the 19th and early part of the 20th century, remains vulnerable to unpredictable twists and turns of the political wheel and, more than other societies, to radical influences.[23] Indeed, at times the words of contemporary Russian commentators appear to come directly from the pages of Huntington's book. What one of

---

[19] Huntington (note 16), p. 88.

[20] Snyder, J., 'Averting anarchy in the new Europe', *International Security*, vol. 14, no. 4 (spring 1990), pp. 5–41. Snyder wrote this article before 1991 and therefore dealt with the Soviet Union, not Russia and the other post-Soviet states: nevertheless, his line of analysis applies still more to them.

[21] Snyder (note 20), p. 21. Snyder's argument extends a by now elaborate German school of thought concerning the *Innenpolitik* sources of late 19th-century German foreign policy. For a convenient English summary of this literature and the counter-view it has inspired, see Lowe, J., *The Great Powers, Imperialism and the German Problem, 1865–1925* (Routledge: London, 1994), pp. 143–49.

[22] Grosser, A., *Germany in Our Time: A Political History of the Postwar Years* (Praeger: New York, 1971), p. 9.

[23] There is no space here to be more specific about the contemporary Russian version of the general phenomenon that is being alluded to. Many of these manifestations are treated in the now rapidly expanding literature on 'political transitions', to which students of post-Soviet politics are contributing vigorously. For one good illustration, focusing on the weaknesses of political parties in Russia and the broad implications of this, see Dallin, E. (ed.), *Political Parties in Russia* (University of California at Berkeley: Berkeley, Calif., 1991).

them mislabels Russia's 'post-communist democracy' is said to be distinguished by 'its lack of social and political authority, aggravated by an unending struggle for power between various governmental branches, and its lawlessness and corruption'.[24] In this context, the author continues, 'the struggle for power is waged first for control over the rules and conditions of play within the system, and second for the means to determine the starting conditions for various groups of the old, managerial, CPSU [Communist Party of the Soviet Union] and state *nomenklatura* in the struggle to acquire [the bulk of state-owned] property'. 'The third coveted prize', he writes in unconscious imitation of Huntington, 'is the right to appeal to the "interests of the entire people" in order to be less vulnerable to popular discontent'. As Russia passes through this phase of its political development, it will be prone to deal with the outside world, particularly the new neighbours, awkwardly, perhaps aggressively, and certainly in a self-preoccupied fashion.

The reasons are profound, even structural or, seen another way, the product of stages of political development. The sobering implications of the German parallel are that: (*a*) pre-democracies do not rapidly evolve into stable, mature democracies;[25] and (*b*) even when the politics of the moment and the foreign policy emerging from them appear moderate and unexceptionable, the deeper structural vulnerability quietly endures. Hence, notwithstanding Bismarck's stabilizing effect or the initial promise of the Weimar Republic, when Bismarck's dextrous leadership was removed in 1890 or the Weimar Republic began to give way under the accumulated weight of its problems in the late 1920s, the underlying vulnerability reappeared and worked its deadly effect.

This is not the only way in which fundamental processes intrude. Beyond the recasting of state and society, nationalism, the powerful cousin of radical political change, is also stirring in Russia and neighbouring states. Modern thinking about nationalism—and, in particular, about the forces that cause nationalism to intensify and, at some point, to become pathological—bears directly on many of these issues. Treated not as a primeval, mystical impulse written into the genetic makeup of societies, but as a social and political construct, invented to a degree, nationalism becomes much more the comprehensible product of certain moments in the development of the state, certain political pressures and needs, and certain calculations on the part of intellectual, cultural and political leaders.[26] Nationalism, conceived not as a force of nature but as an alternative

---

[24] Kliamkin, I., 'The outlook for democracy in Russia', eds R. D. Blackwill and S. Karaganov, Center for Science and International Affairs, Harvard University, *Damage Limitation or Crisis? Russia and the Outside World*, CSIA Studies in International Security no. 5 (Brassey's: Washington, DC, 1994), p. 32.

[25] Huntington explains why it is hard to escape from 'praetorian disunity' into a civic polity. Huntington (note 16), pp. 237–41. Briefly, 'the more complex the society the more difficult it becomes to create integrating political institutions', and 'in [praetorianism's] more complicated forms, the lack of effective political institutions obstructs the development of community'.

[26] For the major works in this literature, see Gellner, E., *Thought and Change* (University of Chicago Press: Chicago, Ill., 1964); Gellner, E., *Nations and Nationalism* (Cornell University Press: Ithaca, N.Y., 1983); Anderson, B., *Imagined Communities: Reflections on the Origin and Spread of Nationalism* (Verso: London, 1983); and Smith, A. D., *Theories of Nationalism* (Duckworth: London, 1983). For an excellent application of their ideas to the Soviet and pre-Soviet example, see Suny, R. G., *The Revenge of the Past* (Stanford University Press: Stanford, Calif., 1993).

standard of loyalty—in this case, to the nation over, say, religion or clan—is the concomitant of the modern nation-state and necessary to enhance its capacities.[27]

Looked at in this way, however, the intensity and perniciousness of nationalism depend on how healthy and well-performing the nation-state is.[28] Thus, for example, aggressive economic nationalism often erupts out of the dislocation and unattended suffering resulting from either rapid industrialization or the shock of rapid moves towards a market economy, whether in the form of international competition or domestic reform. 'Wilhelmine nationalism . . . was stoked by the backlash from farmers, artisans and shopkeepers who demanded protection from the disruptive impact of international economic interdependence on their traditional market niches.'[29] The connection between the economic frustrations and anger of working-class Germans in the Weimar Republic and the direction in which German nationalism veered hardly needs to be pointed out. In Russia, from the first stages of economic and political reform, the crudest forms of nationalism allied instinctively with the fiercest opposition to markets and the price they exacted from different parts of society. To draw even tighter the link between these phenomena and the problem of proto-democracy, as Snyder notes, the weaker the political institutions bearing the burden of 'managing the process' of market reform, the faster and deeper the growth of nationalism.[30]

The two issues are tied together in a second respect. When the institutions essential for tempering and seasoning popular participation in government lack strength—again, institutions such as working political parties and a responsible free press—nationalism increases in strength. This occurs because nationalism becomes both a tool or gambit for threatened élites striving to undermine or co-opt the rising masses and the equally accessible recourse of the new elements who would replace them.

In Wilhelmine Germany, for example, old élites tried to use nationalism to split apart working- and middle-class proponents of political change, while counting on imperial successes to demonstrate the aristocracy's continued ability to govern. Middle-class groups, however, turned these arguments against the Junker ruling class, contending that the aristocratic army was too small and national diplomacy too conciliatory to meet the international threats that the old élites themselves had conjured up.[31]

Instead of a generally informed public, empowered by institutions to deflect extremist factions and discipline adventurist politicians, society becomes the tool of special interests and jingoistic organizations which, as Snyder says, 'use

[27] Suny uses the phrase 'force of nature' in describing the older, now questioned notion of nationalism. Suny (note 26), p. 7.

[28] Here, again, the cue is taken from an argument made by Jack Snyder. Snyder, J., 'Nationalism and the crisis of the post-Soviet state', *Survival*, vol. 35, no. 1 (spring 1993), pp. 5–26.

[29] Snyder (note 28), p. 14.

[30] Snyder (note 28), p. 16.

[31] Snyder (note 28). Snyder bases his point on Wehler, H. A., *The German Empire* (Berg: Leamington Spa, 1985); and Eley, G., *Reshaping the German Right* (Yale University Press: New Haven, Conn., 1980).

nationalism to create a smoke screen of illusory public-spiritedness'. National leaders also find it tempting in this environment to manipulate the public by stirring things up abroad—hence, for example, the Kaiser's telegram to Paul Kruger in the Transvaal in 1896, an attempt to stir German Anglophobia with the aim of enhancing public and Reichstag support for his pet naval project.[32]

There are still other ways in which the limitations of proto-democracy and the power of nationalism intersect, but enough has already been said to suggest that the future of Russian foreign policy does not rest exclusively on the normal interplay of politics, bureaucracy and the daily challenges of a complex world. The impact of the deep, unsteady transformation remaking the country also threatens to play its role. Until Russia has fashioned the critical institutions of a mature democracy and they have been given time to take root, no matter how tame its course at a given moment, the country will remain partial to simple and arbitrary solutions to problems with weaker nearby states. It will often act on hurt pride and suspicion in dealing with the great powers. It will also too easily accept unilateral, illiberal—that is, protectionist and militarized—responses to the challenges posed by the world outside.

Here, again, the example of Germany underscores the larger point. 'The same crisis that "caused" Hitler's rise to power in Germany', Grosser points out, 'led, in the United States, to Roosevelt's victory and the New Deal'.[33] The misery of economic depression and hardship 'increased by tenfold the general longing for a new order' in Germany. 'This longing was also felt in the United States, but there it was canalized by one of the two great parties within an accepted institutional system: the citizens and their leaders alike were confident in the power of democracy to bring about a new economic and social order'.[34] Germany 'presented a very different picture: the country was deeply divided, and the cry for a change from liberal democracy was all the stronger since the regime was of recent date and its leaders had suffered their power gradually to ebb away'.

The current reality in Russia is complex and far too elusive to be predicted by grand theory. Even without strong mediating institutions, the balance of forces in society need not favour impetuous, hypersensitive and aggressive policies. There may be groups, indeed, rather powerful groups, opposed to 'dangerous and costly imperial adventures'. So runs Sergei Karaganov's characterization of regional political élites in Russia, a potentially crucial influence in the increasingly decentralized Russian setting.[35] Nor does it automatically follow that interests such as those of the military, which are normally thought of as nationalistic and conservative, will invariably support reckless foreign policies. Russia's military leadership appears to be among the more sober voices when talk of using force outside Russian borders starts. To this the following considerations should also be added: (a) among contending political forces the centre of gravity seems to converge on a foreign policy that, while jealous of Russia's

[32] Kagan, D., *On the Origins of War* (Doubleday: New York, 1995), p. 132.
[33] Grosser (note 22), p. 10.
[34] Grosser (note 22), pp. 10–11.
[35] Karaganov, S. A., 'Russia's élites', eds Blackwill and Karaganov (note 24), p. 47.

status and special interests, is still concerned to preserve cooperation with the West; (b) President Yeltsin and the remainder of the national leadership seem intent on keeping the country's sentiments, actions and demands within limits; and (c) even the crudest nationalists are not unmindful of the economic straits in which the country finds itself.[36] The effects of deeper structural features, then, do not exclude moderate influences or, indeed, periods of moderate policy. Rather these deep-lying influences are testimony to the constant vulnerability of moderate behaviour.

IV. The international setting: system, order and choice

What happens within Russia itself constitutes only half the story. As always, and never more than with the German parallel, the international context provides the other half. The German Question, after all, was hardly only of German making; the other great powers also played their part.

The point has already been made that the Russian Question should not be seen as historically analogous to the German Question because their content is not the same. In a more abstract sense, however, their implications are. In the 19th century, Germany threatened international stability by the great burgeoning of its power. Contemporary Russia poses the problems of collapsed power. After World War I, a weakened Germany stood in relation to other great powers differently from today's weakened Russia, because it had been vanquished from without, not from within. Whether strong or weak, Germany's challenge to the other great powers was always direct; the Russian challenge is indirect, the product of its relations with its immediate new neighbours. Yet in both—or in all three—cases this challenge was and remains the defining challenge facing the international order. What it has required of the other great powers may have differed from era to era, but these different requirements none the less should form or should at all times have formed the central axis of their foreign policies. To the degree that the great powers mishandled the German challenge from 1890 to 1914 and, again, from 1919 to 1939, in the same measure they brought ruin to the international order. For the great powers of today—and, therefore, for Europe as a whole—the stakes are no smaller.

In this the issue of choice is crucial. Germany, like Russia today, occupied an enormous space, as much political as physical, in the international system. How its leaders chose to play their role did much to determine the tenor and outcome of relations with other nations. Yet, at the same time, how others chose to define and treat the German Question significantly affected the choices made by German leaders. One can and should say the same of Russia today.

Choice does not come easy. From one direction, the pressures and diversions accompanying change within Russia set boundaries to choice, both for Russian

[36] For an analysis of where the 'centre of gravity' is, see MacFarlane, S. N., 'Russian conceptions of Europe', *Post-Soviet Affairs*, vol. 10, no. 3 (July–Sep. 1994), pp. 234–68; and de Nevers, R., International Institute for Strategic Studies, *Russia's Strategic Renovation*, Adelphi Paper no. 289 (Brassey's: Oxford, 1994), especially pp. 30–39.

and for foreign leaders. From the other direction, international realities also place ineluctable constraints on the flexibility of leaders. No Russian leader is a free agent when it comes to designing a national security policy. None can escape the new, tenuous security environment around its borders, the awkwardly large numbers of Russians now resident in foreign countries, the discrepancies between Russia's strength and that of that of the other great powers or the fact that there are now a good many more of them. In addition, everyone, Russian and European leaders alike, must adjust to a world without the structural clarity, the peculiar discipline, and the unique forms of stability and instability of the cold war era.

Still, if the German example has an ultimate application, it is above all else by revealing how significant human choice can be. Circumstance may have brought about the existence of the German Question, but national leaders in Berlin, London, Moscow/St Petersburg, Paris and Vienna determined its shape and malignancy. Policy did not float helplessly on the tides of nationalism or the dictates of a pre-democratic order. Rather, policy greatly influenced the direction and intensity of nationalist trends and, no less, the consequences of the country's political characteristics—sometimes for the better, more often not. In much the same way, whatever may have been the defining features of the international setting, they worked their effect through the interplay of many nations' foreign policies.

Choice, however, begins with circumstance. At the most fundamental level, Russia has a further aspect in common with Germany. Like Germany—and unlike its 19th-century predecessor—Russia is now what Steven Miller calls 'a centrally located continental power'.[37] For most of its history, at least until the last decades of the Soviet Union, Russia existed at the edge of a European-dominated international system. Its strategy, mentality and preoccupations remained those of a frontier state. Faced with no major powers in any direction except to the west, Imperial Russia had no natural reason to worry much about the state of equilibrium among the great powers. When it sought to make common cause with them, it was to protect the domestic and imperial order from contaminating foreign influences, not to steady the international environment. By the mid-1950s, however, with the rise of China and subsequently the resurgence of Japan, tsarist Russia's Soviet successors gradually found themselves surrounded by strong—potentially very strong—states. Russia, its relative power weaker and the variety of threats along its many borders greater, faces this problem to an even greater degree than in Soviet times.

In these circumstances, the wise state seeks to insure against the fusion of threats. Its first task is to see to it that the nations ringing its border, particularly the most powerful among them, feel no urge to unite against it. Bismarck made this objective the essence of his foreign policy. An admiring Henry Kissinger describes his performance in the following terms:

---

[37] Miller, S. E., 'Russian national interests', eds Blackwill and Karaganov (note 24), p. 77.

He wanted peace for the newly created German Empire and sought no confrontation with any other nation. But in the absence of moral bonds among the European states, he faced a Herculean task. He was obliged to keep both Russia and Austria out of the camp of his French enemy. This required preventing Austrian challenges to legitimate Russian objectives and keeping Russia from undermining the Austro-Hungarian Empire. He needed good relations with Russia without antagonizing Great Britain, which was keeping a wary eye on Russian designs on Constantinople and India.[38]

Through a mix of restraint and subtlety, he pieced together an intricate web of alliances that kept the inherent threats at bay. In contrast, in the 20 years after his dismissal Bismarck's injudicious successors 'managed to foster an extraordinary reversal of alliance'.

In 1898, France and Great Britain had been on the verge of war over Egypt. Animosity between Great Britain and Russia had been a constant factor of international relations for most of the nineteenth century. At various times, Great Britain had been looking for allies against Russia, trying Germany before settling on Japan. No one would have thought that Great Britain, France, and Russia could possibly end up on the same side. Yet, ten years later, that was exactly what came to pass under the impact of insistent and threatening German diplomacy.[39]

At the moment, anti-Russian collusion among the other great powers remains only a theoretical, not a practical danger. Instead a more complicated version of the problem confronts Russia. For the time being, the challenge to Russia's security arises not from the military resources and even less from the aspirations of states on its periphery, but rather from the many regions abutting Russia and the array of trouble possible in any one of them, particularly when combined with the risk of trouble erupting in more than one region at a time.[40] After all, Russia belongs to four grand theatres, of which Europe is only one: through East Asia, inner Asia, the Caucasus and the Balkans, Russia is affected by the level of tension, the forms of conflict and the balance of power in each.

When considering the effect of Russia on European security, Europeans must recognize that any sensible Russian leadership will want to protect its options in the other three areas mentioned above and will therefore shy away from involvements in Europe which jeopardize its flexibility.[41] European security ultimately involves some level of Russian integration into European structures and, indeed, even some degree of alignment with Europe's other great powers. These two things will be feasible only if they do not compromise Russia's ability to have independent relationships with key players in the other regions, notably with China, India, Iran and Japan. For Europeans, this may not be

[38] Kissinger, H., *Diplomacy* (Simon and Schuster: New York, 1994), pp. 145–46.

[39] Kissinger (note 38), p. 171.

[40] Steven Miller, who makes a similar point, calls this a problem of 'multiple theaters, simultaneous contingencies'. Miller (note 37), pp. 101–103.

[41] As Sergei Karaganov notes, Russia is 'a country which is eight per cent Muslim in its population and is bordering the Muslim world [and] cannot afford to remain negligent or hostile towards Islam'. Karaganov, S., 'Russia: towards "enlightened post-imperialism"', eds W. Weidenfeld and J. Janning, *Europe in Global Change* (Bertelsmann Foundation: Gütersloh, 1993), p. 124.

easily appreciated, because, in contrast to the way the world looks from Moscow, to them Russia and the rest of what used to be the Soviet Union matter primarily as Europe's frontier. Their priority is simple—to avoid chaos on this frontier: what they want in relations with Russia derives almost entirely from this concern.

Russia's geo-strategic context, however, is still more complex, but for reasons that are the reverse of the German case. After 1866, the integration of the German state determined Germany's relationship with Europe. Since 1991, the disintegration of the Soviet state has determined Russia's. The collapse of the Soviet Union has meant that Russia does not participate simply and directly in any of the four key theatres, including Europe. Instead, it is part of a new sub-system of states arising out of the wreckage of the Soviet Union, which, in fact, is the link to critical theatres beyond. Not only does Russia enter Europe through this sub-system, but its relations with the new post-Soviet states create a seamless web among the dimensions of Russian security—from the problem of internal order within Russia to that of instability on Russia's immediate borders and, from there, to that of threats in the larger world.

Out of this intervening reality comes the first of two parallel imperatives uniting the security prospects of both Europe and Russia. First, security for both depends on their success in preventing these three dimensions, the internal, the regional and the global, or any two of the three from interacting to produce a downward spiral. Both Russia and Europe must most fear the destructive interaction of developments within Russia, the immediate region and the wider European arena. Both should fear the likelihood that things gone awry in any one dimension will with high probability spill over into one or both of the other two. Both have therefore a considerable incentive to seek ways of keeping the dimensions decoupled when and if trouble breaks out at one or another level.

Because nationalist excess, exaggerated mistrust, warped notions of threat and the abuse of power are the forces transporting the effects of tension and instability from one dimension into the next, Russian and European leaders have a second security interest in common: namely, to conceive policies aimed at impeding the integration of reactionary impulses. Although this is alien to traditional notions of defence, national security planners in Western Europe and Russia need to start with the objective of preventing protectionists, nationalists and militarists from making common cause. They need to plot ways of weakening and divorcing the various frustrations inspiring these distinctive sections of society. Because the sources of protectionism tend to be independent of those driving, for instance, militarism, consciously crafted policy can hope to keep them apart. Because genuine security issues do not necessarily overlap with the fate of ethnic kin abroad, policy should be designed to separate these two domains; or, to take another example, to the extent that nationalism run amok leads naturally to imagined foes and the vilification of other states, leaders should take care to see that the professional military is held to a higher standard of level-headedness and that the shabbier claims of politicians are constantly watched and exposed to light.

For Russian and West European leaders, however, the task is not merely to obstruct the potential synergy among reactionary forces in Russia: the same challenge is present in nearly all the post-Soviet states. All are susceptible to nationalism in its dangerous form and for the same reasons as Russia. 'When a whole all-encompassing world view like communism collapses . . . the demise of the holistic structure implied in communism throws people back to their immediate experience in the realms of culture, history and collective memory, and elevates national and ethnic identity as the readily available unifying symbol around which they can anchor their rediscovered yet shattered selves.'[42]

It is a saving grace at present that in the four most important post-Soviet states—Belarus, Kazakhstan, Russia and Ukraine—national leaders have shunned ethnic nationalism in favour of civil nationalism. That is, they are labouring to build the nation not on the basis of ties of blood and language, but by including all who live within their borders. Unfortunately, the shortcomings of pre-democracy leave the state constantly open to a shift towards more dangerous forms of ethnic nationalism, while at the same time also promoting the fortunes of protectionist and militarist elements. Finally, the agonies and dislocations involved in the process of advancing beyond pre-democracy reinforce and unite all three pathologies.

The result is two vicious circles with which policy—Russian as well as West European—must contend. In the first of these, democracy turns out to be the solution to most of the threats to security raised by pre-democracy, but democracy is precisely what is most menaced by these threats. For example, one road to domestic violence, even civil war and ultimately interstate conflict, goes via the fracturing of society along ethnic lines. The fracturing often starts with a minority raising a challenge to the cohesion and integrity of the state and the dominant group striking back. The road away from this unhappy sequence, nearly everyone agrees, is to secure the minority's stake in the state, a goal which can only be reliably accomplished by protecting minority rights and ensuring a minority's access to government through well-functioning electoral institutions.[43] Faced with rebellious ethnic groupings, however, pre-democracies find it still harder to create and defend these democratic forms. To make matters worse, challenges of this sort often heighten ethnic nationalism in the dominant group, and ethnic nationalism as the basis for nationhood requires an authoritarian state capable of repression and discrimination.[44]

The second vicious circle sets state against state. The rise of any of the damaging modern '-isms' in one state feeds the same deformity in neighbouring states. Nationalism in one place, particularly if it contains overtones of ethnic

---

[42] Avineri, S., 'Paradigm change: analytical and conceptual approaches to the post-cold war world', eds Weidenfeld and Janning (note 41), p. 26.

[43] For a clear statement of this proposition from someone who has struggled long and hard with the problem in the former socialist states of Eastern Europe and the Soviet Union, see van der Stoel, M., 'Prevention of minority conflicts', ed. L. B. Sohn, *The CSCE and the Turbulent New Europe* (Friedrich-Naumann-Stiftung: Washington, DC, 1993), pp. 147–54.

[44] Appropriately, the point is made by an insightful East European. Hardi, P., 'Security issues and nation building in East-Central Europe', eds Weidenfeld and Janning (note 41), p. 205.

nationalism, stirs the nationalist pulse of those next door. Militarism reproduces its own kind across borders and, perhaps, intensified nationalism along with it. Protectionism or simply aggressive economic policies also provoke either imitation or one of the other malignant ideologies. Heightening the potency of the process, states caught in such a cycle find it hard to escape by themselves. As two Russian authors observe, because 'for a long time to come, nationalism will still be the determining political force in many republics, whereas democracy will still remain too fragile to resist it successfully', any hope of building stability on the basis of guaranteed rights for ethnic minorities 'will be possible only when powerful pressure is brought to bear from the outside'.[45] Those on the outside, however, especially the great powers of the West, find it hardest to bring themselves to intervene in precisely those cases where the causes of conflict appear to be primal.

Such considerations lead directly to the issue of choice. Russians and West Europeans, whether they mean to or not, will together fashion the security environment in both individual countries and the region. How they do so—whether with forethought or as a matter of course, whether systematically or randomly, and whether with sensitivity to one side's impact on the other or not—will greatly affect the outcome. To this it should be added that it is now rather than later that Russia and Western Europe enjoy their greatest freedom of decision. 'When an international order first comes into being, many choices may be open to it', Kissinger writes. 'But each choice constricts the universe of remaining options. Because complexity inhibits flexibility, early choices are especially crucial.'[46]

Political leaders today begin with advantages (contrary to much contemporary commentary) compared with their 19th- and early 20th-century predecessors. First, in contrast to every other period in modern history, Russian and West European leaders face their task unencumbered by enmities among the great powers. There are no semi-permanent rivalries to complicate the search for European stability, such as those in the last century between France and Germany, Great Britain and Russia, and the Austro-Hungarian Empire and Russia. Second, the disintegration of the Soviet empire has not given way to an intense competition among outsiders over the spoils, as when the Ottoman Empire collapsed, nor, as in the wake of the Austro-Hungarian Empire's demise, to a struggle for influence over the fragile new successor states. Third, the threat of a powerful rogue state preparing to overthrow the existing international order is not on the horizon. To be spared such burdens lightens dramatically the challenge of building European security and also eases the pressure to imitate the errors of the past.

They do, however, have one serious disadvantage uniting them with their 19th-century predecessors. This is the tendency to underestimate the age within which they live; to assume that catastrophe is so improbable that their narrow

---

[45] Benevolenski, V. and Kortunov, A., 'Ethics, integration, and disintegration: a Russian perspective', *Ethics and International Affairs*, vol. 7 (1993), p. 113.

[46] Kissinger (note 38), pp. 26–27.

self-preoccupations can be safely indulged; and to define the challenge of coping with a disintegrating or (in our day's case) disintegrated international order so modestly that no risks need to be run or costs paid.

V. Russia's options

One option for Russia is not considered here, since it is a straw man, although it is still being beaten by critics of the original foreign policy of Yeltsin and former Foreign Minister Andrey Kozyrev. This would be docilely to follow the West, do its bidding, hope to be admitted to the club, and count on self-sacrifice and fealty to elicit Western support in times of trouble. Apart from the fact that not even members of the Western club behave this way, no leadership in pre-democratic Russia, no leadership of a 'centrally located continental power', could or would choose this course. Russia has three basic options when trying to ensure the nation's safety in an uncertain international environment: unilateralism, a balance-of-power policy and liberal institutionalism.

Unilateralism

Russia's real choices begin with the one traditionally pursued by Russian leaders: the path of unilateralism. Russia could decide—indeed, it has already to a degree decided—to deal with potential security threats on its own. The gradual evolution towards a privileged and assertive Russian role in keeping the peace and managing disorder among and within the new neighbouring states represents a strong movement in this direction. So do the closing of the Russian mind to strategic alignments with other great powers as a legitimate recourse open to the country and the reluctance of national security planners to acknowledge limits to Russia's capacity to deal with all possible threats.[47] It is present, too, in the churlish warnings of politicians and diplomats that Russia means to defend its 'special interests', whether others like it or not.

Throughout the 19th century Russia regularly adopted a unilateralist approach.[48] During Russia's Soviet incarnation, unilateralism was more than a proclivity; it was the essence of policy, at least until the regime's last years. The Leninist notion of international politics assumed a level of alienation between East and West that left Soviet leaders little option but to rely on their own devices in protecting the country, and nothing in the character of post-war Soviet alliances diluted the impulse towards unilateralism.

[47] A good illustration is the inter-agency document 'Osnovnye polozheniya kontsepstii natsionalnoy bezopasnosti' [Basic conceptions of national security] summarized in Chernov, V., 'Natsionalnye interesi Rossii i ugrozy yeyo bezopasnosti' [National interests of Russia and threats to its security], *Nezavisimaya Gazeta,* 29 Apr. 1993, pp. 1–3.

[48] This was true in the 1826 ultimatum sent to Constantinople over disputed matters, including passage through the Dardanelle Straits; in the war launched against Turkey in 1828; in the 1833 intervention against the Egyptian rebel, Mehemet Ali; in the lead-up to the Crimean War of 1853–56; in the threatened intervention during the 1876 Bulgarian crisis; in the war against Turkey in 1877 and the dictated Peace of San Stefano; and in 1886 when Russia forced the hand of Bulgaria's Prince Alexander.

Unilateralism is only a particular form of *machtpolitik* or power politics.[49] Even if it starts as something else, this is where it leads. Practitioners of unilateralism, dependent as they are on their own wit and resources, must be willing to bully and threaten and, if need be, use sanctions or force against those whom they want to influence. They cannot shift the burden of blame, rely on notions of 'mutual responsibility' or soften the impact of their demands by hiding them as part of a general settlement. Often, as shown in the case of Germany at the end of the 19th century, unilateralism insists on translating security challenges into military problems, and the solution—greater reliance on military power—brings with it all the consequences of *machtpolitik*. Kissinger's description of Germany's descent into power politics in the post-Bismarck era is of more than passing interest to Russia's contemporary friends. 'What the Kaiser wanted most', he writes:

was international recognition of Germany's importance and, above all, of its power. He attempted to conduct what he and his entourage called Weltpolitik, or global policy, without ever defining that term or its relationship to the German national interest. Beyond the slogans lay an intellectual vacuum: truculent language masked an inner hollowness; vast slogans obscured timidity and the lack of any sense of direction. Boastfulness coupled with irresolution in action reflected the legacy of two centuries of German provincialism. Even if German policy had been wise and responsible, integrating the German colossus into the existing international framework would have been a daunting task. But the explosive mix of personalities and domestic institutions prevented any such course, leading instead to a mindless foreign policy which specialized in bringing down on Germany everything it had always feared.[50]

In Russia's own earlier experience, the lessons of unilateralism are equally pertinent. In almost all instances, Russian unilateralism was undertaken in—indeed encouraged by—a local balance of power that favoured Russia, but in a broader and unheeded context where the balance of power was very much against Russia. As a result, even when Russia prevailed locally, as it often did, the other great powers were drawn closer together against it; and, when the challenge seemed too much to them, they inflicted major diplomatic defeats on the country.

Balance of power

Russia's second choice is a balance-of-power policy. Rather than practise the political 'free hand', sustained by the regular and wilful use of national power, Russia would start with a careful weighing of its strengths and weaknesses, and through a provident policy of restraint and artful diplomacy do what it could to manoeuvre various players into positions which reinforced Russian security.

---

[49] The notion of power politics is used here in the sense employed by Kissinger, as 'the accumulation, threat, and if need be use of armed force as an instrument of policy'. Howard, M., 'The world according to Henry: from Metternich to me', *Foreign Affairs*, vol. 73, no. 3 (May/June 1994), p. 133.

[50] Kissinger (note 38), p. 171.

Russia's earlier efforts to discourage the strengthening or enlargement of NATO and to make the Organization for Security and Co-operation in Europe (OSCE), Europe's key security institution, fit into this kind of approach. So would selective strategic alignment with the West, not in East–Central Europe or the new states of the former Soviet Union, but against instability to the south, on the littoral of the Indian Ocean.[51] So, too, would attempts to balance Turkey against Iran with the aim of preventing either from penetrating into the Caucasus or Central Asia, and so would a desire to keep the USA engaged in East Asia as a hedge against Japanese remilitarization and a buffer against Sino-Japanese competition. Finally, through a subtle mix of reassurance and admonition, a balance-of-power policy would have Russia striving to avoid the formation of anti-Russian coalitions among its immediate new neighbours or between any of them and other powers.

Among many policy analysts in Moscow, a balance-of-power strategy comes closest to capturing the essence of their preferred course. It is also the approach that is most consonant with a long tradition of thinking about the nature of international politics, from Metternich to Kissinger, and in the end probably the closest to the convictions of most foreign-policy analysts. The problem is that a balance-of-power policy is complex, with complexity leading to further complexity, eventually outstripping the capacity of all but the most autocratic governments or imperious leaders. In the chaos of democracies and, in this case, of pre-democracies as well, such a policy is particularly vulnerable, as the fate of both Bismarck's and Kissinger's handiwork illustrates. It is especially likely to degenerate into unilateralism, not least because the skilled application of restraint is difficult both to understand and to sustain.

For Russia, practising a balance-of-power policy in the 'near abroad' without soon slipping into a policy of 'divide and rule' will be particularly difficult. Rather than master the subtle blending of security assurances—beginning with a convincing acceptance of the sovereignty and independence of other post-Soviet states—with the determined use of power to discourage the formation of strategic alliances directed against Russia, in moments of anxiety the temptation will be to exploit the domestic vulnerabilities of recalcitrant leaderships or their disputes with neighbours to bend these leaderships to Russia's will. With currents of unilateralism already running strong in the Russian body politic, this seems a safely predictable outcome; and beneath these currents, at a still deeper level, are the permanent dangers associated with pre-democracy and nationalism.

One policy could easily slide into the other: this is another way in which the different dimensions of Russian security are likely to merge with unhappy effect. At the moment and for the first time in more than a century, Russia is a plausible, even a desirable, potential ally for all the other great powers. Among these states are those, notably China, Germany and Japan, whose burgeoning

---

[51] This notion figured in the concept of Russian security worked out by members of the Russian Council on Foreign and Policy, published in *Nezavisimaya Gazeta*, 19 Aug. 1993, p. 4.

strength may well encourage others to seek the comfort of Russia's support. As Russia plots a path to security in the larger setting, this is an important resource, although not if Russia destroys the confidence and goodwill of the outside world by menacing and ruthless treatment of the lesser powers on its borders. Russia can throw away this advantage in various ways. It need not do so by crudely intervening in the troubles of neighbouring states. It need merely begin to brandish its military strength in bullying ways. In either case, inter-mediate powers—Poland, Sweden, Turkey and so on—will amplify the effect, as they, too, draw their conclusions from Russia's behaviour.

Liberal institutionalism

Russia's third alternative, which has the least foundation in the country's tradi-tions and a shrinking base of support in the present political context, derives from what Western social scientists call liberal internationalism. In this case, Russia would entrust its security, in the 'near abroad' and the 'far abroad', to strengthened multilateral institutions and to increased great-power responsibil-ity for peace and stability at all levels of the international system. The notion comes from the same family as the concept of collective security and, therefore, shares some of its weaknesses.[52] Thought of in less comprehensive or ambitious terms, however—that is, conceived not as the organizational core of a new international order, but as a foreign-policy strategy—the idea of collective action seems less questionable or unlikely and is not so far from what thought-ful Russian analysts are calling for. One of the most thoughtful, Alexei Arbatov, starts with the proposition that Russia does have vital interests in the 'near abroad' and a right to protect them, but not by asserting a 'special role' or claiming special 'responsibilities'.[53] It should seek to prevent the domination of these states by other powers, he argues, but not by substituting its own domina-tion. Rather, the 'first priority of Russia's foreign policy is to support the emergence of independent, stable, peaceful and neutral new states in place of the former Soviet colonial republics'. Because many of these new states are inherently unstable, often in conflict with one another and usually mistrustful of Russia, in attempting to promote stability without straining its resources or miring itself in high-cost interventions, Russia needs the other great powers.

It is in Russia's interest . . . to actively involve the advanced industrial West in creating economic and political networks of stability in these regions . . . Peace-enforcement or peacekeeping interventions should be based on multilateral (UN, OSCE, or [Commonwealth of Independent States] CIS)—decisions and actions. The principal

---

[52] For a recent and trenchant discussion of these weaknesses, see Betts, R., 'Systems for peace or causes of war? Collective security, arms control, and the new empire', *International Security*, vol. 17, no. 1 (summer 1992), pp. 5–43. In simple form, however, the problem is, as Kissinger notes, that among the powers expected to act collectively, 'interests are rarely uniform, and security rarely seamless', making them 'more likely to agree on inaction than on joint action'. Kissinger (note 38), pp. 90–91.

[53] Arbatov, A., 'Russian national interests', eds Blackwill and Karaganov (note 24), p. 62.

Russian role should be that of an active, impartial and creative broker and mediator in settling conflicts and only when sought by others.[54]

To be realistic, Arbatov is not a typical representative of the contemporary Russian foreign policy intelligentsia, nor are his views favoured by the general drift of thinking within the country. He may, indeed, speak for no more than the tiniest minority, and a shrinking one at that. This does not diminish the wisdom of his argument or the benefit it would confer on his country, but it does bear on the practical choices open to West European states and other great powers.

VI. Europe's options

Although it took 130 years, history did ultimately resolve the German Question—as much as and for as long as history ever does. An analogous solution, however, is not yet available in the Russian case. In the German case, the solution was to embed a mature democracy with a vibrant economy in a liberal regional order. Without a democratic Germany and the European Union, the German Question would not be behind us, and German unification, rather than occurring as unremarkably as it did, would have seemed an unthinkable invitation to trouble. Russia, however, has work to do before it is a mature democracy, and Europe's liberal regional order covers only part of the continent. The West European states will therefore have to find another method of making Europe safe from the Russian Question.

More of the same

Like Russia itself, West European states have several basic options. They could continue with their current chosen course of action, which is to try and improve upon the somewhat rickety and misshapen tools and structures left over from the cold war era. This involves limited and largely symbolic steps to ease the frictions within the post-Soviet region, while postponing indefinitely consideration of fundamental issues of the structure of security in Europe and hoping that Russian politics will remain on an even keel, burnishing the hope with modest amounts of aid and generous amounts of advice. In view of the advantages that contemporary European leaders have over their late 19th-century predecessors, this may be adequate. With the basic issue of war and peace pushed into the background, thanks to the absence of great-power rivalry, an ad hoc approach to the lesser security challenges likely to arise in contemporary Europe could well suffice, provided that nothing goes terribly wrong in or among the post-Soviet states. Until now, national leaderships in Russia and the surrounding states, with only a few exceptions—and these of secondary importance—have managed to contain domestic tensions. For leaders in Bonn, London and Paris, with other matters to worry about, the success of the post-

[54] Arbatov (note 53), p. 63.

Soviet leaderships so far in finding ways around the innumerable sources of friction between them makes it easier to believe that this will continue: specifically, it makes it easier for them to believe that what they are doing, when doing more seems to them so difficult, will be enough.

Continuing the present course—that is, continuing simply to improve on the past—carries with it certain risks. First, it has within it an inchoate element relating to spheres of influence. Russia is asking, and with increasing frequency demanding, that Western Europe and the USA recognize as its responsibility all the territory that lies within the former borders of the Soviet Union, something that West European states and the USA have refused to do formally. Their reluctance to engage seriously in the processes under way within the region, including, in particular, Russia's international affairs, results in a de facto acceptance of a Russian sphere of influence, leaving them only able feebly to demand some level of Russian restraint.

If Russia does not meet the standards promoted by the West—and without Western involvement it will be harder for it to do so—the present course could quickly dissolve into what might be called a policy of malign neglect. Frustrated by Russian behaviour, but not feeling an imminent or large-scale threat to themselves, and unwilling to exert themselves on any scale, West European states, joined by the USA, would simply retreat from the problem. Neglect (or complacency) is already an element in current policy, and not much would be required to give it a bitter and mistrustful cast. A policy of malign neglect, in these circumstances, might suit the bulk of the populace in most Western nations, which might give the policy critical popular support but would deny Western Europe any control over Russia's effect on its own fate.

'Neo-containment'

A second option has the same roots as the first, but is more decisive and could be the basis for a more systematic and coherent policy. Western Europe could choose a course of neo-containment. Some observers in the West, primarily in the USA, argue that Russia's aggressiveness towards its neighbours, its obvious difficulty in shedding an imperial psychology and its unpredictable political evolution require the West to act now. According to this analysis Western Europe and the USA have already waited too long: (a) to begin shoring up the vulnerable new states on Russia's rim, particularly Ukraine; (b) to speak frankly with the Russians about their behaviour in the 'near abroad', making it plain that Western assistance and cooperation will depend on Russian restraint there; and (c) to engage in discussions with others, such as China, who also have an interest in containing Russian expansionism. In a phrase, Western Europe and the USA should create 'a felicitous environment for Russia to define itself purely as Russia'.[55]

---

[55] The phrase is Zbigniew Brzezinski's. Brzezinski, Z., 'The premature partnership', *Foreign Affairs*, vol. 73, no. 2 (Mar./Apr. 1994), p. 79.

A neo-containment strategy on the part of Western Europe's great powers, at this stage, is meant to counterbalance a possible Russian threat to Europe before it actually emerges. A strategy of neo-containment would essentially constitute a deterrent strategy, designed to divert Russia from the path of excess before it advances down that route. Advocates of such a policy normally favour the prompt and straightforward enlargement of NATO to include the Visegrad Group of countries,[56] not only in order to secure those four countries against the uncertainties of a shadowy future, but to lay down markers for Russia. If the major powers of Western Europe were to move in this direction, they would be acting as though they knew that the effects of proto-democracy and intensified nationalism were inevitable and best countered by throwing up barriers in advance.

Advocates of neo-containment, however, do not wish to see Russia isolated. Like the balance-of-power policy option discussed for Russia, the other half of neo-containment would feature (West European) restraint, an ongoing dialogue with Russia, a willingness to aid Russia (but no more generously than Ukraine and other key post-Soviet states) and the search for common ground. Rather like its conceptual ancestor, it would urge a mix of inducements and threats as the answer to the old and familiar dialectic of competition and cooperation.

Neo-containment may, at some point, become Western Europe's choice, but not one freely made. Given the extreme unlikelihood that Europe's major powers today would agree on the need for such a course or that any one of them could muster the energy to give it life should it be chosen, it will almost certainly be at Russia's initiative. If Russian unilateralism is bold or crude enough, Western Europe may be galvanized into choosing this second option—not as a deterrent strategy or a way of diminishing the Russian Question, but rather as an involuntary and, most likely, reflexive reaction after the event.

Liberalizing the international setting

Western Europe's third alternative also parallels a Russian option, and it, too, suffers from difficulties. If the German solution cannot be applied to the Russian case, then West European states nevertheless may want to do what they can to promote an approximation to it. In essence, West European states would consciously seek to weave together the security agendas of Europe and Russia. Rather than instability in the region of the former Soviet Union being treated in isolation and as largely Russia's responsibility, inviting only peripheral West European involvement, the evolution of relations among the post-Soviet states would be made a vital extension of European security. As a result, European institutions and structures would be regarded not so much as marginal adjuncts of CIS or Russian mechanisms, but as the superstructure into which these other institutions were carefully integrated. Policies would be designed to address the honeycomb of factors underlying prospective trouble in this region—min-

---

[56] The Czech Republic, Hungary, Poland and Slovakia.

orities, territorial irredentism, military postures, forced migration and so on—not simply to help ease specific clashes as they arise. Russia's central role in the region, while natural and even desirable if played constructively, would be the object of regular deliberation with the other great powers of Europe, and, in turn, the other great powers would be willing to engage themselves in the area politically as well as economically and on a scale enabling Russia to share responsibility.

In this lies the chief objection to NATO enlargement. Thought of in these terms, the error in casting NATO's protective wing over East–Central Europe stems not from the hard feelings that it may generate among Russians, but from the obstacle that it will create to the integration of post-Soviet security with European security. Furthermore, the obstacle will be as much on the Euro-Atlantic side as on the Russian side—as much in the deadening of the West's capacity to deal with security in the post-Soviet region as in Russia's reluctance to cooperate. This does not mean that the problem of a security vacuum in Central Europe should be ignored or finessed. As noted above, grey zones are one of the four hazards to European security, and a grey zone in East–Central Europe has a large Russian dimension. Ways other than NATO enlargement must be found to deal with the problem of security in the post-Soviet region. Otherwise Europe will be trading the solution for one category of threat to European security against another of no less importance.

Intensified political engagement by the West in post-Soviet security arrangements involves many and diverse things. At one level, Western Europe would need to consider the kind of security environment being created among the CIS states, the evolution of threat perceptions in key states, military trends within the region and the nature of the security dialogue among these states, and then act to reverse destabilizing trends. West European governments have already concluded a number of agreements fostering new forms of military cooperation between themselves and individual post-Soviet states. Under this third option, they would work at least as hard to encourage military cooperation, confidence-building measures (CBMs), and arms control between Russia and the other new states.

At another level, Western Europe would look hard at the adequacy of existing machinery for the tasks arising from an enhanced involvement. Are the vehicles for addressing the problem of minorities in the international relations of the post-Soviet region, including the OSCE's High Commissioner on National Minorities, sufficient, and do they enjoy a priority status in the foreign policy of France, Germany and the UK? Is crisis prevention in the former Soviet Union an idea taken seriously by West European states? Bearing in mind that the number of people engaged in crisis prevention under UN auspices is pitifully small and the skills needed to do the work vastly underdeveloped,[57] is there any reason to believe that Europe is doing better in its part of the world, so much

[57] See the article by then Australian Foreign Minister, Gareth Evans, 'Cooperative security and intra-state conflict', *Foreign Policy*, no. 96 (fall 1994), pp. 3–20.

better that it can make crisis prevention an objective in and between the new post-Soviet states?

Finally, for liberal institutionalism to become a viable option for Western Europe in dealing with Russia and the post-Soviet region, the division of labour between institutions and states needs to be consciously and fully developed. Russia talks about a division of labour, but largely in terms of being deputized by the international community to orchestrate and direct peacekeeping in the region. The more essential division of labour concerns the relationship between regional or CIS mechanisms for crisis prevention, peacemaking and peacekeeping, those at the European level (such as the OSCE and NATO) and those at the global level (chiefly the UN). For liberal institutionalism to make a difference, West European states must persuade themselves and Russia that European and Russian security depends on the ambitious and coordinated use of institutions at all three levels.

The OSCE effort in Nagorno-Karabakh provides a model. All the essential elements are present. The international community has accepted a role, without denying Russian primacy. For peacekeeping to work, Russia and the other states of the region must provide the makeweight of resources, but the presence of the OSCE both facilitates the participation of other key regional powers, such as Ukraine, and denies Russia a sphere of influence. A Russian sphere of influence, whether de jure or de facto, would be critically different from Russia's natural and inevitable primacy in the region, because it would remove all alternatives for Russia's immediate neighbours and shut out the other great powers.

Unfortunately, the Nagorno-Karabakh example appears increasingly to be an accident rather than a prototype of a new West European approach to the problem of stability in the post-Soviet region. Nor even as a one-time accomplishment has it retained the interest and active commitment of the great powers. Instead they have been all too willing to pass over the responsibility to Europe's smaller powers, particularly Finland. Indeed, the lack of progress in settling this conflict after the OSCE Budapest summit meeting of December 1994 is spectacular.

To move in another direction will not be easy. By and large, trends in Europe are headed the other way, away from the level of conceptual linkage implicit in the liberal institutionalist option, and even more so away from facing up to significant structural challenges of the kind outlined above. Moreover, Russia is itself less and less inclined to this approach: in that, however, lies the single strongest argument for the option.

Ultimately, the gravest threat to European security posed by Russia is the prospect of Russia turning its back on great-power responsibility for the larger international order—ceasing to concern itself with European security or the way in which developments within its own immediate region bear on European security, and substituting instead a narrow-minded and self-centred approach to national security, including the arrogated right to do as it pleases within what used to be the Soviet Union. Under President Mikhail Gorbachev the Soviet

Union took on the responsibility of promoting a liberal international order as the successor to the post-World War II cold war order. Russia, in the course of repudiating the excesses to which Yeltsin and Kozyrev carried this commitment at the outset, has not merely rejected a policy; it has gradually ceased to concern itself with a great power's responsibility as an architect of a new international order. Much in Russia's petulant and incessant claim to great-power status these days is about only that: status, not responsibility.

Among Western Europe's options, only the pursuit of liberal institutionalism can serve to lead Russia back to this larger sense of responsibility. Drawing lines in the sand or threatening to deny Russia trifling amounts of assistance, as US legislators are wont to do, assuredly will not accomplish it. Therefore, idealistic or impractical though it may seem in the current climate, the stakes are too high not to make the case for a more thorough integration of the mechanisms for security in the post-Soviet region into those for European security as a whole.

The final lesson of the German Question is that Europe's woes began when Germany no longer wished to bear the burden of order and settled for the free rider's role, as in the 1890s, or succumbed to the spoiler's role, as in the 1930s. On neither occasion were the rest of Europe and, in particular, the other great powers innocent in the choices made by the Germans. To repeat: the German Question was not Germany's fault; rather, it was Europe's fate.

Part II

Domestic political developments: the security implications

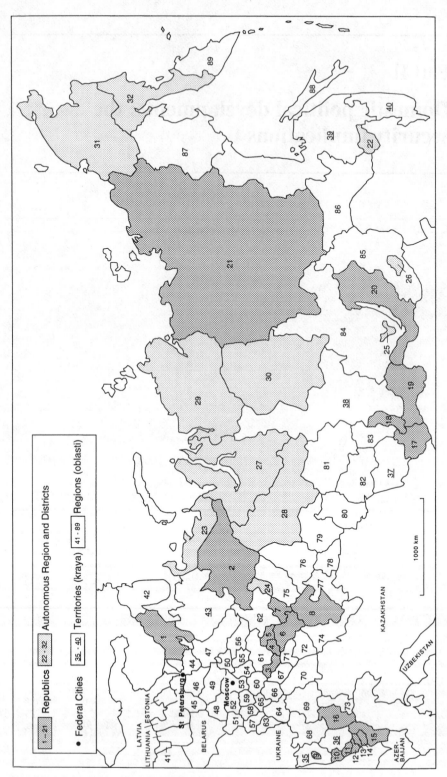

Russia and the subjects of the federation

According to the 1993 Russian Constitution, the Russian Federation consists of 89 'subjects of the federation': 32 ethno-national territories and 57 administrative entities.

Ethno-national territories

Republics

1. Karelia
2. Komi
3. Mordovia
4. Chuvashia
5. Mariy El
6. Tatarstan
7. Udmurtia
8. Bashkortostan
9. Adygueya
10. Karachaevo-Cherkessia
11. Kabardino-Balkaria
12. Northern Ossetia
13. Ingushetia
14. Chechnya
15. Dagestan
16. Kalmykia
17. Gorniy Altay
18. Khakassia
19. Tuva
20. Buryatia
21. Yakut-Sakha

Autonomous Region[a]

22. Yevreysk (Blagoveshchensk)

Autonomous Districts

23. Nenets
24. Komi-Permyak
25. Ust-Ordyn Buryat
26. Aguin Buryat
27. Yamalo-Nenets
28. Khanty-Mansi
29. Taymyr
30. Evenki
31. Chukotka
32. Koryaki

Administrative entities

Federal Cities

33. Moscow
34. St Petersburg

Territories ('kraya')
(numbers underlined on map)

35. Krasnodar
36. Stavropol
37. Altay (Barnaul)
38. Krasnoyarsk
39. Khabarovsk
40. Primorskiy (Vladivostok)

Regions ('oblasti')[a]

41. Kaliningrad
42. Murmansk
43. Archangelsk
44. Leningrad (St Petersburg)
45. Pskov
46. Novgorod
47. Vologda
48. Smolensk
49. Kalinin
50. Yaroslavl
51. Bryansk
52. Kaluga
53. Moscow
54. Vladimir
55. Ivanovo
56. Kostroma
57. Kursk
58. Orel
59. Tula
60. Ryazan
61. Nizhniy Novgorod
62. Kirov
63. Belgorod
64. Voronezh
65. Lipetsk
66. Tambov
67. Penza
68. Rostov
69. Volgograd
70. Saratov
71. Ulyanovsk
72. Samara
73. Astrakhan
74. Orenburg
75. Perm
76. Sverdlovsk (Yekaterinburg)
77. Chelyabinsk
78. Kurgan
79. Tyumen
80. Omsk
81. Tomsk
82. Novosibirsk
83. Kemerovo
84. Irkutsk
85. Chita
86. Amur (Blagoveshchensk)
87. Magadan
88. Kamchatka (Petropavlovsk)
89. Sakhalin (Yuzhno-Sakhalinsk)

[a] Where the name of the region is not that of the capital city, the city is given in parentheses.

Principal ethnic groups in the Russian Federation (1989 census)

Total population 147 400 537: Russian 82%; Tatar 4%; Ukrainian 3.5%; Chuvash, Belarussian and Bashkir c. 1% each; other groups 5% (< 1% each)

Ethnic Russians as a percentage of the total population of Russia/USSR			
1719	1917	1989	1996
71	45	51	82

Background chronology

1990

12 June — The Supreme Soviet of the RSFSR adopts a Declaration of Sovereignty

1991

6 Mar. — An all-Union referendum results in a vote in favour of preserving the USSR as a renewed federation

12 June — Boris Yeltsin is elected President of the RSFSR

19–21 Aug. — Abortive coup attempt by hard-line opponents of Soviet President Gorbachev

8 Dec. — Leaders of Russia, Ukraine and Belarus conclude the Belovezh Agreement abolishing the USSR and establishing a Commonwealth of Independent States (CIS)

21 Dec. — The CIS treaty is signed in Alma-Ata by 11 former Soviet republics (the Baltic states and Georgia are not signatories)

25 Dec. — President Gorbachev announces his resignation

1992

31 Mar. — The Federation Treaty is signed by the constituent parts of the Russian Federation; Tatarstan and Chechnya refuse to sign and a number of other republics attach reservations

2 Nov. — Russia imposes a state of emergency along the border between North Ossetia and Ingushetia and deploys troops to separate armed militias there

6 Nov. — The Parliament of Tatarstan approves a constitution for a 'sovereign state' of Tatarstan: the republic is to be associated with but not part of the Russian Federation

1–14 Dec. — Meeting of the Seventh Congress of People's Deputies gives rise to a sharp dispute between president and parliament over the powers of executive and legislature

1993

11–29 Mar. — Constitutional dispute between the president and parliament intensifies as the Congress of People's Deputies tries to derail a previously agreed constitutional referendum on the powers of executive and legislature and to dismiss Yeltsin

25 Apr. — The referendum gives a vote of confidence to president and government; voters support Yeltsin's economic reform programmes and plans for new elections

21 Sep.–4 Oct. — Yeltsin signs a decree disbanding the Supreme Soviet and Congress of People's Deputies and calls for new elections. The legislature reacts by impeaching Yeltsin on a charge of attempting a *coup d'état*. Armed supporters of Supreme Soviet attempt to occupy the Mayor of Moscow's office and the Ostankino television centre. Troops loyal to Yeltsin shell and capture the parliament building; resistance organizers are arrested

12 Dec. — New federal constitution approved by a narrow (and subsequently disputed) majority in a national referendum; elections to the Federal Assembly result in significant gains in the Duma for conservative and nationalist political factions

1994

13 Feb. — Russia and Tatarstan sign an agreement delineating Tatarstan's autonomy

23 Feb. — The Russian Parliament approves an amnesty for those involved in the Oct. 1993 rebellion against Yeltsin

5 Sep. — Russia places units of the North Caucasus Military District on combat alert following intensification of fighting between Chechen Government forces led by President Dudaev and Russian-backed opposition forces

11 Dec. — Russian ground and air units launch an offensive into Chechnya to put down secessionist rebellion. Intense fighting in the capital, Grozny, results in many civilian casualties

1995

14 June	Armed Chechen rebels storm Budennovsk in southern Russia, taking *c.* 1500 civilians hostage; their release is conditional on the Russian Government's agreeing to negotiate an end to the conflict. Two assaults by the Russian Army to free hostages fail; the government accepts the separatists' demands
30 July	Representatives of the Russian Government and the separatists sign an agreement calling for an end to hostilities and the gradual withdrawal of Russian Army units in exchange for the disarming of Chechen fighters; agreement later breaks down
17 Dec.	Elections to the State Duma: Communist Party of the Russian Federation emerges as the largest party in parliament with 157 seats out of 450

1996

27 May	Yeltsin and Chechen separatist leader Yandarbiev sign an agreement calling for a cease-fire and exchange of prisoners; the decision on Chechnya's future status is deferred for later talks
3 July	Yeltsin wins a majority in the second round of voting in presidential elections
27–30 Aug.	After several weeks of offensive operations by Russian troops, separatist fighters respond by regaining effective control over Grozny. Gen. Lebed, Head of the Russian Security Council, negotiates and signs a controversial agreement with the separatist leadership, declaring the war in Chechnya over and promising to withdraw Russian troops
Aug.–Sep.	Information on Yeltsin's forthcoming heart surgery provokes a new round of acute political struggle in Moscow

4. The vicissitudes of Russian politics

Alexei Arbatov

1. Introduction

There is no question that trends in Russian domestic politics have greatly affected foreign policy decision making and its practical implementation. In this respect, the development of reform in Russia, the country's transition from a totalitarian regime with an over-centralized economy towards a democracy and the establishment of market relations are by far the most important factors. Regrettably this process has ended in formidable failures and distortions rather than impressive achievements and progress.

The real roots of this development are to be found in the fact that, having gained power in August 1991 and finalized its rule in December 1991 by disbanding the Soviet Union and removing President Mikhail Gorbachev and the higher Soviet party–state *nomenklatura*, the new governmental team did virtually nothing to create a solid political and institutional foundation for its rule and the democratic reforms it envisioned.

The end of 1991 was exactly the right time for a referendum on the new constitution, early elections to all branches and levels of Russian state institutions, reorganization of governmental structures, and sweeping changes in the top and middle-level personnel of the state bureaucracy. It was also precisely the time to consolidate the political base of the new leadership by creating a presidential party out of the victorious Democratic Russia movement, by building a broad coalition of liberal to moderate–conservative parties, and by advocating and supporting democratic development and market reforms.

Early elections, reorganization and political consolidation would have been basic principles in a representative democracy, but they were quite alien to the new Russian political leaders. Instead, they relied on the enormous post-August 1991 popularity and charisma of President Boris Yeltsin, counted on disarray and panic in the communist–nationalist camp, and intended to use a superficially reorganized and relabelled but basically intact state bureaucracy as an obedient instrument in their hands. The Democratic Russia movement was quickly forgotten and left without regular access to the president, as were many new liberal consultative and advisory panels. Their support was assumed and taken for granted, and their advice was neither genuinely sought nor followed. The parliament was treated as a decorative body, entitled to rubber-stamp presidential decrees under the management of Yeltsin's then democratic associate and protégé Ruslan Khasbulatov, speaker of the Congress of People's Deputies.

The initial mistakes of the new Russian leaders were not surprising and in some cases quite natural. Their ascent to power occurred quite suddenly, since even as late as July 1991 no one could have expected such a spontaneous and rapid collapse of the Soviet communist regime. They had neither properly worked out programmes of economic and political reform nor enough people to implement them at the centre, still less in the regions. There were no experienced management cadres outside the huge Soviet-era bureaucracy, and the bureaucracy was unenthusiastic about radical reforms and ready to subvert new endeavours. There were no developed political parties in society and no unifying programmes other than opposition to communist rule, which ceased to be a relevant platform after August 1991. Finally, the economic situation was deteriorating rapidly, leaving society faced with the prospect of intolerable food shortages, an energy crisis and general chaos, similar to the situation before the October 1917 Bolshevik coup.

President Yeltsin and his associates were faced with the enormous task of building a new social system within narrow time-limits. With all their goodwill and energy, many mistakes and failures were unavoidable: none the less, some of their blunders should not have happened and cannot be ascribed purely to objective circumstances.

II. Russian reforms: shock without therapy

It is beyond the scope of this chapter to evaluate the economic reforms enacted in January 1992, but one general observation is in order: the shock therapy programme of Yegor Gaidar, acting Prime Minister at the time, was stillborn as a result both of its inherent deficiencies and of lack of public involvement in its elaboration and implementation.

Unlike Poland or any other country in the world, the Soviet Union (of which the Russian Federation was the most significant successor state) had an economy with 70 per cent of its capacity contracted to and funded by the state and not tied to consumer needs. Its core was a mammoth military–industrial complex consuming about 30 per cent of gross national product (GNP) and employing up to 10 million people and 90 per cent of the scientists of the nation. More than 95 per cent of the economy, including agriculture, trade and services, belonged to and was run and priced by party–state bureaucracies at both central and local levels.

The USSR was a state with a highly diverse economic, geographic, ethnic and cultural composition. Following the disbanding of the Soviet Union, Russia did not possess real administrative or economic borders, 40 per cent of the highly integrated subsidiaries of the Russian economy were left stranded 'abroad', and its currency in the form of cash and cheques was shared by 100 million people in 14 other sovereign states.[1]

In contrast to those of the other former communist states, the economy of the USSR was not only distorted or damaged by the management system of

[1] Yavlinskiy, G., *Uroki Ekonomicheskoy Reformy* [The lessons of economic reform] (Epicenter: Moscow, 1993), pp. 51–56, 64–69.

centralized command. The Soviet economy was rather created from scratch during the five-year plans of the 1920s and 1930s. It was designed to be ruled from one place—the Kremlin; it relied on extreme integration and mono-polization and did not use money in the ordinary economic sense of the term. Such a system could be reformed only by consistent and comprehensive state policy; it was impossible to reform it simply by liberalizing prices and adopting other methods from the liberal economic model. Inevitably, instead of pro-moting the emergence of market mechanisms, those methods in a very different sense 'liberated' the Soviet command economy, and in particular the enormous bureaucracy running it from government ministers down to factory directors. This monolithic establishment quickly disintegrated into various branches and regional sections and began to act according to its own parochial interests, com-peting in a legal, financial and institutional vacuum and introducing its own rules of the game and, eventually, its own specific political patterns.

Under all these circumstances the economic model of shock therapy—essen-tially the liberalization of prices and curtailment of credits and subsidies with a view to restructuring the economy and inducing market-oriented growth—could not possibly be implemented using only economic instruments. It could, perhaps, have been carried through by relying on powerful repressive political and administrative mechanisms, foremost among them the armed forces, the internal police and dictatorial rule by the top political leadership. Had this been attempted, the leadership would have had to suppress a public outcry expressed in the form of strikes, demonstrations, pogroms and rampant crime stemming from widespread bankruptcy, unemployment, homelessness and large-scale dislocation of labour. It would have needed to crush all political opposition, impose stringent controls on the mass media, and frighten both the bureaucracy and the population by administering rapid and harsh punishment for corruption, theft and tax evasion. It would have been obliged to ignore (and force others to ignore) the rapid collapse of the former modest but comprehensive social security infrastructure and of subsidized areas such as food and consumer goods, housing, health care, culture, basic research, and so on. On the other hand, particularly bearing in mind recent Russian history and older national traditions, such a regime would by definition have had little interest in making progress towards democracy and developing a market economy. Its natural interests would rather have lain in reviving a totalitarian state operating under nationalist and militarist slogans, rebuilding a powerful military machine, restoring an oppressive empire, expanding outwards to consolidate its holdings and perpetuating hostility to the world outside the sphere of its domination. Clearly, Yeltsin's personal good intentions and the preferences of his team would have been too weak to withstand this. They would either have had to 'convert' or have been thrown out by new totalitarian rulers.

A much more attractive alternative to Gaidar's shock therapy policy would have been not merely a different set of programmes and initiatives, but rather a different method of elaborating, adopting and implementing reforms, based on as broad a democratic political coalition as possible. In this sense there were dozens of options oriented towards the same final goal, but differing in their structure, sequence and time-frame. In a democracy, which Russia was longing to become, means are always at least as important as goals, and strategy should never be allowed to justify the use of dubious tactics. The methods and forms of policy formulation are as crucial as the substance of policy. No ideal democratic reform programme, even if approved by International Monetary Fund (IMF) and World Bank experts, would ever work if not clearly adapted to specific Russian conditions, elaborated with the participation of the main pro-democratic political parties, and reliant on cooperation between all three branches of power for its implementation.

Instead, the reform programme was imposed on an unresponsive and passive society. As was to be expected, it quickly disintegrated under the weight of its inherent inconsistencies, internal sabotage by the bureaucracy and the external opposition of all parties and groups, with the exception of Democratic Russia. The latter made the fundamental blunder of offering political support to a policy it had never chosen and could not affect in any way.[2]

As a result, democratic forces became discredited, confused and split,[3] and the conservatives assumed a virtual monopoly over criticism of the government. No consistent democratic alternative course or alternative leaders existed in the public mind and all the political pressure was coming from conservative or extreme right-wing quarters. This in turn greatly restricted Yeltsin's room for manoeuvre and in particular defined the balance of forces in the parliament.

Within months of the implementation of the shock therapy programme, Russia's whole economic and social structure found itself on the brink of catastrophe. This is the opposite of the view held by many Western observers that the reform programme was gaining momentum.[4] Inflation was in fact slowing down, but at the cost of several months' delay in payment of wages and salaries for the majority of the population. There was, moreover, no mechanism for restructuring the economy or expanding production of consumer goods to avoid massive bankruptcy and unemployment without in turn fuelling inflation.

Under pressure from industrial and rural managers, trade unions and old bureaucratic structures, such as the State Bank, the government began a crash money-printing programme to try to compensate for price rises and to avoid a collapse of the economy and social chaos. The immediate effect was inflation of prices, wages and subsidies, a mounting budget deficit, and rapid deprecia-

---

[2] Petrakov, N., [Some thoughts on Russian reforms], *Moskovskie Novosti*, no. 3 (19 Jan. 1992), p. 14; Arbatov, G., 'Reforma: odin god spustya' [Reform: one year after], *Nezavisimaya Gazeta*, 24 Oct. 1992, p. 4; interview with Grigoriy Yavlinsky, *Nezavisimaya Gazeta*, 14 Jan. 1992, p. 4; and Bogomolov, O., 'Uroki vostochnoy Evropy: doklad Instituta mezhdunarodnykh ekonomicheskikh i politicheskikh issledovanii' [Lessons of Eastern Europe: Report of the Institute for International Economic and Political Studies], *Nezavisimaya Gazeta*, 9 Feb. 1992, p. 4.

[3] Malkina, T., [The Congress of the defeated Democratic Russia becomes an opposition again], *Nezavisimaya Gazeta*, 22 Dec. 1992, p. 1; Mekhanik, A., [Stupidity, or something else?], *Nezavisimaya Gazeta*, 27 Feb. 1993, p. 3 ; Tretyakov, V., [The President plays for high stakes], *Nezavisimaya Gazeta*, 23 Mar. 1993, p. 2; and Parkhomenko, S., 'Diagnoz: politicheskaya distrofiya. Tretiy vozrast Prezidenta' [Diagnosis; political dystrophy. The third age of the president], *Segodnya*, 16 Mar. 1993, p. 2.

[4] See, e.g., Islam, S., 'Russia's rough road to capitalism', *Foreign Affairs*, no. 2 (spring 1993), p. 58.

tion of the rouble. Nevertheless, the recession continued, with private enterprise developing only through trade and profiteering. Investment in production was impossible owing to excessive taxation, sky-rocketing inflation and exorbitant interest rates for commercial bank credit. All this was occurring, moreover, against the background of the disintegration of the social security network, housing, health care, culture, scientific research and public services, to say nothing of unprecedented levels of crime and corruption.

The opposition was gaining momentum, capitalizing on the government's mistakes and joining forces with the centrist and moderate–conservative majority. These factions were disenchanted with President Yeltsin's inflexibility, his confrontational approach to politics, and his apparent unwillingness to work for genuine compromise and share power with other political groups apart from his immediate government team.

III. The regime in crisis

The origins of the constitutional crisis which culminated in the dramatic shelling of the Russian Parliament building in October 1993 were not in the outdated constitution itself, however bad it was. Nor were they simply a 'red–brown' (communist–nationalist) opposition to reforms allegedly being carried out by President Yeltsin.[5] Rather, they were in the Yeltsin Administration's management and political conduct, which created executive chaos and left the president politically isolated in the face of a united front of enemies, consisting of his principal ideological opponents and disappointed or offended former allies. The problem was not the lack of presidential prerogatives, but the absence of a consistent reform programme, along with a reluctance to accept responsibility for major blunders in domestic policy. In the same way, the coalescing of the red–brown opposition to reforms inside and outside the legislature was not so much the cause as the consequence of the failure of reforms and unavoidable owing to the way in which they had been elaborated and implemented.[6]

It is possible that President Yeltsin sincerely believed that after the Supreme Soviet was disbanded a new democratic system would be established through elections to the new parliament in December 1993, presidential elections in June 1994 (as he promised) and the adoption of a new constitution. There were undoubtedly influential persons around him, however, who wanted an authoritarian regime rather than a democratic one in order to continue with the failing

---

[5] It is worth noting that Yeltsin's offensive was against the same Supreme Soviet that in 1990 had elected him chairman, in 1991 supported him as a candidate for the Russian presidency, in Aug. 1991 united around him against the attempted putsch, in Dec. 1991 approved the dissolution of the USSR and establishment of Russian sovereignty, and subsequently granted Yeltsin special powers to implement reforms.

[6] Vasilev, L., 'Yeltsin bez kharizmy' [Yeltsin without charisma], *Novoe Vremya*, nos 2–3 (Jan. 1993), pp. 7–8; 'Vyzhivet li demokratiya i Rossii?' [Will democracy survive in Russia?], *Novoe Vremya*, no. 28 (July 1992), pp. 10–12; and Kohen, S., [Marching on the spot or stepping back], *Novoe Vremya*, nos 2–3 (Jan. 1993), pp. 8–9.

reforms; moreover, there were others who wanted an authoritarian system simply in order to stay in power, reform or no reform. After the October 1993 violence in Moscow, which was clearly provoked by those who did not want a compromise on the basis of simultaneous presidential and parliamentary elections, the president's position quickly drifted away from the idea of establishing genuine democracy for the sake of further reforms. Yeltsin reneged on the promise of an early presidential election, supported an unbalanced and undemocratic draft constitution, and approved manipulation of the rules governing parliamentary elections and the adoption of a new constitution.

The results of the December 1993 election were a shock only to those who did not understand, or were unwilling to recognize, the real sources of domestic economic and political crisis in Russia. Yeltsin's disbanding of the Supreme Soviet dealt only with the consequences and symptoms, not with the causes, of Russia's social malaise. Furthermore, the way in which it was done—politically and then militarily—dealt a heavy blow to public morale and to fragile, newly acquired democratic values. The result was further popular disappointment, disenchantment and disgust with the authorities, their programmes and slogans.

Major electoral gains for communist and nationalist forces, along with the failure of government and opposition democratic parties in the parliament, frightened the leadership, despite the limited real powers of the legislature. It perceived the election results as a reflection of the public mood and especially of the preferences of the armed forces, which heavily supported a radical nationalist candidate, Vladimir Zhirinovsky, and his party. Gaidar, Boris Fedorov and a number of other authors of the shock therapy programme resigned from the government. Moderate–conservatives, led by the new Prime Minister, Viktor Chernomyrdin, expanded their control over policy making with the intention of reviving some form of state regulation of wages and prices, increasing subsidies and support to selected branches of industry and agriculture, and providing for some measure of social security to try to avoid economic collapse and simultaneous social explosion.

However, it proved much more difficult to revive centralized economic management than Chernomyrdin and his ministers had probably expected. Although the new market economy system had failed to materialize, the old command system was also in an advanced state of disintegration. There were no administrative or political instruments left, short of the revival of dictatorship, to elaborate and introduce new controls over prices, incomes and wages. Massive subsidies to the highly monopolized and still state-dependent, quasi-privatized sector of the economy were likely to produce immediate hyperinflation, but promised no guarantee of commensurate overall economic growth—to say nothing of a market-oriented economic revival.

Instead, the government gradually shifted towards endorsing the same economic logic which it was supposed to correct. The policy is again aimed at cutting the budget deficit and thus qualifying for the next instalment of IMF credits at the price of degrading still further the social infrastructure, culture and scientific research. No funding is provided for the restructuring of the economy, conversion of the defence industries, support for productive business or farming or relief and retraining for the unemployed. No serious investment is envisioned in infrastructure, environmental protection or the reallocation of resources to regional projects. Moreover, the budgetary guidelines are based on unrealistically optimistic projections of GNP, inflation and state revenues. The parliament remains largely deprived of the information, time and effective mechanisms needed for it to make sensible amendments to the budget.

Hence, as a result of a combination of inertia and the balancing act between massive unemployment and hyper-inflation which has taken the place of an economic programme for the government, the new economy is emerging as an odd hybrid of three major components.

One component consists of the remaining monetarist tools in budgetary policies, which strangulate what is left of the state's social security functions and undercut legitimate and productive new businesses and farming through excessive taxation and lack of support. Having failed to break up monopolies or introduce competition and private property rights, the government achieved a tough budget policy and the suppression of inflation at the expense of chronic and massive non-payment of state obligations, thus blocking both old state-contracted and new market-oriented production and opening up broad opportunities for financial speculation.

The second comprises several mammoth post-Soviet, and for the most part counter-reformist, sectors of the economy: the military–industrial, fuel and energy, agro-industrial and transport sectors. There are also some powerful regional state industrial groups, as well as the inflated armed forces and security structures, liberated from any tangible political control from the top. All these have a fairly impressive array of levers at their disposal with which to threaten the political leadership and extract additional subsidies and appropriations at the expense of other, less imposing social groups.

The third component is the expanding, criminalized and unaccountable 'black' and 'grey' spheres of the economy, based on unprecedented corruption at the federal and local levels. They are involved in the illegal export of all resources of any value, financial profiteering and international criminal deals of unbelievable proportions.

Since the chance was missed to reform the economy on the basis of a strong democratic state and consistent policy priorities supported by a sufficiently strong domestic political constituency, the 'liberated' and uncontrolled state monopolistic economy began to generate a political system suited to its own particular driving forces and interests, and to give rise to conditions of staggering social stratification and deprivation for the great majority of the population in contrast to the unabashed wealth and unbounded power of a small minority. In this sense Lenin's insights into the nature of state monopolistic capitalism, described by him as 'dying, rotting and parasitic',[7] have been finally proved

---

[7] Lenin, V. I., *Imperialism as the Highest Phase of Capitalism*, Collected Works, vol. 27 (5th edn) (Political Literature: Moscow, 1973), pp. 396–406.

true in many respects, with only one correction: Lenin believed that he was describing the evolution of European capitalism at the end of the 19th century, while in fact he was projecting the development of Russian state capitalism in the late 20th century.

IV. Drifting towards authoritarianism

In the domestic political arena the key development has been the growing reliance of the Yeltsin Government on authoritarian methods and instruments for running the country. Having inadvertently inflicted devastating damage on both society and the economy through the adoption of shock therapy policies and provoked a backlash of anti-democratic, nationalist and communist forces, the leadership then initiated a sharp change of course away from democracy.

Quite probably, both for Boris Yeltsin personally and for some of his associates, staying in power was seen as the way to save democracy and continue reforms, however painful and controversial they may be, and to restore some measure of stability and prevent the most anti-reformist, backward-looking groups and leaders from rising to power by popular vote. Equally clearly, for the majority of the bureaucracy at all levels the sole remaining *raison d'être* is self-enrichment in an environment of comprehensive corruption; indeed, for some individuals staying in office is the only way of avoiding criminal prosecution. This, moreover, is precisely the administrative structure whose duty it is to provide information for and elaborate and implement presidential decrees and governmental decisions.

Under such conditions, control over the bureaucracy becomes of paramount importance. In the Soviet system this was provided by the Communist Party apparatus and the dreaded Committee of State Security (KGB). With these now removed, the only way to control the state bureaucracy is through the division of power, first and foremost through the powerful legislative bodies in existence at all levels, via regular changes of central and local political leaders in elections. The goal of democratic control over the bureaucracy can be furthered by encouraging freedom and openness; constraining the size, secretiveness and prerogatives of the bureaucracy; facilitating active feedback from society into the political process; and developing self-government initiatives.

Meanwhile, the rather authoritarian and certainly controversial new constitution, which was also pushed through in somewhat dubious fashion, has created a considerably weakened legislative branch, not to mention a number of other obstacles to normal democratic procedures. In all probability the authors of the new constitution did not understand that a weakened Duma[8] does not necessarily make the president stronger, but rather renders him more vulnerable to the manipulations of the bureaucracy. Furthermore, the haste with which the election was conducted, arbitrary election rules and numerous violations of the

---

[8] Under the new constitution the Russian Parliament consists of 2 chambers: upper (the Council of the Federation) and lower (the Duma).

rules of vote counting, to say nothing of the effects of earlier policies on public opinion, all affected the composition of the Duma, where democratic forces would otherwise have gained a much greater share of the seats.

Against this background, mechanisms of democracy were steadily downgraded and curtailed by the government in late 1993 and early 1994. A number of presidential decrees directly encroached on the economic and political freedoms of citizens. The rights and responsibilities of security institutions were broadened in some areas to levels comparable to the pre-Gorbachev era. Violations of both the law and the constitution by state agencies have proliferated under the pretext of fighting organized crime and corruption. There is a growing propensity on the part of the executive branch to rule by arbitrary and anonymously elaborated decree, rather than by laws introduced and approved according to the constitution. These decrees are bypassing not only parliamentary and public scrutiny but even that of the cabinet of ministers.

Without the support of democratic institutions or popular support, the president is helpless and vulnerable to the self-serving manipulations and intrigues of the major groups within the bureaucracy. He is screened by them from information and denied innovative ideas and viable political allies for the revival of democratic reforms. Constant tensions between the executive power and the parliament and attempts to compromise, denigrate and further curtail the Duma's authority deprive the president of independent political support and of mechanisms for testing, correcting and adjusting government initiatives according to the real conditions and moods prevailing in society.

The fundamental vicious circle of current Russian domestic politics can be described as follows: to stay in power, fight crime and social disintegration and prevent anti-reformist forces from climbing to the top, Yeltsin's team feels obliged to curtail democracy and rely more and more on executive structures, foremost among them the armed forces. This in turn gives ever growing power to the huge and corrupt bureaucracy and its feuding internal factions, which exerts greater influence on economic and political development than do the legally constituted political authorities through their decrees and laws. That again exacerbates the crisis in society, increases popular disenchantment with the authorities, discredits the very idea of democracy and undermines the search for effective remedies. Meanwhile the opposition capitalize on the deepening crisis by expanding their social base, thereby pushing the authorities into taking further steps to fortify their position through the use of authoritarian methods.

This destructive interaction is further exacerbated by the clear policy of some political figures and institutions of deliberately unleashing and pandering to radical nationalists and even fascists. Their motive is partly tacit sympathy for those groups, but more importantly it expresses the tactic of creating a scarecrow with which to frighten domestic liberals and the West into supporting the present leadership no matter what, in view of the dreadful alternative believed to be lurking in the background. As Gorbachev's experience in 1990–91 showed, this is a dangerous policy, since such tactics tend to get out of control—a relevant consideration in view of the present mood of the army and state security structures. Undercutting attractive alternatives, which has become an important element of political tactics, does not necessarily fortify the position of the incumbent leadership.

The double paradox of the present policy of the leadership is: (*a*) that avowedly democratic reforms are being implemented in highly arbitrary and undemocratic ways without the participation or support of a stable and broad constituency, which means that they have no chance of producing the proclaimed results; and (*b*) that authoritarian methods are ineffective in the post-communist era in view of the absence of fear and discipline in both the bureaucracy and society as a whole and the lack of mechanisms with which to impose decisions from the top. This is the explanation for the tremendous inefficiency and inconsistency of the present policy of the Yeltsin–Chernomyrdin Government.

None the less, in recent years Russians have demonstrated much greater tolerance for hardships and readiness for a market economy and democracy than was previously expected. In fact, many of the new 'democratic' political leaders have proved to be much less prepared than the population at large to accept the freedoms and responsibilities of democracy. Society at large still resists the appeals of reactionaries and does not want to be involved in the infighting of various segments of the political élite or support ambitions of restoring the Soviet or Russian empire. The Russian people have shown a great capacity for adapting to the rapidly changing environment and a willingness to do so in legal and productive ways, if only they can be guided by sensible laws and economic incentives. After decades of communist suppression the new entrepreneurial spirit and desire to work honestly for one's livelihood are truly impressive, especially against the background of brazen corruption in the bureaucracy and systematic enrichment of the criminal business strata.

With all the hardships and despite, not as a result of, the policy choices of the authorities, genuine market forces are developing in various niches of the disintegrating and corrupted state economy. Democratic freedoms have acquired some roots in the country and the people are becoming accustomed to freedom of information, to political and ideological pluralism, to taking care of their destiny without total reliance on the authorities, and to forming and expressing without fear their own views on all events and leaders. Whatever their handicaps, there are freely elected legislative bodies at all levels and a proliferation of political parties and public organizations. The beginnings of civil society are clearly emerging in Russia and welcoming democratic, comprehensible and consistent guidance.

To predict with any certainty whether these healthy processes will eventually overcome the present trends towards disintegration and authoritarianism is impossible, but the likelihood that they will not is enough for serious concern and major policy revisions to be warranted. The vicious circle of vacillation within the Russian political élite may not continue indefinitely; the reserve of patience and perseverance in society, although surprisingly large, is not limitless. This was clearly manifested by the parliamentary election of November

1995, with the notorious defeat of the political forces that supported the president and the considerable success of the communists. Logically, the final outcome of the current impasse can be only one of two things: either the reactionaries will come to power in a legal way (the Weimar Republic model); or the growing chaos and disintegration in society will oblige the leadership to establish an authoritarian regime, discarding the remnants of democracy and relying on the army and security forces to suppress all opposing forces (the 1918 Bolshevik model). In the latter case other reactionaries will gain power from inside the bureaucracy and armed forces.

One-person control over key state institutions and total reliance on the personal loyalty of principal officials in such a situation is too weak a guarantee, as the example of the failed August 1991 *coup d'état* proved with the utmost persuasiveness. In many respects it is amazing to see how many of the mistakes made by Gorbachev in 1989–91 were repeated by President Yeltsin, who otherwise had been creating precisely the opposite image to that of his predecessor. All in all, this is yet further evidence of the enormous powers of self-regeneration of the traditional political system if it is not thoroughly redesigned and managed by no less powerful new people and political methods.

V. Conclusions: second wind for reform

In order to break out of the vicious circle outlined above, which cannot lead to any desirable outcome, it is necessary to do away with several outdated and fallacious political stereotypes still shared by the top Russian leadership, a large part of the liberal intelligentsia and most of the Western supporters of Russian reforms.

The first is the belief that the main danger to the market-oriented reforms and democratization emanates from the communist–nationalists. In reality the greatest threat to reform now comes from the inflated, corrupted and uncontrolled bureaucracy: its self-serving activities are leading to social disintegration and degradation and are creating the conditions for the advent of an authoritarian nationalist regime in one form or another. The most important task is thus to put the bureaucracy under control. What is needed for this is a new programme of reforms, elaborated outside the parochial state structures; new personalities in all key state posts; rapid expansion of all elements of democratic control, checks and balances; and greater discipline and stricter ethics in state institutions. Only such measures might provide a democratic way out and reduce the role of reactionaries inside and outside the bureaucracy. The readiness and the ability of the country's leadership to implement such radical steps will define the future of Russian democracy.

The second fallacy is that Russia is facing a choice between democracy and stability. In reality, it is precisely the lack of democracy, the inadequacy of public participation and feedback in politics and the absence of democratically worked out and implemented reform programmes which generate instability and degrade the economic and political life of society. The growing power and autonomy of the bureaucracy—the only alternative to democratization—will not bring stability or salvage reforms, because the omnipotent Russian 'state–commercial' apparatus (already much larger than that of the whole former Soviet Union) is part of the problem rather than the solution. By definition, existing problems cannot be resolved without tough political guidance and public control. Further curtailment of democracy will only bury the causes deeper and eventually make a reactionary authoritarian regime the only option, but only after a profound crisis which would itself be rife with unpredictable consequences.

The third fallacy is a stereotype which took on immediate political relevance on the eve of the June 1996 presidential election. It assumed that stability requires a strong moderate political centre between the radical reformers in the Yeltsin Administration and the extreme communist–nationalist opposition. In fact, there were no radical reformers left in the government, nor was there any sensible programme of further reforms. The top leadership was probably at the centre of the political spectrum of the society, permanently manoeuvring between liberals and anti-reformists, but gradually shifting in the direction of the latter. As with Gorbachev in 1989–91, such a policy cannot win a stable centrist political constituency. Moreover, it is neither available in a situation of rapid social stratification nor perceived as necessary by the governing nomen-clature, which prefers to rely more on executive structures and above all on their 'forceful elements'.

The massive, indiscriminate and legally dubious (despite the pro-presidential verdict of the Constitutional Court) use of force in Chechnya since December 1994 deprived the Yeltsin Administration of the support of the democratic parties in Russia and of any substantial political base. A powerful campaign during the preparations for the presidential election, aimed at presenting Yeltsin as a stronghold and the only possible guarantor of democracy, is by no means sufficient to restore his democratic credentials. If Yeltsin's regime survives this war politically, by implication it will have to rely more and more on an authori-tarian political system, armed agencies (*silovye struktury*), oppressive methods and nationalistic ideology, with all the dire consequences this entails for Russia's economic and political reforms and its relations with the rest of the world. Hence, the results of the June 1996 presidential election notwith-standing, the real political requirement for the development of democracy and stability in Russia today is the creation not of a 'moderate centre' but of a broad, consistent and active democratic opposition to the policy of the execu-tive power and the propensities of the bureaucracy. In 1989–91 such a demo-cratic opposition to the manoeuvring of Gorbachev was built and led by Yeltsin, and it saved democracy in August 1991. Such a movement is needed now more than ever before inside and outside the parliament, local legislatures and communities.

It could be hoped that it would provide a counterweight to the pressure of anti-reformist forces and halt the drift of the administration towards authoritarianism and conservativism, presenting a viable democratic alternative to both the claims of the backward-looking traditionalists and the mismanagement of the incumbent administration. Under such a scenario there would be some prospect of resolving the disastrous situation in the northern Caucasus and other political and economic problems resulting from five years of Yeltsin's rule.

5. Towards a post-imperial identity

Marie Mendras

I. Introduction

At a time when the nation-state is on the decline in the West, Russia is engaged in the difficult search for its own national identity. To overcome the effects of unplanned 'decolonization' and the subsequent shrinking of the homeland, Russia aspires to be one and whole. More than ever before, it is looking for its centre of gravity and seeking to define its new location on a transformed continent.

With a quarter of the former Soviet territory gone, Russia has formally lost control over two-fifths of the Soviet population, one-sixth of its Russian-speakers and a significant part of Soviet resources, equipment and transport outlets. Its western outpost was the border between the two Germanies; now it is Smolensk, 2000 km to the east. The area of Moscow's dominance has shifted eastward.

From this straightforward, clinical observation of post-Soviet Russia, many conclude that the Russians 'cannot take it'. The political élite in Moscow, almost with one voice and echoed by many foreign analysts and officials, explain that Russians will not, and should not, accept a loss and humiliation of such magnitude. This is one of the arguments boldly used to justify a brutal war in Chechnya since December 1994. The objective of this chapter is to challenge this litany of complaint and propose a demonstration of what Russia gains in jettisoning its imperial self and the Soviet mould.

This chapter is not an analysis of the élite's views and divisions, neither is it a study of the leadership's behaviour and policies. It is an attempt to refute the common assumptions about what divides both the élite and the people of Russia. The question to be examined here is not whether the Slavophiles will win over the 'Westernizers', whether the foreign minister has joined the 'neo-imperialists' in an aggressive nostalgia for past grandeur or whether the government's hard stance over the defence of Russians in the 'near abroad' is legitimate.

The object of this chapter is different. Looking beyond the smokescreen of Kremlin discussions and the bickering between new republican ruling élites, it considers Russia's new political and economic geography and its new position on the Eurasian landmass and in world affairs. The working assumption, in direct contradiction with the litany of complaint, is the economists' golden rule: bygones are bygones. Indeed, the dismemberment of the Soviet edifice, the ruin of the ideology and the fall of the one-party regime and state-run economy have demolished all certainties, broken the safety net of minimal social assistance and left everyone without a compass. Yet it is precisely because everything is open that the reconstruction of the old is not an alternative. The very absence of a new blueprint is in itself a formidable force pushing the country forward into the unknown. Because Russians cannot continue to think of their country in the old terms, they are forced to invent new ones.

It is this Russia, the new 'imagined community',[1] that is sketched here. This chapter argues that the Russia imagined by Russians is a relatively compact and homogeneous land, the population of which is over 80 per cent Russian. It is centred on Moscow and encompasses all the regions of central and northern Russia; its southern lands towards but excluding the northern Caucausus and the Kazakh steppes; the Ural mountains; and western Siberia with its resources and big industrial cities. Eastern Siberia and the Far East are far-away lands, seen more as a reservoir or outlet than as core Russian lands. The war in Chechnya reinforces the argument: Chechens are not Russians, Chechnya is not an indivisible part of the Russian land, and war is exacerbating the estrangement.

The exercise is highly speculative, not only because it makes assumptions about what Russians think but also because it implies that the political borders of the Federation do not necessarily define the imagined community. The argument is that the ex-Soviet national has rapidly come to terms with three big losses—immensity, the enemy and 'Sovietness'—in return for gains which are significant—a more compact nation, secure neighbours (except in the Caucasus) and 'Russianness'.

II. The end of grand design

With a reduced territory, new state borders and no enemy, Russia finds itself in a radically new situation. The tsarist Empire and the Soviet Union never had trusted and trusting allies but always had enemies. Now it has no enemies and is trying to understand the virtue of having partners, if not allies. Since the 15th century, Russia's territory has steadily expanded, with a few exceptions, the last being the years of turmoil generated by World War I and the revolutions of 1917. Successive leaderships fought to establish buffer zones at the periphery of the empire and were never keen to define the borders of the empire. Today's Russia is surrounded by states with internationally recognized borders and has to break with this tradition.

Territory made Russian history. Land, space and resources were for centuries the measure of Russian development. Military might and administrative power expanded to cope with the need to rule new territories, tame nature and subdue non-Russian populations. Immensity, it seemed, compensated for the backwardness and isolation of Russia from the rest of the continent. The philosopher Nadezhdin wrote in 1830 that Providence had manifested itself throughout

---

[1] Borrowed from Anderson, B., *Imagined Communities: Reflections on the Origin and Spread of Nationalism* (Verso: London, 1991).

Russian history since she had allowed Russia to make the most of its geographical immensity and its political and military strength.[2]

Expansion served a quest for security, to protect Muscovy from invasions and secure natural borders (water and mountain) or buffer zones at the periphery of the empire. The tsars and after them the Soviet leaderships worked to conjoin immensity with homogeneity. Tsardom was not to be a patchwork of varied principalities, separated by language, culture and political autonomy. However, with non-Russians forming half of the population at the end of the 19th century, the empire could not hope to homogenize Russia, especially given its size. In remote provinces, even if they were mainly inhabited by Russians, the capital was far away.

In post-Petrine Russia and later in the Soviet Union, the integrity and protection of the territory and administrative centralization prevailed over economic efficiency or liberal principles. The guiding principle was that the centre, Muscovy, could only tame the vast lands of the empire by forging them into one whole. Disparities were perceived as dangerous, threatening to the integrity of Russia. Today as yesterday, ethnic, religious or economic diversity is seen as a weakness. In the view of many in Moscow, the division of Russia into autonomous republics and regions, given the new context of representative democracy, regional assertiveness and local self-government, may lead to fragmentation.

This instinctive distrust of diversity was clearly reinforced by the breakup of the socialist camp in 1989 and of the USSR in 1991. It is still a widely held view in Russian discussions that federalism triggers separatist tendencies. In Ukraine, this sentiment is so widespread that proposing a federal structure for the new constitution is taken as an offence to the state. The idea prevails that, had regional and national identities been denied a political identity, claims to sovereignty would never have surfaced. In other words, federalism and national–regional autonomies in a free society (freed of an oppressive regime) tempt the devil.

Whether Russian rulers are ready to accept it or not, the sheer size of the territory is no longer the measure of Russia's success. What counts is the manageability of the national territory. The empire was impossible to administer from Moscow or St Petersburg unless the ruler resorted to repression. Today, it is clear that a highly centralized administration is not a solution for Russia.

Most politicians, even on the far right or in the ranks of the communists, play with the concepts of local government, regional economic autonomy, and differentiated taxes and subsidies. For the purpose of day-to-day administration, it seems that many Russians have discovered that small may be beautiful. In industrial and agricultural policies, ministries and central administrations in Moscow are now in charge of a more compact landscape, centred on European Russia, the Urals and western Siberia.

---

[2] Quoted by Koyré, A., *La philosophie et le problème national en Russie au début du XIXème siècle* [Philosophy and the national problem in Russia at the beginning of the 19th century] (Librairie ancienne Honoré Champion: Paris, 1929), p. 159.

A number of conversations with officials and managers in Russian provinces[3] suggest that those in charge do not regret the gigantism of the Soviet past. The revival of local identities and *oblastnichestvo* (regionalism) goes with the desire for a more compact Russia, a Russia of human size. Local politics are important. Regions have to rely on their own resources first, on erratic central subsidies second. Elected or nominated by the president of Russia, the governor of an administrative region (*oblast*) or the mayor of a big city is at the head of a political constituency and not simply a fraction of the Soviet complex.

The debate over the status of governors demonstrates the new complexity of regional government. Most heads of regional administrations were nominated by President Boris Yeltsin. Some were elected in 1993, taking the opportunity of a change in legislation, later to be countermanded. Since the adoption of the new constitution in December 1993, the president and central authorities more generally have been very keen to reassert their power over provincial leaders. The dissolution of regional *sovyety* (elected councils) after the October 1993 assault on the federal parliament further discredited representative bodies. In most cases, the new regional *dumy* or councils elected in 1994 exert little influence on regional government.

What ambitious provincial leaders want is executive power legitimated by direct universal suffrage. The election of Eduard Rossel as Governor of the Sverdlovsk *oblast* in August 1995 is a case in point.[4] Other governors, less confident and less interested in popular support or sanction, prefer the neo-Soviet status of commissar of the republic.[5] As a whole, the general impression is that regional awareness and assertiveness are directly proportional to the weakening of central government. The inability of Moscow to provide regular money and support and the lack of clear rules in relations between the centre and the provinces foster an anarchic regionalization where each must fight for his own interest.

Almost all the republics and regions in Russia are 'autonomist', not separatist—anxious to exist as identifiable entities and not to comply blindly with Moscow's directives. Tatarstan is the example of a negotiated arrangement between a republic and the Russian Federation. Chechnya was the exception, as will be seen. The Chechen leader Dzhokhar Dudaev's separatism did not prove contagious, despite the claims of the Russian leadership which used the great threat of the breakup of the Russian Federation as a pretext for the war.

[3] Interviews conducted by the author in Kalouga, Kostroma, Tver and Novosibirsk at various times in 1994.

[4] Rossel was dismissed from his post as head of the regional administration of Sverdlovsk by Boris Yeltsin in 1993, was elected chairman of the new regional *duma* in 1994, and stood for the post of governor against an acting governor who had strong support from the central government. In his own words: 'I need popular legitimacy to act as the president of my region and bargain with Moscow. My ministers will take care of day-to-day management; I will represent our interests outside the *oblast* and steer relations with Yeltsin and central administrations'. Interview by the author, 17 Oct. 1994.

[5] 'The President has chosen me', says Alexander Deryagin, head of the Kaluga *oblast*. 'Moscow has to match some of our demands. Our region is, like many others, heavily subsidized by the central government. It would be better to have our own budget, but who knows when a new fiscal system will provide decent regional revenues?' Interview by the author, Kaluga, 22 June 1994.

The end of the 'capitalist threat' has dramatically reduced the capacity of the central government to dictate economic policies and impose the defence of state interests first. For decades Soviet politics and policies were, explicitly or implicitly, guided by one all-embracing question: 'Who are Russia's enemies?' With the defeat of communism and its corollary, anti-capitalism, with the breakup of the imperial construction, the need for a *positive* definition of Russia is felt very strongly. For many years, Russia's choices were expressed as a negation of other alternatives. The Soviet Union was not a Western-style democracy, not a capitalist society, not an 'imperialist power'. Soviet leaders had more trouble expressing what it was in positive terms. The Khrushchev and Brezhnev years were a long march in quest of new, more convincing descriptions of socialism: 'the state of the whole people', 'developed socialism' and so on. Even more embarrassing was the patched-up dogma of 'internationalism' used to legitimize Moscow's clamp over entire countries.

The West was Russia's rival self. The myth of a hostile and unjust Western civilization legitimized the Soviet Union. Economic policies and political arbitrariness were always justified in terms of the confrontation with the USA and the West. The population had to accept the sacrifices imposed by what was a virtual state of war. The political discourse until the early 1980s never failed to imply that the USSR and the socialist camp lived in a hostile environment. The danger of war was ever-present in the media. The Communist Party and the Soviet state were constantly struggling to 'defend socialism' and protect the Soviet citizen.

The West was not only the convenient scarecrow but also a standard, even a model. The USSR had to do 'better' than the capitalists, to surpass their economic achievements. Competition with more and better-developed countries was the very essence of the Soviet system. Under Brezhnev, the communist Utopia was long dead and only Western achievements gave the Soviets an objective and a sense of purpose.[6] The paradox of the Soviet leadership was that in negating Western civilization it had to constantly refer to it. To use Hegelian logic, the active negation of the rival values reaffirmed the existence of these values.

If the end of the cold war and the loss of the enemy had a disruptive effect both in the USSR and in the West, the disruption is incomparably more profound in Russia. The sense of purpose in capitalist societies may be questioned but this is not primarily caused by the end of the USSR and the fall of communism. The fight against communist states was not the lifeblood of Western societies. In Russia, by contrast, it is the essence of the system that is gone with the end of the confrontation.

Even the socialist specificity is a broken myth. With the policy of *glasnost* after 1987, Soviet President Mikhail Gorbachev unleashed the fiercest criticism of Soviet society's flaws in the press. People were told not only that their

---

[6] Mendras, M., 'The Soviet Union and its rival self', *Journal of Communist Studies,* vol. 6, no. 1 (Mar. 1990), pp. 1–23.

country was in a shambles but also that their counterparts in capitalist societies benefited from better social protection. Had seven decades of socialism been worthless? The sentiment no doubt prevails that time and energy were dramatically wasted. There seems to remain one source of pride and achievement: the victory over Nazi Germany. In many ways, the glorified role of the USSR and the Russian people during World War II, when Stalin invigorated Russian nationalist propaganda, is still a monument that no one dares shatter.

In spite of the numerous blanks in Russian–Soviet history, the attraction of Western civilization has been short-lived. If democracy, the rule of law, private property and profit have become keywords in Russia, Western societies remain distant and alien. They are not foes but their relative success is a threat. To compete with the West and seek its level of prosperity is, to most Russians, a lost cause and it is therefore better not to compete but to find Russian ways out of the slump. Russians prefer to protect themselves from the outside rather than confront it. This does not imply that they will build a new 'fortress Russia' cut off from the rest of the world but that they give priority to self-reliance and minimum dependence on outsiders.

To put it in one image, Russia is cocooning. It is looking inside, not outside. Its quest for security is dictated by internal factors. The ruling élites, both in administration and in business, are primarily concerned with social stability: the economy must provide enough to meet minimal expectations from the population and the administration must ensure a somewhat regulated redistribution of resources and revenues. The ordinary Russian is too concerned about sausage, housing and health care to indulge in political dreams about Russia's grandeur and prestige. What is most astounding in opinion surveys is the belief shared by a large majority that the old system will not be resurrected. Although opinion polls are imperfect, this finding is consistent enough throughout all the polls to indicate clearly that the sentiment is widely shared. The choice for Russians is no longer between slipping back into the recent past and forcing the pace towards a Western-style society and polity. It is rather a question of economic survival on the existing social base. Muddling through may best summarize the average Russian's situation.

Messianism is dying of exhaustion. Populations are tired of grand designs and Utopias. Élites are condemned to seek economic profit, whether by efficient government or by corrupt dealings. Since Russia is struggling to define its own civilization, cultural domination may not be a credible ambition. As to the clash of civilizations or the dominant culture in each region of the globe, the question does not so much concern Russia, which feels strong enough, or specific enough, to be immune from cultural domination, be it US and Japanese capitalisms or Islamic civilization.

If neither the élites nor the population are much concerned about what goes on outside the national boundaries, neither should they be inclined to engender and fuel new ideologies of competition and common sacrifice for a great universal cause.

III. Searching for a national identity

Putting aside for the moment the Russian past, the legacy of the imperial and Soviet periods and even questions about its state borders, what is and where is Russia? Is it possible to define 'authentic' Russian lands? There are no easy criteria. Neither the Russian language nor orthodoxy can serve as sure indicators, still less an improbable 'Russian ethnos'. Can Russia be defined in terms of climate, way of life and economic development? Do previous political borders define a more integrated and consensual Russia? Is history more of a determining factor than national and cultural diversity?

None of these directions is convincing. A more promising, even if highly speculative, approach seems to be some free thinking about how Russians define their Russianness and their national community. What is Russia for a Russian? What sense of the nation or homeland does he have? To put it bluntly, does the ordinary Russian think of the former Soviet Union as his country, the national community to which he belongs? Does he envision the Russian, Belarussian and Ukrainian republics united in one political community? Can the Federation of Russia be the imagined nation?

There may be different ways of addressing the question, and traditional methods of sociological analysis are not necessarily the most helpful. Opinion polls are not always reliable and should not be over-interpreted. Surveys give a picture of what a population expresses as its major preoccupations and dominant opinions about the current situation and declared policies. They do not tell much about the Russian, American or French mind. To look for the answer in official declarations would be even more irrelevant because it would merely revive the litany of complaint and its massive argument: 'What was Soviet was ours, and we have rights over past property'.

What may be more important here is to understand how Russians imagine Russia, how they implicitly define their national political community. This would require a close reading of Russian history and observation of the cultural environment. Russians' self-perceptions have also been strongly affected by the remarkable adjustment of the population at large to recent change, both in Moscow and in the provinces.

First and foremost, Russia is the country of Russians (*Russkie*). Russians think of their country as belonging to Russians and tolerating non-Russians who speak Russian. Non-Russian territories, such as the Caucasus, Central Asia and the Baltic states, where the historical roots are not Russian, belonged to the empire, not to Russia. Russia, contrary to all official qualifications, is not and never was diluted in the empire. Even though the term *Rossiya* is different from the original *Rus* and is to be distinguished from the more ethnic-defining adjective *russkiy*, for the ordinary Russian as for the Russian intellectual—be he Jewish, half-Russian or half-Ukrainian—*Rossiya* is the country of Russians, *Russkie*.

Greater Russia, be it the tsarist empire or the Soviet Union, was a painfully constructed polity, based on a non-national, even anti-national, ideology. It was not an extended Russian nation. The Russian subject worshipped the empire but he did distinguish between himself and the non-Russians. The Soviet citizen was more often than not proud of the Soviet Union, of its might and achievements, yet he did not become a-national; he retained his nationality.

The atavism of Slavic Messianism, combined with the continental continuity of the territory, the patrimonial tradition of the autocratic sovereign and the centralizing strategies, helped to develop the mythology of an imperial nation, of Soviet Man.[7] The latter has not survived the fall of the USSR and communist rule. Recent developments have shown that this vision of the 300-odd million human beings living in the USSR was oversimplified and deceptive. Even if the ordinary Soviet national was a captive of the system, he belonged to communities other than the state—his village or town, his region or national republic, his profession. 'Sovietness' was, paradoxically, a political rather than a sociological reality. To be a Soviet national was to be a subject of the Soviet state. When a Russian, a Ukrainian or a Kazakh visited the West, he would introduce himself as 'Soviet' or 'from the Soviet Union'. In so doing, he would express the fact that he was a citizen of the USSR and that he was *not* French, German or Polish. His nationality was a priori irrelevant in an encounter with a non-Soviet. The Soviet passport indicated citizenship (Soviet) and nationality in an ethnic sense (Russian, Ukrainian, Uzbek, Armenian and so on).

Since the 1960s, Soviet people have lost their respect for the official ideology and have sought to shelter their consciences and families from the state religion that simply ensured the continued domination of one leading group over the entire population. There undoubtedly is a Soviet way of life which has survived the end of the communist regime. It is more difficult to accept the existence and persistence in the future of a Soviet mind, or more modestly of a Soviet community bringing together all former Soviet nationals under one roof and one banner.

The end of the USSR and the sudden emergence of 15 sovereign states in one stroke destroyed the political existence of Soviet Man and forced him to find a new one immediately. For many, the change was swift and welcome. They transformed their nationality under Soviet rule (Armenian or Russian, for instance) into citizenship (citizen of Armenia, citizen of the Russian Federation). For large groups and numerous scattered individuals, the question is still unresolved. Millions of former Soviet citizens have not acquired a new citizenship—Russians in Central Asia, Estonia and Latvia who are neither citizens of Russia nor citizens of their country of residence, and Armenians, Ukrainians and other non-Russians in Russia who cling to their old Soviet passports. Others have a new citizenship but have, against their will, become minority

---

[7] The notion of Soviet Man implies first of all political and psychological self-identification with a Soviet state, imperial in its legacy and authoritarian in its government. It is not to be confused with Alexander Zinovyev's *homo Sovieticus*, a man who had lost all individual conscience and was reduced to a fraction of one big Soviet collective.

groups in new national states. This is the case for a good number of the Russians living in Estonia, Kazakhstan, Latvia or Ukraine. It is also true for some of the Armenians, Georgians and Ukrainians residing in Russia and faced with a difficult choice of citizenship.

By and large, for the great majority of ex-Soviets, the loss of Soviet citizenship has been no trauma. For many non-Russians, particularly in the Baltic and Caucasian republics, it was a 'national victory'. For Russians, by contrast, it reopened the complex and painful question of the Russian national identity in a broken empire which they had dominated.

Under the USSR, the Russian identity was pushed into the background by the ideologically imposed (and largely artificial) Soviet identity. Today it is overshadowed by the concept of 'all-Russian' (*vserossiyskiy*) identity.[8] A Buryat or a Tatar has his own republic in the Federation, the Russian does not. Perhaps out of exasperation with his hybrid nature, he seems to be distancing himself from his Tatar and Cossack antecedents. Dostoyevsky's formula 'Scratch a Russian, you will discover a Tatar' is not in fashion. Russians do not refer to a Russian ethnicity or ethnos, probably because it is a lost battle given the blend of different tribes and peoples down the centuries. They are simply trying to escape from the multinational past and reconquer a Russian identity that they so generously, and often coercively, imposed on others, most notably with Russification.

In their search for Russianness, they leave behind their imperial history. In the words of Valeriy Tishkov, Director of the Institute of Ethnology and Anthropology of the Russian Academy of Sciences, 'Russia is not a "national state" of ethnic Russians. Neither is any constituent part of it the exclusive property of any ethnic group. The realization of these fundamentals can give Russia a chance to move towards a civil society and a democratic state where human rights are respected and the cultural mosaic is preserved'.[9] This is the paradox of today's Russians. They mourn past grandeur but long for a national identity. Pursuing an argument not very different from this one, Roman Szporluk also concludes that 'the Russian nation is not bound to opt for the imperial way . . . simply because the good of Russia and its people calls for attention to matters at home, in the Russian Federation'.[10]

IV. The limits of the imagined community

There is no doubt that the legacy of the past, as well as the demographic realities of the present, affect Russian thinking on ethno-territorial issues. Thus, underlining the complexity of the Russian–Ukrainian relationship, Szporluk

---

[8] The term *vserossiyskiy* is a-national and defines only the geographical boundaries of the Federation of Russia.

[9] Tishkov, V. A., 'What is *Rossia*? Prospects for nation-building', *Security Dialogue*, vol. 26, no. 1 (1995), p. 47.

[10] Szporluk, R., 'Belarus, Ukraine and the Russian Question: a comment', *Post-Soviet Affairs*, vol. 9, no. 4 (1993), p. 373.

recalls that before 1991 'most Russians apparently never took seriously the "Ukrainian Question" and, accordingly, regarded the Ukrainian Soviet Socialist Republic as a fiction. They continued to think of Ukraine as part of a larger and more real Russia. Indeed, for them, the Russian Soviet Federative Socialist Republic (RSFSR) itself was also a fiction, never really standing for Russia *per se*'.[11]

However, this 'extended' Russian thinking is gradually becoming outdated. A rapid evolution has taken place since 1992, reinforcing the political existence and national identity of most republics, despite Moscow's stiffening language of 'reintegration'. What Russians, Belarussians and Ukrainians seem to be most concerned about is free entry to and travel in the former Soviet republics, free exchange and access to goods. What the élites in those countries must be keen to preserve is their new status as national rulers.

On the surface, the cultural, linguistic, geographic and historical proximity of these three Eastern Slav peoples is a strong argument for advocating or predicting a new integration into one polity, but it is by no means a sufficient one. Proximity may even create an incentive to cultivate particularities and defend one's identity and independence. Paradoxically, in this respect the dominance of the Russian language may prove to be more detrimental to Russia's state-building than to Belarus's or Ukraine's. A Ukrainian citizen may speak Russian more readily than Ukrainian but Ukrainian is his national language. For a Russian, the language is not a straightforward symbol of Russianness because it is so extensively spoken by others.

The fact that 25-odd million Russian-speakers now live abroad, in Belarus, Estonia, Kazakhstan, Latvia, Ukraine or Central Asia, is certainly a new phenomenon for Russian thinking and complicates the whole development in the post-Soviet space. Contrary to some over-easy assumptions, however, it is not a daunting problem. Russians are not irredentist about Russian communities outside. The explanation may be that a Russian national community did not exist under Soviet rule. Hence, the 150 million Soviet Russians did not form a solidarity group. They missed a clear sense of belonging to one group and were deprived of most republican institutions. The RSFSR, contrary to the other republics of the Union, did not have its own Communist Party (after 1925), its Academy of Sciences, and so on.[12]

Russian-speakers in the former republics of the Soviet Union pose problems in the state building of the new states, rather than in Russia.[13] Just as the existence of French-speaking communities in Belgium, Canada and Switzerland did

[11] Szporluk (note 10), p. 368.
[12] Mendras, M., *Un État pour la Russie* (Complexe: Brussels, 1992), pp. 21–23; and 'Existe-t-il un État russe?' [Is there such a thing as the Russian state?], *Politique Étrangère*, no. 1 (1992), pp. 25–34.
[13] In the Baltic states, opinion surveys indicate that Russians do not feel mistreated, are prepared to share their host republic's destiny and do not wish to leave for Russia. Russia is not their home. Rose, R. and Maley, W., 'Conflict or compromise in the Baltic states?', Radio Free Europe/Radio Liberty (hereafter RFE/RL), *RFE/RL Research Report*, vol. 3, no. 28 (15 July 1994), pp. 26–35. The situation is very different in Central Asia, where (apart from the northern regions of Kazakhstan) Russians live in a culturally alien environment.

not impede the building of a French nation, the Russians abroad are not a major obstacle to nation building in Russia. Most of them have not changed their place of residence as a result of the breakup of the USSR and will adjust to the new sovereign status of the republic they live in. It will clearly be more difficult for Russians in the states of Central Asia than for those in Belarus or Ukraine.

Non-Russians in the Russian Federation are altogether a different matter. Other Slavs—Belarussians, Poles and Ukrainians—are well assimilated. Non-Slavs pose various problems. Most of these peoples have a titular republic or territory, inherited from the administrative patchwork of the 1920s. The 1993 Russian Constitution stipulates (Article 5, para. 1) that all subjects of the Federation—the republics, *kraya* (territories or provinces), *oblasti* (regions), federal cities, autonomous regions and autonomous districts—are equal (*ravno-pravnye*) but that only republics are 'states' (*gosudarstva*) (Article 5, para. 2). Most republics have adopted their own constitutions.

The north Caucasian republics are a special case. There Russians are a minority and Caucasians a large majority. National assertiveness is present in all the republics but nowhere except Chechnya has it led to open defiance of Moscow.

Chechnya was the exception. Boris Yeltsin, with a few men in the Kremlin, decided in December 1994 to wage a fully-fledged war to do away with the Chechnyan separatists. For the sake of 'territorial integrity', they started the most brutal enterprise of the destruction of a large city, of a small country and of a significant part of its population of one million.[14] To prove that Chechnya was part of its patrimony, the Russian leadership agreed to the systematic destruction of what Yeltsin had that same month called 'a Russian city'. The majority of the 300 000–400 000 refugees or homeless are Russians who had to flee from Chechnya. Approximately 400 000 Russians were permanent residents of the republic before 1994. The war has made Chechnya more Chechen.

As a Russian journalist very aptly wrote, 'if you define Chechnya not as the territory (which can always be "cleansed" of its "armed bandits" but also of all its population), but as the Chechen people, it is clear that this people will be for several generations cut off from Russia, at least in heads and hearts'.[15]

All opinion polls conducted in Russia since December 1994 show a growing dissatisfaction with and condemnation of the war in Chechnya.[16] To politicians and the military, the northern Caucasus may have an important strategic value. To the ordinary Russian, these regions are not part of the homeland, but left-overs of the empire. They are a source of insecurity on the borders of Russia and are outside the imagined Russian community.

[14] Mendras, M., 'Tchétchénie, la guerre du Kremlin' [Chechnya, the Kremlin's war], *Esprit*, nos 3–4 (Mar./Apr. 1995), pp. 111–19.
[15] Burtin, Yu., 'Voyna: predvaritelnye itogi' [The war: first evaluations], *Moskovskie Novosti*, no. 3 (15–22 Jan. 1995), p. 6.
[16] 'Chechenskiy krizis i vybory-96' [The Chechen crisis and the 1996 elections], *Segodnya*, 7 Feb. 1995; and Gudkov, L., 'Vlast i chechenskaya voyna v obshchestvennom mnenie' [Power and the war in Chechnya in public opinion], *Segodnya*, 23 Feb. 1995.

Does Siberia have its place in the imagined Russia? Siberia is not one but many. The cities of the Urals and western Siberia, built in the 17th, 18th and 19th centuries, are an intrinsic part of Russia: the industrial and agricultural development of modern Russia was conditioned by the conquest of those lands and the settlement of Russian pioneers. The southern Siberian border territories are an eclectic group. The Republic of Tuva, incorporated in the USSR only in 1944, remains an outsider, despite heavy Russian immigration and colonization. The other regions, such as Buryatia, are seen by Russians as part of their Siberian lands.

Beyond Tomsk and Kemerovo, however, Russia becomes such a thin line of railway and towns, and the distances from European Russia become so great, that a sense of wilderness and aloofness prevails. Eastern Siberia and the Far East are not core Russian lands but a distant periphery or extended backyard. Vladivostok and Khabarovsk are two far-away outposts in what Russians term 'the Far East', not eastern Russia. Yakut-Sakha and other regions of eastern Siberia and the Far East are rich in resources which Moscow, naturally, does not intend to abandon to local élites. Nevertheless, Moscow's claim over at least a significant part of the resources may reinforce the 'colonial' status, as distinct from 'home', of remote Siberian provinces, even though Russians and other Slavs are far more numerous than indigenous peoples.

The national republics of the Volga are yet another group. Tatarstan, Bashkortostan, Udmurtia, Chuvashia, Mordovia and Mariy El are centrally located in European Russia. Kazan, only 800 km south-east of Moscow, was conquered by Ivan the Terrible in 1552; four centuries have turned it into a part of the core lands of Russia. The Tatars are one of the most urbanized and Russified groups in demographic and social terms. The titular nationalities do not form a majority in any of the six republics, except in Chuvashia,[17] and interaction between ethnic groups is traditionally important, as intermarriage rates indicate, and peaceful. The problem today rests mostly on the republican and national status of the titular group which must combine its 'Tatarness' or 'Bashkirness' with some form of 'Russianness'. The very large majority of non-Russians on the Volga speak Russian and do not question their being part of Russia. If Chechnya or Tuva could physically leave the Federation—it would simply imply a change of border—Tatarstan can only negotiate its political and economic status in Russia and redefine its relations with the central government.

In the Russian mind, the Volga republics belong to the imagined community. This is, however, a sensitive region because it complicates the search for a Russian identity. These republics prove that Russianness is not a strictly ethnic or linguistic notion. The centuries-long cohabitation of Tatars and Volga peoples with the Eastern Slavs and the central position of their national territories are the decisive factors.

[17] According to the 1989 census, Chuvash made up 68% of the population in Chuvashia.

The western limit of Russia is drawn by the borders with the newly independent states of Estonia, Latvia, Belarus and Ukraine. The determination of those countries to stay on the world map is strong enough, with a possible reservation about Belarus, to impress the fact of their existence gradually on people's minds. Regular national elections in these countries have contributed to forging the sentiment of belonging to one's own state community. The reality of these new polities seems to be more easily accepted now by the population of Russia, which is primarily concerned with freedom of communications and exchange between the former Soviet republics. In the aftermath of the collapse of the USSR, the main fear was that independence would mean separation between the countries. However, when it became clear that Belarus, Russia and Ukraine were relatively open spaces, the sense of loss declined. Anyone in Russia may visit relatives in Ukraine without restriction—the high cost of travel being the new limitation.

Russian politicians and strategic experts may argue endlessly about Russians on the other side of the border, about the 'legitimate right' of Russia to its 'historic lands', about the 'artificiality of Belarus', and so on.[18] It is a lost battle. States may be weak inside, with fragile governments and corrupt administrations, but they are recognized actors on the international scene. As a consequence, Russia has to accept that a complete break with imperial and Soviet history has taken place and its state sovereignty now stops at its border. Power and influence are, of course, another matter. Yet the rules of the game are now much better defined and compelling. The new states have entered the world community. It is this community's duty to remember this and remind the Russian leadership of it.

Protesting about lost territories and wealth, from the Baltic to the Black Sea, is a stick with which to beat one's political foes.[19] Talking tough on the Russian 'sphere of influence' is also the product of Russia's concern not to become a junior partner of the West. However, some Russian politicians recognize full well that the empire is lost for ever. Even Gorbachev, in an interview in July 1994, explained that the republics' achievement of sovereignty was irreversible.[20] The last General Secretary of the Soviet Communist Party had at last come to terms with the independence of the former Soviet republics.

V. Concluding remarks

The Russia sketched here is not a nation-state; it is a national community, the limits of which do not have to coincide with the borders of the state. The question whether Russians have come to terms with their new state borders or

[18] See, e.g., Sorokin, K. E., Russian Academy of Sciences, Institute of Europe, 'Rossiya i mnogo-polyarnost: vremya obnimat, i vremya uklonyatsa ot obyatii' [Russia and multipolarity: a time to embrace, and a time to avoid being embraced], *Polis*, no. 1 (1994), pp. 7–32.

[19] The former foreign minister's litany about Russians in the 'near abroad' should be read in this light. See in particular 'An interview with Russian Foreign Minister Andrey Kozyrev', *RFE/RL Research Report*, vol. 3, no. 28 (15 July 1994), pp. 36–42.

[20] *Nezavisimaya Gazeta,* 7 July 1994.

will claim the Belarussian, Ukrainian, Kazakh and Caucasian lands as theirs is certainly an important one. Yet Russians do not generally think in terms of state borders and subjects of international law. Their concern is to belong to a political community, with a national (not necessarily ethnic) identity and a sense of commonness. The forming of this community is closely associated with a search for security, both internally and at the periphery of the community. The imagined Russia is more Russian and more secure than the former Soviet Union with its integrated non-Russian republics and European satellites.

The essential point is that the imagined Russia may be smaller, not larger, than the Federation. In a context of peace, political borders are not as significant today as they were yesterday. The state is no longer the only legitimate and most desired community. As long as borders with neighbouring states are open to people, goods and capital, Russians abroad are not left out. Non-Russians in Russia are not prisoners of a state system because those who wish to be also Russian citizens (*Rossiyane*) may be so (in Buryatia, Karelia, the Volga republics, and so on).

Russia's integrity is, however, called into question by the Caucasian cauldron. The Kremlin's war in Chechnya is the most potent demonstration of the fact that Chechnya is not Russia and that Russians do not regard Chechens as 'theirs'. The leadership in Moscow cannot on the one hand claim a right to protect Russian-speakers abroad, which is a violation of the principle of territoriality, and on the other hand destroy Chechnya and kill a good part of its population to defend the principle of territorial integrity.

Russia cannot be a nation-state in the different 19th- and 20th-century uses of the word. It will have to be both the Russian state (*rossiyskoe gosudarstvo*) and the core of the Russian-speaking world around. Its economic, cultural and geopolitical influence will continue to be important, but to try to integrate all traditionally Russian-speaking regions into the Russian state might undermine its vitality. Today it is surrounded by former imperial lands which are not enemies of Russia, again with the possible exception of the northern Caucasus. No threat to Russian integrity and security is likely to come from Kazakhstan, Ukraine, Belarus, the Baltic states or Finland. Russian politicians prefer to speak of a 'sphere of influence'. In reality, unless oil is poured on the fire, they have gained friendly neighbours.

6. Russia's emerging statehood in the national security context

Aleksei M. Salmin

I. Introduction

The external and internal aspects of national security are inseparable in today's Russia. They form more or less lasting 'crisis complexes', both actual and potential. Most of these complexes are, in one way or another, related to Russia's fundamental problem: the immaturity of its statehood. The question at issue is not only the political system *per se*, but also the new Russian state's self-determination within the geopolitical space of the former Soviet Union and the implications of that for Europe and the international community.

None of the former constituent republics of the USSR at the time of the Union's collapse was a complete state with all the appurtenances of state-hood—frontiers, an army, a monetary system and a state machine. In 1991 the Russian Soviet Federative Socialist Republic (RSFSR) was the least complete state among all the republics, coexisting and competing with the Soviet state (the USSR) and the Communist Party. This seems to have made the disintegration of the USSR easier and, at the same time, weakened the new Russian state first and foremost in terms of its internal structure. Economic and regional interests formerly represented by the totalitarian union centre were gradually organized in other union republics during 1988–91 to counterbalance the centre. There was no matching process in the RSFSR. The formation of the Russian state was thus made difficult at the very outset, and this has aggravated the problem of the maintenance of national security and complicated Russia's relations with its immediate and more distant neighbours.

The historical forms of self-sufficient nationhood have largely been destroyed in Russia and the basic concepts of its national existence and political organization have yet to take shape. By this is meant not only the concept of the constitution, but also sufficiently developed concepts of federalism, inter-ethnic and inter-confessional relations, foreign policy and defence doctrines, domestic security concepts, the philosophy of international alliances, and so on.

Since the collapse of the USSR, the Russian Federation has confronted two main internal challenges to its security and even to its national existence. These challenges might in principle jeopardize European as well as world security in the broadest sense of the word.

The first threat was a crisis of the regime which may result in the rise of extremist and/or (even more likely) nationalist groupings to power in Russia. If they involved the country in a series of home and foreign policy adventures, this could seriously challenge the established order in Europe and the European institutions. After Boris Yeltsin's victory in the presidential election of June 1996, this danger moved slightly aside, although it has not vanished entirely. The second was the prospect of Russia's collapse, following the scenario of 1917–20 or any other, entailing the destabilization of a vast geopolitical zone and radically tipping the balance of power in Europe and the world. The threats analysed in this chapter are not mutually exclusive; in fact, the opposite is the case. They could only materialize in some combination or other.

This chapter explores the domestic aspects of Russia's security. Its security is understood as the ability of the state to ensure the attainment of the following goals: (a) the completion of the ethnic and economic divorce in the best possible way from its neighbours—the former republics of the Soviet Union, which could be expected to lead to the formation of a community integrated in a new fashion and incorporated in the organized European and world system; (b) the safeguarding of regional security at the same time as protecting Russia's national interests and respecting its international commitments; and (c) the maintenance of law and order on Russia's territory and the securing of its integrity within boundaries that are acceptable to the politically decisive nucleus of society and compatible with Russia's international obligations. These goals interpreted as foreign policy objectives imply the establishment and efficient functioning of a political regime which is not at variance with human nature, enjoys authority and is legitimate, does not ignore people's conceptions of history and natural borders, has a clear-cut concept of national interests, and is oriented to joining the world and European communities.

Section II of this chapter considers the emerging political system, its social component and the challenges to social stability that could impinge on political stability. Section III examines the stability of the republics and regions which make up the Russian Federation and the threat posed to its cohesion by different kinds of conflict, while section IV identifies the areas of greatest risk to the security of the Russian Federation and their implications for its international relations. Section V presents some general background considerations and section VI the conclusions that may be drawn.

II. The emerging political system

One of the most dangerous political results of the collapse of the old system was the existence of two autonomous centres of power within Russia during 1991–93: the Congress of People's Deputies and the presidency. They emerged on the political scene at two different times, the former in 1990, the latter in 1991, and both were better suited to the Soviet than to the Russian structure. The continuous conflict between them unfolded within the framework of a constitution whose authority was declining and which was too easy to modify. It is debatable whether or not the tragic outcome of the conflict was inevitable, but it is clear that it was in no way accidental and that it sapped the strength of the state.

This conflict between the two branches of government inevitably increased the degree of uncertainty in Russia's relations with Europe and the rest of the Western world. Foreign policy became a hostage to it. It was feared at the time that the country might take an 'anti-Western' turn if the Congress of People's Deputies won; this fear now appears to have been exaggerated, but the attempt to use the foundations of foreign policy as a tool in internal political struggles was detrimental to Russia's standing in Europe and the world. Certain Russian politicians also entertained hopes, if only implicit ones, that the threat of the ascent of anti-Western forces to power would push the governments of Western Europe and the USA and the international financial institutions to invest (literally and politically) in Russian democracy. This never came about.

The adoption of the new constitution and the election of the parliament (the Federal Assembly) on 12 December 1993 meant that the president and parliament, so long as they both abide by the constitution, no longer have the possibility either to annex central power or to prevent each other from exercising their legitimate powers. The dangerous disagreement between the executive and legislative branches of power, which had become centres of attraction for various political forces, is unlikely to reappear, at least not in the form it took up to the end of 1993. This does not, of course, necessarily mean that Russia now has a sound system of political power, but its groundwork is laid and being gradually reinforced.

To be viable and balanced at the same time, power must also (*a*) win itself reliable support in society, (*b*) develop its functional structures, and (*c*) lay the foundations of consistent and consensual foreign policy.

The sanction of society

Support for the maintenance of power in society today is a combination of dynamism, readiness for compromise, desire for order and orientation to the rule of law. Dynamism is ensured mainly by the broadening of the sphere of personal initiative and personal mobility, which is only partially reflected by the official statistics and, therefore, too often overestimated.[1] As regards the

[1] See reports prepared in 1993–94 by different research centres. Institute of Humanitarian and Political Studies, *Potentsial i perspektivy rossiyskogo federalisma, 1 avgusti 1993* [Potential and prospects of Russian federalism, 1 August 1993] (IHPS: St Petersburg, 1994), p. 23; Gelman, V., *Novaya mestnaya politika* [A new local policy] (IHPS: Moscow, 1994), p. 28; Senatova, O. and Kasimov, A., *Federatsiya ili novy unitarism?* [Federation or new unitarism?] (IHPS: Saratov-Moscow, 1994), p. 11; other materials of IHPS monitoring the situation in the Russian regions; and publications of the Center for Political Technologies: *CHG v srednesrochnoy perspektivoy* [CIS: mid-term prospects (CPT: Moscow, 1994), p. 14; Pappe, M., *Rossiyskie ekonomicheskie elity* [Russia's economic élites: a sketchy description] (CPT: Moscow, 1994), p. 14; and Magomedov, A., *Politicheskie elity v rossiyskikh provintsiyakh* [Political élites in the Russian provinces] (CPT: Moscow, 1994), p. 12. See also Salmin, A., *Postsovetskoe prostranstvo; usloviya i perspektivy integratsii* [Post-Soviet territory: conditions and prospects of integration] (Foundation for Development of Parliamentarism: Moscow, 1994), p. 2; Nesterenko, A., *Byudzhetnye osnovy ukrepleniya rossiyskogo federalisma* [Budget foundation for a stronger Russian federalism] (Foundation for Development of Parliamentarism: Moscow, 1994), p. 2; Council for Foreign and Defence

readiness for compromise, relative tolerance and fear of wars and conflicts were major elements of the psychological atmosphere in Russian society during *perestroika*.[2]

Most of Russian society at present, including the overwhelming majority in the provincial areas—a very important point—is still oriented to maintaining stability. The apparent growth, after the beginning of reforms in 1992, of sentiment in favour of a planned economy and social security is to be seen in the same context of people seeking more order in everyday life. There were two bodies of opinion in Russian society as it was undergoing reorganization: a 'market' point of view and a 'social' point of view. Each of them at different times was in a majority of approximately 60–70 per cent of the population. It is obvious that for a certain section of society the orientation to the market and free enterprise was in one way or another combined with expectations that the advantages of regulated prices, social allowances and so on would continue. Changes in this respect today are mostly the result of experience. This is a complex matter: what is sometimes taken for frustration with market values is in most cases frustration with the inability of the market economy to automatically solve all the problems of society. According to public opinion polls taken during the period of reform, the number of those who are 'frustrated' by the realities of the market economy has grown, but so has the number of those who are against any restraint on private business and market activities. Similarly, concern over the penetration of foreign capital in Russia ('a threat to its independence') has grown, but the proportion of those who support inviting foreign investment has also grown or remained stable.

An Agreement on Public Accord signed on 28 April 1994[3] was a political event in Moscow, but raised interest at the provincial level only to the degree to which people there were concerned with the political battles in the capital. The idea of such an agreement has been of little relevance in most regions of Russia because of the relative stabilization of the social and political situation. Public opinion polls indicated that the immediate demands of survival overrode the developing social and political conflicts.

Finally, society is increasingly oriented to the rule of law. In today's Russia, which has lived through seven decades of totalitarianism and another decade of more or less disorderly development, it is law and not tradition, sacral authority

Policy, 'Strategiya dlya Rossii' [A strategy for Russia], *Nezavisimaya Gazeta*, 19 Aug. 1992, pp. 4–5; Council for Foreign and Defence Policy, 'Strategiya dlya Rossii: II' [A strategy for Russia: II], *Nezavisimaya Gazeta*, 27 Aug. 1993, pp. 4–5; Council for Foreign and Defence Policy, 'Vozroditsya li soyuz? Budushchee postsovetskogo prostranstva' [Will the union revive? The future of the post-Soviet space], *Nezavisimaya Gazeta*, 23 May 1996; Kozhokin, Ye., 'Gosudarstvennaya Duma i Zemskii Sobor' [The State Duma and the Assembly of the land], *Segodnya*, 15 Apr. 1994; Russian League of Industrialists and Businessmen, *Rossiyskie regiony v perekhodny period* [The Russian regions enter a transitional period] (Russian League of Industrialists and Businessmen, Expert Center: Moscow, 1993), p. 103; and Tishkov, V., *Natsionalnye otnosheniya v Rossiyskoy Federatsii* [Nationality relations in the Russian Federation] (Russian Academy of Sciences: Moscow, 1993), p. 72.

[2] *Russian Society: Chaos, Order or Orderly Chaos?* (Center for Political Technologies: Moscow, 1994), pp. 2–7, 11–12.

[3] The Agreement on Public Accord was solemnly signed by dozens of small political parties and social organizations, though not by the Communist Party. *Rossiyskaya Gazeta*, 30 Apr. 1994.

or an abstract idea of justice that is usually the supreme norm regulating political relations. Political figures refer constantly to the law, which represents an immense break both from the pre-revolutionary practice of political life and from official Soviet ideology.[4]

Strengthening the state

Modern Russian society is developing its functional structures very quickly, sometimes even 'overdoing the job', as is typical of bureaucrats. A new, non-ideologized body of civil servants is coming into being. On 22 December 1993, for example, a presidential decree approved an Ordinance on the Federal Civil Service,[5] although a civil service as such is just one element in the system of executive power and its reform will be useless unless the system of power structures and above all of the armed forces and the general and special-purpose police is changed.

Judging by opinion polls, the strengthening of the state has the support of the greater part of the population. On some occasions this support has grown into a demand for the establishment of order, which does not rule out the use of harsh methods. It would, however, be a mistake to identify these feelings with a nostalgic longing for a 'firm hand' as such. Polls also show that the majority does not want any restriction of political freedoms or *glasnost* or a ban on any political parties.

The achievement of social stability can only strengthen the political regime. On the whole, the first period of reforms in Russia, which was marked by the transition to a disorderly market, rapid social differentiation and the replacement of the political élite in 1991–92, did not destabilize society or make the state unmanageable. As a result a relatively stable social and state system emerged in the Russian Federation; some observers even called it 'stagnant'. It is safeguarded by the emergence of a new, integrated and homogeneous socio-political élite, especially after October 1993. Stability is also assisted by a sufficiently high level of social mobility among the most active groups in society and a far higher level of expectations on the part of sufficiently broad social strata. Many social stabilizers such as the family, the enterprise and some social protection mechanisms are also being preserved.

In a few years' time, however, Russia will have to face several new challenges to its internal stability. First, a substantial increase in unemployment, caused by structural changes in the economy, reductions in the armed forces and mass emigration from the successor states of the USSR, is practically inevitable. Of particular concern is the development of areas of permanent high unemployment, where whole towns or even groups of settlements were

---

[4] Russian Academy of Sciences, Institute of Sociology, Socioexpress Center, Moscow, *Zerkalo mnenii: resultaty oprosov obshchestvennogo mneniya rossiyskogo naseleniya* [Mirror of opinions: results of opinion polls of the Russian population], no. 1 (1992–93), pp. 5–7; no. 2 (1992–93), pp. 37–38; no. 3 (1992–93), pp. 12–14; no. 4 (1992–93), pp. 9–13; and no. 5 (1992–93), pp. 17–19.

[5] *Konsultatsionnoe Soveshchanie*, no. 1 (Aug. 1993). pp. 76–91.

formerly oriented to one kind of production only, most often the military industry,[6] and the disproportionate growth of unemployment in the national republics of the Russian Federation, especially in the northern Caucasus. Second, the securities market, which is already large enough to be important, will inevitably become a permanent factor affecting social and even political stability within the country. The underdevelopment of this market in combination with heightened expectations can occasionally produce serious conflict situations and even crises. Third, further growth of marginal groups of the population is highly probable. One-third of the population is already marginalized or on the way to being so: widespread alcoholism and increased drug addiction are increasingly permanently excluding people from the system of social relationships.[7] Efforts to restrain the growth of crime, which according to public opinion polls worries the majority of the population more than anything else, are unlikely to succeed in the foreseeable future. Finally, growing social differentiation, even in a relatively 'safe' environment, will contribute to raising the general level of discontent. A fairly widespread opinion (although this is generally not confirmed by the findings of special studies)[8] that the new business community is of 'non-indigenous' ethnic origin may also provoke inter-ethnic conflicts and increasing chauvinist feeling.

These and other challenges are substantially mitigated by several circumstances. Employment structures are still relatively paternalistic. Factory managers are using every tool they can to avoid open unemployment by resorting to the latent or partial kinds. Factory workers, in their turn, vary the forms of their employment and often keep their jobs only as a symbol of social status. Conditions vary greatly between regions. Combined with the vast territorial expanses, this makes simultaneous organized social action difficult. The state of affairs is relatively better in the capital city and some other major centres, which reduces the probability that social and political tension within the country will develop into a mass social explosion such as could jeopardize the foundation of the regime.

The potential for stabilization can only be realized if the current authorities take into account certain definite requirements. Their legitimacy must be consolidated both through legislation and by abstaining from actions which are explicitly at variance with legal and moral norms. The stability of the élite itself must be ensured, and this must preclude open conflict between its various elements (the top commanders of the army, the Ministry of the Interior, the military–industrial, energy and agro-industrial complexes and so on) whose

---

[6] Numerical estimates are impossible to make in this case because official statistics are extremely unreliable and alternative data sources are fragmentary. According to authoritative experts data concerning the degree of economic recession and information about the state of affairs in the labour market are not trustworthy.

[7] All-Russian Centre for the Study of Public Opinion (VTsIOM), *Ekonomicheskie i sotsialnye izmeneniya: monitoring obshchestvennogo mneniya* [Mirror of opinions . . . Economic and social change: the monitoring of public opinion], no. 1 (1994), p. 1.

[8] Salmin, A. *et al.*, *Politicheskie partii v Rossii v 1989–93: stanovlenie sistemy* [Political parties in Russia in 1989–93: institution of a system] (Nachala Press: Moscow, 1994), pp. 390–92.

interests will in time objectively diverge. The most influential regional élites must be involved progressively in the political process unfolding in Moscow. The inevitable decline in the rate of upward mobility and, correspondingly, in expectations must be compensated through 'levelling up' at least a section of the middle social strata with the new 'top'. A broader political centre must be formed and the extremist (communist and nationalist) political 'flanks' reduced and/or transformed into more moderate political groupings; this objective, like the previous one, is unlikely to be achieved unless the economic 'cake' to be cut up is made bigger.

The achievement of social stability will strengthen the political regime but it will not guarantee the preservation of the regime under any scenario. In a certain sense today the political structure is an inverted pyramid. At the top is the presidency, whose broadest constitutional powers are inadequately counterbalanced by the power of the other branches of government or by the real, established structures of civil society and forms of political self-organization. The absence or deficiency of the latter gives particular, if not extreme, importance to the outcome of presidential elections. Only in these elections can the potential of discontent and protest be released.

Foreign policy

Foreign policy must be pursued in such a way that it neither provides grounds for the regime to be accused of unilateral concessions to any party (particularly to the West) nor leads to the re-establishment of a cordon sanitaire on Russia's western borders and the isolation of Russia that would result.

It is still premature to talk of coherent Russian foreign policy, but some progress has been registered in this dimension as well. The end of the struggle for power in 1991–93 between the parliament and the president reduced the sharp division of opinion between pro-West and anti-West factions, at one stage one of the main manifestations of political struggle, to a vague issue of highly nuanced political positions, mainly those of fractions in the State Duma (the lower house of the parliament). The all-out offensive which communists and nationalists formerly waged against the government's foreign policy has been largely exhausted, and foreign policy has become only a background issue in political struggles. At the same time, the Russian Administration and, to a limited extent, the Cabinet and the Foreign Ministry have accepted the concept of overall protection of the 'national interests of Russia'. This move has deprived the opposition of much of their arguments with respect to the government's foreign policy. The parliamentary election of December 1995 and the presidential election of June 1996 proved at last that Russian foreign policy had become mostly the subject of national consensus. All fractions in the State Duma approved the appointment of Yevgeniy Primakov as foreign minister.

Under these conditions, internal developments will have only a limited impact on the foreign policy of Russia. It is therefore hardly possible at present to imagine an electoral scenario which would result in a substantial and rapid change for the better in relations between Russia and Europe: economic and geopolitical realities, the security structures developed by history and, finally, prejudices stand in the way of a drawing together of the Russian and European states and societies. The actual policy orientation of a particular winning candidate is not likely to play a crucial role. It may, however, affect the overall climate in international relations. Changes for the worse are fairly probable in the event of an extremist candidate winning; in the worst case, this could destabilize the situation in Europe and in the world and bring about a hasty expansion of the system of Western alliances and the technological, economic and political isolation of Russia. It could also encourage the processes of disintegration and separatism.

Perceptions of Russia's place in the post-Soviet space, Europe and the world are today deeply divided. Judging by the opinion polls there is still a good deal of nostalgia for the former 'big country'. Most of the population regards the collapse of the USSR as a wicked deed and a national tragedy. On the other hand, the shock of its collapse is somewhat softened by the realization that the countries of the 'new abroad' are not quite like the traditional foreign countries. The borders between the countries of the Commonwealth of Independent States (CIS) are mostly open and Russians continue to have relations with people living in other CIS countries. The Russian population is becoming increasingly aware of belonging to the Russian Federation; at any rate it is less inclined to sacrifice its economic interests for the sake of a hasty and poorly conceived reintegration. The diversity of the former Soviet Union is no longer a secret or a taboo subject, and is increasingly admitted. The citizens of the Russian Federation are thus increasingly orienting themselves not towards the complete and lasting reintegration of the Union but towards an alliance of three republics—Belarus, Russia and Ukraine—with particular attention to Kazakhstan. Other CIS member states seem not to have attracted public interest.

The dissolution of the Soviet Union has also somewhat cushioned the effect of Russia's withdrawal from the former Warsaw Treaty Organization countries. These countries found themselves out of the focus of public attention and are not causing polarizing controversies. The only aspect of the withdrawal which was visible in the public mind was the redeployment of returning troops on Russian territory. Once they were resettled the acuteness of this problem diminished. It cannot, of course, be ruled out that in the future some issues may be brought back to the arena of domestic politics, for instance the future of former Soviet property in Germany. In the meantime, the possibility of their joining NATO is viewed by all the main political forces as a threat to Russia's security.

In the longer term the combination of objective circumstances and subjective domestic policy stimuli are certain to push the Russian political élite—even though that élite itself may change—towards aligning all aspects of relations with the near and more distant neighbours along three lines—'Western', 'Eastern' (Central Asia) and 'Southern' (the Caucasus).

Along the 'Western' line, the combination of economic, political and geo-strategic imperatives will perhaps encourage the deepest possible integration of Russia with Belarus and Ukraine in parallel with *rapprochement* with the European Union (EU) and a quest for advantageous strategic alliances with the West in general. Setting aside the most extreme scenarios (such as an extremist group coming to power in Russia), historical alliances and loyalties are unlikely to displace the desire to sustain a lasting European balance of power as in the 19th century.

Along the 'Eastern' line the main driving force behind Russian policy is most likely to be an aligning of a system of obligations to ensure Russian military and domestic security and Russia's economic interests within the space of the former Soviet Union 'in return' for Russia's assistance in economic development, state-building and the building up of armed forces in the new independent states. The crossing and even collision of Russian interests with those of the West in the area of what was the Soviet Union will have a predominantly economic, and only secondarily political, character.

Along the 'Southern' line Russia's security interests, including domestic security and territorial integrity, may come into collision with a possible orientation of Turkey, a NATO member which is seeking membership of the EU, towards supporting Azerbaijan in the Transcaucasus and minorities speaking Turkic languages in the northern Caucasus within Russia. This is the place which today presents the greatest danger of an unpredictable and uncontrollable threat both to Russia's security and to that of Europe. The Russian political élite is currently asking itself whether this danger is realized by the EU and whether there is a mechanism to avert it.

The West's interest lies in incorporating Russia into the existing political and security structures and showing it a distant but not impossible prospect of economic cooperation and developing integration. Otherwise the levers which Europe and the West possess for handling threats which could arise from Russia's internal developments are 'sticks' rather than 'carrots', very little different from the sanctions or threat of sanctions of the cold war, and will not influence the nature of the domestic political regime.

III. Regional stability in the Russian Federation

The Russian state is not coterminous with the Russian Federation. Uncertainties and ambiguities persist.

In the first place, the authorities of the Russian Federation have not succeeded in establishing control over the whole territory of the country.[9] This was not only because two constituent republics did not sign the Federation Treaty of

---

[9] At the time the constitution was passed, the Russian Federation consisted of 89 'subjects of the Federation': 32 'ethno-territorial entities' (21 republics, formerly autonomous soviet socialist republics or ASSRs, 1 autonomous region and 10 autonomous districts); and 57 administrative entities (49 regions or *oblasti*, 6 territories or *kraya* and 2 federal cities).

1992[10] and forbade the constitutional referendum of 1993 on their territory, important as those developments were: it was also because neither the new constitution nor the Federation Treaty regulates certain aspects of relations either between the centre and the regions or between the latter. For example, the autonomous districts constitute parts of administrative territories—the regions (*oblasti*) and territories (*kraya*)—but the character of these vertical relations has not been clarified. It is therefore still too early to talk about the federal constitution as a functioning mechanism: many critical elements of it are still missing.

Second, in the Russian Federation there are a number of extraterritorial and quasi-state structures unrecognized by the Russian Federation, not provided for by its constitution and not fitting into its political structure.

Third, there are also structures juridically and actually subordinated to the power bodies of the Russian Federation which are geographically located outside it, and relations between these structures and local authorities are in many ways problematic. These are the Black Sea Fleet in Crimea and border guards and other troops in Central Asian and the Transcaucasian republics. While it is unable to control its own borders, the Russian Federation bears responsibility for guarding the greater part of the former Soviet border.

Finally, in the Russian Federation, as was the case in the former USSR, there is a problem of internal and external borders. Not only do they not coincide with ethnic and historical frontiers (internationally it is the exception rather than the rule for them to coincide fully) but their legal status is also extremely vulnerable. However, while the borders between the former Soviet republics are still guaranteed—problematic as they may be in some instances—by international legal norms, the situation with Russia's internal borders is far more complex.

In the light of all this, there are today four types of theoretically possible conflict, pertaining to the issue of Russia's territorial integrity and its relations with neighbours, relations threatening the state's stability and regional order: (*a*) conflicts caused by the intention of constituent entities to secede from Russia; (*b*) conflicts resulting from the intention of territories outside the Russian Federation to join or associate with it in one way or another against the will of the states of which they are now part; (*c*) conflicts caused by illegal or, more correctly, extra-legal structures operating in the Russian Federation in so far as they try to take power responsibilities; and (*d*) conflicts between the subjects of the Russian Federation which might contribute to general destabilization of the situation in the country, and directly rather than indirectly threaten both its integrity and its good relations with the neighbouring countries.

---

[10] The Agreement on the Prerogatives and Powers between the Federal Authorities of the Russian Federation and Those of the Republics Within the Russian Federation (the official title of one of the three Federal Agreements which together made up the Federation Treaty of 31 Mar. 1992) was not signed by the Chechen Republic or Tatarstan. (Chechnya in turn did not regulate its relations with Ingushetia.) Other autonomies signed it with reservations mainly pertaining to the tax system.

Threats of secession from Russia

The intention to secede has so far been clearly expressed and carried through only by the Chechnyan leadership, which in late 1991 declared its 'non-participation in the affairs of the Russian territories'. The unsuccessful war of 1994–96 against the separatists has only reduced the chances of Chechnya's continuing as a constituent part of Russia.

The position of Tatarstan, the second republic after Chechnya which did not sign the Federation Treaty and did not hold the referendum on the constitution of December 1993, is more nuanced. Its leadership insisted, successfully, on a separate agreement with the Russian Federation, in which the parties would act as equal partners and subjects of international relations.[11] As a result of this agreement, signed in March 1994, Tatarstan acquired a special status within the Russian Federation. Leaving aside rhetorical exaggerations, the Tatarstan leadership's long-term strategy was consistent and simple enough. It insisted on acquiring within the Russian Federation more or less the same status which the former union republics formally had in the USSR—with one stipulation: this should be a real status, apparently including a genuine right to secession. The agreement as it is cannot be taken as a guarantee of the unity of Russia.

After Tatarstan's, special bilateral agreements were concluded with the republics of Bashkortostan and Kabardino-Balkaria which, unlike Tatarstan, had signed the Federation Treaty. Other republics and territories either followed or are to follow these three. It is evident today that the bilateral agreements are not so much the mechanisms of the 'fine tuning' of federal relations, as President Yeltsin once said, but rather a substitute for the Federation Treaty. The proliferation of the new treaties calls into question the long-term stability of the federal construction. The outcome will have less to do with the quality of the agreements themselves than with the general conditions of the development of the Russian Federation, and in particular of its self-determination in the post-Soviet space.

Separatism has not yet become the official position of many republics or territories within Russia. The idea of distinctness and even separation from Russia is being actively supported by more or less influential movements, organizations and some leaders in almost all the republics of the northern Caucasus and in Bashkortostan, Buryatia and Tuva. The issue of independence is being raised even in Siberia, in the Urals, in the Far East (particularly in Sakhalin) and in other places.

While appraising all those heterogeneous movements, positions and declarations, one should bear in mind an important factor. Even the most consistent separatists of the 1991–92 period, the Chechens and Tatars, intended to become independent within the USSR and later the CIS. Their conscious feeling that

[11] Batyrshin, R., 'Mintimer Shaimiev za assotsiatsiyu s Rossiey' [Mintimer Shaimiev for the Association with Russia], *Nezavisimaya Gazeta,* 26 June 1992; 'Net smysla raskhoditsa' [No reason to separate], *Rossiyskaya Gazeta,* 10 July 1992; and 'Organizatsiya obedinennykh natsii . . . Povolzhya' [United Nations of . . . the Volga area], *Russia,* nos 33–34 (1992).

they were 'not Russia' coexisted with their wish to remain within the 'greater union'. This implies two conclusions. First, much in Russia's relations with separatists will depend upon the destiny of the CIS or any other alliance which might gradually replace it. If the CIS stabilizes and transforms itself into an integrated interstate entity or even a state alliance before the Russian Federation integrates more closely, this could stop separatist trends—although not the awareness of being 'not Russia'—in almost all the republics and territories. Second, if the CIS is reduced to a community of equal partners, or preserved merely as a symbolic community, or transformed into an alliance headed by Russia, or if it disappears altogether, the current 'semi-separatists' will be faced with a dilemma. Either they must break with Russia and simultaneously with the 'greater union' mentality, or they must return to the Federation on some condition or other, not necessarily as part of it. Either case will require more definite relations. It need hardly be said that a great deal will depend on the separatist communities' economic situation and the ability of their political élites to preserve domestic stability.

A tendency towards isolationism persists and is even developing in the parts of the Russian Federation. By 1993, when the Russian Federation had no internal customs borders, 23 autonomous entities had introduced their own restrictions on the passage of goods beyond their borders and had established their own customs posts with the help of local interior bodies and voluntary formations. In 1992 beneficial quotas for raw material exports were granted to the republics of Karelia, Komi, Yakut-Sakha and Gorniy Altay, and to the Irkutsk and Tyumen regions. In 1993 the republics of Bashkortostan, Buryatia and Udmurtia and the Amur, Kaliningrad, Murmansk, Yekaterinburg, Chelyabinsk and Chita *oblasti* and Krasnodar *kray* attempted to achieve the same. Tatarstan, Yakut-Sakha, the Chelyabinsk region and the Council of Siberian Regions have decided to establish what is called a one-channel taxation system, by which taxes are collected by the regional authority which then shares a proportion of them with the federal centre.[12] The system of budget federalism looks rather disorganized today. Some territories have special tax conditions; bilateral agreements between the Russian Federation and its constituent territories regulating such conditions are proliferating. Tax burdens differ between different regions.[13] There is a general increase in the number of territories where some movements are working for separation from the Russian Federation or within the framework of the Russian Federation's or at least for the implementation of some special status for their territories.

[12] Neschadin, A., 'Borba v ekonomicheskom prostranstve' [Struggle in the economic space], *Moscow News*, 21 June 1992.

[13] Nesterenko (note 1); and Shirobokova, V., [No real budget federation this year], *Nezavisimaya Gazeta*, 8 Aug. 1994.

Irredentism

A request to join the Russian Federation was officially conveyed to it by the Supreme Soviet of South Ossetia (part of Georgia) in 1991. The issue was also raised in 1991–92 in Abkhazia (part of Georgia) and the Trans-Dniester region (Moldova), has been discussed in Nagorno-Karabakh (Azerbaijan), and is constantly on the agenda in Crimea (Ukraine). The possibility should not be excluded of similar developments in Azerbaijan (in areas populated by the Lezgins), in northern Kazakhstan (in areas populated by Russians), in Narva and Kohtla Jarve (Estonia) with predominantly Russian populations, in eastern Ukraine, in some other regions of the Transcaucasus and even in some areas of Central Asia.

Until now the Russian Government has, at least officially, taken a fairly consistent position and defended the inviolability of the current borders between the members of the CIS, being aware that any other position, whatever the injustice of the existing borders, would call into question the integrity of Russia itself. At the same time, the possibility of a change in its position cannot be excluded—for instance, if communities seeking association with Russia become independent subjects of international law, or if the statehood of their 'home' post-Soviet countries collapses. It should be recalled, for example, that in 1918 Bessarabia was annexed by Romania in conditions of civil war and anarchy in the greater part of the former Russian Empire.

The intention of some external territories to join the Russian Federation cuts both ways. If they destabilize Russia's relations with neighbouring republics or if pro-Russian manifestations receive inadequate support from Russia (or their initiators believe this to be the case), they will lead to centrifugal counter-trends in Russia. For instance, the negative reply from the Russian Government to the South Ossetian leaders' address resulted in the growth of anti-Moscow sentiments in North Ossetia. Russia's 'refusal' to support the Abkhazian secession movement provoked an acute reaction in the northern Caucasus, both from some ethnic organizations and from the authorities in some of the republics. It is quite probable that Russia's 'indifference' towards the destiny of the Lezgin people, divided by the Russian–Azerbaijani border, will strengthen the separatist element in the Lezgin national movement in Dagestan.

It is clear that possible 'moves back' of some territories and ethnic groups to Russia (including northern Kazakhstan) could have the most destabilizing international consequences. Restraint and impartiality will be needed on the part of Russia and of its distant neighbours if the international community is to avoid the error of interpreting these 'moves back' one-sidedly as a revival of the imperial spirit. It should also be emphasized in this context that the tough measures taken by the federal government against the Chechnyan separatists (regardless of the efficiency of those measures) paradoxically changed the general climate in other successor states where irredentist movements existed. Their governments felt reassured when the separatists reduced their demands.

Extra-legal structures

Various forms of ethnic and ethno-cultural organization were started as a reaction to the clear inappropriateness of the state structure to the actual ethnic composition of the state. The establishment of extraterritorial organizations ('associations', 'councils' and 'societies') of dispersed ethnic groups, often without territorial autonomy, began in 1988–89. This process was accompanied by the revival of such ethno-cultural (sub-ethnic) groups as the Cossacks.

In 1991–93 movements for the self-determination of dispersed ethnic communities and associations of kindred ethno-cultural groups formed certain quasi-governmental structures or organizations. The Kurultai (congress) of the Tatar People elects the Millimajlis, a kind of extraterritorial ethnic parliament; the Caucasian Peoples' Confederation (CPC)[14] has a 'parliament' consisting of representatives of the majority of the republics of the northern Caucasus; there are also the Kabarda People's Congress, the Balkar People's National Council and others. Both the CPC and to a lesser extent the Millimajlis are actively claiming power functions in territorial states and have come into acute conflict with the local or central authorities in their republics—in the case of Tatarstan with those of the Russian Federation of which it is a part. The CPC's active role in the Abkhazian–Georgian conflict has also been a major destabilizing factor over the whole Caucasus and became a turning-point in the internationalization of Caucasian conflicts. In late 1993 the CPC moved its capital from Grozny in Chechnya to Sukhumi, Abkhazia, thus becoming a symbol of a structure operating across international borders.

The Cossack movement has resulted in the creation of various organizations, including armed ones. Some of them are trying to find their place in the regular army, and in 1993 they achieved this with the decree of the president setting up special border guard forces, special units and elements in the armed forces;[15] others function as organizations of armed self-defence of the Russian-speaking or non-titular populations in zones of ethnic conflict in the northern Caucasus and other areas. Finally, groups belonging or claiming to belong to a rather motley Cossack movement are beginning to play an even more noticeable role in politics, often in areas far away from those of traditional Cossack settlement.

A vocal and active Cossack movement which acts across not only new but also old boundaries (for instance as 'volunteers' in Kazakhstan, Trans-Dniester and Bosnia and Herzegovina) is a very controversial phenomenon. It is the movement's generic character that gives rise to a security concern. At the same time it is important to distinguish between three different components of the movement: (a) Cossacks as an organic part of the Russian population, be it

---

[14] Previously the Confederation of Caucasian Mountain Peoples (CCMP).

[15] Presidential decree no. 341 'On the reform of the military structures, frontier and interior forces in the northern Caucasus region of the Russian Federation and state support of the Cossacks', *Rossiyskaya Gazeta*, 23 Mar. 1993; Presidential decree no. 17 (1996) 'On questions of the control of the Cossack forces by the President of the russian Federation', *Sobranie Zakonodatelstva Rossiyskoy Federatsii*, no. 1953 (1996); and Presidential decree no. 1173 'On questions of the control of the Cossack forces by the President of the Russian Federation', *Rossiyskaya Gazeta*, 16 Aug. 1996.

within autonomous republics or in some neighbouring states, whose interests in quite a few cases are genuinely suppressed; (*b*) Cossack units of the regular Russian Army; and (*c*) illegal militias, claiming (with or without any grounds) to be Cossacks and acting according to their own will in Russia or abroad.

The objective of practical policy should be to separate the three components. The problem of Cossacks outside Russia is part and parcel of the bigger problem of ethnic Russians who found themselves in the 'new abroad'. As for illegal militias, failure to prevent their formation has been one of the most serious mistakes of the Russian Government. This mistake could have been caused by government weakness and failure to appreciate the substance of rapidly developing processes. In any case, the tackling of all the illegal armed formations, including the Cossack ones, should be a priority.

Conflicts between the constituent territories

Territorial disputes

Almost 50 per cent of the borders in the Russian Federation 'are not confirmed by any legally binding documents'.[16] The new constitution in Article 67, Clause 3, stipulates that 'the borders between the subjects of the Russian Federation can be changed on the basis of mutual consent'.[17] Territorial claims and conflicts actually exist and there have been numerous appeals to Moscow to intervene.

The most severe conflicts at present are ethno-territorial ones in the northern Caucasus, especially those between the Ossets and the Ingush in the Prigorodny district of North Ossetia; between the Chechens, Laks and Avars in the Khasavyrtovsky and former Aukhovsky districts in Dagestan; and between the Kumyks and the Laks, also in Dagestan. Tension still exists and is even growing over possible future frontiers between Kabarda and Balkaria (in the present-day Kabardino-Balkaria) and Chechnya and Ingushetia (in the former Checheno-Ingushetia).[18] Other territorial conflicts between the republics of the northern Caucasus are not at all ruled out for the future and may if they occur differ from the conflicts within those republics only by virtue of the status of the border under dispute. Especially sharp and protracted might be conflicts in multi-ethnic Dagestan. Conflicts between Cossacks and ethnic Caucasians often develop at the local or village level; their specific feature is the Cossacks' orientation towards Russia. The war in Chechnya provided a strong incentive for demands for two districts which were transferred to Chechnya in the 1950s to be returned to Stavropol *kray*.

The emergence of territorial conflicts cannot be ruled out in the Volga area (Tatarstan and Bashkortostan) and in the Buryat national and territorial enti-

[16] Abdulatipov, R., 'Ya dalek ot dogovornoy eyforii' [I am far from euphoric about the treaty], *Rossiyskaya Gazeta*, 13 Aug. 1992.

[17] Constitution of the Russian Federation, published in *Izvestiya*, 10 Nov. 1993.

[18] 'Opasnaya tyazhba u pogranichnogo stolba' [Dangerous litigation near the frontier post], *Rossiyskaya Gazeta*, 28 Aug. 1992.

ties—the Buryat Republic, Ust-Ordyn Buryat and Aguin Buryat autonomous districts.

Conflicts between administrative regions and territories, although possible in principle, are unlikely to take place and if they do will be considerably less sharp than territorial conflicts between the republics, because the latter already have some of the attributes of fully-fledged statehood. It should be noted that, apart from Chechnya, North Ossetia and Ingushetia[19] have some armed formations. Tatarstan has also declared its intention to form a 'national guard'.

Non-territorial inter-ethnic tensions

Conflicts here relate above all to the ousting of one ethnic group by another. The Russian populations are being ousted from the former autonomous entities without any territorial claims being involved because they are scattered and because in the conditions of general demoralization and the crisis of 'imperial' consciousness they are forced to accept the notion that the territory they are leaving in fact 'belongs' to the indigenous population. According to a unique opinion poll carried out in 1991, 37 per cent of the Russians there wanted, for example, to leave Checheno-Ingushetia, 27 per cent to leave Tuva, 10 per cent to leave Yakutia (now Yakut-Sakha) and 5–7 per cent to leave Tataria (now Tatarstan).[20] Scores of thousands of Russian-speakers have left Tuva and Chechnya. In the foreseeable future even greater migration from other republics, first of all from the northern Caucasus, is not ruled out.

The reasons for this (relatively) mass migration of Russians are different. They can tentatively be divided into three groups: (*a*) a direct threat to their security such as inter-ethnic tension or a high level of crime;[21] (*b*) political restrictions on the non-titular population or language discrimination; and (*c*) the deteriorating economic situation and unemployment which, counting in latent unemployment, is extremely high in the republics of the northern Caucasus.

There is a persistent idea of a long-lasting (sometimes 'age-old' or 'historical') conflict, the main victim of which at the present historical stage of the 'collapse of the empire' is the Russian population. It is hardly necessary to stress that among the victims of this kind of conflict there are also representatives of other ethnic groups, considerably less strong numerically and therefore less noticeable against the background of a mass Russian exodus.

Serious inter-ethnic conflicts arise for economic reasons and/or because of crime and the movement of refugees. Tension in the relationship with Caucasians in places where refugees are concentrated, in the cities and towns, has resulted in outbreaks of violence from time to time in the past; similarly,

[19] Felgengauer, P., 'Voyna s "separatistami" v gorakh i na plyazhakh' [War with separatists on the mountains and the beaches], *Nezavisimaya Gazeta*, 9 Sep. 1992.

[20] Zorkaya, N. and Gudkov, L., 'Iskhoda ne budet: prognos migratsii russkikh iz "blizhnego zarubezhya"' [There will be no exodus. The forecast for emigration of Russians from the 'near abroad'], *Nezavisimaya Gazeta*, 31 July 1992.

[21] In Tuva and Checheno-Ingushetia those surveyed mentioned 'enmity to Russians' as a reason for migration almost 1.5 times more frequently than the average in the Russian Federation 'national' republics or in the CIS.

violence against the Gypsies is no new phenomenon. The threat of conflicts with refugees has, however, grown considerably where they are concentrated in particular localities. Until recently the public opinion polls gave no grounds for thinking that there is any hostility towards any particular ethnic group shared by any meaningful stratum of the population.[22] Since the end of 1992, however, anti-Caucasian sentiments have engulfed a considerable part of the population in the large cities. These sentiments are today a major component of right-wing radicalism in Russia.

IV. Prospects for stabilization and zones of risk

National and territorial problems will not, either today or in the foreseeable future, cause the Russian Federation's disintegration and thus additionally and abruptly intensify instability in Europe and in the world by themselves, without a great many heterogeneous factors coinciding. They do not have the 'critical mass' to do this.

The titular ethnic groups have an absolute majority or are the largest single grouping only in approximately one-third of Russia's autonomous entities, basically those located along the Russian Federation's frontiers in the northern Caucasus—Kabardino-Balkaria, Chechnya, Ingushetia, North Ossetia, Dagestan and adjoining Kalmykia—as well as Chuvashia in the Volga area and Tuva in southern Siberia. However, the situation should be considered both statically and dynamically in its demographic, economic and foreign policy aspects. From this point of view today there are five basic 'belts' or 'knots' of actual or potential instability where the national or geopolitical factor could detonate conflict that would threaten the continued existence of the Russian Federation: (*a*) the north Caucasian knot; (*b*) the Volga area knot; (*c*) the Siberian/Trans-Baikal belt; (*d*) the northern belt; and (*e*) the Kaliningrad Region. Each has its own specific features.

The northern Caucasus

With the exception of the Chechnyan leadership, so far, and with some qualifications, there is no clearly visible separatist or anti-Russia trend of any strength in this area. The picture is rather one of long-term instability which could develop into a number of serious conflicts and of progressive distancing from the Russian centre which would be reinforced by the exodus of the Russian population from a number of republics. The eruption of conflict here and there is a more probable scenario than a steady conflict over many years between a few influential forces in this belt.

Analogies with Lebanon have often been made, but can hardly be justified in relation to the northern Caucasus. Before it can become the second Lebanon, the northern Caucasus would first have to unite, which is hardly possible.

[22] *Rossiyskoe Obozrenie*, no. 35 (19 Aug. 1992).

'Lebanonization' in its proper sense means above all the struggle for constitutional legalization of the influence of different communities. This influence and the right to existence itself are not challenged by the main participants in the northern Caucasus. If any similarity with Lebanon can be traced there, it lies first of all in the fact of more or less active participation, particularly secret, of outside forces in local policy making.

Conflict in the region could be precipitated by: (a) the Chechen bloc; (b) the Adygueyan bloc of Kabardinians, Circassians, Adygs, Abkhazians and Shapsugi; (c) the Karachaevo-Balkar bloc; or (d) Ossetia.

The 'mountain unity' which expressed itself in the CPC is a complicated phenomenon and to some extent a form for cooperation in demonstrating or at least protecting common interests against Russia, Georgia and possibly Azerbaijan in the future. Beyond this the consolidation of the CPC will be limited by fundamental differences connected with history, economics or religion: Ossetia is Christian and pagan, the other republics are Muslim, the Imamat tradition is firm in Dagestan and Chechnya but is not influential in the western part of the northern Caucasus, and so on. The CPC is able in principle to help some of its participants to separate themselves from Russia but will not be able to resist Russia strategically. In the northern Caucasus each side, usually the official republican authorities and extraterritorial ethnic movements, fights for itself in the prevailing situation by uniting with others, temporarily, conditionally and not fully, and only for the sake of opposition to Moscow or Tbilisi or against general instability in the region. The coincidence of some interests in conditions of general friability and separation and against a chaotic background explains, on the one hand, the multi-layered character of the political organization in the northern Caucasus (the coexistence on different levels of public authorities, ethnic movements and the CPC) and on the other hand the search for a stable structure across all possible dimensions.

The current war in Chechnya is the only actual instance of secession in the northern Caucasus or the Russian Federation as a whole. The history of the Chechens is unique—the experience of the Caucasus wars over 50 years in the 19th century, the military uprising at the beginning of the 1940s, and finally total deportation in 1944 which only strengthened the Chechens' anti-Russian identity. The formation of the separatist regime took place over a short period of time in the closing months of 1991, at a time when the all-union state institutions no longer existed but those of the Russian Federation had not yet appeared. The late and ineffective attempt to suppress the separatists, undertaken three years later, undermined the prestige of the Russian Administration both inside the country and abroad. The Chechnyan war put back Russia's joining the Council of Europe for a year, strengthened the arguments of the adherents of NATO enlargement eastwards, complicated Russia's relations with some of its neighbours, especially Turkey, and gave rise to serious international problems in spite of the domestic character of the conflict and the solution.

During the period of the conflict the Chechnyan war became an important symbol for Islamic extremism—although for some reason, perhaps purely historical, Russia is not accepted as the main adversary along with the USA and Israel. The influence of the war in aggravating fundamentalist sentiment and movements in Turkey must not be underestimated. Any spread of the conflict outside the country (the territories on the Caspian are closely linked) would have had very seriously negative consequences for peace in the whole of the Caucasus. At the same time it could enhance the significance of political factors in Russia's relations with the trans-Caucasian neighbours, prejudicing economic cooperation.

With the Chechnyan war in the background, the intermittent Ingush-Ossetian conflict takes on the character of a local conflict and is not threatening regional order. The federation government, moreover, is not in this instance on one side in the conflict, but is an intermediary and a guarantor of order, the conflicting parties being too weak to change the situation.

Whatever their outcome, events in the northern Caucasus can hardly threaten the existence of the Russian Federation or its state order. To ensure this, however, the consequences of mass migration, arms proliferation, the permanent involvement of large military forces and so on in the area should be reduced to a minimum and the conflict zone efficiently localized.

The Volga area

The main 'troublemaker' in the area and across the entire Russian Federation was Tatarstan. Its independent and sometimes obstructionist line towards the Federation Treaty, the federal constitution and Russia's centre in general is backed by the position of the Tatars as the second ethnic group in the Russian Federation after the Russian (with about 4 per cent of the population) and the inheritor of an ancient statehood, older than Russia's. In addition, there is common ground for separatism or at least isolationism in Tatarstan and Bashkortostan in their possession of natural resources (oil) and advanced industrial potential (the military–industrial complex, chemicals, electronics and so on). A comparatively moderate level of tension in relations between the two nationalities combined with a long-lasting and widespread conviction in both republics that their exchange with the 'centre' is not equal allow their leaders to conduct broadly compatible policies. Separatism in its present form does not evoke the active resistance of the Russian minority, as the idea of injustice and disadvantages of the status of Tatarstan and Bashkortostan for all citizens has been half-officially advanced and in general accepted for several decades.

The Tatar nationalist movement has been constrained by the following three factors: (a) ethnic, linguistic and religious balance: the population is made up 49 per cent of Tatars and 43 per cent of Russians; (b) the fact that only one-third of all Tatars living in Russia are concentrated in the territory of Tatarstan; and (c) the existence of rather close ties between the two nations, a high incidence of intermarriage (unusual where the Christian and Islamic cultures coexist) and very similar economic structure. In Bashkortostan, a similar constraint results from the relative position of the titular ethnic group, the Bashkirs. It is numerically only third, after the Russians and the Tatars, in the population of the republic, and its share has fallen in the past few years. The Tatars are the second largest group and their share in the total population is noticeably growing. For this reason the Bashkirs' chances of assuming power are less favourable than those of the Tatars, but this same circumstance could sharpen the territorial problem, especially in relations between Tatarstan and Bashkortostan.

A truly explosive situation in the Volga area could develop if the Tatar and the Bashkir nationalist movements were to unite on Pan-Turkic or Islamic grounds. Some elements of such a convergence have been observed since 1994, especially in Bashkortostan. The outcome will depend on less immediate events over a much wider area.

As far as other republics of the Volga area are concerned, the dominance of the Russian population there (except in Chuvashia), their cultural identity (all except Mariy El, where pagan traditions are strong, are Orthodox) and the scarcity of natural resources significantly weaken if not reduce to zero their separatist potential.

Although the forms of Volga area separatism are fairly moderate and relatively 'civilized' at this stage of development, it is potentially threatening to general stability in the country and indirectly to the whole geopolitical zone. It is difficult for public opinion to accept and objectively threatens the existence of Russia as a state since it involves the core of Russia, formed in the 16th century and surrounded by Russian regions. The withdrawal of a republic in the Volga Basin from Russia or any serious destabilization in the region would practically sever the principal transport and power lines running from east to west and north to south and provoke a sharper and more dramatic reaction than any other development. It hardly needs to be said that such a reaction would attract a response in the Turkic–Islamic world, the consequences of which are difficult to forecast.

The Siberian and Trans-Baikal area

The ethno-territorial entities in this region include the republics of Tuva, Buryatia, Khakassia and Gorniy Altay and the Aguin Buryat and Ust-Ordyn Buryat autonomous districts. Tense relations between nationalities in this region and the general crisis in Russia's political development and economy could lead to the growth of separatist aspirations.

Only Tuva has a realistic chance of claiming self-determination within its present boundaries. The titular ethnic group comprises two-thirds of the population; its share has been growing in recent years and the Russian population is in the process of being ousted. Tuva is one of the few territories of the Russian

Federation to have a tradition of independent statehood: it remained independent until relatively recent times and was incorporated in the USSR as an autonomous republic only in 1944. It is, however, relatively poor and lives on federal subsidies. Potential separatism there could hardly seriously destabilize the situation in Russia or even in the region. Such destabilization could come about only if a general imbalance of forces emerged in the entire Siberian and Far Eastern regions, and this is possible only hypothetically—if China disintegrates before the situation in Russia stabilizes. Self-determination in this part of the Russian Federation could in that case reinforce the centrifugal forces among national minorities in the neighbouring regions of China.

The northern belt

This includes a chain of former and present autonomous entities from the Komi Republic and the Nenets Autonomous District in the west to the Chukotka and Koryaki autonomous districts in the east. Prospects for instability in this zone are connected not so much with possible inter-ethnic conflicts (which surfaced in Yakut-Sakha and in other places) as with 'resource separatism': some of the republics and regions are extremely rich in natural resources, and the behaviour of local governments depends very much on the possession of raw materials or industrial production in their territories.[23] The 'raw materials' republics and territories of the north, such as Yakut-Sakha, Komi and the Yamalo-Nenets Autonomous District, may join (and sometimes do) the bloc of more radical separatist leaders of other republics against the centre. Such a bloc, made up of Tatarstan, Bashkortostan and Yakut-Sakha, appeared in August 1991.

In general the northern belt is more capable of intensifying instability than of creating it. Geopolitical considerations render useless any separatism in this area. Its contribution to a possible disintegration of the state could take the form of damaging the financial system or of some circumstance developing at the same time as and reinforcing Siberian or Far Eastern regional separatism.

The Kaliningrad Region

The least obvious problem but the one which most directly concerns European security now is the problem of the Kaliningrad Region, which in 1991 become an exclave of Russia on the Baltic Sea.[24]

Its isolation from the 'mainland', outstanding problems of transit through neighbouring countries (the Baltic states, Belarus and Poland) and its military facilities create many complications. Although no official territorial claims have so far been made to Russia, there are forces in some countries which do not consider the issue settled. Some countries (primarily Germany, Lithuania

---

[23] Shakhray, S., 'Kaliningrad–Königsberg–Krulevetz' [Kaliningrad–Königsberg–Krulevetz], *Nezavisimaya Gazeta*, 26 July 1994; and [Vice-Prime Minister suggested his vision of the Kaliningrad problems], *Segodnya*, 4 Aug. 1994.

[24] See also chapter 15, section V in this volume.

and Poland) are discussing in depth the Russian military presence in Kaliningrad as a potential threat to regional security. The problem of the territory's international status has also been raised (for instance, in the European Parliament in February 1994).

Two opposing points of view are emerging clearly both in Kaliningrad and in Russia: one seeks increased economic and administrative autonomy for the region and even the status of a republic within the Russian Federation; the other stresses its potential status as Russia's military and political outpost in the West.[25] It is quite likely that, as often happens, both approaches will start to work simultaneously under pressure from different forces. The danger lies, first, in a split among the region's population and domestic instability there, and second in the possible destabilizing interference of external forces.

The foreign policy implications

The northern Caucasus is practically the only region in the Russian Federation which could become a source of serious and protracted complications in international affairs. Indeed, the war in Chechnya has demonstrated the relationship between local conflicts and international affairs with great force. It should be noted, however, that the case of Chechnya has also revealed the limits of external interference in what is generally recognized as basically a domestic Russian matter.

In the immediate future developments in the Volga Basin are unlikely to trigger any destabilizing process in Eurasia or to complicate Russia's relations with Europe. The situation may look different, however, in the more general context of the triangular ties between Russia, the West and the Islamic world. Western policy in the Islamic world and the West's ability to build a stable system of long-term relations with it will be a factor, albeit an indirect one, in the future development of the Volga Basin. Siberia, the Trans-Baikal area and the north will not have any meaningful impact on Russia's relations with Europe. The only hypothetical exception is the potential problem of delivery of energy resources, particularly natural gas, if there were to be separatist action among the autonomous regions of eastern Russia. This concern should not be exaggerated: the critical importance of oil and gas exports for Russia's economy will force any Russian leadership to act decisively. Only a very improbable overall collapse of Russian statehood could force the region east of the Urals and the northern entities to seek their own economic and political identities. Interwoven domestic and external problems theoretically make Kaliningrad Russia's only domestic issue that can complicate its relations with Europe. However, this development does not look probable in the near future.

The overall impact of the ethno-territorial conflicts inside Russia on international stability will not be the same as the impact of conflicts in the adjacent non-Russian territories. However, the increasing domestic uncertainty, a deteri-

[25] Tarasov, A., 'Severny predel' [Northern limit], *Izvestiya*, 3 Sep. 1992.

oration of Russia's image in the West, a subsequent worsening of the political and investment climate and increasing migration from Russia taken all together could cause further reservations in Europe's attitudes to Russia and a general deterioration of relations. The states and institutions of Europe could play a positive role in minimizing internal conflicts of this kind in two ways: (a) in restraining those international actors which for cultural or geopolitical reasons are not disinterested in Russia's internal problems; and (b) in facilitating Russia's integration into the multilateral institutions, thus opening for them a real prospect for deepening cooperation, which would enable Russia to appeal to European principles and values in the settlement of those conflicts.

V. General considerations

The incompleteness of Russia's development into statehood so far has given rise to discussions about the possibility of building a nation-state on the basis of the Russian Federation at all,[26] about the Russian Federation's role in the post-Soviet geopolitical space, and about the degree of authoritarianism that is necessary or acceptable in the transitional period. All these discussions have revealed some important concepts which should be taken into consideration regardless of the concrete form the new Russian state takes. Otherwise Russia's stability in building relations with Europe on a conflict-free basis cannot be ensured.

1. The struggle against anarchy and crime is now a task of high priority in the creation of a democratic, federal state based on the rule of law. Society has reacted only sluggishly to the general deterioration of social conditions. A strong state is not necessarily one without checks and balances and guarantees of constitutional rights; and to build a strong state on the basis of the struggle against anarchic and criminal deviations may be more natural, more acceptable and even a more irresistible factor uniting a nation than a strong, total central power directed against the regional authorities.

2. A certain minimum of territorial consolidation of the state is necessary today. Today elements of the former Soviet state machinery (not only military) are under the Russian Federation's jurisdiction but geographically outside Russia, in the former Soviet republics, and their competences and the formal jurisdiction of the new states must be clearly and gradually differentiated. This will imply Russian assistance, including training.

3. The establishment of control over the territory of the Russian Federation itself also requires, in particular, a programme of developing specialized services which would constitute the civil service. Special attention should now be paid to the training of an administrative élite on the basis of strict and uniform requirements. This élite should reflect Russia's ethnic and regional diver-

---

[26] Tishkov, V., 'Rossiya kak natsionalnoe gosudarstvo' [Russian as a nation state], *Nezavisimaya Gazeta*, 26 Jan. 1994.

sity and its natural identity with the overall post-Soviet territory. Opportunities for this already exist today.

4. Russia's general orientation in its relations with the countries of the 'near abroad' should be towards assistance in building up territorial structures in neighbouring countries. The Russian Federation cannot and should not renounce many of its post-Soviet obligations, but it has sensibly minimized and refined them and allowed the maximum delegation to local authorities. This does not exclude but actually presupposes Russia's integration with the former Soviet republics, including the transfer of some specialized and monitoring functions to the supranational level (within the CIS or other associations). The issue today is not a choice between total control over the territory of the former USSR and that of the former RSFSR but rather Russia's ability to create a structured and hierarchic system of authorities and links between them. This would not be to the detriment of state control over the whole post-Soviet territory, although naturally not from a single centre.[27]

This kind of perception of the future political organization of the territory is supported by the existence of the European Union. The emergent structure of Europe, although there are many uncertainties, is of a 'non-classic' character and cannot be equated with that of a single nation-state in a 'normal' two-level federation.[28] A system effectively combining various forms of territorial and functional administration can become, indeed is perhaps already becoming, a new paradigm of political organization replacing the paradigm of the nation-state. It could become the same cultural imperative for modern states as the nation-state was for decades.

5. The prospects for the federalization of the Russian Federation should also be considered in the context of the tendency towards federalization of the whole post-Soviet territory. The classic functional approach to federation, which is of great normative importance (as a rule, it has worked rather well in the USA although not in Canada), implies a high degree of decentralization of power and equality of subjects with the necessary operation of the discretionary principle, that is, direct and two-way connections between the federal authorities, the collective subjects of the federation and the individuals comprising them. This kind of model also implies the existence of certain 'extra-political' circumstances: relative cultural homogeneity over the whole territory (as the founding fathers of the USA knew very well) and relative equality of economic conditions.

In today's Russian Federation these conditions do not exist uniformly if they exist anywhere. The rapid differentiation of living conditions in different parts of the Russian Federation and the differentiation of the climate of ethnic relations have made it harder than before to speak about a uniform approach to the settlement of the national issue in the country. Within the Russian Federation there are territories characterized at one and the same time by a chronic need

---

[27] Salmin, A., 'Soyuz posle soyuza' [A union after the Union], *POLIS*, no. 1 (1992).
[28] Montani, G., 'Micronationalism and federalism', *Federalist*, no. 1 (1993), pp. 9–20.

for subsidies, low levels of economic development and a rapid growth of the 'indigenous' population leading to the ousting of the 'outsiders'—all this against the background of the wish to exist independently.

These facts do not rule out classic federalist formulas; they merely demonstrate that the classic formulas are not sufficient in themselves to re-establish actual control over territories. In particular, the introduction of a special status for some territories, as appropriate, cannot be ruled out—naturally not against their will and on the basis of a universal norm that is greater than the sum total of bilateral deals concluded ad hoc in each case. Even in the USA, a nation of classic federal structure, there existed the status of the federal territory not reflected in the constitution, and Puerto Rico is a 'freely aligned state', a commonwealth associated with the USA since 1952.[29] Different statuses for the component parts of the state should be developed to succeed the now archaic division into republics, autonomous regions and autonomous areas. This can hardly be achieved yet. What is needed is an understanding of the essence of development rather than another constitutional revolution.

The future of the Russian Federation is essentially linked to the prospects of a well-conceived, purposefully carried out integration policy, primarily and particularly economic policy. It is worth remembering again that a national programme of railway construction played a decisive role in overcoming the political and psychological effects of the secession of the South and civil war in the USA.

VI. Conclusions

Today it is only possible to lay out political imperatives in this area which require serious elaboration, legislative effort and institutional guarantees.

First, mass ethnic conflicts and the forced emigration of sections of the population for ethnic and religious motives should be prevented by all possible means. In the territories whose authorities cannot cope with disturbances, federal rule should be introduced. Specialized peacekeeping forces and armed forces with a preventive function have long been needed.

Second, there is a need to work out in advance a migration policy (at present stuck in dispute and discussions) so that minorities (mainly but not only Russian) do not become hostages in the territories where they live. The conditions of minorities should be linked strictly to federal subsidies and to the Federation's political action in relation to its subjects.

Third, the idea of cultural and national autonomy which is gradually becoming popular should not be reduced merely to extraterritorial self-government in culture and education. This version of autonomy is perceived by many, not without reason, as a step back as compared with national and territorial auton-

---

[29] The Jones Act of 1917 defined Puerto Rico as an 'organized but unintegrated territory' whose people had US citizenship.

omy, and is therefore rejected. The essence of cultural and national autonomy is the political representation of ethno-cultural groups on an extraterritorial basis. Initially, a special council (an elected State Committee for Nationalities) could be a federal body for such representation, at least with consultative functions such as France's Economic and Social Council has.[30]

The paradox of the present situation is the absence of a direct threat to the Russian Federation either from an external enemy or from overall domestic collapse similar to that of the Soviet Union. Incidentally, such a situation with all its obvious advantages has an evident demobilizing potential. The 'relaxation' of Russia, an unstable balance between the centrifugal and centripetal forces, may emerge in the long run from a 'loss of quality' and from an inability to deal with any sudden troubles which may be created by the unstable (or as yet still stable) geopolitical environment both closer to and further from home.

The stabilization of the situation in the Russian Federation today and the achievement of a higher level of security are strategic objectives which need comprehensive and systematic approaches. They need an approach which will include the development of a constitutional basis of statehood, forms of inter-ethnic and inter-confessional interaction, and the formation of reliable interstate and regional patterns with countries of the 'near' and 'far' abroad.

At present there are no significant domestic political factors which might directly influence relations between Russia and its European neighbours and the international organizations. In spite of resistance to the idea of NATO enlargement eastwards, there are no traces of serious growth of anti-West sentiment in Russia. (The reservations and disappointments which succeeded the 'pro-West' euphoria of the 1980s and early 1990s were of a quite different character.) It is today more likely that unbalanced actions by the West will affect the development of the internal situation in Russia unfavourably than that Russia's internal situation will influence crisis developments in Europe and the world.

The Chechnyan war has without question complicated Russia's relations with international society. Chechnya has been a challenge for Russia as a member of the Council of Europe (since February 1996) and at the same time a challenge for the Council of Europe. Great care is required if it is not to turn into a factor that unbalances relations in Europe and generates a new round of the cold war. The success or failure of the settlement will determine whether the conflict is an isolated phenomenon or another step in the development of Islamic extremism.

However, even despite the extremely poor performance of the Russian authorities in dealing with the Chechnyan war, it is clear today that the integrity

[30] The idea of the ex-territorial autonomy as an element of the political organization of the state is suggested in Salmin, A. and Zubov, A., 'Optimizatsiya etnopoliticheskikh otnoshenii v usloviyakh "etnicheskogo vozrozhdeniya" v SSSR' [Optimization of ethnopolitical relationships under the "ethnic renaissance" in the USSR], *Rabochiy Klass i Sovremenniy Mir,* no. 3 (1989), pp. 62–84; and Salmin, A. and Zubov, A., 'Soyuz dogovor i mekhanizm novoy etnopoliticheskoy organizatsii SSSR' [Union treaty and the mechanism of the new ethnopolitical organization of the USSR], *POLIS,* no. 1 (1991), pp. 42–57.

of Russia has been strengthened. The danger of its disintegration, even if not altogether removed, is much smaller than it was at the beginning of the decade.

Finally, the main internal factor in Russia influencing the stability of Europe will be the consolidation of its democratic institutions, which is the condition of permanent closer integration with Europe. The parliamentary election of 1995 and the presidential election of 1996, their deficiencies notwithstanding, clearly proved that the electorate voted for democracy. It is the strengthening of democracy, even more than factors such as internal conflict, criminality and so on (important as they are) which be crucial for the future interaction between Russia and Europe.

Part III
Debates on Russia's national interests

Part III

Debates on Russia's criminal interests

Background chronology

1992

15 May   At a CIS summit meeting in Tashkent, leaders of Armenia, Kazakhstan, Kyrgyzstan, Russia, Tajikistan and Uzbekistan sign a 5-year collective security treaty providing for mutual military aid in the event of aggression against any signatory

4 Nov.   The Supreme Soviet ratifies the START I Treaty, making Russia's exchange of instruments of ratification conditional on the other 3 CIS republics with former Soviet nuclear weapons on their territories acceding to the 1968 NPT as non-nuclear weapon states

9 Sep.   President Yeltsin postpones a state visit to Japan amid fierce domestic criticism of his alleged willingness to negotiate the return to Japan of the Kurile Islands

1 Dec.   The Russian Foreign Ministry issues an official document describing the conceptual foundations and basic elements of Russia's foreign policy

15 Dec.   Foreign Minister Kozyrev delivers a controversial 'mock' address at a CSCE ministerial meeting in Stockholm warning the West of the dangers of fuelling growing 'red–brown' anti-Western nationalism

1993

28 Feb.   Yeltsin proposes that the UN grant Russia special status to act as guarantor of peace and stability on the territory of the former USSR

28 Apr.   The Concept of Russian Foreign Policy (in draft since Feb. 1992) approved by the Russian Security Council

15 Aug.   Russia and the USA sign an agreement on cooperation in space. Russia commits itself to comply with the MTCR and to suspend a deal to sell rocket engines to India

25 Aug.   Yeltsin and President Walesa of Poland sign a joint declaration stating that Polish membership in an enlarged NATO would not be detrimental to Russia's vital security interests

15 Sep.   Reversing previous statements, Yeltsin sends a letter to US President Clinton and other Western leaders setting out his objections to an enlargement of NATO to include new member states in East–Central Europe

1994

5 Apr.   Yeltsin signs a decree on the establishment of Russian military bases on territories of some former Soviet republics

22 June   Russia joins the NATO Partnership for Peace Programme

24 June   Yeltsin and EU leaders sign a wide-ranging Agreement on Partnership and Cooperation

5 Sep.   The first combined US–Russian peacekeeping training exercise begins in Totskoe, Russia

1995

3 Apr.   Russia rejects a US request to end negotiations with Iran over the sale of nuclear reactors, which the USA claims would assist a clandestine Iranian nuclear weapon programme

18 Apr.   Kozyrev warns that under some circumstances Russia might have to resort to military force to defend the rights of ethnic Russians living abroad

31 May   Russia signs 2 cooperation agreements with NATO covering arrangements for joint training and exercises and outlining areas of consultation ranging from cooperation in peacekeeping operations to measures to enhance nuclear security and curb proliferation

21 June   Yeltsin submits the START II Treaty to parliament for ratification amid mounting parliamentary opposition to the treaty

8 Sep.   Yeltsin appeals for the establishment of a CIS-based structure similar to the defunct WTO

14 Sep.	Presidential decree on 'Russia's strategic course with respect to the CIS member states'

1996

5 Jan.	Kozyrev resigns
9 Jan.	Yevgeniy Primakov appointed Foreign Minister
28 Feb.	Russia is admitted to the Council of Europe, despite continuing controversy over its human rights record
18 Mar.	The Russian Duma approves two communist-sponsored resolutions asserting that the USSR legally still exists and rejecting the Dec. 1991 Belovezh accords which formed the CIS
4 June	Foreign Minister Primakov tells NATO foreign ministers meeting in Berlin that Russia can accept the political enlargement of NATO but will oppose an eastward extension of its military infrastructure

7. Russian foreign policy thinking in transition[*]

Alexei Arbatov

I. Introduction

Russia's domestic politics after the demise of the USSR have been closely interwoven with the evolution of the country's foreign policy. In this respect, the violent October 1993 crisis in Moscow and the parliamentary elections in December of the same year together formed a clear threshold in Russian developments. Domestically those two events signified the failure of the Russian leadership to implement market economic reforms by way of 'shock therapy' and to establish a functioning democracy to deal with the country's internal and external problems. The foreign policy implications were no less important: the 'romantic', cosmopolitan and Western-centred policy started to give way to a much more Russian-centred and geopolitically defined course of action. At best, the new policy was to become tough and pragmatic, at worst neo-imperial, nationalist and coercive. The evolution of foreign policy is affected by domestic, economic and political developments, the interplay of various groups within the Russian foreign policy élite, the reaction of the 'near abroad', and the policy of the outside world, first and foremost that of the Western powers.

II. Principal groups in the foreign policy élite

The traditional Western description of Russian foreign policy thinkers and players as belonging to three basic groups—reformers, reactionaries and centrists[1]—was not quite correct in 1992–93, and is even less adequate now and for the foreseeable future. At least four major groups were trying to affect Russian foreign policy during the first two years following the demise of the USSR in December 1991. One way to analyse their respective foreign policy positions is to compare their stances on two main general groups of issue: Russia's relations with the former Soviet republics (the 'near abroad') and with the main foreign powers (the 'far abroad').

The first faction, most vividly represented by the Foreign Minister at the time, Andrey Kozyrev, was characterized by conspicuously pro-Western views,

---

[1] See, e.g., Simes, D., 'Reform reaffirmed', *Foreign Policy*, no. 90 (spring 1993), pp. 48–53.

[*] Sections of the material contained in this chapter have previously appeared in the following publications by the author: 'Russia's foreign policy alternatives', *International Security*, vol. 18, no. 2 (fall 1993), pp. 5–44; and 'Russian national interests', eds R. Blackwill and S. Karaganov, Centre for Science and International Affairs, Harvard University, *Damage Limitation or Crisis? Russia and the Outside World*, CSIA Studies in International Security no. 5 (Brassey's: Washington, DC, 1994), pp. 55–76.

with a heavy bias towards economic determinism, universal democratic values and a general neglect of the competitive geopolitical and strategic elements of international politics. Kozyrev's principal support came from President Boris Yeltsin and his close associates, Gennadiy Burbulis, a State Adviser, and Yegor Gaidar, then the Prime Minister. Within the Foreign Ministry those ideas were shared by a narrow circle of ministers' deputies and aides.[2] Their proponents were also to be found in a 'pacifist' faction in the Supreme Soviet, in some academic institutions, among well-known journalists and figures in the arts and culture, and within a segment of the liberal mass media. They dominated the government's formulation and implementation of policy on relations with the West, on arms control and regional problems (the former Yugoslavia, Central America, the Persian Gulf and the Korean peninsula) and on positions in the UN and in the Conference on Security and Co-operation in Europe (CSCE).

The driving idea of Kozyrev and his allies was the urgent economic, political and even military integration of Russia into the West.[3] They did not recognize the enormous obstacles to integration stemming from the uniqueness of Russia's physical dimensions, its current transitional state, its heritage and the implications of its specific geopolitical situation for its national interests. Furthermore, with the world no longer divided by competing ideologies, they did not take into account the possibility of significant differences emerging between Russia and the West on regional and global issues, including arms control and conflict resolution.

At the same time, this group was quite indifferent to and uninterested in Russian relations with the 'near abroad', and especially so with regard to the Transcaucasus and the Central Asian republics. Belarus and Ukraine had cooperated in disbanding the USSR on 8 December 1991; most of the former Soviet republics had endorsed this decision on 21 December 1991;[4] trouble-free relations with those states were thereafter largely taken for granted.

The second faction consisted of moderate–liberal representatives from the governmental, political and academic social strata. Although relatively Westernized in their upbringing and outlook, they were in most cases distinguished by a more cautious and realistic, sometimes even pragmatic attitude towards Russia, the West and the world at large.

They differed from the first group primarily in their emphasis on the necessity of distinctive Russian foreign policy and security priorities, based on the specifics of the country's geopolitical position and transitional domestic situation. This implied according the highest priority to Russia's relations with other former Soviet republics. With some exceptions, members of this group advocated maximum concessions and flexibility in relations with the new states in

---

[2] Shelov-Kovedyaev, F., [In the criticism of Russia's foreign policy we are confronted with dangerous dilettantism], *Nezavisimaya Gazeta*, 30 July 1992, pp. 1, 3; and Nadzharov, A., [The USA and Russia again show that they can come to agreement], *Nezavisimaya Gazeta*, 27 Mar. 1993, p. 1.

[3] Kozyrev, A., 'Prevrashchenie ili Kafkianskaya metamorfosa?' [Transformation or Kafkaesque metamorphosis?], *Nezavisimaya Gazeta*, 20 Aug. 1992, p. 3.

[4] For the text of these agreements relating to the establishment of the CIS, see *SIPRI Yearbook 1992: World Armaments and Disarmament* (Oxford University Press: Oxford, 1992), appendix 14A, pp. 558–62.

order to overcome their ingrained fears of revived Russian imperialism and attempts at domination, the only exceptions being an insistence on the preservation of centralized control over nuclear weapons outside Russia and their urgent elimination.

As for relations with the USA and its allies, these politicians and intellectuals did not doubt the choice of the Western model of economic and political development, and they consistently advocated better and more stable political and strategic relations with both NATO and Japan. At the same time, however, they argued that the improvement of relations with the West did not mean automatically accepting all the positions and proposals espoused by current Western governments. They were, for example, quite critical towards many aspects of US policy in the early 1990s, sharing many of the views prevailing in the US liberal foreign and strategic policy community. They were against too many easy concessions of the kind made by Russia in 1992–93, and argued in favour of more equitable and fairer deals with the USA and other Western powers.

This group was generally sceptical about relying too heavily on promises of Western economic aid and considered sound national security policy as a value in its own right, regardless of the amount of foreign credits it might earn. They were working on the principle that refusal to be misled by unfounded expectations and naïve illusions would help to avoid later disappointments and recriminations.[5]

The third faction, consisting of centrist and moderate–conservative factions, partly associated with the Civic Union, was represented by people such as former Vice-President, Alexander Rutskoy, the former Chief of the Security Council, Yuriy Skokov, and the former Speaker of the Supreme Soviet, Ruslan Khasbulatov. It enjoyed the support of a dominant section of the military high command, industrial managers and the chief echelons of the federal bureaucracy who could not reconcile themselves completely to the demise of the Soviet Union, although they did not advocate reunification by military force. In general it took a tougher stance on relations with Ukraine and other former Soviet republics and advocated pressuring them on territorial, ethnic, economic and military issues of contention.

This faction recognized the many weaknesses of Russia's position in the world and on many international issues was ready to follow the US lead, provided the West recognized Russia's 'special interests, rights and responsibilities' in the 'near abroad'.[6] At the same time, its moderate–conservative supporters suggested considering alternative economic and political partners

[5] Arbatov, A., 'Dogovor dorozhe deneg' [Agreement is worth more than money], *Novoe Vremya*, nos 2–3 (Jan. 1993), pp. 24–27; Arbatov, A., 'Imperiya ili velikaya derzhava?' [Empire or great power?], *Novoe Vremya*, no. 49 (Dec. 1992), pp. 16–18; *Novoe Vremya*, no. 50 (Dec. 1992), pp. 20–23; Baev, P., [Creation of the world with the help of weapons], *Novoe Vremya*, no. 37 (Oct. 1992), pp. 20–21; and Goncharov, S., 'Rossiyskie osobye interesi: kakovy oni?' [Russia's special interests: what are they?], *Izvestiya*, 25 Feb. 1992, p. 3.

[6] Council for Foreign and Defence Policy, [A strategy for Russia], *Nezavisimaya Gazeta*, 19 Aug. 1992, p. 5; and Rutskoy, A., 'Ya tsentrist, derzhavnik i liberal' [I am a centrist, a great-power patriot and a liberal], *Argumenty i Fakty*, no. 37 (Oct. 1992), p. 2.

(China, India and Iran) and called for expansion of the arms trade and exports of nuclear technology and materials as a promising way of earning hard currency.

Finally, the fourth faction consisted of neo-communists and nationalists, some of the latter being former anti-communists and even dissidents (dubbed 'hurrah-patriots' or 'red–browns' by representatives of the first group). On their extreme wing were radical nationalists such as Vladimir Zhirinovsky. More respectable representatives of this group in the Supreme Soviet were organized in the multi-party Russian Unity coalition, while outside parliament they relied on support from the notorious National Salvation Front and various militarist and chauvinist organizations, such as the All-Army Officers' Assembly, Ours and so on. This faction was fully devoted to the goal of revival of the Russian Empire and a superpower role for Russia, on the basis either of communism or of Great Russian nationalism, and combined a fundamentalist version of Russian Orthodoxy with anti-Semitism and a vigorous anti-Western political crusade. It was prepared to reinstate the Soviet Union by military force and advocated economic blockade and open intervention on the side of separatists in the Baltic states, Crimea, Georgia and Moldova. It proposed to resume Soviet-era alliances with all the radical anti-Western regimes—Cuba, Iraq, Libya and North Korea—and advocated the renunciation of UN sanctions and the sending of arms and volunteers *en masse* to Bosnia and Herzegovina and Iraq. Naturally, too, the hard-liners were in favour of a crash military build-up and fiercely opposed to the 1993 US–Russian Treaty on Further Reduction and Limitation of Strategic Offensive Arms (the START II Treaty) and the Treaty on Conventional Armed Forces in Europe (the CFE Treaty), unilateral cuts and withdrawals of Russian troops.[7]

This line of thinking enjoyed popularity among some sections of state–industrial labour (with the exception of miners and oil workers), the impoverished urban lower and middle classes, pensioners, housewives frightened by rampant crime, Russian refugees from other republics, homeless officers from military units withdrawn to Russia from abroad, the backward and passive part of the peasantry, and the new Mafia-type business community, engaged in profiteering and black market speculation. They also had many tacit sympathizers in the ministries of defence, security and internal affairs.[8]

---

[7] [Interview with S. Baburin], *Moskovskie Novosti*, no. 6 (9 Feb. 1992), p. 5 ; Navrozov, L., [A Russian Stalinist's forecasts for 1993], *Izvestiya*, 30 Dec. 1992, p. 4; Gribanov, V., [The dead body of communism is turning into a Nazi vampire], *Nezavisimaya Gazeta*, 6 Nov. 1992, p. 4; and Bragin, V., 'Gde front tam voyna' [Where the front is, there is war], *Izvestiya*, 27 Oct. 1992, p. 4. For the texts of the START II and CFE treaties, see *SIPRI Yearbook 1991: World Armaments and Disarmament* (Oxford University Press: Oxford, 1991), appendix 13A, pp. 461–88; and *SIPRI Yearbook 1993: World Armaments and Disarmament* (Oxford University Press: Oxford, 1993), appendix 11A, pp. 576–89, respectively.

[8] Felgengauer, P., [The Army is neutral for the moment], *Nezavisimaya Gazeta*, 30 Oct. 1992, p. 1; Bespalov, Yu., [The state security service is trying to restore its former power], *Izvestiya*, 16 Mar. 1993, p. 3; and [Report of the RF–Politika Centre: the unfinished coup d'état], *Izvestiya*, 30 Oct. 1992, p. 2.

III. Infantile disorders of foreign policy, 1992–93

During the first two years of the Russian Federation's existence as a sovereign state, the evolution of the domestic situation had the greatest impact on the government's foreign policy.[9]

There is no reason to doubt the good intentions of the policy's authors: they sincerely wanted to advance Russian foreign policy to a new level of relations with the civilized nations of the world and transcend the traditional framework of geopolitics and strategic balances, and they sought to found these relations on common values and international law.

For all its good intentions, however, the course pursued by the Yeltsin Administration and the Foreign Ministry in 1992–93 had several serious and interrelated deficiencies. The architects of post-Soviet policy failed to formulate or even specify in general terms the nature of Russia's new national interests and priorities abroad in a way that would be different both from the scaled-down neo-imperialist version of traditional Soviet ambitions and from utopian slogans like those of Soviet President Mikhail Gorbachev's 'new political thinking'—the 'universal defence of human rights in the world', the 'strategic democratic initiative' and so on. For two years Russia did not put forward any realistic, workable initiative on conflict resolution, arms control or the adaptation of multilateral organizations to the new circumstances of the post-cold war era. On most issues Russia simply followed the Western lead.[10]

One problem stemming directly from this was that Russian foreign policy makers failed to recognize in time that their first priority in the wake of the disintegration of the USSR should be to build good relations with Georgia, Kazakhstan, Ukraine and other republics of the former Soviet Union, however messy and unglamorous they might be. These relations were the key not only to the protection of Russian economic, political and security interests abroad, but also to Russia's relations with the USA, Western Europe and neighbouring states in Asia, and, moreover, to the very prospects of Russian democratic reforms at home.[11] This policy vacuum was quickly filled by other governmental agencies, military commanders, parliamentary factions and political parties, acting independently of each other and all openly challenging the foreign minister and the president.

A second important deficiency was that in dealing with the West the government gave a widespread and mostly justified impression that it was making a never-ending series of unilateral concessions, in particular with respect to UN sanctions on Iraq, Libya and Yugoslavia (Serbia and Montenegro), the provisions of the START II Treaty, missile technology exports to India, the rights of

---

[9] Argovskiy, G. and Rumyantsev, D., 'Faktory vneshney politiki' [The factors in foreign policy], *Nezavisimaya Gazeta*, 9 Mar. 1993, p. 1.

[10] Erlanger, S., 'Moscow stepping in', *New York Times*, 20 May 1993, p. A12.

[11] Portnikov, V., [The Belavezhskiy period in Russia's history is opened], *Nezavisimaya Gazeta*, 16 Mar. 1993, p. 1; Furman, D., 'My i nashi sosedi' [We and our neighbours], *Nezavisimaya Gazeta*, 3 July 1992, p. 2; and Dubnov, A., [Interview with I. Klyamkin: from a strong CIS to strong states, not the other way round], *Novoe Vremya*, no. 38 (Oct. 1992), pp. 14–16.

ethnic Russian minorities in the Baltic states, the South Kurile Islands, and so on. Even such ill-conceived concepts as Russia's joining NATO and participating in the US Strategic Defense Initiative (SDI) found their way into official policy.[12]

Finally, the government's foreign policy did not have the support of any substantial domestic constituency. Foreign Ministry operations were disorderly and distinguished by numerous mishaps. Contrary to expectations, in the crucial founding phase of the new post-Soviet state, and in contrast to the period when Eduard Shevardnadze was Foreign Minister, there was a complete lack of interest in comprehensive analysis of major policy issues involving experts from the Academy of Sciences and the new independent think-tanks and foundations. The decision-making pattern was highly irregular and shielded from public view, and for a long time no serious efforts were made to engage parliament, the mass media or the academic community in an attempt to forge a solid domestic political basis for foreign policy. Even within the Foreign Ministry passive opposition to its leadership became quite strong as a result of disagreements over policy on issues of principle and dissatisfaction with the loss of that ministry's traditional prestige and role.

To make matters even worse, on several occasions Kozyrev (together with other close associates of the president, such as Gaidar, Burbulis and Mikhail Poltoranin) openly involved foreign governments in domestic political clashes within Russia.[13] This exposed them to accusations of conspiring with foreigners against their own people and encouraging Western intervention in Russian domestic affairs. Even at the presidential level, in times of acute domestic crisis US support was sought for actions against the other branches of state power—in March 1993, September–October 1993 and January 1994 and on some other occasions. It is difficult to say what were the leadership's main motivations for seeking Western support—a lack of political culture, a naïve belief in the possibility of intimate relations with the USA or blind hatred of political opponents at home. In reality, of course, nothing could have more thoroughly discredited Russian foreign policy or compromised its authors in the eyes of public opinion. The ground was thereby prepared for a later chauvinistic backlash.

For their part the Western powers were ready to stop considering Russia as an enemy, but politely declined enthusiastic appeals to become instant allies.[14] They bargained firmly on all substantive issues, from economic assistance to strategic arms reduction.

---

[12] Savelev, A., 'SOI i yeshcho raz o besplatnykh zavtrakakh' [SDI and free lunches once again], *Nezavisimaya Gazeta*, 24 Mar. 1992, p. 2.

[13] Nadein, V., [The most tragic mistake could be Western procrastination over support for economic reforms], *Izvestiya*, 7 Feb. 1992, p. 4; Shalnev, A., [The new US Secretary of State promises to increase support for the reforms in Russia], *Izvestiya*, 15 Jan. 1993, p. 2; and Kozyrev, A., 'Partiya voyny atakuyet v Moldove, Gruzii i Rossii' [The party of war is attacking in Moldova, Georgia and Russia], *Izvestiya*, 30 June 1992, p. 3.

[14] Kissinger, H., [Russia's perception of democracy is very special], *Izvestiya*, 1 Feb. 1992, p. 3; and Kissinger, H., 'The new Russian question', *Newsweek*, 10 Feb. 1992, p. 12.

The government's pro-Western policy came more and more to be perceived in Russia as a humiliating course of unilateral concessions, exchanged for very small benefits—all the more so since foreign credits and aid had not been used efficiently—and hence detrimental to Russian prestige and economic, political and security interests. The West, too, perceived it as a policy of concessions and very quickly learned to take it for granted.

During most of the first year of the Yeltsin Administration, apart from relations with the 'near abroad' (in particular, the conflict in Moldova and controversies with Ukraine over Crimea), foreign policy was in the background. By the autumn of 1992, however, it had become one of the major issues in domestic politics. Moreover, moderate–liberals were pushed aside by new players in the foreign policy debates—moderate–conservatives and hard-liners, the former having split from the united democratic front and the latter having recovered after their defeat in August 1991. Both changes were primarily the consequence of the government's domestic economic and political failures, although its international conduct also proved a liability rather than an asset in the balance-sheet of the Yeltsin Administration's first year. The turning-point in the domestic controversies over foreign policy was probably the aborted presidential visit to Japan in August 1992. Mismanagement of the Russian–Japanese territorial dispute by the authorities in Moscow provided an ideal target for right-wing attacks.[15] Yeltsin was forced to cancel the summit meeting at the last moment—the first instance of his obviously yielding to the powerful nationalist political campaign.

The conservative offensive on the government's foreign policy has been gaining momentum ever since. After the Kurile Islands came Yugoslavia, then alleged Russian export losses as a result of the UN-sanctioned embargo on arms sales to Iraq, Libya and Serbia, as well as the curtailment of Russian arms transfers to Cuba and North Korea.[16] At the beginning of 1993 a massive attack against the START II Treaty signed in January that year was in preparation, an attack that was interrupted only by the even more dramatic confrontation over constitutional issues and the April 1993 referendum.

For most of the rest of 1993 foreign policy, with the exception of Russian relations with the 'near abroad', once again largely shifted to the background, and all attention concentrated on the escalation of the domestic political, economic and constitutional crisis. It returned to public attention only after the tragic events of October 1993, and even then in an odd way, via the parliamentary election campaign of Vladimir Zhirinovsky. This marked the beginning of the next phase of the Russian foreign policy debate.

---

[15] Arbatov, A. and Makeyev, B., 'Kurilskiy baryer rossiyskoy diplomatii' [The Kurile barrier in Russian diplomacy], *Novoe Vremya*, no. 42 (Nov. 1992), pp. 24–26.

[16] Felgengauer, P., 'Vse v Rossii khotyat prodavat oruzhie' [Everyone in Russia wants to sell arms], *Nezavisimaya Gazeta*, 1 Oct. 1992, p. 4.

IV. Realignment of domestic foreign policy groups

Even before the crisis of October–December 1993, a major realignment of the parties to foreign policy debates had been taking place, preparing the ground for a significant shift in Russian foreign policy. This shift had several aspects, all leading in one direction.

1. There was a growing mood in favour of Russian self-assertiveness, of finding clear-cut Russian national interests and missions in the world and defending them with all available instruments, including military power.
2. There was an increasing aversion to all kinds of 'universal values', the requirements of international law and other 'idealistic' propositions as guidelines of policy.
3. Anti-Western sentiments started to appear more prominently in both the public mood and political debates.
4. Russian relations with the 'near abroad' came to the foreground in theoretical debates and practical policy making, leaving all other international issues far behind, with the sole exception of obtaining foreign credits and economic assistance.
5. Most importantly, all the above features combined in expanding support for what was called the Russian 'Monroe Doctrine'. This was expressed officially and at a high level for the first time in President Yeltsin's February 1993 appeal at the UN to delegate to Russia the mission of ensuring stability and carrying out peacekeeping operations within the geopolitical space of the former Soviet Union. This line was elaborated by Foreign Minister Kozyrev at a number of ministerial meetings within the framework of the CSCE, the Group of Seven (G7) and the Commonwealth of Independent States (CIS) and during official visits to the Baltic states.[17]

There were a number of reasons for this profound shift. The fundamental explanation was the deteriorating economic and social situation and the growing dissatisfaction of the population with the results of reforms. This made the political leadership more vulnerable to the mounting pressure of nationalist and aggressive moods which was building up not only within public opinion and in the Supreme Soviet but also within the bureaucracy, the military and security establishments, industrial groups and newly established private capital. In addition, the growing political conflict between the executive and legislative powers made the support of military and security institutions much more important, and the rival factions of the new ruling élite attempted to attract that support through neo-imperialist appeals.

The deficiencies of foreign policy in 1992–93 described above also backfired on its architects. Having failed to formulate concrete and imaginative new national priorities, the foreign policy leadership started to succumb to the most

---

[17] Portnikov, V., 'Andrey Kozyrev opredelyaet prioritety' [Andrey Kozyrev defines the priorities], *Nezavisimaya Gazeta*, 20 Jan. 1994, pp. 1–3.

superficial, primitive, 'non-idealistic' formulation of the national interest, with a wide appeal to insulted national pride. This was basically a scaled-down version of the traditional Soviet (and before that Imperial Russian) policy of expanding the imperial perimeter at the expense of weaker neighbouring nations. In this sense it corresponded perfectly both with traditional Russian insecurity as expressed in a bullying attitude and with a dissatisfaction with the new circumstances which easily became nostalgia for idealized past advantages. For all the variations in interpretation, design and justification among individual proponents of the doctrine, its essence is simply revival of the Russian Empire or restoration of the Soviet Union to the extent that this is feasible and possible. This, then, is the newly formulated national priority and mission of Russia in the post-cold war, post-Soviet Union world.

In parallel with the growing popularity and acceptance of this doctrine, the internal dynamics of the various foreign policy orientations and the framework of their debates have also changed. Instead of the four principal groups of 1992–93, by the beginning of 1994 there were only two groups left of any significance. The first, pro-Western group, led by Kozyrev, with few exceptions merged with the moderate–conservative group, as did many within the moderate–liberal faction.[18] Many within the centrist and moderate–conservative grouping shifted closer to hard-liners on the problem of the 'near abroad',[19] while the hard-liners shifted closer to the radical nationalist views espoused by Zhirinovsky.

Most of the professional staff of the Foreign Ministry shifted away from Kozyrev towards the more conservative end of the spectrum. An even more hard-line stance was adopted by the central bureaucracy of the Defence Ministry, while the vast majority of field officers supported radical nationalist views. Even the democratic and liberal factions of the new parliament, to say nothing of the conservatives, communists and nationalists, joined in opposing the Foreign Ministry on the conservative side, a shift expressed in February 1994 by the Duma's condemnation of the newly signed Russian–Georgian Treaty of Friendship, Neighbourly Relations and Cooperation[20] and its enthusiastic support for the newly elected pro-Russian President of Crimea, Yuriy Meshkov.

The crucial difference between the two groups, apart from preferred methods and time-frame (which are circumstantial), is the following. The moderate–conservatives suggest striking a deal with the West, in essence involving the establishment of spheres of influence—the former Soviet 'space' (minus the Baltic states) going to Russia, the rest of the world to the West. The latter group makes no exception for the Baltic states and is ready to restore the empire in

[18] Tretyakov, V. *et al.*, 'Vneshnaya politika Rossii' [Foreign policy of Russia], *Nezavisimaya Gazeta*, 2 Feb. 1994, p. 5.

[19] Migranyan, A., 'Rossiya i blizhnee zarubezhe' [Russia and the near abroad], *Nezavisimaya Gazeta*, 18 Jan. 1994, pp. 4–5; and Lukin, V., 'Rossiya v dalnikh i blizhnikh krugakh' [Russia in far and near circles], *Segodnya*, 3 Sep. 1993, p. 10.

[20] Mikadze, A., 'Georgyevskii traktat 1994 goda' [The Georgievskiy treaty of 1994], *Moskovskie Novosti*, no. 5 (30 Jan.–6 Feb. 1994), p. A-10.

spite of the opposition of the West and at the cost of a new cold war and global 'deadly rivalry'. Their respective views are analysed in more detail below.

Four observations are in order, however. First, several representatives of the moderate–liberal group remain who still publicly express an alternative position.[21] Although they are a small minority, this position is presented below to contrast with the views of the two dominant coalitions. Second, there were probably personal motives worth mentioning in relation to the changed postures of Yeltsin. His more assertive stance may be interpreted as a way to make up for something he felt most vulnerable about, and for which he was criticized by almost everyone—the dismantling of the Soviet Union in 1991, allegedly to get rid of President Gorbachev and take his place in the Kremlin. Third, for Kozyrev the policy of making concessions to hard-liners seemed to be aimed at saving what he valued most—relations with the West—at the same time as deflecting massive criticism of himself by displaying toughness and pragmatism over what he probably considered to be of lesser relative importance— relations with the 'near abroad'. Fourth, the appointment of Yevgeniy Primakov to the position of Foreign Minister in January 1996 was, paradoxically as it may seem, welcomed by practically all the competing factions within the foreign policy community in Russia—something which testifies to the new minister's own professional prestige rather than to any emerging consensus about Russia's external relations.

V. Russian foreign affairs in the 'near abroad'

The first and highest priority for Russia is its relations with some former republics of the USSR, above all Kazakhstan and Ukraine, owing to its very extensive interdependence with them at many levels. Growing instability, conflicts and violence within and among these new states would threaten the security of Russia and Russians and endanger its humanitarian, economic and military interests as well as its democratic economic and political reforms.

Russian moderate–liberals, at least those few who remain true to their initial platform, believe that there are strong, objective attractions—economic, humanitarian, cultural and security-related—between the former Soviet republics, notably Armenia, Belarus, Georgia, Kazakhstan, Russia and Ukraine. Precisely because of their objective nature, however, these ties should not be forced on others by one state. A consistent policy of mutual respect, the recognition of the sovereignty and territorial integrity of other republics, and fair and equal cooperation in various fields would, it is argued, be the best way to prevent the development of centrifugal forces within the territory of the former USSR. Reintegration should start on a new economic basis and only if freely willed by the smaller republics, which are sensitive to any signs of renewed

[21] Arbatov, A., 'Raketno-yaderny prestizh ili realnaya bezopasnost?' [Nuclear-missile prestige or real security?], *Moscow News*, no. 49 (5 Dec. 1993), p. A-4; and Portnikov (note 17), pp. 1–3.

Russian dominance or of Russia's taking on itself the role of arbiter or guarantor of others' security.

According to this logic the first priority of Russia's foreign policy would be to support the emergence of independent, stable, peaceful and neutral new states in place of the former Soviet colonial republics. If these new states are weak and militant, either they will come under the influence of other powers potentially hostile to Russian interests or, to prevent this, Russia will have to establish its own dominance over the former Soviet geopolitical space. The first alternative would be highly detrimental to Russia's foreign policy interests and security; the second would draw Russia into imperial wars, undercut its resources (even the USSR could not bear the costs of empire), and destroy its economic and political reforms. Be that as it may, many of the new states are inherently unstable and in conflict with Russia and each other. Hence it is in the interests both of domestic Russian reforms and of other states to help them achieve at least a minimum of stability and resolve conflicts, without over-stretching Russia's own diminishing resources, while actively involving advanced Western nations in economic and political networks of stability in the area.

Moreover, it is argued that Russia, being by far the largest and strongest of the republics, should exercise much greater flexibility and make bigger concessions on most issues. The only exception is the nuclear legacy of the USSR. Moderate–liberals believe that Russia should be extremely cautious about intervening in the affairs of other republics, even when invited by the local government (as in Tajikistan), so as not to take on responsibilities and waste resources and lives in support of factions in civil wars. Peace enforcement or peacekeeping should be based on multilateral decisions and action initiated by the UN, the Organization for Security and Co-operation in Europe (OSCE)[22] or the CIS. The main Russian role—but only when others wish it—should be that of an active, impartial and creative broker and mediator in settling conflicts.

The OSCE-sanctioned principle of the inviolability of frontiers is to be viewed as the basis of relations between the republics, all of which are now OSCE member states. This means that frontiers may only be changed as a result of peaceful negotiations, not by force. Ethnic separatism within individual republics should be discouraged, and military support by any state of ethnic separatists across the border should be prohibited. Taking into account the specific conditions engendered by post-imperial and post-communist calamities both within Russia itself and in the 'near abroad', exceptions to this rule might include situations where an individual republic itself initiates a revision of its frontiers, for instance by deciding to unite with another state (Moldova with Romania), or if a given republic attempts genocide against an ethnic minority (the treatment of Armenians in Azerbaijan). In these cases a demand from the minority for secession or unification with another republic might be considered legitimate. To protect the rights of minorities, various sanctions would be

---

[22] On 1 Jan. 1995 the CSCE became the OSCE.

warranted, including, as the instrument of last resort, the use of military force. To prevent any abuse of these norms (such as provoking ethnic conflicts to justify military intervention), all the necessary rules and mechanisms should, in the view of moderate–liberals, be established in advance at CIS forums and receive international recognition and negotiated support from the UN and the OSCE.[23]

In contrast to the views of the moderate–liberals, the presently dominant centrist and moderate–conservative group draws different conclusions from the same assumption concerning the deep and multifaceted interdependence of former Soviet republics.[24] It sees Russia as being entitled to a special role because of its size, historic preponderance and other advantages over the smaller republics on the territory of the former Soviet Union and because of its 'out-of-area' strategic and political interests. Preserving and, wherever needed, reinstating its dominant role across the space of the former USSR is the principal goal of their version of Russian foreign policy.[25] This is to be achieved by various means: using the economic dependence of some republics, exploiting the presence of an ethnic Russian population and armed forces on the territory of others, or exploiting ethnic and political tensions within certain states and border conflicts between them. The underlying logic is that the weaker and less stable other republics are, the stronger and better off Russia is.

President Yeltsin in his January 1994 New Year broadcast declared that 'the unconditional emphasis . . . will be the defence of Russia's national interests, of the rights of Russian and Russian-speaking populations within the guidelines of international law and proceeding from the idea of all-national solidarity'.[26] In his notorious January 1994 speech at a conference of ambassadors of the CIS countries and the Baltic states Kozyrev claimed that:

The states of the CIS and the Baltic republics constitute the area of concentration of Russia's principal vital interests. This is also the area from which the main threats to these interests emanate . . . I think that raising the question about complete withdrawal and removal of any Russian military presence in the countries of the near abroad is just as extreme, if not a more extremist suggestion, than the idea of sending tanks to all republics to establish an imperial order there.[27]

Although these statements were, no doubt, motivated to a great extent by domestic political considerations, they nevertheless seriously affected the frame of reference of foreign policy debate and decision making. They are yet another

[23] Arbatov (note 5: 1992), pp. 20–21.

[24] Zubov, A., 'SNG: tsivilizovanny razvod ili novy brak?' [CIS: civilized divorce or a new marriage?], *Novoe Vremya*, no. 36 (Sep. 1992), pp. 8–9.

[25] Chernov, V., 'Natsionalnye interesi Rossii i ugrozi yeyo bezopasnosti' [National interests of Russia and threats to its security], *Nezavisimaya Gazeta*, 29 Apr. 1993, pp. 1–3.

[26] Cited in Dubnov, A., 'Eto velikoe slovo: solidarnost' [This great word—solidarity], *Novoe Vremya*, no. 2 (Jan. 1994), p. 10.

[27] Cited in Pushkov, A., 'Kozyrev nachal igru na chuzhom pole' [Kozyrev has started a game on an alien field], *Moskovskie Novosti*, no. 4 (1 Jan. 1994), pp. 23–30, p. A-13.

element to consider when analysing the real causes and consequences of the October–December 1993 watershed in Russia's political evolution.

The proponents of this policy believe that the preservation of a Russian capability to keep developments under control and rein in smaller republics' propensities towards independence will in due time result in the decline of local nationalism, after which a reintegration process will—with a few exceptions such as the Baltic states—again pick up momentum. They believe that Russia's 'special responsibility and authority' for the former Soviet republics (a new version of the Monroe Doctrine) should be recognized by the West and sanctioned by the UN.[28]

It seems that the new dominant Russian thinking underestimates the power of nationalism and historic grievances in the smaller republics, just as it overestimates Russian resources and the ability of the authorities in Moscow to keep extreme Russian nationalists at bay and to control the escalation of ethnic conflicts. Ironically, the 'democratic' ruling élite, which had come to power as a result of the collapse of the Soviet empire, seemed later to forget completely the lessons of the Soviet eclipse or wrongly assumed that the collapse was caused by the actions of Gorbachev and Shevardnadze and that its lessons thus did not apply to their own policy.

Another feature of the present alignment of factions and patterns of thinking on foreign policy is a blurring of the distinction between moderate–conservative neo-imperialists (calling for 'mild domination' or 'benign activism') and hard-line nationalists and communists, advocating tough policies towards other republics of the former USSR and the routine use of economic blackmail and military force in support of the openly proclaimed goal of reviving the Soviet Union or tsarist Russian Empire. Both groups may unite on many concrete issues of policy and over practical actions to be taken. Actual events, however, will be determined not so much by Russian policies as by the actions of other players in the 'near' and 'far abroad', which might affect the situation and Russian policy more profoundly than the interplay between moderate and hard-line neo-imperialists in Moscow.

The Baltic states

Estonia, Latvia and Lithuania do not wish to reintegrate with Russia and will not do so voluntarily. They gravitate naturally to the neighbouring cultural and economic environment from which they were separated by force in 1939–40. Liberals in Russia advocate restoration of normal economic, trade and political relations with the Baltic neighbours and the conclusion of special agreements with them on the use of port facilities and communications lines, now that the Russian troops have been withdrawn. At the same time they support the use of all available political and in the extreme case economic means to support the rights of the Russian ethnic minorities in these countries if and when they are abused. Moderate–conservatives would freeze relations with the Baltic states

[28] Loshak, V., [NATO: the guarantee from fire], *Moskovskie Novosti*, no. 8 (23 Feb. 1992), p. 3.

until all economic, ethnic and defence disputes between them and Russia are resolved to Russia's liking. Nationalists would go as far as encouraging secessionist activities in Estonia and Latvia and provoking civil violence as a pretext for Russian intervention to dismember the Baltic states or subdue them to Russian dominance as the price of their territorial integrity. More or less the same type of 'alternative' policy is advocated in Russia by this faction in relation to Moldova and the trans-Dniestrian and Gagauz secession movements there.

It is reasonable to hope that the basis of Russia's security relations with the Baltic states will in fact be their neutrality and political cooperation within the OSCE. They present no conceivable security threat to Russia so long as Russia does not push them into military alliances or an anti-Russian orientation by its own hostile policy.

Belarus and Ukraine

Ukraine is by far the most important subject of Russian policy. Moderate–liberals advocate a consistent policy of recognition of its independence and territorial integrity, which would in turn strengthen the position of moderate groups in Kiev. This, according to moderate–liberals, would be the best way to revive fair and mutually beneficial cooperation between the two states and facilitate economic integration and cooperation on foreign policy and defence issues. That would make the borders between the two as insignificant as those between France and Germany or between the USA and Canada. Such a policy, coupled with Russian–US security guarantees and financial help to Ukraine, would be the best way to achieve elimination of nuclear weapons in Ukraine in line with the Lisbon Protocol to Facilitate the Implementation of the START Treaty of May 1992[29] and the Trilateral Statement of the Presidents of the United States, Russia and Ukraine of 14 January 1994.[30]

Conservatives and those liberals who recently joined them would exercise a policy of consistent pressure on Ukraine, for example, by using its vulnerabilities over the Crimean issue (including the Black Sea Fleet and Sevastopol port facilities), exploiting the growing tensions between western Ukraine and the pro-Russian industrial eastern region of the country, manipulating the energy supply, and trying to discredit and isolate Ukraine in Western capitals. This group argues that Ukraine is not viable as an independent state and that economic and social destabilization and disintegration there are quite likely. They advocate a policy of active Russian intervention in Ukrainian affairs to protect Russian economic, humanitarian and security interests there.[31]

In this policy they are encouraged by the recent examples of Belarus and Georgia. The former has never been especially enthusiastic about independence

---

[29] *SIPRI Yearbook 1993* (note 7), pp. 574–75.

[30] Arbatov (note 21). For the full text of the statement, see *SIPRI Yearbook 1994* (Oxford University Press: Oxford, 1994), appendix 16A, pp. 677–78.

[31] Razuavaev, V., 'Krizis na Ukraine i v Rossii' [The crisis in Ukraine and Russia], *Nezavisimaya Gazeta*, 17 Dec. 1993, p. 5.

and neutrality. With few exceptions, it has preserved the old communist élite in power and has not moved forward with economic or political reforms since 1991. With the change in Russian economic policy and the revival of its neo-imperialist foreign posture in early 1994, Belarus initiated the process of moving towards reintegration with Russia. In principle there is nothing wrong with this, since the initiative is coming clearly from Belarus, without any Russian pressure. Unfortunately, the essence of the move is not reintegration on a new economic and political basis, but rather an attempt by the Belarussian authorities to avoid democratic reforms altogether. On the other hand, if Russian democratic reforms continue in a revised, socially oriented version, growing internal tensions and democratic transformation will be unavoidable in Belarus and will create serious problems for its relations with Russia.

Proponents of a tough policy towards Ukraine are not in the least concerned about the effects of such policy becoming a self-fulfilling prophecy and making the situation there worse. The dire implications for Russia itself of destabilization in Ukraine and outside intervention are clearly not entirely recognized or are considered acceptable in view of the prize of bringing Ukraine back into the Russian domain.[32]

On this crucial subject the posture of the nationalist hard-liners differs mostly over tactics, time-frame and final ambitions. They would not be satisfied with subduing Ukraine to Russian economic, political and defence leadership by the threat of dismembering the country and destroying it economically: instead they would strive either for actual annexation of Crimea and eastern Ukraine to Russia or for the incorporation of the whole of Ukraine into the Russian Federation.

Developments in Ukraine since the summer of 1994 have somewhat confused all groups' positions on the issue. For a number of reasons the July 1994 victory of Leonid Kuchma in the presidential election in Ukraine has had a stabilizing effect on its relations with Russia, although it should in no way be taken as implying any retreat from the idea of Ukrainian sovereignty. Kuchma has in fact turned out to be more consistent and rigid on this issue than his predecessor, Leonid Kravchuk, who was more vulnerable in relation to Crimea and eastern Ukraine. Russian conservatives supported Kuchma enthusiastically but are likely to be greatly disappointed in their expectations of Ukraine's rapid return to the Russian fold. If they overreact with expressions of resentment against Kuchma too, Ukraine might move much further away in the direction of the West and of enhancing its state sovereignty than would have been conceivable under Kravchuk.

The Transcaucasus

In respect of the Transcaucasus, the policy of the Russian Federation has on the surface achieved a success. As a result of Russian support of the Abkhazian separatists, in particular in their violation of the Moscow-sponsored truce with

---

[32] Razuavaev (note 31).

Tbilisi in September 1993, and as a consequence of simultaneous civil war, Georgia came to the brink of complete national collapse and disintegration. Having been brought to his knees, Georgian President Shevardnadze agreed to join the CIS and pleaded for Russian military intervention, which defeated his internal rival Zviad Gamsakhurdia and temporarily quelled the fighting on the Abkhazian front. On 3 February 1994 the Russian–Georgian Treaty of Friendship, Neighbourly Relations and Cooperation was signed.[33] Under it Russia acquired the rights to have three military bases in Georgia (a demand rejected earlier by the Georgian authorities) and assumed responsibility for training and arming the national army and protecting Georgia's external borders. Territorial integrity was guaranteed to Georgia, conditional on deep Russian military involvement in managing Georgia's relations with the militant autonomous regions of Abkhazia and South Ossetia.

Clearly, the integrity of Georgia and Armenia is essential to Russian security, specifically in order to contain secessionist movements merged with Muslim fundamentalist tendencies in the Russian territory of the northern Caucasus, a combination which threatens to spread into Tatarstan and Bashkortostan, virtually splitting Russia along the River Volga. In addition Armenia (which would not hold if Georgia disintegrated) is the bulwark separating Turkey from Azerbaijan and thus interrupting geopolitical continuity between Turkey and the Turkic nations of Central Asia.

Right-wing nationalists would probably continue the policy of undeclared war against Georgia until its complete disintegration is brought about, intervening openly on the side of separatists, claiming Russian special interests along the Black Sea shore and aiming at the annexation of Abkhazia, Adzharia and South Ossetia. The question here is whether Georgia would be able to remain an independent state and regain stability following a Russian intervention. If not, instead of being a natural Russian geopolitical ally it would burden Russia with its ethnic, economic and social problems without being at all grateful for Russian patronage. Such an ally would not help Russia either to keep north Caucasian secessionists under control or to contain the spread of Turkish influence in the Transcaucasus and Central Asia. This could have been different if, after Shevardnadze's ascent to the presidency, Russia had helped Georgia to hold together by discouraging Ossetian and Abkhazian separatism. The rights of these minorities and their protection against Georgian hard-liners could have been secured by international guarantees with active Russian participation[34] and, even without Russian military bases, Georgia would have been a much more stable and reliable ally in the maintenance of Russia's geopolitical interests in the region. If needed to counter the emergence of a tangible common strategic threat, the deployment of a Russian military presence would always have been easy to negotiate.

[33] See note 20.
[34] Mutalibov, A., 'Bolshaya smuta na Kavkaze' [Major turmoil in the Caucasus], *Novoe Vremya*, no. 46 (Dec. 1992), pp. 8–10; Payin, E. and Popov, A., [The flame of the Caucasus war is the price for legal and political mistakes], *Izvestiya*, 5 Nov. 1992; and Furman (note 11).

Unfortunately, the simple-minded policy of Russian dominance, the personal hostility towards President Shevardnadze of Russian hard-liners stemming from his role in the Soviet retreat of the late 1980s and early 1990s, and the determination of the military to retain garrisons and facilities at all costs—all these factors defined a very different Russian policy. In the long run the victory of 1994 may turn out to have been a Pyrrhic one. Russia's growing troubles in Chechnya at the end of 1994 were indicative of potential calamities which threaten it with loss of control not only in the Transcaucasus but also in the north Caucasian areas of its own territory.

Both moderate–liberals and moderate–conservatives are shifting in favour of Armenia in its conflict with Azerbaijan over Nagorno-Karabakh. Here, however, they would accord differing priorities to geopolitical, humanitarian and ideological considerations (Armenians are Orthodox Christians, while Azeris are Shiite Muslims). Liberals would be more eager to facilitate a cease-fire between Armenia and Azerbaijan if only they knew how to do so and how in the final resolution of the conflict to reconcile the Armenians' rights to self-determination with the principle of the inviolability of existing borders. Conservatives are less worried about continuing war, provided that neither side wins a decisive victory and there is no military intervention by Iran or Turkey.

Ironically, in spite of the 'Christian' zeal expressed in dealing with Central Asia, many Russian nationalists support Azerbaijan against Armenia on the issue of Nagorno-Karabakh. This is because Armenia has, until recently, had the image of one of the most independent and democratic republics of the CIS, being strongly supported by the Armenian diaspora in the West. On the other hand, the Western position is ambivalent on this issue. Turkey, being a member of NATO and preferable to Iran, strongly supports Azerbaijan. Since as a general rule Russian nationalists give priority to anti-Western over geopolitical or religious considerations, their position on Nagorno-Karabakh is nuanced.

Central Asia

In Central Asia conservatives argue for an active policy of cultivating pro-Russian regimes and supporting them economically and, if necessary, militarily. This is justified by the significant natural resources of the region (oil, gas, uranium and gold), by the need to protect Russians living there (about 3.3 million, apart from the estimated 6.2 million living in Kazakhstan), and by the need to seal the southern border of the former USSR.[35] Kazakhstan is considered to be especially valuable in view of its natural resources and highly developed industrial, scientific and military infrastructure such as the Baikonur space test range, the Sary-shagan anti-ballistic missile (ABM) facilities, strategic weapons deployment sites, the Semipalatinsk nuclear test range and other sites. Since all these facilities were built by the Soviet state, they are considered

---

[35] Playis, Ya., 'Rossiya i tsentralnaya Azia' [Russia and Central Asia], *Nezavisimaya Gazeta*, 19 Jan. 1994, p. 3.

as Russian property, and the goal of conservative policy is to retain and in some cases regain Russian control over them.

Hard-line nationalists go further than this: they do not even consider Kazakhstan a legitimate state. They attack the Kazakh leadership for allegedly abusing the rights of Russians there (the problem exists, but certainly not encouraged by President Nursultan Nazarbaev) while keeping silent on the much worse situation in Tajikistan and Uzbekistan, the governments of which demonstrate political loyalty to Russia. The nationalists attempt to blackmail Kazakhstan with the threat of encouraging the secession of its northern and eastern regions, inhabited predominantly by Russians, and claim unilateral Russian control over the country's industrial and military assets. Since they anticipate that Russia will be transformed into an authoritarian state once more, they see no problem in reviving close political and economic control as well as full-scale military involvement in Central Asia in order to prevent Muslim, Western or Chinese expansionism in the region.

Moderate–liberals are generally reluctant to approve direct Russian military intervention under the slogan of opposing the expansion of Muslim fundamentalism. Some neo-communist feudal regimes may try to secure Russian military support to fight local opposition movements by labelling them as Muslim fundamentalists, and in this way, indeed, push the opposition towards religious extremism. This process threatens to involve Russia in hopeless neo-colonial wars that are against its foreign interests and domestic political preferences. Seemingly, this is what is now happening in Tajikistan.[36]

For liberals, unlike conservatives or nationalists (with a few exceptions), Central Asia is the least important subregion in the former Soviet geopolitical space for Russian interests. If democratic reforms continue in Russia the four Central Asian states will most probably start to move away from the CIS (or whatever may eventually supersede it) and become integrated into the South Asian economic and political sphere. That Russians are fighting in Tajikistan is all the more wrong, since the Tajik and Uzbek leaders have their own policy of intervening in the Afghan civil war.[37] Russia cannot control these policies and in this respect is more a subject of than an active player in the regional game.

Kazakhstan, however, is altogether a different story, being genuinely an area of vital Russian interests for ethnic, economic and security reasons. The spread of nationalism and Muslim fundamentalism would be fatal for Kazakhstan and tragic to the Russians living there. Ethnic violence and a war over the partitioning of Kazakhstan would certainly involve Russia, and might lead to a large-scale war between Russia and a Kazakh state allied with the Islamic regimes of Central Asia and the entire Arab world. Such a war would be catastrophic for Russia, all the more so since the positions of the West and China are far from certain.

---

[36] Panfilov, O., 'Rossiya posylyaet yeshche odin batalion v Tajikistan' [Russia sends another battalion to Tajikistan], *Nezavisimaya Gazeta*, 29 Apr. 1992, p. 3.

[37] Dubnov, A., [Russia has an Afghan headache again], *Novoe Vremya*, no. 5 (Feb. 1994), pp. 24–27.

The strengthening of Russian–Kazakh relations should be the main perspective from which to consider events in Central Asia, including the present war in Tajikistan. Russian military interventions (especially when unsuccessful, as in Afghanistan) create a danger of radical militant movements sweeping away moderate regimes and, finally, reaching Kazakhstan. Russia has to be extremely selective in its military actions in this region, and in most cases restrict itself to economic and political influence. Military actions, if taken at all, should be based on multilateral operations by the Central Asian republics, and always conditional on the approval of Kazakhstan.

VI. The 'far abroad' and Russian global interests

Yugoslavia

Following the Western lead on the former Yugoslavia has done the greatest disservice to Russian interests and the Yeltsin Administration's foreign policy record. Russia has been largely marginalized in international policy making on this issue, in spite of its having a much greater stake (domestic and foreign) in developments in the former Yugoslavia than any of the other major powers. In addition, Russia missed an opportunity to gain the initiative in stopping the war by using its historic special relationships with the Serbs, as it could have done, in order to pressure them to make concessions while at the same time protecting them from discriminatory UN sanctions.

As a result, Russia's presence in the process of peace settlement in Bosnia and Herzegovina was no more than symbolic. All this has made conservatives quite sceptical of multilateral UN- or OSCE-sponsored peacekeeping cooperation with the West. For nationalists, unreserved support for the Serbs against the Croats, the Muslims and the West has become one of the primary international issues.

Multilateral cooperation

The moderate–conservatives would generally be reluctant to participate in multilateral peacekeeping or peace-enforcement operations on the basis of a UN Security Council or OSCE mandate. Indeed, Russia's involvement in the Implementation Force (IFOR) in Bosnia and Herzegovina, which might well be welcomed as the first experience of practical interaction with NATO forces, seemed to be motivated first and foremost by a desire to compensate for Russia's marginal political role in preparing the Dayton Agreements. In a broader sense, one important condition of Russian political (and eventually military) cooperation would be the willingness of the West to respect Russian 'vital interests' and 'special responsibilities' in the former Soviet geopolitical space.

Nationalist and communist hard-liners would certainly do their best to obstruct any collective action if it emanated from NATO, the Western European Union (WEU) or ad hoc Western coalitions (as with the 1991 Persian Gulf War). This line of thinking, although recognizing Russia's inability to oppose the Western actors directly with military force, would advocate doing so indirectly by supplying opponents of the West with arms and other kinds of aid and by sending military advisers and volunteers. This could make Western actions too costly and precipitate a major new confrontation in world politics, further aggravated by the proliferation of nuclear weapons and missile technologies.

Europe

Moderate–liberals argue that within Europe the best guarantee against the hypothetical revival of German expansionism is European integration within the institutional frameworks of the European Union (EU) and the WEU and the strengthening of the OSCE as a mechanism for collective security and collective action against a potential aggressor. One of the instruments for that may be the employment of NATO structures to perform selected missions on behalf of the OSCE or the UN. A residual US political and military presence in Europe within the NATO framework is believed to be a stabilizing factor.

On the other hand, liberals recognize that too active a NATO role or NATO enlargement would provoke a negative Russian reaction and greatly strengthen the hand of hard-liners in Moscow. To avoid that the West needs to pay much greater attention to Russian views and interests and to act on the basis of genuine compromise and consensus, primarily through the UN and the OSCE, so that these bodies do not end up looking like fig-leaves for essentially US, NATO or German actions.[38]

Conservatives and hard-liners do not believe that European integration is in Russian interests. Their policy would be to encourage a split between the USA and Western Europe and between Germany and other European states. They would try to bring about a US military and political withdrawal from Europe and provoke controversy in NATO and the WEU by adopting an uncompromising stance in the UN Security Council and OSCE institutions. Their ideal would be to establish a Russian–German axis to divide Eastern Europe into spheres of influence and to set France, the UK and the USA against each other.

The Middle East and South Asia

Conservatives and hard-liners would here in principle give preference to India, Iran and Iraq over pro-Western Turkey and Pakistan. One of the nationalist extremists' most ambitious and improbable ideas is for Russia eventually to gain access to the Persian Gulf through a strategic alliance with Iraq and to subjugate Turkey and Iran. According to Vladimir Zhirinovsky this would provide Russia with unopposed strategic access to the Indian Ocean, cheap oil for its

[38] Baev (note 5).

domestic needs and exports, and a powerful energy lever on the West and Japan, splitting them away from the USA.[39]

Liberals dismiss such ideas as insane, arguing strongly against any thorough-going Russian involvement in the region extending beyond normal trade relations. Moderate–liberals, however, are much more concerned about what they perceive as Turkish expansionism in the Transcaucasus and the Balkans, claiming that this might bring Russia and Turkey into conflict with each other, with dire implications for Russia's relations with the West, which is allegedly pandering to Turkey's regional activism.

The Far East

In the Far East, according to moderate–liberals, the interests of Russia (in contrast to those of the USSR) may be best served by the maintenance of a US political role and military presence. In the event of a US withdrawal, the Japanese reaction could be no other than remilitarization, in view of the rapid growth of the economic and military power of China. A clash between the two regional giants over the Korean peninsula, Taiwan, Hong Kong or South-East Asia could draw Russia into the conflict as well.

Since Russia will remain weak and vulnerable in the Far East for many years to come, its interests are tied to a more stable regional balance of power. This is impossible without stability on the Korean Peninsula, and in future Russia would benefit more than anybody else from peaceful reunification of the two Korean states on the basis of a market economy and democracy.

The current slant in favour of China could put Russia in a position of one-sided dependence on Beijing. Resolution of the problem of the Kurile Islands with Japan would provide Russia with a much more advantageous political position and greater freedom of manoeuvre in the Western Pacific. Moderate–liberals would approach this controversial subject not from a legal or historical angle, and certainly not in the 'islands-for-credits' mode, as the Russian Government attempted to do in the summer of 1992; they favour returning the islands to Japan in a phased way over a 10–15 year period in the context of agreements on demilitarized zones, deep armed force reductions, limits on anti-submarine (ASW) operations and implementing confidence-building measures (CBMs) in the Far East. (CBMs might, for instance, include all the Kurile chain, the Sakhalin and Hokkaido islands and the Sea of Okhotsk in their area of application.) In this way both parties' security interests would be taken care of, and the territorial agreement would be part of a fundamental revision of political and security relations between Russia and Japan, a change which could be followed by economic cooperation provided Russia creates attractive conditions for foreign investment in Siberia and the Far East.[40]

---

[39] Ivanidze, V., 'Piratskaya kniga Zhirinovskogo' [Pirate book of Zhirinovsky], *Izvestiya*, 10 Feb. 1994, p. 8.
[40] Arbatov and Makeyev (note 15); and *Novoe Vremya*, no. 43 (Nov. 1992), pp. 24–25.

Moderate–conservatives are now influencing Russian policy in the direction of improving economic, political and military relations with China (including large-scale exports of arms and military technologies). Relations with Japan are accorded secondary importance because of an aversion to making any territorial concessions.[41] This group would not put forward new broad schemes but would wait for Japan to show greater flexibility on the issue, hoping that its fear of Chinese expansionism would soften its traditional uncompromising stance.

Nationalists would go much further in siding with China against Japan, and would certainly resume cooperation with North Korea in opposition to South Korea and the USA. This might well further destabilize the situation on the Korean Peninsula and in the Western Pacific in general, as well as accelerate nuclear and missile proliferation in the world at large.

Global issues

Despite the current domestic crisis Russia has important global responsibilities to fulfil. They include its position as a permanent member of the UN Security Council, its role in other international organizations and its participation in peacekeeping operations mandated by UN resolutions.

Russian cooperation is essential for non-proliferation of nuclear and other weapons of mass destruction, for better control over the export of missiles and missile technology, and for the introduction of quotas and restrictions on the arms trade. Russian conservatives encourage exports of nuclear materials and technologies and of all kinds of arms to any state, if they are paid for in hard currency. This policy could very soon create a danger for the security of Russia itself, undermine regional stability and create new areas of tension with the West.

The Western position on these issues is also important. Political restrictions on Russian arms and nuclear exports should be at least partially compensated for by Western economic aid. If not, Russia will fight to expand its share in the world trade in these commodities to earn hard currency. Conservatives and hard-liners are already arguing that Russia is losing much more financially through compliance with UN-sanctioned embargoes (on Iraq, Libya and the former Yugoslavia) and on arms trade restrictions introduced under US pressure (Cuba, India, Iran and North Korea) than it is gaining in credits and economic assistance from the West.[42] The deepening economic crisis, the failure of defence industry conversion and the growing interest of the defence industries in arms exports to compensate for drastic cuts in state contracts are having a tangible effect on Russian foreign policy, with long-term international implications.

In strategic relations with the USA, conservatives have serious reservations about the START II Treaty, while nationalist hard-liners advocate the adoption

[41] See note 25.
[42] Borodenkov, A., 'Proshchay oruzhie' [Farewell to arms], *Moskovskie Novosti*, 28 Jan. 1992, p. 14.

of a first-strike strategy[43] and are adamantly against arms control treaties with the USA. The START II Treaty indeed envisions much more radical, irreversible reductions and limitations for Russian strategic forces and modernization programmes than for US systems.[44]

The moderate–liberal alternative is not to relieve restrictions on Russian forces but to apply some additional limitations to both sides (in particular, restricting sea-based counter-force capabilities and reducing bomber alert rates) to make the START II Treaty more balanced, more strategically stabilizing and less politically vulnerable within Russia.[45] Some proposals have envisioned faster reduction rates by way of unscrewing warheads in advance from the missiles slated for dismantling. Apart from radically lowering alert rates, this would have defused the problem of nuclear proliferation through the nationalization of strategic weapons in Kazakhstan and Ukraine.[46]

As long as moderate–conservatives are dominant in the executive and legislative branches, the chances of START II ratification and implementation are uncertain. Their argument is that the treaty constrains Russian forces too harshly, undermines strategic parity and weakens Russian national security.[47] New negotiations might be needed to ensure implementation of the START I and START II treaties within the framework of more radical cuts and limitations, provided the USA shows greater flexibility and readiness to apply more stringent measures to US forces.[48] Otherwise the two sides would be obliged for several years to take the path of unilateral reductions—an option they are currently exercising, in view of the block obsolescence of their strategic forces and curtailment of modernization programmes. The evolution of the general political and security relations of Russia and the West would then determine the prospects of further bilateral and multilateral arms control and reduction agreements.

There is no question that hard-liners would like to resume strategic nuclear rivalry with the USA and abandon the current arms control regime to restore what they call the central pillar of Russian power and grandeur in the world. None the less, even if their preferences were to gain the upper hand, an all-out strategic arms race would not necessarily be resumed, at least not during the 1990s. Economic and other problems would make it impossible for Russia to

[43] Repin, V., 'Yeshcho raz o strategicheskikh dilemmakh' [Strategic dilemmas once again], *Nezavisimaya Gazeta*, 24 Sep. 1992, p. 2.

[44] Arbatov, A., 'START-2, red ink, and Boris Yeltsin', *Bulletin of the Atomic Scientists*, vol. 49, no. 3 (Apr. 1993), pp. 16–21.

[45] Arbatov, A., 'Rossiyskie strategicheskie dilemmy' [Russian strategic dilemmas], *Nezavisimaya Gazeta*, 28 Aug. 1992, p. 4.

[46] Arbatov, A., 'Yeltsin, Kravchuk i ballisticheskie rakety' [Yeltsin, Kravchuk and ballistic missiles], *Nezavisimaya Gazeta*, 6 Aug. 1992, p. 4.

[47] Georgiev, O., 'SNV-2 ne imeet analogov' [START II has no analogues], *Nezavisimaya Gazeta*, 5 Feb. 1993, p. 4; and Belous, V., 'Politika, ekonomika i razoruzhenie' [Politics, economics and disarmament], *Nezavisimaya Gazeta*, 14 Feb. 1992, p. 4.

[48] 'SNV-2 i natsionalnye interesi Rossii' ['START II and Russia's national interests': report of the Foreign Policy Association], *Nezavisimaya Gazeta*, 23 Mar. 1993, p. 5; and Litovkin, V., 'SNV-2 ukreplyaet bezopasnost Rossii' [START II strengthens Russia's security: interview with G. Berdennikov, V. Dvorkin and A. Arbatov], *Izvestiya*, 10 Apr. 1993, p. 15.

compete with the USA as it did before. The arms control framework, which at this stage requires a great deal of mutual trust and cooperation, would certainly disintegrate, with all the ensuing political tensions and uncertainties.[49] The inevitable deterioration of Russian strategic capabilities might push it towards unstable and provocative strategies, increasing the risks of inadvertent or accidental nuclear war.

VII. Conclusions

Russian foreign policy has shifted from its initial pro-Western stance to a much more conservative one. It has already become more assertive with regard to Russian national interests, identity and position on international problems, and most of all with regard to Russia's special responsibilities in the post-Soviet geopolitical space.

Outside the post-Soviet space, the new policy is not necessarily to be characterized as expansionist or aggressive. It is severely constrained by economic and political problems at home; by the reaction of public opinion, the mass media and parliament; by difficulties and vulnerabilities in relations with neighbouring republics; and by dependence on Western economic aid, credits and investment. It will be restricted by the current multifaceted arms control regime and contained by Western strategic preponderance, as well as by the weakness of the Russian armed forces and the degradation of the defence industries.[50]

Clearly, many issues will become subjects of controversy between Russia and the West: arms and nuclear exports, regional conflict resolution, peacekeeping operations in various parts of the world, arms control compliance and so on. All of these are normal issues of international politics and can be settled by traditional diplomatic bargaining and compromises.

In contrast, Russian relations with other former republics of the Soviet Union may create a genuine and dangerous problem. A policy of preserving and restoring Russian dominance, and for this purpose using the weaknesses and instabilities of neighbouring states, may inadvertently draw Russia into an increasing number of conflicts, undercut its democratic reforms and precipitate a new confrontation with the West. At the time of writing, apart from a few individuals, there is no serious liberal opposition to this policy in the Russian political élite. Such opposition may emerge after major failures, but the cost could be too high and the damage done irreparable.

To prevent this dangerous trend would require active, creative and sophisticated policies on the part of the USA, Western Europe and Japan, and this kind of policy has yet to emerge. Russian attempts to obtain Western recognition of its 'special rights' through a UN or OSCE mandate should not be rejected out of hand, nor should recognition be granted unconditionally. Rather, Russia's

---

[49] Nikolaev, V., 'Strategiya dlya Rossii' [Strategy for Russia: interview with Col-Gen. V. Achalov], *Pravda*, 11 Feb. 1993, p. 2. An All-Army Officers Assembly heard a charge against START II from its chairman, Sergey Terekhov. Interfax, 20 Feb. 1993.

[50] Council on Foreign and Defence Policy (note 6), p. 4.

concern to gain Western acceptance should be used to get the West deeply involved through the international organizations in multilateral peace enforcement and peacekeeping activities in the former USSR. Naturally, this also implies equal and fair Russian participation in conflict resolution in the 'far abroad', together with the USA and European nations, within a broader new framework of a multilateral security system in Europe and the post-Soviet space. A thoroughly reformed and much more effective OSCE might be the best structure for that purpose. The Partnership for Peace (PFP) programme could be one of the instruments of this structure, helping NATO (not just the former communist states) to adapt to the post-cold war environment in Europe and to new peacemaking and peacekeeping missions as opposed to collective defence.

Clearly, all this would require determination, consensus and the investment of substantial resources on the part of the West. There is hardly any other area of international relations, however, that would be as well worth the effort and sacrifice as political developments in Europe and the one-sixth of the Earth that was formerly called the Soviet Union.

Part IV
Military aspects

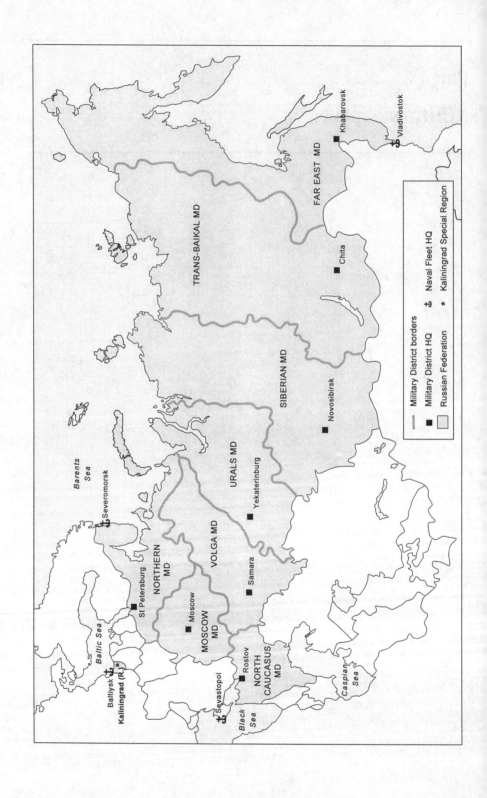

Background chronology

1992

6 May   President Yeltsin issues a decree creating independent Russian Federation Armed Forces including all former Soviet soldiers and military installations on Russian territory, as well as troops and naval forces under Russian jurisdiction based outside the republic. Strategic nuclear weapons remain under the command authority of the CIS Joint Forces

15 May   At a CIS summit meeting in Tashkent, an agreement is signed by Armenia, Azerbaijan, Belarus, Georgia, Kazakhstan, Moldova, Russia and Ukraine re-allocating the former USSR's ceilings of treaty-limited equipment (TLE) set out in the CFE Treaty

1993

3 Jan.   Yeltsin and US President Bush sign the START II Treaty, which mandates cuts in Russian and US strategic nuclear forces to no more than 3500 deployed warheads each and eliminates all multiple-warhead land-based ballistic missiles

15 June Dissolution of the CIS military command announced in Moscow

17 Sep. Yeltsin calls for upward revision of Russia's flank sub-ceilings on TLE under the CFE Treaty

2 Nov.   Russian Security Council approves a new military doctrine which codifies new roles and missions for the armed forces and abandons the Soviet-era pledge not to use nuclear weapons first in a conflict

1994

5 Apr.   Yeltsin signs a decree on establishment of Russian military bases on territories of some former Soviet republics

5 Dec.   At CSCE summit meeting in Budapest, Russia exchanges the START I Treaty instruments of ratification with Belarus, Kazakhstan, Ukraine and the USA, thereby bringing the treaty into force

1995

8 Apr.   To reduce crippling manpower shortages, the Duma extends the period of national service from 18 to 24 months and cuts the numbers of exemptions from conscription

17 Nov. Russia fails to meet the deadline for completing its TLE destruction obligations under the CFE Treaty and is declared to be in 'technical noncompliance'

1996

16 May   Presidential decree abolishing conscription; to take effect in spring 2000

1 June   Yeltsin signs the Law on Defence approved earlier by parliament which delineates the powers and duties of federal and regional bodies involved in Russia's defence and the rights and obligations of Russian civilians

1 June   Agreement reached at the CFE Treaty Review Conference gives Russia 3 more years to meet the flank limits on TLE. It contracts the flank area, thereby allowing Russia to deploy more heavy weapons along its southern and northern borders than would have been permitted under the original terms of the treaty

9 July   The Duma Committee on Defence is reported as having submitted a new draft law 'On military reform' introducing smaller and better-funded armed forces by the year 2005 and setting defence spending at a minimum of 5% of GNP and 25% of the federal budget

18 July Gen. Rodionov appointed Defence Minister following dismissal in June of Gen. Grachev

Key facts

Comparison of Soviet and Russian military power

	1988	1994
Total active armed forces	5 100 000[a]	1 500 000
Troops deployed in Eastern Europe	665 000	0
Main battle tanks	53 300	19 500
Major surface warships	268	150[b]
Main battle tank production	3500	40
Fighter/fighter-bomber production	700	50
Major surface warship production	9	0

[a] Includes *c.* 1 500 000 railway troops, construction troops and civil defence personnel but excludes *c.* 600 000 KGB and Interior Ministry paramilitary troops. [b] Figure is for 1995. *Sources*: International Institute for Strategic Studies, *The Military Balance 1988–1989, 1994–1995, 1995–1996.*

Russian defence budget

1994	43.4 trillion roubles[a]	22% of total government expenditure	5.6% of GDP
1995	59.379 trillion roubles	19.6% of total government expenditure	< 4% of GDP

[a] Does not include mobilization, subsidies to 'closed' towns. *Sources: SIPRI Yearbook 1995,* pp. 404–406; *SIPRI Yearbook 1996,* pp. 333–34.

Because data on inflation, GDP and off-budget items are unavailable or unreliable, determining the true level of Russian military expenditure is problematical.

Percentage shares of the main spending categories in the official defence budgets

	1989	1995[a]
Procurement	42.2	17.3
Operations & maintenance (O&M)	26.1	53.7
Research & development (R&D)	19.8	8.3
Construction	6.0	10.4
Pensions	3.0	8.2
Ministry of Atomic Energy (nuclear weapons)	3.0	1.7

[a] Does not include non-Ministry of Defence budget allocation for mobilization. *Sources: SIPRI Yearbook 1992,* p. 215; *SIPRI Yearbook 1996,* p. 334.

The distribution of the official defence budget allocation has changed significantly since 1989. Weapons acquisition—procurement of new equipment and R&D activities—constituted nearly two-thirds of the Soviet defence budget in 1989 but only slightly more than one-quarter of the 1995 defence budget, a decrease that calls into question Russia's ability to maintain and modernize its military capabilities.

8. The Russian Armed Forces: structures, roles and policies

Roy Allison

I. Introduction

The role of military means in addressing the potential threats to Russia's security in the early and mid-1990s is inherently difficult to ascertain since the military institution and the instruments available to it have become meshed into a complex web of political and economic influences. In other words political, social and economic considerations have come to play as large a part as if not a larger one than strategic and military–technical ones in the debates on the size, structure, basing arrangements, roles and missions of the armed forces. This is also true of the position occupied by nuclear weapons and of the characteristics of Russian military interaction with the outside world more broadly. Much of the effort of the Defence Ministry and General Staff is now devoted to handling immediate crises of military accommodation, recruitment shortfalls or social tensions, to lobbying for greater defence expenditure or to coming to terms with new political currents and ambitions in the military establishment.

To generalize, however, military factors appear to have assumed a growing salience in this period compared to the late Gorbachev years, despite an initial period of shock and despair within the military élite over the collapse of the integrated Soviet military apparatus, and despite the broadening of the security agenda to encompass new issue areas (reflected, for example, in the diverse topics discussed in the Russian Security Council). This reflects the militarization of politics in many of the states of the Commonwealth of Independent States (CIS) and the conflicts erupting within them (as well as within the Russian Federation in the case of Chechnya), which have offered the Russian military new roles and leverage on political leaders in their efforts to bolster stability.

These developments have raised the profile of military factors and Russian military forces with respect to the former Soviet states much more than in relation to states in the 'far abroad'. A number of subjects discussed in this chapter, such as Russian military strength, structure and deployment plans, and related political/economic factors, often therefore impinge only indirectly on European security at large, although they raise questions about the identity and intentions of Russia as a power in Europe.

II. Social, political and economic constraints

Social problems

The cohesion of the new Russian armed forces as an institution has been severely challenged by the chaotic process of reorganization, reduction and redeployment which followed the collapse of the USSR. Social deprivation among officers has resulted in a climate of despair that breeds crime and political radicalism.

Social conditions for the officer corps have been most adversely influenced by a continued high level of homelessness. The housing construction plans for 1993 were not fulfilled, leaving 120 000 officers without apartments; by the summer of 1994 this number had increased to 180 000 and was still growing.[1] The construction programmes financed by Germany for officers withdrawn from eastern Germany may only meet half of the demand for apartments, and the 8.35 billion DM allocated by Germany to build 36 000 flats for servicemen may itself be sharply reduced by Russian state taxation. It is true that a special fund has been created for the payment of benefits to those discharged under the cuts, but separate payments promised to those still in service have mostly not been received and occasional non-payment of salaries has exacerbated tensions.

Large numbers of younger officers are leaving the military where other employment opportunities arise, further undermining the social structure of the armed forces. Some 95 000 officers under the age of 30 left the army between 1990 and 1993.[2] This is hardly likely to be counterbalanced by the small if growing number of officers who have left the armies of the other CIS states to join the Russian officer corps (after the initial mass transfers between these states) lured by higher wages.[3] In the spring of 1994 the ground forces alone faced a shortage of 17 000 junior officers.[4] The declining quality of personnel is also indicated by the fact that educational levels have been steadily falling in the army as a whole. While 93 per cent of all enlisted personnel had a secondary or secondary technical education in the late 1980s, by 1994 the figure was only 76 per cent.[5]

Corruption, theft and even armed robbery have increased within the Russian officer corps. Military links with local mafia networks have developed, which may undermine the discipline of entire units and even pose a threat to society, especially in regions already beset by acute instability. In summer 1994 Prime Minister Viktor Chernomyrdin reportedly decided to order an intensive audit of

[1] *Krasnaya Zvezda,* 23 Mar. 1994; and Report by Defence Minister Grachev to the Defence Committee of the Duma, ITAR-TASS, 11 July 1994, reported in *Summary of World Broadcasts—Former USSR* (hereafter SWB–SU), 2047 S1/3.

[2] Belousov, A. (Col), *Krasnaya Zvezda,* 10 June 1994.

[3] Some 3000 officers from these other CIS armies joined the Russian Armed Forces in 1993. *Moskovskiy Komsomolets,* 25 Feb. 1994, reported in SWB–SU, 1940 S1/1.

[4] According to the Commander-in-Chief of the Russian Ground Forces, Col-Gen. Vladimir Semenov, Interfax, 19 May 1994, reported in Radio Free Europe/Radio Liberty (hereafter RFE/RL), *RFE/RL News Briefs,* vol. 3, no. 21 (1994), p. 5.

[5] Russian Defence Ministry briefing reported in Rubnikovich, O., *Nezavisimaya Gazeta,* 21 Jan. 1994.

military spending to eliminate large-scale theft and corruption, which threatened to implicate the former Commander of Russian forces in Germany, Colonel-General Matvey Burlakov, and other high-ranking officers.[6] Burlakov was nominated to be a Deputy Defence Minister but was suspended by President Boris Yeltsin in November 1994 following public outrage at the assassination of a Russian journalist investigating corruption in the Western Group of Forces (in Germany). Illegal commercial activities were particularly evident among units stationed abroad, creating a new élite of officer entrepreneurs in the armed forces.

An official report of the Acting Chief Military Procurator on military engagement in commercial activities is particularly revealing. A picture emerges of widespread abuse by senior officers of the material resources and funds of the Defence Ministry for personal enrichment. Among other areas this involves 'the unlawful acquisition of weapons by businesses'. Funds allotted directly for financing troops, for wages and military equipment are being siphoned away, which sometimes 'simply paralyses the activities of military units and institutions'. Such abuse was claimed to be acute for the Northern Fleet and no better in the Pacific Fleet, the Siberian Military District (MD) and the Strategic Rocket Forces.[7]

Such military restructuring as has occurred has also raised social tensions by dividing army units into élites and non-élites, effectively producing first- and second-class officers. In turn social divisions are deepening among servicemen between contract soldiers and conscripts. Military sociologists described this as occurring in a general environment of poverty and disillusionment, which was leading to the disintegration of the army as a cohesive social organization.[8]

Necessarily this is reflected in a significant decline in morale. According to one survey in 1993 almost 44 per cent of personnel surveyed claimed that they had at least once refused to obey a commander; 57 per cent of officers stated that they could not provide for their families; 51 per cent said they were overworked on account of personnel shortages. Even more telling, only 18 per cent of conscripts believed that draft dodging is wrong, while 25 per cent approved of it.[9] Another report in the spring of 1994 confirmed that 70 per cent of all officers and warrant officers thought that their units were incapable of performing their missions and that up to 40 000 young officers leave the army each year.[10] Such disenchantment among military personnel also has political implications.

---

[6] 'Generals in business', *Moscow News*, 24 (1994); and Stepanov, S., *Segodnya*, 24 Aug. 1994.

[7] Report from Lt-Gen. of Justice Grigoriy Nosov, published in *Moscow News*, 34 (1994), p. 3.

[8] Deryugin, Yu. (Col), [Army at war with itself], *Nezavisimaya Gazeta*, cited in *The Guardian*, 8 Sep. 1994; and 'Russian army forced on to the defensive', *The Guardian*, 25 Aug. 1994.

[9] Zhilin, A. and Skorobogatko, T., 'Yesli zavtra voyna' [If there were war tomorrow], *Moskovskie Novosti*, 9–16 Jan. 1994.

[10] Kholodov, D., *Moskovskiy Komsomolets*, 22 Mar. 1994.

Political issues

The general failure to integrate the post-Soviet military into society, accompanied by a tendency on the part of political leaders to attribute a special role and functions to the armed forces as a guarantee of stability and social order (particularly since the use of military units by President Yeltsin in October 1993), has helped to politicize the army and encourage divisions among middle-rank officers as well as military leaders at high levels. This further undermines command authority and unit cohesion.

It also distracts more senior officers from their professional duties by encouraging them to consider the benefits of forming coalitions with civilian politicians to advance their corporate and sectional interests and maintain their privileges. This is related to an entrenched institutional inertia in the central Defence Ministry and General Staff apparatus which has hamstrung the process of military reform and restructuring. In the autumn of 1994 the Chairman of the Defence Committee of the Duma, Sergey Yushenkov, went so far as to claim that no effective system of public control of the army existed; that neither the president nor the parliament had the structures for this purpose; and that the Defence Ministry continued to guard its corporate interests.[11]

Some maverick officers have gone further and taken to radical political activity to pursue a broader extreme nationalist political agenda, such as Lieutenant-Colonel Stanislav Terekhov (leader of the unofficial Union of Officers and since 1994 co-founder of the Great Power Party), or Colonel-General Albert Makashov (leader of the ultra-nationalist organization Fatherland). Officers of this kind were denounced by the Russian military command and threatened with forced retirement (Terekhov and Makashov have been retired).[12]

In fact it is only possible to weed out the most vocal and active of the politicized officers and this process may itself be swayed by the political preferences of the high command. It remains to be seen how far an agenda for 'strong-man rule' associated with such people as Alexander Lebed[13] takes root politically among disenfranchised and rootless officers and on some issues even provides support for extremist nationalism.

Indeed, the high command itself sympathizes with many of the positions advanced by nationalist politicians in the Duma (especially on matters such as 'peacekeeping') although formal political coalitions on this basis, even on specific issues such as arms sales, have failed to form. The increased politicization

---

[11] *Rossiyskie Vesti,* 17 Sep. 1994.

[12] In spring 1994 Gen. Grachev specified that the planned discharge of the officer corps would include 'those officers and warrant officers who have simply not got used to present conditions: those who still carry political views and support certain political parties and currents'. Interview on Ostankino Channel 1 TV, Moscow, 11 Apr. 1994, reported in SWB–SU, 1971 S1/4.

[13] Lt-Gen. Alexander Lebed, former Commander of the Russian 14th Army deployed in the Trans-Dniester area of Moldova, who retired from the armed forces in 1995 to become one of the strongest contenders for the presidency at the 1996 election. In June 1996 he was appointed President Yeltsin's national security adviser and Secretary of the Security Council of the Russian Federation, thus becoming one of the most powerful figures in the Kremlin.

of the army means that military policy and the role of the armed forces could give rise to more damaging intra-military debates in the future than those generated principally by different military–professional judgements or traditional service rivalry. So far such debates within the new Russian armed forces have been contained. The official plans of the Defence Ministry and General Staff on the missions and structure of the armed forces, as analysed in this chapter, could be drawn further into political controversy later in the 1990s. They are already fundamentally challenged by current fiscal realities.

Fiscal realities

Soviet military expenditure as a share of gross national product (GNP) was 8.5 per cent in 1989,[14] but its Russian equivalent fell to 4.7 per cent in 1992 and 4.3 per cent in 1993.[15] The implications of this decline were clarified during the acrimonious debate over the 1994 defence budget: in its initial draft of 37.1 trillion roubles (against the initial bid by the Defence Ministry for 87 trillion roubles) it represented some 6 per cent of anticipated GNP but a cut of more than 50 per cent in real terms.

Deputy Defence Minister Andrey Kokoshin listed likely consequences of such a defence budget: the armed forces could become unmanageable; the production of new military equipment in Russia would need to be terminated; over 3000 companies of the military–industrial complex were likely to go bankrupt and four million people would lose their jobs; recruitment of servicemen on contract would have to cease and more than 20 per cent of the armed forces personnel would need to be discharged.[16] Military lobbyists argued that a defence budget of anything less than 55 trillion roubles would bring about the disintegration of the armed forces, while lay-offs in defence plants would mean that Russian society 'will have an army of opponents to the democratic regime'.[17] These alarmist concerns were not allayed by a slight increase in military spending from 37 trillion to 40.5 trillion roubles. During the summer of 1994 strikes by military workers were reported in Severomorsk, the headquarters of the Arctic Fleet, for non-payment of wages. The All-Russian Union of Workers in the Defence Industry also began to develop a programme of collective action.[18]

The seriousness of lobbying by the Russian high command has been shown by their criticism of the existence of 'five armies', of other armed formations, which they claim the Russian budget cannot afford to support: the Federal

[14] *Krasnaya Zvezda*, 10 Feb. 1993; and 19 Aug. 1992.
[15] *Izvestiya*, 19 May 1994.
[16] Felgengauer, P., *Segodnya*, 10 Mar. 1994. These likely outcomes, particularly as regards procurement and the closure of defence enterprises, were confirmed by Col-Gen. Vasiliy Vorobyev, chief of the main department of military budget and funding of the Russian Defence Ministry, in *Krasnaya Zvezda*, 12 Mar. 1994.
[17] Sergey Yushenkov, Chairman of the Defence Committee of the Duma, cited in *Rossiyskie Vesti*, 1 June 1994.
[18] 'Military cuts put Yeltsin under threat', *The Guardian*, 15 June 1994.

Security Service, the Ministry for Emergency Situations, the Federal Agency of Government Communications and the Presidential Guard.[19] This kind of internecine political feuding between the regular military forces and other militarized bodies (even if they are not underwritten by the defence budget) is likely to continue. The then Defence Minister, Pavel Grachev, also brought pressure on other forces which are covered by the military budget, such as the Border Troops, to become an integral part of the armed forces under him as a means of increasing his control over their costs.

However, these financial constraints are only dimly reflected in Russian military planning. Certainly the growing military-related expenses Russia will incur later in the 1990s and the limits on overall defence expenditure make the new Russian focus on a limited mobile force structure rational. But the stubborn attempts of the Russian General Staff to maintain a mass personnel and industrial mobilization capacity, based on obsolescent worst-case planning assumptions, have been divorced from economic (let alone social, ethnic and political) realities. It was not until July 1994 that Yeltsin decreed a reduction in the level of the Russian mobilization capacities and mobilization reserve to bring them into 'conformity with the changed international situation' and to reduce the unproductive burden on the national economy.[20]

The gap between Russian aspirations and potentialities is highlighted by procurement policy. The Russian military leadership is still developing plans to develop the high-technology service branches in the new Russian forces and to furnish them later in the decade with state-of-the-art and high-precision weapons. But it is difficult to envisage political approval in Moscow for the sharp rise in military costs this would entail.

By 1993 military procurement had virtually ceased in some sectors as the military budget was sharply reoriented towards the needs of servicemen. The output of sophisticated equipment, especially for the navy, was most severely curtailed. Kokoshin's views since the autumn of 1993 on the danger of disintegration of the military–industrial complex are relevant here. By 1994 it appeared that procurement for the next few years would need to remain low, forcing the military to survive to a considerable extent on the reserves of weapons and military equipment accumulated over recent years.

While some 10 per cent more of the Russian military budget was allocated to procurement in 1993 than in 1992, expenditure on armaments remained a small proportion of the total military budget. A demand by the Defence Ministry for a 50 per cent increase in procurement orders for 1994 was unrealistic given budget limits and the unavoidable closure of more defence enterprises. A particular concern for military leaders has been the fact that current research and development (R&D) does not promise to supply the Russian professional forces with the high-technology systems planned for the end of the 1990s. R&D is proceed-

---

[19] Complaint by Chief of the General Staff Mikhail Kolesnikov at a meeting of the Duma Defence Committee, *Komsomolskaya Pravda*, 24 May 1994.

[20] Edict issued on 8 July 'On the Reduction of Mobilization Capacity and the Mobilization Reserve'. *Rossiyskaya Gazeta*, 13 July 1994.

ing only on military projects which have been under way for several years and in which the greater portion of planned resources has been invested. In fact there is confusion within the military itself over the relative importance of funding R&D versus procurement. With respect to R&D, Russia can most nearly achieve its plans in the medium term by concentrating on developing high-technology systems and precision weapons (as favoured by Kokoshin) but fielding only limited quantities for further trials with troops. It appears that the limited industrial resources Russia has available may be used to create an infrastructure to enable a 'rapid surge in production' of these sophisticated technologies if and when required.

This sober approach is not yet reflected in military–economic plans. In December 1992 the Defence Ministry approved the principles of a draft programme for weapon development in the army up to 2000–2005, which envisaged growth in capital investment for procurement and R&D as the country's economic situation improved.[21] In autumn 1993 the Defence Ministry developed a new long-term programme up to the year 2015, which was debated together with its request for the 1994 fiscal year defence order. Both plans appeared to be wish lists, based on over-optimistic economic forecasts which failed to take account of the real military-related demands on resources.

A Russian study has indicated that in addition to the costs of providing housing, reforming the army and social protection for servicemen there will be huge extra costs to the 'traditional' military budget in the period to the year 2000, especially for contract military service and for withdrawing the army from other former Soviet republics.[22] Moreover, where Russian forces are not withdrawn back to the Russian Federation and new basing arrangements are negotiated with the CIS states, the costs of these bases and the upkeep of Russian troops abroad (largely borne by Moscow) will be very high. New peacekeeping missions will rapidly increase these costs for the Russian high command.

III. Military reform: social and economic aspects

The social and economic difficulties facing Russian military organization are reflected in basic elements of the military reform effort. This has made it difficult to reach consensus over the appropriate size of national forces or to maintain an effective policy for military recruitment.

---

[21] Drawn up in Dec. 1992. *Krasnaya Zvezda*, 2 Dec. 1992.

[22] The financial burden was estimated in a statement by the Russian General Staff representative Gen. Barynkin on 12 May 1992, as follows: (*a*) withdrawal of troops—347 billion roubles; (*b*) additional sums for contract military service—59 billion roubles per annum; (*c*) decommissioning of nuclear submarines—100 billion roubles; (*d*) destruction of strategic nuclear arms—23 billion roubles; (*e*) destruction of tactical nuclear arms—150 billion roubles; (*f*) destruction of chemical weapons—60 billion roubles; and (*g*) destruction of conventional arms—5 billion roubles. Sorokin, K., 'Vozrozhdenie rossiyskoy armii: blizhayshie perspektivy' [Revival of the Russian Army: the immediate prospects], *Mirovaya Ekonomika i Mezhdunarodnye Otnosheniya*, no. 1 (1993), p. 14.

Controversy over force levels

Russian military leaders have been confronted with a series of problems in planning the level of their future armed forces: the future geographical distribution and deployment needs of these forces are uncertain; their conscription base differs from that of the former Soviet forces (many republics in the Russian Federation itself are imposing restrictions on military service outside their territories);[23] in the absence of a firm consensus on force structures and missions views on military requirements vary widely; and fiscal constraints are ever present.

Military leaders were reluctant to accept that the army and fleet should be cut down to 1.5 million men by 1995 when this ceiling (1 per cent of the state's population) was set in the Russian Law on Defence in September 1992.[24] Even this level of forces, however, threatens an intolerable defence burden driven by the conflict between on the one hand improving pay and living conditions for professional forces and on the other ensuring an adequate programme of weapon development. Russian legislators have argued the case for keeping defence expenditure at less than 4.5 per cent of GNP (an outcome linked to the military budget battle), which in their view would yield a force of 1 million men. In May 1993 Defence Minister Grachev himself advocated an all-volunteer army with less than 1 million men.[25] This could yield ground forces 250 000 strong (as opposed to 360 000–380 000 personnel for a total base force of 1.5 million), which could be translated into some 30 division-sized units at 80–90 per cent strength, if such a higher-readiness structure eventually replaces the former Soviet structure of cadre and mobilization divisions.

Against this background a proposal by Grachev in December 1993 that the statutory strength of the future forces should be over 2 million appeared to defy practical sense. In principle this goal, which Grachev sought to justify by invoking the vast borders of the Russian state, would permit 1.45 million men in the European part of Russia (given the limits embodied in the 1992 CFE-1A Agreement[26]). In practice such a large force could not easily be fitted into combat-capable military structures and the plan implied a longer-term presence and a slower reduction plan—or a freezing of such reductions—in regions such as the Kaliningrad exclave. This could still be said of a statutory force strength of 1.9 million, a compromise offered by the military leadership in March 1994,[27] and three months later Yeltsin reinstated the goal of reducing the army to 1.5 million servicemen.

[23] Interview with Gen. Grachev in *Izvestiya*, 1 June 1992.

[24] The text of the law is reproduced in *Rossiyskaya Gazeta*, 9 Oct. 1992.

[25] Gen. Grachev on the eve of the first anniversary of the Russian Armed Forces, reported by ITAR-TASS, Moscow, World Service 7 May 1993, in SWB–SU, 1684 C2/2.

[26] The 1992 Concluding Act of the Negotiation on Personnel Strength of Conventional Armed Forces in Europe. All parties to the CFE Treaty—the Treaty on Conventional Armed Forces in Europe of 1990—are parties to the CFE-1A Agreement.

[27] *Krasnaya Zvezda*, 17 Mar. 1994. At this time Russian defence officials admitted that, although the nominal strength of the Russian armed forces totalled 2.34 million, the number of men actually in uniform

The intention has been to reduce the Russian forces in phases from their manpower level in May 1992 of 2.8 million. This process began with a reduction of some 220 000 in 1992; some 40 000–50 000 officers should be transferred to the reserve annually. Fiscal demands apart, two factors have compelled a rapid reduction timetable.

First, there has been a strong wish to bring combat units up to full strength, that is, to align the numbers with actual combat-ready structure. The intention has been to redistribute personnel and significantly cut the number of units with low combat-readiness. At the same time wholesale reductions and the disbandment of military units which are unable to obtain a full complement of personnel and which are not strategically significant have been very difficult because of the high cost of destroying or dismantling *matériel* and munitions.[28]

Second, a rapid reduction in forces would also take account of the loss to Russia of draft-age populations in the non-Russian successor states[29] and mitigate the effect of growing draft evasion and other recruitment problems.

Problems of recruitment and contract service

Draft evasion, which reflects the broader social malaise of the armed forces, rose from 30 000 in the spring of 1993 to 70 000 by the autumn of that year.[30] A more serious problem still for the Russian Army, and a critical one by the summer of 1993, was the increase in draft deferral eligibility.

At the end of 1992 the Russian forces were 960 000 soldiers short of the planned level for the current force structure, and by mid-1993 this shortfall had only slightly declined.[31] Some officials raised the prospect of the manpower level of the Russian Armed Forces falling by such spontaneous de facto reductions to 1.2 million—and this would be a force with a very high officer content.[32] By March 1994 figures released by Russian defence officials suggested indeed that the real strength of the army stood at just over 1.4 million.[33] At this time the Russian Army was claimed to face a shortfall of 500 000 new conscripts below the level necessary to maintain combat capability.[34]

---

was only 60% of that figure. If accurate this puts the actual strength of the Russian Army at just over 1.4 million. However, some 800 000 men in military uniform are not under the jurisdiction of the Defence Ministry, including the Border Troops (50 000), Ministry of Interior Forces (350 000) and railway troops (70 000). The Federal Counter-Intelligence Service and the Presidential Guard have also created their own military formations. Interview with Kolesnikov, *Izvestiya*, 17 June 1994.

[28] Boldyrev, O., *Segodnya*, 13 July 1993.

[29] In May 1993, however, the parliament voted to enable the Russian military to recruit citizens of CIS states in which Russian troops are deployed according to interstate treaties.

[30] Defence Ministry briefing reported in Rubnikovich, O., *Nezavisimaya Gazeta*, 21 Jan. 1994.

[31] *Krasnaya Zvezda*, 18 Feb. and 16 Mar. 1993. In July 1993 the shortfall was reported variously as 700 000, by Lt-Gen. V. Bondartsev in ITAR-TASS, 15 July, and *Kommersant Daily*, 16 July 1993, and as 910 000 by Sergey Stepashin, then Chairman of the Committee on Defence and Security of the Supreme Soviet, in *Nezavisimaya Gazeta*, 2 July 1993. See also 'Kadrovoy krizis v rossiyskoy armii' [Personnel crisis in the Russian Army], *Nezavisimaya Gazeta*, 23 Mar. 1993.

[32] *Krasnaya Zvezda*, 9 Dec. 1992. Stepashin issued this warning in *Nezavisimaya Gazeta*, 2 July 1993.

[33] Interfax in *RFE/RL News Briefs*, vol. 3, no. 10 (2 Mar. 1994), p. 3.

[34] Grachev, P. (Gen.), *Selskaya Zhizn*, 12 Apr. 1994, reported in SWB–SU, 1975 S1/1.

This was despite the fact that in the autumn of 1993 military service deferments for many students were quietly revoked. This was expected to relieve the situation by bringing an additional 400 000–450 000 conscripts into the armed forces annually. Although in January 1994 the number of enlisted personnel stood at only 54 per cent of the required level (70–90 per cent in élite units— airborne troops and those for strategic nuclear formations), it was forecast by the General Staff to rise to 85–90 per cent by the end of the year.[35] A decision in 1995 to increase the period of conscription from one and a half to two years was similarly intended to overcome the shortfall in conscript numbers, although the continuation of this extended service period is inconsistent with the effort to increase the role of professionals in the forces.

If draft problems are eventually overcome, the run-down of Russian forces may be eased by developing a mixed professional soldier/conscript military structure for the Russian Army. At the end of 1992 efforts began to recruit 100 000 professional (volunteer) soldiers for 1993, to serve under contract. This target was exceeded and in January 1994 the Defence Ministry was authorized to call up a further 150 000 soldiers on contract service in 1994.[36] At a second stage (1994–95) it was planned to increase the number of contract soldiers to 30 per cent of the forces. The third stage (1996–2000) envisages contract soldiers making up 50 per cent of the forces, which would provide a continuing source of qualified reserve forces for large-scale future mobilization in war.

However, criticism has increasingly been levelled against the quality of contracted personnel—a failing which has slowed down recruitment. The initial recruitment drive began before Russian society and its armed forces were quite prepared for it. The first priority was to recruit for airborne and special forces and other peacekeeping forces, in particular to fill junior commander and technical specialist positions, but this effort to create a new corps of junior officers was poorly planned and implemented. Selection criteria were relaxed and in 1994 Grachev revealed that some 25 per cent of those contracted subsequently had to be discharged.[37] A spate of critical articles appeared about the complications for the armed forces created by the contract process.[38] The neglected social infrastructure of the military, as described above, continues to impede high-quality contract recruitment; these problems need to be tackled as a package.

Moreover, this shift in recruitment principles is highly expensive and its success will depend on sufficient allocations in future annual defence budgets. It was estimated in early 1994 that, if contract service rises from 120 000 (1993) to 400 000 (1994) and 750 000 (1995–97), monthly expenditure in

[35] Report by Kolesnikov, in Felgengauer, P., *Segodnya*, 21 Jan. 1994; and Gen. Grachev in ITAR-TASS, 7 Feb. 1994, reported in SWB–SU, 1919 S1/1. For a critical assessment of the defects of the 1993 draft process, see Falichev, O., *Krasnaya Zvezda*, 25 Jan. 1994.

[36] For the text of the document on the phased transition to contract service, see *Krasnaya Zvezda*, 3 Dec. 1992; for Yeltsin's Jan. decree, see ITAR-TASS, 18 Jan. 1994, in SWB–SU, 901 S1/1.

[37] Interview in *Krasnaya Zvezda*, 7 May 1994.

[38] For example, in *Krasnaya Zvezda*, 22 Dec. 1993. See also Foye, S., 'Manning the Russian Army: is contract service a success?', *RFE/RL Research Report*, vol. 3, no. 13 (1 Apr. 1994), pp. 41–43.

constant roubles will rise from 15–20 billion roubles (1993) to 60–70 billion in 1994 and to about 100 billion roubles in 1995–97. However, in this period the fall in numbers of conscripted servicemen from 1 300 000 (1993) to 75 000 (1995–97) would only result in a corresponding drop in monthly expenditure from 8 billion to 5 billion roubles—a minor saving.[39] The costs of this transition also compete with the major ongoing expense of military redeployments.

Against this background, it is not surprising that serious doubts have been expressed about President Yeltsin's decree of 16 May 1996 abolishing conscription in the armed forces by the year 2000. This will prove to have been nothing more than a campaign manoeuvre on the eve of the presidential election unless very difficult conditions, financial, organizational and political, can be fulfilled.

IV. The redeployment and basing of Russian forces

Almost half of the Soviet general-purpose military assets was deployed outside Russia at the end of 1991. Russia inherited this legacy after it decided in March 1992 to establish fully-fledged national armed forces.[40] A total of some 2.8 million servicemen came under Russian jurisdiction, of which in May 1992 some 600 000 were serving beyond the Russian borders, in Germany, the Baltic states, the Transcaucasus and the Trans-Dniester region.[41]

The traumatic period of Russian military retreat from outside the CIS was virtually over by the summer of 1994. The withdrawal of the Northern Group of Forces in Poland was completed in November 1992 (except for some logistics troops). The Western Group of Forces in Germany was fully withdrawn in August 1994. The North-Western Group of Forces in the Baltic states has left behind only minor residual units, in particular those attached to the radar base in Latvia at Skrunda (which may be used by Russia for a further four years).

Overall, however, since 1992 large-scale redeployments to Russia have confronted the Russian military command with the logistical nightmare of absorbing within its borders numerous often depleted or fragmented military formations without sufficient barracks, training grounds or storage depots. At the same time it has been faced with the organization of large-scale intra-CIS transfers of officers and demobilized servicemen back to their home republics. Officers and servicemen have flooded back into Russia, largely as a result of bilateral intergovernmental agreements with other former Soviet republics.

Despite this, Russian military deployments in certain CIS states are now set to continue later into the 1990s and many of these military units could eventu-

---

[39] Bykov, R., *Argumenty i Fakty*, no. 8 (Feb. 1994), p. 5. The problem is underlined by the fact that in 1993 only 6 billion roubles were allocated for contracting volunteers.
[40] The final decree creating these forces was issued on 7 May. Text in *Rossiyskaya Gazeta*, 9 May 1992.
[41] According to Gen. Grachev, ITAR-TASS World Service, 22 May 1992, reported in SWB–SU, 1389 C2/1.

ally be disbanded rather than redeployed. In the Transcaucasus, for example, many Russian units largely manned by local recruits have simply dissolved. The idea of a comprehensive Russian military pull-back from the Transcaucasus has been abandoned.[42] A withdrawal of this kind was implicit in the decision to create a Group of Russian Forces in the Caucasus in August 1992 (a structure appropriate for Russian troops on foreign soil), based on the remaining units of the Transcaucasian MD. However, Russian leaders have revised their views on military basing and now seek to maintain a grouping of 23 000 servicemen in the Transcaucasus.

This shift in approach is linked to the revival of hopes among many Russian military leaders since the autumn of 1993 that some kind of reintegrated economic and military–political union under Russian leadership may eventually be formed. Given this assumption there is little point in withdrawing troops and undertaking the huge costs over many years of rebuilding border defences on Russian frontiers when these troops could be deployed back in the other CIS states in the foreseeable future.[43] In September 1993 Defence Minister Grachev reportedly revealed in an internal briefing that a decision had been taken in the Russian Security Council not to pull back to Russia's borders, but to maintain the old Soviet borders, especially in Central Asia and perhaps the Transcaucasus.[44] This is consistent with Yeltsin's open description of the Tajik border as 'in essence the border of Russia'—a definition which may also be applied to the outer borders of the Transcaucasian states or even Moldova.

A proposal by Yeltsin in June 1993, that Russia should adopt basing practices similar to those of the USA (on the basis of intergovernmental agreements) to formalize the Russian military presence in Armenia, Georgia and Moldova, as well as in Central Asia, suggests at least a medium-term Russian military presence in these regions. In the spring of 1994 Yeltsin issued a directive endorsing a Defence Ministry proposal to establish some 30 military bases in CIS states, partly based on Russian troops deployed there and partly on key military installations. Russia has proceeded to negotiate long-term lease agreements with many of these states, most prominently with Georgia.[45]

According to the then Foreign Minister, Andrey Kozyrev, Russia had to keep its military presence in former Soviet republics to prevent forces hostile to

[42] For a strong statement of opposition to such a hasty withdrawal by the then Commander of the Transcaucasus MD, Col-Gen. V. Patrikeyev, see *Krasnaya Zvezda*, 19 Mar. 1992.

[43] The Russian border protection concept and associated agreements with CIS states are explained by Lt-Gen. Alexander Tymko, Chief of the Main Staff of the Russian Border Troops, in *Rossiyskie Vesti*, 11 June 1994.

[44] Felgengauer, P., 'Starye granitsy i "noviye" bazy' [Old borders and new bases], *Segodnya*, 16 Sep. 1993.

[45] The Russian Government or Defence Ministry, in addition to the well-known agreements with Tajikistan, has (*a*) concluded an agreement with Armenia on the basing of the 127th Motor Rifle Division in Gyumri and the retention of Russian border troops on the Armenian–Turkish border; (*b*) concluded an agreement with Turkmenistan that Russian troops should remain in this state; and (*c*) concluded an agreement in Feb. 1994 to establish Russian military bases in Georgia at Batumi, Akhalkalaki and Tbilisi and to deploy Russian troops as border guards on the Georgian frontier with Turkey. However, an agreement with Moldova in Oct. 1994 on the status of the 14th Army anticipates its withdrawal over a 3-year period.

Russia from filling the security vacuum.[46] The new military doctrine also confirmed that Russian forces may be based outside its territory jointly with forces of other (implicitly CIS) states or as Russian groupings.[47] However, some Russian analysts have argued that the idea of such bases will have to be abandoned since the enormous sums they will cost Russia will 'inflict greater damage on this country's national security than complete loss of these bases'.[48]

V. Debate on the role and mission of the armed forces

Former Soviet forces could be oriented towards restraining the armies of clearly identified countries and maintaining an influence in specific regions. This approach has been discarded, although a new emphasis on Russian national interests and 'spheres of interest' has emerged. Russian officials have been reluctant to identify specific interests which should be supported by the military instrument outside the geographical confines of the former USSR. However, according to a developing consensus among Russian nationalist politicians the whole geopolitical space of the former USSR (except perhaps for the Baltic states) should be viewed as a zone of Russia's vital interests, to be secured if necessary by force.

The emphasis has shifted to instability in the 'post-Soviet space' and a far-reaching debate in the early 1990s has resulted in a reconfiguration of the strictly military and more traditional roles of the Russian (formerly Soviet) armed forces.

The new military doctrine[49]

Four new features in the 1993 military doctrine should be noted.

1. The post-communist Russian military will in the first place be geared towards controlling regional conflicts. To the extent that such conflicts are expected in practice in 'the south' this tends to downgrade the role of the truncated Russian Navy (which has also lost access to vital coastlines and ports of the former Soviet Union) and emphasizes the need to create mobile rapid deployment forces (including naval infantry).

2. Mobile forces may eventually become an instrument *inter alia* to secure a more controversial mission for the Russian Armed Forces, specified in the 1993 military doctrine: to counteract 'the suppression of the rights, freedoms and

---

[46] Statement on 13 Jan. 1994 in a speech to Russian ambassadors to the CIS and Baltic states, reported in *Financial Times*, 14 Jan. 1994; and *RFE/RL News Briefs*, 10–21 Jan. 1994, p. 3. See also interviews with Kozyrev in *Izvestiya*, 8 Oct. 1993; and *Nezavisimaya Gazeta*, 24 Nov. 1993 (in Russian).

[47] *Izvestiya*, 18 Nov. 1993, p. 4.

[48] Felgengauer, P., *Segodnya*, 8 Apr. 1994.

[49] Excerpts from the military doctrine were published as 'Osnovnye polozheniya voennoy doktriny Rossiyskoy Federatsii' [The basic provisions of the military doctrine of the Russian Federation] in *Izvestiya*, 18 Nov. 1993, pp. 1, 4; and *Rossiyskie Vesti*, 18 Nov. 1993, pp. 1–2. All subsequent references refer to these original sources. *Krasnaya Zvezda* published a slightly longer excerpt on 19 Nov. 1993. A translation into English appeared in *Jane's Intelligence Review*, Special Report, Jan. 1994.

legitimate interests of citizens of the Russian Federation in foreign states'. The previous draft military doctrine of May 1992 had referred to the more intrusive military task of defending 'the rights and interests of citizens of Russia and people linked with it ethnically and culturally abroad' (a much broader and more ill-defined group than Russian citizens).[50] The implication remained, however, that the armed forces should support beleaguered Russians scattered throughout the former USSR. Such a role also tends to reinforce the Russian military system in the various republics of the Federation.

This could become an explosive issue since many of the main concentrations of former Soviet forces (as well as defence industry) are in predominantly ethnically Russian areas (such as eastern and southern Ukraine, eastern Moldova, and northern and eastern Kazakhstan). A Russian Deputy Foreign Minister has suggested specifically that a rapid-deployment force be created specifically to protect the rights of Russian-speaking people outside the Russian Federation.[51] This alarming idea has not been officially endorsed. Yet in the future Russian nationalist politicians and conservative military leaders may be tempted in a number of regions to use Russian military forces to back secessionist movements seeking to set up new Russian republics or territorial exclaves which could eventually be incorporated into Russia proper.

3. The Russian Armed Forces have been accorded another new mission in suppressing conflicts not only on Russian borders but also within the Russian Federation—a change codified in the new military doctrine. Certain formations of the regular armed forces may now assist Ministry of Internal Affairs troops in 'localizing and blockading a conflict region, suppressing armed clashes, and separating the conflicting sides, and also in defending strategically important installations'.[52] In fact the doctrine defines internal threats and the internal function of the armed forces so broadly that the distinction between their role and that of the Internal Affairs troops is blurred. This definition reflects the new perceived demands of 'internal peacekeeping', such as Russian operations in Ingushetia and, more forcibly, in Chechnya.

Yet some Russian critics have argued that legislative codification of possible army intervention in Russian internal affairs 'makes it a very important foreign policy factor that is potentially dangerous for incipient Russian democracy'.[53] It has been claimed that the new clauses on employing the armed forces in internal conflicts stem from Yeltsin's reliance on military units in his clash with Parliament in October 1993 and the initial uncertain military commitment to the president in this crucial confrontation. This is reflected specifically in the decision to provide the new mobile forces (see below) with an independent

[50] 'Osnovy voennoy doktriny Rossii' [The bases of the Russian military doctrine], *Voennaya Mysl*, special issue, May 1992, pp. 4, 7.

[51] Russian Deputy Foreign Minister Sergey Krylov on 3 Dec. 1993: ITAR-TASS report in *RFE/RL News Briefs*, 6–10 Dec. 1993, p. 2.

[52] *Izvestiya*, 18 Nov. 1993. For a comment on this new internal auxiliary role for the armed forces, see Ivanov, Lt-Gen. G., *Krasnaya Zvezda*, 8 Feb. 1994.

[53] Tsygichko, V., *Nezavisimaya Gazeta*, 13 Apr. 1994. Tsygichko is a professor but also a colonel who contributed in significant ways to earlier Russian/Soviet military reform debates.

operational command. In principle this will enable the Russian President and Defence Minister to mobilize directly almost all the combat-ready mechanized infantry and airborne formations, which will be removed from the control of the military districts.[54]

4. The November 1993 document on doctrine has a strong accent on peacekeeping more generally. An important new political mission assigned to the Russian military is participation in peacekeeping operations under the auspices of the United Nations and other international security agencies. Except in this respect, however, the decline in the role of the Russian military outside the former USSR (especially its naval dimension), despite the fulminations of radical nationalist Vladimir Zhirinovsky, is set to continue.

These new principles apparently reflect current concerns of the Russian military leadership.[55] The introversion in military thinking they represent has, however, also been precipitated by a general confusion about the *modus operandi* and purposes of the military organization, which has been reinforced by three factors which were critical in the military debate during 1991–93.

1. Views on the nature of the external threat or principal risk to Russia, if such exists, have been indeterminate. It was not until the spring of 1993 that Grachev was able to define the main near-term danger as arising from the south, and it was not until the November 1993 military doctrine that the language of the cold war was finally dropped from Russian military writings.

This 'southern' threat, which requires a reinforcement of the North Caucasian MD, remains inchoate. It is perceived to arise not only from the spillover effect of ethnic conflict in the Transcaucasus but also, implicitly, from Iran and its sponsorship of Islamic fundamentalism, and to a lesser degree from Turkey and Afghanistan. Yet Russian military planning cannot exclude near- and longer-term threat scenarios from other directions.[56] In particular some Russian military theorists have pointed to the danger of Chinese military pressure applied to the Russian Far East as Chinese national power expands.[57]

2. The role of Russian forces has been complicated by the possibility, although it is still small, of joint military action with CIS allies, perhaps even in combined general-purpose groupings, on the basis of a 'coalition doctrine'. The decree setting up the Russian Armed Forces gave them the role at the outset of defending the interests of both Russia and—within coalition forces—its allies.[58]

---

[54] Bykov, R., *Nezavisimaya Gazeta*, 21 Apr. 1994.

[55] There have been claims that approval for a military doctrine favourable to the armed forces was a trade-off for military support for Yeltsin in his autumn 1993 confrontation with the Russian Parliament, which led the Russian Security Council to favour a version of the military doctrine advanced by the Defence Ministry rather than its own draft. *Segodnya*, 9 Oct. 1993.

[56] Various such scenarios are analysed, for example, in Klimenko, A. (Col), 'Metodika otsenki voennykh ugroz i mery po ikh neytralizatsii' [Methods of assessing military threats and measures to neutralize them], *Voennaya Mysl*, no. 5 (1993), pp. 30–32.

[57] For example, Stepashin, V. (Col), 'Sovremennaya voennaya doktrina Kitaya' [The contemporary military doctrine of China], *Voennaya Mysl*, 1 (1993), p. 68; and Gareyev, M. (Col-Gen.), *International Affairs* (Moscow), no. 6 (1993), p. 8.

[58] Decree of 7 May 1992, in *Rossiyskaya Gazeta*, 9 May 1992.

The option of a limited CIS coalition on the basis of the 15 May 1992 Tashkent Treaty on Collective Security[59] receded when the joint CIS military command was dissolved in June 1993.[60] Despite this, by the spring of 1994, after a renewed emphasis on CIS integration, the national composition of the CIS Defence Ministerial Council had become basically the same as that of the Collective Security Council established on the basis of the Tashkent Treaty.[61] The Secretary of the Defence Ministerial Council spoke of a two- to three-year process of creating a military alliance and claimed that the military commands of most member states of the Council favoured a new defence union.[62] After a CIS summit meeting in April 1994 the Russian Defence Minister called on the member states to unite their armed forces as the first step towards such a union. This prospect remains uncertain, however, and it is likely that Russian military principles would be central to the overall military planning of any military sub-group or broader grouping of CIS states which might arise.

3. Military calculations over the likely scale of future conflict have been modified, but in the teeth of conservative military resistance. While a key premise for Russian military doctrine has been the emphasis on local and low-intensity conflicts,[63] it remains rational for Russia to develop forces for a range of contingencies. For example, Deputy Defence Minister Kokoshin, a civilian who had been one of the key advocates of concepts of non-offensive defence in Moscow in the late 1980s,[64] has advocated forces sufficient to curb rapidly the escalation of a conflict (under a scenario of local or low-intensity conflict). For Kokoshin, however, it is also essential to create centrally based rapid-deployment forces, which 'can be thrown in the shortest possible time into any region of the CIS to repulse external aggression, to end the conflict on favourable terms acceptable to us' (a scenario of possible larger-scale conflict).[65]

Despite this, in the draft military doctrine of May 1992 the Russian high command still paid considerable attention to the scenario of large-scale conventional war, although it was not considered likely. Such a war could arise

---

[59] For the text, see *Izvestiya*, 16 May 1992, p. 3. The original signatories were Armenia, Kazakhstan, Kyrgyzstan, the Russian Federation, Tajikistan and Uzbekistan. By the spring of 1994 Azerbaijan, Belarus and Georgia had also joined.

[60] For a discussion of how a coalition military doctrine could operate, see Klimenko, A. (Col), Department Head, Centre for Operational and Strategic Studies, Armed Forces General Staff, 'CIS military doctrine: what kind should it be?', *Military News Bulletin*, Novosti, no. 1 (Jan. 1992), pp. 1–2. See also Borchev, M. A. (Major-Gen.), 'O voennoy organizatsii Sodruzhestva nezavisimykh gosudarstv' [The military organization of the CIS], *Voennaya Mysl*, no. 3 (1993), pp. 3–9; and the case for coalition rapid reaction forces made by Burutin, G. (Col-Gen.), 'Nuzhny koalitsionnye sily bystrogo reagirovaniya' [Coalition rapid-reaction forces are needed], *Rossiyskaya Gazeta*, 20 Aug. 1993.

[61] *Krasnaya Zvezda*, 26 Feb. 1994.

[62] Lt-Gen. Leonid Ivashov, interviewed in *Nezavisimaya Gazeta*, 17 May 1994.

[63] 'Osnovy voennoy doktriny Rossii' (note 50), p. 5; interview with Andrey Kokoshin on Mayak Radio, 3 June 1992, in SWB–SU, 1400 C2/3; and Gareyev, M. (Col-Gen.), *Krasnaya Zvezda*, 20 Nov. 1992.

[64] For an example of his earlier thinking on the nature of the threat to Soviet security, see the interview in *Trud*, 2 Oct. 1990.

[65] Interview in *Krasnaya Zvezda*, 17 Mar. 1992.

from the escalation of a local conflict or from differences between states in regions adjoining Russian borders.

Russian force requirements

To provide for the contingencies of both local (low-intensity) war and a larger conventional war the military doctrine of November 1993 proposed that the Russian Armed Forces should include at least three components: (a) a limited number of theatre troops in permanent combat readiness would be stationed forward to repel local aggressions; (b) mobile reserves (rapid-reaction forces) would be held further back, capable of deploying rapidly to any region to assist the troops of permanent readiness to repel a medium-level aggression; and (c) strategic reserves would be formed during a period of threat and during wartime to conduct large-scale operations.

This blueprint reflects the growing appreciation in the Russian military command that the traditional Soviet emphasis on tank-heavy ground forces suits the needs of neither local conflicts nor possible future dynamic, large-scale military operations. As conservative resistance has been gradually overcome among Russian commanders this has offered a key role to rapid-deployment forces (mobile forces) in the overall structure of the Russian Armed Forces.[66]

Such forces would be based on airborne troops and marines capable 'of operating autonomously in any sector from which an external threat to the country's security may appear'.[67] They would require appropriate transport facilities and a developed infrastructure, including pre-positioned arms dumps.

Rapid-deployment forces will, however, only be part of the overall Russian force posture. A high-technology vision of the future military structure has been developed, which may turn out to be a mirage if the economic constraints analysed in this chapter continue to apply. Thus for Kokoshin reliable defence for Russia (given the uncertain scale of conflict) may be assured through the use of restructured, high-technology branches of the armed forces, with significantly reduced force levels and radically restructured ground formations.[68] Russian military planning should be based on a highly flexible and manoeuvrable defence, assisted by the development of new models of high-precision weapons. Priority will be accorded to highly mobile troops, air defence and military space facilities, army aviation and command, communication, control and intelligence (C^3I) systems.[69] The development of the Russian Air Force would emerge as a key area if this emphasis on high technology is

---

[66] For the internal Russian debate on military priorities at the beginning of the 1990s, see Blank, S., 'New strategists who demand the old economy', *Orbis*, vol. 36, no. 3 (summer 1992), pp. 365–78. See also Kaufman, S., 'Lessons from the 1991 Gulf War and Russian military doctrine', *Journal of Slavic Military Studies*, vol. 6, no. 3 (Sep. 1993). The latter includes an evauation of the 1992 draft doctrine on pp. 386–93.

[67] Interview with Gen. Grachev in *Krasnaya Zvezda*, 1 Apr. 1992.

[68] Statement in *Rossiyskaya Gazeta*, 8 Apr. 1992.

[69] Report on General Staff Academy conference in *Krasnaya Zvezda*, 2 June 1992.

economically sustainable. However, so far the planned advanced aircraft remains only a blueprint.

In the absence of a clearly identifiable threat the Russian high command has decided anyway to reject total defence along the whole perimeter of the external borders of the Russian Federation.[70] Resources would simply not be available for a Soviet-style system of deeply echeloned defence along borders. Strategic planning and training for the Russian Armed Forces will be carried out instead to repel a local aggression from any axis of threat. The main emphasis here is on the operation of small, highly manoeuvrable groupings, which will be at some considerable distance from the state border (or presumably the CIS outer border—in agreement with the CIS states concerned). In the border zone only operational covering forces will be held, which, together with border troops, will beat off the strikes of the attacker's first-echelon forces.

None the less, Moscow has not renounced plans to repel a potential large-scale aggression. The traditional emphasis on the need to maintain a military framework for mass mobilization coexists uneasily with the 'new thinking' on local wars. The former implies the need to retain reserve military–industrial capacities which can no longer be sustained (as implied by the Russian decree of July 1994 finally to reduce Russian mobilization reserves and capacities) and it is premised on a scenario of war which is not credible in the near to medium term (despite worries over China). It is also inconsistent with recent Russian thinking on the deterrent value of nuclear weapons.

The role of nuclear weapons

Despite the active debate on the roles of the Russian conventional forces, in the new fluid threat environment Moscow is likely to rely on nuclear deterrence as its principal means of defence against large-scale attack, and in the current transitional phase also perhaps to prevent states to the south of the former USSR from incursions in the new Central Asian or Transcaucasian states.[71] This option is reinforced by the belief that nuclear weapons form the most reliable and well-controlled component of the Russian Armed Forces, especially in a period of major restructuring of general-purpose forces and doubts about their combat capability. Moreover, a form of extended deterrence in the form of nuclear guarantees by Russia is likely to cover now at least the Central Asian CIS states, Armenia and Belarus—especially those states which signed the May 1992 Tashkent Treaty with Russia.[72]

[70] Report on parliamentary hearings in *Krasnaya Zvezda*, 14 May 1992.

[71] Felgengauer, P., 'Rossii pridetsa stroit svoyu oboronu na yadernykh strategicheskikh vooruzheniyakh' [Russia must build its defence on strategic nuclear armaments], *Nezavisimaya Gazeta*, 18 Nov. 1992.

[72] See note 59. The possibility of nuclear guarantees is suggested by former Vice-President Rutskoy in 'Voennaya politika Rossii: soderzhanie i napravlennost' [Russia's military policy: content and direction], *Voennaya Mysl*, no. 1 (1993), p. 7. Gen. Grachev talked of Russian nuclear deterrence responding to 'an indeterminate zone of "nuclear risk"' from the south covering the geo-strategic space of Russia and its closest neighbours. He claimed that this arises from the 'semicircle' formed by 'the unadvertised "nuclear club"' around this space. *Nezavisimaya Gazeta*, 9 June 1994.

This is consistent with the Russian decision in its new military doctrine to reverse the former Soviet policy on the non-use of nuclear arms against non-nuclear states. Russia now reserves the right to use nuclear weapons also in response to a conventional attack in certain specified conditions: (a) if a state allied with a nuclear state (such as Turkey, whose interest in the Transcaucasus and Central Asia unsettles Moscow) launches an armed attack on Russia, its armed forces or its allies; or (b) in the event of joint actions by a non-nuclear state and a nuclear state in carrying out or supporting an attack upon Russia or its allies.

One likely object of this doctrinal revision has been to discourage states which have fluid security arrangements and are contiguous to Russia or its CIS neighbours from seeking to enter NATO or the Western European Union (WEU) or from offering rights of passage or bases to support a possible Western intervention in Russia or the 'near abroad'. The change in policy, which also abandons the former Soviet commitment to no-first-use of nuclear weapons[73] and revives the concept of 'limited nuclear war', could equally be seen as a warning directed against Ukraine, at least while its position was more ambiguous before it acceded to the 1968 Non-Proliferation Treaty (NPT) in December 1994. Since Russia also promised not to employ its nuclear weapons against any state party to the NPT which does not possess nuclear weapons (except in the conditions specified above), the former Soviet states were given an additional incentive to accede to the NPT regime.[74]

The change in Moscow's declared policy may also reflect a growing Russian sense of conventional military vulnerability in relation to China and the need to adequately deter China in the absence of the huge former Soviet conventional force. This is a distinct possibility notwithstanding the conclusion of a five-year Russian–Chinese military cooperation treaty in November 1993[75] and an agreement between the two states in the summer of 1994 that they would no longer target each other's territory with nuclear missiles.

The strategic role of nuclear weapons under Russian custody will be influenced by the restructuring of the nuclear force and the major reduction in warheads under the START (Strategic Arms Reduction Talks) treaties.[76] It will also reflect the course of political relationships with other nuclear powers and with Ukraine. Yet statements by Yeltsin that Russian nuclear missiles are no longer targeted against the United States or Britain (while these states have made similar claims on the re-targeting of their missiles away from Russia) leave unclear the nature of the deterrent relationship between East and West. In early 1993

[73] For discussion of the no-first-use issue, see Repin, V., 'Eshche raz o strategicheskikh dilemmakh' [Strategic dilemmas again], *Nezavisimaya Gazeta*, 24 Sep. 1992.

[74] The rejection of the commitment to no-first-use also lends substance to reports of a new draft Russian military doctrine in Sep. 1995, according to which Russian tactical nuclear weapons may be redeployed to Kaliningrad, Belarus and the Baltic Sea in response to a decision to expand NATO eastwards. *Komsomolskaya Pravda*, 29 Sep. 1995.

[75] *Krasnaya Zvezda*, 12 Nov. 1993.

[76] US–Soviet Treaty on the Reduction and Limitation of Strategic Offensive Arms, 1991 (START-I); and US–Russian Treaty on Further Reduction and Limitation of Strategic Offensive Arms, 1993 (START-II).

Yeltsin also promised that Russia would guarantee the integrity of a non-nuclear weapon Ukraine and defend it against nuclear attack. At the time this had a hollow ring in Kiev. A dispassionate debate on the role of residual Russian strategic nuclear forces may only be possible now with the apparent resolution of the contentious 'CIS nuclear arms proliferation' issue.[77]

This could also help clarify Russian strategic thinking behind the renunciation of the Soviet-era policy of no-first-use. On the one hand this change (which also applies to sub-strategic systems) simply brings Russian nuclear policy into line with that of NATO. As noted above, it may also have certain political functions. On the other hand, for Russian military leaders who are keenly aware of the continued unreliability and overstretching of their conventional military means and increasingly worried about the vulnerability of their nuclear forces and strategic command and control (prompting first-strike or launch-on-warning options), it may mark a step back from the general recognition that nuclear weapons are essentially unusable. Russian military specialists argue that under conventional attack conditions could develop in such a way that 'Russia's strategic nuclear forces are forced on pain of destruction to be the first to use nuclear weapons'.[78] Some favour a firm Russian declaration, therefore, that any premeditated attack with the use of conventional weapons on the Russian strategic nuclear force would result in the 'guaranteed start of a nuclear war'.[79]

The emphasis here is still on deterrence. Grachev strongly reaffirmed the deterrent role of Russian nuclear weapon policy and denied that Russia might use nuclear weapons first in a limited conflict.[80] However, the Russian strategist Colonel-General Makhmut Gareyev argues that the practical implementation of the Russian concept of nuclear deterrence requires 'changes in the entire system of nuclear planning and the orientation of the armed forces' training'. He favours reinstating the no-first-use principle and notes that some Russian military experts disagree with Grachev's emphasis, arguing that 'weapons whose use is ruled out cannot be a means of deterrence'.[81] This suggests that a debate in Russia over the 'nuclear threshold' and post-cold war deterrence may develop further.

VI. Russian military organization and structure

Russian military organization and force structure will form an essential component of the emerging European security order. The debate in Russia on military

---

[77] For some discussion of Russian nuclear strategy beyond the START treaties, see Belous, V. (Maj.-Gen., Ret.), 'Tsena bezopasnosti' [The price of security], *Nezavisimaya Gazeta*, 30 Dec. 1992; and Arbatov, A., 'Yadernaya strategiya i politicheskiy vybor' [Nuclear strategy and political choice], *Nezavisimaya Gazeta*, 3 Oct. 1992.

[78] Belous, V. (Maj.-Gen., Ret.), *Segodnya*, 9 Feb. 1994.

[79] Volkov, L. (Lt-Gen.), former chief of the Defence Ministry Central Research Institute, *Segodnya*, 1 June 1994.

[80] *Nezavisimaya Gazeta*, 9 June 1994.

[81] Interview in *Krasnaya Zvezda*, 29 June 1994.

roles and missions helps clarify the options for Russian force structures, but it leaves considerable latitude in determining such structures.

The first obstacle to Russia's developing an effective national force structure has been the loss of key elements of the former integrated Soviet military organization. Grachev lamented that Russian C³I, missile early warning, air defence and logistical support systems were wrecked.[82] Furthermore, Russia acquired second strategic echelon forces so that a high proportion of the most combat-capable units, equipped with the latest arms, were left outside the state, although those in Germany and the Baltic states have been withdrawn back to Russia. Grachev complained that 70 per cent of the equipment Russia inherited with the collapse of the USSR is obsolete. Most fundamentally, the force structure Russia inherited was oriented to operations on a Union-wide basis and to defending the territory of the former Union. The residual Russian forces were both badly deployed according to any reasonable judgement of national defence needs and mostly at low levels of readiness. In the autumn of 1992 Yeltsin complained that Russia had virtually no combat formations in the west and south.[83]

The reorganization of military districts

Despite these weaknesses the organizational cohesion of the Russian forces began to recover by 1993. However, one prerequisite of this recovery has been the reorganization of the former Soviet military districts, which by this time had become obsolete. In so far as the current revision of the military district system reflects a strategic rationale it helps to identify the emerging Russian defence and mobilization posture.

The Leningrad and Moscow MDs have been reinforced by units from the former Western and North-Western groups of forces. It appears that a new army grouping will be formed in the Leningrad MD, which is now viewed as a strategically important border district covering the north-west of Russia. Second, the North Caucasus MD, formerly a rear-echelon district, has emerged as a key front-line 'combat' MD against dangers from the south.[84] It encompasses Russia's only outlets to the Caspian and Black Seas and its borders with Azerbaijan and Georgia. It also borders on Kazakhstan and Ukraine.

Meanwhile the Volga and Urals districts are being reconstituted from rear districts to districts of the second strategic echelon and the interior Volga MD is emerging as a base area for planned mobile forces and the military transport aviation associated with them. It is no longer likely that the western sector in the structure of Russian military districts will resume its position as the main military axis in operational planning.

[82] Speech on 5 Dec. 1992, *Krasnaya Zvezda*, 8 Dec. 1992.
[83] Yeltsin as reported by ITAR-TASS, Moscow World Service, 23 Nov. 1992, in SWB–SU, 1547 C2/2.
[84] Kolesnikov, M. (Col-Gen.), 'Ostanovit voennye reformy nikomu ne pod silu' [Stopping military reform is beyond anyone's capacity], *Rossiyskie Vesti*, 9 Apr. 1993, p. 2.

The MD reorganization also parallels the devolution of political power to regional authorities in Russia. Commanders of MDs are expected to receive full control over all the forces in their districts rather than sharing their authority with Moscow-based service commanders-in-chief. The military supply system is also destined to be decentralized to enhance regional logistical dependence of military units. These steps together are leading towards the replacement of the MD system at some time in the mid-1990s by a system of territorial commands, with potential far-reaching implications (see below).

Russian force restructuring

The military 'losses' Russian forces sustained with the collapse of the USSR have been a stimulus to radical change in their structure. The traditional division of general-purpose forces—ground forces, air force, navy, air defence forces and the Strategic Rocket Forces—is under discussion. Proposals have been advanced to reduce these services to three, which would leave the general-purpose forces (ground forces), air forces (to include the Strategic Missile Forces after the year 2000) and the navy. Such a reform would be aimed at the more efficient control of forces, which would operate in three spheres—ground, air-space and maritime—and at ensuring greater coordination and effective combat employment between them.[85] The reorganization will at least transform the Air Defence Forces into Aerospace Defence Forces.[86] The new force structures will not compete equally in the domestic contest for resource allocation. The navy, for example, which has already suffered heavy reductions in surface vessels and submarines, will probably continue to be accorded low priority (except in relation to its strategic nuclear component so long as it retains this).

Second, a reorganization has been announced from an army/division force structure to a predominantly corps/brigade structure, with the intention of increasing the number of combat-ready combined units.[87] This is also aimed at providing greater operational flexibility and manoeuvrability for the core mobile forces; brigades are also central in the force planning of most of the other post-Soviet states. However, it is uncertain how far this shift in emphasis will proceed.[88]

Third, the Russian General Staff has gained political support in principle for the new configuration of forces outlined in documents on military doctrine: theatre forces in permanent combat readiness; mobile reserves or rapid-reaction forces; and strategic reserves.

[85] Gareyev, M. A. (Gen.), 'On military doctrine and military reform in Russia', *Journal of Soviet Military Studies*, vol. 5, no. 4 (Dec. 1992), p. 550; Nikolaev, A. (Lt-Gen.), *Krasnaya Zvezda*, 10 Mar. 1993; and hearings of the Duma Defence Committee on reform of the armed forces, *Segodnya*, 20 July 1994.

[86] Interview with Gen. Grachev, *Krasnaya Zvezda*, 7 May 1994.

[87] Statement by Gen. Grachev in *Rossiyskie Vesti*, 4 Jan. 1993. For a discussion of possible variants of operational and tactical force structuring for the Russian armed forces, see Dick, C., 'Russian views on future war', Conflict Studies Research Centre, Royal Military Academy, Sandhurst, UK, 8 June 1993.

[88] Interview with Kolesnikov, *Segodnya*, 29 Dec. 1993. Kolesnikov anticipates a more mixed structure including the 'traditional' regiments and divisions of the Russian Army.

From the tripartite force structure envisaged in Russian military plans the key operational role is now assigned to the rapid-reaction or mobile forces, which could assume a status equivalent to a service. This would shift forces and military priorities from the ground forces and reflect the dominance of the paratrooper forces in the debates on military doctrine. However, the establishment of such élite formations as the core of the future Russian Army is being strongly resisted by military traditionalists who favour the existing infrastructure as the model. For example, Colonel-General Vladimir Semenov, the Commander-in-Chief of the Russian ground forces, has argued that combined arms task-force commands and special troops of the ground forces should remain the backbone of the Russian Armed Forces.[89]

At a time of large-scale reorganization of the military apparatus and of force reductions in Russia the creation of mobile forces has been intended partly to compensate for the lack of cohesion and reduced military readiness (linked to manpower shortages) of other 'regular' non-nuclear units and groupings.[90] The mobile forces can address the principal military challenge for Russia in the mid-1990s—low-intensity conflicts in the CIS states and on their peripheries. Among these forces Russia has designated specific military units for peace-keeping or perhaps more appropriately peace enforcement functions.

The initial plan was to create mobile forces with a strength of 100 000 men comprising airmobile regiments, brigades and divisions. They would be based largely (60 per cent) on airborne troops, but would also include some motor-rifle formations equipped with light armaments and capable of being airlifted, naval infantry, military transport aircraft and logistics forces. Light mobile forces that would include about five division equivalents are already in prospect. These could be drawn from elements of a number of airborne divisions.[91] They will be divided according to their operational role. Immediate-reaction troops, on constant alert, would be expected on receiving orders to land in designated areas in less than 24 hours. Rapid-deployment forces in contrast will not be at full strength and their preparation will take up to three days.[92]

By the summer of 1994 the anticipated strength of the mobile forces had been raised to about 200 000 men.[93] However, the creation of this new structure in a militarily efficient form continues to be hampered by the economic, social and infrastructural problems discussed above. The development of the mobile forces has also been set back by the lack of strategic airlift (much of it lost to Belarus and Ukraine), which would make it very difficult to deploy mobile

[89] Semenov, V. (Col-Gen.), 'Sukhoputnye voyska: zadachi i problemy razvitiya' [Land forces: tasks and issues of development], *Voennaya Mysl*, no. 6, 1993, p. 23. See also Blank (note 66).

[90] Speech by President Yeltsin on 23 Nov. 1992 at an expanded meeting of the Collegium of the Russian Defence Ministry, reported in *Nezavisimaya Gazeta*, 25 Nov. 1992.

[91] For detailed proposals for the structure of the mobile forces, see Vladykin, O. (Col), 'Mobilnye sily Rossii' [Russia's mobile forces], *Krasnaya Zvezda*, 18 Dec. 1992; and Ovsienko, S., 'Sily bystrogo reagirovaniya' [Rapid-reaction forces], *Rossiyskie Vesti*, 5 Mar. 1993.

[92] Interview with Ye. Podkolzin, Commander of the Russian airborne troops, *Moskovskaya Pravda*, 31 July 1993, reported in SWB-SU, 1761 C3/3.

[93] Gen. Grachev, describing a draft presidential decree on these forces. Ostankino Channel 1 TV, 1 July 1994, reported in SWB-SU, 2040 S1/1.

units from the Far East and Siberia for potential conflicts in western sectors. To meet the requirements for these forces, units will need to be revitalized, such as those withdrawn from the Baltic states and Germany, and new facilities and bases will need to be constructed.[94]

With the limited resources available Russian military leaders have had to be selective in developing these newly created forces. Initially it was announced that the core of the rapid-reaction mobile forces would ultimately be based in the Ural and Volga MDs. However, the reorganization of the North Caucasus MD into a 'border-adjacent military district' has become a priority[95] and by the summer of 1994 this district was pronounced to be combat-ready. Mobile forces are being developed in the northern Caucasus as a fire-break, on the assumption that the region is likely to remain the most dangerous axis over the next few years and the most obvious target for peacekeeping. The crisis in Chechnya only confirms this. South Russia (Stavropol-Krasnodar-Rostov-Don) has rapidly become the main base area for peacekeeping forces.

Despite the new emphasis on the northern Caucasus it has been suggested in Moscow that compact mobile units may eventually be deployed in all the Russian military districts. For example, a mobile grouping is to be formed from units of the Baltic Fleet and the 11th Guards Army in the Kaliningrad region, which has become a special defence area.[96] This larger goal, however, can only be realized slowly.

The mobile forces occupy a paradoxical position. On the one hand in military planning they are intended to form a 'strategic fist' which can be rapidly directed to any threatened axis to gain time for the deployment of larger forces. On the other they are intended to provide forces as the cutting edge to the rather partisan peacekeeping operations in which Russia will increasingly be involved. The tension between these two roles will be difficult to sustain.

New regional commands

Plans are also being developed for a new Russian regional command structure which would replace the military district structure for the division of troops: the MDs could be transformed into mobilization districts for the Russian forces.[97] Initially, in the spring of 1992, Grachev spoke in favour of creating three strategic groupings of general-purpose forces in the mid-1990s deployed in the Western (European), Southern (Central Asian) and Eastern (Far Eastern) regions of Russia and provided with the strength to carry out their missions

---

[94] Baev, P., 'Russia's rapid reaction forces: politics and pitfalls', *Bulletin of Arms Control*, 9 Feb. 1993, pp. 15–16.

[95] See Yeltsin's edict of 15 Mar. 1993 on the reform of the Russian military in the northern Caucasus, *Krasnaya Zvezda*, 18 Mar. 1993.

[96] Gen. Grachev quoted in ITAR-TASS, 17 Mar. 1994, reported in *RFE/RL News Briefs*, 14–18 Mar. 1994, p. 6.

[97] *Rossiyskie Vesti*, 4 Jan. 1993.

independently.[98] It was suggested that new strategic groupings of this kind could include combined arms formations (each with perhaps between five and seven army corps or their equivalent), logistics troops, military transport aviation and airmobile forces.[99]

By the autumn of 1994, however, it was announced that plans for joint territorial commands envisaged four rather different territorial groups of forces: Northern (the Northern Fleet and troops of the Leningrad MD), Southern (all troops of the North Caucasian MD), Urals–Transbaikal, and Far Eastern. The Urals–Transbaikal group of forces would provide a central reserve for the other three groups.[100]

In fact attempts to establish new regional commands and to reform forces along territorial lines have been delayed, probably because of the manifold problems of military cohesion discussed above. The goal of forming a Far East joint command headquarters in the Komsomolsk-na-Amur area—strengthening the Far East in Russian geopolitical strategy—has been public since the spring of 1993. The intention has been to create a powerful and mobile grouping including troops from the Far East MD, Pacific Fleet forces, air defence and air force units, and combined units deployed in the region. Little progress in this direction has been registered. The creation of a similar joint command incorporating the Transbaikal and Siberian MDs, with its headquarters in Ulan-Ude, also first mooted in 1993,[101] has now been eclipsed by plans for a Urals–Transbaikal command.

Plans for the European axis have been particularly sensitive. The option of a European regional command was first raised in 1993 as a possible response to a further deterioration of the position in the south of the Russian Federation. This structure would be developed on the southern borders of Russia on the basis of the North Caucasus MD and troops deployed both on the borders of and within the Central Asian CIS states.[102] It is significant to note here that the thrust of this 'European' joint command would be south and south-west rather than west, with all this implies for near-term strategic planning. The large-scale Russian military deployments against the rebellious Chechen Republic in December 1994 tend to confirm this future orientation.

[98] Proposed in a paper delivered at the Military Academy of the General Staff, 27–30 May 1992, in *Voennaya Mysl*, special issue, July 1992, pp. 111, 113. Gen. Grachev proposed the transition to a territorial command structure for a 3rd stage of military reform during 1995–96. However, as reported in 'Vooruzhennye sily Rossii: etapy formirovaniya' [Russia's armed forces: the stages of formation], *Krasnaya Zvezda*, 23 June 1992, the 3rd stage described would cover the period 1995–99. This source emphasized the view that the destruction of the current military–administrative structure in the next 1–2 years at a time of economic difficulties would lead to loss of troop control and reduce military readiness.

[99] Kuzmin, F. (Col-Gen.), 'Prednaznachenie, zadachi i sostav Sukhoputnykh voysk' [Destinations, tasks and structure of the land forces], *Voennaya Mysl*, special issue, July 1992, p. 63.

[100] 'Ministr oborony utochnil plany reformirovaniya armii' [Defence Minister specifies plans for the reform of the Army], *Krasnaya Zvezda*, 28 Oct. 1994.

[101] [Report of visit by Gen. Grachev to garrisons in the Far East and Siberia], *Krasnaya Zvezda*, 22 Apr. 1993.

[102] See note 101; and 'Resheno vossozdat territorialnye komandovaniya' [Decision to recreate territorial commands], *Kommersant Daily*, 24 Apr. 1993.

Russian military weaknesses mean that these blueprints may remain just that into the later 1990s, but the possible consequences of their realization should still be assessed. The geographic orientation of these groupings could assist their commands to carry out coordinated operations with the armed forces of neighbouring CIS states. At the same time this kind of new organization would provide Russia with greater flexibility for unsolicited military intervention throughout the area of the former USSR.

Yet the plan for new regional commands carries dangers for Russia. First, its implementation could help unravel central military control if political and economic regionalism grows stronger in the Russian Federation. Certainly it would be likely to provide more authority to the heads of the regional commands at the expense of the service chiefs. These regional commanders may have their own perspectives on regional dangers at odds with military planning assumptions in Moscow. For example, in the Russian Far East these perspectives could reflect the concerns of local authorities with Chinese ambitions in the area. The heads of regional administration cannot yet issue orders to regular military forces in their region, but such an option cannot be ruled out in the future. Second, the effort to build up force groupings capable of independent military action—the underlying logic of the former Far Eastern theatre of military action (TVD)—is likely to generate demands on military resources which the Russian economy simply cannot meet.

Nuclear forces

In creating its armed forces Russia brought the former Soviet Strategic Rocket Forces under its own jurisdiction, but they remained part of the joint CIS armed forces. Once Yeltsin appointed a Russian Commander of the Strategic Rocket Forces, Colonel-General Igor Sergeyev, in August 1992, however, direct leadership of the forces (in relation to combat readiness, training and so on) was entrusted to him.[103] The abolition of the CIS joint command in June 1993 resulted in Russia finally assuming de facto direct operational control over all former Soviet nuclear weapons (despite the equivocal position over nuclear arms on its soil maintained by Ukraine until the end of 1994).

Russian strategic nuclear weapons will be greatly reduced under the START treaties and their structure significantly changed. Andrey Kokoshin claims that these agreements have helped Russia to arrive at a clear idea about the strategic nuclear forces it needs and can possess up to approximately 2010.[104] The main emphasis is likely to be on deploying and maintaining a reliable single-warhead delivery system, most likely the SS-25 intercontinental ballistic missile (ICBM), the Topol RS-12M as it is called in Russia, both in fixed launch silos (perhaps 30–40 per cent) and on mobile launchers (perhaps 60–70 per cent). An

---

[103] Interview with Col-Gen. I. Sergeyev, *Krasnaya Zvezda*, 23 Sep. 1992.

[104] Interview with First Deputy Minister of Defence Andrey Kokoshin, 'Voennaya doktrina Rossii' [Russia's military doctrine], *Nezavisimaya Gazeta*, 3 June 1993: see also Konovalov, A., Oznobishchev, S. and Surikov, A., 'Start II: a treaty logical for Russia', *Moscow News*, no. 19 (13–19 May 1994).

arms development programme has been drawn up for Russia's strategic nuclear forces to the year 2005 but the status of these residual forces has not been fully clarified.[105]

Many Russian officers have been worried about the scale of nuclear reductions codified in the START treaties and suspicious about possible unilateral concessions, even if such concerns have been muted or absent in official military statements.[106] Certainly the goal of comprehensive nuclear disarmament is now little discussed in Moscow. Yeltsin himself, when pressed on this issue in 1992, claimed that he was fully in favour of the final destruction of nuclear weapons 'in the world', but described this as 'a dream'.[107] Despite this, in September 1994 Yeltsin proposed a new 'disarmament and strategic stability treaty' involving further reductions in nuclear warheads below the level of 3500 each for Russia and the USA defined by the START II Treaty[108] and he revived the ultimate goal of full nuclear disarmament. This may have been more public relations than policy. However, a number of Russian politicians and specialists wish to reduce Russian forces to 1000 nuclear weapons, since in their view such a 'minimum deterrence posture' is the only option the country can afford.[109]

VII. The new context of arms control and arms transfers

In any assessment of the military-related interaction of Russia with the outside world arms control has an important place. However, the active period of arms control negotiations of the late 1980s and the beginning of the 1990s has now been displaced. The strategic rationale of the 1990 Treaty on Conventional Armed Forces in Europe (CFE Treaty) is now dubious, with elements open to challenge, and attention has shifted to the Russian arms trade with the attendant problems of the proliferation of missile and other high technology. In the field of nuclear arms the controversy over the Soviet successor states' accession to the NPT appears to have been overcome. The START treaties and agreements on tactical nuclear weapons are being overshadowed in the internal Russian discourse by practical questions related to the reduction of the nuclear production infrastructure, the elimination of excessive nuclear warheads, the safety of nuclear stockpiles and the future of nuclear testing.

---

[105] Litovkin, V., *Izvestiya*, 9 Feb. 1994; Sergeyev, I. (Col-Gen.), 'The Russian missile forces today and tomorrow', *Military News Bulletin*, no. 4 (Apr. 1993), p. 2; and Volkov, L. (Lt-Gen.), *Segodnya*, 1 June 1994. On the configuration and location of these forces, see 'Sekrety, za kotorye sazhali i nagrazhdali shpionov' [Secrets for which spies were imprisoned and rewarded], *Izvestiya*, 20 Nov. 1993; and International Institute for Strategic Studies, *The Military Balance 1993–1994* (Brassey's: London, 1993), p. 99.

[106] See the assessment in Solovev, V., 'SNV-2: vzglyad iz ministerstva oborony Rossii' [START II: a view from the Russian Defence Ministry], *Nezavisimaya Gazeta*, 16 Mar. 1993.

[107] See interview in *Izvestiya*, 24 Feb. 1992.

[108] See note 76.

[109] See the discussion on Russian nuclear doctrine in the Presidium of the Russian Academy of Sciences, *Vestnik Rossiyskoy Akademii Nauk*, no. 2 (1992), cited in JPRS-UMA-92-034, 16 Sep. 1992. See also the proposals by Gen. M. Gareyev reported in *Krasnaya Zvezda*, 29 June 1994, to change the entire system of Russian nuclear planning.

The heyday of multilateral arms control negotiations which helped overcome the cold war confrontation may be past, but certain underlying Russian approaches to the reduced arms control agenda and to the role of international organizations in Europe show some continuity with Soviet military planning concerns of the past. For example, the Russian preoccupation with forward basing issues in the 1950s, which reappeared in the initial phase of the negotiations in the 1980s leading up to the INF Treaty,[110] is reflected again in current Russian concerns over the military implications of NATO enlargement.

Having lost their forward defensive zone in East–Central Europe, Russian generals in search of defensible frontiers increasingly express a traditional geostrategic aversion to Western encroachments and a fear of 'encirclement' in resisting the idea of Western military structures (particularly NATO) approaching the western CIS frontiers. Although the likelihood of direct conflict with Western states in the medium term is viewed as remote by such Russian officers, they continue to highlight the military–technical potential of NATO, specifically in relation to air- and sea-launched cruise missiles and other long-range high-precision conventional weapon systems capable of 'strategic' strikes against Russian targets. At the same time the immediate threats to the Russian Federation have indisputably shifted from the west to the south, a shift which is not reflected in current arms control regimes. This has disorientated Russian arms control policy and resulted in new challenges to the seminal CFE Treaty.

The treaty remains the centre-piece of European arms control, despite its outdated strategic assumptions. Its implementation is integral to continued confidence building as a result of its elaborate inspection regime. Yet its impact on Russia remains controversial. The division of the Soviet allotment of treaty-limited equipment (TLE) under the treaty leaves Russia as the preponderant but not militarily dominant power among the Soviet successor states. Taking into account also the considerable stockpile of combat equipment in the Asian part of Russia, a Russian parliamentary report on the consequences of the CFE Treaty for Russia concluded that the agreement on quotas 'creates no imbalances that endanger Russian interests'. Moscow also understands that the treaty creates 'a legal impediment to any future arms race among the CIS states'.[111] None the less, the new Russian military command, aware that the CFE Treaty obliges the country to have only a fraction of the forces the USSR had (perhaps 20–25 divisions), remains aggrieved over the imbalance which 'Shevardnadze's treaty' codified between Russia and NATO in favour of NATO in the region from the Atlantic to the Urals.

Russia pressed for adjustments in the treaty to better reflect its new perceived north–south axes of threats of regional conflict. In June 1993 Defence Minister Grachev raised the idea specifically of revising sub-limits in the treaty to permit a relocation of arms from one region to another without altering Russian ceilings for TLE. This would enable Russia to concentrate more forces in an

---

[110] The 1987 US–Soviet Treaty on the Elimination of Intermediate-Range and Shorter-Range Missiles.

[111] Report within the Committee for International Affairs and Foreign Economic Ties of the Supreme Soviet of the Russian Federation. *Nezavisimaya Gazeta*, 29 July 1992.

emerging base area in the North Caucasus MD (where sub-limits apply as a flank region in the CFE Treaty) to counter emerging southern threats.[112] One Russian proposal to escape the sub-limits was to reclassify the northern Caucasus from a flank region to a rear region. Alternatively, Russian officials suggested that the Russian units in the Transcaucasus which they designate as peacekeeping forces (loose terminology in this context) should be exempted from the sub-limit figures.

Such revisions to the CFE sub-limits are anathema to Turkey and opposed by all the Western and East–Central European parties to the treaty (although Romania seeks certain revisions of its own) on the grounds that changes to the treaty regime would undermine a central pillar of the post-cold war security system in Europe. This consideration apart, the Russian claim was not so unreasonable. In the early negotiations Turkey itself managed to exclude a considerable portion of its south-eastern territory from the treaty regime on the grounds that it faced southern threats from Syria and Iraq, so that forces here should not be counted in the East–West balance.

Through the autumn of 1995 the Russian military leadership pressed for revisions to the treaty by which the Rostov region and the Stavropol and Krasnodar territories (*kraya*) and the Volgograd region (*oblast*) would be regarded as outside the sub-limit regime for the flanks. Eventually, at the CFE Treaty Review Conference in 1996 it was agreed to give Russia three more years, until 31 May 1999, to meet the flank limits on TLE. Until then Russia will freeze its deployments in the flank zone at their current levels (1897 tanks, 4397 armoured personnel carriers and 2422 artillery pieces). Even after May 1999 Russia will be permitted to deploy significantly more heavy weapons along its northern and southern borders than would have been permitted under the original treaty terms.

The question of Russian military psychology is important here. One danger was that failure to reach an accommodation on the issue of flank limits for the CFE Treaty threatened to engender a 'Versailles' mentality among the Russian military leadership—resentment of an unjust treaty, which failed to codify equal security, forced on a weakened opponent.[113] This could tap a growing anti-Western undercurrent in Russian political life and encourage a more truculent Russian military attitude, which could spill over into other areas of policy such as the implementation of the Partnership for Peace (PFP) initiative or arms transfers.

A military response of this kind was unmistakably present during the debate in the spring of 1994 preceding the final Russian political decision to join the

---

[112] Gen. Grachev in Interfax, Moscow, 2 Mar. 1993, reported in SWB–SU, 1628 C1/2; and *International Herald Tribune*, 12–13 June 1993. According to Lt-Gen. A. Nikolaev, current TLE quotas would permit Russia only around 165 tanks and 10 armoured combat vehicles in the North Caucasus MD. *Krasnaya Zvezda*, 10 Mar. 1993. For detailed assessments, see Clarke, D., 'The Russian military and the CFE Treaty', *RFE/RL Research Report*, vol. 2, no. 42 (22 Oct. 1993), pp. 38–43; Sharp, J., 'Should the CFE Treaty be revised?', *CDS Bulletin of Arms Control*, no. 15 (Aug. 1994), pp. 2–10; and Kolesnikov, M. (Col-Gen.), *Krasnaya Zvezda*, 19 Apr. 1994.

[113] Clarke (note 112), p. 43.

PFP. The Chief of the General Staff, claiming that Western inflexibility over the CFE Treaty flank restrictions had 'driven Russia up a blind alley', stated that Russia 'doesn't sense any partnership with NATO'.[114] Russian military leaders supported the idea of Russia occupying a special, more influential position, alongside the USA, in an arrangement broader than that offered in the PFP proposal. This view that Russia's perceived military prowess as a 'great power' entitles it to a special role in relation to other PFP states remains a bone of contention.

Russian military leaders also tend to agree with those nationalist politicians in Moscow who claim that Western states have sought to constrain Russian arms sales abroad for self-interested purposes. The question of the restoration of Russian arms sales to 'traditional' clients, such as Iran, Iraq (despite the UN embargo) or Syria, could become increasingly contentious. Indeed in many respects the arms trade of the new post-Soviet states in the 1990s is less discriminating in terms of clients and means of trade than that which preceded it. The support and expansion of arms exports are now fostered as top Russian (and Ukrainian) state priorities. It is true that Russian officials claim that they closely regulate the export of arms, military technology, licences for the latter and sensitive materials, but corruption and the high demand for arms through agencies specializing in such trade in the former USSR make control over the final destinations of arms transfers at best loose.

The collapse of the centralized Soviet state and pressures for regional devolution in the Russian Federation have encouraged the 'liberalization' of the arms trade on the former Soviet territory. The sharing out of Soviet military assets among the new states has left the threat of uncontrolled military transfers to unstable regions, both on CIS territory and beyond. The real European security concern here remains the danger of unsanctioned or illicit sales and the leakage from Russia or other CIS states of sensitive military technologies, such as long-range missile components, to destinations further afield.

The volume of official Russian arms sales abroad will be much less than was implied by initial unrealistic projections in Moscow. For example, in 1992 some $2.4 billion of sales were achieved, despite hopes of arms exports in the range of $11–12 billion; in 1993 the value of arms exports was $2.5 billion and the forecast for 1994 was $3.4 billion.[115] Russia hopes that hard currency earnings from such sales may sustain domestic military R&D, help finance defence conversion and provide for the social protection of personnel employed in defence industries. In this respect the prospects of long-term cooperation in military technology with China are considered especially promising. This would make it possible 'to plan the load on the Russian Federation defence industry' from Chinese orders and 'to a certain extent to maintain a number of enterprises in China's interests'.[116] In fact such hopes are probably illusory; the

[114] Kolesnikov, M. (Col-Gen.), Segodnya, 5 May 1994.

[115] Anthony, I. et al., 'The trade in major conventional weapons', SIPRI Yearbook 1995: Armaments, Disarmamant and International Security (Oxford University Press: Oxford, 1995), p. 501.

[116] Krasnaya Zvezda, 18 Aug. 1993; and Kommersant Daily, 12 Aug. 1993.

closure of ever more defence enterprises promises growing instability in the Russian military–industrial complex and society at large.

VIII. Conclusions

The areas of Russian military policy discussed here reflect a state and political order in rapid transition, which has yet to find its bearings firmly in the post-Soviet space and the inchoate post-cold war European security order. It is clear that most of these military dimensions will impinge on the security of Russia's neighbours, especially the states of the former USSR, and Russian nuclear policy and doctrine will have global ramifications. It is not yet clear how far the new internal thrust to Russian military priorities and objectives—whether internal to the Russian Federation or to the territory of the former Soviet Union—will serve to distance the Russian state from the security concerns of Western and East–Central European nations (despite diplomatic forays in Bosnia and Herzegovina). Much here will depend on Russian military expectations in regions contiguous or close to its borders and the broader influence of the Russian military institution in the determination of central policy decisions.

However, in the near and medium term the ambitious plans developed by Russian military leaders will need to be moderated and scaled down, especially with respect to the development of new military technologies. The wholesale restructuring of Russian forces can only proceed slowly. The infrastructural, social and economic challenges to the cohesion and effectiveness of these forces, as reviewed in this chapter, are hard realities which demand the immediate attention of the Russian military command. This suggests that the troubled Russian military establishment will remain preoccupied for a number of years with the struggle to overcome its own shortcomings and financial strains whatever role it seeks to assume on former Soviet territory or further afield.

9. The changing role of military factors

Alexander A. Konovalov

I. Introduction

The necessity of a 'bottom–up review' of the role of military factors in Russian security, foreign and domestic policy became very clear shortly after the breakup of the Soviet Union. The end of the Soviet Union meant not only the dissolution of the huge state but the collapse of the biggest military machine ever to exist. The military legacy of the Soviet Union to Russia bore no relation either to Russia's current geo-strategic position and economic capabilities or to those vital national interests which might need to be defended by military means.

Russia, which represents only slightly above 50 per cent of the territory and population of the former USSR, inherited roughly 80 per cent of its armed forces and defence industry. This, together with deep economic crises, a dramatic decline in gross national product (GNP) and falling industrial production, has predefined a widening gap between the armed forces and the state. On the one hand large sections of the Soviet military machine have not yet become the Armed Forces of the Russian Federation and settled in to their new identity, mission and goals; on the other, the new Russian state is definitely unable to maintain this military heritage and urgently needs to bring the Soviet military legacy into line with its security interests and economic capabilities. In this connection Russia faces an enormous task—the peaceful transfer of the Soviet military legacy into the Russian Armed Forces—in a dangerous transitional period when economic crisis and internal political instability are becoming worse. In these circumstances the successful solution of military problems in Russia is becoming the key issue for international security and stability.

This chapter looks in detail at what has been happening to the armed forces in Russia over the past four years. Section II analyses the changes in the political role of the military that have occurred since the attempted coup of October 1993, examines voting patterns among the military and discusses the warning signs of increasing politicization among the military. Section III considers the new Russian military doctrine of November 1993, its relation to foreign policy, the need for reform of the military and restructuring of the defence forces to date. Section IV examines the nuclear strategy aspects of the new military doctrine, the abandonment of the principle of no-first-use of nuclear weapons and the implications for nuclear arms control; and section V looks at the possibility of joint defence arrangements among the successor states of the USSR and the prospects for a collective security system in the Commonwealth of Independent States (CIS).

II. The politicization of the military

Political preferences

During 1992–93 several steps were taken with the aim of setting up mechanisms of civilian control over the military and providing the military with the legal framework which would define normal civil–military relations. There were broad discussions about the national security concept inside the Defence and Foreign Ministries, the Security Council and the Supreme Soviet. The Supreme Soviet adopted a number of laws related to military matters, the most important one being the Law on Defence of September 1992.[1]

Attempts to establish the kind of civil–military relations that would be normal for a democratic society and to put the military under civilian control were interrupted with the confrontation of powers which directly engaged the armed forces. The events of October 1993 in Moscow and the results of the subsequent parliamentary elections and constitutional referendum raised legitimate questions about the new political role of the Russian military.

During the political confrontation in Moscow the armed forces were faced with a dangerous choice—to decide which orders to accept as legitimate, those issued by the presidential team or those received from the Supreme Soviet. At that time the choice was made in favour of the president, but later developments demonstrated how deep the split was inside the armed forces and how narrow the margins for President Boris Yeltsin and his supporters.

The success of the radical nationalist Liberal Democratic Party of Vladimir Zhirinovsky in the parliamentary elections and the result of the constitutional referendum of December 1993 shocked public opinion in and outside Russia. The reasons for the tremendous success achieved by the radical nationalists is outside the scope of this chapter, but the question for whom the military voted is relevant and important.

There are different assessments of the political sympathies of the Russian military as shown in these elections, in addition to the official view of the Defence Ministry that it was impossible to identify the ballots of the military and their families and that all speculation about the success of Zhirinovsky in the military strata of the electorate was groundless. Overall, however, there is sufficient evidence to conclude that more than 50 per cent of voters in the military gave their sympathies to radical nationalists and communists.[2] It was not

---

[1] The Law on Defence (a) required that the military build-up should be based on an adequate threat assessment; (b) proclaimed civilian control over defence spending and activities of the Defence Ministry and the possibility of having a civilian defence minister; (c) prohibited 'hidden' defence spending; and (d) established a numerical limit on military personnel: 1% of the population. 'The task of the armed forces' is 'to repulse an aggression and to defeat an aggressor and to fulfil the duties following from the international obligations of the Russian Federation.' Any other use of the units and formations of the armed forces is only allowed in accordance with the law or under special decree of the parliament. *Krasnaya Zvezda*, 10 Oct. 1992, pp. 1–2.

[2] The great majority of the military were assigned to civilian electoral districts and their ballots were mixed with those of civilians. Nevertheless independent sources gave interesting and representative statistical analyses. According to the prominent military observer Pavel Felgengauer, support for the Liberal Democratic Party (LDP) in the armed forces was practically the same as among the general public,

accidental that an urgent reorganization of the Manpower Agency (formerly the General Political Agency of the Defence Ministry) which was responsible for the loyalty of the officer corps was launched soon after the election as a kind of punishment for the political opposition demonstrated by the military electorate. The results of the vote demonstrated that the Russian military were deeply dissatisfied with the situation in the armed forces and the unsettled social problems, considered that internal, foreign and military policies did not correspond with the vital national interests of Russia, and were linking their hopes with radical nationalist political forces.

The participation of the military in the October 1993 events in Moscow should therefore not be seen as overwhelming and unconditional support for the president and his policy by the armed forces. The Russian military have not yet become an independent political power and will continue to resist further attempts to engage it in internal political struggle. At the same time, however, there is a clear trend of growing political opposition among the military and a will on their part to influence directly the security, foreign and even economic policy of Russia.

Division and demoralization

The Association of Military Sociologists conducted a study of trends in the Russian Armed Forces. Its results, published in August 1994, picked out three main threats arising from present trends in the military.[3]

First, the professional military and their families were continuing to decline into the poorest strata of Russian society, living below the poverty line. They appeared to be the social group least adaptable to the market economic environment in Russia. For instance, direct payments to officers (in many cases the only source of income for their families because 42 per cent of officers' wives do not work) in the Far Eastern and Trans-Baikal military districts (MDs) were equal to 25–30 per cent of the subsistence level in those areas. Budget shortfalls were added to the dramatic housing problem. The situation was expected to get worse when all troops were withdrawn from Germany and the Baltic states.

The authors of the study considered that the main threat was not internal financial difficulties but the deepening social split inside the armed forces. 'The armed forces of the present are the armed forces of social poles loaded with the latent energy of internal conflicts.'[4] Inside the officer corps the study distinguished at least three social groups with different orientations.

varying between 4.3% in Tajikistan and 18% in the Black Sea Fleet. *Segodnya*, 15 Dec. 1993, p. 3. However, *Novaya Ezhednevnaya Gazeta* reported that almost 70% of the Russian military voted in favour of Zhirinovsky. *Novaya Ezhednevnaya Gazeta*, 12 Jan. 1994, p. 2. At a press conference on 22 Dec. 1993 the president stated that one-third of the armed forces voted for the LDP. *Segodnya*, 24 Dec. 1993, p. 2. An opinion poll organized by the Defence Ministry in the military units shortly after the elections, also reported by Felgengauer, showed that 74% of the military voted for the new constitution. *Segodnya*, 30 Dec. 1993, p. 2.

[3] *Nezavisimaya Gazeta*, 24 Aug. 1994, pp. 1, 2.
[4] *Nezavisimaya Gazeta*, 24 Aug. 1994, p. 1.

The first was the youngest, from lieutenant to captain rank. They were interested in making some initial capital using either access to the armed forces' property or some other activities and to leave the armed forces. This group was not interested in a military career. The second group included officers from the rank of major to major-general (not military bureaucrats but field commanders). They would prefer to continue their military service because it seemed too late for them to start up in business in civilian life. The political preferences of this group were as follows: 50 per cent did not support privatization, 60 per cent were against price liberalization and 40 per cent were strong proponents of radical patriotic ideas. The third group consisted of military *apparatchiks* serving primarily in the Defence Ministry or General Staff and engaged in political games in the capital. An important dividing-line inside the armed forces was defined by the closeness of officers to military property and the proceeds from sales and other forms of realization of capital. The group having access to this source of profit was characterized as the military–commercial clan.

The growing internal divisions of the professional military have resulted in significant demoralization of the officer corps; indeed, according to the study, 42 per cent of officers saw no future in their professional career. The continuation of such trends could increase internal social tensions in the armed forces to the point of social explosion, which does represent a real threat to Russian society.

A second potential threat was the increasing probability of technical accidents and disasters in the armed forces. Reasons for this assessment included the increasing age of weapons, a lack of resources for training and maintenance, and deficiencies in discipline. In particular several explosions had occurred at Pacific Fleet munition stores near Vladivostok, of which the latest had a yield equivalent to that of a small nuclear bomb.

Third, the negative processes going on in Russian society could not but affect the military and lead to even more dangerous consequences. The most grave concern was the very serious criminal statistics. During 1993 servicemen in the Interior Ministry troops were found guilty of more than 2000 crimes, while on duty they prevented and cleared up 300 crimes.[5] During the first nine months of 1993 military courts dealt with 10 000 cases of crime committed by military servicemen.

The study concluded that the Russian Armed Forces were degrading to such an extent that they could change from being the preservers of security into being 'an integrated threat to individuals, society and the state'. Persistent failure to settle the problems of the armed forces would 'encourage their transformation into a "third power" when the generals and the officer corps, more likely from the second echelon, have to undertake decisive action aimed at avoiding the final breakup of the armed forces and pass power to the most capable political forces'.[6]

---

[5] *Nezavisimaya Gazeta*, 24 Aug. 1994.
[6] *Nezavisimaya Gazeta*, 24 Aug. 1994, p. 2.

This conclusion should be accepted as a serious warning signal. The Russian Armed Forces do not yet represent an independent political party and would definitely prefer to avoid close engagement in political games. However, weakness in the Russian political leadership and its inability to settle their problems could provoke active moves on the part of the military, probably not so much to win power as to pass power to 'capable political forces'. In other words, under such circumstances the military, using their specific means, could bring to power political forces with the ability to change the situation. It is evident that such a scenario would call the prospects for democracy in Russia into serious question.

The crisis in Chechnya

These factors were not taken into consideration when the Russian political leaders and top military commanders launched an extremely provocative and destabilizing action in Chechnya. It would be out of place in this chapter to analyse the reasons why this decision was taken, but it had several important consequences in the military–political area.

First, the military adventure in Chechnya led to the dramatic widening of the split between the political leadership of Russia and the armed forces. It was the first occasion in both Soviet and Russian times when high-ranking officers openly opposed and criticized the decisions of political leaders. Policy in Chechnya was sharply condemned by the then Commander of the 14th Army, Lieutenant-General Alexander Lebed, and Deputy Defence Minister Colonel-General Boris Gromov compared the military action there with the Soviet invasion of Afghanistan in the light of its devastating consequences for the vital national interests of Russia.

Second, the polarization of political views inside the armed forces resulted in a deep internal split. There were numerous reports of servicemen, mainly middle-ranking officers, refusing to obey orders. Such incidents are extremely serious warning signals. They demonstrate the extent of the politicization of the armed forces and they call very seriously into question the ability of these split armed forces to perform their duties in the event of a real emergency.

The war in Chechnya led to dramatic changes in the armed forces' attitudes to political struggle in Russia. One result was that Russia found itself with armed forces with a much increased feeling of dissatisfaction, a complete lack of trust of the political ruling circles and an extremely high level of readiness to act as an independent player on the Russian political scene. As before, the armed forces do not have their own positive political and economic programme but they are actively searching for political leaders who would better suit their understanding of the country's national interests.

III. The new military doctrine and reform of the armed forces

Many facts confirmed that the president did recognize the crucial role played by the armed forces in his struggle with his political opponents, but the most impressive demonstration of this took place only one month after the October 1993 coup attempt. On 2 November 1993 the Security Council adopted the Foundations of the Military Doctrine of the Russian Federation.[7] It was brought into force by a special decree signed by the president.[8]

It is interesting to note that no military doctrine ever existed before in such comprehensive form. The Defence Minister at the time, Pavel Grachev, had every justification in saying that it 'is worked out for the first time in our history'.[9] In the Soviet period the military build-up and the military–strategic concepts were based on political guidance provided by the Communist Party and the state leadership of the time. The only document on military doctrine was issued by the Warsaw Treaty Organization (WTO) in 1987.

The conceptual foundations of the national security strategy including the basic elements of the military doctrine had been under discussion for a long time, but the events of October 1993 provided the impulse to give form to the military dimension of the problem.

To the surprise of many specialists involved in previous discussions, the version adopted was the one originating in the Defence Ministry rather than one submitted by the Security Council only a few weeks before the coup attempt. The Security Council's version took into account the views of different state institutions and independent defence analysts and was considered the version most likely to be adopted (with some corrections). The final choice, however, was made in favour of the project submitted by the military, with Defence Minister Grachev being the main speaker at the Security Council meeting. This was the president's special way of paying his debt to the military for their contribution in resolving his dispute with his political adversaries.

The military doctrine appeared before the general concept of the national security strategy was worked out. In other words, the basic foundations of the military and foreign policies were adopted before the vital national security interests of Russia and the risks and challenges which can threaten these interests had been clearly formulated. The military doctrine, furthermore, appeared when the parliament had been dissolved and the new one was not yet elected, and therefore broke the Law on Defence which states that the military doctrine needs parliamentary approval.

At a press conference on 3 November 1993, Grachev introduced the doctrine to the media and recommended them to pay attention to four important elements. First, he stressed that it was based on a new understanding of the secur-

---

[7] *Izvestiya* published extensive excerpts from the military doctrine in 'Osnovnye polozheniya voennoy doktriny Rossiyskoy Federatsii' [The basic provisions of the military doctrine of the Russian Federation] on 18 Nov. 1993 and *Krasnaya Zvezda* published a slightly longer excerpt on 19 Nov. 1993. A translation into English was published by *Jane's Intelligence Review*, Special Report, Jan. 1994.

[8] Decree no. 1833. *Krasnaya Zvezda*, 19 Nov. 1993, p. 3.

[9] *Nezavisimaya Gazeta*, 8 June 1993, p. 5.

ity problem and would be an integral part of the broader security concept of the Russian Federation. Second, it specified how not only the armed forces but also all other types of armed formations could be used for national security needs. Third, it was based on the real political, economic and military capabilities of the state. Fourth, it dealt with the period of transition to the market economy, which completely changed the role of the Defence Ministry in the making and administration of military–technical policy.[10]

Political and military aspects of the doctrine

The military doctrine contained several important innovations. The most significant may be summarized as follows.

First, it rejected the principle of no-first-use of nuclear weapons, which was a key element of the Soviet declared nuclear strategy after June 1982.[11] Second, it stated that the armed forces could be used in international efforts for preserving peace, deployed outside the national territory, and involved in peacekeeping operations[12] in the newly independent states of the former Soviet Union. Third, it stated that units of the armed forces could be used in internal conflicts 'to support the forces of the Interior Ministry of the Russian Federation to localize . . . conflicts, to stop armed clashes and to disengage the conflicting parties as well as to defend strategically important objects'.[13] In this part the doctrine directly contradicted the Law on Defence, which prohibits the use of regular armed forces in internal conflicts inside the country. Fourth, an important innovation was the social guarantees which the state would grant to the military and their families. Traditionally such obligations were never considered as a part of the military doctrine in Russia and their inclusion was assessed by experts as an extra concession by the president to the military and confirmation of their growing political influence. Another point on which the doctrine conflicted with the existing law was that it set no numerical limits to the peacetime manpower of the armed forces, while the Law on Defence limited it to 1 per cent of the population, or 1.5 million men.

The military doctrine proclaimed that Russia did not consider 'any state as a potential adversary' and would not use its armed forces or other armed formations 'against any state for any purposes but collective or individual self-defence in the event of armed attack on the Russian Federation, her citizens, territory, armed forces or the other Russian armed formations or her allies'.[14] Furthermore, the Russian Armed Forces would be used 'to defend the sovereignty, territorial integrity and other vital interests of the Russian Federation in the event of aggression launched against her or her allies . . . to stop armed

[10] *Krasnaya Zvezda*, 4 Nov. 1993, p. 1.
[11] The nuclear-related aspects of the doctrine are discussed in the next section.
[12] Russian political parlance does not distinguish between 'peacekeeping'and 'peace enforcement': *mirotvorchestvo*—literally, peace creation—is the word for both. In this book *mirotvorchestvo* is translated by 'peacekeeping' except where the context clearly indicates otherwise.
[13] *Krasnaya Zvezda*, 19 Nov. 1993, p. 6.
[14] *Krasnaya Zvezda*, 19 Nov. 1993, p. 1.

conflicts or illegal armed violence on the borders . . . or inside the territory of the Russian Federation threatening her vital interests'.

The political part of the military doctrine defined the potential sources of a military threat towards the Russian Federation from outside. They included in particular: (a) territorial claims by other states; (b) existing and potential local wars and armed conflicts, primarily those in direct proximity to the Russian borders; (c) the proliferation of nuclear weapons and other weapons of mass destruction, their means of delivery and modern military technologies; (d) suppression of the rights, freedoms and legitimate interests of citizens of the Russian Federation abroad; and (e) enlargement of military blocs and alliances violating the military security interests of the Russian Federation. The biggest threat, according to the doctrine, was armed conflict unleashed by aggressive nationalism and religious intolerance.[15]

It may at first seem to be a positive and stabilizing factor that Russia did not identify a potential adversary in the new doctrine and saw the realistic challenges and threats to military security in this way. At the same time many items of this doctrine left open the possibility of multiple interpretations of the very important definitions which should form the general concept of national security. These have not yet been formulated by Russia's political leaders: it is not known what they mean by 'vital interests of the Russian Federation', 'military security interests of the Russian Federation', 'legitimate interests of citizens of the Russian Federation abroad' and so on. In the press conference when the Defence Minister introduced the new doctrine to the media no one could answer the question which countries are the allies of Russia. The meanings of all these terms are crucial because they define the situations in which and the reasons why Russian armed forces and other armed formations can act either inside Russia or abroad.

In other words, the military doctrine shows clearly that its political part was prepared and written by the military, who had a very vague perception of the subject. The lack of real political foundations or a general security concept weakens this document significantly and puts its durability into doubt.

The military chapter of the doctrine started with a declaration which identified the view taken of the possible character of future conflicts. 'Under conditions when the danger of global war (either nuclear or conventional) is reduced substantially while is not liquidated completely, local wars and armed conflicts represent the main threat to stability and peace. Their probability in some regions is increasing.'[16] The doctrine then stated that military action could be taken in local wars and armed conflicts by groups of forces deployed in the region of conflict in peacetime. If necessary these groups of forces could be reinforced with units redeployed from other directions (regions). Another article proclaimed the necessity to maintain the combat potential of the groups

[15] Krasnaya Zvezda, 19 Nov. 1993, p. 2.
[16] Krasnaya Zvezda, 19 Nov. 1993, p. 4.

of forces deployed in peacetime at a level adequate to repulse an aggression on local (regional) scale.

It is hardly possible to define such a vague term as 'an aggression on local (regional) scale'. These articles of the military doctrine could therefore be interpreted as meaning that in peacetime Russia should deploy in each region a group of armed forces strong enough to wage and win a local war or armed conflict while it also needs a mobile reserve capable of reinforcing the regional peacetime group of forces. This would leave the military with a free hand in choosing the size of the peacetime armed forces, but does raise the question of affordability.

The doctrine defined a wide variety of forces which could be engaged in operations, from a limited number of units to operational–strategic groups of forces, and the use of all types of weapons from small arms to modern high-accuracy smart weapons. Priority should be given to the development of armed forces 'to deter an aggression and mobile forces and other armed formations . . . capable of being redeployed in a short time and of waging a manoeuvre combat action in any direction (in any region) where a threat towards the security of the Russian Federation can appear'. Furthermore, 'the armed forces of the Russian Federation must be ready for redeployment in a short time to threatening directions and actions, either defensive or offensive, in any variant of . . . armed conflict or wars with modern or possible future weapons being used on a large scale'.[17]

A special provision in the doctrine stipulated that the Russian Armed Forces could be deployed outside the national territory whether this were dictated by the security interests of the Russian Federation or by those of the other CIS states. Their deployment should be regulated by international treaties.

Analysis of this part of the doctrine leaves a sense of internal contradiction. On the one hand it discusses local wars and armed conflicts and their possible escalation on a declaratory political level. On the other hand, when it turns to the practical aspects, means and operational strategic concepts, it reads like a guide to preparing for the possibility of military operations around the globe, implying the need to acquire global-scale sea-lift and air-lift capabilities. All this means a complete rejection of the goal declared not so long ago by the USSR and the NATO countries—'to liquidate the capabilities for launching surprise attack and for initiating large-scale offensive action'.[18] It is unclear why Russia decided to reject this principle when the military–political environment was more favourable and its possibilities of projecting military power were much less impressive than in the Soviet period.

---

[17] *Krasnaya Zvezda*, 19 Nov. 1993, pp. 6, 7.

[18] Stated at a meeting of the WTO Political Consultative Committee in Berlin, May 1987 and at the NATO Meeting of Heads of State and Government in Brussels, 2–3 Mar. 1988. *Pravda*, 30 May 1987, 9 June 1988; and *NATO Review*, no. 2 (Apr. 1988), p. 32.

Military reform

The new doctrine hardly touched on the problem of military reform in Russia. It mentioned only the stages of the restructuring of the armed forces and planned changes in the military posture. The first stage was to last until 1996 and include: (a) the organization of groups of forces on the territory of the Russian Federation according to function; (b) improvement in the structure of the services; (c) completion of the withdrawal of Russian forces stationed elsewhere back to national territory; (d) continuation of the shift towards a combination of conscripts and professionals in the armed forces and a mixed organizational principle; and (e) reduction in numbers to a definite level. The second stage was planned for the period 1996–2000 and included: (a) completion of structural reorganization; (b) a further shift towards the mixed organizational principle; and (c) the organization of groups of forces and the corresponding military infrastructure in the territory of the Russian Federation.

President Yeltsin, speaking about the problems which must be solved in the current stage of the military reform, mentioned: (a) the establishment of a legally proved system of social guarantees for active-duty and retired military and their families; (b) the change to the mixed principle of organization; and (c) the introduction of an alternative service.[19] It seems very significant that the president gave top priority to social guarantees for the military.

The doctrine did not elaborate on how many groups of forces and in which potentially dangerous directions (regions) Russia would deploy in peacetime. The lack of political foundation for the military doctrine left open several crucial questions about the most probable number, geographical location and scale of the conflicts Russia can be engaged in and should be ready to wage simultaneously. Nevertheless some elements of the planned military posture can be extracted from the public statements of the top military officials.

As early as June 1993 Grachev mentioned that two MDs, Moscow and North Caucasus, were now of strategic importance for Russia.[20] The point was underlined later by President Yeltsin, who stated in February 1994 that the Moscow, North Caucasus and Leningrad MDs had changed their postures and became front-line military areas while the Volga and Ural MDs would become bases for the preparation of mobilization resources.

According to Grachev, 'Russia is unable now to deploy military units under each bush along our longest borders. In this situation we can build on rapid-deployment forces only'. By the end of 1993 the idea of establishing rapid-deployment forces had became one of the central points in the discussions of military reform. As the Head of the Military Build-up and Reforms Agency of the Defence Ministry, Lieutenant-General Gennadiy Ivanov, put it:

Changes in the military–political situation and geo-strategic posture of Russia made it necessary to work out new approaches to the organization of groups of forces. It is not

---

[19] *Krasnaya Zvezda*, 25 Feb. 1994, p. 1.
[20] *Nezavisimaya Gazeta*, 8 June 1993, p. 5.

reasonable now to deploy groups of forces along the whole border as was done before. The structural reform is based on the principle of a mobile defence. It presupposes an organization of not so large but sufficiently powerful forces ready to be used operationally at the point where the real threat to the security of Russia appears.[21]

Analysts reported that Russia was planning to organize two types of mobile forces—immediate-deployment and rapid-deployment. The first must have an alert status of 10 hours (that is, be ready to act within 10 hours after getting an order); the second would need several days to arrive and be operational and would consist of motorized rifle divisions and reinforcement units.[22]

It is to be noted that these plans and programmes had not been discussed publicly or adopted by the parliament. Furthermore, when speaking of the plans of his Agency for 1994, General Ivanov underlined the need to work out 'conceptual proposals for changes in previously adopted laws to bring them into line with the new constitution and the new military doctrine'. This meant in particular that the doctrine in the military mind has a much higher status than the laws previously adopted by the Supreme Soviet. In other words, the laws are to be amended, in accordance with a doctrine introduced by presidential decree and never adopted by parliament, to make them more comfortable from the point of view of the military. The Agency had also to prepare new bills which 'are necessary in the defence field'. By and large, it seemed quite clear that the Defence Ministry intended to play a more active role in the legislative process, at least on military-related issues.

Further amendments to the reform plans of the military leadership were mentioned on 8 July 1994 by Defence Minister Grachev:

Plans are corrected by real life and many aspects of the reform of the armed forces should be reconsidered. For instance, nobody could imagine in 1992 that Russia would have to deploy military bases abroad, organize the Kaliningrad special military region, reform the air defence system and strengthen the role of the MDs. Drastic financial restrictions have had an impact on the whole process of the creation of the Russian Armed Forces.[23]

One of the major 'reconsiderations' concerned the number of services in the Russian Armed Forces. Russia inherited from the Soviet Union five armed services: the strategic missile forces, ground forces, air defence forces, air force and navy. It is expected that by the year 2000 the armed forces will consist of four services (at the expense of air defence) and that after that it will be possible to move to a three-services structure—air and space forces, army and navy.[24]

The overall size of the Russian Armed Forces is also a matter of 'reconsideration'. By the end of 1993 the total number of active-duty servicemen was 2.3 million. Grachev stated at a press conference on 29 December 1993 that

[21] *Krasnaya Zvezda*, 8 Feb. 1994, p. 1.
[22] *Nezavisimaya Gazeta*, 30 Dec. 1993, p. 1.
[23] *Krasnaya Zvezda*, 25 Feb. 1994, p. 1.
[24] *Krasnaya Zvezda*, 25 Feb. 1994, p. 1.

'during the coming year the total size of the armed forces will be reduced to 2.1 million active-duty military and will be preserved at this level in the years to come'.[25] Grachev later stated that numbers would be reduced to 1 917 000 active-duty servicemen by October 1994 and shortly after that to 1.5 million (in line with the Law on Defence). At the end of 1994, according to expert assessments, total personnel did not exceed 1.7 million, of whom about 1 million were professional military.[26] At the beginning of 1995, the government in the first draft budget for 1995 included a target of total manpower of 1 469 000 active-duty servicemen.[27] It is also accepted that the capacity of the military colleges and academies greatly exceeded possible demand and that their numbers and structure should be brought into line with demand.

Whatever the plans for military reform might be, their implementation is severely affected by the economic crisis in the country and will depend on the development of the internal economic situation. The armed forces are suffering from the same financial problems as the general economy. First Deputy Defence Minister Andrey Kokoshin stated that in the past the Defence Ministry received its agreed allocation from the Finance Ministry every two months, but in 1993 the funding was divided into 56 stages, putting the military in debt to all their contractors.[28] For 1995 the Defence Ministry requested 111 trillion roubles. The government reduced this request to 45.3 trillion roubles and the Duma authorized 50.9 trillion.[29]

The problem has been exacerbated by the withdrawal of Russian forces from abroad. During 1993 alone Russia withdrew from other countries' territories more than 100 000 men, more than 5000 pieces of armoured equipment and artillery systems, and about 700 aircraft and helicopters. It was a very tight schedule.[30] No less impressive work on the withdrawal and reorganization of the armed forces was planned for 1994: 250 000 servicemen and about 120 000 items of equipment were to be withdrawn to Russian territory during 1994.[31] The total number of former Soviet troops withdrawn from the former WTO member countries, Azerbaijan, the Baltic states, Cuba and Mongolia was 730 000.[32]

The problem of military reform was put at the centre of political discussions as a result of events in Chechnya. President Yeltsin in a speech on 16 February 1995 was strongly critical of the situation in the armed services and stated that 'military reform is going wrong'.[33] In the debate which followed in the press, a

---

[25] *Nezavisimaya Gazeta*, 30 Dec. 1993, p. 1.
[26] *Nezavisimaya Gazeta*, 3 Nov. 1994, p. 5.
[27] George, P. *et al.*, 'World military expenditure', *SIPRI Yearbook 1995: Armaments, Disarmament and International Security* (Oxford University Press: Oxford, 1995), p. 407.
[28] Interview with Andrey Kokoshin in *Segodnya*, 19 Feb. 1994.
[29] *Finansovye Izvestiya*, no. 66 (1995), p. 11. This was the figure authorized by the Duma on 'national defence' and excludes spending by the Ministry of Atomic Energy, the costs of implementation of international arms control treaties, the Border Guard forces, Interior Ministry forces and the Space Agency.
[30] *Krasnaya Zvezda*, 8 Feb. 1994, p. 2.
[31] *Krasnaya Zvezda*, 6 Jan. 1994, p. 1.
[32] *Krasnaya Zvezda*, 25 May 1996, p. 3.
[33] *Nezavisimaya Gazeta*, 17 Feb. 1995, p. 1.

number of urgent problems were highlighted. One of them was putting the organization and training of all the armed formations in Russia on a common basis. This seems to be a major task. Russia has not only the five armed services but also the Border Guard units, Interior Ministry troops, railway troops, units of the Federal Counter-Intelligence Service, troops of the government communication and information system, civil defence troops coming under the Ministry of Emergency Situations, and many other military and guard units. To end this bureaucratic division and to make all the armed forces available and efficient for the purposes of national defence, it was proposed to include (especially in wartime) the Border Guard units and Interior Ministry troops in the Armed Forces of the Russian Federation and to raise the status of the General Staff to make it responsible for all the armed forces and not only for those which are controlled by the Defence Ministry. Several suggestions were made about the establishment of effective political control over the military sphere. It was also proposed to change the functions of the Defence Ministry and put a civilian at its head.[34] A 'coordinating and control inter-agency body able to realize military reform in Russia' was proposed earlier in 1994 in a presidential message to the Federal Assembly.

It is obvious that military reform is to become one of the top priorities of the newly appointed (in July 1996) Minister of Defence, Colonel-General Igor Rodionov. What the practical results will be remains to be seen. The dangerous gap between the economic capabilities and security needs of the Russian state on the one hand and the size and demands of the inherited Soviet military machine on the other persists.

IV. The new Russian nuclear strategy and arms control

The principle of no-first-use

The innovations in nuclear strategy were assessed by analysts as the most radical part of the new military doctrine. Russia clearly showed its intention of making the concept of nuclear deterrence the basic element of both declaratory and practical nuclear policy. At the beginning of its political section the new doctrine proclaimed that 'the goal of . . . policy in the area of nuclear weapons is to liquidate the threat of a nuclear war by the deterrence of aggression against the Russian Federation and her allies'.[35] Thus Russia openly rejected the Soviet Union's principle of no-first-use of nuclear weapons. Commenting on this move, the Secretary of the Security Council at that time, Oleg Lobov, stated: 'In the current situation nuclear war is absolutely meaningless . . . Russia stands for setting up a system of collective security such as would ensure the prevention of war—either nuclear or conventional. But if war against Russia or her

[34] *Nezavisimaya Gazeta*, 27 Jan. 1995, p. 3.
[35] *Krasnaya Zvezda*, 19 Nov. 1993, p. 1.

allies is unleashed we have the right to use all available means to defend our vital interests'.[36]

The new doctrine did, however, include an obligation not to use nuclear weapons against states signatory to the 1968 Non-Proliferation Treaty (NPT) as non-nuclear states, with only two exclusions: (*a*) when such a state which is an ally of a nuclear-weapon state launches an aggression against Russia, its territory, its armed forces or other armed formations or its allies; or (*b*) when such a state acts jointly with a state which has nuclear weapons to support an invasion or an armed attack on the territory of the Russian Federation, its armed forces and other armed formations or its allies.[37] The political section of the doctrine also proclaimed that Russia stood for a comprehensive nuclear test ban and was interested in further reductions in nuclear weapons and their complete elimination in the foreseeable future.

Some other new elements of the new doctrine, as far as nuclear weapons are concerned, look very similar to the Western approaches. The doctrine stated that even limited use of nuclear weapons by one party in a war can provoke the massive use of these weapons in retaliation, leading to escalation and catastrophic consequences. It also declared that the Russian Armed Forces in order to prevent wars and armed conflicts 'must maintain strategic nuclear forces which would guarantee inflicting the necessary damage on an aggressor under any circumstances'. It is interesting to note that the concept of 'unacceptable damage' familiar from nuclear deterrence theory was replaced here with 'necessary' damage. The term was not defined.

These radical changes in Russian nuclear strategy raised different and often contradictory reactions in Russia and abroad. Most Western observers and some in Russia responded positively to these changes. In the West analysts stated that they had never trusted the declaratory slogan of no-first-use and that Russia in its nuclear doctrine had simply brought its nuclear strategy into line with practice. Russian observers said that the principle of no-first-use was based on the overwhelming superiority of the Soviet conventional forces in comparison with those of any other state or alliance. The current and foreseeable capabilities of the conventional forces of Russia are much more modest and Russia may find itself in the situation of having to compensate for its relative weaknesses here with nuclear weapons.

It is an important question whether the rejection of the principle of no-first-use matches the real military–political situation and corresponds to the security interests of Russia. The obligations formulated in the doctrine mean that Russia can, at least in theory, use nuclear weapons first against states which have not yet joined the NPT as non-nuclear states, which is meaningless both in a political and in a military sense. This looks less like a declaration of Russia's real intentions in the military sphere than a political message to Belarus, Kazakhstan and Ukraine aimed at putting pressure on them to get rid of the nuclear

[36] *Izvestiya*, 4 Nov. 1993, p. 1.
[37] *Izvestiya*, 4 Nov. 1993, p. 2.

weapons deployed on their territories. It could, however, create the opposite reaction and prove counter-productive.

Besides the states which have not signed the NPT as non-nuclear weapon states, there are others against which the doctrine by implication reserves for Russia the right to use nuclear weapons first in the event of aggression or if they support an aggression against Russia. These are, implicitly, first of all the NATO member states and China. It is obvious, however, that Russia is not going to use nuclear weapons first against NATO member states and does not consider them as potential aggressors. Any other neighbouring states or think-able coalition of states in the foreseeable future could be stopped and defeated by Russian conventional forces only. The argument that Russia has to com-pensate for the possible conventional superiority of a potential aggressor with first use of nuclear weapons can therefore only have been framed in the light of a hypothetical future conflict with China.

However, at present and for the immediate future Chinese conventional forces do not pose a direct military threat to Russia. As one prominent Russian military analyst, Alexei Arbatov, has commented, if Russia is seriously con-cerned about the conventional military capabilities of China in future, it is irrational for Russia to increase its military exports to China as dramatically as it is doing. No one but Russia is willing to provide China with modern aircraft, air defence missiles, combat ships and so on.[38] If any political message intended for China can be extracted from the new military doctrine, it was sent in the wrong way and at the wrong moment.

Ironically, Russia had officially accepted the simplified version of the nuclear deterrence concept after it had become clear that in its traditional form it no longer corresponded to the new political realities and that it needed to be developed with new ideas. In a report by leading experts in the USA and Russia it was stressed how risky a first-use strategy was in the current situation:

These concrete problems of a 'first use' policy need to be discussed between US and Russian defence experts if we are to avoid stumbling into a new nuclear competition. Such a new competition could be provoked by military preparations against a third country—preparation that included a new buildup in nuclear forces to achieve a 'credible' first-use posture against this country . . . To avert such a deployment, Russia and the United States, in co-operation with other powers, should now seek to reinforce the rule that nuclear weapons must never be used first.[39]

The deterrent function of nuclear weapons will continue to exist until they are completely eliminated. At the same time, as was noted by another Russian expert, Sergey Rogov, 'the model of mutual nuclear deterrence, even if both parties base their policies on this, is not compatible with the idea of strategic

[38] *Nezavisimaya Gazeta*, 3 Dec. 1993, p. 3.
[39] Iklé, F. C. and Karaganov, S. A., Georgetown University, Center for Strategic and International Studies, *Harmonizing the Evolution of US and Russian Defense Policies* (CSIS: Washington, DC, 1993), p. 27.

partnership declared by the top political leaders of Russia and the USA'.[40] In any case, it does not seem reasonable to base the military doctrine on it. On the contrary, it seems that in declaring its commitment to a traditional variant of the nuclear deterrence concept Russia missed a very good opportunity to convince the other nuclear states to join the no-first-use concept and to make it a key element of their nuclear strategies.

The official clarifications which followed the adoption of the new military doctrine were obviously intended to relieve the confusion that resulted. Defence Minister Grachev stated that 'at present and for the foreseeable future there is no single non-nuclear state able to launch unilaterally an aggression which would pose a serious danger' to Russia. Rejection of the no-first-use concept, he continued, 'does not mean a shift towards a concept of pre-emptive use of nuclear weapons . . . We definitely do not have in mind any pre-emptive nuclear strike'. Finally, Grachev mentioned that 'there is serious concern in different countries that Russia could use nuclear weapons first even in a very limited conflict'. He refuted such suspicions and stated that 'Russia is categorically against any, including limited, use of nuclear weapons even by one of conflicting parties'.[41] On all these points Grachev was contradicting the new doctrine in a fundamental way. Indeed, if Russia denies the possibility of a first pre-emptive nuclear strike, is against even limited unilateral use of nuclear weapons and does not see a single non-nuclear state as being capable of launching an aggression against Russia, the strategic rationale for reserving a right to first use of nuclear weapons remains unclear. Proclaiming the possibility of first use of nuclear weapons as an element of official nuclear strategy looks more like a step back than a step ahead.

Nuclear arms control

Non-proliferation of nuclear weapons and reductions in their numbers are the two basic issues of nuclear arms control.

For Russia's policy, the Ukrainian position on nuclear issues was of the utmost importance. In October 1991 the Verkhovnaya Rada (the Ukrainian Parliament) adopted a resolution 'On the Non-nuclear Status of Ukraine'; in May 1992 Ukraine signed the Lisbon Protocol.[42] These obligations did not prevent Ukraine from taking dangerous and provocative steps in the nuclear area. In April 1992 the 43rd Rocket Army (a Strategic Missile Forces unit with 170 launchers of intercontinental ballistic missiles, ICBMs) and the 46th Strategic Air Force Army (43 strategic bombers with 670 nuclear warheads on long-

[40] *Krasnaya Zvezda*, 4 Dec. 1993, p. 3.

[41] *Nezavisimaya Gazeta*, 9 June 1994, p. 5.

[42] Protocol to Facilitate the Implementation of the START Treaty, 23 May 1992, signed by Belarus, Kazakhstan, Russia, Ukraine and the USA. Lockwood, D., 'Nuclear arms control', *SIPRI Yearbook 1993: World Armaments and Disarmament* (Oxford University Press: Oxford, 1993), pp. 550–54. For the text of the Protocol, see *SIPRI Yearbook 1993*, pp. 574–75. The Protocol with accompanying letters from Ukrainian President Leonid Kravchuk formulated a Ukrainian obligation to eliminate all the nuclear weapons on its territory over a period of 7 years and to join the NPT as a non-nuclear weapon state.

range air-launched cruise missiles, ALCMs) were formally included by decree of President Leonid Kravchuk in the Ukrainian armed forces. During 1992–93 the personnel of the nuclear technical units in both these armies were forced to swear allegiance to Ukraine.[43] Finally in July 1993 the Verkhovnaya Rada proclaimed Ukraine the owner of nuclear weapons 'by historical circumstance'.

This led to at least three consequences. First, Russia lost the possibility of maintaining the nuclear warheads deployed on Ukrainian territory, because under the NPT it does not have the right to provide a foreign state with nuclear weapon components, services or technical knowledge. Second, this situation posed a direct threat to the NPT and the non-proliferation regime. It was clear that if Ukraine preserved its nuclear status *de jure* or de facto until the end of 1995 the non-proliferation regime would be destroyed. Third, ratification of START II (the 1993 US–Russian Treaty on Further Reduction and Limitation of Strategic Offensive Arms) by the Russian Parliament would not be possible if Ukraine did not eliminate all its nuclear weapons and join the NPT as a non-nuclear state.

The Moscow summit meeting of January 1994 of the presidents of Russia, Ukraine and the USA and the Trilateral Statement signed there[44] did not solve all these problems. Again Ukraine undertook to join the NPT in the shortest possible time, but the formulation of the Trilateral Statement rendered the Lisbon Protocol impotent because it allowed for multiple interpretations. It was important that Russia undertook in the Annex to the Trilateral Statement to 'provide for the servicing and ensure the safety of nuclear warheads'. It was unclear, however, how Russia could do this while the question of ownership of the nuclear weapons in Ukraine was still open. Furthermore, a week after the Trilateral Statement was signed in Moscow, the commanders of the 43rd Rocket Army, the 46th Missile Division deployed in Pervomaysk and the 19th Missile Division deployed in Khmelnitskiy were put under strong pressure to take the oath of allegiance to Ukraine.[45]

According to the Commander-in-Chief of the Russian Strategic Missile Forces, the unilateral steps taken by Ukraine 'liquidated any possibility of operational control over the 43rd Missile Forces Army . . . In this situation Russia is unable to influence the safety and security of nuclear weapons deployed in Ukraine and their potential unsanctioned use'.[46] The situation was aggravated by the refusal of 900 officers out of the 2300 serving in the 43rd Army to swear allegiance to Ukraine. As a result the units of the Strategic Missile Forces in Ukraine had less than 60 per cent of the officer corps they required. The nuclear technical units directly responsible for technical safety of nuclear warheads

---

[43] In Soviet times and later on in Russia, personnel of nuclear technical units were subordinated to the 12th Main Directorate of the Defence Ministry and were responsible for the technical safety of nuclear warheads.

[44] Trilateral Statement by the Presidents of the United States, Russia and Ukraine, Moscow, 14 Jan. 1994. For the text, see *SIPRI Yearbook 1994* (Oxford University Press: Oxford, 1994), pp. 677–78.

[45] *Segodnya*, 28 Jan. 1994, p. 1.

[46] *Izvestiya*, 22 Feb. 1994, p. 2.

were organized by Ukraine but had less than 50 per cent of the personnel they needed.

Political tensions in relations between Russia and Ukraine, the dispute about the Black Sea Fleet and the situation in Crimea gave radical political forces in Ukraine arguments for considering Russia as the main military threat to Ukraine and for speculating about the need to keep a Ukrainian nuclear arsenal as a deterrent. However, the results of presidential elections and the election of President Leonid Kuchma provided hope for a successful settlement of the 'Ukrainian nuclear problem'.

On 16 November 1994 the Verkhovnaya Rada decided that Ukraine would join the NPT. This decision was accompanied by several amendments and reservations. Ukraine demanded broad security guarantees from the nuclear powers, which might on the surface appear reasonable except that protection against 'economic pressure' on Ukraine was mentioned among these guarantees. The term 'economic pressure' was not defined and allowed very broad interpretation. Another amendment was linked with declared Ukrainian ownership of the nuclear weapons on its territory. The Verkhovnaya Rada decided that these weapons must be dismantled on the territory of Ukraine. This demand was unrealistic and could make the very idea of Ukraine joining the NPT regime senseless.

The removal of all uncertainty about Ukraine's non-nuclear status has required considerable effort. Finally, Ukraine deposited the NPT instruments of ratification at the Budapest summit meeting of the Conference on Security and Co-operation in Europe (CSCE) on 5 December 1994, thus joining the NPT regime. At the same time Russia, the UK, Ukraine and the USA signed a Memorandum broadly responding to Ukraine's demands for security guarantees. By June 1996 all the remaining nuclear charges for strategic forces had been withdrawn from Ukraine to Russia.

For Moscow, settling the Ukrainian nuclear question was the *sine qua non* for implementing the agreements on the reduction of strategic nuclear forces. Russia has already announced its programme of strategic missile forces development up to the year 2005 with numbers which are below the limits allowed by the START II provisions. Russia will preserve in the Strategic Missile Forces the only modernized model of the solid-fuel SS-25 missile in two versions, silo-based and mobile. Because of financial shortages Russia will deploy only 900 launchers (ground-based launchers with single-warhead ICBMs) out of a permitted 1300. It is planned that the ratio of silo-based to mobile systems will be 6 : 4 or 7 : 3.

In considering the further role of nuclear weapons in Russian military policy and possible variants on the Russian nuclear posture, several main scenarios have to be distinguished. The first assumes that the problem of nuclear weapons in the new independent states is successfully settled, the non-proliferation regime is saved and the strategic partnership between the USA and Russia develops. In this case it will be possible to work out together with the USA the advanced model of mutual nuclear deterrence which will be made necessary for some time by the continued existence of large nuclear arsenals. This model should be more stable and less dangerous than what can be achieved by new confidence-building measures, transparency in the nuclear area and a lowered state of nuclear alertness. Furthermore, these measures may be accompanied by dismantling the nuclear warheads from their means of delivery and keeping them in special stores under joint or possibly international control. The last detail is especially important if the non-proliferation regime is to be strengthened.

The second scenario could develop if the nuclear club starts to expand by the eroding of the non-proliferation regime from inside (North Korea) or outside (the appearance of officially declared nuclear powers among non-signatories of the NPT). If this happens the world will find itself very shortly in a situation where nuclear weapons are held in the arsenals of dozens of countries, which will make it imperative to formulate new approaches to international security. For Russia, this would be a matter of special concern. According to Defence Minister Grachev, the states of 'unofficial nuclear status' lie along a tight curve along the south of the geo-strategic area which includes Russia and its nearest neighbours, forming an indefinite zone of 'nuclear risk'.[47]

The third possible scenario is that of enlargement of NATO and the resulting military–political isolation of Russia. Detailed analysis of all the consequences of such a change in the military–political environment in Europe is outside the scope of this chapter, but one aspect should be mentioned. Since almost all the former members of the WTO and some former republics of the USSR have expressed a wish to join NATO, Russia is facing the prospect of having to counterbalance the rest of Europe plus the USA. To achieve this with conventional weapons only is economically unaffordable. It therefore seems likely that the enlargement of NATO might lead to more emphasis on tactical nuclear weapons in Russian military strategy. In bilateral Russian–US relations this would mean a return to some variant of the concept of nuclear deterrence.

V. The possibility of collective defence arrangements in the post-Soviet space

From the moment of the breakup of the Soviet Union and the creation of the CIS there were attempts to set up among the member states some permanent form of cooperation in the defence area. Initially these were the product of an unrealistic desire to preserve Soviet military structures under new names. They resulted in complete failure. The Tashkent Treaty on Collective Security,[48] signed on 15 May 1992 by six CIS member states, was not backed up by the political will of all the parties involved and remained a dead letter. The idea of unified forces for the CIS was abandoned and replaced with a more modest

---

[47] *Nezavisimaya Gazeta*, 9 June 1994, p. 5.

[48] For the text, see *Izvestiya*, 16 May 1992, p. 3. The original signatories were Armenia, Kazakhstan, Kyrgyzstan, the Russian Federation, Tajikistan and Uzbekistan. By the spring of 1994 Azerbaijan, Belarus and Georgia had also joined.

plan to create coalition forces. Their central element would be units of between army corps and field army size (30 000 to 50 000 men), including units of the army, air force, air defence, paratroopers and logistics support.

In the initial stage, while the newly independent states were strengthening their sovereignty, centrifugal trends prevailed in their relations with Russia. In 1994, however, they started to reverse this trend. Ideas of close cooperation in the defence area have become more salient, gradually taking form in concrete plans. As the Secretary of the Council of CIS Defence Ministers, General Leonid Ivashov, put it in May 1994, 'suggestions which were not acceptable a year ago, when many politicians could not think about setting up new defence alliances and real, not declaratory, unified armed forces, are now supported by many defence ministers of the CIS states'. He pointed out that the idea of a new defence alliance was supported by Kazakhstan and the need for close defence cooperation was recognized by Armenia, Kyrgyzstan, Tajikistan and Uzbekistan. Comparing the role of the possible new defence arrangements with that of the WTO, General Ivashov said that 'the Warsaw Treaty [Organization] was a European defence alliance confronting a defined opponent—NATO. The proposed new one should be a defensive alliance of Eurasian countries. Its main function will be linked not with an outside adversary but with the protection of the vital national interests of each member of the CIS'.[49]

The CIS participants instructed the Staff on Coordination of Military Cooperation (SCMC) to work out the concept of a CIS collective security system which would be 'the military doctrine of the Tashkent Treaty member states'.[50] In Russia, the idea was addressed at the highest political level. In June 1994 President Yeltsin stated that 'the setting up of the CIS collective security system is a number one priority'.[51]

According to the SCMC's vision of the collective security arrangements, three forms of cooperation would be most appropriate: (a) a coalition between the states with obligations for a specific period only and no coordination bodies or allied command; (b) a military or military–political alliance with a system of permanent political and military bodies and joint or unified military structures, groups of forces, operational plans and plans for combat readiness; or (c) deep military integration involving coalition structures with supranational authority whose decisions would be binding for the member states, joint (as well as national) defence budgets and armed forces under unified coalition command. In practical terms, the second option was considered as the most appropriate one for practical realization. The CIS collective security system should be based on and include several regional sub-systems, taking into account geographical proximity, the specific character of threats, force deployment and infrastructure. Four regional sub-systems could be set up: (a) an East European region (most of the European part of the Russian Federation, Belarus and the Kaliningrad exclave); (b) a Caucasus region (the northern Caucasus part of the

[49] *Nezavisimaya Gazeta,* 17 May 1994, p. 4.
[50] *Nezavisimaya Gazeta,* 17 May 1994, p. 4.
[51] *Nezavisimaya Gazeta,* 6 July 1994, p. 1.

Russian Federation, Armenia, Azerbaijan and Georgia); (c) a Central Asian region, sub-divided into eastern and western parts (the Ural–Siberia part of the Russian Federation, the western part of Kazakhstan, Uzbekistan, Kyrgyzstan and Tajikistan); and (d) an East Asian region (the eastern part of the Russian Federation and the eastern part of Kazakhstan).[52] The military component of each sub-system should be formed by coalition defence forces which would provide the basis for the unified forces.[53] Their command bodies should be provided with supranational authority in a number of spheres dealing with combat readiness, combat and operational training, and control over the forces in peacetime. Such authorities should be delegated to these bodies by the Council of Collective Security of the CIS and provided for in the national laws of the member states.

The CIS states which had not signed the Tashkent Treaty (Moldova, Turkmenistan and Ukraine) would be welcome to take part in the regional sub-systems of collective security. The level of their engagement in collective security activities could be different from that of the other participants and deal with separate aspects of the security problems such as border guards, air defence, and so on.

In general the system of collective security arrangements must be flexible enough to provide the member states with efficient instruments corresponding to their different security needs. It is exactly for this reason that organizing regional sub-systems might be rational because it would make it easier to adjust the collective security system to the different security priorities of the member states of the CIS. However, even at the theoretical level of discussions, there are many unclear elements of a would-be CIS collective security system. On the one hand, its basic principle should be that 'an aggression against one is an aggression against all';[54] on the other hand, it should be 'much broader than a defensive alliance'.[55]

Of special importance is the issue of nuclear guarantees. It is not clear whether this problem has been discussed at the official level. In the public debates, however, representatives of the Russian military community do not seem to have any doubts that 'the Russian strategic nuclear forces should be the foundation of the collective security system . . . Their task should be to provide strategic stability and security guarantees either for all the states forming the collective security system or for each member state separately under any developments of the world military–political situation'.[56]

Finally, it should be noted that a would-be CIS collective security system is regarded as a kind of actor which might be present in the international arena. The issue was raised in the context of discussions on the Partnership for Peace

---

[52] *Nezavisimaya Gazeta,* 6 July 1994, p. 3.

[53] *Nezavisimaya Gazeta,* 6 July 1994, p. 3.

[54] Samsonov, V., 'O sisteme kollektivnoy bezaposnosti SNG' [The system of collective security of the CIS], *Nezavisimaya Gazeta,* 26 Nov. 1994, p. 3.

[55] Ivashov, L., 'Vozmozhen li voenno-politicheskiy soyuz?' [Is military–political alliance possible?], *Nezavisimaya Gazeta,* 18 Oct. 1994, p. 5.

[56] Samsonov (note 54).

(PFP) programme, which might be harmonized with the development of military cooperation within the CIS. Ultimately, according to this logic, cooperation between NATO and Tashkent Treaty member states might be envisaged in a '16 plus 9' scheme.

The summit meeting of the CIS states held in Alma Ata (Almaty) in Kazakhstan in February 1995 demonstrated that real readiness to set up collective security structures among the CIS states was lagging behind the schemes worked out by the specialists on military staffs. The only collective structure in the military field which they have approved is the restored collective air defence system in the territory which used to be the Soviet Union. Substantial differences in security needs and interests exist between the potential members of the CIS collective security system. The security arrangements inside the CIS will most probably be based on bilateral treaties between Russia and the other partners.

The recognition that relations with the CIS states are of top priority for Russian foreign policy was officially confirmed in the autumn of 1995, when Russia published a document directly addressed to this issue. The document was entitled 'The Strategic Course of Russia in Relations with the CIS Member States' and was approved by special presidential decree on 14 September 1995.[57] Signed by the president, it had the highest administrative status. It stressed the priority of relations with the CIS states as a vital national interest.

It contained several very important points. First, it stated that 'the main vital national interests of Russia in the area of the economy, national defence, security and the protection of the rights of Russians are concentrated in the territory of the CIS states. To ensure those interests is a key foundation of our national security'. The main goal of Russian policy towards the CIS states was defined as 'the creation of a union of states integrated politically and economically and able to become a respected member of the world community'. The same introductory part of the document proclaims as a priority of Russian policy in relations with the CIS states 'strengthening Russia as a driving vehicle of the new system of political and economic interstate relations in the post-Soviet territory'.[58]

The second part of the document was devoted to the issue of economic integration among the CIS states. Russia has moved forward to the idea of a gradual joining of all the CIS states in economic and customs unions. It is supposed that the process will be one of different speeds for the different countries, but the document stated that 'the attitude of our partners towards this model will be an important factor defining the amount of economic, political and military support they can expect from Russia'.[59] In other words, Russia was trying to declare its readiness to use all means available at the time, including the dependence of its partners' national economies on all sorts of links with the Russian economy, to speed up economic integration within the CIS.

---

[57] The text was published in *Diplomaticheskiy Vestnik*, no. 10 (Oct. 1995), pp. 3–6.
[58] *Diplomaticheskiy Vestnik* (note 57), p. 1.
[59] *Diplomaticheskiy Vestnik* (note 57), p. 2.

In the part of the document devoted to national security issues, the first goal of Russian policy was formulated as 'the creation of a collective security system based on the Collective Security Treaty of 15 May 1992 and bilateral treaties between the CIS states'. Russia would also 'encourage the intention of the states participating in the Collective Security Treaty to set up a defence union based on commonality of interests and military–political goals'.[60]

The document also announced the possibility of establishing military bases in the territory of the CIS states, the objective of organizing a unified system of border guards, and joint peacekeeping exercises to prevent conflicts in the CIS states. In respect of peacekeeping, it contained two other points which in many respects contradicted one another. On the one hand, it stated that 'all activities of that kind should be carried out in close cooperation with the UN and the Organization for Security and Co-operation in Europe (OSCE)[61] to ensure the real participation of these organizations in the settlement of conflicts in the CIS states'. On the other, it said that 'in relations with third countries and organizations the idea should be promoted that this region is primarily a zone of Russian interests'.[62]

The very term 'zone of interest' is hardly applicable to relations between sovereign states, and more likely reflects the traditional cliché of the authoritarian mind. It should be mentioned as well, however, that among the concluding remarks summing up the main goals of Russian policy in the CIS states the document mentioned 'preventing the relations between Russia and the CIS states from developing in a confrontational way'.[63]

With all the reservations about the terms used in the document, it shows that Russia recognizes the top priority of its relations with the CIS states, supports the growing integrationist trends and sees the CIS in a long-term perspective as a regional international organization able to ensure political, economic and social stability in the territory which used to be the Soviet Union. It seems quite clear, however, that the development of the CIS in this direction in the military field will not be easy.

---

[60] *Diplomaticheskiy Vestnik* (note 57), p. 3.
[61] On 1 Jan. 1995 the CSCE became the OSCE.
[62] *Diplomaticheskiy Vestnik* (note 57), p. 5.
[63] *Diplomaticheskiy Vestnik* (note 57), p. 6.

Part V
The post-Soviet conflict heritage

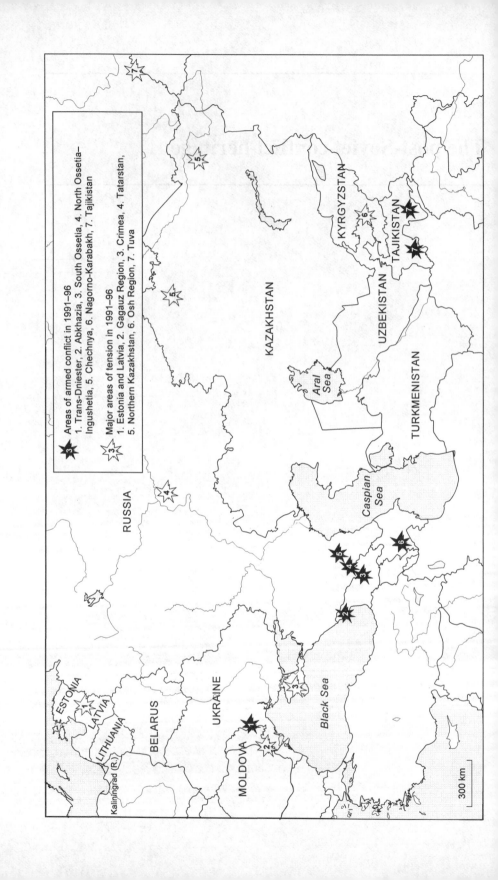

Areas of armed conflict in 1991–96
1. Trans-Dniester, 2. Abkhazia, 3. South Ossetia, 4. North Ossetia–Ingushetia, 5. Chechnya, 6. Nagorno-Karabakh, 7. Tajikistan

Major areas of tension in 1991–96
1. Estonia and Latvia, 2. Gagauz Region, 3. Crimea, 4. Tatarstan, 5. Northern Kazakhstan, 6. Osh Region, 7. Tuva

300 km

Principal categories of conflict on the territory of the former Soviet Union

Territorial
Conflicts over the status of territories and borders in Nagorno-Karabakh (Azerbaijan); Abkhazia and South Ossetia (Georgia); Trans-Dniester area (Moldova); Chechnya, Ingushetia, North Ossetia and Tatarstan (Russia); and Crimea (Ukraine)

Leadership
Use of force in power struggles in Georgia (1992–93); Tajikistan (1992 to the present); and Russia (1993)

Diaspora
Conflicts over the rights of the c. 65 million former Soviet citizens (incl. 25 million Russians) residing outside their titular nations

Economic
Conflicts over compensation for Russian energy sources; the division of the former Soviet debt; introduction of new currencies and customs regulations; and the termination of common prices and financial transfers across the borders of the CIS states

Military
Conflicts over the division of former Soviet military assets (Black Sea Fleet, nuclear weapons, installations and bases) and over Russia's military presence in the 'near abroad'

Background chronology: peacekeeping and related activities

1992

20 Mar.
CIS member states except Turkmenistan agree to create a voluntary peace-keeping force which can be deployed to implement cease-fire arrangements upon request of all parties involved in a conflict

15 May
At a CIS summit meeting in Tashkent, the leaders of Armenia, Kazakhstan, Kyrgyzstan, Russia, Tajikistan and Uzbekistan sign a 5-year collective security treaty providing for mutual military aid in the event of aggression against any of the signatories

24 June
President Yeltsin and Georgian President Shevardnadze sign an agreement to halt the fighting in South Ossetia and establish a Joint Monitoring Commission made up of Russian, Georgian, and North and South Ossetian troops and observers to police the cease-fire

21 July
Yeltsin and Moldovan President Snegur sign an agreement on ending the fighting in the Trans-Dniester area of eastern Moldova. On 29 July a trilateral Moldovan, Russian and 'Trans-Dniester' peacekeeping force begins to operate there

30 Nov.
The defence ministers of Kazakhstan, Kyrgyzstan, Russia and Uzbekistan agree to establish a joint peacekeeping force to be deployed in Tajikistan

1993

28 Feb.
Yeltsin proposes that the UN grant special status to Russia to act as a guarantor of peace and stability on the territory of the former USSR

24 Sep.
Against a background of a deteriorating security situation along the Afghan–Tajik border, agreement is reached at a CIS summit meeting to establish a coalition peacekeeping force of 25 000 troops to be deployed in Tajikistan, with Russia contributing the bulk of the forces

1994

14 May
Georgian and Abkhaz representatives agree to a cease-fire and to deployment of a CIS peacekeeping force to maintain a security zone separating Georgia and Abkhazia. The force, deployed on 24 June 1994, operates under CIS auspices but is made up primarily of Russian troops

16 May
Representatives from Armenia, Azerbaijan and Nagorno-Karabakh sign a Russian-mediated cease-fire agreement in Moscow

5 Dec.
At CSCE summit meeting in Budapest leaders of member states (including Yelstin) agree in principle to send a multinational peacekeeping force to Nagorno-Karabakh

Key facts

Peacekeeping activities on the territory of the former Soviet Union

	Start date	Size of force/ composition	Authorization
Georgia (Abkhazia)	June 1994[a]	3000 Russian[b]	CIS and UN endorsement of peacekeeping mission
Moldova (Trans-Dniester)	July 1992	c. 3000 Moldovan, Russian[c] and 'Trans-Dniestrian'	Bilateral agreement, Moldova and Russia
Nagorno-Karabakh	Dec. 1994	c. 3000 multinational force to be deployed[d]	OSCE authorization
Georgia (South Ossetia)	July 1992	c. 1400 Russian[e], Georgian and South Ossetian	Bilateral agreement, Georgia and Russia
Tajikistan	Sep. 1993[f]	25 000 authorized Russian[g] and small Kazakh, Kyrgyz and Uzbek contingents	CIS peacekeeping operation

[a] CIS mandate approved Oct. 1994. [b] Actual deployment as of Sep. 1996 was 1500. [c] Number of Russian troops c. 1800. [d] No troops yet deployed as of Sep. 1996. [e] Number of Russian troops c. 700. [f] Deployment began Oct. 1993. [g] Actual deployment c. 6000 (of the 201st Motorized Rifle Division) and 10 000–12 000 border control troops. *Source: SIPRI Yearbook 1996: Armaments, Disarmament and International Security* (Oxford University Press: Oxford, 1996), pp. 75–90; and SIPRI archive.

10. Conflicts in the CIS and their implications for Europe

Christoph Royen

I. Introduction

Whatever the initial short-lived illusions about *perestroika* at home and 'new thinking' in foreign policy, the Soviet Union proved unreformable. This was not, as some Western politicians originally thought, because the Soviet leadership would not really try honestly: President Mikhail Gorbachev and his associates tried, but the patient did not survive. The replacement of the Soviet Union by 15 new states, recognized almost immediately by the international community as independent, sovereign entities, although at first surprisingly smooth, caused a structural vacuum. Instead of entering a new order of peace and mutual cooperation the area vacated became the scene of a variety of conflicts, which until then did not exist at all or only in latent form.

In the light of the territorial disputes that have arisen, inter-ethnic conflicts, nationalist intolerance, economic rivalry, mutual recriminations for damages inflicted in the past, and even shocking violence and the use of military force, the question arises whether these conflicts really did not exist before *perestroika* unwittingly initiated the Soviet Union's final phase.[1] Certain categories of conflict could not arise as long as there was a single central power instead of a multitude of competing power centres; probably more important and more numerous, however, are those conflicts which the communist system was able to prevent from appearing openly or to deal with behind closed doors. Regional competition for allocations of funds, for example, must have been a daily preoccupation of party functionaries and government bureaucrats. National animosities or prejudices were likewise certainly high on the agenda of those who were responsible for cadre decisions. In the area of ideological instruction this even became visible when the mass media reported occasionally on the party's stern admonitions to combat 'remnants of the pre-communist past' in the inter-ethnic realm.

In any case, the Soviet leaders succeeded in convincing themselves, their society and even the outside world that real conflicts—in communist jargon 'antagonistic contradictions'—had no place in the socialist system and were characteristics of less advanced stages in mankind's development. Accordingly, when General Secretary Nikita Khrushchev presented the Ukrainian 'brother' republic with the Crimean peninsula in 1954 to commemorate 300 years of

---

[1] A map was published as early as Mar. 1991 showing all the conflicts threatening to disrupt the coherence of the Soviet Union. *Moskovskie Novosti*, no. 11 (17 Mar. 1991), p. 8.

Ukraine's union with Russia, no voice of protest was to be heard. Similarly the numerous decisions changing the status of certain regions or their borders were applauded almost without exception as acts of prudent leadership. As a result the successors of the USSR as well as the rest of the world are confronted now with the fact that no one is adequately prepared to handle these conflicts and to deal with them efficiently. A large part of the 'post-Soviet conflict heritage' consists in just this lack of experience of reality. In describing and analysing the range of problems caused by the demise of the Soviet Union, as well as their implications for Europe, it must be borne in mind that, while the problems may appear conventional, their sudden, unprecedented urgency makes them worse.

Potential concerns that the breakup of the USSR might lead to confusion and conflicting claims with regard to its membership of the UN, especially the Security Council, and in other international organizations, were pre-empted from the outset because the founding members of the Commonwealth of Independent States (CIS) agreed to let Russia continue those memberships.[2] The international community felt relieved and, obviously, went along with this simple solution. Russia also took over, almost without any noise, the buildings of Soviet embassies and other diplomatic representations abroad.

The division of the former USSR's remaining assets and debts seems rather more complicated. The founding documents of the CIS contained a general promise by the participants to guarantee the fulfilment of contractual obligations entered into by the Soviet Union. Three months later the member states agreed on a mechanism for servicing debts and dividing the assets.[3] Since then foreign creditors have engaged in protracted negotiations, apparently conducted by all sides in good faith. The potential for open conflicts over the Soviet Union's heritage is thus fairly well confined to intra-CIS relations.

II. The roots of conflicts

From administrative to international borders

In focusing on border disputes as part of the post-Soviet heritage, one important historical qualification must not be overlooked. Almost none of the present new states existed before 1917. In 1917 the Bolsheviks replaced the empire of tsarist Russia, which was a unitary state: there were no state borders within Imperial Russia. It was in fact Stalin who created national self-awareness and consciousness in many parts of the Soviet Union, using nationalism to rally the masses

---

[2] See the text of the resolution in *Izvestiya*, 23 Dec. 1991, p. 2.

[3] For an extensive exploration of the legal questions connected with the end of the USSR, see Schweisfurth, Th., 'Vom Einheitsstaat (UdSSR) zum Staatenbund (GUS): Juristische Stationen eines Staatszerfalls und einer Staatenbundsentstehung' [From unitarian state (USSR) to confederation (CIS): juridical stages of a state's decay and of a confederation's establishment], *Zeitschrift für ausländisches öffentliches und Völkerrecht*, vol. 52, no. 3–4 (1992), pp. 541–702; and 'Ausgewählte Fragen der Staatensukzession im Kontext der Auflösung der UdSSR' [Selected aspects of states' succession in the context of the dissolution of the USSR], *Archiv des Völkerrechts*, vol. 32, no. 1 (Mar. 1994), pp. 99–129.

under the red flag against the traditional élites, before he switched to a technique of *divide et impera*, constantly rearranging the political map of the union rather arbitrarily. Occasionally even entire populations were uprooted and resettled in another region of the country. It is hence only now for the first time in history that the northern part of Eurasia has real borders between different states, which in turn try to expand or to defend them.

Similarly, inter-ethnic conflicts, the numerous cases of the oppression of minorities by majorities and minorities' attempts to gain independent territory of their own, can be explained by a common denominator. To a great extent they are a diaspora problem, the result of tsarist and even more Stalinist rule which created for vast parts of the empire an incongruence between territory and ethnos.[4]

Deficiencies of the inherited political culture

Young nation-states elsewhere in the contemporary world after winning independence from colonial powers or other dominant empires also appear poorly equipped for the tasks of governing their countries and engaging in peaceful cooperation with neighbours because they lack experienced indigenous politicians and public servants. The post-Soviet states, however, had to start under particularly adverse conditions because the collapse of the previous state structure was accompanied by the simultaneous dissolution of the political system—the monopolistic rule of the Communist Party. The intrinsic identity of the state and a party which insisted on its all-encompassing 'leading role' as the fundamental principle of political life could not provide a political culture of open discussion and common search for compromise between various interests.

Similarly the Soviet political system did not leave an established respect for the rule of law. Laws were obeyed if enforced by the repressive instruments of the state; where there were loopholes the field was open for corruption and arbitrary decisions. Post-Soviet decision makers have preferred to keep silent on the spread of bribery and mafia-type business practices, even if it meant a huge loss of revenue for the state, because racketeers are replacing the internal revenue service and the government tax-collector.[5] Western politicians and many observers, preferring to believe in the firm rule of President Boris Yeltsin and his government of reformers, were hardly aware of the problem,[6] and President Yeltsin and his aides have only lately begun to realize how urgent it

---

[4] See the detailed analysis by Halbach, U., 'Ethno-territoriale Konflikte in der GUS' [Ethno-territorial conflicts in the CIS], *Berichte des Bundesinstituts für ostwissenschaftliche und internationale Studien*, no. 31 (1992) (BIOSt: Cologne, July 1992), pp. 3–10; see also Johann, B., 'GUS ohne Zukunft: Eine Region zwischen Zerfall und neuen Allianzen' [CIS without a future: a region between decay and new alliances], *Interdependenz*, no. 15 (Stiftung Entwicklung und Frieden/ Institut für Entwicklung und Frieden: Bonn, 1993), p. 16.

[5] For an excellent realistic description of how the system of mafia protection works in everyday life, see Dubnov, V., 'Doktor Reket' [Doctor Racket], *Novoe Vremya*, no. 24 (June 1994), p. 4–7.

[6] See, however, the book by a knowledgeable German correspondent in Moscow: Schmidt-Häuer, C., *Russland in Aufruhr: Innenansichten aus einem rechtlosen Reich* [Russia in turmoil: reflections from a lawless empire] (Piper: Munich/Zurich, 1993).

is to tackle this fatal disease.[7] Precious time has been wasted. Without the conviction and confidence of society that its lawmakers are engaged in a meaningful activity and that the courts and law enforcement agencies take their duties under the constitution seriously, not only do the chances of success in the domestic transformations remain minimal: society's trust in political leaders' negotiations and agreements with other post-Soviet governments is undermined and the idea is accepted that force has to be relied on to protect national interests.

Moreover, because the end of the Soviet Union came rather suddenly, new élites did not have time to prepare themselves for the assumption of responsibility, nor did society have a chance to test alternative leaders in advance. Leading functions in government or in the economy continued therefore to be occupied by members of the *nomenklatura* who merely exchanged their communist past for a quickly adopted 'democratic' or nationalistic future.

An additional factor which makes the process of peaceful state-building more difficult is the sheer size of the former empire. Decentralization and the devolution of power to the various regions would have been needed long before the USSR broke up in order to promote responsible engagement in public affairs and make efficient government possible. In fact decentralization was and still is perceived in Russia mainly as a threat of disintegration.

Taken together, all these conditions throughout the different parts of the post-Soviet area make for a strong tendency for political leaders to compensate for their lack of objective qualification for the job and for the sudden disorientation of society by resorting to slogans about their own nation's virtues as contrasted with others' vices. The temptation to blame other nationalities for society's sufferings and to treat the 'strangers' as scapegoats seems to be increasing, as is witnessed, for example, in the Moscow authorities' recent resort to popular prejudice against people from Central Asia and the Caucasian region.

The destruction of cultural internationalism

It has become fashionable, not only abroad but also within the CIS, to use the notion of internationalism ironically or with sarcasm. On an objective reappraisal, however, it is clear that at least in the field of culture and education internationalism was not merely a hollow slogan invented to mask the dictatorial essence of communist rule. Millions of people, especially among the non-Slav nations, benefited from access to Russian and international culture, science and civilization, which were opened to them via the *lingua franca* in the multifaceted Soviet educational network. Moreover, the many missions (*komandirovki*) for Russian specialists to work in other parts of the Soviet Union not only created a layer of privileged, semi-colonialist masters; they also

---

[7] President Yeltsin's inaugural address to the new Russian Parliament in *Rossiyskaya Gazeta*, 25 Feb. 1994, pp. 1–2.

left behind well-documented relations of mutual respect and recognition, often resulting in lasting bonds of trust and friendship.

Regrettably, the processes of urgent nation and state building, combined with rather dubious methods of competition for power among the old and (more importantly) the new élites, have undermined that most positive part of the Soviet heritage.[8] When financial shortfalls are added, it is to be expected—it has happened already—that some groups of the population in the CIS are barred from watching the same television programmes or from reading the same newspapers. Cultural internationalism may appear as a secondary problem, mainly affecting narrow élites and intellectual circles, but experience from other areas of the world indicates the contrary: it is needed to arm people against the chauvinism with which hate-mongers can fill the vacuum of ignorance, and is thus an instrument to preserve peace.

After the severance of economic arteries

The economic heritage of the USSR is another bone of contention. Natural resources, which offer the chance to earn hard currency on the world market for raw materials, cannot be transferred, except by territorial and border changes. Most of this natural wealth is located in Russia, and the other successor states see no possible way to gain a share in it. The situation is different, however, where the possessor state is less powerful. Within Russia, some of the national autonomous units, for example Tatarstan, are basing their aspirations to sovereignty on the 'black gold' under their soil. Whether Tatarstan will be able to defend its oil assets from Russia, which surrounds it, is another matter. In Central Asia neighbouring states have raised competing, potentially explosive claims to a very basic resource—water. Turkmenistan's hopes of becoming a 'second Kuwait' have already been reduced by Russian counter-moves. Azerbaijan, Kazakhstan and others which dreamed of establishing independent pipeline connections with Western customers have had to realize that Russia keeps a keen eye on such endeavours.[9] When Azerbaijan in September 1994 concluded a deal with foreign partners (including the Russian company Lukoil) over oil production from the Caspian Sea shelf, the Russian Foreign Ministry protested strongly.[10] Some observers even attribute Russia's armed attempt to

---

[8] A survey of language policies in the various CIS states is provided by Malek, M., 'Sprachenpolitik in der Gemeinschaft Unabhängiger Staaten (GUS)' [Language policy in the Commonwealth of Independent States (CIS)], *Osteuropa*, vol. 44, no. 8 (Aug. 1994), pp. 743–59. See, however, Emelyanov, V., 'Zdes govoryat po-russki' [Russian spoken here], *Moskovskie Novosti*, no. 3 (16–23 Jan. 1994), p. B10, where the author maintains that the Russian language is gaining ground again.

[9] Payin, E., 'Konsolidatsiya Rossii ili vosstanovlenie Soyuza' [Consolidation of Russia or restoration of the union?], *Segodnya*, 22 July 1994, p. 9; and Zagorski, A., 'Die Entwicklungstendenzen der GUS: Von der Differenzierung zur Konsolidierung?' [Trends in the development of the CIS: from differentiation to consolidation?], *Berichte des Bundesinstituts für ostwissenschaftliche und internationale Studien*, no. 24 (1994) (BIOSt: Cologne, 15 Mar. 1994), p. 12.

[10] Lagunina, I., 'MID RF preduprezhdaet: Volga vpadaet v Kaspiyskoe ozero' [The Foreign Ministry of the Russian Federation warns: the Volga flows into the Caspian lake], *Moskovskie Novosti*, no. 42 (25 Sep.–2 Oct. 1994), p. 4.

force Chechnya back into the federation to Russia's economic interests in the oil pipelines leading through that region.[11]

With regard to man-made productive capacities, the heirs of the Soviet Union have had to learn a bitter lesson: socialist economics did not pay sufficient attention to the need for constant renewal and modernization. Hence most industrial plant is in a deplorable condition and will need massive investment before it can enter international competition. More attention was paid in the old days to adequate maintenance of the defence sector. Here the new governments face another obstacle: large-scale conversion to civilian production is needed. Even the Western economies so far have barely made any progress in finding practicable ways of doing this.

The real conflict potential arising from the post-Soviet economic heritage therefore lies in the sudden destruction of the old union-wide arteries of economic circulation. Whether with the system of supporting transfers to the poorer Soviet republics[12] or the largely guaranteed supply and sale of production in socialist enterprises, once deprived of this constant circulation most post-Soviet states are confronted with acute shortages and, as a consequence, the serious prospect of social unrest and instability. Factories unable to operate any longer are causing increasing unemployment.[13]

The growing disparity between the member states of the CIS is reinforced by differences in the approaches to and speed of economic reform. The more advanced states will try to insulate their hard-won progress from more backward forms of trade and cooperation; the less advanced states will resort to protectionism to save what is left of their assets from superior competitors. In July 1992, Kazakhstan's President Nursultan Nazarbaev attributed 80 per cent of the decline in the CIS states' gross national product (GNP)—on average in the range of 20 per cent compared with the previous year—to the disruption of former ties.[14] If, moreover, the rulers in this second group of countries discover that reforming their economies sooner or later also means repairing the ecological disasters recklessly incurred under the old regime, they will, of course, look for culprits and compensation among the more fortunate co-heirs—which means first of all in Russia.

Until now this part of the heritage has not resulted in open violent conflict, but it will give rise to constant tension and irritation among the members of the post-Soviet community for a considerable time to come. The developed market economies of the West will witness this with concern and frustration. Their

---

[11] Schmidt-Häuer, S., 'Räuber und Gendarm' [Cops and robbers], *Die Zeit*, no. 51 (16 Dec. 1994), p. 6.

[12] Orlowski, L.T., 'Indirect transfers in trade among Soviet Union republics: sources, patterns and policy responses in the post-Soviet period', *Europe–Asia Studies*, vol. 45, no. 6 (1993), pp. 1001–24.

[13] On employment in the Russian defence industry, see Sköns, E. and Gonchar, Ks., 'Arms production', *SIPRI Yearbook 1995: Armaments, Disarmament and International Security* (Oxford University Press: Oxford, 1995), pp. 472–76.

[14] Quoted from Clement, H., *Die Neugestaltung der wirtschaftlichen Beziehungen zwischen der Republiken der GUS* [Economic relations between the republics of the CIS], Working Paper no. 157 (Osteuropa-Institut: Munich, 1992), p. 66. The author also cites another, slightly reduced estimate by the Russian Industrialists' Union, amounting to 60%.

efforts to support economic transformation will have a natural tendency to prefer the more progressive recipients—although even there voices of discontent with the insufficient quantity or with misguided concepts of Western support are gaining ground.[15] By the same token they will contribute to a widening of the gap between the front-runners and the tail-enders.

The fate of military power

In assessing the military power heritage of the Soviet Union, the ambivalent value of that formidable military arsenal must be stressed from the outset. Once the tenets of world revolution had lost their attraction, the USSR's superpower status came to be based almost exclusively on its military potential, and it increasingly lacked the other essential criteria which make for a superpower in the full sense of the term. Nor could the USSR influence the rest of the world by its economic achievements: after earlier attempts to support the decolonized young states in the Third World, Soviet leaders had to tell their partners that they had better look for Western support and models.[16] It did not have a cultural influence comparable to the all-permeating diffusion of American civilization. In trying to keep in shape at least the military foundation of its 'parity' with the other superpower, the USSR got deeper and deeper into trouble, before Mikhail Gorbachev, his adviser Alexander Yakovlev and Foreign Minister Eduard Shevardnadze attempted to stem the tide when they announced a foreign policy of 'new thinking'.

This may be one reason why the post-Soviet successor states were initially not so keen to divide that rather dubious military part of the heritage evenly. Some observers have noted with a tinge of surprise and criticism how quickly Russia, despite its internationally recognized position as the main successor of the Soviet Union, contented itself with the other CIS states having jurisdiction over the parts of the Soviet conventional forces located on their territories.[17]

On closer inspection, such Russian magnanimity (or carelessness) did not change the balance in favour of the other successor states. With the partial exception of Ukraine, all the other CIS members remain militarily weak and can afford to spend only modest shares of their budgets on defence.[18] They seem to have decided in favour of other priorities and treated their shares in the military heritage with neglect. As is seen below, such reluctance has its price.

---

[15] Karaganov, S. A. et al., *Whither Western Aid to Russia? A Russian View of Western Support* (Bertelsmann Foundation: Gütersloh, 1994); and Sidorov, M., 'A bez deneg zhizn plokhaya' [Life is bad without money], *Moskovskie Novosti*, no. 27 (3–10 July 1994), p. 27.

[16] At an international conference of communist parties, workers' parties and liberation movements, Boris Ponomarev, who was responsible for the international communist movement at the Central Committee of the Communist Party of the Soviet Union, was attacked by Third World radicals for the Soviet Union's insufficient revolutionary solidarity. Kridl-Valkenier, E., *The Soviet Union and the Third World: An Economic Bind* (Praeger: New York, 1983), pp. 137–39.

[17] Karaganov, S. A., *Russia: The State of Reforms. Study Report of the Institute of Europe* (Bertelsmann Foundation: Gütersloh, 1993), pp. 36–37.

[18] See in particular Allison, R., International Institute for Strategic Studies, *Military Forces in the Soviet Successor States*, Adelphi Paper no. 280 (Brassey's: Oxford, Oct. 1993).

When threatened by external or domestic enemies, these states—as Georgia and Tajikistan have demonstrated already—have to rely on Russia's support. Even the Ukrainian leaders, after initial serious differences with Russia over the allegiance of former Soviet officers stationed on Ukrainian territory or over the fate of the Black Sea Fleet, seem ready by now to reduce Ukrainian aspirations to become a second conventional military power in the region.

Ukraine's hesitation to give in to combined pressure by Russia and the USA to forgo its nuclear arsenal was probably conditioned by factors other than pure defence motives. Ukrainian politicians had viewed the nuclear weapons on their soil as bargaining-counters and preferred to use them to attract the world's (negative) attention rather than disappearing from the international headlines. Continued possession appeared to be a means to attract Western support against renewed Russian dominance. In addition Ukraine cherished expectations of extracting a good price from Western governments for the eventual decision to dismantle its nuclear arsenal.

Despite the general devaluation of military power immediately after the rupture of the Soviet Union, the trends are now once again pointing in the opposite direction. Above all in Russia the president and the government cannot afford to disregard the interests and demands of the military leaders. Since the dramatic events of 3–4 October 1993, when after some hours of intense prodding the military decided to support the president against his enemies and to crush the rebellion, the opinions of the defence establishment influence Moscow's foreign policy visibly. A good example is provided by the discussions among representatives of the Russian foreign policy élite on the subject of the enlargement of NATO eastward. Hardly anyone has dared to call the military's hostility to such a prospect just what it is—'old thinking'.[19]

Given that peacekeeping or peacemaking[20] in the post-Soviet space is becoming an ever more important topic on the agenda of Russian decision makers and their counterparts in the other CIS states, it is to be expected that energy and resources urgently needed for civil transformation will again be diverted for military purposes. The outside world, and first of all the Europeans, will have to deal with partners bent on promoting national interests, influence, prestige and security primarily by relying on military power.

---

[19] Three dissenting opinions deserve mention: Baranovsky, V., 'Vneshnepoliticheskaya pobeda' [A foreign policy victory], *Nezavisimaya Gazeta*, 8 Dec. 1993, p. 4; Blagovolin, S., 'Est li v etom podkhode mesto dlya Rossii?' [Is there room for Russia on this march?], *Novoe Vremya*, no. 7 (Feb. 1994), pp. 26–28 (for the gist of his argument, see *International Herald Tribune*, 8 July 1994, p. 7); and Trenin, D., 'Budet li NATO rasshiryatsya na vostok?' [Will NATO expand to the east?], *Novoe Vremya*, no. 43 (Oct. 1994), pp. 18–20.

[20] Russian political parlance does not distinguish between 'peacekeeping' and 'peace enforcement': *mirotvorchestvo*—literally, peace creation—is the word for both. In this book *mirotvorchestvo* is translated by 'peacekeeping' except where the context clearly indicates otherwise. See also section IV of this chapter.

III. Organization of the post-Soviet geopolitical space

The CIS: vehicle of Eurasian integration?

When on 8 December 1991 the presidents of Belarus, Russia and Ukraine announced their decision to terminate the USSR's existence and found the Commonwealth of Independent States, it looked for a few days as if they were following Alexander Solzhenitsyn's advice to form an exclusive triangle without the non-Slav parts of the empire.[21] Less than two weeks later, the top representatives of 11 former Soviet republics met in Alma Ata (Almaty) and agreed to participate in the CIS:[22] only Georgia did not attend, and the three Baltic states did not regard themselves as former Soviet republics. Sceptics expected the CIS to be nothing but a device for a 'civilized divorce' of partners bent on seeking a better future as independent sovereign states free from the fetters of an empire or a union.

More than four years have passed and the CIS is still alive. If the Slav triangle might have been expected to form the nucleus, actual developments have taken a different direction: Kazakhstan became Russia's initial main partner. These two states together with Armenia, Kyrgyzstan, Tajikistan, Uzbekistan and (initially with less enthusiasm) Belarus made up the core group of the emerging CIS. Distinctly more cautious and reluctant were the attitudes of Azerbaijan, Moldova, Ukraine and Turkmenistan. The former three distrusted Russia; Turkmenistan stayed aloof because its leaders believed that their huge natural gas reserves would open the road to independent affluence for their nation. Georgia under the late President Zviad Gamsakhurdia took a position of almost total abstention, only exceptionally mitigated by the sending of observers.

This prevalence of non-European partners for Russia gave the CIS from the start a certain Eurasian context, reinforced by developments in East–Central Europe, which contributed to a further geopolitical separation of Russia from the rest of Europe. Western and East–Central Europe took a positive view of such a CIS, since it meant that Russia had to devote its attention to the south and the east, forming together with the southern member states a bastion against real (or imagined) threats emanating from Islamic fundamentalism. From a Russian perspective, in particular for those in the democratic camp who were yearning for a 'return to Europe', this new organization of the post-Soviet space must have been less attractive.[23] Further misgivings were caused by the discrepancy between growing Russian nostalgia for the restoration of the ties binding the various parts of the former empire together and the glaring inef-

---

[21] Solzhenitsyn, A., 'Kak nam obustroit Rossiyu: Posilnye soobrazheniya' [How can we build Russia? Some adequate considerations], *Literaturnaya Gazeta*, no. 38 (18 Sep. 1990), supplement, pp. 3–6.

[22] See the founding documents in *Diplomaticheskiy Vestnik*, no. 1 (15 Jan. 1992), pp. 3–10.

[23] Seen from this angle, therefore, it seems surprising that Russian democrats objected so vehemently to plans for NATO enlargement eastward, which after all would bring democratic Europe closer. Royen, C., 'Rozszerzanie UE i NATO oraz zrastanie sie Europy' [The extension of the EU and NATO and the coalescence of Europe], *Polska w Europie*, no. 13 (Jan. 1994), pp. 77–85 (*83*).

ficiency of the CIS. The mass of resolutions, agreements and treaties produced at the frequent CIS summit meetings stood in stark contrast to action to implement them. Advocates of thorough democratic and economic transformation in Russia regarded its partnership with regimes which showed no similar intentions as downright detrimental to Russia's progress.

Gradually most of the original abstainers came to realize that their hopes for independent affluence were illusory. Since Russia had applied various economic and military forms of pressure, including the encouragement of opposition and separatist forces (as in Azerbaijan and Georgia),[24] by the end of 1993 the CIS comprised all the former Soviet Republics except for the Baltic states. Moreover, the results of the presidential election in Ukraine in June 1994 appeared to indicate that its previously mostly empty chair at CIS summit meetings was also finally to be occupied permanently.

Earlier assumptions that the end of the CIS was imminent[25] were superseded by a flurry of discussions and proposals focusing on the future political shaping of the post-Soviet geopolitical space. Officially the main emphasis was placed on improving CIS structures, above all by the development of an economic union in accordance with the treaty signed in Moscow at the CIS summit meeting in September 1993[26] and by strengthening collective peacemaking efforts.[27] Kazakhstan's President Nazarbaev gained the headlines in March 1994 when he ventured the idea of a 'Eurasian Union' (*Evraziyskiy Soyuz*).[28] Similar initiatives followed from Sergey Shakhray, the leader of the Party for Russian Unity and Accord, who proposed a 'Eurasian Confederation',[29] and from a group around Arkadiy Volskiy, a prominent spokesman of conservative industrialists, which suggested a 'Eurasian Community' (*Evraziyskoe Soobshchestvo*).[30]

For the purposes of the present book, the concrete contents of those proposals or their reception in Russia and the other CIS member states[31] are less important than the ensuing more basic debates in Russia, which can be framed into three questions. Should Russia engage in the reintegration of the former Soviet Union? If so should reintegration encompass all CIS members or only a narrow core group? Should it be based on bilateral arrangements between Russia and the individual CIS countries?[32] Finally, will Russia's objective interests be better served by concentrating on its own domestic transformation before real

---

[24] Zagorski (note 9), p. 20, n. 16.

[25] Among many others, see Zagorski, A., 'Sodruzhestvo, god spustya' [Commonwealth, one year later], *Mezhdunarodnaya Zhizn*, no. 2 (Feb. 1993), pp. 47–56.

[26] For the text, see *Diplomaticheskiy Vestnik*, nos 19–20 (Oct. 1993), pp. 36–41.

[27] Mentioned in the Communiqué of the summit meeting. *Diplomaticheskiy Vestnik* (note 26), p. 33.

[28] The text of a preliminary draft was published in *Nezavisimaya Gazeta*, 8 June 1994, pp. 1–3.

[29] *Nezavisimaya Gazeta*, 5 Apr. 1994, p. 3; and *Moskovskie Novosti*, no. 14 (3–10 Apr. 1994), pp. A6/A7.

[30] *Segodnya*, 21 June 1994, p. 2.

[31] Some expressions of approval of Nazarbaev's proposal may have been motivated by tactics, not by ultimate identity of goals.

[32] The President of Belarus, Alexander Lukashenko, has emerged as the most ardent supporter of *rapprochement* with Russia, although initially on a bilateral basis rather than within a CIS framework.

integration with similarly reformed partners, based on a network of new ties between members of a democratic civil society and participants in fully developed market relations, can be begun?

Russian opinion

The predominant interest of the rest of Europe both in the success of peaceful systemic transformation in Russia and in the political stability of the entire Eurasian space clearly contains some mutually contradictory elements. The second goal—political stability—would seem to imply acceptance of Russian hegemony[33] as long as that means that Russia is preoccupied with Eurasia; the former would stress the priority of domestic reform in Russia and necessarily imply a certain degree of neglect for the conflict-ridden zones in the CIS.

It was only natural that a broad consensus emerged among Russian politicians, their advisers from various research institutes and some prominent opinion formers in the media on the need to strengthen Russia's power and influence in the CIS and possibly even beyond. The general common denominator or the vehicle of that consensus is professed concern for the fate of the 25 million Russians living on former Soviet territory under foreign rule.[34] A more specific concern emanates from the practical problems caused by the increasing numbers (estimates vary widely between one and six million[35]) of Russians returning to the Russian Federation and requiring housing, employment and social services.

This broad consensus has taken some of the heat out of earlier accusations directed at Russia's former Foreign Minister, Andrey Kozyrev, blaming him for disregarding Russia's essential interests in the remaining parts of the former Soviet Union.[36] At any rate, some considerable time before the radical populist Vladimir Zhirinovsky alarmed the political establishment with his triumph at the elections of December 1993, Kozyrev and President Yeltsin himself[37] had

---

[33] For a sardonic Russian commentary, see Shchipanov, M., 'Zapad, kak vsegda, proslushaet i promolchit' [The West as always listens and is silent], *Kuranty*, 6 July 1994, p. 4.

[34] For a breakdown of the figures, see *Moskovskaya Pravda*, 20 July 1994, p. 2.

[35] This figure was given by Dmitriy Rogozin, Chairman of the Executive Committee of the Congress of Russian Communities, during a discussion reported in *Trud*, 9 July 1994, p. 1. For a general overview, see Klatt, M., 'Russia's diaspora in the "near abroad"', Radio Free Europe/Radio Liberty (hereafter RFE/RL), *RFE/RL Research Report*, vol. 3, no. 32 (19 Aug. 1994), pp. 33–44.

[36] See, e.g., widely echoed criticism contained in the report of the Council of Foreign and Defence Policy, which brought together a considerable part of the intellectual foreign policy élites in Moscow, in *Nezavisimaya Gazeta*, 19 Aug. 1992, pp. 4–5. However, unnoticed in Western capitals, as early as Feb. 1992 Kozyrev had distanced himself from Gorbachev's and Shevardnadze's foreign policy almost literally in the same terms as were used by his opponents a little later, when they spoke of the 'romantic' conduct of Russia's international relations and a 'rosy' perception of the West having led to neglect of the human rights of Russians in the post-Soviet neighbourhood. See Kozyrev's speech at a conference in Moscow on the 'Transformed Russia in a new world' in *Diplomaticheskiy Vestnik*, no. 6 (31 Mar. 1992), pp. 33–36. Thus the attacks on Kozyrev may be partly explained less by objective differences than by personal ambition and competition for influence.

[37] On 28 Feb. 1993 Yeltsin declared at a plenary meeting of the moderate opposition alliance Civic Union: 'The moment has come when international organizations, among them the UNO, should provide Russia with special prerogatives [*osobye polnomochiya*] as guarantor of peace and stability in the region

already begun to promulgate and practise a tough attitude on these issues. The claim that such concerns are shared and even required by the Russian public appears rather dubious. Two respected experts[38] have produced the results of separate public opinion polls which showed a marked decline of general interest in developments elsewhere in the CIS. While the 'man in the street' still professes a general desire for peace and tranquillity in Russia's neighbourhood, he is preoccupied with securing the economic survival of his family and, especially among the younger generation, with discovering the new opportunities offered by private business.

A link between this more pragmatic attitude on the part of society in general and the political élites may be discerned. Some camps[39] have given hints and statements in favour of strong integrative ties only within the 'Slav triangle'.[40] Kazakhstan is often mentioned as a fourth component, but on closer examination there appears to be a basic distrust of its titular nation and its Islamic cultural allegiance.[41] With regard to the remaining eight CIS states, a philosophy of 'enlightened egoism' and of 'leadership instead of direct control' recommends reliance on bilateral modes of promoting Russian interests.[42] This does not exclude intensive cooperation and support, for example, for Armenia and Georgia, since Russia is interested in containing unrest in the Muslim areas on its southern borders in the northern Caucasus and in preventing potential Turkish trouble-making there.[43] Official explanations for Russia's armed intervention in Chechnya also contained references to the dangers of Muslim fundamentalism.

Absent on both levels of the discussion is any reflection on Russia's historic responsibility for the fate of the smaller nations under the previous empires. The instinctive reaction to such suggestions is—understandably—recollections that for the maintenance of the tsarist and, much more so, the Soviet empire

---

of the former [Soviet] Union'. Quoted from RFE/RL Research Institute, *Russia & CIS Today, TV & Radio Monitoring*, no. 153 (1 Mar. 1993), p. 9.

[38] Payin (note 9); and Klyamkin, I., 'Integratsiya nachinaetsya "snizu"' [Integration starts 'from below'], *Delo*, no. 30 (July 1994), pp. 1–2.

[39] See, e.g., the second report of the Council of Foreign and Defence Policy (note 36) in *Nezavisimaya Gazeta*, 27 May 1994, pp. 4–5; an interview with Sergey Shakhray in *Obshchaya Gazeta*, no. 14 (8–14 Apr. 1994), p. 1; Arbatov, A., 'Realnaya integratsiya: s kem i kakaya?' [Real integration: with whom and what sort?], *Nezavisimaya Gazeta*, 24 June 1994, pp. 1–2; and Stankevich, S., 'Segodnya v otnosheniyakh mezhdu Rossiey, Ukrainoy i Belorussiey, kak nikogda, neobkhodimo iskrennee zhelanie sotrudnichat' [A genuine will to work together is essential as never before in relations between Russia, Ukraine and Belarus], *Delovoy Mir*, 20 July 1994, p. 1.

[40] Advocates of the primacy of the 'Slav triangle' sometimes overlook the fact that Russia itself has more Muslim citizens than most Arab countries. The Duma Committee on CIS Affairs and Links with Compatriots has correctly drawn attention to this in a report on the CIS's prospects. *Nezavisimaya Gazeta*, 13 July 1994, p. 3.

[41] Arbatov (note 39). An extensive critical assessment of Kazakhstan is also given in Kurginyan, S., 'Soderzhanie novogo integratsionizma: modeli evraziyskogo sodruzhestva i ikh sootvetstvie strategicheskim interesam Rossii' [The content of a new integrationism: models of a Eurasian commonwealth and how they correspond to Russia's strategic interests], *Nezavisimaya Gazeta*, 7 July 1994, p. 5.

[42] See sections 3.6 and 3.7 of the second report of the Council of Foreign and Defence Policy (note 39).

[43] Arbatov (note 39). In this context see also the plea for incorporation of Armenia into the Russian Federation by two Armenian authors. Ter-Mkrtchyan, A. and Ter-Mkrtchyan, D., 'Posledniy shans Armenii' [Armenia's last chance], *Vek*, no. 25 (1–6 July 1994), p. 10.

Russians had to pay a very high price in economic subsidies, war casualties and administrative neglect of their own needs. The reformist opponents of reintegration seem also to strike a sympathetic cord in Russian society.[44] Their main arguments amount to the following. First, as long as Russia's government, legislators and other segments of the political structures have to deal with pseudo-democratic counterparts and unreformed economies in the partner states, Russia's own stabilization of pluralist democracy and economic reform will be constantly hampered. Critics of reintegration point to Estonia's success with economic transformation and Lithuania's laggard performance, explaining the difference partly by the decision of the former to cut the umbilical cord with the former Soviet Union and the latter's hesitation to take such a drastic step. Second, reintegration will inevitably draw Russia into the role of pacifier. This in turn will produce numerous situations where the distinction between democrats and the adherents of Great Russian neo-imperialism becomes blurred.

While the anti-reintegrationists may easily be accused by reintegrationists of being unpatriotic and neglecting their unfortunate compatriots beyond the borders of Russia, the truth is different. While critical of reintegrationist trends, they suggest thoughtful practical measures for supporting compatriots in the former Soviet Union;[45] some of these recommendations were enacted in August 1994 by presidential decree and subsequently as a government programme.[46] Kyrgyzstan's sensible attempts to reduce the high rate of Russian emigration confirms the anti-reintegrationists' result-oriented approach[47] as compared with the declaratory patriotism of some of the ardent defenders of Russia's Cause.

Europe, Russia and Eurasia

Viewing these debates and developments from Western and East–Central Europe, the question occurs whether the prevailing centrist camp of *derzhavniki*, the proponents of great-power status for Russia in the region and in the world, is not subconsciously looking for an escape from failures on the domestic front of transformation. The most frequent justification of this stance is societal pressure and the danger that real chauvinist forces might exploit the

---

[44] Zagorski (note 9); Oleshchuk, Yu., 'Novaya Rossiya i integratsionnye tendentsii v SNG' [The new Russia and integrationist tendencies in the CIS], *Mirovaya Ekonomika i Mezhdunarodnye Otnosheniya*, no. 4 (Apr. 1994), pp. 83–92; Borko, Yu., 'Ideya slishkom khorosha, chtoby toropitsa eyo isportit: razmyshleniya o Evraziyskom Soyuze' [Too good an idea to be ruined by hurrying: thoughts on a Eurasian Union], *Obshchaya Gazeta*, no. 15 (15–21 Apr. 1994), p. 7; Shelov-Kovedyaev, F., 'Staraya model dlya novogo soyuza' [An old model for a new union], *Moskovskie Novosti*, no. 26 (26 June–3 July 1994), p. A8; and Payin (note 9). A stimulating variant is represented by Nikonov, V., at that time Chairman of the Duma Subcommittee on International Security and Arms Control, '"Rossiyskiy neo-gollizm": novaya paradigma vneshney politiki' [Russian neogaullism: a new paradigm in foreign policy], *Nezavisimaya Gazeta*, 24 May 1994, p. 5.

[45] See the report on the work of a team under Emil Payin, member of the Russian President's Advisory Council and Director of the Research Department in the Analytical Centre of the Russian President. *Izvestiya*, 22 July 1994, pp. 1–2.

[46] Decision by the Government of the Russian Federation on 'Measures of support for compatriots abroad', adopted on 31 Aug. 1994: text in *Diplomaticheskiy Vestnik*, no. 19–20 (Oct. 1994), pp. 38–42.

[47] Kliamkin (note 38).

neglected aspirations of the Russian people. This argument is to a great extent self-serving. Following the logic of those who advocate priority for domestic reforms, a different picture emerges: the more the individual member of Russian society gains personal confidence in the permanency of democratic processes and his own role in them, and the more he sees his and his children's economic future secured by working in modern competitive enterprises, the less chance will populist demagogues have to find an audience with chauvinist, neo-imperialist slogans.

As a first sign of improvement among the Russian political mainstream, one verbal, at first glance a minimal, change can be seen in the use of the term 'near abroad' (*blizhnee zarubezhe*). This term, especially when used by official spokesmen and in official documents, has given rise to suspicions that Russia does not regard the other post-Soviet countries as 'normal foreign states' of the 'far abroad'.[48] Gradually, however, a less ambivalent differentiation between the 'old abroad' and the 'new abroad' is gaining ground. This may help to clarify another ominous ambivalence in speeches of Russian political leaders calling for a more forthright pursuit of national interests in 'traditional spheres of Russian influence'. Not only the Baltic peoples but also the Poles had begun to ask whether their country was going to be included in that sphere once again.

An honest appraisal of West European attitudes towards the developments in Russia and in the CIS will have to admit an equal, possibly even more fundamental, ambivalence. Original illusions that the demise of communism without bloodshed had ushered in the healing forces of democracy and free enterprise quickly proved to have been at best naïve. By now, politicians and voters in the Western democracies are fully aware of the need for massive material support and personal engagement in assisting the post-communist states and societies in systemic transformation and for major concessions to enable the young democracies to earn their living by exports to Western markets.

However, awareness may not be matched by action. In addition, support for Russia's preferred concentration on its domestic transformation raises immediately the next three serious questions:

1. Who is taking care of the enormous needs of the other CIS states such as Ukraine? Expectations that Turkey would shoulder a large part of that burden on the southern perimeter of the CIS were viewed with suspicion in Russia. Neither expectations nor suspicions took into account the limited capacity of Turkey to step in where others preferred to stay behind.

2. Can intensification of the integration of the European Union (EU) in accordance with the 1992 Maastricht Treaty and its eventual extension to the

---

[48] When the Deputy Foreign Minister at the time, Vitaliy Churkin, was questioned on this subject at a press conference in Jan. 1994, he conceded in his reply that there was a problem. *Diplomaticheskiy Vestnik*, nos 3–4 (Feb. 1994), p. 34. His assurance, however, that official language had already abandoned the term was still not quite borne out by the facts at that time.

eastern part of Central Europe be reconciled with the EU's engagement and partnership with Russia and the CIS?[49]

3. Last but not least, who in Europe is ready to assume an active role in the prevention or the suppression of open conflicts in the post-Soviet space? Again, Russian interlocutors occasionally like to chide the West for its lack of engagement; yet the impression persists that, if Western governments once began to consider a more active role in post-Soviet conflict resolution, the Russian side would be most uneasy over such intrusion on its turf.[50] In this context it is indicative that Russia suspected the Minsk Group of the Conference on Security and Co-operation in Europe (CSCE)[51] of being merely a tool in the hands of Western powers, including Turkey, which wished to control Russia's actions in the CIS;[52] and, although the relevant resolution adopted at the CSCE summit meeting in Budapest in December 1994 envisaged future multilateral peacekeeping operations in Nagorno-Karabakh, Russia seems still to doubt the efficacy of such 'foreign involvement' in conflicts within the CIS area.

IV. Approaches to the resolution of post-Soviet conflicts

Peaceful prevention and settlement of conflicts

Under normal conditions in the life of states and societies tensions and conflicts may erupt. Before they disturb internal peace and stability fatally, the time-honoured principle of the state's monopoly of force steps in: an efficient police force and an established rule of law set strict limits to turmoil and violence. In functioning pluralist democracies society possesses an additional instrument in the various forms of public dialogue and the habitual respect for compromise solutions. Modern labour conflicts and their settlement provide just one example.

In the post-Soviet states, practically all these prerequisites are lacking or exist, at best, in a rudimentary form. In a 'lawless empire'[53] individuals as well as groups fall back on pursuing their interests without or against the law and the basic method of settling disputes and conflicts, whether on the domestic scene or in relations between states, by negotiations and mediation first of all is viewed by the warring factions as unsuitable. The same is true for forms of settlement based on compulsion by judicial institutions. The only remaining

---

[49] Rühle, M., 'Europa bleibt doch geteilt' [Europe remains divided], *Rheinischer Merkur*, no. 32 (12 Aug. 1994), p. 7.

[50] In this context, see Karaganov, S., '"Rossiyskiy imperializm": ugrozy mnimye i realnye' ["Russian imperialism": threats imaginary and real], *Segodnya*, 3 Aug. 1994, p. 3.

[51] The Minsk Group was set up in Mar. 1992 to monitor the situation in Nagorno-Karabakh. The member countries are at the time of writing (Dec. 1995) Belarus, Finland, France, Germany, Hungary, Italy, Russia, Sweden, Switzerland, Turkey and the USA, plus Armenia and Azerbaijan.

[52] See, e.g., the analysis by Special Ambassador V. Kazimirov, 'Rossiya i "minskaya gruppa" SBSE' [Russia and the Minsk Group of the CSCE], *Segodnya*, 14 Oct. 1994, p. 3; see also Podlesniy, P., 'Komu byt mirotvortsem v SNG?' [Who should be peace-creator in the CIS?], *Moskovskie Novosti*, no. 61 (4–11 Dec. 1994), p. 5.

[53] Schmidt-Häuer (note 6).

peaceful tool, which may be a sufficient deterrent from violence, is economic pressure and sanctions applied by the government or by the stronger party.

This deficiency in the arsenal of peaceful conflict resolution was and still is largely responsible for the recurrent internal crises within the Russian Federation and threatens to lead to the falling apart of Russia. Among the members of the CIS the situation looks identical or rather worse: the CIS has a Statute[54] and numerous other legal documents designed to regulate mutual relations; the Statute even stipulates a CIS Economic Court, whereas other special agreements include arbitration. Their relevance, however, is close to nil. The decisive—indeed, the only—difference which prevents the outbreak of *bellum omnium erga omnes* is connected with Russia's superior economic and military power. Since economic instruments have proved to be not always available or effective, conflict resolution in the CIS necessarily relies to a considerable extent on methods other than peaceful ones.

Armed conflict resolution in the CIS

Peacekeeping and peacemaking

In evaluating the CIS's record of conflict resolution by armed force, three initial considerations must be borne in mind.

In the first place, before 1992 neither the Soviet Union nor the constituent republics had gained practical experience of international peacekeeping. As one Russian author correctly points out,[55] Soviet participation in UN peacekeeping activities was minimal and mostly symbolic.

Second, and still more fundamental, the 'classic' UN peacekeeping model was developed during four decades under global conditions of relative stability, guaranteed by the stalemate between the two blocs and systems. Both blocs were able to limit the resort to arms in their spheres of influence. Where armed conflicts nevertheless broke out, as a rule—except for the cases of the German Democratic Republic (GDR) in 1953, Hungary in 1956 and Czechoslovakia in 1968—they involved either poor countries in the far-away Third World or warring factions too weak to resist a UN resolution providing for a settlement and the stationing of 'blue helmets'. Now, however, it is in the leading power of one of the former blocs that armed conflict is erupting, and no superior external force is readily available to suggest an armistice to be secured by a mere 'keeping' of the induced peace. Instead, the end of fighting has to be enforced; peace has to be made, or, as the term preferred by Russian officials and authors, *mirotvorchestvo*, suggests, be 'created'.[56]

---

[54] Adopted originally in Minsk on 22 Jan. 1993 by only 7 member states. For the text, see *Diplomaticheskiy Vestnik*, no. 9–10 (May 1993), pp. 31–38.

[55] Trenin, D., 'Russians as peacemakers', *Internationale Politik und Gesellschaft*, no. 3 (1994), pp. 257–66; and Trenin, D., 'Russia', ed. T. Findlay, *Challenges for the New Peacekeepers*, SIPRI Research Report no. 12 (Oxford University Press: Oxford, 1996), pp. 68–84.

[56] See note 20.

This terminology occurs frequently where the context would suggest the word for 'peacekeeping'—*podderzhanie mira*. This imprecision does not betray a tendency to violate international law. The UN Charter itself does not use the word 'peacekeeping': Chapter VII speaks of 'measures to maintain or to restore peace and security', if necessary by armed force. Secretary-General Boutros Boutros-Ghali in his Agenda for Peace report to the Security Council defined four modes of UN-guided activities in securing world peace: preventive diplomacy; peacemaking; peacekeeping; and post-conflict peace-building.[57]

A different picture emerges of the rules and standards of the Organization for Security and Co-operation in Europe (OSCE).[58] Because of its peculiar genesis, the CSCE engaged exclusively in peaceful conflict resolution similar to that described in Chapter VI of the UN Charter until the end of the division of Europe into two competing blocs. While its member states recognized in Helsinki in 1992 that they had to do more, they still refrained from going beyond peacekeeping.[59]

The fact that the 'blue helmets' are bound by the existing rules to refrain from combat and to preserve strict impartiality, whatever crimes or attacks may be perpetrated by one or more warring factions, will reduce public support for peacekeeping. Experts are therefore at present deliberating over new, more 'robust' modes of peacekeeping, where impartiality would no longer amount to tolerance of large-scale violations of human rights.[60]

From this the third consideration follows. After more than 40 years of peace most European governments and societies are not ready to go to war unless they themselves feel directly threatened. They are certainly worried about potential spillovers in the form of waves of refugees fleeing their war-ravaged countries or ecological disasters resulting from the accidental or intentional destruction of nuclear power plants in the course of hostilities. These nightmares, however, are not sufficient to produce the resolve to send the boys into actual battle. Instead politicians and ordinary citizens alike watch reports from the former Yugoslavia and from parts of the former Soviet Union on their television screens with horror and disbelief. This attitude in turn will reinforce Russian scepticism with regard to Western participation in CIS peacekeeping and confirm Russian resolve to practise more adequate and flexible 'peace creation'.

---

[57] UN, An Agenda for Peace: Preventive Diplomacy, Peacemaking and Peacekeeping, Report of the Secretary-General, UN document A/47/277, S/24111, 17 June 1992.

[58] On 1 Jan. 1995 the CSCE became the OSCE.

[59] See excerpts from the Helsinki Summit Declaration and section III, paras 17–38, of the Helsinki Decisions in *SIPRI Yearbook 1993: World Armaments and Disarmament* (Oxford University Press: Oxford, 1993), pp. 190–209.

[60] Kühne, W. (ed.), *Blauhelme in einer turbulenten Welt: Beiträge internationaler Experten zur Fortentwicklung des Völkerrechts und der Vereinten Nationen* [Blue helmets in a turbulent world: contributions by international experts to the development of international law and of the United Nations], (Nomos: Baden-Baden, 1993). Allison, R., Western European Union, Institute for Security Studies, *Peacekeeping in the Soviet Successor States*, Chaillot Paper no. 18 (ISS: Paris, Nov. 1994) applies a similar qualified approach to Russian peacekeeping in the CIS.

Russia's role in CIS conflicts: genuine and ambivalent

When the leaders of the Russian Federation met their colleagues from the other CIS states to draft the rules governing the new confederation, they probably not only shared that general European abhorrence of war. They might also have been suffering still from fresh memories of the war in Afghanistan. The Russian representatives encountered a certain distrust among their partners. In any case, one of the first common attempts to organize the future use of the inherited military power resulted in an Agreement on Military Observer and Collective Peacekeeping Groups in the CIS, adopted in Kiev on 20 March 1992.[61] The agreement defined this CIS peacekeeping in accordance with UN rules and the new CSCE standards under preparation by declaring peacekeeping to be applicable only where the parties to the conflict have given prior consent and have already reached an understanding on ending all hostilities. Another essential condition excluded the peacekeeping groups from combat.

Reality, however, soon dictated a different approach.[62] It was not possible to wait for the mechanisms under the agreement to take shape and be implemented: events in South Ossetia and the Trans-Dniester region required urgent action. Reportedly the governments in Georgia and Moldova would have preferred the involvement of the UN or the CSCE,[63] but it was obvious that only Russia was ready and able to take the lead without delay. While the formal basis for the ensuing military actions was contained in bilateral agreements with both governments, in the first case the trilateral forces, comprising Russian, Georgian and South Ossetian units, were none the less clearly dominated by superior Russian contingents. In the case of the Trans-Dniester region, the force structure was even more simple: the units of the former Soviet 14th Army, still stationed in the area, were assigned to suppress hostilities. The troops were able to achieve success in both cases. Clearly, however, Russia was not an impartial actor, nor could those forces possibly act in accordance with the peacekeeping rules as defined in the CIS agreement of March 1992.

The next case where Russia saw a necessity to become actively involved was the conflict between Georgia and secessionist Abkhazia in 1992–93. Here, however, the facts suggest a serious ambivalence in Russia's engagement. Whether on orders from Moscow or on their own initiative, local Russian commanders in the first phase of the conflict supported the Abkhazians, enabling them to defeat the Georgian forces and drive them out of Abkhazia. That defeat motivated the Georgian President, Eduard Shevardnadze, to signal his country's readiness to join the CIS in exchange for Russia's help in stabilizing the military situation. Admittedly, the available data are too incomplete to

---

[61] Text in *Diplomaticheskiy Vestnik*, no. 7 (15 Apr. 1992), pp. 9–11.

[62] For a more detailed account see Amer, R. *et al.*, 'Major armed conflicts', *SIPRI Yearbook 1993* (note 59), pp. 93–107; and *SIPRI Yearbook 1994* (Oxford University Press: Oxford, 1994), pp. 49–51, 169–203.

[63] Kreikemeyer, A., 'Großmacht auf Bewährung: Rußlands Militär zwischen Friedenssicherung und imperischer Restauration' [Big power on parole: Russia's military between securing peace and imperial restoration], *Blätter für deutsche und internationale Politik*, vol. 39, no. 6 (June 1994), p. 725.

allow an unequivocal conclusion. From this time on, however, Russian peace-making at the very least invited the question whether beyond the sincere interest in peace and the avoidance of bloodshed Moscow had a second motive—the restoration of Russian hegemony in the post-Soviet space.

The fourth case, the war in Tajikistan, superficially seems to refute such nagging doubts. So far this has been the only case of units from third CIS parties (Kazakhstan, Kyrgyzstan and Uzbekistan) taking collective action along with Russia. The four states decided to act in conformity with the March 1992 agreement on collective peacekeeping and with the special declaration on Tajikistan, adopted in Bishkek, the capital of Kyrgyzstan, on 9 October 1992.[64] All four dispatched forces. Yet again, the Russian contingents were vastly superior in quantity and quality, while the agreement supported one side of the conflict, which was essentially between hostile Tajik clans. Increasingly Russian spokesmen, including the president himself,[65] maintained that on Tajikistan's southern border with Afghanistan Russia was ultimately defending its own borders.

Each of these actions can be justified as necessary to end the actual fighting, since no feasible alternative from outside or from within the CIS was available. Despite more recent Russian pressure on its associates in the CIS to increase their participation in collective peacemaking, the practical results remain very modest.[66] At the same time the shortcomings and contradictions in Russia's own practice and theory of peacemaking call for some open discussion.[67] Some shortcomings were probably almost unavoidable, like the initial lack of the experienced professional forces required for a complicated assignment combining military capabilities and political and human sensibilities. Less excusable is the absence of pertinent domestic legislation and of a system of civilian control, although it might be partly explained by the well-known tensions between the executive and legislative branches in Russia. The same is true, with potentially dangerous implications, for the uncontrolled role of Cossack units in the areas along Russia's southern borders in the Caucacus and with Kazakhstan, where they might increasingly prevent peace and provoke armed clashes under the banner of Russian orthodoxy.[68]

More ominous are elements of the accompanying justifications and strategic concepts offered by Russia's political leaders. Official statements suggest that the 'Russian people' demand assertive peacemaking by Russia and will vote for

---

[64] *Diplomaticheskiy Vestnik*, no. 3–4 (Feb. 1993), p. 41.

[65] According to the Russian television news programme Vesti, 26 July 1993, 20.00 hours, Yeltsin stated that this border was de facto Russia's, not Tajikistan's: reported in RFE/RL Research Institute: *Russia & CIS Today, TV & Radio Monitoring*, no. 529 (27 July 1993), p. 6. See also Yeltsin's decree of 27 July 1993 'On measures to regulate the conflict on the Tajik–Afghan border and on general normalization of the situation on the Russian Federation's borders', *Diplomaticheskiy Vestnik*, nos 17–18 (Sep. 1993), pp. 3–4.

[66] Bulavinov, I., 'Generaly ne khotyat byt boevymi' [The generals are not eager to fight], *Kommersant Daily*, 19 July 1994, p. 3.

[67] They are almost all presented by Trenin (note 55: 1994).

[68] For official attempts to regulate the revival of Cossack communities and their use in the protection of Russia's borders, see the interview with V. Shchegortsov, *Krasnaya Zvezda*, 20 Aug. 1994, p. 3.

extremist right- or left-wing parties if it does not come about. Available opinion polls[69] tell a different story, similar to the attitudes mentioned above in the context of reintegration. On the theoretical, conceptual level constant references to the 'laws of geopolitics', which supposedly dictate the avoidance of a 'vacuum' to be entered eventually by hostile external forces, smack of a substitute for earlier schemes, when comparable demands and requirements were deduced from the 'laws of the global class struggle between the imperialist and the socialist camp'. Finally, the broad consensus among the political élites in Moscow that Russia must secure its place in regional and world politics as a respected great power makes for an even more intriguing background.

Europe, of course, might still prefer not to scrutinize this mixed balance and let the Russians with the other nations in the CIS sort out the problem themselves. However, at least two considerations warn against such complacency: (a) if peacekeeping and peacemaking really were to be abused in the interests of Russian great-power ambitions, the post-war order of peace in Europe would suffer a second serious blow, after European incompetence and inactivity in the former Yugoslavia have already undermined its credibility; and (b) Russia's leaders themselves demand recognition of their peacemaking as consonant with the standards of the UN and the OSCE and even call for the outside world to share the burden.

Europe's attitude

Preconditions of active involvement

In trying to meet the challenge of the conflicts afflicting the CIS, and given the ambivalent methods of solving them, Europeans in the western and central part of the continent should start from the following proposition. There is no ready solution, but it is nevertheless important and justified to confront their Russian partners with some critical questions as long as this is done for the sake of an open and constructive dialogue as the prerequisite of cooperation.

First, following the 1994 Budapest summit meeting of the CSCE, Russian decision makers have to clarify among themselves and then inform the West whether they prefer to preserve a monopoly in the post-Soviet space in dealing with armed conflicts or whether they are ready to welcome eventual active participation by Western forces too. Until now, Russian statements on this issue have differed. Former Foreign Minister Kozyrev and others liked to emphasize their readiness to cooperate.[70] Others suggest quite openly or by implication

---

[69] Also reported by Trenin (note 55: 1994). See also Kreikemeyer, A., 'Renaissance of hegemony and spheres of influence: the evolution of the Yeltsin doctrine' and Zagorski, A., 'Russian peace support in the CIS: possibilities and limitations of its internationalization', eds H.-G. Ehrhart, A. Kreikemeyer and A. Zagorski, *Crisis Management in the CIS: Whither Russia?* (Nomos: Baden-Baden, 1995), pp. 93–113, 143–56.

[70] Kozyrev, A., 'Rossiya fakticheski v odinochku neset bremya realnogo mirotvorchestva v konfliktakh po perimetru svoikh granits' [Russia is bearing the burden of real peacemaking virtually alone in conflicts on its borders], *Nezavisimaya Gazeta*, 22 Sep. 1993, p. 1; and Trenin, D., 'International institutions and

that they regard the possibility of Western military units on CIS territory with intense suspicion.[71]

Second, the standards of international law guiding post-Soviet peacemaking must be addressed. The argument, although rarely made explicitly, that the 'internal' borders between the CIS states cannot be treated as long-established is hard to accept. It would not only suggest that recognition of their sovereignty and admission to international organizations such as the CSCE might have been premature acts. It would also ultimately confirm that the Russian distinction between the 'far' and 'near' abroad was not completely unfounded. One Russian author, critical both of the political establishment in Moscow and of the West's passivity, warned in this context of a 'new Yalta', this time separating the CIS from the free part of Europe.[72]

It is, however, equally true that to ignore the obvious differences between the new states and their societies on the one hand and the long-established traditional states on the other will result in illusory assessments of international stability. The original CSCE documents consciously created a very careful balance between the stabilizing twin principles of state sovereignty and territorial integrity on the one hand and the revolutionary principle of self-determination on the other. Hardly anyone in 1975 foresaw that less than 20 years later the explosive capacities of the latter principle would threaten the peace in large parts of Eurasia. In the search for a more adequate solution and to restore the balance at least to some extent, a more evolutionary approach might be appropriate.[73] While it has to be admitted that the classic rules of sovereignty, territorial integrity and non-interference in internal affairs are difficult to apply to the new—some even call them already 'failing'[74]—states, the established states should agree that it is their common responsibility to support the newcomers' progress.

Where the legitimacy of peacekeeping and peacemaking in the CIS is concerned, this would mean that the criteria for meeting OSCE standards as designed by the CSCE foreign ministers at their meeting in Rome on 30 November–1 December 1993[75] do not all have equal value. The most impor-

conflict resolution in the former Soviet Union', Draft paper for the research project of the Italian Instituto Affari Internazionali on 'Security in Europe after the cold war: what role for the international institutions?', presented at the Centre for Higher Defence Studies, Rome, 10–11 Dec. 1993, p. 13.

[71] See remarks by the head of Russia's delegation to the CSCE, Vladimir Shustov, quoted by Crow, S., 'Russia promotes the CIS as an international organization', *RFE/RL Research Report*, no. 11 (18 Mar. 1994), pp. 35–36.

[72] Zagorski, A., 'Kontseptsiya "blizhnego zarubezhya" v rossiyskoy vneshney politike: istochniki, tseli, instrumenty, problemy' [The concept of the "near abroad" in Russia's foreign policy: sources, goals, instruments, problems], *Seminar na Temu: Kontseptsiya "Blizhnego Zarubezhya" vo Vneshney Politike Rossii: Sovmestimost s Obshcheprinyatymi Normami Mezhdunarodnogo Prava* [Seminar on the concept of the 'near abroad' in Russia's foreign policy: its consistency with the generally accepted norms of international law, Bonn, 23–24 June 1994] (Moscow State Institute of International Relations/German–Russian Forum: Moscow, 1995), pp. 4–30.

[73] The problem is also emphasized by Baranovsky, V., 'Evropa: ispytaniya na razryv' [Europe: testing to destruction], *Moskovskie Novosti*, no. 3 (17 Jan. 1993), p. A14.

[74] E.g., Marks, E. and Lewis, W., National Defense University, Institute for National Strategic Studies, *Triage for Failing States*, McNair Paper no. 26 (INSS: Washington, DC, Jan. 1994).

[75] *Atlantic News*, no. 2576 (3 Dec. 1993), p. 2.

tant, central condition legitimizing peacekeeping and peacemaking actions would be the strict observance of *transparency* because it would not only enable other members of the international community to control the methods and the purposes pursued by the peacemaker state: it would also promote mutual confidence and allow third parties to participate in designing negotiable positions and offer active support beyond mere peacekeeping in the classic sense. Such active support may come in the form of financial contributions, and Russian decision makers sometimes appear interested mainly in this aspect of sharing the burden of peacemaking. Much depends, however, on how such financial solidarity can be applied in practice. It would clearly not be acceptable for Russia to come up with a lump sum of expenditure based on unverified figures and demand compensation. Financial burden-sharing, furthermore, should not be viewed as a way to avoid the close cooperation connected with actual Western participation.

The Russian–US bilateral peacekeeping manoeuvres carried out in the autumn of 1994 in Totsk near Orenburg and similar plans involving European partners can be regarded as first steps in the right direction. After decades of mutual suspicion, the experience of practical cooperation between soldiers will hopefully start to replace prejudice with mutual esteem.

Civil conflict prevention and peace-building

Ultimately, peacemaking by using armed force is, if unavoidable, essentially not much more than curing the symptoms of a disease but not the disease itself. Not accidentally, in An Agenda for Peace the components of preventive diplomacy and post-conflict peace-building point to the more basic task—addressing the roots of the conflict. Where governments and their citizens, instead of sending troops into conflict zones, engage in promoting the construction of pluralist civil societies, this should be viewed with respect and gratitude. Dissemination of communal and minority-oriented dialogue or practical instruction in the working of the rule of law, especially on the local level, will yield visible results which encourage imitation elsewhere. Another fertile field for working at the grass roots would be to bring historians together in order to revise school textbooks. The German–Polish experience since the middle of the 1970s could serve as a stimulating model. Some of these ideas may receive heightened attention at the regional tables initiated under the Balladur Plan.[76]

Related activities, amounting to something like a new, much more ambitious but urgently needed Peace Corps, might involve individual citizens and private and non-governmental organizations or institutes, including foundations established by political parties, trade unions and churches. Europe, however, already has an interstate institution, whose public presence in the media is inversely proportional to its record of practical work—the Council of Europe. Closer acquaintance with the Council of Europe's programme brings out a simple but

---

[76] Pact on Stability in Europe, June 1993. The text is reproduced in *SIPRI Yearbook 1994* (note 62), pp. 247–49.

often neglected truth: democracy and peace finally rest more on citizens than on presidents, international treaties and armies. It also makes us aware of another truism: peace and democracy depend not only on taxes paid and inter-governmental aid, but equally on the personal initiative and engagement of individuals.

V. Concluding remarks

With hindsight, it is obvious that neither governments and society in Western Europe nor the rulers and the people in the former communist countries were prepared for the scale of the violence that was to be witnessed in Europe after the end of communism. The expectations of a 'new age of peace' nurtured in November 1990 at the CSCE summit meeting and expressed in the Charter of Paris for a New Europe[77] adopted there have turned out to be illusory. Apart from the Balkans, actual concerns are connected with the post-Soviet space. In order to save the continent for future generations, peace must be restored and consolidated.

The response to this challenge cannot consist only in grand institutional schemes covering the entire area from Vancouver to Vladivostok. Instead, attempts to create conditions of cooperative relations among neighbours and of tolerance for minorities should concentrate on developing solutions for smaller subregions. Once the international community achieves a breakthrough in one concrete case, it is to be hoped that this will encourage other conflicting parties to go down a similar path. Ultimately, however, the most important guarantees against the outbreak of conflicts in the CIS rest with establishing a democratic political culture in its member states.

[77] The text is reproduced in *SIPRI Yearbook 1991: World Armaments and Disarmament* (Oxford University Press: Oxford, 1991), pp. 603–10.

11. Post-Soviet conflicts: new security concerns

Victor Kremeniuk

I. Introduction

When the leaders of Belarus, Russia and Ukraine (the chairman of the Belarussian Supreme Soviet, Stanislav Shushkevich, Russian President Boris Yeltsin and Ukrainian President Leonid Kravchuk) met secretly in Belarus in early December 1991 with the purpose of signing a document which effectively buried the Soviet Union, they were not in a position to think much about the medium- and long-term consequences of their decision. They were sure that without destroying the Soviet Union as it had existed since 1922—with a huge all-Union bureaucracy, armed forces and secret police, all of them under the strict control of the Communist Party—it was impossible to hope for any significant progress in changing Soviet society. This argument was the main one behind their official statement on 9 December 1991.[1] At the same time they hoped that the dismantling of the Union would win them strong support from both democratic and nationalist forces within their respective republics.

At the same time, it is hard to believe that they could not foresee that the process of disintegration in a country as big as the Soviet Union would not go painlessly and without conflict. It was evident that the desire of democratic forces to crush the backbone of the communist regime by dissolving the Soviet Union was accompanied by the intention of strong anti-integrationist nationalist forces to seize the opportunity to take complete independence for their republics. The policy of nationalists, especially of those groups such as the Ukrainian Rukh movement with its radical overtones, was for complete separation and the division of all-Union property and accused Russia of having a hidden blueprint to re-establish control over the territory of the former Russian Empire. As should have been perceived at the time, they sought to use the destructive (as regards the Soviet Union) potential of nationalism with the strong anti-communist momentum of the democratic movements and thus to prevail over Soviet President Mikhail Gorbachev and over those foreign leaders who were against the disintegration of the USSR (first among them US President George Bush).

The existence of such forces as these had to be understood as presaging tough battles over issues surrounding the division of the Soviet heritage, as well as emerging territorial and other disputes. The three leaders understood the urgency of this threat and decided to supplement their decision to dissolve the Soviet Union with the creation of the Commonwealth of Independent States

[1] *Izvestiya*, 10 Dec. 1991, p. 1.

(CIS). The idea of the CIS also created a rosy hope that, while the former Soviet republics would enjoy the benefits of independence, and thus greater internal stability, the CIS would take care of resolving emerging conflicts among them, essentially through emphasizing the advantages of cooperation, as opposed to complete isolation, in security, economic, financial and other issues. Belief in the efficacy of this scheme and a desire to jump on the bandwagon were so strong that shortly after the three presidents' decision to form the CIS, taken on 8 December 1991, eight other former Soviet republics declared their wish to join the new Commonwealth.[2]

Numerous conflicts erupted shortly after December 1991 inside Russia, in other former Soviet republics, and in relations between them. Attempts to create adequate conflict-resolution mechanisms through the organs of the CIS have failed, thereby providing additional evidence that the conflict potential in relations between the former Soviet republics was much stronger than could have been foreseen. A spate of conflicts in the post-Soviet space has become a part of European and Asian reality and has significantly changed the strategic situation.

Two questions emerged as a result of this development. First, to what extent have these conflicts, once the previous order was destroyed, shown that the new states had embarked on a new path of development which could threaten the security interests of the other states in Europe and Asia? Second, and closely related, what type of impact could these conflicts have on both the processes of building new nations in the former Soviet space and the security situation in that area and especially in Russia?

II. Conflicts in the post-Soviet space: where, why and when?

The conflicts which have erupted in the aftermath of the disintegration of the USSR can only partly be traced back to the effects of the breakup of the Union, notably in the case of conflicts over territories or over the division of Soviet property. The roots of the majority of these conflicts go far back into Soviet and Russian history and can be explained only in the context of that history. The administration of Soviet rule made it possible, at least for some time, for such conflicts to be kept under control, in a state of hibernation. As soon as the authority of Soviet power was destroyed, they began to grow and multiply. In this way, the residual tensions of Soviet society manifested themselves in the new conditions prevailing after the dissolution of the USSR.

There are numerous overviews and analyses of the conflicts in the post-Soviet space.[3] Taken together they give a good picture of the multiplicity and

---

[2] *Izvestiya*, 25 Dec. 1991, p. 1.

[3] Lebedeva, M., Netherlands Institute of International Relations, *Dealing with Conflicts In and Around Russia: Enforce or Negotiate?* (NIIA: The Hague, 1992); and Kanet, R. E., *Coping with Conflict: The Role of the Russian Federation*, Program on Arms Control, Disarmament and International Security Occasional Paper (University of Illinois at Urbana-Champaign: Urbana-Champaign, Ill., Oct. 1993). See also Kremenyuk, V., *Conflicts In and Around Russia: Nation-Building in Difficult Times*, Contributions in Political Science, no. 341 (Greenwood: Westport, Conn., 1994).

number—over several dozen—of conflicts, each of which is unique and at the same time highly typical for the state of affairs in the post-Soviet world. In Soviet times they developed in conditions of almost complete information blockade (no facts, no positions, no discussion in the media) and in an atmosphere of intensive propagandist brain-washing. Conflicts were declared to be a part of capitalism, not of socialism which could only produce brotherhood and solidarity. In this respect the conflicts once they developed were often treated as something unexpected, abnormal, even illegal. At the same time the history of the collapse of other multinational empires and the Balkan wars of the beginning of the century in fact show that such conflicts between the former parts of the empire or between the metropolis and these parts may be a normal pattern rather than a deviation.[4] In this sense it was only natural to expect that, once the Soviet political and social order was broken, conflicts both within individual successor states and in relations between them would inevitably follow.

Many of the conflicts that appeared in the post-Soviet space after 1991 should be regarded as expressions of a rapidly changing situation which both reveals old grievances, dormant for many years and now brought into life by the changed political and military environment, and itself produces fresh conflicts where the interests of different nations or ethnic groups collide as a result of their search for a new status. In this sense it is useful to note that in the majority of conflicts both sides tended to move very quickly through the first, opening stage of the conflict when negotiation was still possible and did not stop until the 'bridges' back to the pre-conflict situation had been burned. The violent stage of conflict gave the actors much more feeling of legitimacy and self-assurance.

The conflicts in the post-Soviet space fall into three groups.

1. The first group of conflicts can be dated back to pre-Soviet times. They are born of the history of the expansion of the Russian Empire. Some new lands and territories voluntarily joined the empire seeking protection from external enemies. This applies to today's Armenia, Belarus, Georgia, Kazakhstan, Moldova and most of Ukraine. Others were included in the Russian Empire by force—Azerbaijan, the Baltic states, Central Asia, Tatarstan, the western part of Ukraine and the northern Caucasus. It might be assumed that in the case of the first group 'divorce' would be generally peaceful and orderly, whereas with the second group painful historical memories compounded by more recent experiences would create problems for their relations with Russia. This would be an oversimplification. Ukraine voluntarily joined in a union with Russia in 1654 but now because of differences over the distribution of Soviet property has very hard feelings towards Russia; the nations of Central Asia, although they were conquered in the 19th century through war, have managed to preserve reasonably friendly relations with Russia in the process of dissolution of

---

[4] Rupesinghe, K. (ed.), *Ethnic Conflicts, Autonomy and Devolution of Power in Multiethnic States* (Macmillan: London, 1993).

the Soviet Union, at least on the official level. One special case is that of the northern Caucasus. This whole area was conquered by Russia after a long and exhausting Great Caucasian War in the 19th century which finished with the capture of the religious leader, Imam Shamil, in 1867. The crisis in Chechnya revealed the depth of the differences between the ways in which different nations perceive their historic and current relationship.[5]

2. Other conflicts appeared as a result of Soviet rule and of the nationalities policies of the Communist Party. They fall into three sub-groups.

First, some conflicts are the result of the arbitrary drawing of borders which were regarded by the communist authorities as merely administrative lines and were never regarded as possible national or international borders—those between Russia and Ukraine, Russia and Kazakhstan, Russia and Estonia, Russia and Latvia, Moldova and Ukraine, Kyrgyzstan and Uzbekistan, Armenia and Azerbaijan, and some others. A whole range of open or latent conflicts has been produced by the fact that these administrative lines have now become national and international borders.

Second, the territorial status of whole areas has become a source of serious conflict. Predominantly Armenian-populated Nagorno-Karabakh wanted to leave Azerbaijan of which it was an integral part; the predominantly Ossetian South Ossetia decided to leave Georgia and join its brothers in North Ossetia which is a part of Russia; the predominantly Russian and Ukrainian Trans-Dniester region in Moldova demanded autonomous status; and mainly Russian-populated Crimea demanded special status from Ukraine in order either to become completely independent or to join Russia.

These are examples of essentially domestic conflicts which have nevertheless touched relations between neighbouring states. Other Soviet-produced conflicts are predominantly domestic in character, although they may sometimes appear in an international or a CIS context. Among these are the conflict between the federal government in Moscow and Tatarstan over the status of that republic within the Russian Federation; the conflict in Abkhazia where the local government decided unilaterally to revive the constitution of 1925, which gave Abkhazia independent status; the conflict in Moldova with the Gagauz population which demanded autonomy; and domestic conflicts in Azerbaijan between the central authorities and different regions of the republic. The biggest and most important conflict in this group is that between Russia and the rebellious Chechnya, which proclaimed independence from Russia unilaterally and was prepared to defend that independence by force of arms. The conflict which followed amounted to full-scale war. The capital, Grozny, and smaller towns and villages have been destroyed, tens of thousands have been killed or wounded, hundreds of thousands have fled the area of hostilities and there is a clear prospect of continued instability in the future.

[5] Arutyunov, S. A. *et al.*, *The Ethnopolitical Situation in the Northern Caucasus*, Project on Ethnicity and Nationalism Publication Series, Paper no. 1 (International Research and Exchange Board: Moscow, 1994).

The case of Chechnya sheds additional light on the third sub-group of conflicts which are part of the Soviet inheritance—those connected with the issue of 'dislocated nations'. Beginning in the early 1940s, whole nations, first among them the Russian Germans who had their own autonomous republic on the River Volga and then the Crimean Tatars, the Meskhetian Turks, Chechens, Ingush and Kalmyks, were forcibly uprooted and moved to Siberia and Kazakhstan. The usual explanation was collaboration with the Nazi German occupation authorities. Under this pretext whole nations were deprived of their homes and sent into exile and their lands and homes were given to other nationalities. The process of return of these peoples started under General Secretary Nikita Khrushchev in the late 1950s. The Kalmyks, Chechens and Ingush were permitted to come back, and found that some of their historical lands were occupied by newcomers. Conflicts followed. Others (the Russian Germans and Meskhetian Turks) have not been permitted to return and that has contributed to their conflicts with the central authorities. The Ukrainian Government's approval of the return of the Crimean Tatars to Crimea has created tension on the peninsula and there are already signs of conflict between the Tatars and the people who moved in and occupied their lands after 1944.

3. The third group of conflicts consists of those born in the process and as a result of the disintegration of the USSR. In this group belong conflicts over the division of Soviet property, especially of the armed forces; quarrels and debates on the status of Russians and Russian-speaking populations; and internal conflicts on religious, communal and inter-clan relations. They include the Russian–Ukrainian conflict over the Black Sea Fleet; the Russian–Kazakh controversy over the status and future of the Baikonur space launching site; numerous debates between Russia and Estonia, Kazakhstan, Kyrgyzstan, Latvia and Ukraine on the issues of the Russian-speaking minorities there; and some special cases which amount to civil war, such as Georgia and Tajikistan.

This division into three types of conflict, both domestic and international, applies in the analysis of all the instabilities in the area of the former Soviet Union and brings out the historical dynamics of the creation, layer by layer, of all the unresolved issues which have flared up in the process of the collapse of the communist empire. Certain types of conflict were evident 100 years ago—independence movements, religious intolerance, ethnic identification, and so on. The sources of conflict are very often repeated and reveal a host of problems which were never resolved by the Russian or Soviet government. Among the first was the problem of national self-determination for the non-Russian nations and their relations with Moscow or St Petersburg.

There may also be an alternative classification of the conflicts in the post-Soviet space in terms of Russia's role in their development and their implications for Russia's interaction with the outside world in general.

1. There are domestic conflicts in Russia between the centre and some provinces seeking independence or autonomy (Chechnya, Tatarstan, Tuva and

others). If they are not contained or settled, these could have significant international implications for Russia, as with the war in Chechnya.

2. There is a number of actual or potential conflicts between Russia and some of the newly independent states (Estonia, Latvia and Ukraine).

3. Russia is involved to a significant extent in certain other conflicts in the post-Soviet states—Georgia, Moldova and Tajikistan. All have a direct as well as indirect relevance for the process of formation of the new Russian statehood, its domestic and foreign policies, military doctrine, foreign economic relations, legal administration, and so on.

4. There are a few conflicts in which Russia is not participating directly. Examples are the quarrels between Kyrgyzstan and Uzbekistan (in the Osh region) and even smaller communal quarrels in Azerbaijan, Kazakhstan and Uzbekistan. They add to the general state of instability and unpredictability but in reality do not represent a significant threat to the formation of a new order in the area of the former Soviet Union. One special case here is that of Nagorno-Karabakh, both because of the scope of the conflict and because of Russia's political involvement in efforts for a peace settlement.

The conflicts in which Russia is involved directly or indirectly may also be grouped by their origin and source: disputes over the division of the Soviet property, inter-ethnic conflicts, local civil wars and domestic conflicts. However, the relative nature of all characterizations must be kept in mind. The post-Soviet conflicts most often have more than one dimension.

Disputes over Soviet property

The states which succeeded the USSR immediately faced the problem of the division of Soviet property—military forces, the merchant marine, bank assets, foreign debt and so on. The issue of military assets appeared as early as at the first meeting in Belarus where the decision on the creation of the CIS was taken. At that point it was stressed that the greater part of the Soviet military assets would be under the control of CIS organs and would not be subject to division. These included the strategic forces, the air force, air defence forces, the navy and the military academies; the only exception was the ground forces. Ground forces stationed on the territories of the relevant republics would be 'nationalized' on the basis of free choice of allegiance by officers and non-commissioned officers (NCOs). (Up to 85–90 per cent of the officers and NCOs in the Soviet Army were Russians, Ukrainians and Belarussians, which left the other Soviet successor states practically without qualified military personnel.) Later, as a result of the increase in the number of members of the CIS, debates over non-military property and not least the influence of Ukrainian policy, the situation changed and the members of the CIS began the nationalization of the rest of the armed forces and weapons on their territories, including air forces, strategic weapons and navies.[6]

---

[6] 'The giants of yore: the plight of Russia's military', *Newsweek*, 1 Mar. 1993, pp. 18–22.

The Tashkent summit meeting of the CIS heads of state in May 1992 decided to give the troops stationed in the territories of independent states the opportunity to choose their national allegiance, to allow the newly independent states to retain military objects and installations in their territories and to withdraw those troops from their territories which opted to stay in the Russian Armed Forces. Thus many of these conflicts have been successfully overcome by the efforts of the CIS and by political negotiation.

The most important and potentially dramatic conflict involved the nuclear forces which at the time of the dissolution of the USSR were stationed in Belarus, Kazakhstan, Russia and Ukraine. On 23 May 1992 the four governments signed the Lisbon Protocol (with the assistance of the US Administration) which established that Russia would retain nuclear status as heir to the Soviet Union while the other republics adhered to non-nuclear status.[7] On 14 January 1994 Ukraine agreed to sign a tripartite agreement with the USA and Russia which prescribed the process of withdrawal of the nuclear forces from Ukraine to Russia.[8] One extremely important dispute continues—that between Russia and Ukraine over the status and future of the Black Sea Fleet, which could even yet escalate into a serious conflict.

The origins of this group of conflicts were closely connected to problems created by decisions made during the Soviet period, such as the transfer of Crimea from Russia to Ukraine (1954), the occupation of the Baltic republics (1940), the drafting of the 'administrative' borders between republics and some others created by Soviet rule.[9] The impact of these issues could increase if the question of borders were to arise: (a) between Russia and Estonia or Latvia (both the latter consider the existing border unjust); (b) between Russia and Kazakhstan, where significant parts of the northern and north-eastern parts of the territory are predominantly populated by Russians, who are dissatisfied with being left as part of Kazakhstan; or (c) between Russia and Ukraine.[10] The Russian Government denies that there is any territorial dispute with Estonia or Latvia. It has also stated officially that it has no territorial claims on Kazakhstan or Ukraine, but it may be sensitive to strong irredentist movements in northern Kazakhstan and Crimea.

This group of conflicts should be highlighted for several reasons: (a) they are international in nature since they developed between formally sovereign states, and have thus to be resolved on the basis of international law and the arrangements of the Organization for Security and Co-operation in Europe (OSCE); (b) they may in some cases escalate to the level of local wars; and (c) they offer

[7] Protocol to Facilitate the Implementation of the START Treaty (Lisbon Protocol), 23 May 1992. For the text, see *SIPRI Yearbook 1993: World Armaments and Disarmament* (Oxford University Press: Oxford, 1993), pp. 574–75.

[8] Trilateral Statement by the Presidents of the United States, Russia and Ukraine, Moscow, 14 Jan. 1994. Goodby, J., Kile, S. and Müller, H., 'Nuclear arms control', *SIPRI Yearbook 1995: Armaments, Disarmament and International Security* (Oxford University Press: Oxford, 1995), p. 637. For the text, see *SIPRI Yearbook 1994* (Oxford University Press: Oxford, 1994), pp. 677–78.

[9] Tishkov, V., 'Fire in the brain: inventions and manifestations of Soviet ethnonationalism', Paper presented at the annual meeting of the American Anthropological Association, Chicago, Nov. 1991.

[10] *New Times*, no. 27 (July 1991), pp. 6–9.

significant scope for settlement either through CIS mechanisms or through direct bilateral negotiation.

Ethnic unrest and interstate relations

The second important group of conflicts are those which combine unrest among ethnic and other minorities with interstate relations between former Soviet republics. Two aspects are involved: the position and status of Russians or Russian-speaking populations in other former Soviet republics and the status of other ethnic minorities which feel abused by the current territorial division.

The problem of the Russians in republics other than Russia (their number is estimated at 25 million) is a hot issue for Russian domestic politics, where different nationalist movements are vying with each other to be the true defenders of the rights of the Russians in the 'near abroad'. This puts the government of Russia on the defensive and has induced it to raise this painful issue in relations with the Baltic states and other former Soviet republics. In extreme cases tensions in this field may escalate into armed conflicts, as was clearly manifested in the Trans-Dniester region in Moldova. Similar in substance, although with different ethnic components, is the dispute in Nagorno-Karabakh, which grew into a genuine regional war.[11]

Conflicts involving other ethnic minorities involve both ethnic minorities in particular republics attempting to attain self-determination, which can be regarded as internal issues for the independent states arising from latent ethnic divisions, and, very importantly, irredentist movements—ethnic minorities seeking union with their ethnic kin across the border in neighbouring republics. These conflicts are therefore highly complicated; peaceful solutions may require renegotiation of borders, the settling of the status of relevant territories, the resolution of language problems, and so on. These conflicts challenge the wisdom of previous trends and administrative solutions and are directed against the existing system as such, implying sometimes the need for a complete review of the existing territorial arrangements—a demand which inevitably spills over into the sphere of relations between neighbouring states.

Civil wars

Almost all the former Soviet republics are experiencing difficulties connected with the incomplete nature of national self-determination because the natural process of their development was thwarted under communist rule. There are also problems of non-indigenous populations, rivalries between local political or religious groups, and the hardships of democratization and economic development. However, only in a few cases has the complex of these issues accompanied by failure of government brought such dramatic results as in Georgia and Tajikistan. In essence both experienced typical civil wars based on

[11] Husarska, A., 'Stepanakert postcard: burned out', *New Republic*, 24 Jan. 1994, p. 11.

clan, ethnic or provincial differences, threatening the integrity and even survival of those countries.

In Georgia there are several overlapping conflicts which reinforce each other.[12] The turbulence started with mutinous Abkhazia, which wanted a greater degree of independence. It grew into a struggle between several sides—the supporters of the former elected president, Zviad Gamsakhurdia, against supporters of the current president, Eduard Shevardnadze, and the central government against Abkhazian and South Ossetian separatists. The situation was significantly aggravated by general disorder and economic collapse. The unresolved conflicts continue to impede the formation of statehood in Georgia.[13] In Tajikistan, the war between two different groups or clans, one of them looking to its ethnic kin in neighbouring Afghanistan, the other to Russia for help, has continued unabated since 1992. It has passed through several stages, each of which has brought significant losses and refugee problems. The situation continues to be complex with little hope of settlement but with a strong possibility of Tajikistan being dragged into the civil war in Afghanistan. The current situation in the country is far from stable and shows every sign of turning into an endless war.

Domestic conflicts

An account of the structure of conflicts in the former Soviet Union is not complete without reference to the various conflicts within Russia itself, especially in relations with its most mutinous minorities, and within other former Soviet republics.

Almost all—in Azerbaijan, Georgia, Kazakhstan, Moldova, Ukraine and Uzbekistan, to name the most salient examples—possess restive minorities—ethnic, religious and historical—which feel either ignored or betrayed by the new governments and are anxious for what they call historical justice. Within Russia there are the cases of the Chechens in the northern Caucasus or Tuvinians in the Tuva Republic in the Russian–Mongolian borderlands. In Ukraine there is the case of the Crimean Tatars, in Moldova that of the Gagauz, in Georgia that of the Meskhetian Turks, and in Uzbekistan the Karakalpaks. Each of these groups has its claims and grievances which demand some response from the central authorities of the post-Soviet states. 'The Union has disintegrated, but the inter-ethnic conflicts remain': so ran the conclusion of one of the first reports on the situation in the former Soviet Union.[14]

The importance of these conflicts is enhanced by the background of failing economies, the growing paralysis of the central authorities, political instability and growing crime. The state of the economy in the majority of the former Soviet republics continues to be one of recession, with falling industrial and agricultural production, double-digit inflation and a seemingly irreparable

---

[12] For an analysis of the various conflicts in and around Georgia, see chapter 20 in this volume.

[13] Mikeladze, A., 'Vechnaya voyna?' [An eternal war?], *Moscow News*, no. 39 (26 Sep. 1993), p. 4.

[14] Mukomel, V., Payin, E. and Popov, A., 'Soyuz raspalsya: mezhnatsionalnye konflikty ostalis' [The Union has disintegrated, the inter-ethnic conflicts remain], *Nezavisimaya Gazeta*, 10 Jan. 1992, p. 5.

budget deficit. The governments have appeared incapable of finding ways of arresting the drop in production and encouraging investment. Foreign investors are discouraged from making deals by an inadequate legislative framework and unimaginable corruption. Practically the only thing these governments are trying to do is to keep their economies afloat in the faint hope that the natural way of things will somehow reverse the trend and that the result of privatization of large sectors of the economy will bring some measure of economic revival. Almost all government spending is directed at maintaining the budget deficit at tolerable levels without fuelling further inflation. This is typical of most of the successor states of the Soviet Union. The exceptions are the Baltic states, Turkmenistan (because of its gas reserves), Kazakhstan if it finally finds ways to put its gigantic oil reserves into production, and possibly Russia which, if it moves fairly quickly through a difficult period of economic transition, may also achieve a level of acceptable economic and social stability.

Because of the extremely hard economic situation, the governments of the former Soviet republics cannot allocate enough resources to help reduce ethnic and nationalist tensions.[15] Nationalist propaganda presents the poor state of the economy and of living standards as a consequence of the central authorities' neglect of the needs of minorities, which generally exacerbates the situation. Economic hardships also put pressure on the relationship between labour and the authorities, thus adding a new element to inter-ethnic and nationalist controversies. In these conditions an outside involvement in conflict management is sometimes crucial, and Russia as the largest of the former Soviet republics is certainly better placed to play such a role than any other state. However, the economic and financial burden of conflict management may be too heavy even for Russia, especially bearing in mind its attempts to deal with some conflicts militarily, as in Chechnya.

III. The Russian response

Russian history is replete with conflicts and wars. It can be argued that the contemporary transformations are typical of the upheavals that have been the turning-points of Russian history. Cases in point include the period following the Tatar–Mongol domination (13th–15th centuries), the Time of Troubles (early 17th century) and the period of the 1917 Revolution and the Civil War (1918–22). Each of these periods of upheaval was in some way connected with the destruction of the previous political and social order and the emergence of a new one. From the point of view of Russian history, then, the current conflicts are perceived as bearing the seeds of the new Russia and are often regarded as inevitable birth-pangs. In this sense, the current situation in and around Russia may be treated as a part of the traditional pattern of conflict during transition.

---

[15] Payin, E. et al., *Nationalities and Politics in the Post-Soviet World: 1993*, Project on Ethnicity and Nationalism Publication Series, Paper no. 2 (International Research and Exchange Board: Moscow, 1994).

Russia is at a very serious juncture in its political and social development. The new constitution, approved in December 1993 by national referendum, concentrates almost all executive power in the hands of the president and his staff, leaving the government in the curious position of searching out the areas of competence left to it by the constitution. In these conditions the parliament (the Council of the Federation as the upper chamber and the Duma as the lower chamber) is either reduced to secondary responsibilities or split between the two largest groups of nationalists and ultranationalists at one end of the political spectrum and the democrats at the other. The centre is so insignificant that it cannot be a basis for consensus in the parliament.

Without significant and active support from the legislature, the executive is trying to take urgent measures against rising crime and social upheaval, including worker and ethnic unrest, the illegal trade in arms and drugs, growing corruption in the bureaucracy and other evils which, while they are the results of the current situation, at the same time significantly complicate and aggravate it. The practical results of this effort to date are less than encouraging, but it is an important element in the general state of affairs, both domestically and internationally, in relation to conflicts in the post-Soviet space.

Political and security dimensions

The first thing which deserves consideration in the study of post-Soviet conflicts is their relation to the existing political and administrative order.

In some cases these conflicts may be regarded as the direct offspring of the official policy of ignoring or underestimating the importance of the nationalist claims of some local political movements or governments. Examples here are Chechnya and Tatarstan. There are serious grounds for considering this type of conflict, in which the centre and a part of the federation cannot find a compromise on the issues of sovereignty, as one where the policies of the central authorities have given much ground for the development of the confrontation. Currently, it seems, the most dangerous stage in relations with Tatarstan is past, and the bilateral treaty between it and Russia of February 1994[16] provided an example of the possibility of political settlement of conflicts arising from different approaches to sovereignty of the members of Russian Federation. Even so, the conflict cannot be considered completely and definitely solved.

The case of Chechnya is much more complicated. The then Chechnyan President, Dzhokhar Dudaev, when he proclaimed full independence for Chechnya was taking literally President Yeltsin's words in 1991—'take as much sovereignty as you can bear'. The basis of his policy was that the increasing problems for Russia in the northern Caucasus and beyond the moun-

---

[16] Tatarstan refused to sign the Federation Treaty of 13 Mar. 1992 and successfully insisted on signing a special Treaty on the Delimitation of Spheres of Authority and Mutual Delegation of Powers between the Agencies of State Power of the Russian Federation and of the Republic of Tatarstan, 16 Feb. 1994. For the text, see *Rossiyskaya Gazeta*, 17 Feb. 1994. On the background to the treaty, see Teague, E., 'Russia and Tatarstan sign power-sharing treaty', Radio Free Europe/Radio Liberty (hereafter RFE/RL), *RFE/RL Research Report*, vol. 3, no. 14 (8 Apr. 1994), pp. 19–27.

tains, in Georgia and Abkhazia, opened up significant opportunities for independence from Russia. Dudaev also actively supported the resurgence of Islam in the area as a means of resisting Russian 'expansion'.

In late 1994 Moscow started military operations against Dudaev, aiming to 're-establish constitutional order in Chechnya'. The conflict, including the bombing and artillery shelling of the towns and villages of Chechnya, caused thousands of fatalities, most of them civilian.

The war in Chechnya provides significant additional material for the analysis of the role of purely domestic conflicts for the current and future position of Russia itself. Because the general state of affairs in the country, whether in the economy, security, social matters or further democratization, is far from satisfactory, these conflicts play a major role both as obstacles to the further progress of society and as challenges to the policies of the current government. They divert attention from more urgent needs of economic reform and political stability, consume time, energy and resources, and create pockets of instability and fighting, all of which works against the prospect of stabilization and increases the influence of radicals in domestic politics and the role of the military.

In fact the war in Chechnya has revealed a more general problem—the absence of efforts either by the government or by the parliament to create a better basis for economic and political conflict settlement. Indeed, until recently there has been no sustainable and comprehensive policy towards conflict resolution in Russia. Instead different twists and turns in the policy of both president and parliament have contributed to the creation of such conflicts and prevented the search for a solution. Very often these conflicts were simply regarded as pawns in the Great Game between the branches of the Russian state. From time to time the various actors, in quest of wider political support, would encourage separatists and secessionist movements, usually alleging the promotion of democracy or preservation of the balance of relations between the centre and the periphery; very often, however, they played into the hands of those who were working against territorial integrity.

The whole problem of federalism in Russia is part of the background to this lack of sustainable policy. Difficult negotiations on the principles, forms and methods of federalism have been constantly accompanied by confrontations and mutual grievances. The Federation Treaty of March 1992 did not satisfy all the members of the Russian Federation and may be questioned at any time, as is shown by the case of Tatarstan. It should also be noted that the conflicts happened at places and times when there were no legal mechanisms to deal with the source of conflict or when existing legal mechanisms did not work. There were discussions about the need to create special bodies and agencies in order to deal with current and future conflicts, but this was not supported by the law enforcement agencies and 'power ministries' or by the parliament. Developing collisions or confrontations were for this reason often not checked at the right time and were allowed to go beyond the stage at which they could still be contained.

These points can help to explain the possibilities of growing conflicts in Russia and of their escalation, but none of them can explain completely the reluctance of the Russian authorities to deal with conflicts properly and in due time. This requires a different explanation. First and foremost, there was (and still is) a widespread belief that military or paramilitary force is a good guarantee against any escalation of conflict and even against its evolution to a violent stage. This was reflected both by the inclusion of the idea of using military force against domestic disorders in the text of the new Russian military doctrine[17] and by the use of armed forces in the conflict between Ingushetia and North Ossetia (autumn 1993) and against Chechnya. Second, there is also a widespread belief that dealing with domestic conflicts is a domestic affair which should not in any way be used by foreign governments against Russia. In this sense the evolution of the conflict in Chechnya and especially the indiscriminate bombing of the civilian population in Grozny and other Chechen towns and villages, which produced so much protest in the world, were regarded as exclusively the area of responsibility of the Russian Government. Third, sometimes in the attitude of the Russian Government towards domestic conflicts with an ethnic element there have been elements of nationalistic and even chauvinistic approaches which were used to forge 'national integrity'.

The Russian Government's policy towards its domestic conflicts has contributed to their developing in the direction of violence and reduced the chances of peace. It can be similarly concluded that the unresolved conflicts have become an important factor in promoting the further evolution of the general situation in Russia in the direction of increasing instability and greater violence.

One of the side-effects of domestic conflicts for Russia is the possibility of interference by neighbouring countries. Until now Russia has had to assume the Soviet legacy in fighting Afghan volunteers in Tajikistan, thereby eliminating the possibility of retaining good-neighbourly relations with Afghanistan. It is possible that Russia will run into a conflict of interests with Turkey as a result of the Nagorno-Karabakh and Azeri–Armenian conflicts, which has serious implications since Turkey is a member of NATO and could complicate the Russian–NATO dialogue. There has been some Russian–Romanian friction because of events in Moldova. None of these was a purely Russian conflict.

Not only do these conflicts create an image of Russia as an unstable, chaotic society, thereby diminishing its international standing and its chances of attracting solid foreign investment. They also create a situation where, in the absence of a serious external threat, both the Russian Government and society still feel concerned about their security and have to continue to retain a large standing armed force and allocate a significant part of the national budget for military purposes.

---

[17] *Izvestiya* published extensive excerpts from the military doctrine in 'Osnovnye polozheniya voennoy doktriny Rossiyskoy Federatsii' [The basic provisions of the military doctrine of the Russian Federation] on 18 Nov. 1993 and *Krasnaya Zvezda* published a slightly longer excerpt on 19 Nov. 1993. A translation into English was published by *Jane's Intelligence Review*, Special Report, Jan. 1994. For a fuller discussion see chapters 8 and 9 in this volume.

Russia as a peacekeeper

Russia's active involvement in the 'near abroad' takes various forms—the roles of supplier of a number of vital resources, source of financial aid and major regional 'peacekeeper'. The latter role has been institutionalized both through domestic institution building (the creation of special intergovernmental agencies to deal with threats to security within the CIS such as drug trafficking, terrorism, illegal arms shipments and the protection of nuclear warhead silos) and by enhancing Russia's role in the CIS through new commitments and obligations. In its turn, this has produced growing aspirations on the part of some Russians for the revitalization of the idea of a 'Greater Russia' (as, for example, with the Russian Empire before 1917) and a ground swell of protest among other sections of population who challenge the wisdom of Russia's taking on a new 'imperial burden'.

After some initial hesitation in 1991–92, the Russian Government seemed to conclude that its role in the conflicts which had emerged as a result of the disintegration of the Soviet Union was crucially important both for the Russian national interest and for the way the country was perceived in the West. Most importantly, according to this thinking, Russia's great-power role in the world would first of all depend on its performance in organizing the geopolitical space of the CIS. Hence, although reluctant to play its peacekeeping role in 1992, it reacted with jealousy when the Conference on Security and Co-operation in Europe (CSCE)[18] or the UN demonstrated interest in some of the conflicts within the former Soviet Union. It was not very enthusiastic when the CSCE involved itself in Nagorno-Karabakh and viewed with suspicion the activities of UN bodies and missions in Abkhazia and Tajikistan, although this has never been stated officially—on the contrary, Russia as a rule 'welcomed' the international community's interest in these conflicts.

It must be stressed that hidden Russian scepticism about UN activities had a sound basis. The actions of UN peacekeeping forces in Somalia and the former Yugoslavia have provided enough evidence since then not only of their incapacity to deal with such conflicts even when UN forces had a visible military edge over local insurgents (as in Somalia) but also of the UN Secretariat's inability to formulate policy goals clearly and distinctly and to render them acceptable to member countries.[19] So, being rather sceptical about the peacekeeping role of the UN in other parts of the world, Russia could not agree easily to entrust to it the same functions in the CIS. On the other hand, Russia wanted to avoid accusations of neo-imperialist activities and demanded a UN mandate for its peacekeeping actions.[20]

---

[18] On 1 Jan. 1995 the CSCE became the OSCE.

[19] Kremeniuk, V., 'OON i podderzhanie mira: fiasko v Somalii' [The UN and peacekeeping: fiasco in Somalia], *Moscow News*, no. 30 (25 July 1993), p. 7.

[20] Allison, R., Western European Union, Institute for Security Studies, *Peacekeeping in the Soviet Successor States*, Chaillot Papers no. 18 (ISS: Paris, 1994); and Russia, Foreign Ministry, 'Ob osnovnykh polozheniyakh kontseptsii vneshney politiki Rossiyskoy Federatsii' [On the main foundations of the concept of the foreign policy of the Russian Federation], Moscow, Apr.–May 1992.

It is impossible in a single chapter to track every stage in the evolution of Russian attitudes towards the conflicts in the former Soviet Union. Simply stated, what was once perceived as a more or less easy task that could be solved either through diplomatic efforts backed up by the promise of Russian raw materials (oil and gas supplies) or through a limited military operation has in the long run appeared as a specific and quite difficult area of domestic and foreign policy, elevated in importance to deliberation at the level of the Russian Security Council.

The first sign of official confusion over the significance and role of conflicts in and around Russia may be found in the initial draft of the Concept of the Russian Foreign Policy, worked out by the Russian Foreign Ministry under urgent pressure from the Supreme Soviet in 1992.[21] This document was widely circulated in Moscow and was subjected to different critical analyses. In that part of the draft which formulated Russian policy goals in the CIS, the focus of attention was very much on the process of institution building (which has, incidentally, since proved very cumbersome), with the problem of conflicts treated as something temporary and of lesser importance. The document simply stated that Russian policy in conflict-affected areas will consist of 'friendly assistance' to independent nations in overcoming their difficulties. What aroused particular criticism on the part of the government's conservative and nationalist critics was the attempt by the authors of the draft to avoid identifying such important issues as the 'Russians abroad' as a special problem, particularly in relations with the Baltic states, Azerbaijan and the Central Asian states. The draft was recognized as unsuccessful and the Foreign Ministry continued to work on it for another year until a revised draft was accepted in June 1993 by the Russian Security Council as a basis for policy planning.

The Foreign Ministry's approach to the problem of domestic conflicts has injected a significant new diplomatic element into peacemaking efforts within the CIS. A host of high-ranking Russian diplomats, almost all of them with the temporary title of Special Representative of the Russian President, were assigned to try to bring about cease-fires in the conflicts in Abkhazia, Moldova, Nagorno-Karabakh and Tajikistan. On some occasions these efforts were coordinated with the military commanders of locally stationed Russian forces, who provided support to the diplomats. There were also cases when the efforts of different agencies of the Russian Government—diplomatic and military, justice and interior—were not coordinated or worked in different directions, for instance in Abkhazia. Russian foreign policy also progressed in negotiating agreements on troop withdrawals from the Baltic states and similar efforts were initiated with Moldova. Russia signed agreements with Armenia and Georgia on military cooperation and an agreement on the Baikonur space-launching site with Kazakhstan. These agreements made it possible to avoid conflicts which could have developed because of the unspecified status of Russian forces in the

---

[21] Russia, Foreign Ministry (note 20); and Kremeniuk, V., 'Vneshnyaya politika Rossii: nuzhny orientiry' [Russia's foreign policy: guidelines are needed], *Nezavisimaya Gazeta*, 17 Aug. 1993, p. 5.

former Soviet republics and to push forward talks on military cooperation with those republics which opted for the presence of Russian troops or military experts on their territories.

The Defence Ministry, in contrast to the Foreign Ministry, its traditional rival, was quick to develop additional avenues to make the peacekeeping effort one of its main objectives. In June 1992 it issued for public discussion a document entitled 'A Draft of the Russian Military Doctrine'.[22] This draft policy document paid much more attention to the problem of conflicts in the former Soviet republics. First, it stated that the status and destiny of Russians abroad had become one of the concerns of the ministry: a large number of military veterans were left in the Baltic states and a number of other former Soviet republics where the Defence Ministry had encouraged them to settle upon retirement. Second, conflicts in the 'near abroad', where the lives and property of Russians were endangered, were defined as one of the priorities of Russian defence policy. Third, the draft prescribed the creation of special forces which were to be assigned to playing a peacekeeping role in the former Soviet republics. The draft intentionally introduced the term 'peacemaking [*mirotvorcheskie*] operations', which occasioned a sarcastic comment from the Foreign Minister at the time, Andrey Kozyrev, to the effect that this was a special type of operation unknown to the Russian military.[23]

This 'advance' by the Russian military was based on the considerable measure of experience achieved by the Russian forces in 1992 in Moldova, South Ossetia and Tajikistan. In Moldova, the intervention of the newly appointed Commander of the 14th Army, General Alexander Lebed, played a perceptible role in putting an end to hostilities between the Moldovan Army and the 'volunteer forces' of the Trans-Dniester region, hostilities which led to hundreds of civilian deaths in the region in early summer 1992. In South Ossetia, where armed clashes developed between the Georgian Army and South Ossetian paramilitary forces, trilateral troop units (Georgian, Ossetian and Russian) occupied the buffer zone between the adversaries following agreement between Georgia, Russia and South Ossetia in June 1992 and contributed to the freezing of the conflict. In Tajikistan, the intervention of the Russian 201st Motor Rifle Division which had been deployed in the area since Soviet times put an end to open hostilities in a civil war which had left almost 50 000 dead and thousands of refugees.

These acts by the Russian military can hardly be described as peacekeeping in the UN sense. In some cases the decision to intervene was prompted by a desire on the part of the local Russian commander to stop the bloodshed (and later blessed by Moscow, as in the case of Moldova). Sometimes the decision was taken in Moscow and only later coordinated with the local government.

[22] 'Ob osnovakh voennoy doktriny Rossii' [On the basics of the Russian military doctrine] (Krasnaya Zvezda Publishing House: Moscow, June 1992).
[23] [Interview with Foreign Minister Kozyrev], *Izvestiya*, 15 Nov. 1993. On the Russian terminology of peacekeeping, see chapter 9, section III, and chapter 10, sections II and IV, in this volume; and Trenin, D., 'Russia', ed. T. Findlay, *Challenges for the New Peacekeepers*, SIPRI Research Report no. 12 (Oxford University Press: Oxford, 1996), pp. 70–71.

This was the case in Tajikistan where two rival governments were fighting each other and Moscow decided to support one of the two sides, issuing relevant orders to the local commander. Only in Georgia can Russia's military action be called peacekeeping in the strict sense, because it was negotiated with both sides of the conflict, a cease-fire was achieved and only then did the Russian troops move in. With all these nuances, the fact was that armed intervention by Russian troops helped to pacify the situation, at least temporarily. It should be added, however, that at later stages of the conflict the residual Russian troops sometimes played a provocative role in prolonging the confrontation.

The cases when the military helped to stop hostilities whereas Russian diplomacy had failed to impose peace or even a cease-fire have been interpreted as proof that military force can be a useful instrument in dealing with some intra-CIS conflicts. This has had profound significance for the Russian military since it came at a time of heated debate over military procurement, defence expenditure and the feasibility of conversion—debate which might result in the Russian military losing a significant part of its customary sphere of power and influence. Underscoring the importance of peacekeeping operations has helped the military to retain a significant share of its human and material resources, opening up a completely new sphere of potential missions under the banner of 'saving Russians abroad'.[24] In a more general sense it has contributed to an assessment of the importance of conflict-control policies, a fact that has gradually led to a significant change of focus in Russian policy towards the 'near abroad'.

Both diplomatic and military peacemaking efforts have raised serious concerns within Russia proper, in the CIS and in the world at large. In Russia, strong opposition appeared in the Duma since decisions to send Russian peacekeeping forces to CIS countries were taken without the legislature being consulted, and it was feared that casualties would cause a wave of popular opposition. Some political forces in the CIS countries also opposed the idea of Russian peacekeeping and peacemaking initiatives, arguing (a) that they would constitute interference in their domestic affairs, and (b) that Russia cannot be regarded as a neutral force and that its involvement would support one side in the conflict against the other. Wherever it has intervened—in Tajikistan, for example—this has happened.

Equally, Russian peacekeeping activities met with some concern and suspicion in the West and at the UN. Taken together with the concept of the 'near abroad', Russian peacekeeping looked like the continuation of a traditional Russian imperial role within the territory of the former Soviet Union. The perpetuation of the traditional practice of controlling information, foreign visitors and even overflights through other countries' airspace (as in Abkhazia) added to the impression that what was happening in reality was Russian military expansion and build-up under the guise of peacekeeping.

---

[24] 'Osnovy voyennoy doktriny Rossii' [The foundations of Russia's military doctrine], brochure published by *Krasnaya Zvezda*, Jan. 1994.

To neutralize this impression, Russia has worked actively both through diplomatic channels and through the contacts of the CIS parliaments to create a solid legal basis for its peacekeeping operations. At the CIS summit meetings in 1993 and 1994 and at the meetings of defence ministers of the CIS countries, Russia agreed that all its peacekeeping operations in the former Soviet Union would be conducted on behalf of the CIS and in the presence of UN and CSCE invited observers. It also insisted that other countries which had signed the Tashkent Treaty on Collective Security of 15 May 1992[25] should participate actively in peacekeeping operations in Tajikistan and Nagorno-Karabakh.

With all these qualifications about Russia's peacekeeping capabilities, it is evident that Russia and its armed forces have been oriented towards an active policy in local conflicts. It would be premature to discuss Russia's role in conflict resolution, however, since almost no conflict in its immediate surroundings in which it is involved directly or indirectly can be regarded as solved.

IV. A security challenge for Europe

Two questions were formulated at the beginning of this chapter.

The general answer to the first question is fairly positive. The new nations which appeared on the territory of the former Soviet Union are going through a painful process of national self-determination (which in some cases has been developing for centuries but only now become possible) at the same time as searching for a new political and economic order. Some of their problems can therefore be solved through conflicts—conflicts with what they see as the remnants of the Russian role (the Russian diaspora, dependence on the Russian economy, the need to rely on Russia in matters of security, and so on), with the supporters of the old conservative traditions, or with separatism and criminal activities. Basically, these conflicts are contained within national borders and could not be perceived as an external threat were it not that the weakness of the new institutions, of the economic base and of mass support has led to the need for foreign involvement—Russian, Western and international. It is this that carries a real threat of internationalization of these conflicts and of their evolving into a source of international crisis.

The answer to the second question is that, while these conflicts are regarded sometimes as unavoidable, even constructive in the sense that they clear the ground for modernization, they cast a serious shadow over the prospects for survival of the new nations. They threaten to turn the evolution of these countries in the direction of permanent chaos and disorder and in this sense have become a focus of interest in European security and Russian–Western relations.

---

[25] For the text, see *Izvestiya*, 16 May 1992, p. 3. The original signatories were Armenia, Kazakhstan, Kyrgyzstan, the Russian Federation, Tajikistan and Uzbekistan. By the spring of 1994 Azerbaijan, Belarus and Georgia had also joined.

It seemed for some time that, once the threat of a major war in Europe was removed following the end of the East–West military confrontation, a solid basis for peaceful and stable development in Europe was finally established. It was expected that, while the West would continue to develop along the path of economic prosperity and integration, the Eastern part of the continent would undergo a period of economic reform and social change and that the foundations for an all-European order based upon East–West cooperation and a comprehensive security system would thus be laid.

The growing instability in the post-Soviet geopolitical space has significantly dampened such hopes. The number and intensity of the conflicts in the former Soviet Union, coupled with the evident inability of the authorities to deal with them and keep them under control, have significantly altered the attitudes of the Western alliance. Among Western reactions to the consolidation of President Yeltsin's power after the Supreme Soviet of Russia was forcibly dismissed in September 1993, there were some concerned voices which appealed for greater caution and prudence in approaching conflicts in and around Russia and their implications for European security. In particular, it was stressed that the turmoil in Russia had revealed the weaknesses of the political regime, the growing distance between the centre and the regional authorities (there were even predictions of the further disintegration of Russia),[26] and the fact that conflicts in the former USSR have become an unavoidable backdrop for political events in Europe and Asia. The situation in the former Soviet Union and former Yugoslavia has become a standard item on the Western lists of threats to security.

It is often said in Europe that, while five or 10 years ago the threat to the continent emanated from the ideologically based policies of the USSR, now it is Russia's unexpected weakness which constitutes a threat.[27] Unpredictability, volatility and controversy over what is currently happening in Russia have turned the country into an almost unknown variable in the European equation. At the same time, it is well understood that, even with its present reduced status, Russia continues to be one of the largest military forces in the world, the largest oil producer and exporter, a major exporter of gold, and one of the leading nations in military research and development. The extent of the threat it presents to Europe can only be assessed in the light of its size and its weight in international affairs.

To summarize emerging Western anxieties and concerns stemming from the continuing conflicts in the area of the former Soviet Union:

1. These conflicts appear to be the manifestation not only of a transitional period but of a seemingly permanent form of relations both between Russia and some of its neighbours and within some of new post-Soviet nations.

---

[26] 'Perceptions of the Finnish political élite', *Yearbook of Finnish Foreign Policy* (Finnish Institute of International Affairs: Helsinki, 1994), pp. 24–59.

[27] This was one of the major conclusions reached at a conference on 'New Trends in Security Orientations in Central and Eastern Europe', held in Bratislava, 18–19 Feb. 1994.

2. Post-Soviet conflicts are often latent and long-lived and their sources many and deep.

3. Conflict-resolution efforts are far from adequate and the conflicts in question tend to develop in the direction of growing violence and the use of a wider arsenal of weapons, including heavy artillery, armour and air power.

4. Russia, which is assuming the role of a peacekeeping force in the former Soviet Union, is itself far from stable and can hardly be regarded as a reliable partner.

5. The West could very easily face a new situation in the eastern part of Europe which could develop into regional wars.[28]

In this sense the conflicts in and around Russia can be regarded as one of the major channels of the Russian impact on European politics at present.

1. They bring a significant amount of instability and unpredictability into the emerging European order. For example, if the Russian conflict with Estonia and Latvia over the status of Russian minorities there were to escalate into military confrontation, the potential consequences for the whole of Nordic Europe are self-evident. The same could be said of the possible Russian–Ukrainian conflict, although in this instance the consequences would perhaps be less visible.

2. Russian attempts to play a monopolist peacekeeper role in the region are also regarded with suspicion and mixed feelings. For some Europeans, the Russian desire to play a policing role in this volatile region is treated as something akin to a blessing, since it is hard to imagine that European governments would be eager to send their own troops and pay for policing actions in the region. Other Europeans regard it with deep suspicion, interpret it as a rehearsal for Russian domination over the eastern part of the continent and argue that through such peacekeeping operations Russia would be able to re-establish military control over the neighbouring territories. In this sense, the February 1994 Russian–Georgian Treaty of Friendship, Neighbourly Relations and Cooperation[29] is often mentioned as a pattern, giving Russia significant military leverage in the Caucasus region (and, incidentally, causing serious concern in neighbouring Turkey).

3. The spectre of conflicts in the former Soviet Union raises old fears that the West may in the long run be put in the position of the Roman Empire, besieged by barbaric tribes and eventually overrun by them. This fear is underlined by the evident fact that, even after the end of the cold war and the erasure of the traditional lines of ideological confrontation, Europe continues to be deeply divided into two worlds: the world of stability and affluence in the West and the world of conflicts and poverty in the East. It is this which could be the most serious threat to the rich world.

---

[28] Huber, K., 'The CSCE and ethnic conflict in the East', *RFE/RL Research Report*, vol. 2, no. 31 (30 July 1993), pp. 30–36.

[29] 'Rossiysko-gruzinskiy dogovor o druzhbe, dobrososedstve i sotrudnichestve' [Russian–Georgian Treaty of Friendship, Neighbourly Relations and Cooperation, Tbilisi, 20 Feb. 1994], *Rossiyskaya Gazeta*, 21 Feb. 1994.

This line of analysis prompts two differing sets of conclusions for European governments. One of them, which has become much more influential of late, upholds the view that Europe should aim to enhance its security through the North Atlantic Alliance. According to this line of thinking, the enlargement of NATO eastwards into East–Central Europe would permit it to preserve and increase stability on the continent. Russia as a comparable military force should not be antagonized and could become a viable partner in the security dialogue with NATO.

The second set of possible conclusions is much less oriented towards military security. It takes into consideration the fact that historically Russia has played an important role in containing the 'Wild East' and keeping overspills of violence away from the European heartlands. It played the role of European bread-basket for almost two centuries and supplied almost all the continent with cheap, high-quality raw materials. In the new conditions, then, it can be argued, Russia should be encouraged to play the same role as previously and, primarily through peacekeeping operations in its immediate vicinity, prevent the spread of disorder and violence into Europe.

Part VI

The Slav triangle: challenges and opportunities

Background chronology: Russia's relations with Belarus and Ukraine

1991

8 Dec.
Meeting in Minsk, the leaders of Belarus, Russia and Ukraine declare that the Soviet Union has ceased to exist and sign an agreement establishing a new association, the Commonwealth of Independent States (CIS)

1992

6 May
Ukraine announces completion of withdrawal to Russia of the former Soviet tactical nuclear weapons based on its territory

23 May
Leaders of Belarus, Kazakhstan, Russia and Ukraine sign a protocol with the USA (the Lisbon Protocol) committing themselves to adhere to the former Soviet Union's obligations under the START I Treaty ; Belarus, Kazakhstan and Ukraine pledge to become non-nuclear weapon states under the terms of the Non-Proliferation Treaty

4 June
Amid mounting tension between Russia and Ukraine, the Ukrainian Rada (parliament) approves a resolution rejecting the previous month's vote by the Russian Supreme Soviet to annul the 1954 decree transferring Crimea from Russia to Ukraine

23 June
In Dagomys President Yeltsin and Ukrainian President Kravchuk agree to draw up a wide-ranging treaty aimed at improving bilateral relations; the issue of Crimea is left off the agenda. They agree to remove the Black Sea Fleet from the CIS strategic forces and make it a joint Russian–Ukrainian fleet, the assets of which are to be divided later

1993

3 Sep.
Yeltsin and Kravchuk reportedly agree at a summit meeting in Massandra (Crimea) that Ukraine will sell its share of the Black Sea Fleet and lease Sevastopol to Russia in exchange for a reduction of Ukraine's debts to Russia; considerable confusion and acrimony arise when the Ukrainian Government subsequently denies that it has reached any specific agreements with Russia

1994

14 Jan.
In Moscow the presidents of Russia, Ukraine and the USA issue a Trilateral Statement that agreement has been reached on completion of withdrawal to Russia of the former Soviet strategic nuclear weapons based in Ukraine and on compensation for Ukraine for the value of the fissile material they contain

12 Apr.
Prime ministers of Belarus and Russia sign a controversial treaty on monetary union. The treaty grants the Russian central bank the sole right to issue currency and conduct monetary policy for the union

1995

17 Mar.
Ukrainian Rada abolishes presidency and constitution of Crimea on the grounds that they violate Ukrainian law

1 Apr.
Ukrainian President Kuchma issues a decree placing Crimea under direct presidential rule

9 June
Yeltsin and Kuchma sign an agreement dividing the ships and other assets of the former Soviet Black Sea Fleet (Ukraine agrees to sell Russia a significant portion of its share of the fleet), but the two sides remain divided on the long-term status of Sevastopol as the main base of the fleet

9 Dec.
Representatives of Russia and Belarus sign a series of agreements intensifying their military cooperation, including measures for joint air defence and the use of military infrastructure in Belarus by Russia

1996

2 Apr.
Yeltsin and Belarussian President Lukashenko sign a union treaty forming a Community of Sovereign Republics and providing for deeper integration between Belarus and Russia

1 June
Ukraine announces that it has fulfilled its pledge to become a non-nuclear weapon state with the completion of the transfer to Russia of the remaining former Soviet strategic nuclear warheads based in Ukraine

Key facts

Ukraine is the second largest state in Europe (600 000 km^2), with a population of 52.2 million (18% of the total population of the former USSR). Belarus, with a total territory of 200 000 km^2, has 10.4 million inhabitants.

Ukrainians and Belarussians are ethnically and lingustically close to Russians; ethnic Russians make up respectively 22% and 13% of their populations; Russian is generally spoken (in Belarus predominantly). The proportion of Russians in the population is especially high in the eastern and to a lesser degree the southern areas of Ukraine; in Crimea (which was administratively transferred from the RSFSR to the Ukrainian SSR in 1954) they constitute 67% of the total 1.7 million population. Five million Ukrainians live in Russia; one-third of officers and subalterns in the Russian armed forces originate from Belarus and Ukraine. The Orthodox confession is predominant in both countries although there are significant numbers of Greco-Catholics in western areas.

There is a high level of economic interdependence between the three countries. Belarus cannot function self-sufficiently. Russia and Ukraine are each other's largest trading partners, with a total turnover of over $13 billion. Ukraine and Belarus are heavily dependent on gas and oil exports (up to 75–90% of consumption); their debts to Russia in mid-1996 were estimated at $6 billion and $1.2 billion, respectively.

Ukraine and Belarus inherited from the USSR significant armed forces (700 000 and 130 000 troops, respectively) and a considerable number of modern weapons. Reduction and restructuring (under financial constraints and in order to abide by the Conventional Armed Forces in Europe (CFE) Treaty) are under way. Both states inherited nuclear armaments from the USSR and pledged to accede to the Non-Proliferation Treaty as non-nuclear weapon states. All nuclear warheads (c. 3000 tactical and 2000 strategic warheads) were withdrawn from Ukraine to Russia by June 1996; the last nuclear warheads were withdrawn from Belarus to Russia on 27 Nov. 1996. The status of the Black Sea Fleet has been one of the most contentious issues in Russian–Ukrainian relations.

12. The East Slav triangle

Vasily Kremen

I. Introduction

The peoples of the three Slav states—Belarus, Russia and Ukraine—are ethnically, culturally and spiritually close; they have a shared history centuries long and strong traditions of a common state system. The ethnic differences between Russians, Belarussians and Ukrainians are insignificant; moreover, millions of Russians live in Belarus and Ukraine and millions of Belarussians and Ukrainians in Russia, most often without preserving a strong ethnic identity. The three countries are economically very interdependent. Belarus and Ukraine are in the sphere of Russia's nearest geopolitical interests and Russia is therefore extremely interested in preserving its decisive influence on the developing social and political processes there. For Russia they are a gateway to East–Central and Western Europe; relations with them can be regarded in a sense as relations with Europe. At the same time, the establishment of relations with the independent Belarussian and Ukrainian states has become one of the most serious challenges for Russian democracy and for the country's ability to join the world community on the basis of the accepted norms of international relations.

This chapter analyses the state of Russia's relations with its immediate Slav neighbours. It begins by assessing the new East Slav states' long-term prospects for survival. Section III analyses the possible geopolitical orientations of Belarus and Ukraine and Russia's place in these and describes the essential features of the present transitional state of their relations. Section IV addresses some security aspects of the 'East Slav triangle' and examines the advantages of forging a coordinated foreign policy among the East Slav states, arguing that such coordination would lead to closer integration with Europe and the world community and that this is the best guarantee of their security and independence. Section V presents conclusions.

II. The viability of the new Slav states

During the past few years multinational states such as the USSR, Yugoslavia and Czechoslovakia have ceased to exist. More than 20 new states now occupy their place, making it possible to speak of the emergence of a partially new state system in Europe and Central Asia. Unlike many previous historical developments of this kind, the changes were not the result of large-scale military operations and the corresponding redistribution of spheres of influence among conflicting parties; rather, they came about for reasons quite often invisible from the outside.

Many observers point to the failure of communist social practice and ideology as the principal reason for the disintegration of these multinational states and the emergence of new ones. While there is no doubt that this failure has played a part, it is also important to take into account the fact that in Soviet times communist ideology succeeded in becoming the basis for state integration and adapted itself to the East Slav genotype.

As it developed in Russia, communism became a state ideology functioning primarily to protect the state system and which facilitated the formation of a totalitarian system of power.[1] The whole history of Russia shows that the state has played an important part in every field of Russian social, economic and political life. It was precisely in this respect that Russia, having adopted much of the cultural tradition of the Byzantine Empire, differed from Western civilization.[2] The state mechanism was a superstructure which carried out the functions of generating social and economic structures. This made it possible, within the limits of certain ideological doctrines, to mobilize the potential of the whole country—whether that of the Russian Empire or of the USSR—for consolidating and reinforcing the state.

Like any other highly centralized state system, the more it realized its purposes, the less stable and effective it became.[3] Having met the challenge of industrial modernization which demanded a maximum concentration of the efforts of the whole state, the Soviet system was unable to respond appropriately to the challenge of the post-industrial society, the key to which was not so much the external motivation and organization of a production process but the stimulation of the individual interest of a worker. The world of high technology requires not a state mechanism of compulsion but a social system able to unleash the creative potential of every person. It was precisely this social and economic aspect—not a mere generally humanist, propagandist and idealistic aspect, as is often thought—which caused communism of the East European model to give way to Western individualist civilization.

However, communist ideology and the Communist Party were not only symbols but also essential elements of the Soviet social organism, the foundations that supported the whole system. Just as the collapse of the tsarist autocracy in 1917 resulted in a temporary disintegration of the Russian Empire, the failure of the Communist Party of the Soviet Union resulted in the disintegration of a great power.

Criticism today of the disastrous consequences of the Belavezh Agreements[4] by a significant part of the Russian intelligentsia (which had fought actively against the communist system) is not simply a reflection of nostalgia for the past. It is also a recognition that their recent conception of the essence of the

---

[1] Guravleva, V. (ed.), *Na Doroge Krizisa* [On the way to crisis] (Politisdat: Moscow, 1990), pp. 135–36.

[2] Maslin, M. M. (ed.), *Russkaya Ideya* [The Russian idea] (Respublika: Moscow, 1992), pp. 316–17.

[3] Djilas, M., *Litso Totalitarisma* [The face of totalitarianism] (Novosti: Moscow, 1992), p. 192.

[4] Agreements on the dissolution of the USSR reached between Belarus, Russia and Ukraine at a secret meeting on 7–8 Dec. 1991 at Belavezh, near Brest, Belarus.

Soviet state structure and of the role that the state plays in the destinies of the peoples of Russia was oversimplified. It is no accident that various political parties in the post-Soviet states have started to search more actively for some common national doctrine that could become a state ideology to replace both autocracy and proletarian internationalism.[5] Remarkably, this process is being initiated not only by those who seek the restoration of a united state. Ruling quarters in all the countries of the Commonwealth of Independent States (CIS) are looking for a state ideology, even if without manifesting it.

This process did not start from nothing. Indeed, it is difficult to imagine what could have happened to the former Soviet Union if, at the moment of the collapse of communism, it had been a united, unitary power—if there had been no union republics and other national and territorial units with frontiers established by Lenin and Stalin, or if there had not been a local élite who had grown up in Soviet times with an established grip on the economic potential of 'their' territories and who knew how to keep their populations under ideologically repressive control.[6] Evidently, in spite of all the costs, a more or less peaceful 'divorce' of the republics of the USSR would have been impossible, as would their international recognition. The disintegration of the USSR therefore not only resulted from an exhaustion of the old totalitarian system facing the problems of a post-industrial future, but was made possible by so-called Soviet federative democracy, which from the very beginning marked the lines along which the centralized state and all-Soviet control mechanisms broke up.[7]

It was furthermore no accident that the lesson of this breakup made the greatest impression on the political élites of the new independent states. In order to stop the process of division there too, it is necessary to prove that the fragments of what used to be a single country possess a genotype which could provide a basis for their independent development. The central authorities of the new states react with pain to any attempt to give real autonomy to the 'autonomies' or to grant 'special status' for constituent parts of their territories. Their suspicions extend to local government, which they interpret as a threat to the centralization and concentration of economic and political power.

This only increases the danger for the future of the new democracies in conditions of growing social and economic crisis and a slow rate of reform, as in Belarus and Ukraine. The genesis of President Boris Yeltsin's regime showed once more how superficial the democratic processes in Russia are and how subordinated they are to the more traditional priorities of Russian social life. Watching these processes warily from Kiev or Minsk, no one could exclude the possibility of a repetition of this scenario in other states of the CIS.

The disintegration of the USSR, although caused by objective factors, was not inevitable. The thirst for complete independence of the peoples of the con-

---

[5] See, e.g., Kurginian, S., 'Politicheskie osnovy gosudarstvennogo stroitelstva' [The political foundations of state-building], *Rossiya–XXI*, nos 9–10 (1994), p. 13.

[6] Volkov, V. K., 'Etnokratiya: nepredvidenny fenomen posttotalitarnogo mira' [Ethnocracy: the unforeseen phenomenon of the post-totalitarian world], *Politicheskie Issledovaniya*, no. 2 (1993), p. 47.

[7] Dragunskiy, D. V., 'Navyazannaya etnichnost' [Imposed ethnicity], *Politicheskie Issledovaniya*, no. 5 (1993), p. 26.

stituent republics in 1991 should not be overestimated, except in the cases of the Baltic states and perhaps Georgia. Most of these populations were confronted by the accomplished fact of the collapse of the USSR resulting from the struggle for power among the Moscow political élite. Soviet President Mikhail Gorbachev's regime believed strongly in spreading ideas of democracy and freedom in the USSR, but proclaimed imperishable values instead of trying to adapt them to real social, economic, political and historical conditions. As a result, the mechanism of the Union was functioning worse and worse. The swings from one extreme to another in both the political and the economic fields only led to growing distrust of the central authorities and intensified their conflicts with local élites. Against the background of deep popular disenchantment with Gorbachev's economic policy, there formed the necessary prerequisites for redistributing real power from the centre to the provinces.

The greatest interest in this process—excluding the Baltic republics—was taken by the authorities of the most powerful of the Soviet republics, that is, the Russian Federation. They took the national movements in other republics to be their natural allies in their struggle against the 'Empire centre'. The Belavezh Agreements forced the republics to withdraw from the Union, thus de facto liquidating the discredited but still legitimate Union centre.

This could not but raise a number of new questions. The most substantial concerns the future of the new post-Soviet states: Are they capable of independent existence? Indeed, an assessment of the long-term prospects for the survival of Belarus and Ukraine as states is basic to understanding the present situation and the future of the Slav triangle. A number of factors in each of these states affect in both positive and negative ways their future as independent entities.

The objective conditions under which the consolidation of the Ukrainian state system is taking place are less favourable than those in Russia. In terms of its economy, the destruction of the common economic complex of the former USSR has had severe consequences for Ukraine, which specialized in energy-consuming industries. With much of the coal and virtually all the oil and gas resources on its territory already exhausted, Ukraine is almost totally dependent on external supplies (mainly from Russia and to some extent from Turkmenistan). It also lacks significant gold reserves and its industry is to a great extent geared to meet military demands.

The import content of Russia's gross national product (GNP) is estimated at 16 per cent while only 11 per cent is exported. If Russia halted its trade with the countries of the CIS and the Baltic states, it would be able to maintain its GNP at 65 per cent of its present level, while if it abandoned its imports from the 'far abroad' the figure would be 86 per cent. In the same situation Ukraine would be able to maintain only 15 per cent of GNP, and Belarus 4 per cent. The asymmetrical interdependence of these economies is also evident in estimates that

Russian imports are involved in the production of 67 per cent of Ukrainian GNP while Ukrainian imports are involved in only 1 per cent of Russian GNP.[8]

Clearly, the 'Ukrainian fragment' of the former all-Union economic complex cannot function without radical reconstruction. This underlies Ukraine's urgent need for investment and modern technologies. With debts reaching billions of dollars and in a situation of chronic financial instability, the satisfaction of these needs is at present impossible.

At the same time there are factors which favour the creation of an effective national economy—favourable natural conditions; the largest areas of *cherno-zem* (black earth) in the world; great scientific and industrial potential; highly developed mechanical engineering, metallurgy and chemical industries; rich mineral resources; and an industrious, well-educated labour force. However, the development of the political system is impeded by the lack of strong traditions of Ukrainian statehood and by the low level of national self-awareness among a large part of its population.

The population of Ukraine is not homogeneous. As a result of the division of Ukrainian territory between different countries over long periods of time (Russia, Poland and the Austro-Hungarian Empire), different regions have developed considerably different mentalities and social and political attitudes. Three main regions are usually identified: the east together with the south, the centre and the west. The differences between them are evident in their political orientations towards foreign countries. Data collected in September 1994 by the Social Monitoring Centre of the National Institute for Strategic Studies show that, while 73.4 per cent of the inhabitants of eastern regions favour the unification of the republic with the CIS, the corresponding figure in Crimea is 67 per cent; in the central areas, including Kiev, 36.7 per cent; and in the west 19.8 per cent. As a rule, specialists distinguish between Ukrainians and Russians, but it is more reasonable to point out three main groups which are approximately equal in size: Ukrainian-speaking ethnic Ukrainians; ethnic Russians; and Russian-speaking ethnic Ukrainians. There are other nationalities as well, but they are much less numerous. Attempts made during the first years of independence to impose the values accepted by some of the inhabitants of Ukraine on the whole country and excessive haste in linguistic Ukrainization resulted in the considerable alienation of the eastern and southern regions from the political capital, and this, along with the worsening of the economic situation, is responsible to a large extent for the abrupt decline in the prestige of the idea of the nation-state. This decline was evident in the results of the parliamentary and presidential elections held in 1994.

The Ukrainian state can sustain and develop itself only by balancing the interests of the inhabitants of every region and by elaborating a mechanism for securing vitally important links with Russia. Against a background of deep economic crisis, any tendency to take into account the interests of a single region

---

[8] Kupryanov, A. V., *Novye Politicheskie Kontseptsii Ekonomicheskikh Svyazey Rossii i Ukraini* [The new political concepts of the economic links between Russia and Ukraine] (Lotos: Odessa, 1994), p. 23.

while ignoring those of other groups of Ukrainian citizens can provoke confrontations not only between the regions and the centre but also among the regions.

The future of the Ukrainian state depends to a great extent on the all-national integration and consolidation of the society. This is made more difficult by the lack of political parties with significant support all over the country. There are 37 political parties in Ukraine representing the whole political spectrum. Some of them, the left for instance, are popular in the eastern and southern regions but less so in the central regions; others, the social democrats, draw significant support in the western regions, less in the central regions and none at all in the east and south.[9] With the exception of President Leonid Kuchma, there are no nationally popular political leaders.

Geographical conditions, however, favour the strengthening of the state system of Ukraine. The country has land frontiers with seven states and an outlet to the Black Sea, which makes it possible to use alternative sources of energy supplies.

On the whole, conditions in Belarus are less favourable to the strengthening of the state system. The country has practically no tradition of statehood. Over the centuries the national political élite occupied only a marginal position in the former Lithuanian, Polish and Russian state systems. The level of national consciousness is even lower than that in Ukraine. The Belarussian language and culture have a much more limited field of functioning: the 1994 census showed that only 12 per cent of the population speaks Belarussian fluently.[10] Its geographical conditions are less favourable than Ukraine's: in particular it has no outlet to the sea. Finally and probably most importantly, its industry is even more dependent on Russia and other republics of the former USSR. It is true that Belarussian industry consumes less power than Ukraine and is more directed to consumer needs. Also, like Ukraine, Belarus has well-developed scientific and educational systems and a fairly cheap and well-trained labour force. Overall, however, it is in greater need of ties with Russia than is Ukraine.

III. Russia in the foreign policies of Belarus and Ukraine

With the achievement of statehood, both Belarus and Ukraine have had to confront the challenge of working out their own foreign policy concepts. This has been a difficult task, since neither has previously been an independent state in the modern international system, and they have become such at a time when their geopolitical situation is altering considerably.

---

[9] Bazovkin, E. G., *Politicheskie Partii i Obshchestvennye Dvizheniya v Sisteme Sovremennoy Demokratii: Sravnitelny Analiz Ukraini i Rossii* [Political parties and popular movements in the system of contemporary democracy: a comparative analysis of Ukraine and Russia] ([Crimean Council of Ministers]: Simferopol, 1994), p. 153.

[10] Levyash, I., 'Russkie v Belarusi: doma ili v gostyakh?' [Russians in Belarus: at home or guests?], *Sotsiologicheskie Issledovaniya*, nos 8/9 (1994), pp. 139–40.

In theory, several possible broad foreign policy lines are open to Belarus and Ukraine, each of them professed in some form by different power groupings.

The first, and perhaps the most popular during the initial stage of independence, is one in which neither Belarus nor Ukraine will join any bloc but both will rather construct their foreign policy on the basis of bilateral agreements with different countries. However, this option would be open only for a country whose economy does not depend upon a single state, which is an organic element of world economic relations, which has old and strong traditions of a state system, and which enjoys a stable domestic political situation. The present situations of Belarus and Ukraine are such that this does not seem to be a real option for them.

The second option is for these countries to pursue rapid integration into the community of Western nations in the hope of receiving investment and new technologies and of raising living standards. However, the experience of the first four years of independence has demonstrated that neither Belarus nor Ukraine is in the front rank of those countries which might realistically expect to forge strong links with the West; the countries of East–Central Europe (ECE), being closer to Western Europe territorially, economically and historically, are ahead of them. It is also clear that the West is not ready for massive investment in countries where the infrastructure is only embryonic and that the new states themselves are not ready for close integrating links.

The third variant is based on the idea of establishing a bloc with the Baltic countries and certain ECE countries—a Black Sea–Baltic community or Inter-Sea.[11] However, this strategy would not allow Belarus and Ukraine to realize their economic interests, which are for access to raw materials and markets.[12] It is also far from clear whether the political rationale for such a bloc—which would be to unite states which have the common aim of confronting the power of their eastern neighbour—would be strong enough to create a durable alliance. Moreover, Russia regards the idea of the Black Sea–Baltic community as an attempt to construct a cordon sanitaire between Western Europe and itself.

Putting aside even less realistic ideas of forming a bloc in a southern direction, above all with Turkey, there remains only one realistic foreign policy option for Belarus and Ukraine: namely, alliance with Russia and other CIS countries. The public mood in Belarus and Ukraine favours such an alliance, and this sentiment is growing all the time. As research from the National Institute for Strategic Studies in Kiev shows, 20.8 per cent of Ukrainian citizens supported the policy of uniting the CIS republics into a common state in 1992, 30.7 per cent supported it in 1993 and 47.4 per cent supported it in 1994.

---

[11] 'Zadla spilnoi mety' [For the sake of the common purpose], *Politika i Chas*, no. 4 (1994) (in Ukrainian). See also chapter 15 in this volume.
[12] See, e.g., Kolomiec, P., 'Vid haosu do osmislenith dij' [From chaos to comprehensive action], *Politika i Chas*, no. 7 (1994), pp. 24–25 (in Ukrainian); and Kyrashik, V., 'Bilorysi lishaaytsia optimistami' [Belarussians remain optimistic], *Politika i Chas*, no. 9 (1994), p. 4 (in Ukrainian).

This foreign policy line gives Belarus and Ukraine the possibility of realizing many of their principal national interests. First, alliance with Russia is natural, since the three states are components of an organic entity that has been forming for centuries. The disintegration of the USSR destroyed the state but did not eliminate the strongest links between its components, and the new states in the difficult process of finding their social and economic identities have to adapt their relations to these basic interdependencies. Second, this option would give Belarus and Ukraine a chance to make maximum use of their industrial potential and to restore natural markets and raw material supplies. Third, it would create the conditions for a gradual reconstruction of their economies, which would move them in the direction of being able more fully to satisfy the principal needs of their citizens. Finally, it is precisely the economic nature of an alliance with Russia that would serve as the basis for a compromise acceptable to each of the East Slav partners, promote the stabilization of the social, economic and political situations in Belarus and Ukraine, and help to secure the indivisibility of their national territories.

It should be noted, however, that the disintegration of the USSR in 1991 initiated a new phase in Russia's relations with Belarus and Ukraine. The principal change was the transition from relations of dependence and subordination within the territorial boundaries of a superpower—the Soviet Union, which can be considered as 'Greater Russia'—to relations of cooperation between formally equal independent states. This transition has been unstable and has revealed considerable differences of interest. From time to time, particularly in relations between Russia and Ukraine, there has been a danger of direct confrontation.

Mutually beneficial integrating links have not been created at the interstate level. This has resulted in the destruction of the positive gains that had been made during the previous historical period and has hindered the development of the state systems of Belarus, Russia and Ukraine.

The dynamics of disintegration complicated the situation in every field of national life in the three states. In the economic realm, it revealed itself in disastrous falls in production caused by the breakup of cooperative links and chains of many technological processes and the destruction of a common market and financial space that had been functioning for a long time.[13] In politics, rule from a single centre and lack of political freedom were replaced by political rivalries and confrontation between new states whose home and political affairs were in serious disorder. In the social field, guaranteed—if minimal—living conditions gave way to a struggle for survival, an unusual problem for most former Soviet citizens. In the realm of spiritual life and morality, the discredited values, including the sense of pride in being a citizen of a great power, have not yet been replaced by a new system of values.

---

[13] Popovkin, V., 'Uroki ekonomichnoi eklektiki' [Lessons in economic eclecticism], *Viche*, no. 7 (1994), pp. 3–4 (in Ukrainian).

A number of problems have emerged that are producing stresses and conflicts in Russia's relations with the other Slav states. They are: (a) the debts and assets of the former USSR, the division of its property abroad and the future of the Black Sea Fleet; (b) relations between Ukraine and its component part, Crimea, which before 1954 was part of the Russian Federation; (c) contacts between the inhabitants of frontier regions; and (d) transport problems. These conflicts can be settled in a civilized way only within the limits of cooperation between subjects enjoying equal rights.

Many factors impede the development of more equal and cooperative relations between Belarus and Ukraine on the one hand and Russia on the other. The development of the Belarussian and Ukrainian nation-states is not complete. A number of important institutions are lacking or underdeveloped. Their economies are over-integrated into the Russian economy, especially with respect to energy supplies. The feeling of national identity is not strong enough among a considerable proportion of the Belarussian and Ukrainian populations and there is something of a 'younger brother' complex vis-à-vis Russia. The Western countries are having difficulty working out a policy towards Belarus and Ukraine. Russia continues to occupy a privileged position in the relations of the West with the CIS countries.

One obstacle to putting interstate relations in the East Slav triangle on a more equal footing is the continuing perception of Belarus and Ukraine as organic parts of Russia. The Slav closeness of the peoples favours the growth of this sentiment. After the elation following the August 1991 confrontation, part of Russia's population is increasingly inclined to see the disintegration of the USSR as an enormous loss. It considers the concept of the Russian Federation's independence from the USSR to be a political absurdity. In turn, most of the ethnic Russians and Russian-speaking Ukrainians in Ukraine have become aware of the disastrous consequences of an ideal of self-sufficiency and independence: not only the social and economic interests but also rather sensitive aspects of the national, linguistic and spiritual self-identification of that considerable part of the population which is not separating itself from Russia are being sacrificed to this idea. Moreover, despite numerous failures and the high cost of reforms in the Russian Federation, the standard of living there is still much higher than in Belarus and Ukraine. This has demoralized some groups of the population that had hoped for higher rates of growth compared to those of Russia.[14]

Certain subjective factors have a considerable influence on Russia's relations with Belarus and Ukraine. To a decisive extent these factors are conditioned by the position of élite groups within the three countries. In this regard there is an essential difference between Russia on the one hand and Belarus and Ukraine on the other.

---

[14] Nebogenko, V., 'Socialna naprugenist: upovilnena mina chi vasil samoporjatunku' [Social tension: a ticking bomb or the key to self-preservation], Viche, no. 11 (1994), p. 36 (in Ukrainian).

Russia inherited the old Soviet élite, with its varied history, multiple experience of functioning at the state level and long-established close contacts with élite groups in other countries. The Russian élite is not homogeneous, however. With respect to its views and positions on relations with Belarus and Ukraine, there are two main groups discernible within this élite: one recognizes the legitimacy of the new states and accepts the need to form relations with them on the basis of equal rights between sovereign states; the other group denies the very right of Belarus and Ukraine to exist as independent states and considers them to be accidental and temporary phenomena.

The political élites of Belarus and Ukraine can be categorized according to their pre-independence activities into two main groups: former government officials and those recruited from more or less active opponents of the previous regime. The first group is more realistic and pragmatic about relations with Russia, while the second quite often takes absolutist positions based upon the national idea; its representatives are characterized by a kind of romanticism and political impatience. It was the second group which largely determined the ideological and political positions of Leonid Kravchuk when he was President of Ukraine, especially in 1991–93. They were responsible for his government failing to find a middle course between the dangerous extremes of uncompromising nationalist positions on the one hand and dependence on Russia on the other.

There are also significant regional differences in the views and preferences of the Ukrainian élite about relations with Russia. If political leaders in eastern Ukraine favour Russia, those in western Ukraine favour the West.

Nevertheless, the general tendency of the public mood in Ukrainian society now favours closer contacts with Russia. This was evident in the parliamentary and presidential elections in 1994. The results of these elections showed that any obstacles of a subjective nature to establishing friendly and equal relations with Russia have been removed from the Ukrainian side.

The ascendancy of President Kuchma is symptomatic in this regard. He was elected not only thanks to a wave of popular discontent caused by low living standards, but also because of his position on relations with Russia, which garnered considerable support among Russians and other Russian-speaking nationalities. Kuchma drew most of his support from the eastern and southern regions, while in western Ukraine he was eclipsed by Leonid Kravchuk. Many, especially in Russia, expected with hope, but in Ukraine with fear, that Kuchma would force reintegration with Russia, which seemed to be the logical outcome of his views. However, this did not happen. To the disappointment of a certain part of the Russian public, he launched a policy of mutually advantageous and rational cooperation.

There is only one objective explanation for this: the notion of Ukraine as an independent state has gained a firm enough hold in public opinion, and especially élite opinion, for the actions of a nationally elected leader to be unable to go against it. Moreover, the fact that it was Kuchma, a politician with a more realistic and pragmatic policy approach free of myths and Utopianism, who was elected president cut the ground from under the feet of critics of the nation-state system. Ukraine thereby gained additional opportunities to consolidate its independent status.

The international factor also affects Russia's relations with Belarus and Ukraine. From early 1994, the USA paid greater attention to the two countries, moving away from its previously exclusive focus on relations with Russia. However, it is clear that relations with Russia will still be the highest priority for Western countries because of Russia's position in the world, its potential and its possession of nuclear weapons. It is doubtful whether the USA and the West European countries would take extreme measures to restrain Russia's geopolitical appetites in the space of the CIS. This situation would change radically only in the event of a sudden growth of Russian aggressiveness directed westward; however, the probability of such a course of events in the immediate future is very slight.

At the same time, it is quite possible that under certain conditions the relations of Belarus and Ukraine with the Western countries could be used by the latter to put pressure on Russia. The ruling quarters in the Russian Federation realize this, and the result is a noticeable Russian suspicion about the development of Western institutional links, above all those of NATO, with Belarus and Ukraine.

The strengthening of trust on a bilateral and multilateral basis, including through the Organization for Security and Co-operation in Europe (OSCE), the UN and other international institutions, would promote the development of neighbourly relations of mutual benefit between the Russian Federation and its two Slav neighbours. The security guarantees and pledges to respect territorial integrity granted to Ukraine after its parliament voted in November 1994 to ratify the 1968 Non-Proliferation Treaty (NPT) created a real basis for alleviating the issue of nuclear weapons as a potential source of conflict in relations between Russia and Ukraine.[15] There are reasons to think that the continuous strengthening of Ukraine's economic cooperation with the Russian Federation will help to solve the problem of the future of Crimea and will increase the prospects for settling the problem of the Black Sea Fleet on mutually acceptable terms. The degree of *rapprochement* between Belarus and Russia in the past two years has in particular been considerable.

At the same time, there exists a certain anxiety in Ukraine, and to a lesser extent in Belarus, about getting closer to Russia.[16] This reflects a fear of their falling again into total economic and political dependence on Russia, a concern which derives from considerations of the great difference in potentials, the literal size of their states and their genuine inequality, as well as the nature of public opinion in Russia. Hence, an economic alliance with Russia would require strict specifications concerning its functioning if these states wish to

[15] Goodby, J. E., Kile, S. and Müller, H., 'Nuclear arms control', *SIPRI Yearbook 1995: Armaments, Disarmament and International Security* (Oxford University Press: Oxford, 1995), pp. 638–39.

[16] Konvay, B., 'Ekonomicheskiy souz ta interesi Ukraini' [Economic union and the interests of Ukraine], *Rozbudova Dergeavi*, no. 10 (1994), p. 16 (in Ukrainian).

secure their economic sovereignty and their rights to develop contacts of mutual benefit with third parties.

IV. Problems of security and strategic perspectives

Many aspects of relations between Belarus, Russia and Ukraine are directly connected with the problems of security in this area and in the wider— European and world—arena, and the significance and specific weight of security problems in relations between the three countries will grow, especially between Russia and Ukraine, as the new states develop their statehoods and separate themselves from the former common defence system.

Russia's 'loss' of Belarus and Ukraine as a result of the disintegration of the Soviet Union—the use of the term 'lost' is justified, in the view taken here, because the USSR can be considered as Russia post-tsarism—greatly complicated its security problems because it reduced Russia's defence and industrial potential, human resources and territory. Now a distinctive new corridor of states has appeared between Russia and the ECE countries. On the one hand, this circumstance can be considered favourable to the solution of Russia's security problem, because the country is thereby separated territorially from those bodies which were its traditional rivals and opponents and from the NATO bloc. On the other hand this 'buffer' is not so important because of the range of modern missiles. Moreover, there are no hard guarantees that the new states or some of them will not join the traditional potential enemies of Russia, which is why Russia is extremely concerned to block the enlargement of NATO eastwards and the inclusion of Ukraine and other new states in its sphere of influence.

This is a factor of increasing importance in relations between Russia and Ukraine, and to a lesser extent between Belarus and Russia. Belarus not only has a pro-Russian policy, but is ready for integration to the extent that it might cease to exist as an independent state, first de facto, then *de jure*.

Ukraine has taken the opposite position. It aspires to keep strictly to its proclaimed policy of neutrality, which presupposes no association with the military blocs. That is why it reacts negatively to any proposal that might lead to the amalgamation of the military potential of the former Soviet republics. At the same time it has taken steps to cooperate with the NATO bloc, above all within the framework of the Partnership for Peace (PFP), but has not stated a wish to join the bloc, being aware that such a step would seriously complicate the maintenance of European security and does not correspond to its own national interest in present conditions. Ukraine is moreover constantly aware of the open or hidden pressure of Russia in the economic, political and information spheres, which it cannot possibly ignore given its position of essential dependence on its neighbour—especially in energy supplies.

In Russia's security thinking, the significance of Belarus and Ukraine cannot be overestimated. For Russia the most important, if not decisive, condition of maintaining its own traditional geopolitical space and thus of aspiring to the role of a superpower is keeping Belarus and Ukraine in its sphere of influence. This pattern may, however, prevent their consolidation in the world community and hamper the natural processes of national self-identification. There is reason to think that the present policy of Belarus is fraught with precisely this danger. At the same time, if they attempt estrangement from Russia or fail to understand or ignore Russia's legitimate interests, their security may be threatened from Russia's side. A policy of close and mutually beneficial relations on the basis of mutual and equal cooperation is therefore the optimum one. The present leadership of Ukraine states that it aspires to precisely this.

However, there are a number of security obstacles to establishing cooperation between equal partners. Apart from Russia's general desire to keep Ukraine within the common defence area, there are the problems of the Black Sea Fleet and of the nuclear weapons on Ukrainian territory.

The importance of the Black Sea Fleet for Russia's security is doubtful. Its capabilities and the peculiarities of its basing make it effective only on the Black Sea, where Russia has no potential enemies. The problem of the Black Sea Fleet is rather a political one. To keep its bases in Crimea will make it possible on the one hand to exert a certain influence on that part of the Ukraine, and on the other hand to relax to some degree the nostalgic feelings of some Russian citizens and politicians about the 'lost' territory. Ukraine has been obliged to go along with Russia's demands concerning the Fleet, but the fact that the problem was resolved under pressure from the Russian side, that the latter evaded compensation for basing its navy on Ukrainian territory, and attempts to interfere in Crimea—that is, in the internal affairs of Ukraine—have greatly damaged the prospects for establishing good-neighbourly relations and strategic partnership.

The resolution of the problem of nuclear weapons in Belarus and Ukraine is of paramount importance for security in the East Slav triangle. They committed themselves to dispose of the nuclear weapons on their territories and are carrying this out. By May 1992, all the tactical nuclear charges (c. 3000 in total) had been transferred from Ukraine to Russia. Approximately 2000 of these had been destroyed by June 1996. During 1993–94, 40 RS-18[17] intercontinental ballistic missiles (ICBMs) were removed from their battle positions in Ukraine. In accordance with the Trilateral Statement of the presidents of the Russian Federation, Ukraine and the USA of 14 January 1994,[18] all 46 of Ukraine's very modern RS-22[19] ICBMs were deactivated—a major reduction in the level of readiness. By June 1996, the transfer of strategic nuclear charges (c. 2000 in number) was complete. Ukraine continues to prepare to carry out the extensive work of actual destruction of weapons provided for under the START I Treaty (the 1991 Treaty on the Reduction and Limitation of Strategic Offensive Arms). In the first stage of destruction of strategic nuclear arms, that

---

[17] SS-19s according to the US classification.
[18] Goodby (note 15), pp. 636–37.
[19] SS-24s under the US classification.

is, up to the end of 1998, 130 launchers for the RS-18 missiles remain to be destroyed. The process of removal of nuclear charges from Belarus was expected to be complete by the end of 1996.[20]

The liquidation of these countries' nuclear weapons will mean that their armed forces are brought into line with their proper potential, and will thus objectively promote the security of the region and indeed the world. For Russia it will mean the relaxation of tension in its relations with Belarus and Ukraine, but only if they manage to maintain independent policies. If Belarus enters a confederative or other type of union with Russia, the latter may then be interested in basing nuclear weapons on Belarussian territory to reinforce its own potential, and in this event Ukraine might then be interested to look again at the fate of its nuclear weapons. In this connection, it seems that there is no alternative to the decision by Belarus and Ukraine to destroy their nuclear weapons on their own territory with the help of the world community.

How will the problems of security in the East Slav triangle be resolved? The answer depends on many factors, and first of all on the fate of the new states. If the situation is examined as a whole there is a case for saying that the sides and the angles in this triangle are not all equal. It is very clear that Belarus is not capable of a level of national self-identification that would ensure its existence as an independent state. The possibility of its being swallowed up by Russia under the guise of reunification may well be realized. Security problems will then be decided within the limits of one or other type of military alliance or versatile CIS structures.

The relationship between Russia and Ukraine will be decided differently. The development of the domestic political processes in Ukraine bears witness to the increasing steadiness and internal stability of the state, regardless of its economic difficulties. The most probable foundation of Ukraine's security will be cooperation with Russia. On a wider scale, Ukraine is interested in the creation of a system of security that would integrate Europe and Russia. This is conditional on many factors, one of which is the geopolitical situation of the country and the external policy orientations of the populations of the different Ukrainian regions.

A strategic analysis of Russia's relations with Belarus and Ukraine should take into account that all three countries are interested in strengthening their relations with the West, at the same time trying to preserve their most important essential features and peculiarities.

All three countries face a need to break out of the old, confrontational pattern in relations with the West and replace it with cooperative interaction. However, the 'drift' of these countries westwards could take one of two forms. They can move together, in more or less coordinated fashion, without breaking links that have been formed historically and have proved to be rational; or they can move separately, without taking into consideration their mutual interests.

---

[20] See also Kile, S. and Arnett, E., 'Nuclear arms control', *SIPRI Yearbook 1996: Armaments, Disarmament and International Security* (Oxford University Press: Oxford, 1996), pp. 615–16, 628–30.

For Belarus and Ukraine, the first model is important not least because it means that there are options other than the very crude and possibly destructive choice between an eastward and a westward geopolitical orientation. It would give them the opportunity to retain their links to Russia and would allow them to secure public peace, integrity and even statehood. Particularly in the case of Ukraine, it would reconcile the different orientations of the inhabitants of the eastern, western and southern parts of the country and reduce confrontation. It would also eliminate the division of Europe and Eurasia and prevent the emergence of a new 'iron curtain' on the eastern or western frontier of Belarus and Ukraine—developments either of which would be detrimental for both countries. The possibility that this divide would cut through Ukraine itself cannot be excluded.

There is no doubt that closer cooperation with Belarus and Ukraine promises advantages for the Russian Federation as well. It could help Russia to remain one of the centres of modern civilization and strengthen Russia's position considerably in protecting its legitimate interests in Europe and the world. By contrast, alienating these states and ignoring their interests would diminish the Russian Federation's influence and the role it plays in the world.

Furthermore, in the opinion of some analysts, an alliance between Belarus, Russia and Ukraine could weaken a potential threat from Islamic fundamentalism. This threat is perceived as having increased both because of a weakening of Russia itself and because of a uniting of pro-Islamic forces in the country and abroad.[21]

Finally, coordinated action by the three East Slav states would give each of them an opportunity to join the European and world communities on more beneficial terms and, it may be hoped, reduce the time needed for them to achieve equality with the countries of Western Europe not only in the political but also in the economic sense.

Within the Moscow–Kiev–Minsk triangle, relations between Russia and Ukraine are the most important. It is increasingly evident that neither in cultural, economic, political nor military respects are there sufficiently serious reasons for tension in Russian–Ukrainian relations. All three states are tending towards European values and social norms. The methods and means of social modernization chosen by them are almost identical. The reasons for strained relations can be defined as the phenomenon of a 'residual ideological effect'. On the Ukrainian side, there are moods of national romanticism and provincial complexes, while on the Russian side there is a tendency to treat Ukraine as a 'younger brother'.

The principal task of these relations in the present conditions is the development of a reliable interstate mechanism that can secure as fully as possible the three countries' national interests in so far as they relate to their relations with each other. Large-scale economic, financial and humanitarian cooperation

---

[21] Kudrov, V., 'Mesto novoy Rossii v mire' [The new Russia's place in the world], *Svobodnaya Mysl*, no. 6 (1994), p. 56.

based on national interests can become the most fertile basis for these relations. This doctrine can be defined as one of rational partnership, one in which economic interests are undoubtedly dominant.[22] A partnership of this kind will provide each of the parties with the desired freedom of action, including the possibility of establishing contact with third countries.

Russia's policy, if based on this approach, will be supported by Belarus and Ukraine. Its relations with the two will develop at different speeds, since their rates of internal development, geopolitical situation and so on are different and they have different interests and potentials for cooperation with Russia and each other.[23] Both, however, support the formation of interstate organs to coordinate economic cooperation and facilitate procedures for trade flows and payments and for the free movement of labour, which is especially plentiful in Belarus and Ukraine, in contrast to Russia. However, an organizational and economic mechanism for integration should be worked out anew. In the former USSR this used to occur along vertical lines: a certain system of relations was dictated from above and even interactions between the constituent republics were mediated by the centre. Under present conditions, horizontal connections between productive and commercial structures are the most significant.[24]

Closer cooperation and coordination can be expected in science, education, public health and social security, and culture. To achieve this, both multilateral and bilateral structures can be formed. In the immediate future Ukraine will probably participate more actively in the work of the Parliamentary Assembly of the CIS (Belarus is already a full member), which will open up new opportunities both for the assembly and for Ukraine.

More coordinated action between the three states is already possible. Where Russia's political influence favours the realization of democratic principles and the ending of regional conflicts, it can be expected to be supported by Belarus and Ukraine. On the other hand, they will move away from Russia if it should take any expansionist steps—a possibility which cannot be excluded.[25]

There still remains a real possibility that Russia will try to establish a pattern of relations with Belarus and Ukraine in which it plays the dominant role. This approach is based on the enormous economic dependence of these two states on Russian energy and raw materials supplies, as well as on their need for access to the commodities markets of the Russian Federation. Furthermore, Russia has made greater progress in reforming its own economic system, and a new social group—that of the entrepreneurs—is emerging which is beginning to feel constrained within the limits of the Russian Federation's frontiers. By contrast, radical economic reforms have been slow in coming in Belarus and Ukraine. As

[22] Pirozhkov, S., Basovkin, E. and Kremen, V., *Strategii Rozvitku Ukraini: Vikliki Chasu ta Vibir* [Strategies for the development of Ukraine: challenges of time and choice] (Kiev, 1994), pp. 72–73 (in Ukrainian).

[23] 'Interesi Rossii i SNG' [Russia's interests and the CIS], *Mezhdunarodnaya Zhizn*, no. 9 (1991), p. 15.

[24] Kirichenko, V., 'O tendentsii k ekonomicheskoy reintegratsii v SNG' [On the tendency towards economic reintegration in the CIS], *Svobodnaya Mysl*, no. 9 (1994), p. 13.

[25] Pugachev, B., *Rossiya: Politicheskoe Sostoyanie* [Russia: its political state] (Moscow, 1994), p. 19.

a result, business in both countries is weak, labour is comparatively cheap (although still sufficiently highly trained), and internal tax and investment laws are uncoordinated and conflicting. These conditions have attracted the expansion of rather aggressive Russian businesses into their territories.

The representatives of Russian capital are much better adapted than those of Western capital to the turbulent conditions of the 'Wild East Slav market' and, as a rule, have numerous stable contacts with the local establishment at different levels; they already influence many different aspects of domestic policy. The recent tendency to form transnational corporations is of mutual benefit for all three states; however, it will strengthen the domination of Russian business if the process of economic reform in Belarus and Ukraine slows down. It remains an open question whether Russia will gain significant political benefit from these developments. In any case, it is clear that the level and quality of relations within the Slav triangle will be determined primarily by the dynamism and effectiveness of the economic reform programmes that have been proclaimed by Presidents Kuchma of Ukraine and Lukashenko of Belarus with the consent of the leaderships of the political parties in their respective countries.

Belarus and Ukraine seem to have chosen different patterns of relations with Russia—on the one hand integration which may eventually lead to incorporation, and on the other a kind of rivalry or competition. In both cases an important factor will be comparative living standards. At least some of their populations supported independence only for economic reasons, that is in the expectation that it would improve standards of living. The wave of national–democratic movements generated unreal expectations. After four years of independence, these expectations have turned out to be vain, and most people have not managed to maintain their previous living standards. This has been the main reason for disappointment with the idea of national independence. A serious, long-term decline in living standards in Belarus and Ukraine compared with those in Russia is perhaps the greatest threat to the independence of both.

Such a turn of events would mean an historic opportunity for Russia to unite Belarus and Ukraine peacefully under its authority, in one way or another, if not in a unitary or federated state then in a confederacy or within the CIS. The active *rapprochement* of Belarus with Russia has indicated a trend. However, relations between Russia and Ukraine do not follow this pattern. The action of Russia in Chechnya, the participation of Russian troops in the frontier conflicts of Tajikistan, the Russian presence in the Transcaucasus, Russia's own instability and other factors discourage any aspirations on the part of the citizens of Ukraine for union with Russia, while the more pragmatic and balanced policy of President Kuchma has favoured a realistic interpretation of the Ukrainian state system as opposed to the mythical, nationalist and radical interpretation. A new version of the Pereyaslav Rada which joined Ukraine to Russia 340 years ago is not to be expected.

V. Conclusions

Belarus, the Russian Federation and Ukraine, like other countries of the CIS, contain many conflicting tendencies and forces. On the one hand, disintegration processes are going on. The shell of the old unity has broken up. This is true not only of the 'large' geopolitical space, that is, the total area of the former USSR, but also of the 'small' one, the nucleus of the previous state—the Slav triangle. One aspect of the unity of the republics of the former USSR—the organizing function of Moscow—is fading into the past. Russia has certainly played an outstanding part in securing and extending their territories and forming their way of life. Expectations once directed at Russia, however, have now given way to expectations directed at Europe.

Belarus, Ukraine and other constituent republics of the former Soviet state have became the subjects of international law, even though the processes of their political, social and economic self-identification and of their definition of national interests are proceeding with difficulty and at considerable expense. At present the Russian Federation remains by far the leading country in the post-Soviet space. However, its way of influencing other peoples, including those in the East Slav triangle, should be changed. The principal changes should be to consolidate the interstate relations between the three countries and for Russia to respect the statehood of Belarus and Ukraine.

At the same time the Belarussian and Ukrainian state systems cannot be alienated completely from that of Russia. The interconnections between the three peoples are such that the Belarussian and Ukrainian societies must be seen not as independent social systems but as sub-systems of the larger system that was previously called the Soviet Union. If these interconnections are not reflected in specific mechanisms of interaction, it will be extremely difficult if not impossible to secure their state systems.

The East Slav countries are destined to be neighbours and to cooperate. To a decisive degree the character of their relations will depend on Russia, which has considerable advantages over Belarus and Ukraine in all the main indexes of state power. In this lies the crucial importance of the future nature of the Russian Federation's domestic political system. If it is a democratic one, the process will develop in a civilized manner; if it is not, then the most dangerous cataclysms are possible, including the destabilization of the political situations in Belarus and Ukraine from abroad.[21]

However, if events develop in this way, Russia itself will be doomed to instability and violence, and its peoples will be involved in a steadily widening and potentially endless long-term conflict which clearly does not accord with their fundamental interests. Only a commitment to strengthening mutual trust and observing the norms of international law can show the new independent states the right way to the future.

---

[21] Brzezinski, Z., 'Vne kontrolya: globalny besporyadok nakanune XXI veka' [Out of control: global confusion on the eve of the 21st century], *SShA: Ekonomika, Politika, Ideologia*, vol. 4, no. 9 (1994).

13. Russia and the Slav vicinity

Sergei Karaganov

I. Introduction

Relations with Belarus and Ukraine are clearly the key element of the overall relationship of Russia with states of the former Soviet Union. Belarus, Russia and Ukraine for centuries formed the core of Russian tsardom and then the Russian Empire. Their relationship has been characterized by the profound interpenetration and interdependence of their economies. The Russian Empire and later the Soviet Union were ruled mostly by the representatives of these three republics, especially Russia and Ukraine.

The three countries are culturally very close. Belarus and Ukraine still keep nuclear weapons on their soil. For Russia the other two republics play a key role in its communications with the West. Most trade routes and most pipelines connecting Russia with the West run through them. They also have one thing in common in the Russian mind: many, if not most, Russians simply refuse at a deep level to understand that they are and will continue to be something different from Russia. At the same time the acuteness of this feeling is decreasing. Time is healing. The growing gap between the living standards of Belarus and Ukraine on the one hand and Russia, whose economy is declining much more slowly and has a better chance of recuperating eventually, on the other also makes many Russians wonder whether reunification would actually be in Russian interests.

After noting the features which are common to Russian relations with the two Slav republics, however, it must be said that in most aspects they differ. Russian policies towards Belarus and Ukraine are developing along different lines, which could eventually create two of the main models for Russia's relationships with most of the other countries which emerged out of the ruins of the Soviet Union.

II. Ukraine

Ukraine is obviously the most difficult challenge for Russia. After the disintegration of the Soviet Union the feeling of loss was particularly acute in the case of Ukraine. What is now Ukraine was the cradle of the Russian nation. The history of Kievan Rus was the early history of Russia. Many in Russian political circles were afraid that the loss of Ukraine would undermine the economy of Russia and were concerned that Ukraine could eventually pose a serious geopolitical challenge for Russia, creating anti-Russian alliances with neighbouring countries or being used by the West to counterbalance the weight of Russia.

These fears, which later (predictably) proved to be largely unfounded, were to a great extent provoked by some voices in the West, first of all that of Zbigniew Brzezinski, calling for the creation out of Ukraine of some kind of buffer zone between Russia and the rest of Europe, if not a semi-belligerent counterweight.

During the first year of Ukrainian independence there was no Ukrainian policy in Moscow.[1] Contacts were very few if any. The political agenda of relations between two countries, in so far as one existed, was dominated by issues which were of secondary importance precisely because of the absence of policy on the Russian side, and also because the Ukrainian leadership probably came to the conclusion that it could not build a new statehood without the creation of an enemy image. Divisive issues therefore dominated the agenda: the fate of the former Soviet fleet in the Black Sea, the fate of Crimea, the attempts of some Russian political forces to question the borders of Ukraine, and so on.

Interestingly enough the issue of nuclear weapons did not play a prominent role on the interstate agenda at that time. This was partly because the issue was managed relatively successfully with the help of the US Administration and also because the Russian military were sure that Ukrainians would not be able to obtain effective control over the nuclear potential. The only really dangerous (from the point of view of proliferation) part of the nuclear potential on Ukrainian soil—tactical nuclear weapons—was withdrawn relatively quickly thanks to the combined and largely coordinated efforts of Moscow and Washington. The remaining weapons, mostly of a strategic nature, were more or less 'doomed' for withdrawal because Ukraine simply lacked the technical and especially the financial means to keep this potential. An attempt to convert some of these weapons into crude bombs and/or to create new launching platforms for them would have cost even more politically than an attempt to retain the existing weapons in their present form. In the end the Ukrainian leadership yielded to the inevitable and agreed to withdraw all nuclear weapons from the country.

Overall, the first 12–18 months of Russian–Ukrainian relations were marked largely by low-key hostility on the level of rhetoric caused by the Ukrainian search for identity, by a combination of insensitivity, the sense of a divided nation and a feeling of superiority on the part of many Russians, and by the virtual absence of any systematic and regular political and diplomatic exchange between the two nations. That mix was pregnant with future crisis. However, a combination of good luck and caution on the part of the leaders of the two countries meant that a flare-up was avoided.

After the first year of Ukrainian independence, the agenda of Russian–Ukrainian relations started to change, largely because of changes in Ukraine. If during the first year of Ukrainian independence it looked as if Kiev was suc-

---

[1] It is noteworthy that before the Dagomys and Yalta summit meetings in June and Aug. 1992 Russia even tried to solve problems of bilateral relations within the forums of the CIS.

cessfully building up its statehood and had a chance of getting by economically, by the end of 1992 or beginning of 1993 the situation started to change.[2]

More and more people in Ukraine and in Russia started to acknowledge that the Ukrainian economy was sliding towards catastrophe. This was the result of the refusal of the Ukrainian élite to start economic reforms, partly because of the domination of the government by former communist leaders, who in general had been more conservative than their Moscow counterparts, partly because of their decisions as to national priorities. The building up of statehood and not economic reform was made the first priority. In comparison with Russia, Ukraine was also much less well-endowed with natural resources.

One of the reasons for the catastrophic downturn of the Ukrainian economy was the start of reforms in Russia. These reforms succeeded at least in one direction—the introduction of a reasonable price system, which set prices in Russia closer to world prices. It became clear almost immediately that for years Russia had been a net exporter of resources within the former Soviet Union, an economic colony—the opposite of what had been believed in Ukraine and many other republics of the former Soviet Union.

With more realistic prices for oil, gas and other natural resources Ukraine was no longer competitive in the West or on the Russian market. Even Ukrainian food started to lose in competition with food exported from other countries. These developments were exacerbated by the absence in Ukraine of competent economic and technical élites able to run a modern economy or manage modern reforms. That was the result of the fact that for decades if not centuries these élites have been concentrated in Moscow: the Communist Party leadership, for example, was clearly dominated by Ukrainians or Russians of Ukrainian origin, very few of whom returned to Ukraine.

The year 1993 was a critical one for Ukraine because Russia started to curtail the subsidization of the Ukrainian economy by providing resources, and especially oil and gas, at prices considerably lower than those of the world market. In 1992 Russian direct subsidies to republics of the former Soviet Union amounted to $17 billion. At least one-third of that sum went to Ukraine.

By the end of 1993 or the beginning of 1994 it began to be clear that the crisis in Ukraine was taking on a comprehensive and uncontrollable character.[3] The economy was slowly sliding down. Kiev was losing control over it. At the same time new market mechanisms and incentives were not being created, or if and when they were set up they lagged far behind the rate of disintegration of the old mechanisms. To a great extent Ukraine was moving towards a socialist economy without socialist planning or control and was getting the worst of both worlds, in the same way as the Soviet Union was doing during the last Gorbachev year—the model it abruptly, although not totally successfully,

---

[2] According to official Ukrainian sources, in 1992 inflation was 2150%, there was a 30% fall in production and national income fell by 14% as compared to 1991. *Ukrainskiy Vestnik* (Moscow), Feb. 1993, pp. 13, 15.

[3] For an analysis of this crisis, see Razuvaev, V., 'Krizis na Ukraine i Rossiya' [The crisis in Ukraine and Russia], *Nezavisimaya Gazeta*, 17 Dec. 1993.

abandoned when the reforms of then Prime Minister Yegor Gaidar started. The information system and transport links were deteriorating and there were increasing signs that the armed forces were following suit. The only bright spot was that regional leaders were increasingly taking control into their hands; but this has also contributed to the creeping disintegration or, rather, dissolution of the country and to the deterioration of large technical systems.

Given this kind of situation, realistically minded leaders in Kiev started to appreciate that they could not afford the continuation of this low-key confrontation.

Under these circumstances the result of the presidential election of 10 July 1994 was predictable. It was a vote of no confidence against both the economic non-policies of the previous leadership and the policies of economic and political estrangement from Russia. It seemed, however, that many Ukrainians voted for Leonid Kuchma in the vague hope of the restoration of the *status quo ante*—the situation when Russia was de facto the economic donor to Ukraine.

The coming to power of the Kuchma Government did not, as some politicians in Russia hoped, signify a vote for reintegration. However, it partly solved one problem facing Russia—the possibility of conflagration during the period of economic deterioration in Ukraine and Russia. The new government with its clear leaning towards closer and better ties with Russia is unlikely to initiate a crisis. The benevolent attitude of Moscow towards this leadership makes it likely that Moscow, which is not interested in a crisis anyway, will be much more relaxed and flexible about possible trouble-spots.

This does not mean that the horizon of Russian–Ukrainian relations is completely unclouded. Almost all the major problems of the preceding years persist. Bilateral negotiations on the division of the Black Sea Fleet have remained unsuccessful, mainly because of basic differences in approaches to the problem: Russia believes that it would be in its interests to base the two navies separately and station the Russian forces in Sevastopol, and Ukraine obviously fears that this could lead to Sevastopol taking on extra-territorial status and loss of control over the city. Even after agreement was reached between the two presidents on 8 June 1995 in Sochi on some basic principles of division of the Fleet it is still doubtful whether the countries will be able to agree on all the details.[4]

Another issue, closely connected with the previous one and which contributed greatly to the growth of conflict potential in the two countries' relationship, was the Crimean problem. Contrary to what many analysts in the West think, since the election of President Yuriy Meshkov in Crimea in January 1994 and especially since the summer of 1994 Russian policy towards Crimea has manifested goodwill and an intention to improve relations with Ukraine. Russian interference can hardly be traced in the development of the situation on the Crimean peninsula. The main evidence for this is that President Meshkov lost his powers and his reform team was replaced by the old *nomenklatura*

---

[4] See also Baranovsky, V., 'Conflicts in and around Russia', *SIPRI Yearbook 1996: Armaments, Disarmament and International Security* (Oxford University Press: Oxford, 1996), p. 274.

government, headed by a close relative of Kuchma, Anatoliy Franchuk; later, a centrist speaker of the Crimean Parliament, Sergey Tsekov, was substituted by a pro-Kievan, Yevhen Supruniuk. Generally speaking, the Crimean problem seems to be approaching a solution on terms advantageous to the Ukrainian Government and at least for a while will cease to affect relations acutely. However, the psychological legacy of this controversial issue will be a constituent part of the relationship.

The attitude of the Kuchma Administration towards cooperation within the framework of the Commonwealth of Independent States (CIS) is only slightly different from that of Kravchuk's government, especially in military–political matters. Apparently fears that Russia might try to use the CIS as an additional lever to undermine Ukraine's independence and that Ukraine's active policy within the CIS would reduce its chances of moving westwards still dominate the thinking of Ukrainian leaders. This leads to some inconsistencies in policy: on the one hand, Ukraine has signed the agreement on a common CIS air defence system;[5] on the other it has intensified its military contacts with Western countries, which cannot please Russia in the present circumstances when one of the major challenges to Russian security is allegedly the possibility of NATO enlargement eastwards.

The coming to power of a less nationalistic leadership may thus have dispelled immediate dangers, but the core problems endangering Russia and Ukraine have not been solved.

These are, first, the danger that economic stagnation and deterioration in Russia could make thinking and policy more chauvinistic, more inclined to look for outside adventures and threats in order to provide a pretext for the lack of progress at home. Second and more imminent is the danger of continuation of the economic and social degradation of Ukraine. Its government has shown great ambivalence about a course of radical reform. Indeed, reforms including the deregulation of most prices were courageously introduced by the Kuchma Administration. At the same time, however, there were more and more signs that the government was heading towards an attempt to reinstate some kind of centralized control over the economy, pumping money into sectors in collapse and thus most probably only speeding up economic deterioration. Third, Russia is still unable, both bureaucratically and intellectually, to devise a coherent policy towards Ukraine. This vacuum has been creating uneasiness in both capitals and provides, at least theoretically, fertile ground for all kinds of unexpected turns.

At this juncture four scenarios for the development of Ukraine look plausible. The first is the gradual deterioration of the economy, living standards and social order, a creeping dissolution of the country, making it the sick man of Eastern Europe, migration spreading out to other countries, technological disasters, and so on. The second scenario is the catastrophic degradation of the economy, bringing disintegration of the state and a civil war, started by nationalists of the

[5] Baranovsky (note 4), p. 271.

western part of the country. Third would be the coming to power in Ukraine of a strong man, supported by the industrialists and parts of the new bourgeoisie. Most probably such a strong man would push his country towards a close relationship with Russia. The fourth would be successful economic and political reform in the direction of federalization and marketization, creating after an almost inevitable authoritarian stage a viable democratic economy and society.

The analysis of the political forces in Ukraine and the assessment of the state of the Ukrainian economy make this most optimistic scenario the least probable one, at least for the near future. None of the other three scenarios looks attractive for Russia. The worst is the second. The first and the third are the most likely.

If only recently Ukraine looked like a possible geopolitical challenge for Russia, that challenge is now taking on a different dimension. The Ukrainian economy and the Ukrainian state are threatening Russia with mass migration, provoking a nationalistic reaction from Russia. The possible disintegration of Ukraine involves an even more threatening challenge—that of certain southern or eastern Ukrainian provinces calling for reunification with Russia. Most of these provinces are in a terrible economic state. Thus the biggest threat which emanates from Ukraine is the threat of the country's disintegration drawing in Russia directly or indirectly, economically and even militarily and thus grossly complicating Russian democratic development and reform.

Ukraine could also become a major source of trade in narcotics and, if the Ukrainian Army started to disintegrate, of a flow of arms to Russia. Needless to say, the disintegration of Ukraine would face Russia and other countries with loss of control over nuclear weapons, with all the consequences that can be anticipated.

The crisis in Ukraine also has the potential of complicating Russian relationships with the West. The West does not know what to do with Ukraine. It does not want it to lose its independence, but it has no will to help it to get out of its crisis. The aid offered after the introduction of reforms was minuscule in comparison with the country's needs.

If Ukraine starts to lose its statehood because of economic and social catastrophe, Russia could be blamed for that,[6] all the more so because the weakening of the Ukrainian state could be used by some of the groups in Russia which are nostalgic for the Soviet Union and are willing to create a crisis between Russia and the West. These forces could play on Russian nostalgia and create a drive towards reunification with parts of Ukraine, if and when it starts to fall apart.

The tragic developments in Ukraine have transformed the country within one or two years from a jewel in the crown of the empire into the largest single challenge and threat to Russian economic and political security.

[6] Some Western analysts seem to suppose a priori that Russia is an imperialist power in its relations with Ukraine. Zbigniew Brzezinski, for example, believes that without Ukraine Russia ceases to be an empire, but if it subjugates Ukraine, exploiting disruptive processes there, it will automatically become an empire. Brzezinski, Z., 'Prezhdevremennoe partnerstvo' [The premature partnership], *Nezavisimaya Gazeta,* 20 May 1994. A translation of the article appeared in *Foreign Affairs,* vol. 73, no. 2 (1994), pp. 67–82.

This relatively gloomy assessment of developments in Ukraine does not necessarily preclude a fairly calm development of relations between the two countries. Both capitals lack the resources and the political will for a confrontation, and could hardly afford one. Thus in the end they tend to avoid crises. These could happen more because of mismanagement rather than because of ill will. The poor governance of the two states and especially the level of social hardship and distress objectively provide the conditions for all kinds of crises in the foreseeable future. However, the roots of tension will be relatively shallow unless it is artificially exacerbated by policies aimed at further deepening the divide between the two countries and their peoples in the political, economic and human fields.

III. Belarus

There are some basic differences between the situation in Belarus and that in Ukraine. First of all, the drive towards independence in Belarus had relatively narrow support. The national identity was comparatively weak and the history of statehood short. Nationalist movements in Belarus, although spread more evenly over the country, enjoyed less support among the population. Its economic decline in the first post-Soviet years was slower than that of Ukraine or even Russia. Belarus is more or less governed by the younger generation of the previous leadership. That is true for all states of the former Soviet Union, although the change in Russia was somewhat greater. However, because of historical factors this leadership has been originally less ideologically conservative than the Ukrainian Communist leadership and more pragmatic.

The Belarussian leadership has openly called for close reintegration, if not reunification, with Russia. At the same time the leaders wish to retain some of the privileges which they acquired with the dissolution of the Soviet Union and are most probably not ready for full reunification. They prefer to be a part of Russia in terms of gas prices, but at the same time continue to exercise control over the state, getting personal economic benefits from their positions of power in Minsk.

The unexpected (for most Russians) election to the position of president of a populist leader, Alexander Lukashenko, caused a stir and made the situation less predictable, at least in the eyes of Moscow, but most probably did not change the basic direction of Belarussian politics. The bureaucracy is too well entrenched to be defeated. The new president very soon forgot about his anti-corruption drive. He deregulated some prices and cut some subsidies, but stopped halfway. Faced with the disillusionment of the population and with a backlash from the press and the parliament, he had started by the end of 1994 to resort increasingly to authoritarian methods of government and to attack the freedom of the press much more directly than any of the leaders of the three Slav republics. The prospects for the economic and social development of Belarus look rather bleak and the assessment of the Belarussian National Center for Strategic Studies East–West seems to be accurate: 'Belarus is faced with a deepening of the crisis . . . and with the strengthening of authoritarian tendencies'.[7]

Strategically Belarus is far more important for Russia than even Ukraine. Most of the invasions from the West came through Belarus and most of the major trade routes connecting Russia with Europe cross Belarussian territory. Although Belarus does not border the Kaliningrad exclave, close relations with Belarus are the key to keeping Kaliningrad a part of the Russian Federation. They are also of key importance for Russia in order to prevent the theoretical possibility of the creation of a second buffer zone from the Baltic states to the Black Sea, thus isolating Russia, and for regulating the Russian relationship with Ukraine. With Belarus on its side the Russian position *vis-à-vis* Ukraine is strengthened. Ukraine could become a challenge for Russia only if it were to lead an alliance of former western republics of the USSR and some of the East–Central European states. Without Belarus such an alliance would be nothing but a pipedream, and Ukraine, if it chooses to become belligerent (which is highly unlikely), would be profoundly isolated. Ties with Belarus are also an important element in treating the Russian syndrome of being rejected and alone, the syndrome of a divided nation.

The relatively small size of the Belarussian economy, which is heavily dependent on Russia,[8] makes it in principle possible for Russia with a comparatively small investment of capital to tie Belarus to the Russian economy. This seemed a clear tendency until the beginning of 1994. The two countries had agreed in principle on the unification of their monetary systems, putting them under the effective control of Moscow, on a customs union, on the signing of a new political treaty emphasizing the special relationship between the two countries, and on a number of other steps to be taken in this direction. The Belarussian leadership had agreed to sell industrial assets in exchange for debt forgiveness. It looked highly likely that the countries were moving rapidly towards a strong confederation, if not a weak federation. However, by late spring 1994 this movement started to slow down, even before the election of President Lukashenko. The reasons for this were partly the general inability of the bureaucracies of the two countries to work effectively, partly the desire of some of the Belarussian leaders to keep as much economic freedom as possible, and, probably most important, a growing appreciation in Moscow of the costs of merger with Belarus with its essentially non-market economy. The election of the new president not only provoked new doubts, but most likely provided an excuse for a further slow-down.

President Lukashenko came to Moscow on his first foreign visit with essentially the same approach as his predecessors—asking for money and pledging

---

[7] *Narodnaya Gazeta*, 12 Oct. 1994.

[8] According to some estimates, Belarus can independently produce only 4% of its total output. In 1992, 87% of its finished products used supplies from Russia. Fadeyev, D. and Razuvayev, V., 'Russia and the western post-Soviet republics', eds R. D. Blackwill and S. Karaganov, Center for Science and International Affairs, Harvard University, *Damage Limitation or Crisis? Russia and the Outside World*, CSIA Studies in International Security, no. 5 (Brassey's: Washington, DC, 1994), p. 119.

loyalty and willingness for integration. He was treated correctly, but largely cold-shouldered. On his return he had to say that in spite of mammoth aid 'Russia would not be solving all our problems for us and Belarus has to rely on its own efforts first of all'.[9] Soon his Foreign Minister, Vladimir Senko, while emphasizing very close cooperation with Russia, was excluding for the time being unification of the three Slav republics.[10]

It seemed that the semi-turn of Belarus towards a slightly more independent stance was caused partly by the appreciation of the new élite of its new international status and its unwillingness to lose it, partly by subtle pressure from the West, but predominantly by the understanding that Russia is not ready to pick up most of the bills.

This slowing down of the process of integration did not, however, rule out the possibility of its being invigorated. A resumption of the movement towards closer formal integration was made possible, if not probable, by the combination of Belarus' strategic, political and economic significance, the relative size of the country and its economy, the willingness of the Belarussian leadership and population to keep close relations with Russia, and the fact that Belarus would very probably be unable to survive economically without very close links to and aid from Russia. .

Integrationist expectations increased again as a result of the bilateral treaty, signed by Presidents Boris Yeltsin and Lukashenko in Minsk on 21 February 1995, which envisaged that the two countries would coordinate their foreign and security policies, border control and some aspects of economic policy and establish a customs union. A referendum in Belarus in 14 May 1995 further produced 80 per cent support for the building up of economic cooperation with Russia. On 2 April 1996 the two states concluded a treaty establishing a Community of Russia and Belarus and providing, at least theoretically, for deeper economic and political integration. There is therefore a solid legal basis for a Russian policy towards Belarus which will be qualitatively different from its policy towards Ukraine. The choice is largely Russia's.

IV. Conclusions: Russia's choices

Until 1993 Russia theoretically had several choices with respect to its policies towards most of the former Soviet republics, including Belarus and Ukraine. One was forceful reintegration by a combination of economic and direct military pressure or even invasion, using the help of forces within these republics which stand for the reunification of the former Soviet Union. That choice was supported by Russian communists and ultra-nationalists, at least some of them.

Another choice, widely popular in 1992, was isolation. Neo-isolationism was advocated by many of radical democrats, who feared that ties with former

[9] *Zvyazda*, 12 Aug. 1994.
[10] *Zvyazda*, 7 Sep. 1994.

Soviet republics, most of which were economically much more backward and politically much less democratic, would slow down Russian development along capitalist and democratic lines and also hinder the Russian *rapprochement* with the West. It was also supported by some of the ultra-nationalists, 'Russia Firstists', who were driven partly by racist considerations.

There was also a 'soft' reintegration option: by using economic levers and the interest of the local leaders in keeping the welfare of their states on a certain level, Russia could aim for something vaguely resembling the European Community (EC) model, with relatively open borders and few if any impediments to the free flow of capital, goods and people. Under this model Russia would have played the role of Germany in the EC or of the USA in NATO—the role of the strongest partner among equals.

By the end of 1993 or the beginning of 1994 the policy choices for Russia had changed. Complete isolation from other countries of the former USSR was not an option any more. More and more Russians started to understand that it is impossible to seal the country off from potential conflicts in the 'near abroad'. These conflicts have shown a tendency to expand and spill over, threatening stability in the adjacent Russian regions. At the same time the forcible reintegration option started to look even less plausible than it had a year before.

Even a peaceful and entirely voluntary reintegration into a new state-like structure of some kind began to look more and more remote, at least from the point of view of this author. This conclusion may seem strange against the background of the popular feeling for some kind of integration which has been visibly increasing since late 1993 in many, if not most, of the republics of the former Soviet Union and of the vogue for integrationist rhetoric in Russia proper, where even those who applauded or had prepared the 1991 Belavezh agreement on the dissolution of the Soviet Union are joining the ranks of the more vocal integrationists *en masse*.[11]

Several considerations support this conclusion. The first is the fact that the decline of the economies and the weakening of the state structures in most of the republics of the former USSR make reintegration even costlier for Russia than before and prohibitively expensive. Most thinkable regimes in Moscow will not be interested in ruining Russia economically and in taking the responsibility for running their ruined economies and turbulent societies off the shoulders of the local élites. If closer integration came about, Moscow could be blamed for the evils as it had been before.

Second, the Russian economy and the economies of other countries of the former Soviet Union are developing at different speeds and even in different directions. They are gradually becoming less and less structurally compatible. That increasing incompatibility makes it less and less profitable for Russia to integrate with most of them.

---

[11] See, e.g., Vladislavlev, A., 'Vneshnaya politika Rossii' [Foreign policy of Russia], *Nezavisimaya Gazeta*, 6 May 1994; and Petrov, Yu., 'Reintegratsiya post-sovetskogo prostranstva: Mif ili realnaya perspektiva' [Reintegration of the post-Soviet space: myth or reality], *Nezavisimaya Gazeta*, 12 July 1994.

Third, the tendency towards speedy integration is slowed by the weakness of the Russian state and the ineffectiveness of the Moscow foreign policy apparatus, which is unable to implement decisions even if and when they are made. Thus integrationist rhetoric ends in de facto disintegrationist policies.

The relative strengthening of Russia, especially when and if it starts to come out of its crisis situation in the next few years, against the background of the continuous decline of other economies, will most probably lead to a relationship with most of the countries of the CIS which could be compared to that of USA with the countries of Central and Latin America in the 1950s and 1960s. Ukraine, if it survives, and depending on how it survives, will be playing the role of Mexico or of Canada. The CIS countries could serve as supplies of cheap labour and cheap goods to the Russian economy, creating a circle of dependent states around its perimeter, where Russia would play a dominant economic role.

Belarus and Ukraine offer two models for the development of the relationship between Russia and other former republics of the USSR. One is offered by the Russian–Belarussian relationship. It involves speedy reintegration of the economies while the states remain politically independent and most probably a close security union, a customs union, open communications and common transport systems. The first steps in this direction could include monetary union or even unification of monetary systems, the entry of these states into the rouble zone and the acknowledgement by them of the industrial and technological primacy of Moscow and the Russian Central Bank. This model offers some benefits to the countries which choose it, above all direct access to cheap Russian resources and to the relatively large Russian market. It would also involve deep interpenetration of capital and the creation of transnational corporations involving private and state businesses on both sides.

This option is relatively costly for Russia. While being hesitantly offered to Belarus, it is hardly applicable even theoretically to most of the other republics of the Soviet Union, although it could be offered to certain regions of some countries, especially if the processes of regionalization there continue.

The other model of relationships is probably being developed between Russia and Ukraine as well as some other republics. On this model Russia will not invest much in the well-being of its neighbours, selling them goods at world prices while trying to save only those industries which are valuable for the Russian economy.[12] These countries will of course keep their formal political independence, but at the same time will be getting much less benefit from their economic interaction with Russia than the countries (or country) in the first group. The countries in the second group in the end could become economically more dependent on Russia than countries which chose to integrate to it.

---

[12] In June 1994 Russia and Ukraine agreed to set up a joint venture producing pipes for a pipeline running through Ukrainian territory. *Segodnya*, 7 June 1994. There are also plans to establish a transnational corporation for processing Russian oil in Ukraine, which would permit Ukraine to repay some of its debts. *Segodnya*, 7 June 1994, 22 June 1994.

There would be other models of relationships, in particular a Baltic model. The Russia–Kazakhstan relationship will probably develop simultaneously along the Belarussian and Ukrainian lines.

As has been stated above, the Russian–Belarussian relationship will most probably be the exception rather than the rule. Even the US–Latin American model, however, will develop only if neighbouring countries and especially Ukraine are able to keep themselves as viable entities. If Ukraine disintegrates (which now looks unlikely) then the relationship between Russia and what by that time is Ukraine will develop along different lines. Most probably under these circumstances parts of Ukraine will be fully integrated into Russia, at great loss to the Russian economy and its prospects of democratic development. This would be the worst outcome for both Russia and Ukraine.[13]

In a way the relationships which will be evolving will be fair—you get what you can pay for—but they will not be seen as fair by many of the citizens of the countries involved. No appreciably better model for these relationships can be seen, however, at least at the present juncture.

Things will get even worse if Russia moves towards a stagnant authoritarian model. In the present situation it faces an unpleasant choice: either it moves along 'progressive'—aimed at development—semi-authoritarian lines, or it moves towards authoritarian stagnation. That will make for even worse conditions for the neighbouring countries and profound 'Latin-Americanization' in the worst sense of the word of the whole space of the former USSR, with very few chances for most countries to break out of this pattern in the coming years, as many of the Latin American countries are finally breaking out.

It can, of course, be argued that the Slav affinity of these three former Soviet republics could provide a special model for their relationship. That is only partly true. At present at least political and social factors seem to play a much more significant role than national identity or religion.

---

[13] On possible scenarios of relations between Russia and Ukraine (and its successor states), see also Moshes, A., 'Nuzhen li Rossii razval Ukrainy?' [Does Russia need the disintegration of Ukraine?], *Nezavisimaya Gazeta*, 19 Mar. 1994.

Part VII

The Baltic dilemma and relations with Nordic Europe

Key facts

Ethnic Russians in the Baltic states, 1994

Estonia	436 600	29.0% of total population
Latvia	849 000	33.1% of total population
Lithuania	316 000	8.5% of total population

Source: Europa World Yearbook 1995.

Citizenship laws in the Baltic states

Estonia   Adopted June 1992. Grants citizenship to pre-1940 Estonian citizens and their descendants; others may apply individually for citizenship if they have been residents of Estonia for 2 years and pass an Estonian language test. An amendment to the citizenship law approved in Jan. 1995 extended the minimum period of residence in Estonia required for naturalization from 2 to 5 years. At the beginning of 1996, *c.* 400 000 of Estonia's 1.5 million residents did not hold Estonian citizenship

Latvia   Adopted July 1994. Grants citizenship to those who were Latvian citizens before 1940 and their descendants; others born in Latvia may apply for citizenship from 1996 (persons who have moved to Latvia may apply for citizenship from 2003) if they have been residents of Latvia for 10 years and demonstrate knowledge of the Latvian language. A proposed quota for the naturalization of non-ethnic Latvians born outside Latvia was removed from the final citizenship legislation following criticism from the Council of Europe, other European bodies and Russia. At the end of 1995 *c.* 30% of Latvia's inhabitants were non-citizens

Lithuania   Adopted Dec. 1991. Allows all permanent residents of Lithuania, regardless of ethnic origin, to apply for citizenship. By early 1993, more than 90% of non-ethnic Lithuanian residents had been granted citizenship

Status of Russian armed forces in the Baltic region

Estonia   Total Russian armed forces personnel early 1992: 23 000. Withdrawal of Russian troops completed 31 Aug. 1994. *c.* 200 Russian advisers remained to supervise dismantling of nuclear submarine training reactors at Paldiski withdrawn in Sep. 1995

Kaliningrad   Kaliningrad Special Region established 1994. There were *c.* 38 000 Russian ground troops in 1995; the headquarters of the Baltic Fleet is at Baltiysk. Transit of Russian military personnel and cargoes to and from Kaliningrad is regulated by a Nov. 1993 agreement between Russia and Lithuania; Lithuania has refused to codify the agreement formally in a treaty

Latvia   Total Russian armed forces personnel early 1992: 48 000. Withdrawal of Russian troops completed 31 Aug. 1994. Under the terms of an Apr. 1994 agreement with Latvia, Russian personnel are to operate an early-warning radar installation at Skrunda for an additional 4 years, followed by an 18-month dismantlement period

Lithuania   Total Russian armed forces personnel early 1992: 43 000. Withdrawal of Russian troops completed 31 Aug. 1993

Key facts

The Soviet/Russian Baltic Fleet, 1980–95

	1980	1991	1992	1993	1994	1995
Submarines	36	30	20	15	10	9
Surface combatants						
Cruisers	5	4	4	1	3	3
Destroyers	12	4	3	2	3	2
Frigates	28	34	32	24	26	18
Other surface ships						
Patrol and coastal	164	160	140	140	60	65
Mine warfare	100	77	60	60	50	55
Amphibious	43	21	21	20	21	15
Support and other	..	120	120	110	100	102

The Soviet/Russian Northern Fleet, 1990–95/96

	1990/91	1991/92	1992/93	1993/94	1994/95	1995/96
Submarines						
Strategic (SSBN)[a]	37	36	34	32	30	37
Tactical	106	96	85	78	67	71
Large surface combatants						
Carriers (conventional)	2	2	3	2	2	1
Cruisers	16	15	11	9	8	8
Destroyers	8	8	9	8	8	9
Frigates	34	42	38	37	30	29
Other surface ships						
Patrol and coastal	40	30	25	25	10	10
Mine warfare	65	56	40	40	40	45
Amphibious	15	17	12	12	13	10
Support and other	190	190	190	190	180	182

[a] Nuclear-powered, ballistic-missile submarine. *Sources:* International Institute for Strategic Studies, *The Military Balance 1980–1981; 1990–1991; 1991–1992; 1992–1993; 1993–1994; 1994–1995; 1995–1996.*

Kaliningrad force levels and weapon holdings

	1990	1995
Tank divisions	2	1[a]
Motor rifle divisions	1[b]	2
Artillery divisions	1	–[c]
Airborne brigades	1	–
Tanks	802	893
Armoured combat vehicles (ACVs)	1 081	1 156
Artillery	677	495
Attack helicopters	48	52
Combat aircraft	155	32

[a] Plus one independendent brigade. [b] Plus one brigade redeploying from Czechoslovakia. [c] Three brigades remain. *Sources*: International Institute for Strategic Studies, *The Military Balance 1990–1991, 1995–1996.*

14. Russian policy in Northern Europe

Lena Jonson

I. Introduction

What determines the foreign policy of a government, its strategy for guaranteeing the security of the state and for asserting its interests in dealings with the rest of the world? Are enduring factors like geopolitical location and size the determining ones that will make the country return to one and the same policy towards its immediate external environment? Or are there more variable factors pertaining within the state—in its culture, politics and economics—that are decisive and explain changes of foreign policy? The problem has been thrashed over by decision makers and in studies on international relations. It is discussed in this chapter in the context of Russian policy in Northern Europe since the end of the cold war and the disintegration of the Soviet Union.

Over the centuries, Russia has sought to secure its access to the sea in the West—to the Baltic Sea and the Barents Sea.[1] These interests were secured with the help of traditional power politics.[2] With a strong military and with recourse to military expedients, Russia achieved dominance and control.

In the Baltic region, this created not only a problem for Russia's neighbours but also a dilemma for Russian policy. After having granted the Baltic countries their independence in 1918, Russia attempted to reclaim territory by force. In 1940, after the settlement with the Germans formalized in the Molotov–Ribbentrop Pact, the Baltic states were occupied, and after the war they were incorporated into the Soviet Union.

The Soviet conquest of the Baltic states together with the massive build-up of Soviet military potential in the area was of decisive importance for the foreign and security policy stances adopted by all the Nordic countries after World War II.[3] The security policy pattern that emerged in the Nordic region after the war reflected the proximity of the great power. Those states which were furthest away from the Soviet Union (Norway and Denmark) became members of NATO; Sweden proclaimed its non-aligned status but oriented itself entirely

---

[1] By the Treaty of Nystad of 1721 Peter the Great expanded Russian territory along the Baltic coast.

[2] Fuller, Jr, W. C., *Strategy and Power in Russia 1600–1914* (The Free Press: New York, 1992).

[3] The low profile adopted by the Swedish Government on the question of the Soviet occupation of the Baltic states in 1940 and after the war can be explained with reference to the pragmatic approach which small states in the shadow of a superpower are forced to adopt. Carlgren, W., *Sverige och Baltikum: från mellankrigstid till efterkrigsår* [Sweden and the Baltic: from the inter-war years to after the war] (Publica: Stockholm, 1993). The same applies to the preparations by the Swedish Government following World War II for military cooperation with the USA in the event of war. Sweden, Commision on Neutrality Policy, *Had There Been a War . . . Preparations for the Reception of Military Assistance, 1949–1969: Report of the Commission on Neutrality Policy* (Statsrådsberedningen: Stockholm, 1994), SOU 1994:11. The Nordic countries are Denmark, Finland, Iceland, Norway and Sweden.

towards the West; and Finland, restricted in its foreign policy by the Treaty on Friendship, Cooperation and Mutual Assistance with the Soviet Union from 1948, tried to uphold an independent neutrality policy.

Northern Europe was seen as a peaceful corner of Europe during the cold war and bilateral relations between the Soviet Union and the Nordic countries were stable. The division of Europe into blocs, however, split Northern Europe into a western part, consisting of the Nordic countries, and an eastern one which was part of the Soviet Union. Interaction between the two parts was extremely limited. The Soviet military build-up in the Barents Sea in the post-war years and especially during the 1970s and 1980s was witnessed with unease by the USSR's Nordic neighbours.

When Soviet President Mikhail Gorbachev attempted to establish *détente* in Northern Europe through increased cooperation and exchange with those neighbours, the Baltic dilemma for Soviet policy became evident. Gorbachev failed to improve relations because he did not accept demands for Baltic independence and did not carry through his commitment to arms reduction on the Kola Peninsula. His attempt to lower the level of tension thus met with little response in the Nordic countries. Distrust for the Soviet Union did not abate.[4]

While still Chairman of the Supreme Soviet of the Russian Soviet Federative Socialist Republic (RSFSR) before the collapse of the USSR, Boris Yeltsin presented a policy for Northern Europe that contained a possible solution to this dilemma.[5] He supported Baltic aspirations for independence and played down the military aspect. He introduced a new Russian security strategy in Northern Europe, and in his settling of accounts with the old Soviet policy he went further than Gorbachev.

However, with the independence of the Baltic states, the dissolution of the Soviet Union and new state borders, Russia's geo-strategic position radically changed. What remained after 1991 of Russian access to the Baltic Sea was the area around St Petersburg deep in the Gulf of Finland and the Kaliningrad exclave. From this situation new problems followed with consequences for Russian national security.

In this chapter Russian policy towards Northern Europe after the breakup of the Soviet Union is analysed. A major question to be discussed is whether the Russian leadership has accepted Russia's new reduced or withdrawn position on the Baltic Sea or not. The Russian Government has not published any documents in which a policy or security strategy for Northern Europe is outlined. Instead the analysis is based on the government's actions and statements concerning the problems, the vulnerability of the north-western border and its changed notions of Russia's role in the world.[6]

---

[4] Jonson, L., 'Soviet policy towards Sweden and the region of Northern Europe under Gorbachev', *Cooperation and Conflict*, vol. 25, no. 1 (1990), pp. 1–19.

[5] Jonson, L., 'The role of Russia in Nordic regional cooperation', *Cooperation and Conflict*, vol. 26, no. 3 (1991), pp. 129–44.

[6] A number of ideas are thought to be central in the formation of a state's foreign policy. Blum, D. W., 'The Soviet foreign policy belief system: beliefs, politics, and foreign policy outcomes', *International Studies Quarterly*, vol. 37 (1993), pp. 373–94. Compare with the technique described by Alexander

In the next two sections of this chapter, Russian attempts to come to grips with the new problems for its security in the area are analysed. Section IV discusses Moscow's claim to an international role and its consequences for Russia's North European policy, and section V the importance of military defence to Russian security strategy. The final section examines the question to what extent Russian policy in Northern Europe has actually changed.

II. National security strategies and the Russian debate

The national security policy of a state contains features of different strategies and combinations of different foreign policy instruments. The decisive question when assessing the policy is to find where its emphasis on strategies and on instruments is actually placed.

In the Russian foreign policy debate, two main tendencies have conflicted with each other since Gorbachev opened up the debate at the end of the 1980s. They can be called the 'revisionist' and the 'traditionalist' strategies. The revisionist strategy is based on Gorbachev's emphasis of a new security policy thinking with a broader security concept, and it emphasizes international cooperation and non-military instruments. It is based on the insight that the great-power position of a particular state in the world of today rests on a strong economy and a high level of technological development, not first and foremost on military strength. The traditionalist strategy can be equated with a traditional power policy. It emphasizes Russia's aspirations as a global power, describes its interests as opposed to those of the West, depicts a threat emanating from the West and advocates the use of the instruments of power (military or economic sanctions) to secure Russian national interests. Between these two main tendencies, a political battle is being waged in Russia.

Russian President Yeltsin and his Foreign Minister Andrey Kozyrev not only followed in the footsteps of Gorbachev after the breakup of the Soviet Union, but went further in arguing that international cooperation and non-military instruments are important elements in guaranteeing the security of the country and its international status. Kozyrev stressed that only by allying itself with Western countries could Russia count on one day joining the club of highly developed industrial nations with economic strength and international influence.[7] The new government sought economic integration with the West and tried to transplant the Western market economies. It developed further the partnership image of the West and emphasized common interests. It sought acceptance and recognition by the West and the international community by conforming to international law. Yeltsin and Kozyrev tried to modify earlier foreign policy aspirations for influence and control. Kozyrev argued that Russia

---

George as 'an indirect, logic-of-the-situation pattern of inference' which can be used to infer the policy recommendations of different political tendencies in a hidden debate. Cutler, R. M., 'The formation of Soviet foreign policy: organizational and cognitive perspectives', *World Politics*, vol. 34, no. 3 (1982).

[7] Andrey Kozyrev quoted in *Izvestiya*, 31 Mar. 1992; and *Nezavisimaya Gazeta*, 1 Apr. 1992.

had become a 'normal' great power in the sense that it asserted its interests without claiming special rights or an historic mission.[8]

After an intensive foreign policy debate in 1992 and growing criticism of Yeltsin's policy, during 1993 Russian foreign policy behaviour became more assertive. The dissolution of the Soviet Union had been followed by a certain confusion concerning relations with the outside world. When the relations were sorted out, the balance of domestic political forces inside Russia was already changing. Several liberal commentators claimed in early 1992 that the democrats would have to formulate a new cultural–historical paradigm of the 'Russian idea' to correspond with democratic values and international law and to constitute a breakaway from the Russian 'imperial tradition'.[9] The democrats' inability to do so gave the national patriots a considerable advantage in 1992 and 1993 in the struggle over how to define national values and interests. The national patriots clung to the imperial tradition, which sees Russia as an empire and a great power with an historical mission. Given the strength of the tradition, their political line made headway. Yeltsin came under considerable pressure from the opposition, and when the government began to define Russia's national interests he retreated, one step at a time, in the direction of the old and well-established view of what Russia is. With the elections to parliament in December 1993, the Duma was taken over by an overwhelming majority of nationalistic critics embracing most of the political spectrum. Even if the formation of foreign policy is above all the prerogative of the president according to the new Russian Constitution, Yeltsin must be responsive to voices raised within the parliament to be able to implement his policies.

Thus by 1994 it was the view of many foreign and Russian observers that the tide had turned in Russian foreign policy. It was said to be harking back to the tradition of power politics. 'In significant ways, Russia's foreign policy has become hard-nosed and aggressive, taking on precisely the character that President Yeltsin and Foreign Minister Kozyrev had vocally resisted in 1991 and 1992', a Western analyst wrote in the spring of 1994 on Russia's relations with its 'near abroad'.[10] Yeltsin seemed to have slid over into a traditionalist strategy.

In the last years of the Soviet Union's existence Yeltsin had actively encouraged the Baltic Soviet republics in their struggle for independence while suggesting at the same time cooperation in the form of a voluntary confederation between all the Soviet republics. His support for Baltic freedom intensified as the conflict between the RSFSR and the central Soviet authorities intensified. The RSFSR attempted to establish direct contact with the Nordic governments

---

[8] Kozyrev, A., *Novoe Vremya*, no. 3 (1992).

[9] See, e.g., Khoros, V., 'Russkaya ideya na istoricheskom perekrestke' [The Russian idea at a historical crossroads], *Svobodnaya Mysl*, no. 6 (1992).

[10] Crow, S., 'Why has Russian foreign policy changed?', Radio Free Europe/Radio Liberty (hereafter RFE/RL), *RFE/RL Research Report*, no. 12 (May 1994).

and the Nordic Council as early as 1991 in order to further cooperation and exchange.[11]

Until September 1991, when the Baltic states regained their independence, Yeltsin never mentioned a withdrawal of troops or military facilities from the Baltic republics. When the independent Baltic governments demanded that a military withdrawal be completed before the end of 1991, Yeltsin replied by suggesting a gradual pull-out. After the new Russia had shouldered responsibility for the troops of the former USSR stationed in foreign countries, a Russian delegation visited the Baltic capitals on 31 January 1992 to begin negotiations on troop withdrawal. By 1 September 1994 the withdrawal was completed.

Whether or not forced to this by circumstances, Yeltsin had introduced a new and important component in the Russian strategy in Northern Europe. With his support for Baltic aspirations for independence and acceptance of military withdrawal, Russia seemed to be accepting a reduced position on the Baltic Sea. The Russian Government also kept a low profile, refraining from making any official declarations or statements regarding the issue of Russian strategic or military interests in the Baltic states. Yeltsin made no statements on the military build-up on the Kola Peninsula before the collapse of the Soviet Union. With his proposals in October 1991 for further reductions of strategic nuclear forces, his policy seemed to accord less importance to military expedients.[12] Kozyrev, who actively sought to establish cooperation with the Nordic countries in the Barents region, continued to make statements more directly in favour of a cut in the level of armaments on the Kola Peninsula: 'the Arctic will cease to be a theatre of military competition'.[13]

Yeltsin's foreign policy in general and in the Baltic states in particular was questioned after the breakup of the Soviet Union by proponents of a traditionalist strategy. Voices were heard in the Congress of People's Deputies in April 1992 insisting that Russia's strategic interests in the north-west had to be secured.[14] Many were acutely conscious of the fact that Russia 'will have virtually the same ports as . . . when Peter the Great came to power'.[15]

With Yeltsin's foreign policy under change, are there signs that his 'revisionist' strategy in Northern Europe has been abandoned in favour of a more 'traditionalist' one?

[11] Jonson, L., 'Russia in the Nordic region in a period of change', eds M. Kukk, S. Jervell and P. Joenniemi, *The Baltic Sea Area: A Region in the Making* (Europa-programmet: Oslo and Baltic Institute: Karlskrona, 1992).

[12] In Oct. 1991 Yeltsin proposed further and more radical reductions of strategic nuclear forces than had been stated in the 1991 US–Soviet Treaty on the Reduction and Limitation of Strategic Offensive Arms (START I) signed by Gorbachev in July of that year. *Izvestiya*, 9 Oct. 1991.

[13] Reuter/BBC Monitoring Service, 11 Jan. 1993.

[14] Astafev, M., *Rossiyskaya Gazeta*, 27 Apr. 1992, p. 5.

[15] *Moscow News*, no. 41 (1991).

III. New problems in the north-west: a more exposed border?

The Russian Government had to face new problems for its security following the breakup of the Soviet Union. Four aspects of the new situation are discussed here: a reduced military presence; access to the sea; rules of transit and control of the new Russian state border; and the situation of Russians living in the 'new abroad'.

A reduced military presence

Russia's military presence in Northern Europe changed as a consequence of several factors: (a) Russian military withdrawal from the independent Baltic states; (b) international agreements on arms reduction; and (c) Russia's strained economy and limited financial resources.

Russian troops left Lithuania by 31 August 1993 and Estonia and Latvia by 31 August 1994. The negotiations on troop withdrawals from Estonia and Latvia were delayed by the issue, brought up by Russia, of the status of retired or demobilized Russian officers. The agreement with Latvia was signed on 30 April 1994.[16] With Estonia there was disagreement until the last minute before the agreement was signed on 26 July.[17] From having demanded, in early negotiations with Latvia, that three 'strategically important objects' should remain under Russian control, Russia in the end laid claim to only one, the Skrunda radar station, on which the two parties were able to reach a compromise in March 1994, and a series of agreements was signed in June.[18] The compromise gave Russia the right to use the radar station for four more years and to withdraw subsequently over the course of 18 months. Russia is obliged to pay an annual rent of $5 million. Russia is left with two naval bases for its Baltic Fleet, Baltiysk/Kaliningrad and Kronshtadt/St Petersburg. The possibility of constructing an additional military port connected to a new civilian port outside St Petersburg has been discussed.[19]

The Kaliningrad Region remains a Russian exclave and naval outpost. The Russian leadership has repeatedly stressed that Kaliningrad will remain vital to the country's security interests. In 1994 it acquired special status in terms of military organization as the *Kaliningradskiy Osoby Oboronitelny Rayon* under the Commander of the Baltic Fleet, Admiral Vladimir Yegorov, and the General Staff in Moscow. However, the location is vulnerable and its military importance is considered to have diminished. In April 1993 the Commander-in-Chief of the Navy, Feliks Gromov, claimed that the wartime importance of Baltiysk has declined since it runs the risk of being cut off from support and communications by independent Lithuania.[20] However, with growing demands

---

[16] *Diplomaticheskiy Vestnik*, nos 11–12 (June 1994).

[17] *Diplomaticheskiy Vestnik*, nos 15–16 (Aug. 1994).

[18] The other two 'strategic objects' claimed by the Russians in Latvia in 1992 were the naval harbour in Liepaja and radar installations in Ventspils. *RFE/RL Research Report*, no. 29 (17 June 1992), p. 58.

[19] Gromov, F., [Commander-in-Chief of the Navy], *Rossiyskaya Gazeta*, 15 Apr. 1993.

[20] Gromov (note 19).

from the neighbouring countries, Lithuania and Poland, for the demilitarization of Kaliningrad, in 1995 Gromov upgraded its importance and downgraded that of the ports of St Petersburg, thereby indicating the vulnerability of the ports deep in the Gulf of Finland. Because of the shallow common waters of the Gulf, egress for Russian ships is dependent on the goodwill of Estonia and Finland.[21]

The navy had formed the backbone of the armed forces in the erstwhile Soviet Baltic area. The Baltic Fleet has been drastically cut over the past three years and is now assigned to limited missions only. Admiral Yegorov said in June 1993 that the strength of the fleet would be reduced of necessity, as would its sphere of activities, with a change in priorities taking place.[22] This 'necessity' has to do with strained financial resources and the consequent lack of resources for the repair and maintenance of existing ships and construction of new ships. In the Barents region, cuts in the military budget following from the economic crisis have affected the Northern Fleet, which has been cut. The backbone of the Russian nuclear strategic defence, the sea-based missiles, is still intact.

A reduction of the ground forces and of military material had to be completed in the Leningrad Military District (MD) under the 1990 Treaty on Conventional Armed Forces in Europe (CFE Treaty) by 1 November 1995. However, parts of the forces withdrawn in the early 1990s from Central and Eastern Europe have been stationed in the Leningrad MD. The transfer of these entailed both an increase in the numbers and a modernization of main battle tanks and armoured vehicles. One regiment of attack helicopters was transferred to the north of the Leningrad MD and another to the south of the district. From the Russian side these transfers were explained as nothing more than a consequence of the practical problems associated with finding a location for the forces; for the Finnish Government, the transfer implied a reinforcement in the vicinity of the Finnish border.

As a consequence of Russia's changed geo-strategic situation, the Leningrad MD has become a 'first strategic echelon district', as then Defence Minister, Pavel Grachev, said in April 1993.[23] This demands a qualitative restructuring of the district to increase the level of military preparedness in line with its new status.

The Russian military has withdrawn from the Baltic states and a process of quantitative arms reduction is taking place in the Leningrad MD and in the Baltic and Northern fleets. However, with the Leningrad MD now considered a frontier MD, a military restructuring of the district is in prospect.

---

[21] Gromov, F., [The importance of the Kaliningrad Special District for the defence capability of the Russian Federation], *Voennaya Mysl,* no. 5 (1995).

[22] Reuter/BBC Monitoring Service, 26 June 1993.

[23] According to Defence Minister Pavel Grachev. Reuter/BBC Monitoring Service, 7 Apr. 1993.

Access to commercial ports

The loss of trade ports in Tallinn, Riga and Ventspils has caused problems for Russia. However, the way the Russian Government is dealing with this problem indicates that it accepts the situation.

In March 1993 the Russian Government presented a plan for the expansion of its port capacity in order to avoid cargo being shipped via foreign ports. According to this plan, 14 new Russian ports are to be constructed by 1998.[24] Until 1998, up to 14 million tonnes of cargo are to continue to go through ports in neighbouring countries; 5.5 million tonnes of coal, metal, imported grain and other goods from ports in the Baltic states are to be re-routed to St Petersburg, Vyborg and Kaliningrad; and a further 2 million tonnes to Murmansk and Arkhangelsk. Between the years 2000 and 2005, Russian ports will begin to handle all Russian cargo.[25] Included in the plan was the construction of a major new port outside St Petersburg, and in May 1993 Prime Minister Viktor Chernomyrdin signed a decree calling for private investors to build new facilities in the Gulf of Finland outside St Petersburg.[26] Since 1993 different projects for new port complexes outside St Petersburg have competed. Three ports are to be built: Ust-Luga, Bay Batareynaya and Primorsk.[27] The existing ports of St Petersburg will be reorganized to increase capacity. Projects for the construction of new ports in Kaliningrad started to be discussed in 1993. A Russian–German joint stock company was planning to use part of the naval base for a ferry terminal.[28]

Thus the Russian Government sought solutions to the loss of access to the sea for merchant goods but opted for the extremely costly alternative of building its own new ports, which will limit cooperation with ports in the Baltic states.

Transit and control of the new state borders

The new Russian state borders with the Baltic states, which were neither demarcated nor controlled, had to be regulated by agreements. Disagreement between Russia and Estonia and Latvia as to where the borders should be drawn delayed a solution to the practical problems of demarcation and control. Estonia claimed the Pechory district and a slice of land east of the Narva River, referring to the Treaty of Tartu of 1920. Latvia claimed the Abrene region (Pytalovskiy district). In September 1993 the Russian authorities decided unilaterally to establish a border zone of up to five kilometres along the border with Estonia.[29] In August 1994 demarcations were erected and armed patrols began.

[24] Reuter, 1 Apr. 1993.
[25] Reuter, 1 Apr. 1993.
[26] Reuter, 29 May 1993.
[27] 'Ekspertiza' [Scrutiny], Izvestiya, 5 Oct. 1994, p. 13.
[28] 'Russia: special report: Baltic ports and shipping. Company plans to build port at Baltiisk', Lloyds List, 11 Feb. 1994.
[29] Izvestiya, 3 Sep. 1993, p. 6.

The territorial dispute with Estonia intensified early in 1994, and the Russian press reported that the Estonian Government had offered Estonian citizenship to inhabitants of the disputed area around Pskov and that there had been several border incidents.[30] The head of the border guard troops, Andrey Nikolaev, at the beginning of 1994 described the situation on the border as difficult. He drew attention to dangers of conflicts flaring up along the Russian–Estonian border and itemized territorial demands made by nationalistic organizations in Estonia.[31] Defence Minister Grachev had claimed as early as April 1993 that Russia's new state borders were vulnerable, making references to territorial claims and disputes with Estonia, Latvia and Ukraine.[32]

The problems following from the sudden appearance of new state borders concerned not only territorial conflicts but also their transparency and lack of control, which made illegal transit of goods and people possible. Nikolaev identified it as a central task of the border guards to put a stop to violations of the border by criminal groups.

Uncontrolled cross-frontier traffic, both into and out of the country, poses a major problem for Russia. Much of the illegal export of raw materials from Russia takes place via Estonia. Estonia, for example, has become the fifth-largest exporter in the world of non-ferrous metals, in spite of the fact that it has no copper or molybdenum mines.[33] In 1991–92 Estonia and Latvia also became leading exporters of non-ferrous metals such as aluminium and nickel, neither of which they produce. These cross-frontier transactions also entailed enormous economic losses for Russia because the proceeds of illegal exports were usually deposited in foreign bank accounts. Senior Russian politicians have accused the Baltic states of involvement in such activities: Prime Minister Chernomyrdin, for example, said on a visit to the border town of Pskov in July 1993: 'We are happy to trade with the Baltic states on a civilized basis, but will not tolerate being robbed and Russia being plundered'.[34] In November 1994 Yeltsin said in Pskov that strict border controls were needed to stop the smuggling of non-ferrous metals out of Ukraine and the funnelling of illegal arms on to Russia's vast black market.[35]

New visa and transit regulations introduced by the Baltic states made it more difficult for Russians living in these countries to travel into and out of Russia. Russian protests over Baltic visa and transit regulations resulted in the rules being modified.[36] The question of Russian military transit to Kaliningrad over

[30] *Izvestiya*, 15 Jan. 1994; and 25 Feb. 1994.

[31] ITAR-TASS World Service, Moscow, broadcasting in English 14 Jan. 1994 at 17.44 GMT. Reuter/BBC Monitoring Service.

[32] Reuter/BBC Monitoring Service, 7 Apr. 1993.

[33] *Izvestiya*, 15 Feb. 1994, p. 3.

[34] Reuter/BBC Monitoring Service, 29 July 1993.

[35] Reuter, 23 Nov. 1994.

[36] For example, non-citizens living permanently in Latvia do not need a visa for re-entry into the country according to an agreement from June 1994. In Dec. 1994 the passage of people and goods across the border between Russia and Latvia was regulated by agreement. Reuter, 19 Dec. 1994.

Lithuanian territory is the main problem.[37] According to an agreement of November 1993, Lithuania accepted transit but with restrictions and the right to charge a fee.[38] Negotiations on a new treaty were complicated by Lithuania seeking to limit and control transport further and Russia demanding a 'corridor' without restrictions. A compromise was reached in January 1995, prolonging the old agreement. This reduced tensions, but further incidents and increased domestic criticism of the agreement could give rise to tension again.[39]

Russians outside the Russian Federation

Of the new problems following from the Baltic states' achievement of independence and the dissolution of the Soviet Union, the situation of the Russian minorities is the politically most sensitive question.

In contrast to all the other former Soviet republics which opted for a 'zero option' in their legislation on citizenship—that is, all residents in the particular territory have the right to citizenship—Estonia and Latvia set strict conditions for citizenship. The Russian Government early became a target of severe criticism.[40] At the Congress of People's Deputies in April 1992 it was criticized for not defending the interests of Russians in these countries.[41] Since then the parliament on several occasions has demanded political and economic sanctions against the Baltic states in order to force them to change their policy or legislation on the Russian population in these countries. Yeltsin and Kozyrev dismissed these demands; however, their rhetoric on this issue became sharper. At the beginning of 1992 the situation of Russians in the former Soviet republics was characterized by the Russian Government as a 'violation of human rights'. In February 1992 Kozyrev raised the question at the UN Commission for Human Rights, in March 1992 at the Council of Baltic Sea States[42] and after that at the Conference on Security and Co-operation in Europe (CSCE).[43] The language used by top Russian officials became sharper and even included terms such as 'apartheid' and 'ethnic cleansers'.[44]

The Russian Government has not denied that it possesses instruments of coercion in the form of sanctions, threats and warnings in relation to the Baltic states on the issue of Russian minorities.

---

[37] Oldberg, I., *Kasern, handelsplats eller stridsäpple: Kaliningradområdets framtid* [Barracks, market-place or apple of discord: the future of the Kaliningrad region] (Försvarets forskningsanstalt: Stockholm, 23 Mar. 1995).

[38] Under the agreement, Russia needs permission from the Lithuanian authorities and has to apply 12 days in advance. Russian troops are not allowed to leave the trains or to carry weapons. The trains cannot be stopped nor wagons decoupled. Lithuania has the right to inspect the transports and to charge a fee.

[39] Oldberg (note 37).

[40] Tsipko, A., *Izvestiya*, 1 Oct. 1991.

[41] See the records from the Congress published in *Rossiyskaya Gazeta* in Apr. 1992.

[42] Founded in Mar. 1992 and currently composed of Denmark, Estonia, the European Union, Finland, Germany, Iceland, Latvia, Lithuania, Norway, Poland, Russia and Sweden.

[43] *Izvestiya*, 14 Feb. 1992.

[44] Interview with Kozyrev, *Newsweek*, 14 Feb. 1992, p. 5; and *Nezavisimaya Gazeta*, 7 Mar. 1992, p. 5.

By February 1992, Kozyrev had been alluding to the possibility of using sanctions—based on international law—against the Baltic states. Speaking at the UN Commission for Human Rights in Geneva, he advocated the granting of the right to impose economic and military sanctions against countries that violated the human rights of minority groups.[45] At the Congress of People's Deputies in April 1992 he asserted that it should be made possible to employ 'sufficiently severe' (*zhestkie*) and powerful (*silovye*) methods to defend the rights of Russians in accordance with international law. He also stated that levers other than economic and trade measures could be used against the states affected.[46] However, Kozyrev at that time distanced himself from any use of military force to solve conflicts with other former Soviet republics. Such views stood in stark contrast to those of his opponents, including the centrist Sergey Stankevich, who in June 1992 in direct polemic with Kozyrev stressed the significance of military expedients.[47]

Since then the Russian authorities have become more outspoken on the use of sanctions and coercion in defence of Russians in the 'near abroad'. In a draft plan of the Foreign Ministry from February 1992 on support of Russian minorities, economic sanctions and cuts in deliveries of gas and oil were recommended as weapons to be used against the countries concerned.[48] The use of military force has been reserved for crisis situations. The draft of the military doctrine published in May 1992 declared the right of the Russian Army to intervene in order to defend Russians living in former Soviet republics.[49] The doctrine as signed by Yeltsin in November 1993 was modified on this issue but stated that the Russian Army will act if Russian freedom, rights and legitimate interests are violated.[50]

When Kozyrev in April 1995 declared that the Russian Government was prepared to use all necessary means, including military, to defend Russians abroad, this was not a change of policy. However, Kozyrev added a new emphasis on expedients of force and coercion.

There is evidence of two different approaches by the government to the problem of Russian minorities. On the one hand it turns to international organizations, international conventions and international law. On the other hand it regards it as its obligation and right to intervene directly in other states in defence of Russians who legally are not Russian citizens.

In spite of these declarations, rhetoric, warnings and threats, Russia in its defence of Russians in the Baltic states has followed a policy of negotiation and

---

[45] *Izvestiya*, 14 Feb. 1992, p. 5.

[46] *Rossiyskaya Gazeta*, 21 Apr. 1992, p. 3.

[47] *Izvestiya*, 7 July 1992, p. 3.

[48] *Izvestiya*, 17 Feb. 1994.

[49] The draft military doctrine was published in *Voennaya Mysl*, special issue, May 1992.

[50] *Izvestiya* published excerpts from the military doctrine in 'Osnovnye polozheniya voennoy doktriny Rossiyskoy Federatsii' [The basic provisions of the military doctrine of the Russian Federation] on 18 Nov. 1993 and *Krasnaya Zvezda* published a slightly longer excerpt on 19 Nov. 1993. A translation into English appeared in *Jane's Intelligence Review*, Special Report, Jan. 1994. For a further discussion of the new military doctrine, see chapters 8 and 9 in this volume.

agreement.[51] The disparity between the harsher tone adopted by the Russian Government to the governments of the Baltic states and its more moderate behaviour indicated a lack of clarity in its intentions. It also raised concerns that words would be backed up by deeds.

A changed international environment and Russian threat perceptions

During the first half of the 1990s, important political reorientations took place in Northern Europe, not only in the Baltic countries but also in the Nordic countries. How were these understood by the Russian Government? They could be seen as opening up new possibilities. However, from a 'traditionalist' perspective, they could also be understood as detrimental to Russian interests.

The political reorientation of Northern Europe followed from two processes. The first followed in the wake of the dissolution of great-power confrontation and of military blocs in Europe. This made it possible for Finland to have its treaty with the Soviet Union from 1948, which had restricted Finland's options in foreign policy, replaced by a treaty of cooperation with Russia in 20 January 1992.[52] In this treaty the old clauses on consultations between Russia and Finland in the event of aggression against Russia over Finnish territory were removed. Sweden and Finland followed the example of Denmark and joined the European Union (EU). Sweden had applied for membership as early as July 1991 and Finland in March 1992; both became members on 1 January 1995. In the long term, membership may entail security cooperation with NATO, and both Finland and Sweden are thus thought to have abandoned the restrictions which their former policies of neutrality had imposed on them.[53] In May 1994 both countries signed the cooperative venture initiated by NATO, the Partnership for Peace (PFP). With Russia itself waiting for an agreement with the EU (which followed in June 1994 in the shape of the Partnership and Cooperation Agreement[54]), the Russian Government had no official comment on the Nordic reorientation. It kept a low profile also when the possibility of NATO membership for Finland and Sweden was discussed. The statements by the Russian Ambassador to Finland, Yuriy Deryabin, warning Finland of the consequences if it joined NATO,[55] were an exception.

---

[51] An agreement on the status of military pensioners was signed between Russia and Latvia together with the agreement on Russian troop withdrawal in 1994.

[52] *Keesing's Record of World Events*, Jan. 1992, p. 38737.

[53] Leifland, L. and Åström, S., *Historiskt vägval: följderna för Sverige i utrikes-och säkerhetspolitiskt hänseende av att bli, respektive inte bli medlem i Europeiska Unionen (Betänkande)* [Historic crossroads: the consequences for Sweden's foreign and security policy of joining or not joining the European Union], (Regeringskansliet: Stockholm, 1994), SOU 1994:8, p. 8. The Social Democratic government which returned to power in Sweden after the election of Sep. 1994, however, attempted to stick to the old rhetoric on Swedish neutrality.

[54] European Communities, Commission, Proposal for a Council and Commission decision on the conclusion of the Agreement on Partnership and Cooperation between the European Communities, of the one part, and Russia, of the other part, COM(94)257 final, Brussels, 15 June 1994; and Diplomaticheskiy Vestnik, nos 15–16 (1994).

[55] See, e.g., 'Derjabin varnar för NATO' [Deryabin warns about NATO], *Wasabladet*, 5 Mar. 1995.

The second process followed from the fear entertained by the independent Baltic states of Russian intentions for the future. As a consequence, Lithuania applied for NATO membership in January 1994, followed by the other two states. The three Baltic states signed the PFP at approximately the same time in early 1994.

Russia regarded the enlargement of NATO to the east with increasing concern. In 1991 and 1992, individual representatives of the government had expressed a positive view of NATO in vague terms. The draft of the military doctrine[56] already provided a hint of a more negative attitude in May 1992. In September 1993, in a letter to the leaders of France, Germany, the UK and the USA, Yeltsin stated Russia's opposition to NATO membership for the Central and East European or Baltic countries.[57]

The Russian military doctrine, signed by the president in November 1993,[58] mentioned the following sources of possible conflicts: (a) the expansion of military blocs and alliances to states in the vicinity of Russia and detrimental to Russian interests; (b) the deployment of foreign military forces on neighbouring territory; and (c) a military build-up along Russia's borders undermining the 'existing balance of forces'. Threat scenarios depicting local conflicts between Russia and a neighbouring country were also described. Of these, four can be regarded as relevant to the Baltic states: (a) violations of the rights of 'Russian citizens in foreign countries'; (b) attacks on military sites or members of the Russian armed forces located in foreign countries; (c) involvement in and destabilization of Russian internal affairs; and (d) attacks on objects and armaments along the border, border conflicts and armed provocations.

To summarize, the reorientation in the Nordic countries towards closer integration in Europe was not commented on by Moscow. Whether this was a result of passivity or of acceptance was unclear. The reorientation of the Baltic states and the possibility of their becoming members of NATO were described as a threat to Russia. Russian notions of threat included local conflicts, and this applies directly to the Baltic states.

Perceptions of threats to Russian security in the Barents region changed after the dissolution of the Soviet Union. Cooperation developed between Russia and its Nordic neighbours, the tension between Russia and the USA diminished and the Russian military considered the risk of a direct attack on Russia by the West as 'significantly reduced'. However, the risk of a global war with the participation of the USA was not excluded and the Barents area with its strategic location and the deployment of Russia's main strategic sea-based nuclear force in the Northern waters preserved old threat perceptions. These perceptions were also nourished by attention from US submarines close to Russian waters outside Murmansk, as pointed out by Russian intelligence.

---

[56] See note 50.
[57] Reuter, 30 Sep. 1993.
[58] See note 50.

IV. The international role of Russia

Russia after the breakup of the Soviet Union was burdened with a major identity problem and had difficulties establishing its international role. Yeltsin faced the task of defining a role that promoted the interests of Russia abroad and expressed a consensus within the country.

The international environment of Russia can be analysed as concentric rings around a Russian core, the innermost circle being formed by the 'near abroad' and comprising the former Soviet republics, the circles to the west of it representing Central and Eastern Europe, Western Europe and then the USA.

At the time of the dismantling of the Soviet Union, Yeltsin emphasized that Russia had no aspirations to special status within the former Soviet Union. In his support for independence for the Soviet republics and his proposal for a confederation, he expressed no pretensions to a leading role for Russia. In January 1992 Kozyrev coined the term 'normal great power', stressing that Russia was a 'normal' great power in the sense that it pursues its state interests, but without laying claim to any historic mission or task to fulfil. Its great-power status was based on the size of the country, its economic potential, history and culture.[59] This 'revisionist' position served as the point of departure for the government's policy *vis-à-vis* the 'near abroad' and Europe.

A reassessment subsequently took place. Russia sought to regain a leading position within the former Soviet territory. This was evident when Yeltsin in February 1993 laid claim to Russia taking responsibility for maintaining peace and stability in the whole of the former Soviet Union.[60] This was in line with the idea of a Russian 'Monroe Doctrine' introduced earlier by Yevgeniy Ambartsumov, Chairman of the Foreign Policy Committee of the Supreme Soviet in August 1992: Ambartsumov had expressed the view that Russia had to define all of the former USSR as its sphere of interest and that the international community had to accept Russia's role as a guarantor for peace and stability in the region. Moreover, he wanted Russia to be granted financial assistance from abroad to enable it to handle such commitments.[61] In the course of 1993 the Russian Government applied to the international community (the UN and the CSCE) to grant Russia an international mandate for peacekeeping efforts in the former Soviet Union.

It was in relation to the 'near abroad' that the Russian Government started to define its strategic interests, to speak of spheres of influence and to express concern about a possible power vacuum. During the autumn of 1993, Kozyrev started openly to express the idea that a power vacuum was likely to arise along the borders of Russia in the event of a Russian military withdrawal from these states.[62] This power vacuum, he said, might be filled by 'other powers, which

[59] Kozyrev, A., *Novoe Vremya*, no. 3 (1992).
[60] Yeltsin in a speech to the Civic Union coalition on 28 Feb. 1993.
[61] *Izvestiya*, 7 Aug. 1992.
[62] *Nezavisimaya Gazeta*, 24 Nov. 1993.

are not friendly and could even be hostile to Russian interests'.[63] In line with this, in February 1994 the Russian Government announced plans to keep Russian soldiers in the 'near abroad' by constructing almost 30 military bases out of existing military units located on these territories.[64] It became obvious to foreign observers that Russia, seeking to assume an international great-power role, intended to regain it primarily by carving out a leadership role for itself within the former Soviet Union.

The Baltic states, however, are not treated in the official language of the Russian Government as part of the 'near abroad'. Their status is considered to be different from that of the members of the Commonwealth of Independent States (CIS).[65] That is why there was a strong international reaction when Kozyrev blurred the distinction in a speech on 18 January 1994, claiming that 'we shouldn't withdraw from areas which have long been spheres of interaction, spheres of Russian interest' and maintaining that it would be wrong to withdraw Russian troops entirely. The Russian news agency ITAR-TASS reported the statement as having referred to the Baltic states as well; however, this was later denied by the Russian Foreign Ministry.[66]

That Russia is a great power and should bring its foreign policy into line with such a role was the main theme of President Yeltsin's speech to parliament on 24 February 1994.[67] At about this time, Russia started to stake a claim to an international role, that is, a role outside the space of the former Soviet Union. New concepts of 'strategic partnership' and 'real partnership' were formulated to express claims to a position equal to that of the USA in world politics.[68] Kozyrev wrote in the US press that Russia will not accept a subordinate global role.[69] Russia was thus back on the scene, not only firmly decided to be the regional leader within the former Soviet Union but also with claims to global power status.

Against this background of Russian concern about its international role, the Nordic–Baltic region as a whole and Russian policy towards the Nordic countries have seemed to be rather low on the agenda in Moscow. References to this have been made in the Russian press. As early as the summer of 1992, the international reorientation of the Nordic countries was pointed out by the correspondent of *Novoe Vremya* in Sweden.[70] In March 1995 one Russian analyst stated that 'In many respects it was thanks to the passivity of Russian diplomacy that the preconditions arose for the gradual departure of countries such as Sweden and Finland from their traditional neutrality'.[71]

---

[63] *Nezavisimaya Gazeta*, 24 Nov. 1993.

[64] *Aftenposten*, 9 Feb. 1994.

[65] Churkin, V., Deputy Foreign Minister, 27 Jan. 1994, reported in *Diplomaticheskiy Vestnik*, nos 3–4 (Feb. 1994), p. 34.

[66] Reuter/BBC Monitoring Service, 20 Jan. 1994.

[67] *Rossiyskaya Gazeta*, 25 Feb. 1994.

[68] *International Herald Tribune*, 19–20 Mar. 1994.

[69] Kozyrev, A., *International Herald Tribune*, 19–20 Mar. 1994, p. 5.

[70] *Novoe Vremya*, no. 25 (1992).

[71] Petrova, N., *Nezavisimaya Gazeta*, 17 May 1995.

V. The role of military defence

The role of military defence in the north-west of Russia has always been central to Russia's Baltic dilemma. Given the fact that the Baltic states were now independent and a foreign and security policy in Moscow which stresses non-military expedients, the role of the military in this area could be expected to decrease. As mentioned above, the Leningrad MD was declared a first-echelon district in 1993 but the role of the Baltic Sea region to Russia's strategic defence has been drastically diminished.

The case is different with the Barents region. The area offers harbours free from ice all year round and direct access to the ocean and is home base to the Northern Fleet and to the main part of the Russian sea-based nuclear force. The future of the Barents region depends on the structure and priorities of the Russian defence.

Nuclear weapons are to remain the backbone of Russian strategic defence according to the 1993 military doctrine. A revision was made in the declaration, dating back to Soviet times, that the country would never be the first to use nuclear weapons; the Russian Government now has the option of doing this.[72] It can be assumed that the greater the cuts in the defence budget, the more the Russians will rely on nuclear deterrence as a last resort.

The relative importance given lately to nuclear weapons and to sea-based nuclear armaments does not in any way reduce the importance of the Barents region. Furthermore, the START treaties,[73] under which Russia committed itself to reducing its strategic nuclear weapon arsenal by the year 2003 to approximately one-third of its 1991 level, affect land-based intercontinental missiles above all.[74] As a consequence, the relative importance of those based at sea will increase.[75]

The Northern Fleet is more modern than the Pacific Fleet, boasting the latest submarine carriers and systems. It is also accorded greater strategic significance than the Pacific Fleet. Not only the strategic, but also the political, importance of the Northern Fleet was stressed by the First Deputy Commander-in-Chief of the Navy, Admiral Igor Kasatanov, in November 1993: 'The Northern Fleet has been, is, and will continue to be our Number One fleet. This is a fleet which even now has the mightiest material base, guaranteeing the support of sea-based strategic nuclear systems . . . the Northern Fleet, with its ballistic mis-

---

[72] Grachev, P., *Nezavisimaya Gazeta,* 9 June 1994, pp. 1, 5.

[73] The 1991 US–Soviet Treaty on the Reduction and Limitation of Strategic Offensive Arms (START I) and the 1993 US–Russian Treaty on Further Reduction and Limitation of Strategic Offensive Arms (START II).

[74] International Institute of Strategic Studies, *The Military Balance 1993–1994* (Brassey's: London, 1993).

[75] This fact was underlined by Col-Gen. Mikhail Kolesnikov, Chief of the General Staff, who pointed out in Jan. 1993 that with START II Russia had increased the specific importance of its submarine-based nuclear weapon forces. *Svenska Dagbladet,* 8 Jan. 1993.

siles, guarantees both the security of Russia's borders and proper respect for it (*dolzhny avtoritet*)'.[76]

The future importance of the Barents region will depend on the importance Moscow accords the navy. It is at present in a very serious state. Criticism of the major build-up of the Soviet Navy in the 1970s, combined with the economic and financial crisis, has pointed in the direction of more limited objectives for it. None the less, statements by top navy officials stress the need for a blue-water navy to defend Russia's military, political and economic interests.[77] After 1993 Defence Minister Grachev, Commander Gromov and his deputy Kasatanov tried to defend the interests of the navy by pointing out its importance for a great power. Several statements by top military officers indicated that the experiences of the Persian Gulf War had influenced Russian defence thinking because they demonstrated the importance of air attacks from the sea.[78] The political role of the navy was strongly emphasized by Gromov in the spring of 1993, when he referred in an article to Piotr Stolypin, Prime Minister at the beginning of the century: 'No world power can fail to take part in world policy, fail to take part in political schemes and give up the right to have its say in resolving world events. The fleet represents a lever for exercising that right; it is the attribute of a great power'.[79] Gromov explained that every time Russia has tried to strengthen its statehood, as it is doing today, the people and leadership have inevitably found it necessary to re-create the navy as the most important military and foreign policy element in guaranteeing the security and defence of national interests at sea. Representatives of the navy also emphasized its role in protecting and guaranteeing the economic interests of Russia (in which, as Gromov has pointed out, the richest resources are to be found at sea and on the continental shelf) and maritime transport. Discussing Russia's economic interests at sea, Gromov also referred to the defence of Russia's maritime borders, shipping and fisheries and to the need to combat smuggling and terrorism.

The Barents region continues to be dominated by the military instruments of the state.

VI. Conclusions: an altered strategy in Northern Europe?

How did Russian policy in Northern Europe change after the collapse of the Soviet Union? Yeltsin had sketched the main lines of a new strategy before the USSR had entirely ceased to exist. This strategy has here been called 'revision-

[76] *Krasnaya Zvezda*, 30 Nov. 1993.

[77] Jonson, L., 'Russia as a seapower', eds B. Huldt and J. Prawitz, Naval Disarmament, Unpublished report, 1993.

[78] Chernavin, V., *Sovetskaya Rossiya*, 9 Jan. 1992; Gromov, F., *Rossiyskaya Gazeta*, 15 Apr. 1993; the draft military doctrine of May 1992 (see note 49); Tritten, J. J., 'The changing role of naval forces: the Russian view of the 1991 Persian Gulf War', *Journal of Soviet Military Studies*, Dec. 1992, pp. 575–610; and Holcomb, J., 'Russian military doctrine: restructuring for the worst case', *Jane's Intelligence Review*, Dec. 1992, p. 533.

[79] *Rossiyskaya Gazeta*, 15 Apr. 1993.

ist' and entails, apart from a commitment to international cooperation and less emphasis on military expedients, Russian acceptance of a reduced position on the Baltic Sea.

Are there, then, any signs that Russia no longer accepts this withdrawal from the Baltic Sea? Russian troops are now out of the Baltic states. A series of measures is being taken to deal with the new situation. At the same time, it is possible to see from Russian statements that the Russian leadership has become increasingly conscious of the problems following from this situation. In the first place, the question of the status of Russians in the Baltic states has assumed an even more prominent position in the Russian domestic political debate. More attention is also being paid to what are referred to as geopolitical interests in the Baltic area.

The Russian border in the north-west along the Baltic Sea is considered to be exposed and vulnerable. Russian perceptions of the West have changed since 1991–92 and become more complex. Distrust of the West has been more clearly expressed, and the possible eastward enlargement of NATO is described in terms of a threat to Russia. Statements by the Russian Government on Russia's international role have become clearer since 1991. Russia now expressly considers itself to be a great power with responsibilities, rights and obligations within the entire area of the former Soviet Union. Since the autumn of 1993, the Russian Government has spoken in terms of strategic interests and the necessity of a Russian military presence outside Russia to prevent a power vacuum from arising.

The Baltic states have been viewed as a special case. The Russian Government has avoided directly and openly making statements pertaining to Russian strategic interests in the area. However, claiming Russian interests in the 'near abroad' creates a certain ambiguity with respect to the Baltic states. Thus Andrannik Migranyan, political commentator and adviser to Yeltsin, claimed that Russia had geopolitical and military–strategic interests in the Baltic states including ports, communications, agreements on troops and bases, beyond, of course, a responsibility to defend the status of the Russian populations in those countries.[80]

In terms of action taken, there has been no change in policy. Russia acts as if its withdrawn position on the Baltic Sea has been accepted. However, there is a growing disparity between words and deeds. Russian statements reflect altered assessments of its national interests in relation to those of the West, to its international role, to the question of the vulnerability of the north-western border and to the problems arising from its new situation on the Baltic Sea. With a still turbulent domestic scene, there is still a risk that Yeltsin's 'revisionist' strategy in the Baltic may be abandoned in favour of a more 'traditional' one.

---

[80] Migranyan, A., 'Rossiya i blizhnee zarubezhe' [Russia and the 'near abroad'], *Nezavisimaya Gazeta*, 12 Jan. 1994.

Russian relations with the Nordic countries improved considerably during these years.[81] Exchange grew and former enemy images of Russia in those states weakened and gave way to growing interest in Russia. The major disputes in bilateral relations were, however, not resolved, such as the dispute between Norway and Russia over the boundary in the Barents Sea and on the continental shelf. The Nordic countries became more actively involved in the future of the Baltic states. The then Swedish Prime Minister, Carl Bildt, pointed out in November 1993 that Swedish neutrality policy should no longer be considered an obstacle to Swedish support for the Baltic states in the event of their independence being threatened.[82]

The military–strategic importance of the Barents region to Russia will continue to be considerable, given the renewed Russian emphasis on a great-power status and continued reliance on strategic nuclear weapons and Russia's interest in a blue-water navy for the future. A Russian military build-up at any time in the Barents region would cause concern among the Nordic countries.

What would a return to a 'traditionalist' strategy entail for Northern Europe? It would have consequences, above all, for Russia's relations with the Baltic states and could involve Russia attempting, through economic sanctions (such as interruptions to gas supplies) or the threat of military force to press through concessions in its favour, to allow it to use base and port facilities in the Baltic states or to change the status of the Russians living there. A return to a 'traditionalist' strategy need not entail the military occupation of the Baltic states, but it would mean Russia forcing its demands to be met unilaterally and with force or the threat of force.

Russia, Europe and the rest of the world have, however, changed considerably during the past five years. The exercise of Russian power in the Baltic states would probably meet with a strong international reaction. Countries in the East have allied themselves with the rest of Europe in a burgeoning all-European network composed of the Organization for Security and Co-operation in Europe (OSCE),[83] agreements with the EU, the North Atlantic Cooperation Council (NACC) and the PFP. For Russia, which has once again become part of Europe, the price of a power policy pursued against the Baltic states would be too high to pay. The Soviet state was able to turn its back on the rest of the world, with varied success, at different times. Given the current state of the world, however, with society built on advanced information technology and

---

[81] On the part of the Russians, isolated indications of political sensitivity in relation to the Nordic countries could be noted. During the Finnish presidential campaign in Jan. 1994, a Russian protest was suddenly issued to the Finnish Foreign Ministry over 2 small Finnish nationalist organizations having demanded a revision of the Finnish–Russian border. See also chapter 15 in this volume. The protest was received with surprise in the Nordic region as the organizations were insignificant and the protest as such was reminiscent of old-fashioned Soviet power diplomacy; it was viewed by the Nordic countries above all as a temporary error in the work of the Russian Foreign Ministry. It should be noted that it reflected a view similar to that expressed by the commander of the Russian border troops, expressed at about the same time.

[82] Bildt, C., *Sverige och de baltiska länderna* [Sweden and the Baltic countries] (Swedish Institute of International Affairs: Stockholm, Nov. 1993).

[83] On 1 Jan. 1995 the CSCE became the OSCE.

economic interdependence, it would be extremely costly for Russia to even try: discontent within Russia could then explode.

To continue a 'revisionist' policy, on the other hand, would entail seeking solutions to problems through negotiation and on the basis of mutual trust. A 'revisionist' policy has to be built on the insight that the great-power position of a state in the world of today must be based on a strong economy and high level of technological development and not first and foremost on military strength. This means that Russia's need for access to commercial ports along the Baltic Sea and transit and communications across Baltic territory must be met with recourse to negotiation and on a commercial basis. From a 'revisionist' perspective, naval bases (in the vicinity of St Petersburg in particular) would be sufficient for Russian defence and there is no need for military bases, port rights or air defence sites in the Baltic states. For a relationship based on confidence between Russia and the Baltic states, Russia would respect Baltic independence and be confident that Baltic territory would not be used as a deployment area against Russia. The most sensitive issue in Russian–Baltic relations is the status of the Russian populations, but there can be no question that most of these people want to continue to live and work in the Baltic states.

There has been over the years a 'Baltic dilemma' for Russian policy in Northern Europe. The more force Russia exerted to secure its interests in the Baltic area, the more vulnerable it became as a result of reactions from the rest of the world. In today's world, a withdrawn position from the Baltic Sea and respect for Baltic independence seem to be the better guarantee of Russian security in the Baltic area.

There are certain enduring factors in Russian policy in Northern Europe. It has always been, and will always be, in Russia's interests to secure its access to the sea—to both the Baltic and the Barents seas. Nor will any Russian government be able to shirk responsibility for defending the interests of the Russian populations in the Baltic states. However, how Russia's national interests are defined and by what means these interests are to be secured will be determined by Russia's domestic political balance of power.

15. In search of a new strategy in the Baltic/ Nordic area

Alexander A. Sergounin*

I. Introduction

The purpose of this chapter is threefold: to examine the role of the Baltic/ Nordic region in Russian foreign policy interests; to identify progress and problems in Russian relations with the region; and to outline opportunities for cooperation between Russia and the Baltic[1] and Nordic[2] countries and propose some solutions to existing problems. In section II it considers the importance of the region for Russia. Section III examines Russian–Baltic/Nordic military relations, including the issue of the safety and maintenance of Russian nuclear weapons and arms control. Section IV discusses the problem of Russian-speaking minorities in the Baltic and Nordic countries, and section V existing territorial disputes. Section VI summarizes the conclusions.

II. The region through the prism of Russian national interest

Both the Baltic and the Nordic countries are moving up the Russian foreign policy priority list, for the following reasons.

1. In geopolitical terms there have been major changes. With the collapse of the USSR Russia lost direct access to Central and Western Europe. Russia now has a land frontier only with two North European countries—Finland and Norway—and one East–Central European country—Poland—in the Kaliningrad *oblast* (region). Numerous barriers (tariffs, the lack of coordination between customs services and border guards of different countries, organized crime and others) prevent normal communications through Belarus and Ukraine. The Baltic and Nordic countries might again assume the role of a 'window on Europe' which they have had since the time of Peter the Great.

The region is also an important transport junction by sea, land and air. As a result of Russia's loss of its main ports on the Black Sea (Odessa, Nikolaev, Sevastopol, Kerch, Sukhumi and Batumi) and on the Baltic Sea (Riga, Klaipeda and Tallinn) which formerly connected Russia with the West, the role of the Kaliningrad, St Petersburg, Murmansk and Arkhangelsk harbours has become crucial.

---

[1] Estonia, Latvia and Lithuania.
[2] Denmark, Finland, Iceland, Norway and Sweden.

* The research on which this chapter is based was supported by a grant from the Centre for Peace and Conflict Research, Copenhagen.

The new geopolitical situation influences greatly the development of Russian land and sea transport infrastructure. Moscow is planning to develop the above-mentioned ports and transport in northern Russia—for example, to build a high-speed railway between Moscow, St Petersburg and Murmansk.[3] Since the time of President Mikhail Gorbachev the Soviet Union and subsequently Russia has been appealing to the Nordic countries for development of the Northern Sea Route.[4] Moscow is also trying to get free access to the railways and highways going through the Baltic states' territories.

2. In strategic and military terms, the Russian political and military leadership emphasizes the need to protect the most important industrial and administrative centres of north-western Russia, which have become more vulnerable since the emergence of independent states, the separation of Kaliningrad from Russia and the shift of the border close to St Petersburg, Pskov and Novgorod.

Despite disarmament and US–Russian *rapprochement*, the north is still important for Russia from the strategic defence point of view. The Arkhangelsk Air Defence Sector is crucial for the prevention of surprise attack over the North Pole. The Norwegian Sea is the main launch area for Western seaborne attack, so the Russian Navy is still concerned about the readiness of its anti-submarine forces in the Arctic. Northern Russia is one region which has accommodated troops withdrawn from former Warsaw Treaty Organization (WTO) countries and Soviet republics. The same is true for the navy: the Baltic Sea Fleet faces the problem of redeployment of vessels and facilities from the Baltic states to Kaliningrad and Kronshtadt (near St Petersburg). For example, in 1992–93 the 11th Guards Army, a naval brigade, shore defence elements, a division of internal troops and other 'special units' were redeployed into the Kaliningrad Region.[5]

Paradoxically, the arms control process increases the military significance of the north for Russia. Under the 1991 US–Russian Treaty on the Reduction and Limitation of Strategic Offensive Arms (the START I Treaty)[6] Russia should eliminate the greater part of its intercontinental ballistic missiles (ICBMs). The role of airborne and sea-based missiles will therefore be enhanced. The Kola Peninsula and White Sea coast have the biggest submarine bases in Russia: 60 per cent of Russian nuclear-powered, ballistic-missile submarines (SSBNs) are based here. The main areas of submarine activity are the Barents Sea, the Kara Sea and the Arctic Ocean. The north-western Arctic coastline constitutes a

---

[3] Nordic Council, *Cooperation in the Baltic Sea Area: Second Parliamentary Conference on Cooperation in the Baltic Sea Area. Report from a conference arranged by the Nordic Council at the Storting, Oslo, Norway, 22–24 Apr. 1992* (Nordic Council: Stockholm, 1992), pp. 23–24.

[4] *International Challenges*, vol. 12, no. 1 (1992), pp. 23–38, 84–98.

[5] Woff, R., *The Armed Forces of the Former Soviet Union: Evolution, Structure and Personalities* (Carmichael & Sweet: Portsmouth, 1995), vol. 2, part 2, p. F1-4.

[6] For details, see Lockwood, D., 'Nuclear arms control', *SIPRI Yearbook 1994* (Oxford University Press: Oxford, 1994), pp. 644–46; and Karp, R. C., 'The START Treaty and the future of nuclear arms control', *SIPRI Yearbook 1992: World Armaments and Disarmament* (Oxford University Press: Oxford, 1992), pp. 13–37. For excerpts from the text, see *SIPRI Yearbook 1992*, pp. 38–63.

vital forward operating and refuelling area for Russian long-range strategic bombers *en route* to continental North American targets.[7]

The Baltic and the Arctic are still a field of NATO–Russian naval confrontation. Both sides have reduced their naval activities in the region but they are still fairly dangerous. 'Submarine incidents' occur from time to time. Naval intelligence operations have become even more active: NATO and Russia are still interested in each other's intentions.

The significance of the region has increased following the redeployment of Russian nuclear and space facilities. In August 1991, Kazakhstan decided to ban nuclear tests at Semipalatinsk. Novaya Zemlya is now the only Russian testing ground, and would therefore be extremely important for Moscow if the present pressure from the military to resume tests were to succeed.[8] After Kazakhstan became an independent state Russia resumed the launching of missiles from the Plisetsk space terminal in the north of Russia.

3. Politically, Russia has different approaches to the Baltic and the Nordic states. Relations with the former are important if Moscow is to keep its influence in the subregion and protect Russian-speaking minorities. As regards the Nordic countries, Russia hopes to use them: (*a*) as a vehicle for Russia's participation in the European economic, political and military institutions;[9] (*b*) in the diplomatic game against any potential rival in Europe (e.g., Germany, France or the UK); and (*c*) to avoid isolation on the European continent.

4. In economic terms, Russia looks to the Nordic countries as a possible source of investment, advanced technology and training assistance and as a promising trading partner. Geographically the Nordic countries are closer to it than other Western countries. Russia hopes to attract Nordic attention to the development of adjacent regions—the Kola Peninsula, St Petersburg, Kaliningrad, the Northern Sea Route, the autonomous districts on the Arctic coast and so on. For the Baltic states, Russia hopes that they will retain their interest in its natural resources and be a promising market for Russian industrial goods.

5. There are two important humanitarian issues in Russian relations with the Baltic/Nordic region. The first and most acute is the rights of the Russian-speaking minorities in the Baltic states. This is very important from the points

---

[7] Heininen, L. and Käkönen, J. (eds), Tampere Peace Research Institute, *Arctic Complexity: Essays on Arctic Interdependence,* Occasional Papers no. 44 (TAPRI: Tampere, 1991), p. 13; Nieminen, T., *Flank or Front: An Assessment of Military–Political Developments in the High North* (War College: Helsinki, 1991), pp. 11–15; and Heisler, M. O. (ed.), *The Nordic Region: Changing Perspectives in International Relations,* Special Issue of the *Annals of the American Academy of Political and Social Science,* vol. 512 (Sage Publications: Newbury Park & London, 1990), p. 26.

[8] The last test was conducted by the USSR on Novaya Zemlya on 24 Oct. 1990. This was the last nuclear explosion on former Soviet soil. Russia has since observed the moratorium on nuclear testing announced by President Gorbachev on 5 Oct. 1991. For further detail, see Skorve, J. and Skogan, J. K., Norwegian Institute of International Affairs, *The NUPI Satellite Study of the Northern Underground Nuclear Test Area on Novaya Zemlya: Summary Report of Preliminary Results,* NUPI Research Report no. 164 (NUPI: Oslo, 1992).

[9] Russia may be expecting the Nordic states to be more tolerant of and responsive to its intentions than other European countries. At the same time it has to keep in mind their sensitivity to Russian pressure on the Baltic states. Furthermore, they may be more intransigent with respect to violations of human rights and democratic principles by Russia.

of view both of foreign policy (Russia's international authority) and of domestic policy (the confrontation between the government and opposition, the issue of refugees and displaced persons and so on).

The second issue is cultural cooperation between the related (Finno-Ugrian) nations of the north. The Russian leadership understands the need for this cooperation and favours the establishment of cultural ties between, for instance, Finns and Karelians, Mordva, Saami, Komi, Mansi and others.[10]

The importance of the Baltic/Nordic region for Russia has clearly increased. According to official documents, the Baltic states are included in the first, most important circle of Russian national interests.[11] The Nordic countries are also mentioned among the chief priorities in Europe. Russian foreign policy thinking recognizes the similarities and dissimilarities between the Baltic and Nordic problems. Russia takes different approaches to regional problems and particular countries.

However, the Russian leadership, being preoccupied with other problems, has sometimes underestimated the importance of the region. For example, the Nordic countries were not identified as a priority in the early drafts of the Russian foreign policy doctrine.[12] The Baltic states are perceived predominantly through the prism of military and human rights issues while political, economic, environmental and cultural aspects are often ignored. Russian leaders prefer strong language regarding the Baltic states instead of quiet diplomacy. This incomplete view arises from failure to define the basic concepts of Russian diplomacy towards the Baltic/Nordic countries. The doctrinal principles of Russian strategy must be defined before a proper intellectual framework for shaping Moscow's policy in the region can be set up.

First of all, there are serious grounds for perceiving the Baltic states and the Nordic countries as a united, indivisible region with its own historical traditions and basic characteristics rather than as two separate regions. Although the Baltic states are not officially considered as belonging to the 'near abroad', current Russian strategic thinking includes them in the first circle of foreign policy interests; the Nordic countries are seen as part of 'far Europe' (the second circle of national interests). This approach ignores the emergence of a new region consisting of both the Baltic and the Nordic countries.

Second, there is a strong case for Russia identifying itself as part of this region-in-the-making and not as an external power. For Russia to view its Baltic/Nordic policy solely as policy *towards* the region is not adequate. It is conducted *within* the region as well.

---

[10] *Nordic Council of Ministers Newsletter,* no. 1 (Jan. 1993), p. 3; and Osherenko, G. and Young, O. R., *The Age of the Arctic: Hot Conflicts and Cold Realities* (Cambridge University Press: Cambridge, 1989), pp. 84–86.

[11] 'Kontseptsiya vneshney politiki Rossiyskoy Federatsii' [The foreign policy concept of the Russian Federation], *Diplomaticheskiy Vestnik,* Jan. 1993, p. 13.

[12] 'Kontseptsiya vneshney politiki Rossiyskoy Federatsii' [The foreign policy concept of the Russian Federation], Russian Ministry of Foreign Affairs, 1992. This was an unpublished brochure circulated among the deputies of the former Russian Supreme Soviet.

Third, somewhat emotional attitudes to Baltic problems hitherto have led to exaggeration of the significance of the Baltic issues and to a vision of the Baltic states as 'a source of threat to Russia'.[13] The Baltic states, incidentally, are very skilful in using Russia's blunders to present Moscow as being in the wrong in the conflict.

Fourth, in dealing with its Baltic/Nordic problems, Russia acts from a unique place in the world security order. Russia's role will be crucial in the maintenance of order and stability within the Eurasian strategic space as well in establishing a link between the European and Eurasian security complexes. Russia is in the process of changing its security role and image from being a force threatening European countries to being a mediator and guarantor. Russia's politico-military potential and great-power status can be instruments for the consolidation of the security order on the continent, not for winning unilateral advantages. The Baltic and Nordic countries in fact constitute a border region between the European and Eurasian security complexes. This entails a special responsibility for Moscow and a need for balance and restraint.

In fact, a new Baltic/Nordic security sub-system is emerging now in the region as a part of the European security complex. This is natural as the countries of the region draw increasingly close for economic and political reasons. There is much discussion of its status, identity, orientation, role and concrete form in a contemporary scholarship[14] but the existence of the sub-system is a matter of fact, which every regional actor should take into account.

It appears that Russia wishes to contribute to the development of this security sub-system and to be a recognized member of it. To be realistic, it will not be simple for the Baltic and Nordic countries to accept the participation of Moscow. It will only be acceptable if Russia abandons its imperial traditions and interprets its membership in the security community as a duty rather than a natural privilege. Clearly, this cannot be realized immediately. Moscow should change the foundations of its foreign policy in order to put right former misperceptions among the countries of the region and to provide its diplomatic and military undertakings with a solid economic basis.

To summarize, a special and clearly pronounced Russian doctrine for the Baltic and Nordic countries is needed. A coherent regional strategy is at present lacking.

The sections which follow consider the main aspects of security politics in the region.

[13] Statement of then Russian Foreign Minister, Andrey Kozyrev, 19 Jan. 1994.

[14] Kukk, M., Jervell, S. and Joenniemi, P., *The Baltic Sea Area: A Region in the Making* (Europa-programmet: Oslo and Baltic Institute: Karlskrona, 1992), pp. 211–38; Joenniemi, P. and Vares, P. (eds), Tampere Peace Research Institute, *New Actors on the International Arena: The Foreign Policies of the Baltic Countries,* TAPRI Research Report no. 50 (TAPRI: Tampere, 1993), pp. 1–31, 39–65; and Øberg, J. (ed.), *Nordic Security in the 1990s: Options in the Changing Europe* (Pinter: London, 1992), pp. 20–26.

III. Military issues

Recent developments in Russian military policy towards the region have given rise to both hopes and concerns in the Baltic and Nordic states. There were three main problems in Russian–Baltic/Nordic military relations: (*a*) the withdrawal of Russian troops from the Baltic states and related issues; (*b*) Russian military activities in the region; and (*c*) the safety and maintenance of Russian nuclear weapons.

Withdrawal of Russian residual forces

There were three main problems concerning withdrawal: (*a*) political—the linkage with human rights; (*b*) financial—the costs of redeployment of forces and dismantling of military installations; and (*c*) technical—the future of Russian military property in the Baltic states and accommodating the troops withdrawn in Russia. Unfortunately, financial and technical issues were often hostages of grand policy and quiet and pragmatic diplomacy was the victim of political chance and nerves.

Initially Russia, Estonia and Latvia had quite different views of the problem. Russia had three main conditions: (*a*) the Baltic states must guarantee the civil rights of the Russian minorities; (*b*) the final date for withdrawal should be determined by the ability of the Russian Defence Ministry to accommodate the withdrawn forces; and (*c*) the Baltic states should provide the Russian military with access to the bases and with transit rights. The Baltic states, however, insisted that withdrawal should be a precondition for negotiations on other problems.

Lithuania adopted citizenship legislation which satisfied Russia. The two reached agreement on withdrawal of the residual forces relatively quickly and Russia completed withdrawal from Lithuania by 1 September 1993. In January 1995 the two countries exchanged diplomatic notes by which Lithuania agreed to extend the existing rules for Russian military transit to the Kaliningrad Region until the end of 1995 and Russia stated that the agreement giving Lithuania 'most favoured nation' status, signed in November 1993, had come into force.[15] Despite some contradictions, bilateral relations, including relations involving military issues, are satisfactory for both sides.

It was more difficult for Moscow to conclude agreements on troop withdrawal with Estonia and Latvia. Both sides, under pressure from domestic public opinion and hoping to gain more advantages, used tough tactics instead of a pragmatic search for a compromise.

---

[15] A formal bilateral agreement was politically impossible because of opposition in Lithuania. *Baltic Independent,* 27 Jan.–2 Feb. 1995, p. 1; and van Ham, P. (ed.), Institute for Security Studies, Western European Union, *The Baltic States: Security and Defence After Independence,* Chaillot Papers no. 19 (1995) (ISS: Paris, 1995), pp. 15–16.

For some time a tactic of 'linkage' between the issue of minorities and that of troop withdrawals was a main instrument of Russian policy towards Estonia and Latvia. In 1993–94 Moscow postponed troop withdrawal several times, linking its decision with Russian-speaking minorities and financial issues.[16] However, its pressure on Estonia and Latvia had contradictory consequences. On the one hand, both conceded some liberalization of their citizenship and language legislation and resolved the problem of retired Russian servicemen. On the other hand, it became apparent that Moscow's power to affect the Baltic countries' policy towards Russian minorities is limited, and Russian pressure evoked irritation and countermeasures. This cast doubt on the effectiveness of the tactic. The linkage tactic also proved to be very harmful for future Russian–Baltic relations. The Baltic states perceive Moscow's current policy as a continuation of Russian (or Soviet) imperial policy. They do not believe that the new Russian foreign policy is truly democratic in character.

The failure of the linkage tactic suggests that in pursuing its foreign policy goals Russia should use other means to influence the Baltic states (or other former Soviet republics) which do not hurt their national self-respect.

Quite apart from the ineffectiveness of the linkage tactic, two other factors changed the Russian position: Western pressure and Western promises to cover some of the expenses connected with force withdrawal. In July 1994, for example, when President Boris Yeltsin declared a postponement of the withdrawal from Estonia, the US Senate amended a bill which would have provided $839 million in aid to Russia conditional on the departure of all Russian troops from Estonia and Latvia by 31 August.[17] On the other hand, at the Vancouver summit meeting of the Group of Seven industrialized countries (G7) in April 1993 US President Bill Clinton promised Yeltsin $160 million to pay for housing Russian troops leaving the Baltic states.[18] At the same time the USA, the UK, Germany and the Nordic countries exerted pressure visibly and behind the scenes on the Baltic states to make them more flexible in negotiating with Moscow.[19]

Finally, after lengthy and difficult negotiations, Russia concluded agreements with Latvia (30 April 1994) and Estonia (26 July 1994) and had withdrawn its troops from both countries by 31 August 1994. Small Russian contingents remained to maintain the Skrunda radar station in Latvia for another five years and to dismantle nuclear reactors at the submarine training base in the Estonian port of Paldiski.[20]

The Baltic states are still concerned about the future of Russian military property left behind after force withdrawal, about the environmental consequences of the former Russian military presence in the region, and about the

---

[16] *Krasnaya Zvezda*, 25 Dec. 1993.
[17] *Baltic Independent*, 22–28 July 1994, p. 1.
[18] *Baltic Independent*, 17–23 Feb. 1995, p. 1.
[19] *Baltic Independent*, 6–12 May 1994, p. 1.
[20] *Baltic Independent*, 6–12 May 1994, p. 1; 29 July–4 Aug. 1994, p. 1; and 5–11 Aug. 1994, p. 1.

several thousand Russian servicemen still residing in Estonia and Latvia and waiting for housing to be built for them in Russia.[21]

To summarize, compromise was finally reached on the basis of mutual concessions. Russia had failed to force Estonia and Latvia to grant citizenship automatically to all Russian-speaking inhabitants, to prolong troop withdrawal for years, to get compensation for its military property and to keep strategically important naval bases in the region. Estonia and Latvia had had to agree to guarantee the social rights of Russian military pensioners and to provide them with residence permits, to give Moscow some limited access to base facilities (the Skrunda radar station), and to abandon their claims to financial compensation for the ecological damage caused by the Russian military.

Russian military activities

The Russian military has considerably reduced its activities in the region, motivated both by political and by economic considerations.

The Baltic Military District (MD) has been abolished. The Leningrad MD has been provided with a more defensive configuration. Over the period 1990–95 the number of motor rifle divisions in the MD fell from 11 to 6, the number of tanks was reduced from 1200 to 950, and the numbers of artillery, multiple rocket launchers and mortars fell from 2140 to 1000. Over the same period the Baltic Fleet reduced the number of its submarines from 42 (2 strategic and 40 tactical) to 9 tactical submarines and the number of surface ships from 450 to 260; and in the Northern Fleet the number of submarines fell from 153 to 109 and the number of surface ships from 370 to 294.[22]

Most of Russia's strategic submarines are no longer on the alert and are stationed at their bases. They often have no fuel to stay out at sea. At the same time the navy's operational capacity has been reduced. According to some reports, only 30 per cent of its needs for repairs and ship maintenance can be met.[23] Military shipbuilding has been reduced or in some cases stopped.

This has reduced Baltic and Nordic concerns regarding a Russian military threat. However, the Russian military presence and activities in the region are still fairly intensive.

Russia is to expand its naval facilities at Baltiysk in the Kaliningrad Region in a plan linked to the withdrawal of warships from the Baltic states, according to Admiral Vladimir Yegorov, Commander-in-Chief of the Baltic Fleet. The naval presence at Baltiysk will be expanded to include more conventional submarines and new barracks to house a 1100-strong maritime border guard unit.[24]

---

[21] Baltic Independent, 17–23 Feb. 1995, p. 1.

[22] International Institute for Strategic Studies, The Military Balance 1990–1991 (Brassey's: London, 1990), pp. 39–40; and The Military Balance 1995–1996 (Oxford University Press: Oxford, 1995), pp. 116–17.

[23] Dellenbrant, J. Å. and Olsson, M. O. (eds), Centrum för Regionalvetenskaplig Forskning, University of Umeå, The Barents Region: Security and Economic Development in the European North (CERUM: Umeå, 1994), p. 168.

[24] Jane's Defence Weekly, 13 Mar. 1993, p. 14.

Some Nordic military experts believe that the lack of cohesion and precisely defined military purpose makes these considerable forces useless in a military sense.[25] However, most Baltic/Nordic leaders consider their potential sufficient to create a significant threat to Baltic/Nordic security in the event of possible tension.

The Russian military doctrine

Moreover, some provisions of the Russian military doctrine by Yeltsin in November 1993[26] (for example, the assumption of use of military force for the protection of Russian citizens abroad and repeal of the principle of no-first-use of nuclear weapons) have aroused Baltic/Nordic concerns once again.

In particular, they are worried about Russia's abandonment of the principle of no-first-use. There are two exceptions from Russia's promise not to use nuclear weapons against any state party to the 1968 Non-Proliferation Treaty (NPT): if '(a) a state which is connected by an alliance agreement with a nuclear state attacks the Russian Federation, its territory, armed forces and other services or its allies, [or] (b) such a state collaborates with a nuclear power in carrying out, or supporting, an invasion or an armed aggression against the Russian Federation, its territory, armed forces and other services or its allies'.[27] In one way or another all the Nordic and Baltic countries, and especially the NATO members, Denmark, Iceland and Norway, may come into these categories.

Their reaction was contradictory. On the one hand, they considered this change to a Western concept of deterrence as evidence of a greater inclination towards openness and frankness in military matters on Russia's part: few in the West took seriously the old Soviet doctrine of no-first-use. They understood that Russia's new nuclear doctrine reflected its intention to rely mainly on nuclear deterrence to compensate for its conventional weakness and keep its great-power status. On the other hand, they perceived this change as a clear message to them, especially to the Baltic states, that they might be the objects of retaliation if they joined NATO or the Western European Union (WEU) or supported any Western intervention in Russia or the 'near abroad', for example, by giving rights of passage or providing bases.[28]

On 29 September 1995 the Moscow-based newspaper *Komsomolskaya Pravda* published an article on a new defence doctrine, which it claimed had been drawn up by the Russian General Staff, and according to which Russia will immediately invade the Baltic states should they join NATO.[29] Despite

[25] Interview with Lt-Col Michael H. Clemmesen, Professor, Danish Armed Forces Academy, Copenhagen, 7 Apr. 1993.

[26] *Izvestiya* published excerpts from the military doctrine in 'Osnovnye polozheniya voennoy doktriny Rossiyskoy Federatsii' [The basic provisions of the military doctrine of the Russian Federation] on 18 Nov. 1993 and *Krasnaya Zvezda* published a slightly longer excerpt on 19 Nov. 1993. A translation into English appeared in *Jane's Intelligence Review,* Special Report, Jan. 1994. For a further discussion of the military doctrine, see chapters 8 and 9 in this volume.

[27] *Jane's Intelligence Review* (note 26), p. 6.

[28] *Jane's Intelligence Review* (note 26), p. 2; and *SIPRI Yearbook 1994* (note 6), p. 648.

[29] *Komsomolskaya Pravda,* 29 Sep. 1995.

official denials that such a draft existed, the Baltic states summoned the Russian ambassadors to explain their country's new aggressive stance.[30]

These concerns have in turn stimulated discussions of different variants of a common defence—Nordic, Baltic or Nordic/Baltic—and on joining NATO.

Nuclear weapon security and maintenance

The problem of nuclear weapon safety and maintenance is the dominant aspect for the Baltic and Nordic countries. Several thousand nuclear warheads and rockets intended for use at sea, in the air and on land are reportedly located in the Murmansk and Arkhangelsk regions. Accidents have occurred on several occasions during the handling of missiles on board submarines, but it is not known whether this has involved any danger of atomic explosion. Accidents or near-accidents of this type tend to lead to leakage of poisonous missile fuel. Such leakage is said to have come from a submarine in Severomorsk in February 1991; and in September the same year there was an accident with a test missile during shooting exercises on board a Typhoon submarine in the White Sea. Submarine reactor incidents are also very dangerous. In 1989 the nuclear submarine *Komsomolets* went down in the Arctic Ocean near Bear Island (which belongs to Norway) with the loss of 42 crew members. A few weeks later a serious reactor incident occurred off the Norwegian coast involving an Echo II submarine.[31]

The Baltic and Nordic countries are especially concerned by the lack of centralized control over nuclear weapons and materials. They are afraid of leaks of nuclear materials and technologies and of the outbreak of nuclear terrorism.[32] Thirty-two per cent of Finnish respondents surveyed in 1991 believed that this menace is very serious, 44 per cent that it is fairly serious, 17 per cent that it is fairly harmless and 2 per cent that it is totally harmless.[33]

Security options

It seems that the dominant concern behind all initiatives in the military field has been the development of the new security complex on the basis of the present low level of the military balance and the prevention of new threats.

Withdrawal of the residual Russian forces was only an initial step in shaping the new security system in the region. The Baltic and Nordic countries are particularly anxious about their security. There are three strands to their concern. First, they hope that the West will protect them. Second, it has been proposed, for instance by former Lithuanian President Vitautas Landsbergis and former

---

[30] *Baltic Independent,* 6–12 Oct. 1995, p. 2.

[31] *International Challenges,* vol. 12, no. 4 (1992), pp. 33–35; and *International Herald Tribune,* 22–23 May 1993.

[32] Clemmesen (note 25); and answers of Mrs Mette Vestergaard, Secretariat, Nordic Council, to author's questionnaire, 25 Mar. 1993.

[33] *Yearbook of Finnish Foreign Policy* (Finnish Institute of International Affairs: Helsinki, 1992), p. 29.

Ukrainian President Leonid Kravchuk, that a Black Sea–Baltic confederation should include military cooperation.[34] Third, the idea of a Nordic defence pact is being discussed in the Nordic countries.[35]

Joining NATO or quasi-NATO institutions cannot be the solution because it would not eliminate the basic source of insecurity—the mutual distrust of the Baltic states and Russia.

It would also be impossible to provide regional security within any form of Black Sea–Baltic union. Potential members of that union (or confederation) simply do not have the military and economic resources to deter potential threats. Moreover, they do not agree in the most important question, which is who poses the main threat to their security? Fear of Russian retaliation in response to a possible future defence pact has discouraged some of these countries from participation in such a confederation as well. The Landsbergis–Kravchuk idea has therefore not been realized. However, this has not prevented bilateral military cooperation between Ukraine and the Baltic states. In July 1994, the Latvian and Ukrainian Defence Ministers signed an agreement to increase their defence cooperation. The terms of the agreement provide for participation in joint exercises, exchange of information and personnel, consultations on security policy and discussions on the Partnership for Peace (PFP) programme.[36]

It is doubtful whether the idea of a Nordic Defence Community is either relevant or realistic. There is no real military threat to the Nordic countries that could call a defence pact into being. The most serious challenges to Nordic security (environmental issues, migration, organized crime, and so on) do not require a response by military means. The rise of a new subregional defence pact could complicate the current strategic situation in the European security complex, adding to existing uncertainties such as the NATO identity crisis and the relationship between NATO and the WEU, and worsen relations with Russia. Consensus on the functions, powers and responsibility of a defence pact is unlikely to be reached between the Nordic countries and their political parties, and NATO, the WEU and the great powers are likely to resist its emergence. It may be more expedient for them to strengthen bilateral and multilateral defence cooperation and to concentrate efforts on peacekeeping operations than to create a formal defence pact.

[34] van Ham (note 15), p. 11.

[35] Initially, the idea of a Nordic defence community was discussed by Denmark, Norway and Sweden in 1948–49. However, they failed to reach consensus about the purposes, nature and scope of the pact. Øberg (note 14), pp. 3–4; and Sweden, Commision on Neutrality Policy, *Had There Been a War . . . Preparations for the Reception of Military Assistance, 1949–1969: Report of the Commission on Neutrality Policy* (Statsrådsberedningen: Stockholm, 1994), SOU 1994:11, pp. 61–77. Since the end of the Warsaw Treaty Organization and the decline of NATO there has been a revival of the common Nordic defence idea. Hettne, B. *et al.*, *Norden, Europe and the Near Future: Report From the Directors of Nordic Peace Research Institutes*, PRIO Report no. 3 (International Peace Research Institute: Oslo, 1991), p. 43. Public opinion is favourable to the strengthening of Nordic defence cooperation. A poll in Feb. 1993 showed that 51% of respondents in Norway and 54% in Denmark preferred the idea of a common Nordic security and foreign policy while an overwhelming majority in both countries were against the idea of a unified parliament and currency. *Nordic Council of Ministers Newsletter*, Mar. 1993, p. 4.

[36] *Military and Arms Transfers News*, 29 July 1994, p. 11.

A partial solution to the case of the Baltic states could probably be found if all interested sides—NATO, the Nordic Council,[37] the Council of Baltic Sea States[38] and Russia, not just one country or alliance—made joint efforts to strengthen their security.[39] On Russia's side, a valuable next step in the formation of a more stable security system in the region would be an effort diplomatically and psychologically to calm the fears of at least those Baltic states which worry about a Russian military doctrine which foresees the use of military force to protect ethnic Russians in the 'near abroad'.

In September 1994, Russia offered the Baltic states bilateral security agreements like those signed that month with Denmark, Finland and Norway. According to the Russian Defence Minister at that time, Pavel Grachev, another possibility was one multilateral security agreement signed by the three Baltic states and Russia.[40] However, the prime ministers of the Baltic states, meeting in Riga on 13 September, had earlier rejected such a proposal as premature and said that old problems should be resolved first.[41]

Security and arms control

These measures could be complemented by intensification of the arms control process if governments combined to push the arms control issues through the negotiation agenda of the Organization for Security and Co-operation in Europe (OSCE) and through the meetings of Nordic foreign ministers, the Baltic Council[42] and the Barents Council.[43] The first problem is naval arms which are mostly excluded from the negotiation process. Unilateral measures were taken for the reduction of naval armaments and naval activities, especially under the Gorbachev Administration, but they related to obsolete weapons and were compensated for by the development of up-to-date systems such as sea-launched cruise missiles (SLCMs).[44] It will be important to relate arms control initiatives mainly to conventional weapons and forces in order to avoid raising strategic

---

[37] Denmark (including the Faeroes and Greenland), Finland (including Åland), Iceland, Norway and Sweden.

[38] Founded in Copenhagen in Mar. 1992. The membership is currently Denmark, Estonia, the EU, Finland, Germany, Iceland, Latvia, Lithuania, Norway, Poland, Russia and Sweden.

[39] Clemmesen (note 25) suggests that NATO and Russia should provide the Baltic states with security garantees.

[40] *Baltic Independent*, 16–22 Sep. 1994, p. 2.

[41] *Baltic Independent*, 23–29 Sep. 1994, p. 2.

[42] Established at a meeting of the heads of government of the three Baltic states in Talinn on 13 June 1994. The members are Estonia, Latvia and Lithuania. van Ham (note 16), p. 33.

[43] Part of the Barents Euro-Arctic Council, established by the Kirkenes Declaration in Jan. 1993, of which the other members are Denmark, the EU, Finland, Iceland, Norway, Russia and Sweden. The other component of the Barents Euro-Arctic Council is the inter-regional Barents Regional Council—a mechanism for cooperation between regional authorities in Finland, Norway, Russia (including the Autonomous Republic of Karelia) and Sweden. The Reional Council was initiated by a protocol signed at Tromsø in Apr. 1992. Krohn, A. (ed.), *The Baltic Sea Region* (Nomos: Baden-Baden, 1996), p. ?? For their respective memberships, see *SIPRI Yearbook 1996: Armaments, Disarmament and International Security* (Oxford University Press: Oxford, 1996), pp. xxxiv–xxxv.

[44] Heininen and Käkönen (note 7), pp. 7–8; and *Nordiske lands utenriks-og sikkerhets-politikk i et nytt Europa* (Norwegian Ministry of Foreign Affairs: Oslo, Apr. 1992), p. 16.

issues which could complicate the achievement of an agreement. Regional initiatives so far have ranged from the numbers and location of troops on the Kola Peninsula and in the Baltic Sea area, to the deployment of forces withdrawn from Eastern Europe and the former Soviet republics, to submarine activities on the Baltic Sea (this is especially important for Sweden) and the prevention of military incidents.

The famous regional initiative in the past for a Nordic Nuclear Weapon-Free Zone (NNWFZ)[45] is unlikely to be successful now. The idea was valuable in the cold war period as a confidence-building measure (CBM), but now confidence and security in the region can be achieved by other means. Perhaps the only aspect of the Zone idea that is still feasible is the withdrawal of Russian tactical nuclear weapons from the Baltic and Arctic seas. This weaponry is not so important for Russia, so its withdrawal could be realized as a unilateral measure to demonstrate goodwill and to secure peace in the region.

Negotiations on CBMs at sea could be a useful addition to these initiatives. Coordination of naval exercise schedules or essential naval activities by NATO, Russia and the non-NATO Nordic countries, exchanges and visits between military academies or discussions of naval doctrines and force postures among all sea powers of the region could contribute to mutual understanding. Russia could amend these initiatives by analogous steps regarding land forces, in the way, for instance, it has already given the forces of the Leningrad MD a more defensive configuration. An important point for the future negotiating agenda is the issue of accident assistance. At a minimum, assurances ought to be exchanged that help will be provided and accepted when needed. This could be codified in special agreements between Arctic countries or it could be done as an expansion of or in a protocol to the US–Russian Incidents at Sea and Prevention of Dangerous Military Activities agreements.[46] It might prevent or reduce the risks of accidents like the *Komsomolets* disaster.

The first signs of Russian–Nordic cooperation in the military field have appeared already. There were joint NATO–Russian Northern Fleet naval exercises in 1993. In June 1994, the USA led a flotilla of 42 warships from 15 countries in multinational exercise manoeuvres on the Baltic.[47] Three months later Lithuania, Poland, Russia and Sweden and the naval forces of NATO countries took part in Cooperative Venture '94, a naval exercise in the North Sea and Norwegian Sea.[48] Danish Defence Minister Hans Haekkerup visited his Russian counterpart Pavel Grachev (for the first time in the history of Danish–Russian relations) in March 1993 and concluded an agreement for exchange

---

[45] Heininen and Käkönen (note 7), pp. 25–37; Heisler (note 7), pp. 44, 164–65, 167, 169; Lodgaard, S., *Nordic Initiatives for a Nuclear Weapon-Free Zone in Europe* (SIPRI: Stockholm, 1982); and *Nordic Nuclear-Weapon-Free Zone: Report of A Working Group appointed by the Minister of Foreign Affairs* (Ministry of Foreign Affairs: Helsinki, 1987).

[46] The texts are reproduced in Fieldhouse, R. (ed.), SIPRI, *Security at Sea: Naval Forces and Arms Control* (Oxford University Press: Oxford, 1990), pp. 147–57, 278–85.

[47] *Military and Arms Transfers News,* 17 June 1994, p. 11.

[48] *Baltic Independent,* 23–29 Sep. 1994, p. 2.

visits involving naval fleets and military cadets.[49] On 11 September 1994, Defence Minister Grachev signed agreements on military cooperation with Denmark, Finland and Norway during a visit to Copenhagen.[50]

However, a number of factors make negotiations and the implementation of arms control and confidence-building initiatives impossible. First, the Baltic states do not trust Russian promises and guarantees and prefer to rely upon the protection of NATO and the Nordic countries. Second, because Russia has no consistent foreign and military policy towards the region, threats follow goodwill initiatives and vice versa. Third, in the past three years Moscow's attention has turned from arms control issues to national conflicts on the southern and south-western borders of the former Soviet Union at a time when the West has been preoccupied by peacekeeping in the former Yugoslavia and other problems.

IV. National minorities

Russian-speaking minorities are a serious problem for two of the Baltic states. The same countries which have accused Russia of violating the rights of national minorities have now themselves set up several restrictions on non-citizens.

There are several arguments in support of those restrictions that are common to all the Baltic states. First, according to Baltic constitutional and legal thinking, all Soviet legislation on citizenship and human rights since 1940, that is, from the beginning of 'Soviet occupation', is illegal. The restoration of Baltic citizenship legislation therefore meant a choice between the '1940 option' (citizenship would be granted automatically to those who were Baltic citizens before the occupation and their descendants) and the 'zero option' (citizenship would be granted automatically to all inhabitants of the three former Soviet republics). Estonia and Latvia chose the 1940 option, Lithuania the zero option. Second, the Baltic states point to the Russian imperial legacy and authoritarian nationalism. Baltic politicians emphasize that there are many chauvinistic leaders even in democratic Russia. If they came to power the Russian communities in the Baltic states could become both a pretext for intervention and a 'fifth column'. Third, the Baltic states worry about their national cultures and identities, which were very much under attack during the Soviet era. According to Baltic perceptions, the Russians have very limited knowledge of Baltic languages, history and culture and are a threat to the national cultures.[51] This in turn serves as an excuse for discrimination on the basis of language.

The nature of the restrictions varies from country to country. Under Estonian legislation persons who took up residence there after it was incorporated in the Soviet Union in 1940 and their descendants (474 000, or 30 per cent of the

[49] *DanNews* (Copenhagen), 16–23 Mar. 1993, p. 2.
[50] *Baltic Independent,* 16–22 Sep. 1994, p. 2.
[51] Joenniemi and Vares (note 14), pp. 140–42.

population)[52] were not permitted to participate in the constitutional referendum or the elections and do not have the right to an Estonian passport because they are not citizens. A law of February 1992 covering naturalization requirements provided for a requirement of two years' residence followed by a one-year waiting period and knowledge of the Estonian language.[53] According to the Estonian Department for Citizenship and Migration, by the beginning of 1995 nearly 50 000 people had been naturalized. According to the Russian embassy in Tallinn, approximately 60 000 people have taken Russian citizenship.[54]

On 19 January 1995 Estonia passed a second, stricter citizenship law which stipulates five years' residence plus a one-year waiting period to process applications and a test on the basics of the constitution and the citizenship law, in addition to the language test. According to Estonian experts, the law, which took effect on 1 April 1995, has no retroactive force. This means that the changes would not affect the country's present non-citizen population.[55] The authorities established a deadline of 12 July 1995 for applications for work and residence permits. About 80 per cent of non-citizens have applied for permits. In June 1995 the parliament again extended the deadline for applications by another year.[56]

Although discrimination on the basis of race, sex or other grounds is prohibited by the Estonian Constitution, relationships between Estonians and the large ethnic Russian population remain tense. Non-Estonians, especially Russians, have continued to allege discrimination in jobs, salaries and housing based on language requirements.

On 21 February 1995 Estonia adopted a new language law. It left unchanged the system of language testing and categorization by which non-Estonians qualify for citizenship and work permits and added a declaration that Estonian is the only official language. It provided for the regulation of public signs and announcements, specifying fines for the use of foreign or irregular (ungrammatical) language, and prohibits the use of foreign languages without an Estonian translation on television and radio broadcasts unless a programme is clearly targeted at a foreign-speaking audience (as the Russian-language news programmes are).[57] The new legislation met with an angry reaction from noncitizens and from Moscow.

In Latvia ethnic Latvians now make up only 52 per cent of the population, and none of the country's seven largest cities has an ethnic Latvian majority.[58]

---

[52] *Vestnik Moskovskogo Universiteta*, no. 5 (1992), p. 67.
[53] US Department of State, *Country Reports on Human Rights Practices for 1992:* Report submitted to the Committee on Foreign Relations of the US Senate and the Committee on Foreign Affairs, US House of Representatives by the Department of State (US Government Printing Office: Washington, DC, Feb. 1993), p. 765.
[54] *Baltic Independent*, 27 Jan.–2 Feb. 1995, p. 1.
[55] *Baltic Independent*, 27 Jan.–2 Feb. 1995, p. 1.
[56] *Baltic Independent*, 23–29 June 1995, p. 1; 21–27 July 1995, p. 3; and 4–10 Aug. 1995, p. 3.
[57] *Baltic Independent*, 3–9 Mar. 1995, p. 4.
[58] *Mirovaya Ekonomika i Mezhdunarodnye Otnosheniya (MEMO)*, no. 12 (1993), p. 134; and *The Baltic States: A Reference Book* (Estonian Encyclopaedia Publishers/Latvian Encyclopaedia Publishers/Lithuanian Encyclopaedia Publishers: Tallinn, Riga, Vilnius, 1991), p. 92.

The possibility that non-Latvians who entered the country during the Soviet period could control the balance of political power made citizenship and naturalization issues particularly contentious here as well. Under the citizenship act passed by parliament in October 1991, only those who were citizens before 17 June 1940 and their direct descendants could claim citizenship. The citizenship status of other residents of Latvia, including those who arrived or were born there during the Soviet period, was unresolved.

In 1994 a revision of this citizenship act became a hostage of political debate on withdrawal of the Russian troops: the parliament passed a law that Latvia would not naturalize new citizens until the Russian Army had left. On 21 June 1994 the parliament passed a tough citizenship law including a controversial quota system[59] which gave rise to concern both in Moscow and at the Council of Europe and was amended after the Council of Europe gave some hints that it could prevent Latvia's joining the Council. Most applicants will thus now be naturalized by the year 2003.[60] Latvia became a member of the Council of Europe in February 1995. Finally, on 12 April 1995 the parliament passed a long-awaited law applying to citizens of the former USSR who were permanent residents of Latvia before 1 July 1992. It outlined non-citizens' freedom to choose their place of residence, leave and re-enter Latvia and preserve their language and culture in Latvia, established that non-citizens cannot be expelled except under special circumstances and safeguarded their personal security. Non-citizens over the age of 16 will now be eligible for a non-citizen's passport which permits travel to and from the country.[61] The implementation of the law has led to new controversies. Human rights organizations and some members of the Latvian Parliament have criticized the Citizenship and Immigration Department for repeated abuses of power, including unlawful confiscation of passports, the issuing of subsequent deportation orders, and demands for documents not actually required by law from persons applying for citizenship.[62]

Even some Baltic observers admit that Estonian and Latvian legislation on citizenship, official language and civil rights based on the majority rule principle is not fully in conformity with democratic standards. They make at least three reservations: (a) there is a considerable difference between formal law and justice; (b) majority rule is not the only principle of democratic legislation; and (c) the citizenship laws are in a sense retroactive legislation.[63]

Unlike the other Baltic states, Lithuania passed a citizenship law[64] which is fully in line with European standards except for a residence requirement of 10 years. As a result over 90 per cent of the ethnic Poles, Russians, Bela-

---

[59] Non-citizens born in Latvia (the number was estimated at 230 000) could gain naturalization from 1 Jan. 1995 until the year 2000. After the turn of the century there would be 500 000 remaining non-citizens who under the quotas were estimated to gain naturalization at a rate of 2000 per year. *Baltic Independent*, 24–30 June 1994, p. 1.

[60] *Baltic Independent*, 29 July–4 Aug. 1994, p. 4.

[61] *Baltic Independent*, 21–27 Apr. 1995, p. 4.

[62] *Baltic Independent*, 28 Apr.–4 May 1995, p. 2.

[63] Joenniemi and Vares (note 14), p. 134.

[64] US Department of State (note 53), p. 835.

russians, Ukrainians and Jews who make up 20 per cent of the Lithuanian population were granted citizenship. The reason for this tolerance is fairly simple: non-Lithuanians do not threaten control over power in the country where native inhabitants essentially outnumber others.

The Yeltsin Government was heavily criticized by Russians in the Baltic states and by nationalists in Russia itself for neglecting the human rights situation in the Baltic states in 1991–92. As a result Yeltsin changed his policy. On 1 October 1991 the Russian State Council declared that the Russian leadership was responsible for all Russians living in the former Soviet republics. In February 1992 the then Foreign Minister, Andrey Kozyrev, made it clear in a speech at a UN conference on human rights that Russia regarded this issue as a very high priority in its foreign policy.[65] In 1992–94 Russian officials, contrary to declared government policy, referred several times to the issue of national minorities as a reason to delay withdrawal of the remaining forces. Following the demands of Russia and international human rights organizations, the Council of Baltic Sea States[66] in its meeting in Helsinki in March 1993 decided to appoint a High Commissioner for Human Rights and Minorities who would monitor the situation not only in Estonia and Latvia but in all 10 member countries.[67]

The problem of national minorities has damaged Russian–Baltic relations, delayed Russian troop withdrawal and destabilized the whole regional system of international relations.

What steps could Russia take to improve the human rights situation in the Baltic states? It has limited resources to influence them. The use of force is ruled out. Russia has only diplomatic and economic instruments at its disposal as a last resort to prevent discrimination against Russians there. The resolution (or non-resolution) of this complex problem depends mainly on the Baltic states themselves, their wisdom, moderation and goodwill. However, Russia can assist to some extent in solving the problem, by continuing its efforts together with the Nordic and other European countries, on a bilateral basis and through the international institutions, to stimulate Estonia and Latvia to complete the process of naturalization of non-citizens, to soften the authorities' attitude to dual citizenship, to guarantee the right of national minorities to cultural autonomy and to observe human rights standards.[68] That could create favourable conditions for the achievement of social consensus and the integration of national minorities into society.

---

[65] Kukk, Jervel and Joenniemi (note 14), pp. 99–100.
[66] See note 38.
[67] *Baltic Independent,* 19–25 Mar. 1993.
[68] Anker Jørgensen, a member of the Danish Parliament and a former Prime Minister, pointed out in an interview on 14 Apr. 1993 that the Nordic countries are deeply concerned about the human rights situation in the Baltic states and pressing them strongly, although in an informal and gentle way, at official level, to change their policies.

V. Territorial issues

There are various causes of territorial conflicts in the region—historical, economic, ethnic, political and technical. Some are old, others relatively new.

Russia and Norway

Discords between Russia and Norway belong to the economic type of conflicts and arise from the past. At present there are two major jurisdictional disputes in the northern waters. First, the two countries disagree over where the boundary should lie between their continental shelves and 200-mile economic zones in the Barents Sea.[69] A very large area (155 000 km² or more than the Norwegian part of the North Sea) is disputed. The area could hold considerable petroleum resources and is rich in fish and marine life, and is thus of great economic significance. The middle part of the Barents Sea is also of great strategic importance given the posture of the Russian Navy and air defence. In 1978 both sides accepted as a temporary measure the Grey Zone agreement, largely in order to protect cod and other fish stocks,[70] but the dispute remains because Norway is dissatisfied with the agreement, claiming, with some justification, that it favours Russia.

Second, there is a difference of opinion between Norway on the one hand and Russia and some other states on the other as to whether the 1920 Paris Treaty on Spitzbergen, particularly its provisions giving all the parties to the Treaty equal rights to exploit Svalbard's economic resources, applies to the waters and seabed around Svalbard.[71] The Svalbard situation is complicated by the fact that there are two Russian mining communities there and only one Norwegian. The Russian population outnumbers the Norwegian by two to one.[72]

These disputes were relatively unimportant during the cold war when all the Arctic states were preoccupied by strategic–military issues. In the near future, however, if there is no solution to the disputes, it will probably not be possible to maintain their low-key nature indefinitely because pressure will almost certainly build up in time to exploit the seabed resources of the areas in dispute.

In October 1992 Norwegian Foreign Minister Thorvald Stoltenberg declared that as long as the dispute on the continental shelf was unresolved cooperation would be focused on land areas. Moscow is conscious of the obstacle that the dispute with Norway constitutes. In 1992–93 both Yeltsin and Kozyrev

---

[69] Mottola, K. (ed.), *The Arctic Challenge: Nordic and Canadian Approaches to Security and Cooperation in an Emerging International Region* (Westview Press: Boulder, Colo., 1988), pp. 108–109; and Sollie, F., *The Soviet Challenge in Northern Waters: Implications for Resources and Security* (Norwegian Atlantic Committee: Oslo, 1988), pp. 27–30.

[70] Heisler (note 7), pp. 168–69; and Archer, C. (ed.), *The Soviet Union and Northern Waters* (Routledge: London/New York, 1988), pp. 47–48.

[71] Mottola (note 69), pp. 109–11.

[72] Flynn, G. (ed.), *NATO's Northern Allies: The National Security Policies of Belgium, Denmark, the Netherlands and Norway* (Rowman & Allanheld: Totowa, 1985), pp. 195–96.

promised that it would be given priority with the aim of finding a solution.[73] However, the domestic political crisis has prevented Russia from finishing negotiations with Norway.

Karelia

The Karelia issue is also old. It has both a historical and an ethnic background. The Karelians are a nation related to the Finns and only a small minority of 10 per cent of the population in their eponymous republic. Karelia developed as a part of Finland from the 14th century, Finland itself being first a part of Sweden and then of Russia. Shortly after it achieved independence, in 1918–20 Finland occupied a part of Karelia belonging to Soviet Russia, was defeated and was forced to sign the Tartu Peace Treaty (of 14 October 1920) which legitimized the division of Karelia.[74] The repressive national and agricultural policy of the Soviet authorities in Soviet Karelia led to a rebellion in 1921–22, supported by Finland and cruelly suppressed by the Red Army, as a result of which many Karelians migrated to Finland. Under the Moscow peace treaty of 12 March 1940 which followed the Soviet–Finnish war of 1939–40, the rest of Karelia (including Vyborg) and the western and northern coasts of Lake Ladoga were transferred to the Soviet Union. The subsequent Soviet–Finnish agreements (the 1944 Moscow armistice and the 1947 Paris peace treaty) confirmed the status of Karelia as an autonomous republic of the Russian Soviet Federative Socialist Republic (RSFSR).[75]

There has been much discussion on the Karelia question in Finland during the past few years. The collapse of the Soviet Union, the restoration of the independence of the Baltic countries, and the negotiations between Japan and Russia concerning the return of the Kurile Islands to Japan served as an additional spur to the discussion. Finland has taken a rather negative attitude towards the idea of initiating official negotiations on the return of Karelia. In December 1991, the Finnish Government officially renounced all claims to Karelia[76] although some groups in Finland and the Karelian Association in the Karelian Autonomous Republic have continued to press both Helsinki and Moscow for Karelia to be returned to Finland.

It should be emphasized that it is impossible for Russia even to recognize officially the existence of the question. Any negotiations on territorial problems with other countries could undermine Yeltsin's domestic political position; and the Russian leadership is cautious about generating a 'chain reaction' in the region. If Russia recognizes the existence of the Karelia issue it could seem to lend legitimacy to other claims. During his official visit to Finland in July 1992

[73] Dellenbrant and Olsson (note 23), p. 173.

[74] Sukianen, I., *Karelskiy Vopros v Sovyetsko-finlyandskikh Otnosheniyakh v 1918–1920 godakh* [The Karelia issue in Soviet–Finnish relations, 1918–1920] (Petrozavodsk, 1948).

[75] Szajkowski, B. (ed.), *Encyclopaedia of Conflicts, Disputes and Flashpoints in Eastern Europe, Russia and the Successor States* (Longman: Harlow, 1993), p. 41.

[76] Szajkowski (note 75), p. 170.

Yeltsin made it clear that there was no such issue. Finland stated that at that point the question would not be raised but at the same time reminded President Yeltsin that the principles of the Conference on Security and Co-operation in Europe (CSCE)[77] made it possible to change borders by peaceful means. The Russian Ambassador, Yuriy Deryabin, stated that in reality the future position of Karelia called for discussion, but instead of changes to the border the aim should be to lower the level of border controls.[78] Russia prefers to develop direct ties between Finland and Karelia rather than to recognize the problem officially.[79]

Kaliningrad

The origins of the Kaliningrad issue lie in decisions taken after World War II. By decision of the Potsdam Peace Conference (1945) a part of former East Prussia, including its capital, Königsberg, was given to Russia. In 1946 the Kaliningrad Region was formed as a part of the RSFSR. Ethnic Germans were moved away from this territory and the region was populated mainly by Russians, who today make up 80 per cent of the population. The overall population of the region is now 900 000 civilians plus an unspecified number of military personnel and demobilized soldiers (estimates range from 60 000 to 400 000).[80] Ten per cent of the population are Belarussians. According to some accounts, in 1994 approximately 17 000–18 000 Germans were resident in the region, although their passports often state that they are Russian or Ukrainian (the official figure was 6000).[81]

A completely new situation has arisen following the collapse of the Soviet Union and the Baltic states' achievement of independence, which separated the Kaliningrad Region from Russian territory. Some German politicians (and even some Russian leaders before German reunification) have considered the exclave as a possible place for the creation of a German autonomous area in Russia in order to prevent further German emigration from Russia.[82] This is resisted by the present inhabitants of the region, although they favour German assistance to the region and the development of a free economic zone. Some extremist groups in Germany claim the return of Königsberg to the *Vaterland*.[83] Although officially Germany does not support these proposals they make Moscow nervous because the issue is very sensitive for Russians. A number of German organizations in Russia have proposed solutions to the Kaliningrad issue. Freiheit (Freedom), an association which emerged in the spring of 1993

---

[77] On 1 Jan. 1995 the CSCE became the OSCE.

[78] *Yearbook of Finnish Foreign Policy* (note 33), pp. 30–31.

[79] Nordic Council (note 3), p. 43.

[80] Szajkowski (note 75), p. 163; *SIPRI Yearbook 1994* (note 6), p. 177; and *Jane's Intelligence Review*, Dec. 1994, pp. 572–73.

[81] *Jane's Intelligence Review*, Dec. 1994, p. 573.

[82] Blanc-Noel, N., *Changement de cap en Mer Baltique* [A change of direction on the Baltic] (Fondation pour les études de défense nationale: Paris, 1992), pp. 62–63; and Szajkowski (note 75), p. 165.

[83] Calabuig, E., 'Quand les Allemands retournent à Kaliningrad–Königsberg' [When the Germans return to Kaliningrad–Königsberg], *Le Monde Diplomatique*, Aug. 1991.

as a radical voice for the interests of Russian Germans, decided to press for the formation (between 1995 and 1997) of a sovereign Baltic German republic under Russian jurisdiction in the Kaliningrad Region. At the same time the association stated that 'it should not be ruled out that this territory will eventually again be incorporated into Germany'.[84] The Society of Old Prussia, set up in 1990 and comprising activists of several nationalities including ethnic Germans, aims to restore the pre-Soviet traditions and in the long run achieve independence for the region.[85]

Interestingly, in contrast with Moscow, the Kaliningrad authorities are not afraid of a possible influx of Russian Germans from the territory of the former Soviet Union. According to some experts, there is sufficient room for 100 000 Germans in the Kaliningrad Region.[86] However, Germany has refrained from highlighting Kaliningrad in its official assistance to ethnic Germans in Russia. This programme is restricted to selected regions, and Kaliningrad is not one of them.

Russia's policy is to stimulate economic and cultural contacts and tourism between Kaliningrad and Germany as well as with other countries of the Baltic Sea region and at the same time to prevent a mass migration of Germans to the strategically important region. In November 1991, President Yeltsin issued a decree granting the city of Kaliningrad the status of a free economic zone. Under the Russian scenario, the area could become a West–East trade bridge, Russia's Hong Kong. Several hundred joint ventures have been registered (45 per cent of them with German companies), mostly small service operations.[87] However, there is a difference of opinion between Moscow and the Kaliningrad local authorities about the status of the region and the prospects for its economic cooperation with foreign countries. The regional government has proposed to make the whole region a free economic zone. Russian officials, however, have complained that foreign investors there get significant tax and other concessions while investing insignificant amounts of money. As of 1 September 1994, a total of 885 enterprises with foreign investments were registered in the Kaliningrad Region, 239 of them fully foreign-owned. Foreign investors accounted for less than $2 million.[88] The region was allegedly being turned into a channel for the export of raw materials, including strategic resources, and for the creeping expansion of foreign influence in the economic and ethnic spheres, with the prospect of the creation of a 'fourth independent Baltic state'.[89] The Russian Deputy Prime Minister, Sergey Shakhray, proposed, instead of making the whole of the region a free economic zone, to create limited zones of free trade activity near ports and main roads in the

---

[84] Szajkowski (note 75), p. 118.
[85] Szajkowski (note 75), p. 393.
[86] *Jane's Intelligence Review*, Dec. 1994, p. 573.
[87] Szajkowski (note 75), p. 164.
[88] *Baltic Independent*, 4–10 Nov. 1994, p. 5.
[89] *Baltic Independent*, 4–10 Nov. 1994, p. 5.

region, stressing that 'we have again to declare clearly the priority of Russia's military–strategic interests in the Kaliningrad *oblast'*.[90]

The concentration of the Russian military in Kaliningrad (although substantially reduced in recent years) is another matter of concern for neighbouring Poland and Lithuania. According to *The Military Balance,* in 1995 Kaliningrad hosted 24 000 ground forces equipped with 870 tanks, 980 armoured combat vehicles, 410 artillery pieces, 16 SS-21 missiles, and 52 attack helicopters. Air defence had 28 Su-27s and 75 surface-to-air missiles.[91] Baltiysk (50 km from Kaliningrad) is the main naval base for the Baltic Sea. Admiral Yegorov told the *Jane's Intelligence Review* correspondent that, despite the speculation of foreign specialists, there were only about 60 000 military stationed in the Kaliningrad Region.[92]

Lithuania, which is especially concerned with the Russian military potential in Kaliningrad, has demonstrated its understanding of the strategic importance of the exclave for Russia. It was thus possible for military transit agreements to be agreed between the two countries in 1993 and 1995.[93] At the same time the Baltic states and Poland have repeatedly proposed the demilitarization of the region. For example, in November 1994 the Baltic Assembly, the parliamentary body of the three Baltic countries, adopted a resolution called for an international round-table conference on the demilitarization of Kaliningrad.[94] Russia interprets such appeals as open interference in its internal affairs, stressing that 'the Russian side will never and with no one discuss in this context the "future" of the Kaliningrad Region and its status'.[95]

To summarize, the Russian leadership still considers Kaliningrad as an important military–strategic outpost of Russia in the Baltic region and will keep the Russian military presence at a significant level.

The Baltic states

Other disputes have been generated or reactivated by the Baltic states' achieving independence. Estonia and Latvia consider their existing borders unjust and have claims on neighbouring territories.

Some of these claims are political in nature and are being used as bargaining-counters. For example, Estonia points out that under the Tartu Peace Treaty of 2 February 1920 approximately 2000 km² east of the Narva River and the Pechory (Petseri) district, part of the Pskov Region, should belong to Estonia. Estonia included reference to the Tartu Treaty in its 1992 constitution.

The Estonian authorities issued thousands of passports for the ethnic Estonians resident in the Pechory district. Russia suspected it of intending to

---

[90] *Baltic Independent,* 4–10 Nov. 1994, p. 1.
[91] *The Military Balance 1995–1996* (note 22), p. 118.
[92] *Jane's Intelligence Review,* Dec. 1994, p. 572.
[93] See note 15.
[94] *Baltic Independent,* 18–24 Nov. 1994, p. 1.
[95] *Baltic Independent,* 18–24 Nov. 1994, p. 1.

create a 'critical mass' of Estonians in the district to lay the legal foundations for calling a referendum and subsequently annexing the territory. The Estonian border regulations are considered in Moscow to be unjust to Russians; maps have been issued which indicate some Russian territories as being under Estonian jurisdiction and Russia has threatened Estonia with retaliation. Russia has refused to discuss territorial issues with Estonia, officially declaring the principle of the status quo.

In the summer of 1994, following a presidential decree, Russia began unilateral demarcation of the border in the Pechory area. 'This border was, is and will be Russian, and not a single inch of the land will be given to anyone', President Yeltsin declared at the newly constructed border checkpoint on 23 November 1994. He said the border had to be made a 'reliable shield' against 'smugglers from the Baltic's and foreign intelligence services'.[96]

Estonia tried to raise the issue in the OSCE but failed to attract any serious attention to the problem.[97] As a result of Russia taking unilateral measures and of lack of international support, the majority of the Estonian political parties have begun to be inclined to compromise with Russia over the border issue. At the end of 1994, Prime Minister Andres Tarand said that Estonia was prepared to make concessions on the border if Russia agreed at least to recognize the Tartu Treaty as the basis for relations between the two countries.[98] According to Russian Foreign Ministry officials, Russia was prepared to recognize the historical importance of the treaty, but that is all.[99]

Latvia also has some territorial disputes with Russia. In January 1992 the Latvian Supreme Council adopted a resolution 'On the Non-Recognition of the Annexation of the Town of Abrene and Six Districts of Abrene by Russia in 1944' and confirmed its adherence to the borders established under the 1920 treaty with Russia.[100] However, Latvia has not made the claim officially and has not insisted on putting the issue on the Russian–Latvian negotiation agenda. Instead, in December 1994, Latvia and Russia signed four agreements to simplify border regulations.[101]

In Russia's relations with the Baltic states there are also conflicts of a technical nature connected with disputable border demarcations. For instance, in January 1992 the Lithuanian Cabinet of Ministers indicated that Lithuania had to mark its sea border with the neighbouring Kaliningrad Region. In addition, a bilateral commission was formed to set and mark the border with Belarus. Further negotiations with the Kaliningrad Region were based on the 1928 German–Lithuanian agreement delimiting the border along the Nemuras and Sesupe rivers, which corresponds to the present situation: there is disagreement only over a few localities. The land border was negotiated by mid-1992,

---

[96] *Baltic Independent,* 25 Nov.–1 Dec. 1994, p. 1.
[97] *Baltic Independent,* 19–25 Aug. 1994, p. 2.
[98] *Baltic Independent,* 9–15 Dec. 1994, p. 3; and 10–16 Feb. 1995, p. 4.
[99] *Baltic Independent,* 10–16 Feb. 1995, p. 4.
[100] *Boundary Bulletin,* no. 4 (May–June 1992), p. 43.
[101] *Baltic Independent,* 23 Dec. 1994–5 Jan. 1995, p. 4.

but the problem remains how to delimit the sea border so that Lithuania does not lose areas rich in fish.

Although the territorial disputes are not so important as other problems (military or humanitarian) they are a potential source of dangerous tensions. There is no doubt that they undermine the security order in the region and that it would be better to settle them alongside other regional problems.

Approaches to the resolution of these problems depend on the nature of the conflicts themselves.

The economic and technical conflicts—the Russian–Norwegian disputes and the Russian–Baltic boundary demarcation problems—are open to discussion and could be resolved through negotiation, even if there is no simple solution. It might be appropriate to create commissions of arbitration for the resolution of these conflicts within the existing subregional institutions (the Nordic Council, the Baltic Council and the Barents Council).[102] The European Union, the International Court of Justice in The Hague and the UN could be valuable mediators if these problems cannot be resolved at bilateral and subregional levels.

Where the Karelia and Kaliningrad issues are concerned, official recognition of the problems and their inclusion on the negotiating agenda could destabilize the situation. For that reason, the principle of the status quo is probably the best option for the time being and in the near future. It is clear that the benefits of self-restraint would be considerably greater than those to be gained by simply appeasing nationalistic feelings. Fortunately, all interested parties (Finland, Germany, Lithuania, Poland and Russia) are refraining from any actions which could have a destabilizing effect.

The promotion of direct economic and human contacts between Karelia and Finland and between Kaliningrad and Germany would probably ease tensions. Free economic zones and the liberalization of the visa regime (which has partly happened already) could be appropriate instruments of such a policy.

VI. Conclusions

This analysis of Russian policy towards the Baltic/Nordic region shows that:

1. Russian relations with the countries of the area have become less confrontational and more friendly in recent years, except for two of the Baltic states. The countries of the region no longer perceive each other as global enemies.

2. There has been a change in the nature of the threat. A military threat is being replaced by environmental and social ones. The Baltic/Nordic security system is not yet ready to meet the new challenges properly.

3. In contrast with the past, all sides are demonstrating increased flexibility and goodwill. This facilitates the search for optimal decisions.

[102] See note 43.

4. At the same time, the internal instability in Russia, the burden of former prejudices and the concentration of the Nordic countries on their own problems make the resolution of all problems difficult—even those which apparently should be straightforward.

5. It is now time for all countries of the region to assess their foreign policy interests thoroughly and develop a common political course through dialogue and cooperation.

Russia, the Baltic states and the Nordic countries could take responsibility for the creation of the new Baltic/Nordic security sub-system as a part of the European security complex. A democratically transformed Russia has a chance to contribute to the formation of this new security order.

Part VIII

Russia and East–Central Europe after the Warsaw Pact

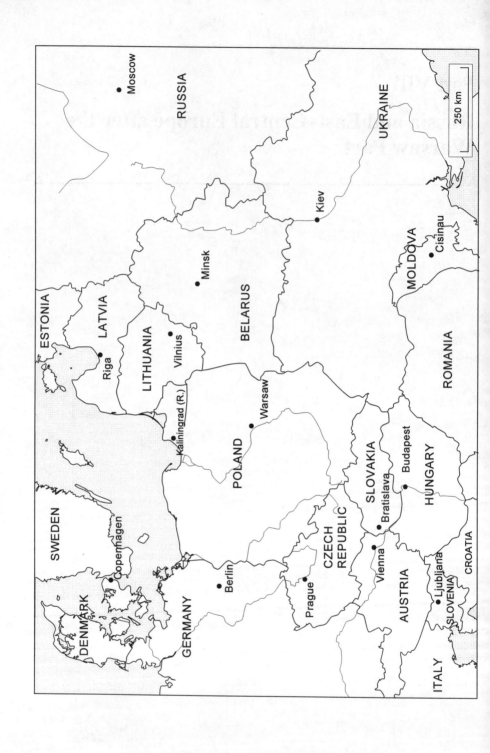

Background chronology

1988
7 Dec.   In a speech before the UN General Assembly, President Gorbachev in effect renounces the 'Brezhnev doctrine' when he recognizes the right of a nation's people to freely choose its social and political system

1989
9 Nov.   Following massive pro-democracy demonstrations in several East German cities, the communist authorities open the Berlin Wall to allow free transit between the eastern and western parts of the city

1991
19 June   USSR completes withdrawal of its remaining troops based in Hungary
28 June   Member states of the CMEA vote unanimously to dissolve the foundering 42-year old organization
30 June   Withdrawal of Soviet troops from Czechoslovakia completed
1 July   Member states of the WTO sign a protocol that terminates the 1955 Treaty of Friendship, Cooperation and Mutual Assistance, thereby dissolving the WTO
8 Nov.   NATO invites heads of government of former WTO member states, the Baltic states and the USSR jointly to launch the proposed NACC
7 Dec.   USSR and Hungary sign a treaty of friendship and cooperation but the accord is not ratified by the Russian Parliament because it contains a recognition of the USSR's responsibility for the 1956 intervention in Hungary
21 Dec.   NACC holds its inaugural session with the participation of the 16 NATO members and Bulgaria, Czechoslovakia, Estonia, Hungary, Latvia, Lithuania, Poland, Romania and the USSR

1992
10 Mar.   Russia and 9 other CIS states become members of NACC
1 Apr.   Russia signs a 10-year treaty of friendship and cooperation with Czechoslovakia
22 May   Russia and Poland sign a treaty of friendship and cooperation
4 Aug.   Russian–Bulgarian treaty of friendship and cooperation signed
28 Oct.   The last former Soviet combat unit stationed in Poland leaves Polish territory

1993
25 Aug.   A joint Polish–Russian declaration, signed by Presidents Yeltsin and Walesa, states that 'Poland's intention to join NATO . . . does not go against the interests of other states, including the interests of Russia'
26 Aug.   Russia signs treaty of friendship and cooperation and a bilateral military cooperation agreement with Slovakia
15 Sep.   Reversing previous statements, Yeltsin sends a letter to US President Bill Clinton and other Western leaders in which he sets out his objections to NATO enlargement

1994
9 May   Bulgaria, Hungary, Poland, Romania, Slovakia, the Czech Republic and the 3 Baltic states become associate partners in WEU
22 June   Russia joins the NATO PFP Programme but fails to gain special status *vis-à-vis* NATO
1 Dec.   The North Atlantic Council adopts a decision to begin the 'process of examination inside the Alliance to determine how NATO will enlarge, the principles to guide this process and the implications of membership'

1995
28 Sep.   NATO releases a study explaining the goals and principles of a possible enlargement of the alliance and the principles that new member states must observe; it does not set out a timetable for enlargement or specify likely candidates for membership

1996

4 June   Foreign Minister Primakov tells NATO foreign ministers meeting in Berlin that Russia can accept the political enlargement of NATO but will oppose an eastward extension of its military infrastructure

16. Russia and East–Central Europe: strategic options

Wojtek Lamentowicz

I. Introduction: the legacy of the past in the search for identity

Both Russia and East–Central Europe (ECE) look to their history and their present geography in order to understand what it is they have that others lack, what constitutes their specific identity. A continuous search for identity has profound geo-strategic implications. However, there is no consensus on the fundamental question whether Russia as an ethnic and cultural entity belongs to Europe or to Asia, nor is it clear which nations make up Central Europe. In addition to Czechs, Hungarians, Poles and Slovaks, many Belarussians, Lithuanians and Ukrainians and perhaps some Germans and Austrians would claim that they are Central Europeans.[1]

This chapter focuses on relations between Russia and the ECE, defined as the Czech Republic, Hungary, Poland and Slovakia, the four members of the Visegrad Group. The four countries share some basic characteristics.

In the first place, these small powers were dominated by three empires—the Prussian, Russian and Hapsburg—with some influences from the Ottoman Empire in the distant past, and by the Soviet empire after 1945. Both the borders and the very existence of these states have changed repeatedly in the course of the past 200 years. They share the tragic experience of not having been independent states for many years until the end of World War I. In fact, they were never united by their own efforts and free choice, but by default, the result of the conflict between three empires and their eventual collapse. Later they were caught in between two totalitarian systems created by the German variety of fascism (Czechoslovakia and Hungary) and the Russian variety of communism (Czechoslovakia, Hungary and Poland).

Second, these countries have the sad privilege of having been at the centre of the most dramatic conflict developments in modern Europe. They have been 'long the locus of disputes and uncertainties that fuelled the 20th century's three great European wars—one of which remained "cold"—from 1914 to 1989'.[2]

---

[1] 'The reason why the participants cannot agree about which part of the historical and social landscape should be denoted Central Europe is simply that Central Europe is created as a function of the debate itself.' Neumann, I. B., 'Russia as Central Europe's constituting other', *East European Politics and Societies,* vol. 7, no. 2 (spring 1993), pp. 349–50.

[2] Hunter, R., 'Enlargement: part of a strategy for projecting stability into Central Europe', *NATO Review,* no. 3 (May 1995), p. 3.

Third, they were and still are in the centre of Europe: 'while subsumed in one of the three great multinational empires . . . [they] none the less preserved major elements of Western traditions: for example, Western Christianity, the rule of law, some separation of powers, a measure of constitutional government, and something that could be called civil society'.[3] They are, however, underdeveloped and, as Pierre Hassner put it, have been always on the periphery.[4] Formerly on the periphery of the Soviet empire, they have now become a periphery of the Western 'centre'. During the 'short 20th century'[5] The ECE, because of its exclusion, has been exposed to the rise and fall of two kinds of totalitarianism and has been the ground for radical and unsuccessful experiments in modernization. Both leftist and rightist totalitarian experiments failed but the region is still on the margin of the European mainstream and unable to catch up with the West.

Finally, the ECE perceived itself as a meeting-point of many religions and ethnic cultures—the Catholic, Orthodox, Protestant and Judaic.[6] Thus the Polish lands located on the periphery of the Christian West and on the trade routes coming from Byzantium were doomed to be a crossroads of cultural traditions.[7] A multicultural heritage and the well-known troubles of the nation-state are a shared experience of all Central Europeans.

These countries' 'community of destinies', as Bruno Bauer described supranational identity, never made them into a homogeneous geopolitical entity. They were disunited and heterogeneous (which contributed greatly to their dependence on Nazi Germany and the Soviet Union). The ECE was caught not only *under* foreign imperial superpowers but also *between* distinct cultures and civilizations. Its geopolitical identity was and is based on a cultural duality, on the hope of being accepted into the West and on the fear of being dominated by East. The ECE shares many traditions, experiences, values and interests, but the pluralism of cultures and its inability to unite its efforts make many experts uncertain whether it is a genuine community or an imagined community only.

Views of the West and of Russia in the ECE are contradictory: the West is viewed as superior, which could produce an inferiority complex, and Russia is viewed as inferior, which could lead to a superiority complex. As Russia was and is obviously stronger in military terms than all the ECE countries put together, the sense of cultural superiority and the fear of being dominated by force could become a deeply entrenched attitude of both citizens and policy

---

[3] Garton Ash, T., 'Reform or revolution?', ed. T. Garton Ash, *The Uses of Adversity: Essays on the Fate of Central Europe* (Random House: New York, 1989), p. 250.

[4] Hassner, P., 'Das Zentrum als Peripherie' [The centre as periphery], *Transit: Europäische Revue*, no. 7 (1994), p. 17.

[5] From World War I to the 1990s. The phrase is adapted by Ivan T. Berend, a Hungarian historian, from Fernand Braudel's famous phrase 'the long 16th century' which covered a century and a half. Berend, I. T., 'Central and Eastern Europe in the short 20th century', *Tarsadalmi Szemle*, no. 3 (1990).

[6] Many distinguished Polish artists and politicians (such as Mickiewicz, Kosciuszko, Moniuszko and Orzeszkowa) were born in Belarus or Lithuania, which used to belong to Poland.

[7] Bogucka, M., 'Between the West and the East: the outline of the Polish cultural identity formation till the end of the 18th century', eds R. Grathoff and A. Kloskowska, *The Neighbourhood of Cultures* (Polish Academy of Sciences, Institute of Political Studies: Warsaw, 1994), pp. 53–61.

makers in the ECE countries. This is the background to the return-to-the West strategy that re-emerged after the end of the Warsaw Treaty Organization (WTO).

Russia has built its geopolitical identity by several hundred years of territorial expansion in Europe and Asia. 'Since the time of Peter the Great, Russia has had no experience of living as anything other than an empire. The need to maintain and strengthen the empire, the pride of being a great power, the multi-ethnic composition of the ruling élite united by devotion to a vast and mighty state became key components of Russian political culture.'[8] This definition seems acceptable to many in ECE countries, where Russia is widely perceived as a 'one-dimensional superpower' whose identity is based on a fatalist view of historical necessity and on fascination with military might.

This distrust of Russia has been founded on painful historical experience. However, after the dissolution of the Soviet Union in 1991, Russian experts to some extent confirmed this judgement on the imperial identity of the Russian Federation. Sergei Karaganov, an influential security adviser and an outstanding expert in international affairs, has put it aptly: 'There is a Versailles syndrome, which is visibly growing among the population of the Russian Federation. Most people were able to adapt easily to the loss of the "external" empire. It is much harder to adapt to the dissolution of the country itself, which was considered theirs and which was inherited from the Russian Tsars of the 16th, 17th and 18th centuries and then renamed in 1721 as the Russian Empire'.[9]

Russian policy is guided in the long run by the fear of being surrounded by an unregulated security space close to its borders. A variety of forward defence has been viewed by many Russian security experts as indispensable and as the justification for a continuous enlargement of the territory controlled by the Russian armed forces.

Russia has a very peculiar position *vis-à-vis* its own empire. On the one hand the empire was built and organized by Russians themselves; on the other hand it was dismantled by the Russian leadership of the Soviet Union. If it had not been for actions taken by Russia under President Boris Yeltsin, the Soviet communist empire would still be in place. Its collapse was not the result of a military defeat, as was the case with the Austro-Hungarian and Ottoman empires in 1918, nor was Russia involved in many civil wars, as happened in the former Yugoslavia, nor did it have to conduct a costly military struggle against independence movements, as did Belgium, Britain, France, Portugal and Spain with their colonial empires. Russia would have had little difficulty keeping the Baltic republics and Slav countries of the 'near abroad' under control if it had had the political will to do so. Even the withdrawal from Germany and the ECE was not the result of ineluctable necessity.

[8] Simes, D. K., 'America and the post-Soviet republics', *Foreign Affairs*, summer 1992, p. 78.
[9] Karaganov, S. A., King's College, London, Centre for Defence Studies, *Russia: The New Foreign Policy and Security Agenda. A View from Moscow*, London Defence Studies no. 12 (Brassey's: London, 1992), p. 8.

Despite various excesses and local civil wars, and despite the failed coup, the fact is that the Soviet empire was not demolished by force; there was no revolution. The disintegration process could perhaps be likened to an impassioned, at times dramatic, but on the whole orderly divorce within the existing legal framework. Precisely a state that had so often been accused of having little or no legal culture consummated its own dissolution within legal structures.[10]

It was to a great extent a non-violent dismantling of the largest empire in the world. 'The Soviet Union can be said to have been dissolved by treaty, Czechoslovakia to have been dissolved by legislation, and Yugoslavia to have been dissolved by civil war and violence.'[11]

This remains true despite the fact that after the dissolution of the Soviet empire there are still many conflicts—fights over land and natural resources, struggles for independence and clan warfare. Some experts believe there are more than 200 ethnic flash-points in the former Soviet Union that could produce open armed conflict.[12] If it is remembered how great the existing conflict potential is, how deeply rooted certain traits of the humiliated Russian national feelings are and how widespread poverty and uncertainty are in everyday life, the domestic conflicts are perhaps less intense than might have been expected.

The centrality of the Russian contribution to the dissolution of the Soviet empire is hardly acknowledged by ECE policy makers. Many of them believe that the Russians were simply acting under pressure of dissident movements in the ECE and were compelled to withdraw their troops and political influence from the region because they were unable to face a Western challenge. Russian democratic reformers expected some gratitude from the ECE countries and are in general disappointed by a good deal of the anti-Russian behaviour which followed the dissolution of the Soviet Union.

ECE and Russian perceptions of the collapse of Soviet empire are and will remain divergent. The fall of communism brought the ECE countries political independence, civil liberties, democratic government and the prospect of prosperity through joining the market economies of integrating Europe. What was liberation to the ECE must have been to Russia a bitter experience of humiliation, of weakness and of the loss of superpower status. At the beginning of the democratic transition, expectations in the ECE countries were much higher than in Russia.

---

[10] Schmid, K., *Untergang und Entstehung von Staaten in Mittel- und Osteuropa* [Decline and rise of the state in Central and Eastern Europe], Berichte des Bundesinstituts für ostwissenschaftliche und internationale Studien no. 34 (BIOSt: Cologne, 1993) p. 40.

[11] Schmid (note 10), p. 39.

[12] Szajkowski, B. (ed.), *Encyclopaedia of Conflicts, Disputes and Flashpoints in Eastern Europe, Russia and the Successor States* (Longman: Harlow, 1993); Szajkowski, B., 'Bantustanisation of Russia', *Swedish Journal of Political Science*, no. 3 (1993); and Payin, E., 'Types of Ethnic Conficts in Post-Soviet Societies', Unpublished manuscript, Aug. 1993.

II. Strategic choices

The ECE countries were not united even before the elegant divorce of the two parts of Czechoslovakia at the end of 1992. Central Europe was reinvented after 1989 by some dissident intellectuals such as Milan Kundera, Milan Simecka, Vaclav Havel and Mihaly Vajda, became a reality after 1989 and remained an imagined community of common hopes. The individual countries wanted to be independent of Russia/the Soviet Union and to be included in West European institutional frameworks—the European Union (EU), the Western European Union (WEU) and the Council of Europe—and eventually the Atlantic alliance, and once again they started their separate efforts towards good bilateral relations based on new treaties with their new neighbours, first of all with a Germany that was in the process of reunification and a Soviet Union which was in the process of being dismantled. 'Even where interests and strategies were perceived to dovetail, as in the case of policy *vis-à-vis* the European Community, cooperation was not entered into, but had to be imposed by what was effectively the third party, the EC.'[13]

It was the European Community which replaced the former USSR as a unifying factor when the Russian rulers slowly but surely withdrew their influence. Western Europe and the USA were inclined to regard the ECE countries as a single entity in order to hold in check the competition between them to be the first to join NATO and the EU. Regional cooperation was attractive to the ECE countries only to the extent that they could believe that it was their 'return to Europe' and an additional guarantee against military and/or non-military threats from the East.

The strategic options of these three countries and later, with some hesitation, of the Slovak Government were built on their search for identity and on their perception of the Russian geo-strategic identity. Instead of staying somewhere in between Germany and Russia, the ECE started its new political dynamic.

The menu of strategic options was rather narrow. It may be described as follows.

1. *Decisive Westernization.* Its advocates assumed that it was imperative to move as quickly as possible towards the West and cut ties to Russia and/or other Eastern neighbours on the grounds that Russia was dangerous, unstable, unpredictable and unable to build a sustainable democracy and a non-imperial form of government; when strong enough it might be in a position to threaten the ECE and prevent it from joining NATO, the WEU and the EU.

2. *Reluctant Westernization*—some movement westwards but in such a way as to provide an open and friendly bridge between Russia and the West, assisting Russia in its efforts to become a Westernized, modern and democratic society and come closer to the Euro-Atlantic community.

---

[13] Neumann (note 1), p. 364.

3. *The in-between option*—a certain *rapprochement* with the West and some distancing from Russia with a view to staying somewhere in between. Within this strategy, Russia, even if it had no room for liberal democracy and a market economy, should be helped to find a 'third way'.

4. *Easternization*—a return to Russia in such a way as to avoid provoking the anxiety of the West, grounded on the belief that Russia would in any case reintegrate its former 'inner' empire and recover its position as a superpower or great power.

After very short-lived temptations to choose the third strategy (for example, debates on neutrality in Czechoslovakia in 1990 and a tendency to look for a third way in foreign and domestic policy in Slovakia in 1993), all the countries of the region started to drift between strategies of the first and second types. They are clearly competing among themselves for special or differentiated status within the frameworks of NATO, the WEU and the EU. Their efforts *vis-à-vis* Western multilateral institutions over the past four years seem to be reducible to two simple principles of international behaviour: 'me first' if possible and 'me too' if some other country gets something first. This peculiar 'mini-max' strategy views Russia as an external factor that could become a stumbling-block on the road to Westernization.

The experience of governments in the region has made it clear that centre-right coalitions (such as the governments of Hannah Suchocka in Poland and of Vaclav Klaus in the Czech Republic) are more inclined to choose the first option, of decisive Westernization, and the centre–left coalitions (such as the governments of Gyula Horn in Hungary and of Waldemar Pawlak in Poland) are rather more keen to follow the reluctant Westernization strategy.

The Russian post-communist élites were uncertain in the early 1990s how the security of the ECE was linked to Russian security. They therefore paid little attention to the region in the aftermath of the dissolution of the Soviet Union in 1991. Relations with the USA and Western Europe have been kept very high on Russia's priority list. The problems of the ECE have been seen by many as being of secondary importance:

The military withdrawal from East Central Europe has done away with the posture of direct military confrontation, which was generally useless and counterproductive. It was useless because there was no threat or possibility of a Western conventional attack and the buffer zone was no protection against nuclear weapons—nor was there any Western intention to use such weapons. It was counterproductive because it solidified the Western front and fuelled the arms race in the West, and thus put additional pressure on an already ineffective Soviet economic system whilst strengthening the militarists and conservatives in the ruling Soviet élite.[14]

This assessment of the WTO and of the buffer zone is of course in contradiction with the traditional arguments of Russian imperial policy of forward defence. It

[14] Karaganov (note 9), p. 4.

reflects the way of reasoning of the early stage of the post-Soviet security debate among democratic reformers in Russia.

This does not, however, mean that the Russian approach to the ECE region has been a passive adjustment to Western challenges and to the region's efforts to join NATO, the WEU and the EU. Beginning in 1994 Russian analysts and policy makers started to turn their attention to the ECE as they felt that the region was getting closer to Western institutional structures.

The Russian leaders have a much bigger menu of strategic options towards the ECE. They can be put into three broad categories—post-imperial, non-imperial and neo-imperial.

1. A *post-imperial policy* was adopted by President Yeltsin after the failure of the *coup d'état* of 1991 when he formally gave his assent to the dissolution of the Soviet Union. It is to be understood as a combination of old imperial habits and new non-imperial aspirations. Some old assumptions about military threats and enemies are still alive, so that there is a great deal of mistrust of NATO, an extended US military presence, and so on. On the other hand there is a new desire to become an open, trustworthy and reliable partner in security, cooperating in friendly fashion with old enemies (such as NATO) and former victims of empire (such as the ECE countries). Post-imperial policy is inconsistent but usually based on goodwill. This explains why at this stage Russian policy makers began to say that there were no immediate threats to Russian security, there were no enemies in the West or in Asia and there was no need for a policy of manipulation by *divide et impera*.

That stage proved to be transitory. Russia was contemplating membership of NATO, but it was not clear that it was serious about this. If the NATO commanders and their political superiors had been able to arrange for bilateral agreements between NATO and former WTO members in 1992 instead of two years later there would have been no Russian veto and perhaps no claim to special status.[15]

2. A *non-imperial policy* would be an entirely new approach to security, freedom and democracy with no visible remains of the imperial tradition and military thinking. Non-imperial thinking, which has so far been evident only in the intellectual debate among Russian democrats, is based on the honestly held assumption that Russia will have no military enemies if it belongs to the community of democratic nations and that it need not try to become a global superpower because it will be recognized by all as a great power contributing to stability and peace among nations. Non-imperial thinking does not spring from anxiety that some small countries (such as those of the ECE) will isolate the Russian Federation or the Commonwealth of Independent States (CIS).

---

[15] The author suggested as early as the winter of 1990 a set of bilateral security agreements between NATO and WTO members, including the then Soviet Union. Lamentowicz, W., 'Future political structure of Europe seen from an Eastern point of view', ed. NATO Defense College, *Future Political Structure in Europe and the Transatlantic Link* (NATO Defense College: Rome, 1990), pp. 34–48.

This second type of policy can take at least three forms: (*a*) approaching Western Europe and the USA, which would imply *friendly cooperation* with the ECE, using it as a stable and democratic bridge leading to the West; (*b*) highlighting the specific Eurasian features of the Russian identity, which would imply staying between Asia and Europe and to a certain extent moving away from the latter; or (*c*) becoming in the future an active member of the prospective community of the Pacific Rim. If a non-imperial policy of the second or third type is adopted in the future, there is a high probability that Russian policy towards the ECE region will be one of *benign neglect* based on good but rather cool and distant relations and declining mutual interaction in the political and economic realms.[16]

3. A *neo-imperial policy* came to the fore on the eve of the Russian parliamentary elections in December 1993 and was significantly different from the country's previous floating position between post-imperial and non-imperial strategies. It was based on the assumptions that Russia must be treated as a great power with global interests. Russian policy now focused on efforts to reintegrate the inner security space of the former Soviet republics around the Russian hard core, increased penetration of some CIS members by Russia, a claim to strategic partnership with the USA, a new assertiveness *vis-à-vis* the West and the ECE, and a policy of preventing the ECE states from joining NATO without Russia—something Russian policy makers tend to perceive as an exacerbation of Russia's isolation. This may be called a policy of *preventive engagement*. It is therefore not surprising that Russia in 1994 claimed special rights while negotiating the Partnership for Peace (PFP) agreement with NATO and expected approval from the international community for very specific peacekeeping operations on former Soviet territory.

As the political future is still undecided, all three options for Russian policy towards the ECE are open—friendly cooperation, benign neglect and preventive engagement. It is self-evident that an ECE choice in favour of either decisive or reluctant Westernization would be compatible with two of the potential Russian strategies, but benign neglect would be less welcome than a policy of friendly cooperation.

Whether Russia will continue its neo-imperial policy in general and the policy of preventive engagement towards the ECE in particular remains uncertain. If it does there must come an open confrontation of interests between an ECE which is willing to move westwards and a Russia which is claiming its *droit de regard*.

III. An uncertain future

The uncertainty of public life in the emerging democracies should not be equated with the uncertainty characteristic of liberal democracies. In a stable

---

[16] The term 'benevolent negligence' has been put forward by Sergei Karaganov. See note 9.

democracy and an established market economy there are procedures and rules such as majority rule, the norms of market competition, constitutional order and the rule of law which are fairly certain and predictable. Only the results or outcomes of human action remain uncertain. In the new democracies of the ECE and Russia the uncertainty is 'dual, embracing both procedures and results'.[17]

In the realm of international relations the level of uncertainty may be even higher than in the fairly unstable domestic frameworks. Domestic conditions are visibly more stable and reliable in the ECE countries than in Russia and its closest neighbourhood. Both forms of government and protection of human rights seem to be much more certain in the ECE than in Russia and economic reform and performance are also better.

The economic gap between Russia and the ECE has increased and may well continue to increase. Economic relations between them are on the decline as Germany has replaced the Soviet Union as the first trading partner of all the ECE countries. The German share in their foreign trade—on average more than one-third today—may well grow as the German recession comes to an end.

It can be assumed that some residual links between Russia and the ECE countries will be kept in the near future. Cultural exchange and political discourse will remain rather limited because interest in developing closer and warmer relations is low on both sides: there is a high probability of mutual neglect based on 'do not disturb' reasoning. On the other hand the ECE will continue its efforts to sell as much as possible on the Russian market in order to be able to import oil and gas and some weapons, military equipment and relevant spare parts. ECE governments are trying to increase their trade with Russia—a package of proposals was tabled by the Polish Foreign Minister in January 1994, for example—but legal uncertainties, the lack of bank guarantees, the penetration of the mafia and other factors are preventing them from successfully trading in the East. The share of all the former Soviet republics together in the foreign trade of Poland fell to almost 10 per cent in 1994.

The most crucial factors in determining the future relations of Russia and the ECE are political in nature: (*a*) domestic political developments in Russia, and (*b*) the debate in both the West and the ECE on extended responsibility for NATO and the feasibility of its enlargement, and the Russian reaction to this debate.

There are three fundamental areas of uncertainty in Russia's domestic politics with enormous implications for its foreign and security policy.

1. Will the democratic evolution of Russia continue and will its government stay democratic? What will happen if Russian democrats lose in a democratic vote and are replaced by nationalist or left-wing radical coalitions?

[17] Bunce, V. and Csanadi, M., 'Uncertainty in the transition: post-communism in Hungary', *East European Politics and Societies*, no. 2 (spring 1993), pp. 266–67.

2. Is it possible to keep the Russian armed forces under civilian control and to make them loyal to democratic values, at least to some rudimentary democratic characteristics of the present Russian Constitution?

3. Is it feasible to plan for almost full reintegration of the former Soviet republics around the Russian core of the inner empire, and what are the strategic implications of successful reintegration, bearing in mind the economic and military dependence of the non-Russian republics on Russia's potential?

The strategic discourse of Russia and the ECE at present seems to be based on divergent views of future security arrangements and guarantees.

The origin of these divergent concerns is the definition of the ECE itself. The people of the ECE tend to look upon their homelands as a tragic region victimized in the past by stronger countries (mostly Russia and Germany) and betrayed by the Western allies in Yalta in 1945. On the other hand Russian policy makers still believe that the ECE is a traditional area of legitimate Russian presence and/or penetration. The more the new assertiveness enters Russian thinking the more strongly they stress that 'Russia might provide interlocking security guarantees for the ECE countries jointly with Western nations . . . Russia should be recognized as a great power with legitimate interests, including security interests beyond its borders'.[18] The mere wording 'beyond its borders' does not necessarily mean that Russia will consider the ECE as its 'near abroad', but it is quite clear that it insists on its right to guarantee the security of the ECE despite the unwillingness of those countries to accept this.

Both the societies and the political élites of the ECE countries expect full membership of NATO. Russian policy makers assert that:

We will consider an enlargement of NATO as an unfriendly move towards Russia. In this respect the idea of NATO enlargement with simultaneous conclusion of a special NATO–Russia partnership agreement must be considered as unrealistic. That is the understanding not only of many State Duma members, but also of the President, the Government, the Ministry of Foreign Affairs and the Ministry of Defence of Russia, and that understanding has been repeatedly expressed on both the domestic and the international level.[19]

Not all Russian politicians think in the same way about ECE aspirations to join NATO; not all stress the sense of being isolated by the possible enlargement of NATO. Yegor Gaidar, the prominent democratic leader, said in January 1995:

Until recently my party considered as improper any enlargement of NATO in Central Europe that did not provide a guarantee of security and simultaneously is convenient for Russian nationalists as it justifies their assumptions of a Western plot against

---

[18] Text of the response from the head of the Russian delegation to the North Atlantic Assembly, V. Viktorov, in Draft Special Report of the Working Group on NATO Enlargement to the Parliamentary Assembly of NATO: Correspondence between Karsten Voigt and Associate Delegations, May 1995, Annex III, p. 32 (mimeographed).

[19] Mityukov, M. A. in Draft Special Report of the Working Group, Annex III (note 18), p. 30.

Russia. Today, in conjunction with Russian actions in Chechnya, I would not dare to advise someone not to join NATO and not to build its own security.[20]

In another interview Gaidar made it clear that his party understands well that 'Russia has no veto right' in decisions about enlargement of NATO.[21] Grigoriy Yavlinskiy, a popular presidential candidate, made his point against NATO enlargement in a softer way than the ruling group around President Yeltsin:

Russia must say decisively and clearly that she will not build either military or political alliances with Ukraine, Belarus or Moldova. With nobody. If I become president I will avoid such alliances, even if Ukraine asks for it. What would be the purpose of it? There is no Western threat to Russia. Such a policy may encourage the West to reconsider whether there is real need for enlargement of NATO eastwards.[22]

Those opposition voices contributed to a certain degree to making Russia's policy more nuanced. Although the present rulers of the Russian Federation still insist on the transformation of NATO, which they perceive as an alternative to its enlargement, there were many moderate voices in the Russian authorities. Ivan Rybkin, then Speaker of the State Duma (the lower house of the Russian Parliament), suggested in Brussels in February 1995 that Russia could become a member of NATO on 'French' terms, that is, participating in decision making but not being integrated into the military structures, stating that Russia wished to be integrated into the political structures of NATO and to contribute to the security of the area from Vancouver to Vladivostok. In talks in Washington at the end of February 1995 Deputy Foreign Minister Georgiy Mamedov suggested some limiting conditions on NATO enlargement. He suggested that new members from the ECE could join NATO on condition that: (*a*) they did not deploy nuclear weapons on their territories; (*b*) they did not allow deployment of military forces of other member states on their territories; (*c*) they did not join the military structures of NATO but remained in a position similar to that of France or Spain; and (*d*) a standing consultative committee of NATO and Russia was formed. The comments of experts after Mamedov's talks were more optimistic, as if Russia had switched from a 'no' policy to a 'yes, but' negotiating position. One month later, on 30 March 1995, Oleg Lobov, then Secretary of the Russian Security Council, gave an interview to the Interfax press agency and repeated the point made by Rybkin in February: there was only one way in which NATO enlargement was feasible, and that only in the long term, because Russia itself should join NATO if the ECE countries were admitted to full membership.

Russian policy makers requested a strategic partnership within the Euro-Atlantic community as a substitute for NATO enlargement. Thus Russia proposed 'a genuine division of labour between the CIS, the North Atlantic

[20] Interview in the Polish weekly *Wprost,* 22 Jan. 1995, p. 43.

[21] Gaidar, Ye., 'Duma Bolszewikow' [The pride of Bolsheviks], *Polityka,* 18 Mar. 1995, p. 19.

[22] Yavlinskiy, G., 'Bede mówit tylko minute' [I shall speak just one minute], *Polityka,* 25 Mar. 1995, p. 11.

Cooperation Council, the European Union, the Council of Europe, NATO and the Western European Union, with the CSCE [Conference on Security and Co-operation in Europe] playing a coordinating role'. The reactions of NATO and the ECE to Russia's various requests were hardly enthusiastic. This was reciprocated by Russia's reluctance to approve the PFP Individual Partnership Programme on the grounds that it would put Russia into the same category as the small and medium-sized ECE and Balkan states.

On 31 May 1995 at the Noordwijk meeting of the North Atlantic Cooperation Council (NACC) Russia finally signed its Individual Partnership Programme, although it again expressed its opposition to NATO enlargement. On the other hand, the ECE countries were disillusioned with the PFP because it came too late and brought too little. It was far less than a clear promise of future NATO membership. Many politicians in the ECE tend to believe that the PFP is a variety of a 'partnership for postponement' as it does not entail criteria and a timetable that could eventually lead to full NATO membership.

It is clear that the reasons for the discontent of Russia and the ECE were as different as their views on security as summarized here.

IV. Conclusions

It seems quite clear that Russian and ECE views on NATO, the Organization for Security and Co-operation in Europe (OSCE)[23] and other institutional frameworks will remain divergent in the years to come. If in this period Russia reintegrates its inner security space (which seems feasible and more probable now than it did some time ago),[24] its government is more influenced by the neo-imperial way of thinking and its frustrated armed forces become more outspoken, the troubled neighbourhood of Russia and the ECE may enter a new, more difficult stage of development.

However, it will hardly be feasible or desirable for Russia to restore its former position in the ECE if Western Europe and the USA are decisive enough in their strategy of peaceful enlargement of both NATO and the EU. If this comes about, Russia may become just a bigger and stronger regional great power vis-à-vis the ECE without being provocative towards the West. There is an opportunity for the ECE to do its best to help Russia in its efforts to become a more Western-like country if Russia is able to accept its policy of reluctant Westernization. This might be a fair deal: security for the ECE within the broader European framework would be compensated for by more substantial aid for the Russian transition to a non-imperial policy as a reliable and predictable great power.

The ECE would not pose an external challenge to Russia even if the ruling élites of these countries wanted to, but Russia is big and strong enough to be a

---

[23] On 1 Jan. 1995 the CSCE became the OSCE.

[24] Recent developments in Belarus and Ukraine suggest that there is little room for those countries to become fully independent of Russia.

genuine threat whether or not its rulers want to return to an imperial policy. Even a minor error in political judgement in Moscow could victimize the ECE. It can only be hoped that both Russian and ECE strategy makers will continue to bear this in mind.

Many Russian politicians are aware of one unique Russian asset. 'Because of its geographic location Russia is a potential link between the three developing trade and economic super-regions—Europe, Asia, and North America.'[25] In order to use this unique opportunity, Russia is interested first of all in good relations among the great powers, which could easily lead to benign neglect of small countries. If this reasoning is not completely wrong Russia may become less engaged in the ECE than it has been at any time in the last 200 years.

At present, however, a Russian strategy which is more beneficial to stability cannot be ruled out. There is still some room for a policy of friendly cooperation between Russia and the ECE in bilateral relations and of increasing the participation of Russia and the ECE in broader European structures such as the OCSE and NATO. Russia does not object to East–Central Europe joining the EU and WEU and this may provide an opportunity for compromises in both political and security matters.

In the long run Russia will do better to control itself and not other countries in order to restore its position as a great power.

[25] Lukin, V. P., Center for Strategic and International Studies, Georgetown University, 'Russia and its interests', ed. S. Sestanovich, *Rethinking Russia's National Interests* (CSIS: Washington, DC, 1994), p. 115.

17. Russian security and East–Central Europe

Yuriy Davydov

I. Introduction

The traditional Russian vision of East–Central Europe (ECE)[1] was conditioned by two geopolitical circumstances. The first is a conviction that Russia's security zone begins with the ECE countries: from there Russia was invaded by the Teutons, Poles, Swedes, French and Germans. The two world wars and the cold war began there. The other is a belief that from the point of view of security the region is more important for Russia than for Western Europe. Russia and the USSR have therefore been tempted, as Russia is still, to view the ECE as its sphere of influence. The countries of the region were considered as objects, not subjects, of the European order.

After the collapse of East European socialism, the disintegration of the USSR and the weakening of the Russian position in Europe, this scheme no longer applies. Russia's zone of security has shifted, and the West now takes it as a premise that the ECE is as important for its security as it is for Russia's, if not more so. As for the countries of the region themselves, they are ready to join Western security structures. The new outlines of a European security system which are emerging as a result and the role designed in it for Russia do not entirely suit Moscow. Disputes over this and the lack of vision in the approaches of all three sides to their own and regional security seem to be leading to a new division of Europe. As at the beginning of the cold war, the shaping of a new system of security depends not on the challenges facing Europe but on the character of Russian–ECE relations. Lack of mutual confidence on security matters and a common tendency to solve issues not on a bilateral basis but through a third party (which has its own interests) are becoming major obstacles to the creation of a more stable and secure Europe.

II. The end of the Yalta system

After World War II, East–Central Europe was not only a prize the Soviet Union was awarded at Yalta for its decisive contribution in the defeat of Germany. The region has been considered by Moscow as an area of vital and prevailing interest, for at least two reasons.

One reason is ideological: the socialist ECE countries had to demonstrate to mankind the universal and not specifically Russian nature of communism and the objective character of its expansion round the world. The other was a secur-

---

[1] The Czech Republic, Hungary, Poland and Slovakia, the countries of the Visegrad Group.

ity reason: Stalin considered the existence of the belt of socialist states along the Soviet borders as the best guarantee against anti-Soviet activity.[2] The region was seen by Moscow as a forward-based security system. The USSR's principal aims were to stop a hypothetical Western attack against the Soviet Union as far as possible from its frontiers (to divert a threat) and to have its own springboard to attack the West if necessary (to create a threat).

The socialism imposed by the Soviet Union and its political and military presence in the region were a source of latent but growing tension between the superpower and the ECE societies for years. Sometimes this resulted in open resentment and popular uprisings against the communist (Soviet) system—in the German Democratic Republic in 1953, in Hungary and Poland in 1956, in Czechoslovakia in 1968 and in Poland in 1980–89; sometimes this resentment was transformed into anti-Russian feeling by nationalistic leaders such as Nicolae Ceausescu in Romania and used by them to consolidate their power positions. That is why the supposed Soviet forward security belt was actually a belt of instability and insecurity: the region could have been the detonator of a major East–West war.

Both these reasons have ceased to apply. The ECE states have stopped being obedient socialist vassals of the Soviet Union and follow their own line in internal and external affairs. Even the USSR under President Mikhail Gorbachev not only tolerated the changes going on there but even to a certain extent facilitated them, by its own example, moral support for the forces of renewal and *perestroika* in the region. Gorbachev's tolerance has been accounted for by his hope of saving the system by means of reform: his ideal was 'socialism with a human face'. He had no intention of giving up Soviet leadership in the European zone of socialism but rather hoped to control the pace of events there; nor did he intend to dismantle the bipolar world system.[3] All these schemes were buried by the 'velvet revolutions' in the ECE countries. Gorbachev's Soviet Union was compelled to promise to eliminate its military presence in the region. That was the end of the Brezhnev doctrine[4] and the end of the Yalta system of international relations.

The new Russian leaders made several gestures of goodwill aimed at wiping clean the historical slate. They recognized the responsibility of the Soviet People's Commissariat for Internal Affairs (NKVD) for the murder of Polish officers at Katyn, condemned the Soviet intervention of 1956 in Hungary and the Warsaw Treaty Organization (WTO)[5] invasion of Czechoslovakia in 1968 (pointing out at the same time that it is the Soviet Union, not Russia, that bears

---

[2] Tito's Yugoslavia and Mao's China proved, however, that it was not so much socialism as Soviet control of 'fraternal states' which ensured their loyalty.

[3] The Soviet–Romanian Treaty, signed in 1990, prohibited each side from joining any alliance considered as hostile by the other; this treaty, however, was never ratified.

[4] Many analysts have identified the end of the Brezhnev Doctrine with the speech of Soviet President Mikhail Gorbachev at the UN on 7 Dec. 1988. Gati, C., *The Block that Failed* (Indiana University Press: Bloomington, Ind., 1990), pp. 161–62.

[5] Formed in 1955 and disbanded in 1991. It consisted of Albania, Bulgaria, Czechoslovakia, the German Democratic Republic, Hungary, Poland, Romania and the USSR.

responsibility) and handed Prague secret documents from the Soviet archives revealing the names of those who invited WTO forces to crush the attempts to build socialism with a human face. As the culmination of this period of relations with its former allies, Russia concluded treaties of friendship and good-neighbourly cooperation with Hungary in December 1991,[6] Czechoslovakia in May 1992 (later with Slovakia[7]) and with Poland in May 1992.[8]

III. The alienation of former allies

After the velvet revolutions, Russia and the ECE in many ways followed parallel courses, although at different speeds, tackling identical problems: the democratization of social and political life, the creation of a civil society and the transition to a market economy. They had to combat similar difficulties and such as they had never known in their socialist past—rapid and severe social polarization, unemployment and public demand for health care, social security and education—all accompanied by a sharp decline in the income of the state sector, unprecedented inflation, the disappointment of hopes for a substantial infusion of Western money into their economies, political instability and social frustration.

At that time Russia was enjoying the 'romantic' period of its foreign policy and believed that the common social, political and other values it shared with the West and the new free ECE would naturally produce an identity of national interests in different spheres, security included, and ensure a friendly approach towards each other. The collapse of the old system of relations provided an opportunity for a fresh start, leaving the hate and distrust of the past behind and reconstructing relations on the basis of mutual respect, complete equality of rights and understanding of each other's needs. The disbanding of the WTO and the Council for Mutual Economic Assistance (CMEA)[9] and the withdrawal of Soviet (Russian) troops from the former WTO member countries closed the old era of relations between the former 'big brother' and his 'juniors'. Russia and its former allies might have been expected to combine their efforts and experience in order to cope better with common problems.

This, however, has not happened. In closing down the old era in Russian–ECE relations, Russia has not—all solemn declarations notwithstanding—opened a new one. On the contrary, relations have begun to cool. A feeling of alienation, albeit not one of confrontation, is growing between Russia and the ECE states. Russia has yielded its influence in the region—not to the USA, with which the clash over the ECE had initiated the cold war, but to Germany,

---

[6] This treaty was never ratified by Russia.

[7] In Aug. 1993. The Czech Republic considers itself as the successor state of Czechoslovakia and as inheriting all its obligations so long as they are not inconsistent with its constitution.

[8] Larrabee, F. S., *East European Security after the Cold War* (RAND Corporation: Santa Monica, Calif., 1993), pp. 12, 45; and Oltary, E., 'Hungary: political fragmentation and economic recession', Radio Free Europe/Radio Liberty, *RFE/RL Research Report*, vol. 3, no. 1 (7 Jan. 1994), p. 79.

[9] By 1990 the membership of the CMEA was Bulgaria, Czechoslovakia, the German Democratic Republic, Hungary, Poland, Romania, the USSR, Cuba, Mongolia and Viet Nam.

which has been considered by Russia as its most generous cooperation partner.[10] Step by step, the ECE has been downgraded to one of the lowest priorities for Russia's foreign policy, and there is no sign of this situation changing in the foreseeable future.

Both sides, whatever their excuses, bear a share of the blame for this process of alienation. Neither side hurried to make a fresh start. Russia has failed to work out a new strategy towards its former allies which could proceed from its and their new national interests. The ECE political leaders were satisfied with the disintegration of the USSR but are now interested in limiting Russia's influence in Europe. In the last analysis they would like the impossible—a weak but stable Russia. This vision and Russia's overreaction to it have led to mutual irritation, exploited by nationalist extremists on both sides. Moreover, the process of overcoming the common past has been complicated by mistakes and wishful thinking on the part of politicians and by the emotional mood of the societies involved. Numerous subjective and objective factors and unforeseen turns in the development of the internal and external situation in the countries concerned have made a significant contribution to the growth of alienation.

There is no doubt that a revival of historical prejudices, enhanced by the experience of compulsory 'socialist friendship', has played an important role. For centuries Russia has been seen by the peoples in the region as an empire, suppressing their freedoms. Politicians on both sides have used history for their own ends. At the same time the painful experience of domestic reform has focused the attention of Russian citizens overwhelmingly upon what is happening in their own country or in the other post-Soviet states where they still have relatives and friends. In recent years, moreover, the attitude has taken root that Russia's foreign policy activity brings the country nothing but losses. While many people in the ECE believe that the former USSR pitilessly exploited the countries of the region (and they can undoubtedly find much evidence for this) the Russian public has come to believe the contrary—that Russia paid too high a price for the loyalty of its European allies. According to some estimates made by Russian experts and shared by many Western economists, its former allies cost the Soviet Union about $10–15 billion per year.[11] That is why Russia is most of all indifferent towards the former 'friends' in the region, who are paying Russia back in its own coin. Neither side intended to perpetuate the former situation: they preferred to keep themselves at a distance. All this has inevitably led to mutual suspicion.

The degrees of alienation between Russia and different ECE countries vary. Two cases deserve special mention.

---

[10] In 1989, for instance, 60% of Poland's imports from Western Europe came from the Federal Republic of Germany; the figures for Czechoslovakia and Hungary were 57% and 50%, respectively. Asmus, R. D., *German Unification and its Ramifications* (RAND Corporation: Santa Monica, Calif., 1991), p. 43.

[11] Marrese, M. and Vanous, J., *Implicit Subsidies and Non-Market Benefits in Soviet Trade with Eastern Europe* (University of California Press: Berkeley, Calif., 1983), pp. 121–27. These estimates were prominently reported in the *Wall Street Journal*, 15 Jan. 1982; and *Time*, 18 Jan. 1982.

Relations between Russia and Poland are the most strained. This is accounted for mainly by the historical background and by the failure of both sides to understand that they are doomed to live together as independent and inter-dependent entities. At the same time, the potential for *rapprochement* is per-haps much greater than it is between Russia and other ECE countries. Polish politicians cannot help understanding that Russia continues to be the most reliable guarantor of the post-war territorial integrity of the country—that if there were a new division of Europe Poland would become a front-line state with all the attendant negative implications for its development. Poland is inter-ested in maintaining the present status of the Kaliningrad Region. Russia in its turn cannot help understanding that its posture in the ECE and Europe as a whole will to a great extent depend on the character of its relations with Warsaw. It is noteworthy that both countries are trying to increase their present collaboration in the economic field and in the cultural sphere.[12]

The relationship between Russia and Slovakia is less strained and more ben-evolent. Slovakia may be less confident about the prospects for Westernization than other countries of the region, but the burden of the historical legacy of its relations with Russia is less painful. Besides the Treaty of Friendship and Cooperation, the two sides have signed an Agreement on Military Cooperation, which reflected to some extent the identity of their approach to security issues.[13] Slovakia is also interested in finding allies which could be reliable mediators in the dispute over the Hungarian minority in Slovakia, and hopes that Russia could be one of them.

IV. A turn to the West

The shift in Russia's foreign policy priorities was facilitated by the exclusively pro-Western orientation of the Russian democratic leaders. They tied their hopes for reconstruction of the economic system, the raising of social output and the development of private enterprise and an efficient market to interaction with the West. The former Soviet allies, from which they could neither borrow experience nor obtain capital and new technology, were no longer either impor-tant or interesting. The élites of the ECE countries regarded Russia in the same way, the only difference being that they hoped to continue to use Russia as a supplier of cheap raw materials and energy. That situation changed when CMEA prices were adjusted to world levels and payment systems switched over to hard currency. From the point of view of elementary logic, it made no sense for Russia to spend hard currency on mediocre East European equipment or foodstuffs when it could easily obtain goods of better quality and even at lower prices from the European Union (EU) or the USA. Similarly, the ECE

---

[12] The volume of trade between Poland and Russia rose by 30% in 1994; the 2 countries cooperate actively in the Kaliningrad area; and they have agreed to build a new pipeline to deliver Russian gas to Western Europe through Polish territory. Cultural exchange between Poland and Russia in 1994 was 3 times more extensive than during the communist years.

[13] In Aug. 1993. Larrabee (note 8), p. 46.

could obtain everything it needed on the world market, thereby escaping dependence upon Russia's caprices and protecting itself from the growing chaos in the Russian economy. As a result both sides came to the conclusion that they did not need each other to reform their respective economies.

Ballpark figures indicate that in the 1970s and 1980s roughly half of total Soviet trade by value was accounted for by the CMEA countries. Of total CMEA trade turnover, about 40 per cent was with the USSR and about 25 per cent with the industrialized West.[14] In 1993 Russian trade with the West was 5.2 times higher than that with the former CMEA.[15] In 1992 Western countries were the purchasers of around 70 per cent of Hungary's and Poland's exports and 57 per cent of Czechoslovakia's. In 1993 about 70 per cent of the ECE's trade was with the West, one-quarter of this amount with Germany.[16]

Moreover, the general and simultaneous turn of the former allies to the West has given rise to a certain rivalry between them for Western goodwill, aid, credits and preferences. For objective reasons the West paid more attention to Russia and directed to it the bulk of its aid and credits. In 1990–93 the total sum of Western aid commitments of different kinds, including loans and loan guarantees, to the countries of the former Soviet Union was $113.9 billion. Of this $53.6 billion came from Germany. For the ECE countries, the equivalent total Western commitments amounted to only $52.4 billion[17] and some of their leaders reacted painfully to this. They stressed that Russia could hardly become a European country in the foreseeable future; that it embodied a different civilization; and that its current loyalty to the West was tactical in nature. Sometimes the anti-communist attitude of the new political leaders in a number of countries quickly turned into anti-Russian propaganda, all the more so because Russian leaders, nurtured by the old system, although trying to present themselves in the West as democrats, behaved in the ECE, if not in imperial style, at least with the condescension of the discoverers of the next bright future.

On the other hand the success of economic reform is more evident in the ECE countries than in Russia, and this has made the region more attractive than Russia for foreign direct investment, which is more important for economic development than aid. Hungary attracted $5.6 billion over the period 1990–93 ($1.2 billion in 1993 alone, or $130 per capita); Poland and the Czech Republic attracted $2.0 billion and $1.94 billion respectively over the period 1990–93 and about $600 million each in 1993. In Russia, the political risks for foreign direct investment are much higher: it attracted only $1.4 billion during 1990–93 and $660 million in 1993, or less than $5 per year per capita.[18] In 1994 the

[14] Gati (note 4), p. 117.

[15] *Central European Economic Review,* winter 1994; and *Wall Street Journal,* 23 Feb. 1994, p. 13.

[16] *Central European Economic Review,* winter 1994, p. 14; and Pichugin, B., 'K perspektivam torgovo-ekonomicheskikh otnoshenii Rossii s Evropoy' [Prospects for the trade and economic relations of Russia and Europe], *Mirovaya Ekonomika i Mezhdunarodnye Otnosheniya (MEMO),* no. 2 (1994), p. 71.

[17] *Stability and Integration: Security Relations with Central and Eastern Europe* (Netherlands Atlantic Commission: The Hague, 1995), p. 26. Precise figures on how much of the money earmarked was actually paid out are not available. Some sources believe that it was 30–55%, depending on country.

[18] 'Emerging market indicators', *The Economist,* 18 June 1994, p. 156; and *Central European Economic Review,* winter 1994, p. 226.

pendulum swung to Russia but not enough to close the gap between it and the ECE.

All the ECE countries have become associate members of the EU and some of them hope to be full members before the end of the century. Russia signed an Agreement on Partnership and Cooperation with the EU in June 1994,[19] but will take two years at least to ratify it, and has no chance of joining the EU in the foreseeable future. These distinctions are caused by objective reasons but in Russia they are sometimes seen as a preference on the part of the West for the ECE at its expense. The Kremlin prefers to put the blame for this on the ECE countries. All this has contributed to the further cooling of the relationship.

The growing alienation from its former allies has created an unfavourable environment for the Russian security posture in Europe. First, this alienation, according to some views in Russia, could be used by outside forces hostile to Russia to draw the ECE into anti-Russian activities, to play balance-of-power games with their differences.[20] Second, it has led some conservative political groupings in Moscow to suspect the ECE countries of aiming to create an anti-Russian coalition; the tentative attempts to set up security cooperation in the framework of the Visegrad Group[21] are viewed by military experts in Moscow as being directed against Russia, even though the Visegrad countries are losing interest in integration among themselves and have a clear preference for joining the EU and NATO. Third, there are apprehensions that some post-Soviet states, such as the Baltic states, Moldova and Ukraine, could be involved in such a coalition, which is why Russia seems very suspicious about contacts between countries of the ECE and the 'near abroad'. Fourth, the growing unfriendliness of the region's political élite to Russia's aim of engagement is often seen in Moscow as an endeavour to isolate it from Western Europe, to build a cordon sanitaire between them, to reduce Russia's international role to the containment of Islamic fundamentalism in Central Asia, and in the last analysis to have the ECE replace Russia in the economic, political, cultural and security aspects of European politics. Finally, all these possible developments could be exploited actively by extreme nationalist and pro-communist forces in Russia to accuse reformers of ignoring the national interests of the country and sacrificing Russia's security posture on the continent and its influence all over the world.

No one in Russia except extremists sees the ECE as a threat to the security of the country. Nevertheless some possible actions of or developments in the ECE are seen by certain political forces as a potential challenge to Russian security. For instance, the involvement of an ECE state or states in the Commonwealth of Independent States (CIS) area, especially in any dispute between Russia and its partners in the post-Soviet space, could be pictured by hard-liners as an unfriendly move aimed at undermining Russia's influence. The ECE itself is

---

[19] European Communities, Commission, Proposal for a Council and Commission Decision on the conclusion of the Agreement on Partnership and Cooperation between the European Communities and their Member States of the one part, and Russia, of the other part, COM(94) 257 final, Brussels, 15 June 1994.

[20] Advocates of this view usually refer to Brzezinski, Z., 'The premature partnership', *Foreign Affairs*, vol. 73, no. 2 (1994), pp. 67–82; and Brzezinski's commentary in *New York Times*, 29 June 1994.

[21] See note 1.

not immune to ethno-political conflicts which could draw in Russia: the most notorious problem is that of the Hungarian minorities in Romania, Serbia and Slovakia which could eventually complicate relations between Hungary and these countries. Even Poland, the most ethnically homogeneous state in the region, has its own Belarussian, German, Lithuanian and Ukrainian minorities and its latent aspirations are unknown. The Czech Republic might once again face pressure from the Sudeten Germans to return their property if not their land. All these issues could have crisis potential. Furthermore, as experience in the former Yugoslavia shows, Russia under the pressure of circumstances or of an internal power struggle can be compelled to take sides in a conflict. Volunteers or mercenaries from Russia can participate in a conflict on one side or another. Russia can participate in an arms embargo imposed on a conflict area or abstain: any choice can be provocative because all the countries of the region are equipped with Russian (or Soviet) weapons. Given the growing alienation between Russia and its former allies, involvement of such a kind could lead to the emergence of challenges to Russia's security.

In the last analysis it is of vital importance to Russia to prevent the ECE area from becoming a source of danger to Russian security. The best way, in the view of some strategists in Moscow, to guarantee Russia against such eventualities is to make sure that it is not separated from the security arrangements covering the area—indeed that it is itself involved in such new arrangements. However, misunderstanding between Russia and its former allies is beginning to grow precisely in the field of security.

V. Remaining interdependence

Do Russia and the ECE countries still have enough common ground and is the area of their remaining interaction sufficiently broad to build a common security arrangement adequate to their new interests?

Since the velvet revolutions, the nature of economic relations between Russia and the ECE has to some extent contributed to the destabilization of the economic situation on both sides. Their economic relations were clearly not effective or adequate to modern demands. To change this the partners had two alternatives: to curtail relations drastically or to transfer them step by step to a new basis taking into account the traditions, structures and experience of cooperation. Both sides chose the first alternative.

This trend had started even before the collapse of the USSR. The share of the CMEA countries in the total volume of Soviet exports fell from 35.3 per cent in 1990 to 22.7 per cent in 1991. The share of CMEA countries in total Soviet imports fell from 36.5 per cent in 1990 to 24.4 per cent in 1991 and the volume of Soviet imports from these countries fell that year by 62.5 per cent.[22] The trend continued in 1992: the general volume of the trade of the former Soviet republics with the former CMEA states fell by 43 per cent as compared with

[22] *Ekonomika i Zhizn*, no. 6 (Feb. 1992), p. 16.

1991; that with Hungary and Poland fell by 40 per cent and that with Czechoslovakia by 50 per cent. The share of the former CMEA partners in Russian foreign trade was 18 per cent in 1992 as compared with 24 per cent in 1991.[23] In 1993 Russian trade with the former CMEA countries fell by 28.1 per cent as compared with 1992.[24] As a result, entire mutually dependent branches of the Russian and ECE economies found themselves in a vacuum. For instance, the Soviet Union drastically reduced oil shipments to Poland and was to cover only 30 per cent of that country's requirements in 1991.[25] On the other hand in 1990–92 the Russian people suffered severely from shortages of cheap medicines which had previously been imported from the ECE. According to some estimates one-third of the fall in industrial production in the ECE in 1990–92 was accounted for by the reduction in or complete halting of exports to the former Soviet Union.[26]

Bilateral intergovernmental economic agreements between Russia and the ECE countries no longer function, because privatized enterprises have become independent of state control. At the same time market relations are only just taking shape on the national level. Each side has manifested an inability to guarantee meeting its supply obligations to the other. At least three implications of this turmoil for Russian–ECE relations are evident: growing tension caused by mutual accusations about the collapse of economic cooperation; a reluctance to restore economic ties even in areas beneficial to both sides; and the reduction of the basis for positive reciprocity.

There are experts on both sides who believe that Russia and the ECE are doomed to develop economic cooperation because their low-quality goods and prices cannot find a niche on the world market. Unfortunately the idea has no relation to reality. In post-communist societies supply exceeds demand and in a situation of comprehensive innovation poor-quality goods have very limited chances. People in the ECE countries prefer used Western cars to new Russian ones, and Russian shops are full not of ECE but of Western food.

There are at least two aspects of the current economic relationship between Russia and the former Soviet allies which have special significance for the security of the ECE. The first is the flow of energy, oil and gas from Russia to ECE countries. Hungary and Poland, according to some estimates, get almost 90 per cent of their oil from Russia. Russia's share in ECE gas consumption is about 80 per cent,[27] 93 per cent in the Czech Republic and Slovakia, 63 per cent in Poland and 50 per cent in Hungary.[28] In spite of disparaging statements ('we can sell everywhere—we can buy everywhere') this energy transfer is beneficial to both sides. Russia has a stable market and the ECE countries save

[23] *Ekonomika i Zhizn*, no. 4 (Jan. 1993), p. 15.

[24] *Business Segodnya*, 25 Jan. 1994.

[25] Deutsche Bank, *Rebuilding Eastern Europe* (Deutsche Bank: Frankfurt, 1 Mar. 1991), p. 86.

[26] Pichugin (note 16), p. 71.

[27] Larrabee, F. S., *Democratization and Change in Eastern Europe*, RAND/RP-112 (RAND Corporation: Santa Monica, Calif., 1992), p. 155.

[28] *Business Segodnya*, no. 22 (10 Mar. 1994).

a good deal of money on the transport of oil and gas by pipeline.[29] This transfer brings with it a degree of interdependence which, depending on circumstances, can be positive as well as negative. ECE countries are uneasy about reliability of supply and many politicians and economists in the region were concerned about the effect the violent events in Moscow of October 1993 might have on the energy supply of their countries; Russia, however, depends on this trade for the foreign exchange earnings it assures. Russian gas, moreover, is delivered to Western Europe via the territories of some ECE countries (a new pipeline is to be laid across Poland). Russia prefers to see mainly the positive aspects of the interdependence, whereas ECE leaders are more worried about the negative ones. Interdependence demands stable and predictable economic relationships, which are difficult to expect in dealing with Russia at present. The attempts of some ECE countries to overcome this significant dependence upon Russia and diversify their energy supply are justified from the political and economic points of view. In Moscow, however, they are often seen as proof of the intention of the ECE to detach its economic security from Russia's. That is why this aspect of interaction is unlikely to be viewed by either side as a basis for *rapprochement*.

The second aspect of security interaction is arms transfers. Indeed, the armed forces of all the ECE countries are mainly equipped with Russian (Soviet) weapons.[30] In 1987–93, Czechoslovakia, Hungary and Poland bought Soviet (Russian) weapons worth $10 billion—mainly tanks, aircraft, helicopters, missiles and communication systems. Military procurement from the West during these years accounted for only 2.5 per cent of this volume.[31] In 1993 Hungary decided to buy 27 MiG-29 fighters in Russia. Maintenance of these weapons in working order entails a need for spare parts, renewal of arsenals and training. For years to come the ECE countries will need to cooperate with Russia in this field. Arms transfers could to some extent be a basis for a security partnership between Russia and the countries of the region.

At the same time they all hope to join NATO in the end. One of the consequences of this could be modernization of their arms to NATO standards. That means that the ECE will turn to the West to purchase new weapons. No doubt the process of rearmament will take years, but even so the reorientation will gradually but inevitably narrow the sphere of security arrangements between Russia and the region. Most probably this process will be seen differently in Moscow and the ECE capitals. The latter will see it as a natural effort to diversify their arms supply and to get rid of all-round reliance on one country. In Moscow it might be viewed as an intention to separate the security of Russia from that of the region as a whole.

---

[29] The price of Russian gas is two-thirds that of Norwegian gas.

[30] *SIPRI Yearbook 1992: World Armaments and Disarmament* (Oxford University Press: Oxford, 1992), pp. 311–14; and *SIPRI Yearbook 1993: World Armaments and Disarmament* (Oxford University Press: Oxford, 1993), pp. 479–82.

[31] See note 30.

There are other non-military aspects of security which are growing in importance in the post-cold war world and where cooperation between the ECE countries and Russia would be helpful. These new challenges include the threat of nuclear terrorism, smuggling of radioactive materials, accidents at nuclear power stations, other environmental disasters, ethnic intolerance, the possibility of large-scale migration and in particular growing concern about crime and the integration of national mafia structures. Russian mafias and their partners in the 'near abroad', the ECE and the West, unlike governments, easily find a way towards each other. No one knows how much 'dirty money' from abroad is laundered in Moscow or how much Russian dirty money is laundered in the ECE or the West.[32] Neither side has the structure or the tools to meet the challenges.

Unfortunately at the moment the political leaders of both Russia and the ECE are interested in cooperation on these non-military security issues in a limited way only. Both sides prefer to deal on these matters with the West rather than with each other. Even bilateral security problems are solved not by direct negotiations between the partners but in a roundabout way: the West is invited to be a judge or mediator. That leads to the further diminution of the area of Russia's and the ECE countries' security interaction.

VI. The new triangle: ECE–NATO–Russia

Even in a new situation the burden of the past or differences in political culture influence the attitudes of Russia's and the ECE countries' élites on security issues. Russia's attempts (often controversial) to find its new role in the post-Soviet space, to generate a process of integration there on a new basis or to be more active in peacekeeping in Eurasia are interpreted by the ECE political élites as a dangerous revival of Russian imperial thinking. Political leaders in the ECE contend that security in the region cannot be based on Russia's proclaimed intention because of the uncertain situation in the country and the manifest inclination of the Russian leadership to resort to force. The violence of September–October 1993 in Moscow and the war in Chechnya confirmed their fears. ECE analysts are compelled to proceed from the worst possible scenarios. The most important fact is not that Russia is ready to halve its armed forces to 1 500 000 servicemen,[33] but that the Russian Army will remain the largest in Europe, superior to all the ECE armed forces put together. That is why, in the security sphere as in the economic one, the ECE states are reorienting themselves to the West and trying to separate themselves from Russia. For instance,

---

[32] Journalist and investigator Yiriy Shchekochikhin argues that c. $17 billion have been deposited privately by unknown Russian citizens in US banks and c. $10 billion in Stockholm banks alone. See his interview in *Obshchaya Gazeta*, no. 36 (9–15 Sep. 1994).

[33] Grachev, P., 'Voennaya doktrina i bezopasnost Rossii' [The military doctrine and the security of Russia], *Nezavisimaya Gazeta*, 9 June 1994. See also chapter 8, section III, in this volume.

the Czech Republic, Hungary and Poland undertake joint military exercises with France, Germany, Sweden and even Ukraine but never with Russia.[34]

For many politicians in Russia it is difficult to acknowledge that, despite the process of democratization, new political thinking, its support of the velvet revolutions and its obsession with domestic problems, it can be viewed by the former Soviet allies as a possible threat. Russia cannot understand that in a situation of political turmoil and lack of civilian control over the army its forces might be seen by others as a danger. Russian politicians have traditionally neglected the ECE states' security needs and regarded the region as an integral part of a broader Russian security area. They believe that the position of Russia must be a decisive factor (some experts mean by this that it must have a right of veto) in all ECE security arrangements. Moreover, Russia believes that from the point of view of European (and world) security Russia is so important for the West that the latter is ready to disregard the ECE's own security concerns for the sake of better relations with Russia.

It is only natural that Russia views the whole problem of European security from the point of view of its own interests. It seems ready to take into account West European and US interests, to consider the prospects of its own relationship to NATO and to manifest pan-European thinking. In these schemes, however, there is no place for the ECE and its interests: they are omitted, forgotten, ignored, just as there was no place for the ECE in Gorbachev's 'common European home' which was to be built on two pillars—the Soviet Union and Western Europe. Is this a vestige of the arrogance of the Soviet *nomenklatura*, a manifestation of traditional imperial thinking or a lack of foreign policy professionalism? It is most probably the result of all these and it leads to a paradox— a complete lack of understanding of the fact that European security for Russia begins with the establishment of friendly, constructive, cooperative relations with the ECE countries. This is why, when the latter showed anxiety about their own security, concluded that in the present circumstances their security had to be bound to the West and decided to join NATO, the Russian establishment and public opinion responded with confusion or shock reminiscent of the panic behaviour of the Soviet *nomenklatura* when the problem of German unification emerged.

The intense debates in Russia on how to meet this challenge have concentrated on a number of essential questions: (*a*) whether the ECE countries will join NATO with Russia or without it; (*b*) whether membership of NATO for the ECE countries will jeopardize Russia's security; (*c*) whether membership of NATO will make the ECE (and NATO) more friendly or more hostile towards Russia; (*d*) how to make others respect Russia's security interests in the area; and (*e*) whether the West or the ECE would be more favourable to Russia's requirements.

There are no convincing answers to these questions. Moreover, Russia's stand on the issue of NATO membership for the ECE countries is very contro-

---

[34] Poland did exercise with Russia in Co-operative Venture '94.

versial, even on the official level,[35] not to mention that of public opinion. As a whole Russian society, being indifferent to world affairs, pays little attention to NATO and its enlargement, but the issue is often exploited by the political élite in the power struggle. The process of decision making goes on sometimes under the impact of factors which have nothing to do with the essential nature of the problem. For many politicians, the problem of the ECE is a good opportunity to demonstrate their devotion to the national interests of Russia simply by fearlessly defaming its former allies. In the legal sense, of course, Russia cannot object to the desire of independent ECE states to join NATO or stop them doing so; and politically the price of doing so would be too high. Russia would spoil its relations both with the ECE and with the West for years to come.

It is evident that at the moment Russia itself cannot become a full member of the alliance, if it ever could. There are also many internal and external reasons against its seeking to join NATO. There is no consensus on the issue in society at large or among the political élite. Generals fear that joining NATO would lead to the democratization of the army and increased civilian control over it. Some democratic experts see NATO as an organization without a future.[36] The West is very dubious about Russia's joining because it has no desire to take all Russia's troubles on its shoulders.

Some politicians and experts emphasize the other side of the issue. They contend that the enlargement of NATO to include the ECE countries and later, perhaps, Ukraine and the Baltic states is aimed against Russia, and draw the conclusion that Russia's security will once again have to be taken care of by expensive unilateral efforts. Furthermore, the absence of Russia from the defence community would mean that the threat, supposedly originating in Russia, would be tackled not in cooperation with it but by isolating it. Its security and its future would be separated from those of Europe. NATO's enlargement without Russia could lead to a situation in which the EU and the Western European Union (WEU) would also expand without Russia. It is the fear of being cut off from Europe that is behind Russia's stand on ECE membership of NATO.

The strategic and military objections to the ECE countries' joining NATO have been developed in a number of articles published by Russian analysts.[37] The most coherent were presented in the report on 'Prospects of NATO expansion and Russia's interests' prepared by the Foreign Intelligence Service and

---

[35] During his meeting with Lech Walesa in Aug. 1933, Boris Yeltsin actually accepted the principle of Poland's entry into NATO, but a month later he disavowed his own statement. Rerlez, J., 'Yeltsin seems to accept Polish bid for NATO', *New York Times*, 26 Aug. 1993; and Cohen, R., 'Yeltsin opposes expansion of NATO in Eastern Europe', *New York Times*, 2 Oct. 1993.

[36] Migranyan, A., 'Zachem vstupat, esli mozhno ne vstupat?' [Why join if it is possible not to?], *Nezavisimaya Gazeta*, 15 Mar. 1994.

[37] See, e.g., Chernov, V., 'Moskva dolzhna podumat dvazhdy' [Moscow must think twice], *Nezavisimaya Gazeta*, 23 Feb. 1994; Poklad, B., 'Partnerstvo dlya SShA' [Partnership for the USA], *Pravda*, 6 Apr. 1994; and Vlasov, Yu., 'Podobnoe partnerstvo ne dlya Rossii' [Partnership like this is not for Russia], *Pravda*, 15 Apr. 1994.

released in November 1993.[38] The authors of the report concluded that the entry of ECE countries into NATO would be contrary to Russia's national interests in general. They underlined that the prospects for the long-term development of NATO remain unclear and that there is no clear understanding within the alliance of its place and role after the cold war. According to the authors' view, many of Russia's concerns caused by ECE intentions to join NATO could be removed or softened if there were signs that the process of functional change in the alliance could precede its geographical expansion. The report points out that Western proposals to Russia about cooperation with the alliance do not amount to the emergence of a security structure adequate to the new conditions.

The costs for Russia of ECE entry into NATO are seen as follows. First, the approach of the world's largest military bloc up to Russia's borders would necessitate a reconsideration of all Russia's defensive concepts, the structure of its armed forces, the installation of additional infrastructure, redeployment of troops, and changes to operative plans and training. Second, implementation of these measures would naturally place strain on the military budget at the expense of some urgent programmes, generally weakening the country's security. Third, Russian military reform would be put in jeopardy and social tension in the armed forces would increase. Fourth, nationalist and anti-reformist forces will intensify their campaign against the ECE and the West. Finally, the 1990 Treaty on Conventional Armed Forces in Europe (the CFE Treaty) would become irrelevant because the ECE countries' joining NATO would change the balance of power in Europe fixed by that treaty.

The advocates of these views contend that the inclusion of the ECE countries in NATO and their feeling more confident as a result would strengthen their anti-Russian potential. Moreover, they may actuate anti-Russian sentiment in the alliance itself. Many of these arguments are convincing for a significant part of Russian society, especially for those who share the view that after the disintegration of the Soviet Union the country's national interests have been neglected by many international actors, former 'loyal allies' included.

The politicians and experts of European (liberal) orientation, looking for closer cooperation with Western security structures, see no serious objections to the ECE's entry into NATO. They point out that Russia already has a common border with NATO in the northern part of the Kola Peninsula; the Soviet Union had a common border with Turkey. Even if the ECE countries join NATO there will be a belt of states (the Baltic states, Belarus, Moldova and Ukraine) which constitute a buffer zone between Russia and the alliance. A new possible and limited common border with NATO in the Kaliningrad area will not change the situation radically. They maintain that the inclusion in NATO of some ECE countries which see an unstable Russia as a danger can reduce their fears and relieve them of their inferiority complex and deep distrust towards their huge neighbour. They may feel more confident and be more willing to cooperate

<hr>

[38] 'Opravdano li rasshirenie NATO?' [Is NATO expansion justified?], *Nezavisimaya Gazeta*, 26 Nov. 1993.

with Russia on equal terms in different spheres, security included. Russia cannot be isolated from Europe; everything that is going on in Russia directly affects the situation on the continent.[39] Few European problems can be solved if Russia is opposed and Europe will not aim to separate itself from Russia because it has a direct interest in influencing its modernization. At the same time liberals point out that the ECE countries' entry into NATO will make sense only if Russia and NATO share responsibility for the security of Europe. The building of the new security structure takes time, which is why advocates of this view would prefer their joining NATO to be postponed.[40]

How far do the arguments of the two sides affect the official line? The refusal of Russia's Foreign Minister in December 1994 to sign the Russia–NATO protocol on cooperation in the framework of the Partnership for Peace (PFP) programme made it manifest that Russia had decided to do its best to block or at least to delay the process of the ECE joining NATO. The Protocol was signed in May 1995, but at the same time Moscow confirmed that the signing did not mean that Russia had ceased to oppose the enlargement of NATO. Moreover, it tried to create the impression that NATO enlargement would suspend Russia's participation in the PFP.

This double stand is a consequence of an internal power struggle and the growing weakness of a government in retreat under pressure from the hard-liners: it is not a balanced choice. Any government strong enough to ignore a power struggle could change Russia's approach to the issue. Unfortunately Russia's approach to security relations with the ECE is being shaped not by a clear assessment of national interests, the objective needs of defence or a sound understanding of the region's role in Russia's European policy, but under the influence of this power struggle, and its relations with the ECE, in the security field as in others, follow all the zigzags of internal politics. That is why it would be premature to expect good sense to prevail in Russia's approach to security relations with the ECE.

At the same time it is important for the outside world to realize that in general there is a certain consensus within Russia as to the undesirability of the ECE joining NATO at the moment. To hold out the prospect of NATO expanding to include the ECE countries would require simultaneous attempts to address Russia's real and alleged concerns about the future of European security. Otherwise the stated assumptions of all Western security policies—that Russia

---

[39] The technical accident at the nickel-steel plant in Norilsk in Dec. 1994 led immediately to a leap in nickel prices on the London Stock Exchange.

[40] Kozin, V., 'Moskva dolzhna prisoedinitsya k "Partnerstvu vo imya mira"' [Moscow must join the Partnership for Peace], *Nezavisimaya Gazeta*, 15 Feb. 1994; Davydov, Yu., 'Rossiya mozhet "prodat" svoe soglasie na rasshirenie NATO' [Russia can bargain on NATO enlargement], *Segodnya*, 24 Mar. 1995; Gaidar, Ye., 'Rossiya XXI veka: ne mirovoy zhandarm, a forpost demokratii v Evroazii' [Russia in the 21st century: not a world policeman but a pillar of democracy in Eurasia], *Izvestiya*, 18 May 1995; Ryzhkin, E., 'Protiv rasshireniya NATO vozrazhaet menee poloviny oproshennykh moskvichey' [Less than half of respondents in Moscow are against NATO enlargement], *Segodnya*, 9 June 1995; Chistov, A., 'NATO kak fenomen kultury' [NATO as a cultural phenomenon], *Segodnya*, 14 June 1995; and Fedorov, B., *Vpered, Rossiya! Liberalny plan dlya Rossii* [Forward, Russia! A liberal plan for Russia] (Dvizhenie 'Vpered, Rossiya!': Moscow, 1995), pp. 19–20.

is in some meaningful sense a security partner and that substantial decisions affecting its security should therefore not be made without full consideration of Russian interests, including detailed consultations with Moscow—could be considered in Russia as meaningless.

Whether it is actually possible to isolate Russia or not is another matter. One thing is clear: an isolated or self-isolated Russia would inevitably slip into authoritarian rule and be more dangerous to its neighbours and Europe than one which is involved in cooperative international structures. If providing security is important to enhance the ECE democracies, then the same must be true for Russia's fragile democratic experiment. Assistance in democratizing Russia should be one of the West's top strategic priorities. If democratic changes succeed in Russia, then there is no legitimate reason to keep it outside a united Europe. A close security partnership with democratic Russia could be one of the strongest guarantees of the prosperity and stability of the ECE itself.

VII. Conclusions

The lack of cohesion between Russia and the ECE states on security issues and attempts, perhaps unconscious, by some ECE political leaders to divide the homogeneous European security space into two halves could lead to a result very different from that expected. Even the discussion on this issue has widened the misunderstanding between Russia and the countries of the region. Meanwhile, security relations between Russia and the ECE are vital not only for them but for the whole of Europe and Eurasia in general.

It is clear that this security dilemma cannot be solved against Russia, without Russia or at the expense of Russia. It is also evident that it cannot be solved on a bilateral (Russia–ECE) level. The lack of a common understanding and security arrangements between Russia and the ECE leads to lack of understanding and security arrangements between Russia and the rest of Europe. The problem could become the main obstacle to the emergence of an all-European (or Eurasian, with US and Canadian participation) security system.

Perhaps the solution can be found in a broader security context which could emerge from an eventual *rapprochement* between all the security structures in Europe. One possible choice which might meet the security needs of all participants could be the following. The ECE countries, after a period of adaptation, could join NATO as full members. Simultaneously Russia and a renovated NATO would sign a treaty which could be based on mutual security guarantees and adequate mechanisms for close cooperation in the political and military spheres and joint action when necessary. At the same time Russia could develop and consolidate its own collective security arrangements with some post-Soviet states who would like to join it on the pattern of the security relationship between the USA and Latin America. Ukraine, if it disagrees with such a choice, could find its own way to participate in the new security structure. The Organization for Security and Co-operation in Europe (OSCE) could operate as a political umbrella for the broad security system. In the last analysis the realization of this scheme could pave the way for the emergence of a comprehensive security zone in the northern hemisphere in the framework of which all other controversial national and regional security problems (such as that between Russia and the ECE) would have better chances of solution.

Part IX

The Balkan connection

Background chronology: Russia and the former Yugoslavia

1991

31 July   The Soviet and US presidents issue a joint declaration on Yugoslavia calling for respect for the principles of the Helsinki Final Act

25 Sep.   The UN Security Council votes to impose an arms embargo on all warring parties in the former Yugoslavia

1992

6 Mar.   In response to the UN Secretary-General's request, Russia agrees to contribute 900 airborne troops to the UN peacekeeping force in the former Yugoslavia

30 May   In a shift in policy towards Yugoslavia, Russia votes in UN Security Council in favour of imposing economic sanctions against Serbia

28 June   Russian diplomatic efforts to mediate between Serbia and the UN Security Council result in the Security Council deciding not to consider delivery of a military ultimatum to Serbia

5 Aug.   Russia recognizes the independence of the Former Yugoslav Republic of Macedonia despite Western reluctance to do so

1993

23 Feb.   Russia puts forward an 8-point proposal to resolve the Yugoslav crisis, calling for a halt to all fighting, adoption of the Vance–Owen Plan, the lifting of sanctions against Serbia and support for the establishment of a multinational UN-sponsored force. It suggests that it would consider sending troops to support the force and would agree to NATO's involvement

27 Apr.   In an effort to pressure the Bosnian Serbs, President Yeltsin states that Russia 'will not protect those who set themselves in opposition to the world community'

29 June   Together with France and the UK, Russia blocks (by abstaining) a vote in the UN Security Council to lift the arms embargo on the Bosnian Government

12 Nov.   Russian Deputy Foreign Minister Churkin begins intensive shuttle diplomacy between the leaders in Belgrade, Pale, Sarajevo and Zagreb

1994

21 Jan.   Russian State Duma passes by a wide margin a resolution opposing NATO air strikes in Bosnia and calling for the lifting of sanctions against Serbia

17 Feb.   Following a NATO ultimatum to the Bosnian Serbs and to prevent NATO air strikes against their positions, Russian peacekeeping troops are moved to the heavy-weapon exclusion zone around Sarajevo and Bosnian Serbs begin withdrawing weapons from the zone

26 Apr.   The Contact Group (France, Germany, Russia, the UK and the USA) is formed to coordinate international efforts to settle the Bosnian conflict

2 Dec.   Russia vetoes extension of the sanctions against the Bosnian Serbs in the UN Security Council

5–6 Dec.   At the CSCE summit meeting in Budapest, Russia blocks the introduction into a final document of a statement on Bosnia assigning guilt to the Serbian side in the conflict

1995

21 Nov.   After several weeks of intense US-sponsored negotiations in Dayton, Ohio, leaders of the 3 warring parties in Bosnia initial a comprehensive peace plan

28 Nov.   Russian and NATO defence officials agree to an arrangement under which 1600 Russian troops will participate in the NATO-led Implementation Force (IFOR) to enforce the Dayton peace agreement; they are to operate under US rather than NATO command

1996

27 Feb.   Serbia and Russia sign an agreement on military–technical cooperation to come into effect upon the lifting of international sanctions against Serbia

Background chronology: Russia and the conflict in Moldova

1990

3 Sep.   Separatists in the Trans-Dniester region proclaim secession from the Moldovan SSR and declare it a new republic within the USSR

1992

1 Mar   Fighting erupts on left bank of Dniester River when armed separatists attack Moldovan police stations

22 June   Town of Bendery recaptured from Moldovan forces by Trans-Dniestrian insurgents with help from units of Russia's 14th Army

21 July   Russian President Yeltsin and Moldovan President Snegur sign accord to end fighting in eastern Moldova; accord envisages granting special status to the Trans-Dniester area and reaffirms inviolability of present borders

29 July   Trilateral Moldovan, Russian and 'Trans-Dniestrian' peacekeeping force begins to operate in Moldova

1993

15 May   Yeltsin and Snegur reach agreement in principle on the withdrawal of the Russian 14th Army from the Trans-Dniester region

1994

8 Apr.   Moldovan Parliament ratifies membership in the CIS

21 Oct.   Russia and Moldova sign an agreement for the withdrawal of Russian armed forces from Moldova within 3 years; agreement awaits ratification

1995

27 June   Moldovan officials rule out allowing Russia to establish a military base in Moldova

24 Dec.   Voters in the Trans-Dniester region overwhelmingly approve a new constitution that proclaims the region an independent state

---

Key facts

Separatism in the Trans-Dniester region of Moldova

The area of land on the left bank of the Dniester River had the status of autonomous republic within the Ukrainian Soviet Socialist Republic until 1940, when it was united with Bessarabia following the USSR's annexation of the latter from Romania. The status of the new entity was upgraded and Moldavia became one of the constituent republics of the USSR in 1944. Approximately two-thirds of Moldova's population consists of ethnic Romanians. After the collapse of the USSR in 1991 the issue of whether Moldova should join Romania quickly moved to the top of the local political agenda. Popular demands within Moldova for unification with Romania fuelled a strong separatist movement in the Trans-Dniester region, the population of which has a considerably higher proportion of ethnic Slavs (25% Russian and 28% Ukrainian). Separatist sentiments in the Trans-Dniester region have been further spurred by the efforts of local élites to preserve their privileged positions.

Russian troops in the Trans-Dniester region

From the 30 000 Soviet troops that were stationed in Moldova, the strength of Russia's 14th Army deployed in the Trans-Dniester region has dropped to *c*. 6000 troops. Units of the 14th Army (renamed the Operational Group of Russian forces in summer 1995), which are manned primarily by local inhabitants, viewed the separatist activities in the region sympathetically and were accused by the Moldovan Government of aiding them. Russia has agreed in principle to withdraw its forces, contingent upon a satisfactory political settlement in the Trans-Dniester region. At the same time Russian officials have raised the question of establishing a Russian military base in Moldova.

18. Russia and the Balkans: old themes and new challenges

F. Stephen Larrabee

I. Introduction

Historically the Balkans have been a major focal point of Russian policy.[1] In the 19th century, especially after the Crimean War, Russia actively strove to increase its influence in the Balkans as part of the growing rivalry with Austria and, to a lesser extent, Germany. This strategic rivalry was given a strong impetus and emotional overtone by the growth of pan-Slavic sentiment in Russia and throughout the Balkans.

With the end of the cold war the Balkans have resurfaced as a focal point of Russian concern. Russia has begun to define its own national interests and develop its own 'Russian' foreign policy. Developments in the Balkans, especially the former Yugoslavia, have played a central role in this process. Indeed, policy towards the former Yugoslavia has been an important issue in the Russian foreign policy debate.

This chapter examines Russia's recent policy towards the Balkans. It focuses in particular on Russian involvement in the Yugoslav conflict and the role that conflict has played in the Russian internal debate over foreign policy. The final section analyses the broader implications of Russia's Balkan policy for the country's relations with the West.

II. Russian interests in historical perspective

Current Russian policy in the Balkans must be viewed against the background of Russia's historical role and interests in the region. Historically Russia has had two main interests in the Balkans. The first has been strategic. Tsarist leaders saw the Balkans as essential to Russian security and the stability of its frontiers. They sought to obtain both a favourable frontier in Bessarabia and a dominant position in the south, including control of the Dardanelle Straits. By the middle of the 19th century, moreover, the Dardanelles had become important to Russia's commercial and economic development, particularly for the shipment of surplus grain to world markets. At the same time Russia sought to

---

[1] For a discussion of the historical dimensions of Russian interest in the Balkans, see Jelavich, C., *Tsarist Russia and Balkan Nationalism* (University of California Press: Berkeley and Los Angeles, Calif., 1962); and Geyer, D., *Russian Imperialism: The Interaction of Domestic and Foreign Policy, 1860–1914* (Yale University Press: New Haven, Conn. and London, 1987), especially pp. 49–121.

block the expansion of other powers, especially Austria–Hungary and Germany, into the region.

The second interest was religious and cultural. In the 1870s, largely because of pan-Slav agitation and the ongoing disintegration of the Ottoman Empire, Russia developed a strong interest in the fate of the Balkan Slavs and Christians. While pan-Slavism was never the dominant driving force behind Russian policy in the Balkans in the 19th century, it exerted a considerable influence on many intellectuals and found support in some official circles. Strategic interests—above all a desire for control of the Dardanelles—remained, however, the main driving force behind Russian policy.[2]

Russian interest in the Balkans continued after the Bolsheviks seized power in October 1917. While the Soviet regime jettisoned the previous tsarist emphasis on pan-Slavism and Orthodoxy, it continued to seek control over the Dardanelles. In the discussions that led up to the Hitler–Stalin Pact signed in 1939, Soviet Foreign Minister Vyacheslav Molotov claimed that the Dardanelles were part of Russia's 'security zone' and demanded the right to establish land and naval bases in the vicinity of the Bosphorus Sea and the Dardanelles.[3] These demands were raised again by Stalin after World War II.

Stalin's demands on the Straits were part of a larger effort to exploit the geopolitical vacuum in the region after World War II in an attempt to expand Soviet influence in the Balkans. This effort was reflected in the attempt to establish Soviet control over Bulgaria and Romania; the raising of claims against the Turkish provinces of Kars and Ardahan; and the support for the communists in Yugoslavia and Greece.[4] Stalin's policy, however, was motivated more by considerations of power politics than by ideology. He wanted obedient clients who would subordinate their interests to those of the Soviet Union, and did not trust movements or leaders—whether communist or not—who were not under strict Soviet control.

He therefore gave only limited support to the Greek communists and advocated the ending of the Greek Civil War (1946–49), fearing that it would provoke US intervention and diminish his chances of consolidating his hold on those parts of the Balkans (Bulgaria and Romania) where Soviet power, backed by the Red Army, was already firmly entrenched.[5] Similar concerns guided Stalin's attitude towards the idea of a Balkan federation, which would include Bulgaria and Yugoslavia. Initially Stalin favoured the idea, but he later changed

---

[2] Lederer, I. J., 'Russia and the Balkans', ed. I. J. Lederer, *Russian Foreign Policy* (Yale University Press: New Haven, Conn., 1962), pp. 417–52. See also Jelavich, B., *The Ottoman Empire, the Great Powers and the Straits Question* (Indiana University Press: Bloomington, Ind. and London, 1973).

[3] Lederer (note 2), p. 423.

[4] For background, see Brown, J. F., *Nationalism, Democracy and Security in the Balkans* (Aldershot: Dartmouth, 1992), pp. 3–16.

[5] In Feb. 1949, for instance, Stalin told a group of Yugoslav communists that the Greek uprising 'had no chance for success at all' and 'must be stopped'. Djilas, M., *Conversations with Stalin* (Harcourt, Brace: New York, 1962), p. 182. For a discussion of Stalin's policy towards Greece at this time, see Stavrakis, P. J., *Moscow and Greek Communism 1944–1949* (Cornell University Press: Ithaca, N.Y., 1989).

his view, fearing that such a federation would be dominated by Yugoslavia and would thereby strengthen Tito's influence.

Tito's increasingly independent course led to a growing conflict with Stalin and to Yugoslavia's expulsion from the Cominform[6] in 1948. Thereafter the USSR sought to consolidate its hold over the Balkans, stepping up the Sovietization process in Albania, Bulgaria and Romania. These efforts, however, ran counter to the growing trend towards nationalism within the communist-ruled parts of the Balkans in the late 1950s and early 1960s.[7] Albania defected from the Soviet camp in 1961, becoming a de facto Chinese client state. Romania began to pursue an increasingly autonomous foreign policy after 1964, while Yugoslavia openly joined the Non-Aligned Movement. Thus by the mid-1960s only Bulgaria remained firmly within the Soviet sphere of influence in the Balkans.

The decline of its influence in the Balkans after 1960 increased the USSR's interest in maintaining a tight hold over Bulgaria. The USSR poured an enormous amount of economic aid and assistance into Bulgaria over the following two decades.[8] This assistance was primarily designed to bind Bulgaria closely to the Soviet Union and ensure the country's support for broader Soviet foreign policy objectives. The strategy was largely successful. Until 1989, when Bulgarian communist leader Todor Zhivkov was ousted from power, Bulgaria remained a loyal and obedient Soviet client, acting, in effect, as the USSR's 'cat's paw' in the Balkans.

In particular, Bulgaria served as a useful proxy for putting pressure on Yugoslavia, especially through the 'Macedonian Question'.[9] The Macedonian Question was often a good barometer of Soviet–Yugoslav relations. When relations were good, the polemics between Bulgaria and Yugoslavia over Macedonia tended to subside; when they were strained, the polemics picked up. It would be misleading, however, to imply that the polemics were totally directed from Moscow. Bulgaria had its own interests in Macedonia. The Macedonian issue served as a useful outlet for the expression of Bulgarian nationalism and a means to increase the Bulgarian regime's legitimacy. However, the polemics

---

[6] The Communist Information Bureau.

[7] For a detailed discussion of the impact of nationalism on the communist Balkans at this time, see Lendvai, P., *Eagles in the Cobwebs* (Anchor Books: New York, 1969).

[8] For a detailed discussion, see Brown, J. F., *Bulgaria Under Communist Rule* (Praeger: New York, 1970), especially pp. 297–300.

[9] Macedonia, parts of which lie in Bulgaria, Greece and the former Yugoslavia, has been a source of discord in the Balkans for centuries. At various times, Bulgaria, Serbia, Greece and Albania have all laid claim to all or parts of the area. For a good historical overview of the Macedonian question, see Barker, E., *Macedonia: Its Place in Balkan Power Politics* (Royal Institute of International Affairs: London, 1950); and Palmer, S. and King, R. L., *Yugoslav Communism and the Macedonian Question* (Shoestring Press: Hamden, Conn., 1971). For more recent treatments, see Kaplan, R., 'History's cauldron', *Atlantic Monthly*, June 1991, pp. 92–104; and Perry, D., 'Macedonia: a Balkan problem and a European dilemma', Radio Free Europe/Radio Liberty (hereafter RFE/RL), *RFE/RL Research Report*, 19 June 1992, pp. 35–45. For Greek perspectives, see Kofos, E., *Nationalism and Communism in Macedonia* (Institute of Balkan Studies: Thessaloniki, 1964); and selections in *Macedonia, Past and Present* (Institute of Balkan Studies: Thessaloniki, 1992).

could hardly have continued if the Soviet Union had not felt that they served its larger strategic interests.

At the same time the Soviet Union never completely gave up hope of being able to woo Yugoslavia back into its orbit. It had two main interests. The first was strategic—to gain access to Yugoslav ports in the Adriatic—but Soviet policy also had an important ideological dimension. Yugoslavia, with its system of self-management and emphasis on non-alignment, represented an alternative model of socialism and posed an ideological challenge to the USSR, one which the Soviet leadership feared might find appeal in Eastern Europe. With the intensification of Yugoslavia's economic difficulties after Tito's death, however, the attractiveness of the Yugoslav model declined significantly—as did the danger that the Yugoslav 'virus' might infect the rest of Eastern Europe.

The Soviet threat played an important role in internal Yugoslav politics. To a large extent, it acted as the 'glue' that kept Yugoslavia together. Whenever ethnic differences or separatist pressures threatened to get out of hand—as during the Croatian crisis in 1970–71—Tito invoked the threat of possible Soviet intervention.[10] This had a sobering impact and served to dampen separatist pressures. However, Soviet President Mikhail Gorbachev's more flexible foreign policy deprived the Yugoslav leadership of the Soviet threat as an instrument for maintaining internal cohesion and control. Once this threat could no longer be credibly invoked, separatist pressures quickly escalated, leading eventually to the country's disintegration in 1990–91.[11]

III. Moscow and the Yugoslav conflict

With the end of the cold war and the disintegration of the former Yugoslavia, the Balkans have re-emerged as a focal point of Russian interest. Russia's policy in the Balkans cannot, however, be seen in isolation. The debate there on policy towards the former Yugoslavia has been part of a larger debate over

[10] The Croatian crisis had its origins in the disappointment in Croatia with the results of the economic reform introduced in Yugoslavia in the late 1960s. Many Croats came to believe that the reform had not benefited Croatia but simply led to the concentration of economic power in Belgrade. Disappointment with economic reform spilled over into the cultural and political arena during 1970–71 and led to a revival of Croat nationalism, which soon infected the top leadership of the Croatian League of Communists, headed by Savka Dabcevic-Kucar and Miko Tripalo. Under pressure from the Serbian party leadership and conservatives within the Croatian party leadership, Tito intervened in Dec. 1971 and purged the top leadership of the Croatian party. For a good discussion of the crisis and its background, see Ramet, S. P., *Nationalism and Federalism in Yugoslavia, 1962–1991* (Indiana University Press: Bloomington, Ind. and Indianapolis, Ind., 1992), pp. 98–135.

[11] A discussion of Yugoslavia's breakup and its causes is beyond the scope of this essay. For a detailed analysis, see Cviic, C., 'The unmaking of a Federation', ed. F. S. Larrabee, *The Volatile Powder Keg: Balkan Security After the Cold War* (American University Press: Washington, DC, 1994), pp. 89–118. For more detailed treatments, see Glenny, M., *The Fall of Yugoslavia* (Penguin: London, 1992); Denitch, B., *Ethnic Nationalism: the Tragic Death of Yugoslavia* (University of Minnesota Press: Minneapolis, Minn. and London, 1994); and Lukic, R. and Lynch, A., SIPRI, *Europe from the Balkans to the Urals: The Disintegration of Yugoslavia and the Soviet Union* (Oxford University Press: Oxford, 1996), pp. 144–73.

Russia's national interests.[12] The outcome of this debate is likely to have a significant impact on Russia's foreign policy orientation over the next decade, especially its relations with the West.

Initially the Soviet Union adopted a low profile in the Yugoslav crisis. The Soviet leadership was preoccupied with its own internal problems and like the USA it was prepared to allow the European Community (EC) to take the lead in trying to resolve the crisis, especially since the USA showed little inclination to get deeply involved. In fact, during this period a strong coincidence of interests existed between Moscow and Washington. Both feared that the disintegration of Yugoslavia would set a dangerous precedent that could have a destabilizing impact elsewhere, especially in the USSR. As a result, both countries cooperated closely behind the scenes in an attempt to prevent the collapse of Yugoslavia and contain any possible spillover.[13]

The collapse of the USSR did not initially have a significant impact on this cooperation, which continued during the first six months of 1992. The high point of the cooperation was reached with the Russian support of UN sanctions against Serbia on 29 May 1992. Russian support for Western policy on Yugoslavia, however, provoked a strong backlash within Russia. Many nationalists, as well as some democrats, openly criticized Russia's cooperation with the West, accusing the then Foreign Minister, Andrey Kozyrev, of betraying Serbia, a traditional Russian ally. [14]

The attacks on Kozyrev's policy towards Yugoslavia were part of a larger domestic struggle between the Foreign Ministry and the Supreme Soviet over the control of Russian foreign policy. Many members of the Supreme Soviet were highly critical of Russia's support for UN sanctions against Serbia. Among the strongest critics was Yevgeniy Ambartsumov, the Chairman of the parliament's Committee for International Affairs and Foreign Economic Relations. In June 1992, for instance, Ambartsumov took Kozyrev to task for slavishly following the US line. 'It would hardly seem obligatory', he asserted, 'that Russia, which naturally has its own interests, duplicate the US position in all aspects'.[15]

Together with Oleg Rumyantsev, the Executive Secretary of the parliament's Constitutional Commission, Ambartsumov conducted his own parallel foreign policy designed to bolster support for Serbia and put pressure on the Russian

[12] For a detailed discussion of this debate, see Crow, S., 'Russia debates its national interests', *RFE/RL Research Report*, 10 July 1992, pp. 43–46; Rahr, A., 'Atlanticists vs. Eurasians in Russian foreign policy', *RFE/RL Research Report*, 29 May 1992, pp. 17–22; and Crow, S., 'Competing blueprints for Russian foreign policy', *RFE/RL Research Report*, 18 Dec. 1992, pp. 45–50.

[13] For a detailed discussion of Russian and US policy during this period, see Larrabee, F. S., 'Washington, Moscow and the Balkans: strategic retreat or re-engagement', ed. Larrabee (note 11), pp. 201–18.

[14] For details, see Lynch, A. and Lukic, R., 'Russian foreign policy and the wars in the former Yugoslavia', *RFE/RL Research Report*, 15 Oct. 1993, pp. 25–29; Crow, S., 'Reading Moscow's policies toward rump Yugoslavia', *RFE/RL Research Report*, 6 Nov. 1992, pp. 3–19; and Crow, S., 'Russia's response to the Yugoslav crisis', *RFE/RL Research Report*, 24 July 1994, pp. 31–35.

[15] *Izvestiya*, 29 June 1992. For a broader discussion of Ambartsumov's role and influence on Russian foreign policy during this period, see Crow, S., 'Ambartsumov's influence on Russia's foreign policy', *RFE/RL Research Report*, 7 May 1993, pp. 36–41.

Government to pursue a more openly pro-Serb policy. In August 1992, just before the UN vote on the use of military force to guarantee the delivery of humanitarian aid (13 August) and the International Conference on Former Yugoslavia in London (26–28 August), Ambartsumov and Rumyantsev visited Serbia, where they had talks with all major Serb leaders. On his return Ambartsumov disparaged Western reports of concentration camps in Serbia, dismissing them as 'myths' and efforts to sow disinformation designed to discredit the Serbs.[16]

Ambartsumov's criticism was part of a broader debate on Russia's foreign policy orientation and national interests. Two broad schools of thought have emerged in this debate. The first emphasizes the importance of Russia's long-standing ethnic, cultural and religious ties with the peoples of the Balkans, especially the Serbs; the second stresses the importance of good ties to the West and integrating Russia into a broader Euro-Atlantic framework. The debate reflects themes that date back to the disputes between pan-Slavists and Westernizers in the late 19th century. Like their predecessors, modern pan-Slavists constitute a small but vocal minority. They argue that Russia's policy in the Balkans, and the former Yugoslavia in particular, should be guided by assistance to Russia's Slav brethren, especially the Serbs, rather than cooperation with the West. Moreover, like their pan-Slavist predecessors, they see Germany and Turkey as key rivals which are intent on expanding their influence in the Balkans.

The most vocal spokesman of the pro-Serb pan-Slav lobby has been Vladimir Zhirinovsky, the ultra-nationalist leader of the Liberal Democratic Party. During a visit to Serbia at the end of January 1994 Zhirinovsky bluntly warned that any attack on Serbia would be tantamount to an attack on Russia itself and called for a union of Slavic peoples from 'Knin to Vladivostok'.[17] He also advocated a radical revision of the territorial map of Europe, especially in the Balkans; in this conception, the new order in the Balkans would be based on a 'Slavic pyramid'. Bosnia and Herzegovina would be divided between a Greater Serbia and a Greater Croatia. A Greater Macedonia would be created with its capital in Sofia, and Greece would be given parts of European Turkey. Hungary would also get back Transylvania.[18]

Kozyrev, the main proponent of the 'Atlanticist' school, tended to play down the idea of Russia as the protector of the Slavs in the Balkans. Initially he emphasized the importance of cooperating with the West and explicitly rejected a policy based on ethnic and religious ties. However, from mid-1992, under pressure from the nationalists and some influential democrats such as

[16] Crow, S., 'Competing blueprints . . . ' (note 12), p. 14.
[17] Pomfret, J., 'Bosnian Serbs hail Russian nationalist', *Washington Post*, 2 Feb. 1994; and 'Vladimir Zhirinovski, chantre de la "Grande Serbie"' [Vladimir Zhirinovsky, enthusiast of a 'Greater Serbia'], *Le Monde*, 2 Feb. 1994.
[18] Zhirinovsky's interview in *Globus* (Zagreb), 4 Feb. 1994, pp. 8, 47. Reprinted in Foreign Broadcast Information Service, *Daily Report—Eastern Europe (FBIS-EEU)*, FBIS-EEU-94-024, 4 Feb. 1994, pp. 39–41; and the map of the 'New Europe' drawn and signed by Zhirinovsky in *The European*, 4–10 Feb. 1994, p. 1 and reprinted in *Le Monde*, 29 Jan. 1994.

Ambartsumov and Vladimir Lukin, Ambartsumov's successor as head of the Foreign Affairs Committee of the Russian Duma, Kozyrev was forced to moderate his pro-Western policy and show greater deference to Serb interests.

The shift in Russian policy towards the former Yugoslavia has been part of a broader shift in Russian policy, since mid-1992, in a more nationalist direction.[19] This shift has been reflected, in particular, in Russia's policy towards the 'near abroad'. Indeed, many of Kozyrev's statements in 1994–95 sounded like caricatures of his controversial speech at the Stockholm Council Meeting of the Conference on Security and Co-operation in Europe (CSCE) in December 1992, when to the shock of his Western counterparts he made a highly belligerent and nationalist presentation, which he later recanted, saying that it had only been a joke designed to warn his Western colleagues about the dangers they would face if the nationalists gained ascendancy in Russia.

The more nationalist tone adopted by Kozyrev was dictated largely by the shift in the domestic centre of gravity in Russia in a more nationalist direction. This shift cut the ground from under Kozyrev's Atlanticist policy and forced him to adopt much of the rhetoric—and at times, some of the substance—of the nationalists' agenda, not only on Bosnia and Herzegovina but on other issues as well, particularly policy towards the 'near abroad'. Behind the scenes, however, Kozyrev continued to try to find a middle ground between his earlier unabashed Atlanticism and the more extreme demands of the nationalists, in order to avoid an open break with the West over Bosnia and Herzegovina.

In effect, the Bosnian issue became a political football in the domestic struggle for power in Russia. The nationalists used the issue as a weapon to attack President Yeltsin in an effort to weaken him politically.[20] Kozyrev became the lightning conductor for their attacks and a symbol in their eyes of Russian weakness and capitulation to the West. At the same time Kozyrev's increasingly nationalistic pronouncements undermined his credibility in the West and reduced his effectiveness. Kozyrev was finally forced to resign in January 1996. His replacement, Yevgeniy Primakov, the former head of the Foreign Intelligence Service and a skilled bureaucratic inflighter, has proved more capable of conducting a coherent foreign policy.

Russia's policy towards the conflict in the former Yugoslavia has had several broad objectives: (a) to prevent Russia's diplomatic isolation and avoid an open break with the West; (b) to defuse and deflect pressure from both the nationalists and the pro-Serb lobby in the Duma; (c) to ensure that Russia remains a major player in the Balkan game; (d) to prevent NATO from 'imposing' a solution that would exclude Russia; (e) to ensure that the UN, where Russia is a member of the Security Council, is the main international forum for discussion

---

[19] For a good discussion of the reasons behind this shift, see Pushkov, A., 'Russia and America: the honeymoon's over', *Foreign Policy,* winter 1993–94, pp. 76–90.

[20] As Sergei Karaganov, a member of Yeltsin's Presidential Council, put it, 'Almost nobody is interested in Serbia here, but the opposition is playing it up to make things difficult for the administration and the administration has to bow to that'. Cited in Gowers, A., 'Russia attacks UN vote on Serbs', *Financial Times,* 20 Apr. 1993.

and implementation of policy towards the former Yugoslavia; and (*f*) to prevent a spillover of the fighting.

The main objective, however, was to avoid diplomatic marginalization and prevent a NATO-imposed solution to the conflict. NATO's ultimatum of 10 February 1994 establishing a 20-km radius heavy-weapon exclusion zone around Sarajevo, for instance, put President Yeltsin in a very difficult position domestically. The ultimatum caused an uproar in the Duma and was sharply condemned not only by the nationalists but also by many moderate democrats. This left Yeltsin little choice but to initially oppose the ultimatum. The Russian Government's opposition, however, was not primarily motivated by pro-Serb sympathy but by the fear of exclusion. Russia objected to the fact that the air strikes would be carried out *by NATO*, which virtually ensured that Russia would have no role in the decision-making process.[21]

In short, Russian diplomacy was aimed not so much at blocking the air strikes *per se* but at ensuring that they were carried out under the auspices of the UN, where Russia had a voice and veto through membership in the Security Council, rather than under NATO control. As Anatoliy Adamishin, then Russian First Deputy Foreign Minister, bluntly put it, 'This is not a matter for NATO. It's a task for the UN'.[22] Once it became clear that the strikes would take place under the overall authority of the UN, Russia eased its opposition.[23]

The subsequent Russian mediation effort, which resulted in the Bosnian Serbs' agreement in late February 1994 to comply with the ultimatum in return for the dispatch of 800 Russian peacekeeping troops to Sarajevo, must be seen against this background. The mediation effort was a clear diplomatic triumph for Russia. It offered the Serbs a face-saving way of complying with the ultimatum and avoiding retribution. At the same time, it avoided a dangerous open split between Russia and the West. Above all it demonstrated that Russia was a player in the Balkan game and had to be taken seriously.

The Serb onslaught against Gorazde in April 1994, however, underscored the limits of Russian influence. Despite a last-minute mediation attempt, Russia was unable to repeat its February success. Instead of halting their attacks and withdrawing their heavy artillery behind the agreed exclusion zone, as they had promised, the Bosnian Serbs continued shelling Gorazde, leaving Russia feeling betrayed and humiliated. The Bosnian Serb intransigence left the Yeltsin Government little choice but to support the air strikes or face diplomatic isolation. At the same time it revealed important divisions within the Russian Government. Whereas Foreign Minister Kozyrev advocated a tougher stance towards the Bosnian Serbs, including qualified support for air strikes, Defence

---

[21] Erlanger, S., 'Yeltsin says Russians must be heard on Bosnia', *New York Times*, 16 Feb. 1994; and Shapiro, M., 'Yeltsin warns against excluding Russia from a Bosnian settlement', *Washington Post*, 16 Feb. 1994.

[22] 'Forcierte Proteste Moskaus gegen die NATO' [Moscow's forced protests against NATO], *Neue Zürcher Zeitung*, 12 Feb. 1994.

[23] Erlanger, S., 'Russian official softens country's stand on Bosnia air strikes', *New York Times*, 14 Feb. 1994.

Minister Pavel Grachev openly opposed such strikes, arguing that the Serbs should not be held solely responsible for the attacks on Gorazde.[24]

Russia's approach to the Yugoslav conflict must, moreover, be viewed within the larger context of its strategic relationship with the West and its concerns about NATO. Russia viewed the NATO air strikes in Bosnia and Herzegovina as yet another example of the West's attempt to make NATO—rather than the Organization for Security and Co-operation in Europe (OSCE)[25] or the UN— the core of a new European security order. Russia opposed this effort because it would have effectively excluded it and deprived it of a major say or role in the creation of a new post-cold war security order in Europe.

Russia's approach to Bosnia and Herzegovina was increasingly linked to its broader concerns about NATO. One of Russia's key objectives was to limit and constrain NATO's role in Bosnia and Herzegovina because it fears that greater NATO involvement could strengthen the alliance's role as the dominant security manager in post-cold war Europe—which would undercut Russia's efforts to build up the OSCE. Russia thus continually opposed any independent military action by NATO that was not directly authorized by the UN, where it has a veto by virtue of its permanent seat on the Security Council.[26]

However, since late 1994 Russia has found itself increasingly marginalized and shunted onto the diplomatic sidelines as the USA has seized the diplomatic initiative. Russia played virtually no role in the working out of the Dayton Agreement ending the Bosnia conflict and had to settle for a minor role in the NATO-led Implementation Force (IFOR). Indeed, the Dayton Agreement made it clear that it was the USA, not Russia or Europe, that was the real power broker in the Balkans.

IV. The wider Balkan stage

Elsewhere in the Balkans as well Russia has not been unfortunate in establishing a foothold, with the partial exception of Bulgaria. Relations with Bulgaria stagnated after Zhivkov was ousted in November 1989, but have subsequently improved. During President Yeltsin's visit to Sofia in August 1992, a new Treaty of Friendship and Co-operation was signed.[27] While the new treaty does not include provisions for mutual assistance—as Russia initially wanted—it does envisage close consultations in case of threats to peace in Europe and the Black Sea region and calls for expanded cooperation in non-security areas.

---

[24] 'Bosnien-Querelen in der russischen Regierung' [Rifts over Bosnia in the Russian government], *Neue Zürcher Zeitung,* 23 Apr. 1994; Bohlen, C., 'Russian defense minister opposes air strikes against Serbs', *New York Times,* 26 Apr. 1994; and 'Kritik Gratchows an den NATO-Drohungen' [Grachev critical of NATO air strikes], *Neue Zürcher Zeitung,* 27 Apr. 1994.

[25] On 1 Jan. 1995 the CSCE became the OSCE.

[26] In early Dec. 1994, Russia vetoed a UN Security Council resolution calling for an embargo against the Bosnian and Croatian Serbs—one of the rare occasions since 1989 when Russia has exercised its veto right in the Security Council. A few days later it blocked the adoption of a declaration on Bosnia at the CSCE summit meeting in Budapest because it condemned the Bosnian Serb attack on Bihac.

[27] Crow, S., 'Russia and the Macedonian question', *RFE/RL Research Report,* 13 Nov. 1992, pp. 36–38.

The victory of the Bulgarian Socialist Party (BSP—the former communists) in the December 1994 parliamentary elections has opened up new diplomatic opportunities for Russia in the Balkans. While the BSP has not changed Bulgaria's domestic or foreign policy radically, it has pursued a less overtly pro-Western policy—especially regarding NATO membership—than the previous governments headed by prime ministers Filip Dimitrov and Lyuben Berov. It has also sought to establish closer ties to Moscow, particularly in the economic field.

A too overtly pro-Bulgarian policy, however, could conflict with Russia's efforts to forge closer ties to Serbia because of the historical antagonism between Bulgaria and Serbia over Macedonia. Balancing these two competing interests has often proved difficult for Russia: its support for the creation of a Greater Bulgaria in 1878, for instance, deeply angered Serbia, which had looked to Russia for support. Similarly, tacit Soviet support for Bulgaria's position on the Macedonian Question was a source of tension between Yugoslavia and the USSR during the cold war era.

These enduring dilemmas have not proved any easier to resolve in the post-cold war era, as Russia's hasty decision to recognize Macedonia in August 1992 illustrates. The move, announced during President Yeltsin's visit to Sofia, caught many observers—and Russian diplomats—by surprise and was clearly calculated to win favour with Bulgaria, which has close historical ties to Macedonia. However, the decision caused an outcry among nationalists in Russia, who regarded it as a betrayal of the Serbs.[28]

The move also created strains in relations with Greece. Since then, however, relations between Moscow and Athens have visibly improved. The communiqué issued at the end of Yeltsin's visit to Greece in July 1993 emphasized the 'strong spiritual and cultural links between the two countries, united by the Christian Orthodox religion'.[29] During the visit the two countries also signed a Friendship and Cooperation Agreement and a series of economic and technical accords. Greece has also expressed an interest in purchasing arms from Russia.[30]

This is not to suggest that a new 'Moscow–Athens axis' is about to form in the Balkans. However, an important coincidence of strategic interests between Greece and Russia does exist. Both countries have strong historical ties to Serbia and they share a common interest in preventing an expansion of Turkish influence in the Balkans. This coincidence of strategic interests could lead to closer cooperation between the two countries in the future, especially if Greece's relations with Turkey continue to deteriorate.

Russia has also recently sought to improve relations with Albania, which was a Soviet client state until it defected to the Chinese camp in 1961. However,

[28] Crow (note 27).

[29] 'La Grèce et la Russie affirment leurs positions communes dans les Balkans' [Greece and Russia affirm common position on the Balkans], Le Monde, 3 July 1993; and 'Offizielles Besuch Jelzins in Griechenland' [Yeltsin's state visit to Greece], Neue Zürcher Zeitung, 2 July 1993.

[30] RFE/RL Daily Report, no. 142 (28 July 1994); and 'Engere militärische Zusammenarbeit' [Closer military cooperation], Frankfurter Allgemeine Zeitung, 26 July 1994.

these efforts have had little visible success. Russia has been reluctant to support Albania on the Kosovo question—the key foreign policy concern for Albania—for fear of alienating Serbia. Moreover, Russia's own economic difficulties limit its ability to offer what Albania needs most—massive economic aid.

From a strategic point of view, Russia's effort to foster close ties to Serbia makes a great deal of sense. Indeed, a strong coincidence of interests exists between Moscow and Belgrade. For Serbia, close ties to Russia offer an important means of escaping isolation, while for Russia close ties to Serbia provide it with a means both of maintaining a presence in the Balkans and of remaining a player in the Balkan game. A strong Serbia also acts as an important counter-weight to Turkish influence in the Balkans.

However, Russia must be careful not to overplay its hand. A too overtly pro-Serbian policy could drive Bulgaria into the arms of Turkey. Bulgaria and Turkey have been traditional enemies. Since 1990, however, relations have significantly improved, especially in the military field.[31] A strongly pro-Serb policy on Russia's part could give this *rapprochement* new impetus. The same is true in the case of Albania, which has also strengthened ties with Turkey of late.[32]

Russia's policy towards Moldova, much of which once belonged to Romania, poses a stumbling-block to better relations with Romania. The latter has viewed with concern Russia's increasing economic and political pressure on Moldova to join the Commonwealth of Independent States (CIS) and grant Russia basing rights there.[33] While the agreement to withdraw Russian troops from Moldova, signed in August 1994, helped to alleviate some of these concerns, the Moldovan issue is likely to remain a source of discord in Russian–Romanian relations and inhibit any far-reaching *rapprochement* between the two countries in the near future.

The prospects for unification between Moldova and Romania in the near future, however, are dim. The overwhelming majority of Moldovan citizens want independence, not unification with Romania. This fact has come as something of a rude shock to many Romanians, who had expected that Moldovan independence would lead to rapid unification of the two countries, and has forced Romania to alter its policy towards Moldova. While Romania has not entirely given up hopes for unification in the long run, it recognizes that this is unlikely to occur in the near future and has concentrated instead on improving cultural and political ties with Moldova on the basis of the existence of two independent Romanian states.

---

[31] Engelbrekt, K., 'Relations with Turkey: a review of post-Zhivkov developments', *Report on Eastern Europe*, 26 Apr. 1991, pp. 9–10.
[32] Zanga, L., 'Albania and Turkey forge closer ties', *RFE/RL Research Report*, 12 Mar. 1993, pp. 30–33.
[33] Socor, V., 'Isolated Moldova being pulled into Russian orbit', *RFE/RL Research Report*, 17 Dec. 1993, pp. 9–15.

V. Russia and Turkey: the new geopolitics

The emergence of turmoil in the Balkans has also contributed to an intensification of geopolitical rivalry between Russia and Turkey. This rivalry has deep historical roots. In the 19th century, Russia emerged as the main defender of the Slavs in the Balkans as they sought to break away from Ottoman rule.[34] The collapse of the Ottoman Empire led to the withdrawal of Turkey from the Balkans. Thereafter, Turkey adopted a low profile in the region, especially in the post-World War II period.

With the end of the cold war, however, Turkey has begun to pursue a more active policy in the Balkans. Ties to Albania and Bulgaria have been strengthened, especially in the defence area. Turkey has also been active within the Islamic world in drumming up support for Bosnia and Herzegovina. In May 1992, it joined Algeria and Iran in calling for a special meeting of the Foreign Ministers of the Organization of the Islamic Conference to discuss the situation. In early 1994 the then Turkish Prime Minister, Tansu Ciller, and Pakistani Prime Minister Benazir Bhutto made a highly publicized visit to Sarajevo to dramatize the plight of Bosnian Muslims in the besieged city.

At the same time, the disintegration of the Soviet Union has opened up new opportunities for the expansion of Turkish influence in Central Asia and the Caucasus.[35] Many of these countries look to Turkey, a secular Muslim state with an expanding market economy, as a model for their own development. While Turkey has been relatively cautious about exploiting these new opportunities, its expanding ties to the former Soviet republics in Central Asia and the Caucasus have made Russia nervous and sparked a new, albeit muted, struggle for influence in the region.

This muted struggle for political influence has been lent greater intensity by economic factors, particularly the desire for access to the energy resources in Central Asia and the Caspian Sea basin.[36] Turkey's key objective is to obtain access to these resources. It has sought to build a series of pipelines that would link Central Asian oil and natural gas reserves, through Azerbaijan, with its own domestic pipelines. This would ensure Turkey's domestic needs and allow the export of energy from Turkish ports. Russia, in turn, fears that Turkish economic influence, above all control of the area's energy resources, would allow Turkey to dominate the region politically and eventually lead to an anti-Russian 'pan-Turkic alliance'.

Russia has responded to the new geopolitical challenge posed by the expansion of Turkish influence in the region by strengthening political and defence

---

[34] On the historical roots of this rivalry, see in particular Jelavich (note 1).

[35] For details, see Fuller, G. E., *Turkey Faces East: New Orientations Toward the Middle East and the Old Soviet Union*, R-4232-AF/A (RAND Corporation: Santa Monica, Calif., 1992).

[36] For a good discussion of the energy issue in Russian–Turkish relations, see Lombardi, B., *Turkish Policy in Central Asia*, Project Report no. 709 (Canadian Department of National Defence: Ottawa, Dec. 1994), pp. 30–44; and Forsythe, R., International Institute for Strategic Studies, *The Politics of Oil in the Caucasus and Central Asia*, Adelphi Paper no. 300 (Brassey's/IISS: London, 1996).

ties with Georgia and Moldova, stepping up assistance to Armenia in its war with Azerbaijan[37] and calling for revisions of the 1990 Treaty on Conventional Armed Forces in Europe (CFE Treaty) that would allow Russia to station more forces and equipment on the flanks. All these moves have been designed to strengthen Russia's influence and military presence in the Caucasus and block the expansion of Turkish—and Iranian—influence there.

Russia has also stepped up economic and political pressure on Azerbaijan. Turkish officials are convinced that Russia had a hand in the coup there in May 1993 which overthrew President Ebulfez Elcibey. Elcibey had pursued a strongly pro-Turkish, anti-Russian policy. His ousting and replacement by Geidar Aliev, a Brezhnev-era communist *apparatchik*, dealt a strong blow to Turkey's hopes of expanding its influence in the region. However, Aliev has proved to be less of a Russian puppet than many in Moscow had expected. He has resisted pressure to station Russian peacekeeping troops on Azerbaijani soil and skilfully managed to play Russia and Turkey off against one another.

The danger is that this growing geo-strategic rivalry between Russia and Turkey in Central Asia and the Caucasus could be transposed to the Balkans, where both countries have strong historical interests. Turkey has already made important inroads in Albania, Bosnia and Herzegovina, Bulgaria and Macedonia. This has begun to worry Greek officials, who have expressed increasing concern about the emergence of a 'Muslim arc' on Greece's northern border.[38] Serbia shares similar concerns. These concerns could lead both countries to forge closer ties to Russia in order to block the expansion of Turkish influence in the Balkans. Renewed rivalry over the Dardanelle Straits could also contribute to greater regional instability. Turkey's adoption of a more restrictive policy on the passage of large tankers through the Straits has important geo-political implications. All Russian tankers sailing from the Russian port of Novorossiysk must pass through the Bosphorus on their way to world markets. The new restrictions give Turkey important leverage over Russia's ability to transport Central Asian oil and over the overall development of the energy sector in Central Asia.

These restrictions have contributed to new strains in Russian–Turkish relations.[39] At the same time, they give Russia a stronger interest in closer economic and political cooperation with Bulgaria and Greece. In October 1994 Russia signed letters of intent with the two countries for the construction of a 350-km pipeline projected to run between the Bulgarian port of Burgas on the Black Sea and the Greek port of Alexandroulis on the Aegean Sea. The possi-

---

[37] In Apr. 1993 Turkish officials released tapes and transcripts of battlefield intercepts which reportedly showed heavy Russian involvement in the fighting between Azerbaijan and Armenia. 'Turk says Russia is tangled in Caucasus war', *New York Times*, 15 Apr. 1993.

[38] Valinakis, Y., *Greece's Balkan Policy and the 'Macedonian Issue'* (Stiftung Wissenschaft und Politik: Ebenhausen, Apr. 1992).

[39] The official reason for the restrictions was to prevent ecological damage. While ecological factors undoubtedly did play a role, geo-strategic factors appear to have been far more important. 'Kalte Winde über dem Bosphorus' [Cold winds over the Bosphorus], *Neue Zürcher Zeitung*, 4 July 1994; and Lombardi (note 36), pp. 40–41.

bility of constructing a gas pipeline running from Bulgaria, through Serbia, to Western Europe is also under consideration.[40] If such plans are realized, Russia will be able to circumvent Turkey's ability to exercise economic leverage over its energy policy and exports.

Thus Russia's larger strategic interests in Central Asia and the Caucasus give it a strong incentive to remain engaged in the Balkans. These interests extend beyond vague feelings of Slav solidarity with Serbia. They involve important geopolitical and economic interests associated with Russia's broader goals in Central Asia and the Caucasus. At the same time, for reasons of their own, Bulgaria and Greece are likely to see Russia as a useful counterweight to Turkish influence in the region.

VI. Prospects for the future

This does not mean that the Balkans will again become a major Russian policy concern or sphere of influence, as they were in the 19th century. Russia's main foreign policy priority is, and is likely to remain, its relations with the successor states of the former Soviet Union. That is the area where Russian national interests are most directly involved. The Balkans are likely to be of secondary, even tertiary, importance. Moreover, even if Russia had the interest, it lacks the economic resources to try to carve out a dominant position in the region.

Some Russians do see the Balkans as a major foreign policy priority—Zhirinovsky among them—but they are in the minority. For most nationalists Bosnia and Herzegovina and the Balkans are a weapon in the larger domestic struggle to topple President Yeltsin rather than a major foreign policy priority in their own right. Slav solidarity, in other words, is a residual factor as opposed to a driving force in Russia's policy in the Balkans. Moreover, the Dayton Agreement has changed the political dynamics in the Balkans, strengthening the position of the USA, which has emerged as the key power in the region, and weakening that of Serbian President Slobodan Milosevic and the Bosnian Serbs. Thus Russia may find it more difficult in the future to exert the same influence on developments in the former Yugoslavia as it has had in the past.

Russia's prospects elsewhere in the Balkans are not much more promising. Relations with Turkey are likely to be marked by the growing strategic rivalry over the Caucasus and Central Asia, while Moldova remains an impediment to any far-reaching accord with Romania. Relations with Greece have warmed recently, but Greece's future lies with the European Union, not close association with Russia. Only with Serbia and possibly Bulgaria are prospects for close cooperation promising. Even in the case of Serbia, Milosevic is likely to want to keep the channels open to the West in order to maximize his chances of receiving Western economic assistance, which he will need in order to rebuild his war-torn country.

---

[40] Robinson, A. and Troev, T., 'Black Sea states see the trade tide turning', *Financial Times*, 21 Oct. 1994.

19. The Balkans test for Russia

Nadia Alexandrova-Arbatova

I. Introduction

Having supported national movements for independence in the Soviet republics in the 1990s, Russia emerged on the international scene after the demise of the USSR completely uncommitted to the former foreign policy of the Soviet Union, including its Balkans policy. The leadership of independent Russia entered the international community with a very pronounced desire to become part of the civilized world. The Strategic Democratic Initiative launched in early 1992 by the Foreign Minister at that time, Andrey Kozyrev,[1] and some other radical steps, such as Russia's proclamation of its intention to join NATO,[2] had to compete with the 'new political thinking' of former President Mikhail Gorbachev and Foreign Minister Eduard Shevardnadze and their more cautious *rapprochement* with the West.

However, concentrating as it was on the idea of rapid integration with the West and relying only on its lead in international affairs, the Russian leadership neglected the development of a distinctive foreign policy and security priorities based on the specifics and the new challenges of the post-Soviet period.

The Balkans policy of Russia was no exception, even though new developments in this region directly affected Russia's interests. Compared with the Balkans policy of the USSR—regional competition with the West on its southern flank and maintenance of the unity of the socialist camp because of the Yugoslav factor—Russia's policy in the region acquired new meaning. First, the Yugoslav conflict became a test for the emerging post-cold war security system and posed the question of Russia's place in this system. Second, the post-communist developments in the Balkans became a catalyst for political and ideological infighting in Russia between democrats and nationalists. Third, the growing regional role of Turkey was becoming a strong challenge to Russia in the Black Sea–Caspian Sea area. Fourth, the post-Soviet conflicts which affected Russia's interests increased regional interdependence, having involved some of the Balkan states.

---

[1] Kozyrev called on Russia and the West to defend democracy and human rights all over the world. Events in Chechnya since Dec. 1994 seem to cast a different light on this initiative, however. Arbatov, A., 'Imperiya ili velikaya derzhava?' [Empire or great power?], *Novoe Vremya*, no. 49 (Dec. 1992), p. 16.

[2] Kozyrev, A., 'Rossiya obrechena byt velikoy derzhavoy' [Russia is doomed to be a great power], *Novoe Vremya*, no. 3 (Jan. 1992), p. 23. In commenting on the notorious misprint in President Yeltsin's message which stated that 'Russia is ['not' alleged to have been missed out by a typist] raising the question of becoming a member of NATO', Kozyrev said: 'Yes, we pose this question, but not right now, later'.

This chapter analyses the main convolutions of the Balkans policy of Russia from the angle of its national interests, hidden factors and driving forces. Section II examines the geo-strategic and historical background. Section III looks at the possible parallels between Russia and the former Yugoslavia, and section IV considers Russian policy on the conflict there. Section V considers Russian policy with respect to the Trans-Dniester area of Moldova, and the final section looks at the foreign policy implications of the Balkans situation for Russia and the West.

II. New challenges for Russia

The Mediterranean heritage of the USSR

Soviet policy in the Balkans was a part of its Mediterranean policy, which had long historical traditions. Imperial Russia and then the Soviet Union took an understandable interest in the nearest warm waters. 'Imperial Russia's numerous clashes with Turkey almost invariably raised the Bosphorus and Dardanelles as an important problem, while the major powers of Europe were concerned about not letting Russia gain a major outlet into the Mediterranean.'[3] However, up to the end of World War II the USSR had neither the strength nor the possibility to penetrate the region.

After World War II, East–West confrontation spread to the Mediterranean and the USSR began seriously to consider the possibility of expanding Soviet influence geographically. After its clash with Yugoslavia, Soviet policy showed an interest in a presence in Albania, and in 1950 the USSR started to use the strategically important island of Saseno and the port of Vlorë.

The post-Stalin policy was part of a different general evaluation of the world and the USSR's place in it. On the one hand, Moscow demonstrated its interest in normalizing relations with some countries in South-East Europe—in the first place with Yugoslavia and Turkey. On the other hand it wanted to gain access to the Mediterranean with a view to demonstrating its naval possibilities and competing with the West. From the 1960s, when the USSR established its presence on a permanent basis, Soviet policy objectives—support and aid to regimes that were strongly anti-USA and anti-Western and the weakening of US influence—were supplemented by military–strategic objectives: (a) to offset the presence of the US Sixth Fleet and restrain its operations in crisis situations; (b) to defend naval and air bases, industrial centres and other shore targets from nuclear and conventional strikes by the US Navy and from amphibious assaults; and (c) to be in a position to interrupt or close Western sea lines of communication.[4] The above missions might be termed the 'maximum

---

[3] Vucadinovic, R., *The Mediterranean Between War and Peace* (Medunarodna Politika: Belgrade/Institut za zemplje u razvoju: Zagreb, 1987), p. 55.

[4] Alexandrova-Arbatova, N., 'Naval arms control in the Mediterranean: a Soviet perspective', eds A. Furst, V. Heise and S. Miller, SIPRI, *Europe and Naval Arms Control in the Gorbachev Era* (Oxford University Press: Oxford, 1992), p. 196.

task' of the Black Sea Fleet and were not linked directly to the Balkans. The 'minimum task' was (a) blockading the Black Sea Straits; (b) control of the Black Sea; and (c) support for land operations against Turkey and in Greece.[5] This would have affected the Balkans.

With the end of the bipolar world, Russia's task was to reduce to a common denominator its national interests and the goal of cooperation with the West both inside and outside the international institutions. In the new context, three foreign policy priorities can be discerned.

The search for a stable environment

Clearly the first foreign policy priority of Russia, which found itself in an absolutely new geopolitical situation, stems from its interest in maintaining stability in the post-Soviet space and along the perimeter of the former Soviet Union. In contrast with the past when the Balkans had been part of the 'foot-in-the-door policy' of the USSR in the Black Sea–Mediterranean region, after the demise of the Soviet empire the region gained new importance for Russia. Romania and Turkey began to be involved directly or indirectly in post-Soviet conflicts. Moldova's proclamation of independence raised the question of eventual reunion with Romania. This was opposed by the Russian minority and led to their proclamation of the Trans-Dniester Republic with the objective of reunification with Russia. The conflict in Trans-Dniester confronted Moscow with a very difficult problem, similar to that which Krajina, the Serb-dominated area of Croatia, presented for Serbia. The Russian leadership, however, did not formulate any distinctive position on this issue or on problems related to Russian minorities in the 'near abroad'.

The challenge from regional powers

Another serious challenge for Russia's foreign policy became the emergence of regional centres of power, which could expand their influence over the unstable zones of the post-communist world—Germany, Iran and Turkey. Thus the second foreign policy priority is to prevent or to minimize any negative outcome for Russia of this possible expansion.

This challenge has major repercussions for Russia's policy on the Balkans, although only Turkey may be considered as a 'pure' regional force. Germany's involvement in the Balkans, and in the conflict in the former Yugoslavia in particular, was a chance after reunification to declare its assertive role in European politics and to back its traditional allies in the region—Croatia and Turkey. The role of Iran, which is competing with Turkey in the Muslim

---

[5] Alexandrova-Arbatova (note 4), p. 200.

republics of the former USSR and in Bosnia and Herzegovina,[6] stems from its ambitions and commitments in the Muslim world.

Turkey's role in the Balkans, as it is seen by Russia, has to be assessed against a broader background. The demise of the USSR and Russia's relative economic, political and in some respects military weakness opened up to Turkey the possibility of re-establishing its influence in the region and expanding it to the post-Soviet areas with Muslim/Turkic populations (including Tatarstan, which is part of the Russian Federation, and the Muslim community in Crimea, part of Ukraine). 'Since the end of the Gulf War and the disintegration of the Soviet Union, Turkey has emerged as a major regional power. From the Adriatic to the Caspian, and from the Black Sea to the Gulf, Ankara is marketing itself, with considerable success, as a secular democratic model for all Muslim people.'[7] This policy has been supported by the West and in particular the USA, which perceives Turkey's role as that of a bulwark against the re-emergence of anti-Western powers in the Middle East and as the vehicle through which the Central Asian republics could be linked to the Western world, blocking Iranian influence in this region.

There are, however, serious doubts as to whether Turkey is in a position to operate as an obstacle to the trends of Islamic fundamentalism, as the West expects it to do. Domestic developments in the country are worrying, pointing as they do to the growing role of religious nationalists.[8] In the worst case, this could result in a repetition of the Algerian pattern; but even under a more favourable scenario the possibility remains that Turkey will take a more assertive course under pressure from fundamentalist and nationalist forces. In fact, this is already happening. These forces are already pushing for the new government to play the ethnic and religious card.

Turkey's democratic image has been considerably damaged in particular by the atrocities inflicted by it on the Turkish Kurds. The Turkish leadership condemned Serbia for its anti-Albanian policy in Kosovo, but deployed one-third of its army in the south-eastern part of Turkey to fight its own Kurdish minority, who were seeking the same thing as the Kosovo Albanians. 'Such is the value the West is attaching to Turkey's importance that it is prepared to ignore Ankara's well-documented record of human rights abuses in Turkish Kurdistan, where the struggle against the Kurd separatists is on the verge of degenerating into a full-scale civil war.'[9]

It would be naïve today to explain Russia's suspicions and concerns in respect of Turkey purely by negative historical experience (although historical memory counts when the present is precarious) or by sincere concern for the

---

[6] According to one report, c. 400 radical Islamic paramilitary groups, formed in Iran of citizens of different Muslim countries, came to Bosnia and Herzegovina to support the Bosnian Government. United States Information Service, Moscow, *News Bulletin,* ERF508 (6 Mar. 1994), p. 8.

[7] Goldstein, L., Kokhinides, T. and Plesch, D., *Fueling Balkan Fires: The West's Arming of Greece and Turkey,* BASIC Report 93:3 (British American Security Information Council: Washington and London, 1993), p. 6.

[8] Nesin, A., 'Retsidiv tmy' [Relapse of the dark], *Novoe Vremya,* no. 40 (Oct. 1994), p. 29.

[9] Amnesty International, *Report 1992* (Amnesty International: London, 1993), pp. 257–60.

secular state and democratic values. Far more important in Russia's perception of Turkey are geopolitical considerations. If the Central Asian republics, with the exception of Kazakhstan, are an area of secondary importance to Russia, the Caucasus region is the soft under-belly of the Russian Federation and a major concern. Turkey is seen as becoming a pole of attraction for those Muslim peoples in the Caucasus who are for different reasons hostile to Russia and who are looking for a strong ally to join on an anti-Russian platform. The risk is far from purely theoretical. If Turkey became a real vehicle for integration between the Muslims of the Caucasus, Russia might be confronted with the emergence of a hostile coalition of states with a strong anti-Russian bias. Turkey is currently extremely active in this region, using not only its traditional ties with Azerbaijan but also a 'stick and carrot' policy to drive a wedge between Georgia and Russia. Numerous facts in the Russian media on Turkey's indirect involvement in Abkhazia and even in Chechnya coupled with the Turkish diplomatic game over the transport of Caspian oil, which affects the interests of both Georgia and Russia, have reinforced Russia's concern about Turkish economic and political expansion.

Another potential threat to Russia's interests involving Turkey, which may become the biggest challenge to the integrity of the Russian Federation, is future developments in Tatarstan. Matters of potential concern are the actively developing cultural and religious contacts between Turkey and Tatarstan, radio broadcasting from Turkey to Tatarstan allegedly encouraging nationalists there,[10] and emphatic elements of Turkism in the political activity of the Ittifak Party of National Independence, which is the most radical secessionist party in Tatarstan. 'It should be recognized that at the centre of the Russian Federation we are seeing the emergence of a confessional enclave which will without question be seeking self-assertiveness in culture, politics and way of life.'[11]

Being interested in consolidating Ankara's position, the West is ready to bless any Turkish policy whatever and encourages Turkey's involvement in the conflict-resolution process in the Transcaucasus and the Balkans. Thus Turkey, being a patron of Azerbaijan, has already intervened as a tough mediator in the conflict between Armenia and Azerbaijan over the disputed enclave of Nagorno-Karabakh. The West is backing Turkish policy in the conflict in the former Yugoslavia regardless of the concerns of some regional states, including Greece, its other ally in the Balkans. The key question is whether the West will be able to keep Turkish policy under control and, if not, whether its policy of encouraging Turkey can be considered expedient or productive.

The West may hope to strengthen the moderate tendencies in the Turkish regime by giving Turkey *carte blanche* in its foreign policy, but Russia cannot depend on Turkey's good intentions. It is very illustrative in this respect that the Turkish Government, being aware of Russia's traditional sensitiveness

---

[10] Reported by Galina Starovoitova, former adviser to President Yeltsin, at the Seminar of the Moscow Centre of the Carnegie Endowment, 16 May 1996.

[11] Malashenko, A., 'U porogov tatarskikh mechetey' [On the thresholds of Tatarstan mosques], *Nezavisimaya Gazeta*, 12 Mar. 1996, p. 2.

about the Black Sea Straits, has already tried unilaterally to review the article of the 1936 Montreux Convention on the regime of the Straits.[12]

Russia, however, seems to have failed in working out an effective response to the 'Turkish challenge'. The goal of its diplomatic efforts should have been to minimize the prospect of a hostile environment for itself developing. In this respect Russia's natural allies in the Caucasus are Armenia and Georgia, sandwiched between Azerbaijan, Iran, Turkey and the Muslim republics of the North Caucasus. Its natural allies in the Balkans are Greece and Bulgaria. In both cases, Russia's policy has been inconsistent and even counter-productive.

The Russian leadership was not able to present itself as an authoritative, efficient mediator from the beginning of its involvement in the conflicts between Armenia and Azerbaijan and between Abkhazia and Georgia, and has disappointed all parties. It has ignored the necessity of establishing new relations with the former members of the Warsaw Treaty Organization (WTO) and the Council for Mutual Economic Assistance (CMEA) after the demise of the USSR, and has given its former allies like Bulgaria and Romania the impression that they could rely only on the West, thus actually blessing the enlargement of NATO eastwards. It cast a shadow over its relations with Greece by its hasty recognition of the Republic of Macedonia under that name, while the USA recognized the country under the name of FYROM (the Former Yugoslav Republic of Macedonia) on 9 February 1994.[13]

Great power or a Greater Russia?

The unconditional support that Turkey is receiving from the West, and from Germany and the USA in particular, in the Balkans and first of all in the conflict in the former Yugoslavia has revived old suspicions. It is part of a more general concern on the part of Russia, which seems to be very sensitive to any attempts to limit the international role as a great power which it inherited from the USSR. To maintain this status is the third foreign policy priority of Russia.

The Russian political leadership has underlined the point on many occasions,[14] having gradually shifted from initial extreme pro-Westernism towards a more self-assertive and more Russia-centred foreign policy.

---

[12] There may be different interpretations of the Turkish decision on the Straits. See, e.g., Potskhveriya, B., 'Interesi Rossii v Chernomorskikh prolivakh' [Russia's interests in the Black Sea Straits], *Nezavisimaya Gazeta*, 30 Nov. 1994, p. 4. Potskhveriya proves in his article that there were no violations of the Montreux Convention by Turkey. The opposite view is presented in Kalinin, A. (Rear-Adm.) and Morozov, G., 'Puti reformirovaniya Chernomorskogo flota' [Ways to reform the Black Sea Fleet], *Nezavisimaya Gazeta*, 17 Nov. 1994, p. 5. What is more important is the way the Turkish Government acted: instead of calming down Russia's suspicions it completely ignored its concerns. This gave the impression that the Turkish leadership deliberately intended to demonstrate its dissatisfaction with Russia's policy in the Yugoslav conflict and to influence Russia, which will be involved in the transport of Caspian oil for export, to use pipelines running through Turkish territory.

[13] Munuera, G., Western European Union, Institute for Security Studies, *Preventing Armed Conflict in Europe: Lessons From Recent Experience*, Chaillot Papers no. 15–16 (ISS: Paris, June 1994), p. 50.

[14] For instance, opening the Moscow meeting on the preparation of multilateral negotiations on the Middle East on 28 Jan. 1992, Kozyrev said: 'Moscow is a successor to Madrid and Washington . . . We are free from imperial ambitions. But it is true also that Russia does not refuse and will not refuse its

With respect to the Mediterranean and the Balkan region, the vacuum in the field of foreign policy priorities and objectives has gradually been filled by more traditional thinking, including that of academic and military experts, who still stick to the former 'foot-in-the-door' policy in this region. The old spectre of a 'Turkish threat', aggravated by the Islamic resurgence, the growing Westernization of the former allies, Bulgaria and Romania included, national conflicts in the Transcaucasus, the fact that the Commonwealth of Independent States (CIS) industrial centres are still within the range of missiles of the US Sixth Fleet—in the eyes of the Russian military all these factors have made the task of defending Russia's and the CIS southern maritime borders all the more vital.[15] The advocates of this approach call for the building of a military pillar in the Black Sea 'near abroad' in order to re-establish the former grandeur of the USSR in the Mediterranean, expand Russia's geopolitical influence to the far Mediterranean and make Russia count.[16]

III. The Yugoslav paradigm

In some respects, Russia's role in the disintegration of the former USSR was similar to that of Croatia or Slovenia in the federal Yugoslavia. However, after the demise of the USSR Russia identified itself more and more with Serbia. The Yugoslav case provided it with many parallels which cannot be ignored in the analysis of Russia's foreign policy.

First, after the collapse of ruling ideologies in both 'empires' there was an outbreak of local nationalisms, including anti-Serbian and anti-Russian sentiment, which started to fuel each other.

The bulk of responsibility for all the sins of the communist regimes in these multinational states has been put on two nations—the Russians and the Serbs. This may be partly explained by the fact that Moscow and Belgrade, which were the embodiments of imperial power, were the capitals not only of the Soviet Union and Yugoslavia but also of the Russian Federation and Serbia respectively. Russia's sense of grievance at anti-Russian moods in the republics of the former USSR, and above all in the Baltic states, was aggravated by the fact that it and in particular the majority of Russians living there had supported national liberation movements in these republics, but had been betrayed by the new leaderships after their victory. Although Serbia's position on the disintegration of the Yugoslav Federation was the opposite of that of Russia, there is some similarity between the position of Russian minorities and that of the Serbs in Krajina, who had supported Franjo Tudjman for the presidency of Croatia.

Second, the demise of both multinational entities highlighted the biggest problem for the newly born states—the fact that almost all of them are also

international responsibility as a great power and UN Security Council member'. *Diplomaticheskiy Vestnik*, nos 4–5 (Feb./Mar. 1992), p. 37. See also Kozyrev (note 2), p. 21.

[15] Kalinin and Morozov (note 12).

[16] Sorokin, K., [No further retreat], *Nezavisimaya Gazeta*, 2 Nov. 1994, p. 4. See also N. Alexandrova-Arbatova's polemic with Konstantin Sorokin in *Nezavisimaya Gazeta*, 19 Nov. 1994, p. 4.

multinational. This appeared to have two aspects: the rights of a minority out-side its home republic (the Serbs in Krajina and Bosnia and Herzegovina; the Russian minorities in the Baltic republics, Kazakhstan, Moldova and Ukraine); and the rights of foreign minorities inside an individual republic (Albanian domination of the province of Kosovo for Serbia; and the threats to the terri-torial integrity of the Russian Federation in Tatarstan, Tuva and especially Chechnya). There may be another problem for Russia, which in future could be compared with that of Kosovo, although it is not so evident for the time being. During recent years several million Chinese have illegally inhabited Russian territory in the Far East. This migration may in time create further tensions between Russia and China which could be similar to those in the Serbia–Kosovo–Albania triangle.

Third, Russia, with whatever justification, began to draw parallels between its position within the USSR and that of Serbia in federal Yugoslavia. The Yugo-slav Federal Constitution of 1974, created by Tito, was seen as discriminatory against Serbia and became the prime target of the Serbian intelligentsia after Tito's death.

The constitution was seen as a protection for Croatians, Slovenians and the Albanians of Kosovo, who 'were fearful of Serbian hegemonic ambitions'. However the consti-tution prompted the development of a sense of real grievances among Serbians that was not addressed effectively until Milosevic rose to power in 1987 . . . Serbia was divided into three constitutional units, allowing Vojvodina and Kosovo to become de facto republics. In addition, the constitution . . . allowed Kosovo and Vojvodina a say in Serbian affairs while Serbia had no say in the affairs of its former provinces.[17]

After the demise of the USSR, with tensions growing between Russia and some of the republics of the former Union, and in the first place with Ukraine, Russians started to experience a similar sense of grievance. Khrushchev's transfer of Crimea, which had been part of Russia, to Ukraine in 1954 became the main apple of discord between the two independent states. Several clashes between the Russian and Ukrainian military occurred, in Crimea threatening to spill over into actual armed conflict. The paradigm of the Croatian war was clearly seen in the growing tensions between Moscow and Kiev during 1993 and the first half of 1994, and could have had considerable repercussions on Russian and Ukrainian policy.

These similarities between the former USSR and the former Yugoslavia and the problems which emerged in the process of their disintegration are very illustrative. For Russia, the mirror effect of the Yugoslav conflict was in general positive: in bloodshed, destruction and an atmosphere of hatred and mistrust Russia saw its own probable future. There was, however, another factor that helped Russia to avoid a repetition of the Yugoslav scenario: the USSR was immediately succeeded by the CIS, which served as a structure for the relatively civilized divorce of the former Soviet republics. No institution of

[17] Griffiths, S., *Nationalism and Ethnic Conflict: Threats to European Security*, SIPRI Research Report no. 5 (Oxford University Press: Oxford, 1993), p. 41.

this kind was established in the former Yugoslavia because of the resolute refusal of Croatia and Slovenia.

IV. Russia's policy

There was no continuity between the USSR's policy on the Yugoslav conflict and that of Russia. In contrast with the cautious leadership of the USSR, Russia joined almost without hesitation all the decisions on Yugoslavia taken by the West and the main security institutions during 1992 and 1993, and consequently shared all the responsibility for their blunders and mistakes.

Recognition of independence

The most serious mistake was the manner in which the international community recognized the independence of the former Yugoslav republics. The international community had to demand certain guarantees from all the post-Yugoslavian states for the national minorities living in their territories. When in December 1991 the European Community (EC) acknowledged criteria for recognition of the new states in the former Soviet Union and other socialist countries (in particular guarantees of the rights of ethnic and national groups[18]), the war was going on in Croatia. The recognition of Croatia meant that the EC was not respecting its own criterion. In Bosnia and Herzegovina, the deliberate boycott by Bosnian Serbs of the referendum on independence should have been not a pretext for the West to neglect Serbian aspirations but a clear warning against hasty, irreversible steps.

The legal basis for recognition is of great importance, because it affects such serious issues as territorial integrity, self-determination and rights of national minorities, which are closely intertwined with and focused on the dilemma of 'how to encourage the nascent democracies without encouraging separatism'.[19] The Russian leadership should have been interested in the elaboration of such principles, because it had and still has similar problems in the space of the former USSR. However, the Western position on recognition of the former Yugoslav republics was never criticized or even analysed on an official level in Russia. This may be explained by two facts. First, after years of confrontation unity with the West came to be the major priority for Moscow. It did not want to cast a cloud over its new relations by introducing any objections or disagreements. Second, it wanted to persuade the West that Russia was a more reliable partner than the USSR. Foreign Minister Kozyrev missed no opportunity to underline the point.[20]

The ill-conceived recognition of Bosnia and Herzegovina made inevitable not only the war in the republic but also its future demise. Having ignored the will

[18] *Diplomaticheskiy Vestnik*, 15 Jan. 1992.
[19] Zametica, J., International Institute for Strategic Studies, *The Yugoslav Conflict*, Adelphi Paper no. 270 (IISS/Brassey's: London, 1992), p. 60.
[20] See, for example, Kozyrev's speech (note 14), p. 37.

of one ethnic group in Bosnia and Herzegovina, the international community doomed it to fall apart. Although the West forced Bosnian Croats and Muslims to coexist in one state and was trying, jointly with Russia, to put pressure on the Bosnian Serbs, the fabric of the federation is artificial and no one believes in its viability.

Sanctions

From November 1991, the first economic sanctions were applied to Serbia and Montenegro, against whom the international community was subsequently to invoke Article 41, Chapter VII of the UN Charter.[21] This was counter-productive. 'Sanctions hit a great many innocent people—which is not the objective—while, at the same time, they considerably reinforce the positions of the regime against which they were imposed—which also cannot be the objective.'[22] The policy stemmed from a very strong desire, perhaps uncon-scious, to punish Serbia for initiating the conflict, which is understandable emotionally but unacceptable politically. The preconceived policy of the inter-national community towards Serbia left the people living there with the percep-tion that the whole world was against them and that they had nothing to lose.

Russia's modest attempts to change this situation were disregarded by its partners. It is appropriate here to quote Vitaliy Churkin, then Deputy Foreign Minister:

I'll repeat the same thing that I have said many times to my foreign colleagues: if the international community had responded in an adequate way to the firing on the Italian aircraft with humanitarian aid . . . which was shot down in fall 1992 obviously not by the Serbs, if the international community had responded in an adequate way to the murder of French soldiers of the UN contingent in Sarajevo, killed obviously not by Serbian sharpshooters . . . we would have avoided encouraging the other belligerent parties to continue the bloodshed.[23]

Until the autumn of 1994 Russia supported all the resolutions of the UN Security Council, the only exception being in April 1993 when it abstained from voting on new sanctions against Yugoslavia (Serbia and Montenegro). This case is very illustrative. The Security Council received wrong information on the situation around Srebrenica and immediately put the question of sanc-tions to the vote without any verification of its information, violating an agree-ment with Russia not to raise the issue till 26 April. As Churkin pointed out at a press conference on 19 April, it was not the first time important questions had been put to the vote on the basis of unreliable information.[24] Explaining why Russia had not vetoed the resolution, Churkin said, in particular, that Russia

[21] UN Security Council Resolutions 770 (18 Aug. 1992), 816 (31 Mar. 1993) and 836 (4 June 1993).
[22] Petkovic, R., 'International impact of the crisis in the former Yugoslavia', *Review of International Affairs* (Belgrade), vol. 14 (1 Apr. 1994), p. 2.
[23] *Diplomaticheskiy Vestnik*, nos 9–10 (May 1993), pp. 23–24.
[24] *Diplomaticheskiy Vestnik*, nos 9–10 (May 1993), p. 23.

had its own foreign policy priorities and it must not quarrel with the international community only because the parties in Bosnia and Herzegovina could not agree upon the borders.[25]

Peacekeeping and settlement efforts

The greatest failing of the settlement efforts in the former Yugoslavia is that the international community did not subordinate individual interests, preferences and dislikes to the goal of conflict resolution. From the early beginning of the conflict Western countries took sides: Austria, Germany and then the EC on the Slovenian and Croatian side, the USA on the side of the Muslims. Yugoslav conflict management took second place to the objectives of European unity and the special interests of the United States in the Balkans.

The Russian leadership accepted this state of affairs and limited its own role to occasional mediation. Kozyrev made one attempt at mediation in May 1992, visiting all the successor states of the former Yugoslavia without any far-reaching results. At the London Conference in August 1992, which was intended to relieve the EC of the burden of sole responsibility, it was decided to divide up the mediation work, concentrating EC efforts on the Croats and Muslims and making Russia responsible for the Serbs.[26] This decision was a precursor to the more active involvement of Russia, the height of which was the 'shuttle diplomacy' of special envoy Vitaliy Churkin in early 1994. With the NATO ultimatum on Sarajevo of February 1994 Russia stepped in and declared itself one of the main actors in the Balkans.[27] Immediately after its diplomatic success in Sarajevo, Russia made a *faux pas* when it tried, under pressure from the West, to convince the Bosnian Serbs to join the Bosnian federation of Croats and Muslims. In April 1994 Russia failed to solve the Gorazde crisis: Churkin interrupted his mediation and came back to Moscow infuriated with the stubbornness of the Bosnian Serbs. NATO's air strikes in response to the escalation of fighting around Gorazde undermined Russia's mediatory role and cast a shade over Churkin's previously successful shuttle diplomacy.

Russia's contribution to peacekeeping in the former Yugoslavia followed from its foreign policy and domestic evolution. First, its low-profile policy in the Yugoslav conflict left all initiative and the responsibility for conflict management to the EC and then the UN. This factor, apart from other reasons,[28]

---

[25] *Diplomaticheskiy Vestnik*, nos 9–10 (May 1993), p. 24.

[26] Baev, P. *et al.*, Western European Union, Institute for Security Studies, *The Implications of the Yugoslav Crisis for Western Europe's Foreign Relations*, Chaillot Papers no. 17 (ISS: Paris, Oct. 1994), p. 41.

[27] On the NATO ultimatum of 10 Feb. 1994, see Zucconi, M., 'The former Yugoslavia: lessons of war and diplomacy', *SIPRI Yearbook 1995: Armaments, Disarmament and International Security* (Oxford University Press: Oxford, 1995), p. 217.

[28] On several occasions, then Defence Minister Pavel Grachev stated that he was against Russian participation in UNPROFOR, using the argument of the Afghanistan experience. Vitaliy Churkin stated at a press conferecce that high-ranking Russian military did not wish to participate because they wished to avoid the contacts between Russian and Western soldiers and officers that would result. Grachev only

aroused the opposition of the Russian military, who were against Russia contributing to the UN mission (the UN Protection Force, UNPROFOR) without having any say in the conflict settlement. Second, growing tensions and conflicts on the post-Soviet space increased Russia's involvement in conflict resolution in its 'near abroad' and consequently the reluctance of the military leadership to provide troops for UNPROFOR. Thus the deployment of a Russian battalion of 900 as a part of UNPROFOR in Krajina, the Serb-populated enclave in Croatia, which was taken for granted in the West, was the subject of intense domestic struggle.

Russia had previously, in May 1993, stepped forward with an initiative to introduce a massive contingent of European, Russian and US troops under the auspices of the UN to ensure the implementation of the Vance–Owen Plan.[29] This was not supported by the West, which was not inclined to deploy large ground forces for real peace enforcement. It was trying to find a substitute for this risky and politically unpopular measure, which would have been the only effective one, and found it finally in the NATO air strikes against Bosnian Serb positions.

The events of October–December 1993 in Russia formed a clear threshold in its foreign policy and consequently in its policy towards the Yugoslav conflict. This shift towards a more self-assertive and Russia-centred course was predetermined by the failures of the Russian leadership in both domestic and foreign policy. The idealistic pro-Western course of the Kremlin was completely discredited in Russia, which had by now failed to become an equal partner of the West. Furthermore, it had encouraged Russian nationalists who had been capitalizing on the government's mistakes.

It would therefore be wrong to explain the shift in Russia's policy on the former Yugoslavia by nationalistic feelings or 'the call of the blood' according to Samuel Huntington's paradigm.[30] It was 90 per cent political. Having accepted the lead of the West in the early stages of the Yugoslav crisis and having ignored its own interests in this issue, the Russian Government had earlier tried to distance itself from the Yugoslav and Serbian leaderships. The initiative had been picked up and shared by moderate–conservatives and the 'red–browns'. They used the Balkans issue to encourage Russian separatists in the Baltic states, Crimea and Moldova and to raise awareness in Russia. Public opinion became very sensitive to the issue, having seen a striking resemblance with the Yugoslav case. It is important to underline that, having failed on the path towards democracy, the Russian leadership itself became very responsive to such feelings.

changed his position after persuasion by the Foreign Ministry and after Ukraine decided to support UNPROFOR.

[29] On the Vance–Owen Plan, see Claesson, P. and Findlay, T., 'Case studies on peacekeeping: UNOSOM II, UNTAC and UNPROFOR', *SIPRI Yearbook 1994* (Oxford University Press: Oxford, 1994), pp. 75–76; and Erlanger, S., 'Moscow stepping in', *New York Times*, 20 May 1993, p. A12.

[30] Huntington, S. P., 'The clash of civilizations?', *Foreign Affairs*, vol. 72, no. 3 (summer 1993), pp. 22–49.

In this respect it is very illustrative that after Russia's diplomatic success in February 1994 its military leaders demonstrated readiness to send additional troops to Bosnia and Herzegovina: it was a chance for them to make an individual contribution to re-establishing Russia's great-power status in international affairs.

The Sarajevo crisis and the first NATO ultimatum in February 1994 were a turning-point in Russia's Yugoslav policy. The initial evident diplomatic success of Russia raised contradictory feelings in the USA and in other NATO countries. On the one hand, it was positive and helped the West to reach its goal—to raise the siege of Sarajevo—without military intervention; on the other, it was a demonstration of a more independent and active foreign policy, which irritated the USA. 'The Russian action provided a face-saving excuse for Serb compliance with NATO's order to withdraw the artillery or to hand it over to UN peacekeepers, and a pattern of sometimes inharmonious US–Russian diplomatic collaboration began to emerge.'[31] The first signs of discord over the Yugoslav conflict in Russian–Western relations appeared. They were a sign of more profound problems which are analysed in the final section of this chapter.

Starting its course of a more active policy in Bosnia and Herzegovina, Russia contributed to the work of the Contact Group.[32] It succeeded in including in the peace plan on Bosnia and Herzegovina the 'mirror rights', as they were called, for all ethnic groups there. This meant that Bosnian Serbs have a right (like Bosnian Muslims and Croats in their agreements on Bosnian federation and confederation with Croatia) to form a confederation with Serbia. Under pressure from Russia, Serbian President Slobodan Milosevic took the decision to dissociate his position from that of the Bosnian Serbs over the issue of a peace plan. At the same time Russia promoted the decision of the international community of October 1994 to review economic sanctions against the former Yugoslavia and to attach Belgrade more closely to the process of conflict resolution. Moscow succeeded in encouraging negotiations between the Croatian Government and Krajina. In November 1994 these negotiations were interrupted by the escalation of the Bosnian conflict. In general the shift in Russia's policy in the former Yugoslavia was positive. One negative factor, however, was that this was done under the pressure of conservative forces.

The accent on NATO as a main instrument in the conflict-resolution process in the former Yugoslavia put the Russian leadership in a false position. Being a partner of the West, Russia had to share all responsibility for the policy it had never approved of or been asked to approve. From the time of the first NATO ultimatum, the Russian Government was never consulted on NATO air strikes on Serb positions in Bosnia and Herzegovina. The shift of the West to a unilateral solution of the Yugoslav problem combined with its neglect of Russia increased the growing tensions between the former partners. In fact it was part

---

[31] Dean, J., *Ending Europe's Wars: The Continuing Search for Peace and Security* (Twentieth Century Fund Press: New York, 1994), p. 146.

[32] Established in Apr. 1994 and consisting of France, Germany and the UK (these 3 representing the European Union), Russia and the USA.

of a broader dispute between Russia and the West over the new world security system and Russia's place in this system.

On 2 December 1994 Russia for the first time since the demise of the USSR vetoed a resolution on new sanctions against the Serbs of Bosnia and Herzegovina and Krajina in the UN Security Council. This meant that the USA, the European Union (EU, as it now was) and Russia were now on different sides in this conflict despite all previous attempts to maintain unity.

The evolution of the situation in Bosnia and Herzegovina in the summer and autumn of 1995 drastically changed the foundation of the peacemaking operations in the former Yugoslavia. The UN leadership came to a decision to withdraw UNPROFOR from Bosnia and it had to be replaced by NATO forces— IFOR, the Implementation Force, intended to ensure implementation of the Dayton Agreement.[33] This presented a problem for the Russian leadership in respect of Russia's participation in IFOR: on the one hand, it did not want to leave the former Yugoslavia, both for foreign policy and for domestic reasons; on the other hand, the NATO framework for peacemaking operations raised the question of the command and operational basis for a Russian division within NATO's structures. The solution was found in a complicated double system of subordination for the Russian peacemakers in the US brigade. This formally avoided the question of NATO's command over the Russian division, which had attracted much criticism inside Russia. The key question, however, is whether Russia was right in accepting NATO's invitation. The short answer may be 'yes'. Any demonstrative gestures such as shutting the door on partnership would have been short-sighted and counter-productive. The long answer is less unequivocal. The future of the NATO–Russia partnership is now at stake in Bosnia and Herzegovina. If it is successful, the IFOR operation will promote this partnership. If it is not, new confrontations will ensue. Whatever 'fig-leaves' it may try to use, NATO is henceforward responsible for the lives of 1600 Russians and for any decisions which lead to casualties or to negative consequences in Bosnia or the former Yugoslavia. In this respect, instead of accepting NATO's rules of the game the Russian leadership should have stood out for a two-pillar peacemaking structure with NATO and Russia under the auspices of the United Nations. This would have avoided the most damaging complications in Russia's relationship with NATO.

V. The Trans-Dniester apple of discord

Russia's policy in the Balkans has to be assessed in a broader context, including, *inter alia*, developments in the Trans-Dniester conflict. It emerged in 1989, when economic depression and the failures of the Gorbachev programme of *perestroika* became the catalysts of a national movement for independence.

---

[33] General Framework Agreement for Peace in Bosnia and Herzegovina, Paris, 14 Dec. 1995. The text and extracts from the annexes are reproduced in *SIPRI Yearbook 1996: Armaments, Disarmament and International Security* (Oxford University Press: Oxford, 1996), pp. 232–50.

Even before Moldova declared independence in 1991, the national movement took on a clear Romanian tinge, as expressed in the People's Front slogan of reunion with Romania. This slogan and the idea of the priority of the interests of the indigenous nation could not but have an affect, given the complicated ethno-national composition of Moldova,[34] and provoked strong opposition from the Russian minority. On 3 September 1990 its leaders proclaimed the Trans-Dniester Soviet Socialist Republic[35] a part of the USSR. The Supreme Soviet of Moldova then declared these decisions unconstitutional. The first clashes took place in Dubossary district on 2 November 1990 and 25 September 1991, the local authorities there having supported the proclamation of the Trans-Dniester Republic. Soviet armed forces were not involved in the confrontation. President Gorbachev intervened in the dispute and issued a decree on measures to normalize the situation in Moldova, to which no one paid any heed.

Having inherited the Trans-Dniester issue from the USSR, Russia was not ready to formulate its position on the territorial integrity of Moldova and the Trans-Dniester secession. In all probability after the demise of the USSR the conflict in Moldova could have been solved by political means if the Russian leadership had declared at this stage that Russia recognized the territorial integrity of Moldova in its present borders and that in the event of reunification with Romania the people of Trans-Dniester would have the right to decide their own future.[36] This would have deprived nationalists on both sides of the pretext either for secession from Moldova or for reunification with Romania. It would have discouraged the United Democratic Convention in Romania which was proclaiming the goal of restoration of the Romanian territories within the 1938 frontiers.

However, having achieved its goal of dismantling the USSR, hastened by the August 1991 *coup d'état*, the Russian leadership began to identify itself more and more with the former centre in its relations with the republics of the former Soviet Union. On this logic Russia was not interested in limiting its diplomatic manoeuvres in the post-Soviet space by formulating a clear position on the Trans-Dniester conflict, as this might have had considerable repercussions on other conflicts. The principle of the territorial integrity of Moldova was only confirmed by Russia in the Russian–Moldovan agreement in July 1992 after much bloodshed during the three months of fighting, from March to June 1992, known as the Trans-Dniester war.

---

[34] The major ethnic groups of Moldova are Moldovans (65%), Ukrainians (14%), Russians (13%), Gagauz (3.5%) and Bulgarians (2.5%).

[35] On the left bank of the River Dniester it included the Kamen, Dubossar, Rybnitsa, Grigoropol and Slabodzey districts and the towns of Tiraspol, Rybnitsa and Dubossary, and on the right bank the town of Bendery.

[36] Russia's hesitation may seem all the more strange if it is remembered that in the early stages of the conflict the Russian leadership, encouraged by radical democrats (Gennadiy Burbulis, Galina Staro-voitova, Fyodor Shelov-Kovedyaev and others), supported independent Moldova and President Mircea Snegur and saw the Trans-Dniester Republic as the last stronghold of communism. Moreover, in Russia's opinion Snegur embodied those political forces in Moldova which were against reunification with Romania.

Military action started on the left bank of the Dniester on 24 March 1992 and became especially bitter in Bendery by 20 June 1992. According to official data, during the first days of the fighting more than 500 people were killed and 1500 wounded while 80 000 of the 150 000 inhabitants of the town fled. A massive artillery bombardment of the towns and more heavily populated districts was carried out with heavy howitzers which Moldova had acquired from the Soviet Army. MiG-29 aircraft, helicopters, tanks and mortars were also used. It was alleged that soldiers and advisers of the Romanian Army took part in the military operations on the Moldovan side. It was also admitted that some officers of the Russian 14th Army, which should have maintained a position of neutrality, took part in the defence of the town together with the Trans-Dniester Guards.[37] The problem was aggravated by the 14th Army threatening to intervene in the conflict if it was not settled by the Moldovan and Russian political leaders.

Russia tried to solve the problem of the status of the 14th Army through the CIS structures. Marshal Yevgeniy Shaposhnikov, then Supreme Commander of the CIS Armed Forces, proposed to President Mircea Snegur of Moldova that the 14th Army units be used to separate the belligerent parties under the control of military observers from the CIS countries. This proposal was rejected by the Moldovan leadership, which was afraid that it could lead to 'foreign military intervention'.[38] Instead, soon after agreement on a cease-fire was reached in June 1992,[39] President Snegur signed a protocol on the activity of military observers and collective peacekeeping forces of the CIS states in zones of conflict. However, this was superseded by another plan, promoted by Russian military leaders, for the deployment of 'disengagement forces' from Russia, Moldova and Trans-Dniester.[40] Russia had succeeded in eliminating possible competitors on the scene—Romania and Ukraine.

Russia also insisted on bilateral negotiations. The Moldovan authorities failed to provide for the fully-fledged participation of observers from the Conference on Security and Co-operation in Europe (CSCE) in negotiations with Russia,[41] although the CSCE mission opened in Cisinau in September 1992 was involved in elaborating recommendations for conflict settlement. The negotiations were aimed at resolving two problems: (a) the political status of the Trans-Dniester region, and (b) the modalities of the withdrawal of the 14th Army, 'the last Russian army located on the territory of a foreign state, with the exception of peacekeeping missions governed by mutual agreements'.[42] Between August 1992 and September 1994, 10 rounds of negotiations between Russia and

[37] The 14th Army, based in Trans-Dniester, had been put under Russian jurisdiction in Apr. 1992, which immediately created a problem concerning its legal status on the territory of the foreign state.

[38] 'The Moldovan Government rejected Marshall Shaposhnikov's proposal', ITAR-TASS, 5 Apr. 1992.

[39] On 24 June 1992 in Istanbul the presidents of Moldova, Romania, Russia and Ukraine reached an agreement on a cease-fire. The state of emergency was not lifted until 19 Aug. 1992.

[40] Allison, R., Western European Union, Institute for Security Studies, *Peacekeeping in the Soviet Successsor States*, Chaillot Papers no. 18 (ISS: Paris, Nov. 1994), p. 3.

[41] Baranovsky, V., 'Conflict developments on the territory of the former Soviet Union', *SIPRI Yearbook 1994* (note 29), p. 190.

[42] Viets, S., 'Moldova pullout pact unrealistic, says Lebed', *Moscow Times*, 25 Oct. 1994, p. 4.

Moldova were held to find a solution. By October 1994 the two sides had agreed that the withdrawal of Russian troops from Moldova should be completed three years after the agreement on the legal status of Russian military formations came into force and synchronized with the political settlement of the Trans-Dniester conflict and the definition of the special status of the region.[43]

The issue of withdrawal of the 14th Army was complicated by the fact that 80 per cent of its personnel, including its officers, were local inhabitants. According to General Alexander Lebed, then Commander of the 14th Army, 'more than half the officers are ethnic Slavs, born and raised in Moldova. They have apartments here and jobs, but back in Russia they have nothing. There is a fear as well that if they pull out, their families will fall victim to a new round of inter-ethnic fighting'.[44] A further aspect was the future of the military arsenals of the 14th Army, which in May 1995 consisted of 49 476 firearms pieces, 805 artillery pieces, 3535 vehicles, 43258 t of munitions and a large quantity of military equipment with a total weight of 58467 t. According to General Lebed, it would be detrimental to conflict management in the post-Soviet space to lose control over these arsenals.[45]

The political status of the Trans-Dniester region is at the time of writing still to be defined. In all probability it will acquire a status of autonomy with special rights within the Moldovan state comparable to the status of Åland, a Swedish autonomy inside Finland.[46] It would be expedient to maintain peacekeeping forces under the auspices of the Organization for Security and Co-operation in Europe (OSCE)[47] in Trans-Dniester for a transitional period agreed between the authorities of Moldova, Russia and the Trans-Dniester region.

General Lebed's reservations about the Russian–Moldovan agreement of 21 October 1994[48] weighed heavy, first of all because of his immense popularity in the area, his open criticism of both sides in the conflict and of the policies of President Boris Yeltsin, then Defence Minister Pavel Grachev and other senior military officials.[49] He accused the local authorities of Trans-Dniester of corruption and criminal connections; at the same time he warned the Moldovan side that the neutrality of the 14th Army would be an armed neutrality. His independent and even arrogant position cost him the displeasure of both the Moldovan and the Russian leaderships; but when in August 1994 the government tried to remove him under the pretext of reorganization of the command of the 14th Army the Russian Counter-Intelligence Service warned

[43] Agreements on the legal status, method and timing of withdrawal of the military formations of the Russian Federation temporarily deployed on the territory of Moldova were signed by the Russian and Moldovan governments on 21 Oct. 1994. Viets (note 42), p. 4.

[44] Viets (note 42), p. 4.

[45] Krutakov, L., 'General Lebed snimet mundir' [General Lebed takes off his uniform], *Moskovksie Novosti*, no. 44 (25 June–2 July 1995), p. 6.

[46] Nantoy, O., 'Kishinev uchitsa u Helsinki' [Cisinau learns from Helsinki], *Moskovskie Novosti*, 19–26 Feb. 1995, p. 10.

[47] On 1 Jan. 1995 the CSCE became the OSCE.

[48] Gen. Lebed claimed that the agreement was 'unrealistic and little more than an attempt to win time to think through a better solution'. Viets (note 42), p. 4.

[49] See, e.g., Lebed, A., 'U Rossii est armiya, no armiya li eto?' [Russia has its army, but is it the Army?], *Nezavisimaya Gazeta*, 16 Nov. 1994, p. 3.

the Russian leadership that this might result in the 14th Army refusing to obey the orders of the Ministry of Defence.[50]

Lebed retired in mid-1995, apparently both under pressure from Grachev and with the intention of entering 'big politics'. His retirement was presented as facilitating implementation of the agreements on the withdrawal of Russian military formations of October 1994.[51] The 14th Army Command was transformed into the Operational Group of Russian troops in Trans-Dniester, and the talks on the fate of the military arsenals seemed to take on a more routine, less complicated character. The Moldovan Government, which no longer wanted to be dependent on the goodwill of General Lebed, seemed to be satisfied with this.

Nevertheless, it would be short-sighted to overestimate the emerging consensus between Moscow and Cisinau. The future of military arsenals is only one part of the issue of the Russian armed forces in Moldova, and the latter is only one part of the Trans-Dniester problem. The visit of President Snegur to Brussels at the end of November 1994, immediately after the conclusion of the agreements on the 14th Army,[52] and his negotiations with the NATO leadership, who promised to support peaceful developments in the situation in Moldova, also testify to the fact that Moldova does not want to rely only on Russia and shows interest in international guarantees and involvement. On the other hand Moldova's suspicions of Russia and its assertive diplomacy may fuel Russian mistrust and concern.

The solution of the Trans-Dniester problem, however, does not depend only on official Moscow, Cisinau and Tiraspol: it is still dependent on various nationalist factions in Russia, Moldova and Romania, which may easily cause a chain reaction and destabilize the situation. It will take great effort and diplomatic skill from all the parties involved in the conflict as well as from the West not to destroy the agreements that have been reached.

VI. Conclusions: implications for the West and Russia

Recent developments in the Balkans and their vicinity have confronted the West and Russia with certain dilemmas and lessons.

1. It is evident now that Russia will be actively involved in the Balkans. It has its own interests and responsibilities there both because of its historical ties with the nations of the region and because of its own precarious geopolitical situation.

One of the main questions is how Russia will be involved in the conflict-resolution process—as an indispensable partner of the West or as its rival.

---

[50] 'Kreml ne risknul vstupit v otkrytuyu konfrontatsiyu s komanduyushchim 14-oy armii' [The Kremlin is not risking open confrontation with the Commander of the 14th Army], *Nezavisimaya Gazeta*, 30 Aug. 1994, p. 1.

[51] Prikhodka, N., 'General Lebed poekhal v Moskvu za pobedoy' [General Lebed went to Moscow to win], *Nezavisimaya Gazeta*, 24 May 1995, p. 2.

[52] *Diplomaticheskiy Vestnik*, nos 21–22 (Nov. 1994), p. 46.

Cooperation between the West and Russia is essential for ending the Yugoslav conflict as well as for resolving other problems of the post-bipolar period. Moreover, internal developments in Russia will be influenced by and dependent on the policy of the USA and Europe towards Russia's role in the Balkans and in international relations in general. The Western policy of unconditional support for the Russian leadership, whose democratic image had been taken by the West on trust, sometimes regardless of its evident anti-democratic stance, came to be counter-productive because it fuelled anti-Western feeling and nationalism. The opposite course, of neglecting Russia and treating it as a loser, brought about the same result. If it is continued, it will be detrimental both for Russia and for the West. Russia should not be left on its own; it should be treated by the West as an equal partner with all the attendant responsibilities.

In 1996 and further into the future, Russia's foreign policy, including its policy on the Balkan area, will evolve as a compromise between the leading political forces. It will be closer to a new version of the Soviet foreign policy of Gorbachev's time, adjusted to the new realities and taking into account the need for pragmatic cooperation with the West. The appointment of new leadership at the Foreign Ministry is a first sign of this trend.

2. NATO enlargement eastwards (two Balkan states, Bulgaria and Romania, are also looking for membership) would mean a new division of Europe and stimulate negative trends in Russia's policy both towards the former republics of the USSR and towards its former allies.[53] Enlargement could bring greater security for a few more nations but at the cost of repartitioning the continent of Europe into Western and Russian spheres of influence. However, even if the process of NATO enlargement is irreversible, it is still possible to limit the damage by making it more gradual, enhancing military relations between Russia and NATO and promoting NATO reform and cooperation between it and other security institutions.

3. The NATO air strikes in Bosnia and Herzegovina proved completely ineffective in spite of a widespread opinion that they played a decisive role. Moreover, there is a danger that they will be perceived as NATO's biggest success and be tried again in post-communist conflict resolution.

It should be remembered that NATO started to bomb Serbian positions in April 1994 and that the new air strikes brought no visible results apart from further escalation. They began to be 'effective' only in 1995. At that time the Croatian Government and the Bosnian Muslims had launched almost simultaneous offensives against the Serbs in Banja Luka and in Bosnia and Herzegovina; Milosevic, encouraged by the West to be obedient, had preferred to wash his hands of the Serbs in Krajina and Bosnia and Herzegovina; Russia was involved in the bloody mess in Chechnya, losing thereby all moral right and

---

[53] If this happened, the impact on the precarious Russian domestic balance, on the messy conflicts in the former Soviet space, on US–Russian relations and on European politics in general can be imagined. A new cold war could inadvertently be brought about and would not be confined to relations between the West and the Serbs, even though few political groups in Russia would advocate a new deliberate split with the West for the sake of defending the Serbs.

any influence over the events of August 1995; and the international community, sick and tired of the war in the former Yugoslavia and of the stubbornness of the warring parties, had closed its eyes to the biggest 'ethnic cleansing' of the whole Yugoslav tragedy—in Krajina. Without these factors the NATO air strikes would never have defeated the Serbs.

One of the lessons of this crisis is that the new problems of conflict resolution and peacekeeping in Europe require new international mechanisms, policies and methods. The cold war organizations, biases and contingency planning cannot be simply adjusted to new tasks without a great risk of reviving past confrontations and dangers. In this respect it would be wise to come back to Russia's initiative, taken in response to the NATO-centred security policy of the West, to reform the OSCE structure in order to make it the core of a new security system in Europe.

4. In respect of the conflict-resolution process in the former Yugoslavia, any compromise peaceful settlement would be better than fighting and bloodshed prolonged indefinitely. The greatest deficiency of Western policy[54] towards Yugoslavia has been that the West has been trying to reach two incompatible goals—to punish the Serbs and to put an end to the bloodshed. As for Russia, it is responsible for having subordinated the goal of international cooperation in conflict resolution to the goal of maintaining unity with the West at any cost.

5. The international community should choose between real peace enforcement in the former Yugoslavia and its previous policy of self-deception. The most resolute self-serving ultimatums and air strikes cannot substitute for a wise, consistent and unbiased policy in conflict resolution or for risky, costly and politically unpopular deployment jointly with Russia of large ground forces for real peace enforcement.[55] It should be remembered that the Dayton peace agreement only became possible when the USA, its main architect, recognized the need to communicate directly with Slobodan Milosevic, who finally took responsibility for the behaviour of the Bosnian Serbs, and deploy ground forces (IFOR) in Bosnia. The idea of establishing direct contacts with Milosevic, however, was not a new one. It had been proposed many times by different countries, including Russia, and been rejected by the USA only because of its anti-Serbian bias. As for the deployment of ground forces, Russia's initiative of May 1993 to introduce a massive contingent of European, Russian and US troops under the auspices of the United Nations in order to ensure implementation of the Vance–Owen Plan had not been supported by the USA or its allies. Instead, the West had been trying to find a substitute for this risky, politically unpopular measure—in fact the only possible effective one—and found it in NATO air strikes. The US leadership therefore had to come back at Dayton to

---

[54] Although the very notion of the West is relative, because the EU position on particular aspects of the Yugoslav conflict differed from that of the USA (e.g., on the question of lifting the embargo on arms deliveries to Bosnian Muslims), it is nevertheless possible to speak about the general approach of the West towards the conflict.

[55] 'The fighting in Yugoslavia did pose a long-term threat to Western security in the sense that the collective reluctance of the major Western allies to commit themselves on the ground revealed serious weaknesses in the concept of multilateral peacemaking.' Dean (note 31), p. 149.

those measures it had rejected earlier, but now after great bloodshed and destruction.

6. It might seem that the main dilemma for Russia is the choice between following the Western lead in international affairs and pursuing its own genuine foreign policy. It is in fact a false dilemma. Russia proved by its diplomatic activity in Sarajevo and in many other 'hot spots' that it can play a very important and positive role in parallel and in addition to the West, which obviously does not mean against the West. On the contrary, a subservient policy on the part of Russia will not lead to international stability and security. A new Russian foreign policy strategy, based on Russian national interests and compatible with the goal of cooperation with the West, is badly needed if a new division of the world is to be prevented.

One more lesson should be drawn from the Yugoslav case by Russia: it should learn to treat the republics of the former Soviet Union not as its 'near abroad' and 'the post-Soviet space' but as completely independent sovereign states. That will be the best guarantee against the repetition of the Yugoslav disaster.

The Balkan turmoil provided the international community with a golden opportunity to prove that a genuine new world order can be built by joint efforts, at least in post-communist Europe. This chance has been lost, but there is still a chance to prevent various relapses into the cold war mentality, wherever they remain or reappear—in Croatia, Serbia, Russia or the USA.

Part X

Challenges from the south

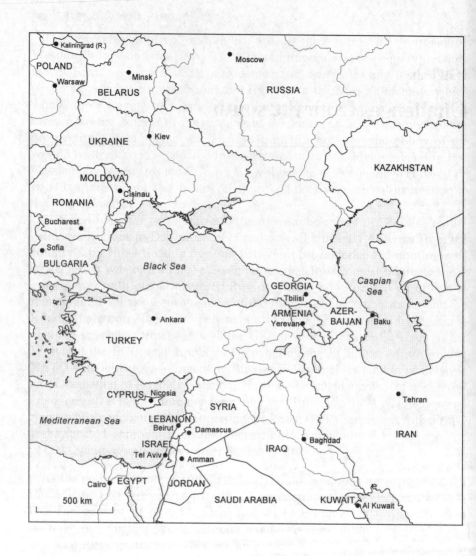

Summary of the principal armed conflicts in the Caucasus

Nagorno-Karabakh (Azerbaijan)

Separatist grievances in this largely Armenian-populated enclave, transferred in the 1920s to the administrative control of the surrounding Azerbaijan SSR, erupted in violence in 1988. The collapse of the USSR turned the conflict into full-scale war. Armenian-backed Karabakh militiamen achieved near-total victory over Azerbaijani forces in the enclave by mid-1992 and established control over surrounding territory (nearly 20% of the total territory of Azerbaijan). Russian mediation produced a cease-fire agreement in May 1994. Negotiations mediated by the CSCE/OSCE (Minsk Group) began in Mar. 1992. In Dec. 1994 the CSCE approved a multi-national peacekeeping force for Nagorno-Karabakh; this was not yet deployed as of late 1996.

South Ossetia (Georgia)

Ethnic tensions between Georgians and the Ossetians (approx. two-thirds of a population of c. 100 000) in the Georgian *oblast* of South Ossetia prompted the Georgian Government to abolish the autonomous status of South Ossetia in Dec. 1990. Ossetian separatists, demanding that South Ossetia be allowed to unite with neighbouring North Ossetia and thus leave Georgia to join the Russian Federation, sparked armed revolt in spring 1992. As inter-ethnic fighting intensified, direct negotiations between presidents Shevardnadze and Yeltsin led to a cease-fire agreement in June 1992, followed by the deployment of a joint Russian–Georgian–Ossetian peacekeeping force the following month. Efforts to find a solution continue.

Abkhazia (Georgia)

Growing tension between Georgians and Abkhazians (who in 1991 made up < 20% of the population of their titular republic within Georgia) culminated with Abkhaz separatists issuing a declaration of independence from Georgia in July 1992. Deployment of Georgian Government forces there was followed by armed clashes punctuated by short cease-fires. In Sep. 1993, combined Abkhaz and North Caucasian militias, reportedly with logistical assistance from the Russian Army, captured the Georgian-held Abkhaz capital, Sukhumi. In Oct., under pressure from this defeat and from renewal of armed rebellion by militias loyal to deposed President Gamsakhurdia, Georgian President Shevardnadze requested direct Russian intervention to quell the fighting. In May 1994 government officials and Abkhaz separatists signed a Russian-mediated cease-fire agreement which provided for deployment of Russian peacekeeping troops.

Chechnya (Russia)

The strong separatist movement in Chechnya is rooted in the turbulent history of tsarist Russian and Soviet policy in the region. In Nov. 1991, after the failed coup in Moscow, a newly elected Chechen leader, Dzhokhar Dudaev, proclaimed Chechnya's sovereignty. The Russian Government's political efforts to rein in the breakaway republic were unsuccessful; Moscow decided to eliminate Dudaev's regime by military action. In Dec. 1994 Russian Army units moved into the republic to 'restore constitutional legality, order and peace', resulting in large-scale fighting, heavy civilian casualties and protests both in Russia and abroad. Negotiations to end the fighting broke down and the conflict settled into protracted low-intensity warfare. On 27 May 1996 a cease-fire agreement was reached envisaging withdrawal of the federal armed forces and eventual negotiations to settle Chechnya's future status. After unsuccessful attempts at a new offensive and the capture of Grozny by the separatists, Russia in Sep. 1996 was forced to accept the withdrawal of troops. Chechnya's status was to be settled within 5 years.

North Ossetia–Ingushetia

Tensions between the two neighbouring North Caucasian peoples were fuelled by the demands of Ingush leaders for the return of territory from which Ingush residents had been deported in 1944 and which was subsequently incorporated into North Ossetia. Fighting between Ingush and Ossetian militias erupted in the autumn of 1992; Russian troops were dispatched to halt the fighting in Nov. 1992; a state of emergency was imposed in the region but rescinded at the beginning of 1995. In Nov. 1995 the presidents of North Ossetia and Ingushetia signed an agreement renouncing territorial claims; the issue of the return of refugees (c. 60 000 in 1992) remains unsettled.

Key facts

The 'Russian factor' in the ethnic composition of the Caucasus, 1994–95

Figures are estimates.

	Total population (millions)	Ethnic Russians (%)	Russophone population (%)
Armenia	3.6	1.6	2
Azerbaijan	7.3	5.6	7.5
Georgia	5.6	6.3	8.9
Northern Caucasus[a]	5.5	28.3	28.9

[a] Consists of 7 autonomous republics of the Russian Federation: Adygei, Chechnya, Dagestan, Ingushetia, Kabardino-Balkaria, Karachai-Circassia and North Ossetia. *Sources*: Trans-Caucasus: A Chronology, vol. 5, no. 7 (Email version received 20 July 1996 from: Internet giragosi@essential.org); Coppieters, B. (ed.), *Contested Borders in the Caucasus* (Vrije Universiteit Brussel: Brussels, 1996), p. 95; and *Novaya Rossiya, 1994: Informatsionno-statisticheskiy almanakh* (Vsya Moskva: Moscow, 1994), pp. 139, 140, 143, 145.

20. Russia in the Caucasus: interests, threats and policy options

Maxim Shashenkov

I. The Caucasian security complex

Since the breakup of the USSR in December 1991, the Caucasus[1] has been one of the most turbulent and unstable regions of the former Soviet Union. The situation there has been marked by a high degree of fluidity and uncertainty. Political turmoil, economic collapse and inter-ethnic and territorial conflicts have become dominant features of recent developments in all but a few areas of the Caucasian region. Long-suppressed historical, ethnic and religious grievances, rivalries and contradictions have burst into local politics, challenging the existing frontiers, territorial integrity and domestic arrangements of the Caucasian states.

In Georgia, violent confrontations with non-Georgian minorities in the autonomous republics of Abkhazia and South Ossetia threatened to accelerate the complex process of fragmentation of the country. In the autumn of 1991 then Georgian President Zviad Gamsakhurdia moved to abolish the autonomous status of the South Ossetian Republic, and the Ossetian conflict gained further momentum in the first half of 1992, forcing large numbers of South Ossetians to flee to Russian North Ossetia. This danger of Georgia fragmenting was increased by the activation of the supporters of ousted President Gamsakhurdia in the western part of the country (Mingrelia) and by serious splits within the Georgian political establishment.

Tensions in Abkhazia between the Abkhaz and the Georgians[2] produced an upsurge of pro-Abkhaz feeling in the northern Caucasus and contributed to the rapid political mobilization of various mountain peoples. In August 1989 representatives from various north Caucasian informal groups gathered in Sukhumi, the capital of Abkhazia, had proclaimed the creation of the Assembly of Mountain Peoples of the Caucasus. In 1992 the escalation of the conflict in Abkhazia gave a renewed purpose to the Assembly, which in October 1992 was renamed the Confederation of Caucasian Mountain Peoples (CCMP) and later became the Caucasian Peoples' Confederation (CPC). The creation of a separate Caucasian Federal Republic with its capital in Sukhumi was asserted to be the ulti-

---

[1] The 3 Transcaucasian states (Armenia, Azerbaijan and Georgia) and the north Caucasian republics of the Russian Federation (Adygei, Dagestan, Ingushetia, Kabardino-Balkaria, Karachaevo-Cherkessia and North Ossetia) together with the self-proclaimed republic of Chechnya, which in Nov. 1991 unilaterally declared independence from Russia.

[2] According to the 1989 Soviet census, the Abkhaz constituted slightly more than 17% of the population of the Autonomous Republic of Abkhazia and the Georgians *c.* 46%.

mate goal of the CCMP. The Abkhaz and Ossetians in Georgia and the Lezgins and other smaller groups of mountain peoples in Azerbaijan were promised political and military protection and assistance.

In the spring of 1992 the conflict over the Armenian-held enclave of Nagorno-Karabakh escalated into a full-scale war between Armenia and Azerbaijan. Disasters at the front brought about several changes of government in Azerbaijan.

Political instability and conflicts in the Transcaucasus, and especially in Georgia, exercised direct influence on the Russian northern Caucasus. By far the most serious problems for Russia have been those posed by developments in the north Caucasian republics of the Russian Federation.

The armed clashes between the Ingush and Ossetians in the autumn of 1992 were the most violent and disruptive within the Russian Federation's borders since the breakup of the USSR. The essential bone of contention between the two mountain peoples was the question who should control the Prigorodny district adjacent to the North Ossetian–Ingush border and the eastern part of the North Ossetian capital Vladikavkaz. This district belonged to the Ingush until 1944, when they and several other north Caucasian peoples (but not Ossetians) were accused by the Soviet authorities of collective collaboration with the Nazis and deported to Central Asia. Past injustices were only partly corrected by General Secretary Nikita Khrushchev, who reinstated the Chechen–Ingush Autonomous Republic in 1957 but left the Prigorodny district and the entire city of Vladikavkaz in the possession of the Ossetians. The Ingush had never given up their hope of regaining the 'lost' territory and renewed their efforts to recover the lands in the aftermath of the USSR's collapse. The speed and scale of the Russian response (11 000 troops were quickly sent to quell the conflict) testified to Russia's determination to prevent the conflict from spreading further and to restore stability in the area. This military deployment, however, could not offer a long-term solution to the conflict.

In Chechnya, in the wake of the abortive August 1991 coup in Moscow, the former communist leadership was accused of giving tacit support to the instigators of the coup attempt and dismissed by the National Congress of the Chechen People. In late October 1991 General Dzhokhar Dudaev was elected president of the self-styled Chechen Republic, which was intent on asserting its independence from Russia. Awkward attempts by the Russian authorities in late 1991 to introduce a state of emergency and to deploy interior troops in the restive republic failed to achieve their objectives and only strengthened Chechnyan opposition to outside interference. Despite an economic embargo and military–political pressure, Chechnya refused to sign the Federation Treaty of 1992 which gave constitutional form to the Russian Federation. More alarmingly for the Russian authorities, General Dudaev embarked on an active Caucasian policy, trying to enlist the support of other nationalist and pro-independence parties and groups in the region. Chechnya has clearly emerged as one of the leading forces in the CPC, giving this organization a strong anti-Russian colouring.

This brief review of post-Soviet security developments in the Caucasus clearly reveals the high conflict potential of this region. In addition to the most salient conflicts described here, there are a great many other potential and so far less violent sources of instability in the Caucasus. The nationalist movements of the Lezgins in the north and the Talysh in the south-east of Azerbaijan are very worrying for the Azeri authorities.[3] Some nationalist Lezgin politicians aspire to unite the Lezgins from Dagestan, which is part of Russia, and from northern Azerbaijan into one Lezgin state. The Lezgin problem distantly resembles that of the Ossetians, divided between the territory of the Russian Federation and Georgia. In Georgia, the relations between the titular nationality and the Azeri minority scattered in the eastern part of the republic are unstable. The northern Caucasus contains something like 37 areas in which territorial and ethnic conflicts could occur.[4]

Two fundamental trends in local security dynamics seem to be of special relevance for an analysis of the Caucasian security complex.[5]

The first is the growing interdependence and interaction between different layers of instability. The inter-ethnic complications of the Caucasus and the fragility of the newly independent states have worked to blur distinctions between internal and regional instabilities. Internal strife and conflicts have invited deeper involvement of neighbours, often with corresponding minorities located in crisis-stricken areas, and thus have tended to acquire distinct regional dimensions. At the same time, successes and failures in regional wars have rapidly become the principal factor in the domestic politics of the Caucasian states. Similar strong links between and interdependence of internal and regional security problems have been evident in several conflict-stricken areas around the world. In the Caucasus, however, this merging of domestic and regional politics is reinforced by the region's history, geopolitics and complex ethnic mix.

The second destabilizing trend in the geopolitics of the Caucasus is the steady growth of conflicts involving powerful currents of ethnic nationalism, domestic state structures and existing frontiers. An apparent dichotomy between the bewildering mosaic of Caucasian peoples and the historical patterns of amity and enmity among them on the one hand and rigid state structures and often artificial and arbitrary borders on the other is a serious complicating factor in building a stable security order in the region.

---

[3] Fuller, E., 'Caucasus: the Lezgin campaign for autonomy', Radio Free Europe/Radio Liberty (hereafter RFE/RL) *RFE/RL Research Report*, vol. 1, no. 41 (16 Oct. 1992), pp. 30–32; and 'Regional survey: Azerbaijan', *Russian Briefing*, vol. 2, no. 1 (1993), pp. 9–10.

[4] This figure was given by the Chairman of the North Ossetian Parliament, Akhsarbek Galazov. *Krasnaya Zvezda*, 27 Nov. 1992.

[5] The term was first suggested by Barry Buzan in Buzan, B., 'A framework for regional security analysis', eds B. Buzan and G. Rizvi, *South Asian Insecurity and the Great Powers* (Macmillan: Basingstoke, 1986), pp. 3–13. A security complex presupposes that distinct and significant relations exist among a set of states locked into geographical proximity. The main security perceptions and concerns of states within a security complex are so interlinked that their national security problems cannot reasonably be analysed apart from one another. Cultural and historical ties further the coherence of a security complex and its durability and promote the notion of intense interdependence.

To be successful, Russian strategy in the Caucasus needs not only to address these growing linkages between different aspects of the instability in the Caucasus, but also to be based on a clear understanding of how the local situation is influenced by history and geopolitics. One of the central questions to be answered is why the Caucasus, rather than, for example, Central Asia, has emerged as the most unstable and volatile region of the former Soviet empire. In this regard, several key factors directly related to the discussion of the regional security issues can be mentioned briefly.

A land bridge between the Black and Caspian seas and a natural link between the Eurasian steppes and the Near East,[6] the Caucasus has long been an area where civilizations crossed, mixed and clashed.[7] The centuries-old competition between Persians, Ottomans and Russians has left a bitter legacy of 'outside patron–Caucasian client' relations: each power sought to cultivate its own support base among local nations and ethoses. Religious and cultural affinities, ethnic amities and enmities, old rivalries and feuds—all counted for external powers which tried to enlist the support of local peoples.[8] As a result, foreign competition for influence promoted and contributed to the internal divisions and fragmentation of the Caucasus.

The nature and geography of the Caucasus were a source both of strength and of vulnerability. On the one hand, the high mountains served as a natural obstacle to would-be external conquerors and were a convenient refuge for those fleeing from foreign domination and oppression. On the other, mountains, valleys and river basins sheltered many ancient and distinctive Caucasian peoples, who fiercely defended their unique cultural inheritance. The terrain has perpetuated a complex ethnic, linguistic and religious mosaic in these areas. It separated peoples, permitting them to live in relative isolation and self-containment and fostering the development of many distinctive dialects: close neighbours often spoke different languages and dialects.[9] A cohesive national consciousness has been emerging only very slowly in the northern Caucasus, many parts of modern Georgia and Azerbaijan. Clan–tribal structures and strong

---

[6] In this chapter, the Near East is defined as Iran, Iraq, Turkey and the immediately surrounding region.

[7] In the past, the region has known only a few centuries of comparative peace. Most of the time the region, in particular the Transcaucasus, has been a theatre of perpetual warfare and conflicts between various peoples and empires. Over the centuries, the Transcaucasian peoples and principalities, sandwiched between large and powerful empires (Sassanid and Byzantine; later, Ottoman and Persian) remained divided and often reduced to the status of buffer nations between rival powers of the East. In the 18th and 19th centuries, tsarist Russia entered the area and after prolonged clashes with the Ottomans, the Persians and various Caucasian peoples conquered the whole of the modern Caucasus.

[8] The Russians often relied on the support of Christian Armenians and Georgians. In the 19th century, the Georgians were the keystone of the Russian position in the region. At the same time, the western parts of Georgia (Imeretia and Guria) preserved strong links with the Ottomans and often sided with them against the tsarist armies. The hostility of Muslim peoples of the northern Caucasus to Russian military penetration made them a valuable asset to the Turks. See, e.g., Henze, P. B., 'Fire and sword in the Caucasus: the 19th century resistance of the North Caucasian mountaineers', Central Asian Survey, vol. 2, no. 1 (July 1983), pp. 8–10. Finally, Persia enjoyed substantial influence among the Azeri Shia population.

[9] The Arabs aptly named the Caucasus 'the Mountain of Languages'. Dagestan alone today is composed of more than 30 different nationalities, and people living in nearby villages speak very different dialects.

regional identification, which fractured wider ethnic identities, have always been an important factor of political life in many parts of the region. By implication, Islam or Christianity rather than the claims of ethnicity often served as a rallying and uniting point for the Caucasian peoples. All these factors have made the Caucasus particularly vulnerable to external manipulation. In few other regions of the world or of the tsarist/Soviet empire was the policy of 'divide and rule' so easy to apply to local conditions. In even fewer regions was it to have such explosive and tragic consequences.

Contemporary Russian policy makers would do well to remember that the more recent legacy of tsarist and Soviet rule in the Caucasus contains many tragic and brutal episodes. These have made their marks on the historical consciousness of local peoples and have actively influenced Caucasian politics since the decline of tight Soviet control over the region. The tsarist imperial advance into the region met with a sustained campaign of resistance among the north Caucasian tribes.[10] It took several decades to 'pacify' the mountain-dwellers and to establish full control over the Caucasus in the mid-19th century. The spirit of defiance, however, never died.[11]

General Secretary Joseph Stalin's reign had perhaps a stronger disruptive effect on the ethno-political structures of the Caucasus than on any other Soviet region. Whole nationalities (Chechens, Ingush and several others) were accused of collective collaboration with the Nazis and deported to Central Asia. Frontiers, largely of an arbitrary nature, were drawn and re-drawn, and territorial units were frequently reshaped. It would not be an exaggeration to state that there are more real and potential sources of border disputes, inter-ethnic conflicts and historical grievances in this region than anywhere else in the territory of the former Soviet Union, including the much larger Central Asian region. The scope, intensity and violent heritage of past conflicts in the Caucasus resulted in their quick revival once the freezing effect of Soviet rule gradually eased after the demise of the USSR.

The abundance of 'hot spots' on the map of the Caucasus was, however, only one manifestation of the challenges from the south with which Russia had to cope. Another probably no less acute problem for the Russian Government was the emergence of a powerful anti-imperialist or anti-Russian trend in local politics.[12] Both Zviad Gamsakhurdia, who was elected President of Georgia in

---

[10] A series of charismatic leaders, among whom Sufi Sheikh Shamil is probably the best known, organized large-scale guerrilla campaigns against the imposition of Russian control. Russian armies suppressed any rebellions with particular brutality. Entire tribes and villages were exterminated, and land and cattle were often confiscated. The prevailing attitude towards indigenous peoples was characterized by arrogance and contempt. See, e.g., Pokrovskiy, M. N., *Diplomatiya i Voiny Tsarskoy Rossii v XIX Stoletii* [Diplomacy and wars of tsarist Russia in the 19th century] (Krasnaya Nov: Moscow, 1924), pp. 195–229.

[11] Uprisings were common and attempts to assert independence occurred regularly. The most salient examples are probably the self-styled Mountain Republic of the Northern Caucasus, established in 1918, the frequent cases of 'collaboration' with invading German troops in World War II and the recent attempt by Chechnya to break away from the Russian Federation.

[12] In this regard, the situation and pattern of decolonization in several Caucasian states contrasted sharply with the picture presented by neighbouring Central Asia. It is significant that the current rulers of the Central Asian republics were 'reluctant liberators' who did not fight for the rapid collapse of the USSR. 'Anti-metropolitan' counter-élites and anti-Russian political currents were not strong in Central

May 1991, and Ebulfez Elcibey, who became President of Azerbaijan in June 1992, were determined to lead their countries out of Russia's orbit and to distance themselves from Russia and the Russian-led Commonwealth of Independent States (CIS).[13] Both tried to consolidate their domestic positions by playing on the danger of renewed Russian domination. The Russian authorities' fear of the emergence of a strong anti-Russian political current in the region was further increased by events in Chechnya within the borders of the Russian Federation. From the Russian perspective, the apparent *rapprochement* between Gamsakhurdia and Dudaev in late 1991 pointed to the dangerous possibility of a consolidation and realignment of anti-Russian élites in the region and a further upsurge of pro-independence sentiments in the northern Caucasus.[14] Indeed, Gamsakhurdia's vision of a future 'Caucasian commonwealth' of the Transcaucasian and north Caucasian states had a clear anti-Russian flavour and promised to encourage the fragmentation of the Federation itself. Similarly, the shrill anti-Russian (and pro-Turkish) line of President Elcibey, in particular in the early period of his presidency, did not win favour among Russian policy makers.

Whether or not Russia was somehow involved in the toppling of the 'ex-dissident' presidents of Georgian and Azerbaijan,[15] the truth remains that this change of guard clearly corresponded with Russia's larger interest in having more 'benign', flexible and predictable political leaders in neighbouring Caucasian states.[16] Although the two new presidents, Eduard Shevardnadze in Georgia and Geidar Aliev in Azerbaijan, are by no means 'Russia's men', they are certainly more inclined to apprehend and accommodate the Russian Feder-

---

Asia. By contrast, the Georgians, Azeris and Armenians, who all have traditions of genuine independent statehood and have developed strong nationalist feelings, became actively involved in forceful campaigns for independence in the late Gorbachev period. The bloody crack-down on nationalist demonstrations in Tbilisi (Apr. 1989) and Baku (Jan. 1990) by the Soviet Army and the dynamics of the local 'anti-colonial' struggle strengthened the popular appeal and influence of the nationalist politicians and movements which later came to power in Georgia and Azerbaijan under the banner of complete severance from Russia and Russia's 'sphere of influence'.

[13] Significantly, the 2 men had very similar backgrounds and similar reasons to dislike the Soviet/Russian domination. Both Gamsakhurdia and Elcibey were dissident intellectuals who had spent some time in Soviet gaols for 'anti-Soviet' activities. Both later emerged as charismatic leaders in their countries' national movements. In the pattern of their political careers and social origins they stood closer to post-communist leaders such as Czech President Vaclav Havel in East–Central Europe than to the majority of communist-turned-nationalist presidents of the CIS countries.

[14] On the Gamsakhurdia–Dudaev axis, see Fuller, E., 'Georgia, Abkhazia and Checheno-Ingushetia', *RFE/RL Research Report*, vol. 1, no. 6 (7 Feb. 1992), pp. 6–7.

[15] Western assessments of Russia's role in the internal politics of the Transcaucasian states range from direct involvement through covert operations (e.g., Goltz, T., 'Letter from Eurasia: the hidden Russian hand', *Foreign Policy*, no. 92 (autumn 1993), pp. 92–116) to turning a blind eye to certain actions of the Russian military.

[16] It is significant that the 'ex-dissident' presidents were replaced by ex-*nomenklatura* politicians, Eduard Shevardnadze and Geidar Aliev, respectively. They had very similar career patterns—a party career in their native republics, periods of work in 'force structures' (the Interior Ministry or Committee for State Security, the KGB), and long periods in Moscow in the higher echelons of the Soviet political establishment. It is symptomatic that these leaders were also more in tune with the product of 'Soviet decolonization' in more pro-integrationist Central Asia—a communist-turned-nationalist political leadership with a good network of personal contacts and ties in Russia.

ation's interests in the Caucasus.[17] More significant, however, is the fact that the departure of nationalist leaders associated with a strongly anti-Russian political current was much more a reflection of the geopolitical and economic realities of the first several years of post-Soviet Eurasia than the successful result of 'sophisticated' Russian policy. This reality was aptly described by the American–Iranian scholar Mohiaddin Mesbahi:

Why can Russia, in the midst of its own deep political and economic crisis, still count on the preservation of its historical interests and influence in Central Asia and the Caucasus? The answer to this question lies in the enduring military, economic and political legacies of the Soviet Union. On all three levels, military, economic and political, while the Russian 'centre' has been severely weakened, it still outweighs the Central Asian and Caucasian 'periphery'. Between the Russian 'centre' and its Asian 'periphery' there exists a level of *structural dependency/ interdependence* that will not be overcome overnight.[18]

Other potential influences are Iran and Turkey, but the economic and social structures of the newly independent Caucasian states were not yet ready for effective cooperation with them. Moreover, the substantial constraints on freedom of political and military action in the Transcaucasus for Turkey (a member of NATO) and Iran (dependent on Russian arms supplies, afraid of Azeri separatism at home and preoccupied with security in the Persian Gulf) limited the ability and the desire of these countries to provide full-scale assistance to any nationalist Caucasian politician facing strong opposition at home or to challenge Russian dominant influence in the region.

In other words, both Gamsakhurdia and Elcibey failed because their political philosophy of a rapid overall reorientation away from Russia came into conflict with the realities both in their countries and in the region as a whole. At the early stage of post-Soviet development, society (in particular influential interest groups—economic, military, industrial and so on) has much more to lose than to gain from the severance of ties with the north. In the final analysis, the best hope for stability and order in the Caucasus seems to be a more steady transformation of the political and economic landscape which: (*a*) allows for progressive consolidation of new intra-regional and extra-regional ties; (*b*) reduces Russia's security sensitivities and concerns; and (*c*) provides some form of geopolitical continuity for the transitional period of Russia's partial disengagement from the area.

[17] Despite their concern for good relations with Russia, both Shevardnadze and Aliev are eager to diversify external political and economic ties. Azerbaijan will certainly have greater room for manoeuvre and even under ex-Politburo member Aliev will work to maintain a more balanced policy, sometimes by exploiting contradictions between the main regional powers (Iran, Russia and Turkey).

[18] Mesbahi, M., 'Russian foreign policy and security in Central Asia and the Caucasus', *Central Asian Survey*, vol. 12, no. 2 (1993), p. 209.

II. Russia in the Caucasus: interests and threats

The evolution of Russian policy

The central development in Russia's strategic thinking since the breakup of the Soviet Union has been the crystallization of a mainstream consensus on the need for the Russian Federation to reassert its geopolitical influence within the territory of the former USSR. Significantly, Russia's perceptions of threats and dangers emanating from the 'near abroad' were among the most important determinants of a shift towards a more proactive approach to the ex-Soviet states. A steadily growing realization that potential challenges and spillover effects cannot be contained by a 'hands off' approach led Russian strategic analysts and policy makers to the conclusion that only preventive diplomacy, advance troop deployments and assertive peacekeeping can maintain the security of the Federation. The preponderance of security considerations was particularly visible in the evolution of the Russian approach to the Caucasus.

Until mid-1992 Russian foreign policy towards the region had been passive, reactive and, often, conducted on an ad hoc basis. Although domestic debates on Caucasian issues were gaining momentum, the prevailing mood favoured disengagement and withdrawal:

The geopolitical importance of the Caucasus is, from Russia's perspective, marginal. Russia's economic interests are also marginal . . . That is why fewer and fewer Russians favour continuous involvement in the area and for the present the dominant mood is to neglect its problems. Troops are being withdrawn from Karabakh and Russian politicians, including Vice-President Rutskoi, openly called for comprehensive troop withdrawals from the free republics. This is perfectly sensible, considering that the continuous presence of troops there leads to their own demoralization and to massive proliferation of conventional weapons in the area.[19]

The views of Russian strategists, however, underwent a serious revision towards the end of 1992. Clearly, it was events in Abkhazia which became the main catalyst for a greater appreciation of the region's importance for Russia and Russian security. The evolution of that conflict has revealed two crucial geopolitical realities and dynamics. First, it has become obvious that the Russian Federation will not be in a position to seal its southern borders and to prevent the spread of instability from the Transcaucasus into the northern Caucasus. The merging of the inter-ethnic violence in Georgia and, at least potentially, in Azerbaijan with the turbulent politics of the northern Caucasus was stimulated by strong historical, ethnic and cultural links between the mountain peoples on both sides of the Russian border. Any attempts by the Russian authorities to hamper the penetration of north Caucasian volunteers into Abkhazia would only serve to increase anti-Russian sentiment and

---

[19] Karaganov, S. A., King's College, London, Centre for Defence Studies, *Russia: The New Foreign Policy and Security Agenda. A View from Moscow*, London Defence Studies no. 12 (Brassey's: London, June 1992), p. 19.

separatist trends among the north Caucasian peoples, many of whom felt strong emotional attachment to the Abkhaz cause. In other words, Russian policy makers realized that security and stability in the Russian northern Caucasus and the Transcaucasus were interdependent and closely interlinked. Second, it has become clear to Russia that internal stability in places like Georgia will not come automatically, at least not in the foreseeable future.

From a Russian perspective, therefore, a speedier and less violent solution to the critical question of Georgian statehood—i.e., the reconciliation of Georgian nationalism with the defence of minority rights—required greater, not less, involvement on the part of the Russian civilian and military authorities. The ultimate conclusion of 18 months of dealing with the 'near abroad' was that in order to reform and to keep its own house in order Russia has to organize and stabilize its 'outer' geopolitical space. In the unstable and fluid Caucasian region in particular, Russia was not to remain an indifferent bystander but to emerge as the principal shaper of the region's political and military development.

From a Western perspective, Russia's involvement in Georgia has often been seen as an additional (if not the main) source of instability in that country. In particular, the Russian military was (often legitimately) accused of assisting the Abkhaz separatist forces. Many in the West believe that the complete withdrawal of the Russian Army and the cessation of Russia's 'meddling' in domestic politics will speed up the stabilization of the region. However, as the example of Afghanistan has demonstrated, withdrawal from an internally unstable and fragile state does not automatically lead to peace and order: intensified civil war may instead succeed fighting against the external intruder. Azerbaijan and Georgia are not Afghanistan. Nevertheless, the removal of Russian troops and influence will simply change the parameters of the local conflicts, and will not necessarily lead to their overall resolution or bring peace and tranquillity to the region and the borderlands of the Russian Federation. Russian strategists believe in the existence of a 'power vacuum' and potential 'arc of instability' in the ex-Soviet south, which requires certain security commitments and obligations from the country. From this point of view, Russia's fear that by withdrawing it will not bring stability to its borders but rather lose the chance to influence the situation there is understandable.

The threats to Russia's interests

Developments in the Caucasus have been particularly salient in demonstrating several of Russia's security predicaments.

1. The total dissolution of the old Soviet empire and Russia's 'imperial disengagement' are important preconditions for the transformation of the Russian Federation into a liberal, democratic nation-state. On the other hand, there is also an indirect threat to the territorial integrity of the Russian

Federation itself. Too quick an abandonment of the 'outer' empire might ultimately involve the disintegration of the Federation itself. In the longer run, one potential threat is that instability and separatism in the northern Caucasus could spur other restive Muslim nations, such as the Tatars and Bashkirs, towards a more radical nationalism and greater political assertiveness.

2. The refugee problem is high on the agenda. Although the Russian diaspora in the Transcaucasus is relatively small[20] (in comparison, for example, with that of Central Asia), the flow of refugees from the Transcaucasus has very destabilizing implications. Along with ethnic Slavs, Armenians, Azeris and Georgians constitute a substantial portion of those who flee the region. Many tend to settle in southern areas of the Russian Federation (the Rostov *oblast,* or region, and the Krasnodar and Stavropol *kraya,* or territories),[21] where inter-ethnic relations have seriously deteriorated since 1992.[22] It is in Russia's fundamental interest to prevent the destabilization of these highly important food-producing areas. The whole framework of Russian–Transcaucasian ethnic relations is also placed under additional strain. This is a very negative development in view of: (*a*) the potential boomerang effect on Russians living in the Caucasus; (*b*) the presence and growth of politically high-profile Armenian, Azeri and Georgian diasporas in the Russian Federation; and (*c*) the worsening of the 'Caucasian problem' in Russian cities, which will definitely grow if the inter-ethnic situation in the south of Russia deteriorates any further.

3. The situation is further complicated by the fact that these southern regions of the Federation have historically been an area of Cossack settlement (the Don, Kuban and Terek regions) and a cradle of the Cossack movement, which in the past served as a key instrument of Russian colonial expansion and a formidable defensive barrier along the Asian frontier forts. Today Cossack revivalism creates both an opportunity and a problem for the Russian authorities. Loyal, self-contained Cossack communities with a strong tradition of military service and community discipline could be of great strategic advantage in the areas adjacent to the turbulent and unpredictable Caucasian region. At the same time, some fiercely nationalistic groups within the still fragmented and internally divided Cossack revival movement could easily foment inter-ethnic clashes

---

[20] In 1991, Russians accounted for 7.5% of the population in Georgia, 6% in Azerbaijan and only 2% in Armenia. Fuller, E., 'The Transcaucasus: war: turmoil, economic collapse', *RFE/RL Research Report*, vol. 3, no. 1 (Jan. 1994), tables on pp. 52, 53, 56. Altogether, Russians numbered only about 900 000 (there are probably fewer now) in the whole of the Transcaucasus. Moreover, in Armenia and Georgia 50% of local Russians were born in these republics and *c.* 25% have lived there for several generations. Generally, local Slavs are more keen to stay than are the Slavs in Muslim republics of the former USSR. Terekhov, V., 'Kak predotvratit katastrophu?' [How to prevent a catastrophe?], *Nezavisimaya Gazeta*, 12 Jan. 1992, p. 4.

[21] Around 70% of all refugees in Russia are now concentrated in the southern regions (North Ossetia, Krasnodar, Stavropol and Rostov). Terekhov (note 20).

[22] See, e.g., an interview with the head of administration of the Krasnodar *krai* (territory), Nikolay Yegorov, in *Argumenty i Fakty*, no. 49 (1993), p. 5. He pointed out that the authorities of the southern Russian regions were pushing in Moscow for the closure of the southern frontiers to refugees from the Transcaucasus, and described the inter-ethnic situation in his *krai* as very tense and fraught with numerous conflicts, which in his view would increase if the flow of refugees continued.

within the borders of the Federation or become instrumental in involving Russia more deeply in outside regional conflicts.[23]

4. Another negative dimension of the Caucasian refugee problem is the progressive exodus of ethnic Russians from the northern Caucasus itself. In the short run, this shrinking of the Slav community (which in the early 1990s accounted for something like 1.7 million, or approximately one-third of the whole north Caucasian population) has negative repercussions for Russian–mountain people relations, disrupts local economies and creates additional problems for the Russian authorities. In the longer run, the decline of the Slav element in these areas will lead to the development of a more ethnically homogeneous and, probably, more Islamicized northern Caucasus,[24] which will require from the Russian authorities a more subtle and flexible strategy of keeping these areas within the Federation.[25]

5. The instability in the southern areas of the Federation has also emerged as an important factor in Russian domestic politics. The deepening north–south divide of the Russian electorate has become one of the most important phenomena in Russian elections.[26] The areas where President Boris Yeltsin's opponents are strongest stretch in a belt along the entire southern perimeter of the country from Krasnodar, Rostov, Stavropol and Astrakhan to the areas bordering Kazakhstan and China. Here the population is particularly responsive to the 'national question' and in general is more inclined to support nationalist–patriotic parties and slogans. What clearly follows from this is the fact that a far-sighted, flexible and successful Caucasian policy is now increasingly needed for domestic Russian consumption.

6. Closely related to these issues is concern over the well-being and security of the local Russians and Russian-speaking populations still remaining in the Caucasus. Clearly, the present Russian authorities have to heed substantial domestic constraints in formulating their position on the issue of Russian nationals abroad and cannot tolerate their harsh treatment in the Caucasus. Ideally, it would be in the Russian authorities' long-term interest for local Russians to adjust to life in the newly independent Transcaucasian states and to emerge as yet another factor in favour of closer cooperation with Russia.

---

[23] As suggested by the conflicts in Abkhazia or Moldova, some groups of Cossacks, or calling themselves Cossacks, are mobile and inclined to develop paramilitary formations, which are difficult to place under the firm control of the Russian authorities. More serious, perhaps, is the problem of the Cossacks in the northern Caucasus. In the Soviet era the local Cossacks, who actively supported the Whites in the Civil War (1918–20), were persecuted and deprived of some of their 'historical lands' in the region. The danger is that the ongoing deterioration of relations between Cossacks and mountain peoples will lead to Cossack calls for territorial reunification with nearby Russian regions and attempts to claim back some of the 'lost' territories. Dzutsev, H. V., 'The Cossacks in North Caucasus: ethnopolitical situation', Paper presented at the Conference on the Contemporary North Caucasus, School of Oriental and African Studies, University of London, Apr. 1993.

[24] Not in terms of political radicalism, but in terms of an Islamic way of life and cultural proximity to the traditional centres of Muslim civilization in the Near East.

[25] In all probability, the region's economic affiliation will play a crucial role in the future. As long as Russia recovers and reforms its traditional economic links with the region faster than the region reorients itself towards the south, Russia still has an important trump card to rely on.

[26] *The Economist*, 25 Dec. 1993–7 Jan. 1994, p. 44.

Among other things, such a scenario presupposes the resolution of violent conflicts and the creation of multi-ethnic liberal states, tolerant to their numerous minorities. Even under a more realistic scenario of a continuing exodus of Russians, the government in Moscow has to prepare to project mobile forces into crisis-stricken areas where attacks on Slavs or ethnic Russians take on particularly dangerous forms or proportions.

7. Military considerations also play a significant role in emerging Russian perspectives on the Caucasus.[27] Other, more specific Russian security concerns in the region include the infiltration of terrorist groups from the Middle East, the spread of organized crime and the rapid criminalization of some parts of the Caucasus, the security of communication links and arms smuggling.

8. There is the further fear that escalation of local ethnic, territorial and religious conflicts (the Armenian–Azeri dispute over Nagorno-Karabakh in particular) will invite deeper penetration and involvement of Near Eastern powers and politico-religious groups (Iran, Turkey, the Afghan Mujahideen and different Islamicist volunteer fighters) in the politics of the Caucasus.[28]

Russia's overall interest is in having stable Transcaucasian states, secure within their current borders and well-disposed towards Russia. During the painful period of internal transformation and sorting out of regional politics in the Caucasus, Russia is seeking to establish itself as a dominant power, guaranteeing regional security, continuity of political experience and existing borders in the region. The strategic goal is to prevent the use of the Caucasus as a platform for threats and a channel for political pressure on the Russian Federation, and to assist instead in the future transformation of the region into a bridge outwards from Russia.

Russia's security perceptions, especially in the western and southern directions, have long been based on the notion of buffer zones. Since the 18th century, the Russian 'mainland' has felt secure behind the barrier of semi-independent principalities, colonies or Soviet republics in the Caucasus. Naturally, it is difficult for Russian strategists to reconcile themselves to the prospect of losing this buffer or, worse, to the penetration of external influences

[27] Russia's military treaty with Georgia (Oct. 1993) came as the final touch to a successful campaign to convince the government of Georgia to accept the deployment of Russian troops in the region. Russian soldiers were to remain on the CIS external frontier. This military–strategic structure was seen as necessary: (a) to guarantee Russia's strategic access to the Black Sea; (b) to solve the problem of the de facto absence of a proper southern border of the Russian Federation; and (c) to provide for advance troop deployments in a southerly direction. Russia has also been successful in promoting its military presence in Armenia, though not in Azerbaijan.

[28] The emerging consensus on these policy objectives resulted in the apparent activation of Russian diplomatic efforts and initiatives in the Transcaucasus. Russia was noticeably dissatisfied with the effectiveness of mediation efforts of the Conference on Security and Co-operation in Europe (CSCE) in Nagorno-Karabakh and inclined to arrogate to itself the leading role in mediating in the Karabakh conflict. Fuller, E., 'Russia's diplomatic offensive in the Transcaucasus', *RFE/RL Research Report*, vol. 2, no. 39 (1 Oct. 1993), pp. 30–34; and Mlechin, L., 'Konflikt Rossiyskoy i Amerikanskoy diplomatii iz-za Nagornogo Karabakha' [Clash of Russian and American diplomacy over Nagorno-Karabakh], *Izvestiya*, 23 Nov. 1993.

perceived as rival or hostile.[29] In the final analysis, Russian disengagement from the Caucasus largely depends on Moscow's view of potential threats to Russian interests from Iran, Turkey and the Near East as a whole.

The previous boom in discussion of the 'Islamic threat' in the Caucasus has been in noticeable decline in recent Russian security debates.[30] It is true that in the past Islam served as the main unifying force for the ethnically heterogeneous peoples of the northern Caucasus. At present, however, the level of Islamicization among the majority of the mountain peoples, brought up in the secular Soviet society, is not sufficient to become the basis for a political movement with a strong Islamic political underpinning.[31] In this regard it is significant that the Chechen campaign for independence has a mainly nationalist as opposed to Islamic flavour. In all probability, Islamic religion and culture need first of all to restore their traditional position of influence and prestige before any powerful and large-scale Islamicist movement can take root in these areas. Furthermore, the consolidation of the north Caucasian peoples under an Islamic banner presupposes the emergence of a common, clear-cut threat to their very survival (as during the brutal Russian conquest of the region in the 19th century).

III. 'What is to be done?': Russian policy options

Theoretically, following the demise of the USSR Russia had four policy options in the Caucasus. In this chapter they are defined as: (a) total disengagement; (b) partial disengagement; (c) active engagement; and (d) constructive engagement. This section examines briefly the advantages and disadvantages of each of these policy scenarios and elaborates on the constructive engagement option.

As was revealed by the turbulent events of the first years after the end of the USSR, the disengagement options have steadily lost much of their attractiveness for Russia. In 1993 and 1994 Russian analysts increasingly articulated the available choices in the Caucasus not in terms of whether or not Russia should commit itself to the region, but rather in terms of what the most beneficial, pragmatic and cost-effective means of maintaining stability and Russian

---

[29] One such scenario is considered by Marie Bennigsen Broxup, a leading Western authority in north Caucasian studies: 'A future North Caucasian confederation or federation . . . would entertain strong economic ties with Azerbaijan, and would naturally look for alliances with Turkey, Iran and the Middle East, gradually escaping from the Russian sphere of influence, and possibly changing the balance of power in the region'. Broxup, M. B., 'After the putsch, 1991', ed. M. B. Broxup, *The North Caucasian Barrier: The Russian Advance towards the Muslim World* (Hurst: London, 1992), p. 238. This is precisely the kind of scenario that the current Russian leadership will work hard to avert.

[30] See, e.g., an article by Kamalludin Gadjiev which argues that Islam is very unlikely to become a unifying force in the northern Caucasus in the near future: Gadjiev, K., 'Geopoliticheskie perspektivy Kavkaza i strategiya Rossii' [Geopolitical prospects of the Caucasus and Russia's strategy], *Mirovaya Ekonomika i Mezhdunarodnye Otnosheniya*, no. 2 (1993), cited from *Rossiya i Musulmanskiy Mir*, no. 5 (Moscow, 1993), p. 21.

[31] Some Western students of the region will object to any argument referring to the strong influence (even in the Soviet era) of the Sufi *tariqats* (orders) in the Caucasus. The influence of Sufism on the politics of the northern Caucasus is certainly weaker than feelings of ethnic solidarity.

influence in the region might be. The security and well-being of the Russian Federation have proved to be inseparable from the relative degree of stability, inter-ethnic accord and economic revival of the Caucasus. Tied to its former 'colonies' by countless threads, Russia can hardly afford to abandon its commitment to the Caucasus during the first crucial years of post-Soviet transformation. A more realistic option is to modify this commitment. Hence this chapter argues that a strategy of constructive engagement is the best available option for Russian policy in the Caucasus.

The disengagement options

Total disengagement

Both disengagement scenarios partly reflected the intellectual climate of the isolationist, Western-oriented and 'romantic' period in the development of Russian democracy at the end of 1991 and for most of 1992. A strategy of total disengagement, often mentioned in Russian policy debates in early 1992, envisioned a radical option of withdrawing from the Caucasian mountains and the 're-creation along Kuban and Terek of an earlier fortified border similar to the Caucasian lines of the 18th and 19th centuries'.[32] The emphasis here was on getting rid of the 'Caucasian problem' altogether and building up a new 'ethnic frontier'. This policy option rested on the belief that Russia would quickly repatriate the remaining Russian nationals from the region, manage more or less successfully to seal its newly created southern border and pursue a low-profile policy in the Caucasus.

A few advocates of this strategic option (found, as a rule, among the radical democrats) pointed to a number of long-term advantages and potential gains inherent in such a 'hands off' approach. First, it could allow the country to concentrate on the urgent task of reconstructing its own economy and society. Second, it would save Russia from spending too much money, energy and resources on a region which promises little in terms of economic development (Azerbaijan excepted) and political stability. Russia, argued the supporters of total disengagement, might be simply sucked into local conflicts and feuds and would gain little in practical terms in the end. Furthermore, they argued, Russia would become so much preoccupied with playing the role of regional policeman in the south that its capability for strategic manoeuvre in the more promising western or eastern directions could be severely hampered.[33] Finally, it represented an early and in a historical perspective less painful implementation of

---

[32] Felgengauer, P., 'My vstupayem v Kavkazskuyu voynu?' [Are we getting into a Caucasian war ?], *Nezavisimaya Gazeta*, 7 Nov. 1992. In this article, Felgengauer describes this strategic option and assesses its advantages and disadvantages.

[33] Some observers would even claim that the West will lose nothing if a more assertive and pro-activist Russia becomes tied up in numerous conflicts in the Caucasus and Central Asia. A 'strategic preoccupation' with the south, it can be argued, would probably reduce Russia's increasing pressure on Ukraine, Moldova and the Baltic states. Interestingly, in the past both Napoleon and Hitler tried a policy of diverting Russian strategic expansion to the south.

what was inevitable anyway—the creation of new southern borders for the Russian Federation. In the longer run (10–20 years), the advocates of total disengagement argued, the demographic trends, geopolitical dynamics and social evolution of both the Central Asian and the majority of the Caucasian Muslim societies would eventually force the Russian authorities to reject the current principle of transparent frontiers with the ex-Soviet southern republics.

Whatever the strong points underlying this kind of geopolitical thinking, as early as 1993 it was clearly no longer on the agenda in Russian policy debates. The logic of domestic politics and political survival placed formidable constraints even on the most liberal circles within the Russian political establishment, who might otherwise have been more favourable towards the total disengagement scenario. That policy can no longer be sustained domestically.[34] Furthermore, Russia's ability to seal the new southern border of the Federation is doubtful. Would refugees be halted at gunpoint? Would a well-fortified frontier be enough to keep out the creeping instability which would be certain to follow from a total Russian withdrawal? In other words, the short-term disadvantages of a total disengagement strategy heavily outweighed the longer-term benefits.

Partial disengagement

The second policy option—partial disengagement—emphasized the territorial integrity of the Russian Federation and keeping the northern Caucasus within the Federation. Significantly, advocates of this approach also insisted that the current Russian–Caucasian border was probably the best available one from a military–strategic point of view. 'The Main Caucasian range', wrote Pavel Felgengauer, 'is a physically impenetrable barrier and is therefore quite suitable as the natural frontier of Russia at this difficult time'.[35] The strategy of partial disengagement suggested that the Russian authorities should work to seal the Russian–Transcaucasian border and mitigate the effects of the spillover of violent conflicts or ethnic frictions in Georgia and Azerbaijan to the politics of the Russian northern Caucasus. In the northern Caucasus itself, Russia should reassert its control, if necessary by the use of force.[36]

Although some of these arguments are quite sensible, the partial disengagement strategy has a number of inherent weaknesses. It is easy to agree with the Gorbachev Foundation expert Vladimir Kuvaldin that it would hardly be pos-

---

[34] There are powerful interest groups (the military and certain industrialist groups) which strongly object to this policy. It is also obviously not in line with the growing national–patriotic sentiments in the administration and among the Russian public. See, e.g., Cherechnia, A., 'Mir ili mech' [Peace or sword?], *Nachalo*, no. 35 (1993), cited from *Rossiya i Musulmanskiiy Mir*, no. 3 (1993), p. 6.

[35] Felgengauer (note 32).

[36] Again, the article by Pavel Felgengauer is interesting in understanding the geopolitical thinking behind this approach. He points out that the northern Caucasus is a 'sphere of vital Russian interests, and order there should be restored, but for this political and diplomatic efforts should be supplemented by a sufficient military force'. Felgengauer (note 32).

sible to fence off war-ridden Transcaucasus from the northern Caucasus.[37] Indeed, from the historical, ethnic and political point of view the Russian Caucasus and the Transcaucasus appear to be an integral whole. Any Russian move to stand between the mountain peoples of the northern Caucasus and Georgia–Azerbaijan would introduce an additional complicating factor into the already tense relations between the Russian Administration and various north Caucasian parties and groups, above all the CPC. Russian soldiers might be caught in the crossfire and become the visible object of accusation and blame on both sides of the Caucasian range. It would also be counter-productive under this scenario for Russia to try to buy the loyalty of the mountain peoples by siding openly with the Abkhaz, South Ossetians or Lezgins. If Russia really seeks to preserve the territorial and political status quo in the region, it should cultivate rather than undermine the awareness of a common Russian–Georgian–Azeri interest in the maintenance of the existing interstate borders in the Caucasus.

Finally, the substantial political limitations on the use of military force in the northern Caucasus have already been demonstrated by Russia's unsuccessful attempt to introduce a state of emergency in Chechnya and the numerous short-comings of Russian military intervention there. Complicated and delicate ethnic problems cannot be solved by force alone, and political compromise with the Chechens should be reached sooner or later. The Chechnyan situation was one of those terrible problems for which a happy outcome seemed almost inconceivable. To let Chechnya go was not a realistic policy option for the Russian leadership. The departure of Chechnya from the Federation threatened a subsequent secession of Russia's Caucasian fringe and could spark off the further fragmentation of the country. The erosion of Moscow's grip on Chechnya could eventually undermine Russia's influence in the whole of the Caucasian region and endanger the important communication lines between Russia and the Transcaucasus. The turmoil in the breakaway republic also threatened Russia's access to Caspian Sea oil and jeopardized Moscow's argument that the Russian pipeline outlet from the Caspian Sea was the safest and most cost-effective option for the transport of Caspian oil, whose exploitation was then being negotiated with an international consortium. For most Russian strategists, therefore, the issue at stake was not whether Russia should act in Chechnya, but how it should handle the situation there in such a way as to further its own strategic aims.

While it is true that President Yeltsin had no good options, political or military, in Chechnya, the one he chose—full-scale use of military force—was bound to incur punitive costs. Since bloodless and rapid victory was not possible, the war against the Chechen secessionists appears to have done more damage than good to Russia from the point of view of its political stability, its economic recovery and its relations with the West and the Islamic world. Even

---

[37] Kuvaldin, V., 'Kavkazskiy vykhod dlya Rossii i Gruzii' [A Caucasian way out for Russia and Georgia], *Moskovskie Novosti*, no. 43 (25 Oct. 1992), p. 9.

if the Russian Army is able to 'teach the Chechens a lesson', it is still unclear how this will be interpreted in other regions of the Federation and in the 'near abroad'. More dangerously, a protracted guerrilla war in the Chechen mountains could undermine the broader objectives of Russian policy in the region—stability on the southern borders and the preservation of safe strategic, communication and transport links with the Transcaucasus.

The integrity of the Russian Federation cannot be assured by a 'big stick' alone. In the final analysis, the future of Russian–north Caucasian relations will be decided not by the number of Russian troops in the area but by the ability of the Russian leadership to co-opt new types of local élites, to accommodate their political aspirations and to link their economic interests to Russian markets. Hence the overwhelming priority of the Kremlin's policy should have been to prevent its actions against the Dudaev regime from evolving into what could be viewed as war against the Chechen people. In 1994 there were plenty of indicators that the separatist sentiments that produced the Chechens' declaration of independence three years before were running into the wall of reality. Chechnya is linked to the Russian mainland by millions of economic, geographical and social ties; it has no capacity to survive on its own, nor does it have anywhere else to join. Long before the Russian military attack on the breakaway republic the realization that the Chechens had no option but to find some form of accommodation with Moscow had begun to assert itself over the pro-independence euphoria of the first post-Soviet years. In other words, time and a good prospect for Russia's economic recovery were working in favour of the Russian Government and Chechen moderates. The Russian authorities appeared to have enough space for political manoeuvre—time and regional and international support—to out-perform Dudaev without the large-scale use of force and the near-total destruction of Grozny. However, this option has turned out to be considerably more difficult after the atrocities of what has turned out to be a protracted war such as could only reinforce Chechnya's drive for secession.

The engagement options

While both the engagement scenarios emphasize Russia's continuing commitment to the whole of the Caucasus, they nevertheless imply two fundamentally different approaches to the region.

Active engagement

Active engagement implies primarily an assertive neo-imperialist policy in the whole of the Caucasus. The core of such a policy is domination through increased dependency of local regimes on Russian security guarantees. Its goal is the creation of a belt of satellite states in the Transcaucasus, closely tied by enforced economic, military and political links to their mighty northern neighbour. Under favourable conditions, the recasting of these relations into some sort of union (not exactly the former Soviet Union, but more than the present CIS) is seen as a desirable option.

The most debated issue in this scenario is not so much Russia's overall strategic goals and the desired institutional structure of Russian relations with the region, but rather the means and methods which are to be used to achieve those goals. The integrationist trends in most of the successor states of the USSR are a very positive phenomenon for the long-term interests of the Russian Federation. They should be encouraged by demonstrating the substantial economic, political and strategic benefits of closer association of the ex-Soviet republics with Russia. Integration, however, should by no means be forced on Russia's neighbours. The history and geography of the Caucasus have created a wealth of opportunities to apply a classic 'divide and rule' policy. Russia can easily play off one people against another; it can skilfully play on the tacit threat of dismemberment of those states that wish to leave Russia's orbit; it can try to manage local conflicts and to contain them at a level where both sides will be in need of Russian military supplies and political support. A direct integrationist policy will only destroy the natural integrationist trends on the territory of the former Soviet Union and backfire against Russia.

Apart from Russian ultra-nationalists, few people in Moscow argue in favour of active engagement. The real danger is that Russia will not so much intentionally embark on a course of neo-imperial expansion in the Caucasus as be pushed along that course by the whirl of events and by the dynamics of its military involvement in local conflicts. Still, the chances of active Russian engagement remain relatively low as long as the present Russian authorities continue to hold power. A shift towards a more nationalist leadership in Moscow, on the other hand, would most probably strengthen the neo-imperialist elements of Russian policy in the Caucasus.

Unfortunately, the more insecure the Russian Federation feels within its current borders, the more tempting it is to turn to an active engagement policy in the Caucasus. In a sense, this strategy would be an attempt to contain the mounting security problems for the Federation as far from its heartland as possible.

Although the policy would be correct in the sense that Russia needs a preventive and proactive policy in the Caucasus, active engagement would be fraught with serious risks and uncertainties. The biggest risk, perhaps, is that the means and methods of implementing this policy could easily undermine its long-term goals. The most important function of Russian foreign policy is to create a security environment for the Russian Federation which remains as benign as possible. A 'belt of good-neighbourliness' is often described as the ideal geopolitical surrounding, but 'good-neighbourliness' imposed by the methods inherent in a policy of active engagement is not likely to last long. The logical conclusion of a policy of active engagement would be an attempt to freeze, often by military means and political and economic pressure, whatever strategic and political combination was believed to be most in Russia's interests. In this situation, Russia would be very likely to fall into the danger of confusing long-term stability with the perpetuation of a particular regional order. The final results of this might well prove negative, for three reasons.

First, the Caucasian region, like many other parts of the former USSR, is undergoing a period of profound change, transformation and readjustment of regional relations. Leaders, governments and élites will come and go. In the northern Caucasus in particular, the emergence of new leadership structures —national, religious and other—is undermining the legitimacy of ex-Soviet local élites, which are open to charges of betrayal of the 'national interests' of the mountain peoples and collaboration with the most conservative elements of the Russian establishment.

The direction of the current changes remains unpredictable and will remain beyond the complete control of the Russian Government. In this situation, Russia is better off having permanent interests, not permanent friends. The rigid framework of an active-engagement security order might be inadequate to withstand the rapid flux of events in the region. Moreover, an active-engagement policy would inexorably draw Russia into deeper and more frequent military involvement in the region either on the side of its clients or against anti-Russian forces. This would carry the obvious risks inherent in thorough-going Russian intervention in the domestic politics of regional states. It would also provoke anti-Russian sentiment among certain elements and political groups in the Caucasus, which are certain to seek support beyond the CIS.

Second, in the long run, such developments would be detrimental to another fundamental Russian interest—strategic denial of third countries in the region. The more obvious, assertive and forceful the Russian military engagement in local conflicts, the stronger the pressures and impetus for Iran, Turkey and various Islamic groups to become actively involved in the Caucasus. By associating itself entirely with certain parties, regimes or groups in the region, especially in times of crises, Russia would provide an opening for different political influences from the Near East.

Third, active engagement would be costly. It would place a substantial economic, military and political burden on Russia, which needs a breathing space in which to concentrate on itself. Full-scale engagement in the region would certainly require substantial economic aid to maintain any degree of social stability in this crisis-stricken area. There are also questions about the ability of the Russian Army to police all the potential conflicts in the region as well as sustaining peacekeeping operations in several other 'hot spots' in the 'near abroad'.

Russia's interest is in slowing down rather than accelerating the disruptive process of ethnic and religious self-definition in the Caucasus. In any case, Russia should retain enough space for political manoeuvre to allow it to pose as a more neutral power broker, and occasionally to distance itself from both sides in a conflict. This manoeuvrability will be substantially reduced if Russia embarks on a policy of active engagement.

Constructive engagement

In contrast to an active neo-imperialist approach, constructive engagement values long-term stability as a key Russian priority in the Caucasus. It aims at skilful encouragement of voluntary integrationist trends by paying the utmost attention to local sensitivities and concerns. Its other main objective is to reduce the risk of the emergence in the Caucasus of openly hostile regimes or political trends closely linked to or supported from the Near East. The constructive-engagement model is based on the thesis that Russia's attempt to shape the geopolitical situation in the Caucasus should be adjusted both to the realities of the region and to the parameters of overall change in this part of the world. Russia would aim to emerge as a leading power for stability and the main external guarantor of a regional security order, while carefully managing and occasionally restraining the natural desire for change.

In contrast to the 'enforced stability' of the active-engagement scenario, constructive engagement presupposes that close security relations between Russia and the Transcaucasian states will evolve through a collaborative effort. The regional states should not be forced into such relations (as happened in Georgia) but, if possible, persuaded into them by the clear advantages of Russian security guarantees. In addition, local initiatives in relation to the structures, forms and mechanisms of bi- and multilateral security arrangements in the Caucasus should be carefully studied and encouraged. If possible, representatives of the Caucasian states should be assigned commanding roles in preparing, drafting and implementing these initiatives. Only such collaborative effort could assure Russia's continuing and long-term role as a major security provider for the Caucasus.

To master the techniques of constructive engagement, Russia should utilize the tremendous experience of other ex-colonial powers (France in francophone Africa in particular) in the field of managing security relations with its former colonies. Despite fundamental differences between the French overseas empire and the Soviet landmass imperial formations, the French example is very helpful in shaping the philosophy of Russian imperial disengagement. The crux of French strategy was to maintain a strong influence in francophone Africa while preserving its ultimate freedom of action.[38] A network of military–strategic agreements between France and African states has assured France exclusive military action in parts of Africa and served as a deterrent to any aggression inimical to French interests.

Following the pattern of French and British colonial disengagement (which lasted for decades), Russia should emphasize that it does not aim at reconquering the Caucasus, but rather aspires to steady imperial disengagement at a pace corresponding to the interests of Russian security and the requirements of regional stability. The presence of Russian troops would be temporary,

---

[38] Chipman, J., International Institute for Strategic Studies, *French Military Policy and African Security*, Adelphi Paper no. 201 (IISS: London, 1985); and Chipman, J., *French Power in Africa* (Basil Blackwell: Cambridge, Mass., 1989), pp. 114–85.

intended to continue for 10–15 years, and one of their main roles would be to prepare and train local armies. Similarly, it is desirable to establish a clear link between the Russian commitment to the southern borders of the Transcaucasus and the pace of creation of indigenous border troops in Armenia, Azerbaijan and Georgia.

A policy of constructive engagement relies on two premises.

First, Russia needs a comprehensive, coherent and long-term pan-Caucasian strategy. Most of the time, different upheavals, conflicts and disturbances in the region cannot be dealt with in isolation, but require a complex approach. Russia should address the growing linkages between different aspects of the instability in the Caucasus. The inevitable interaction of political developments in the Russian and non-Russian Caucasus will require from Russia an ability to influence the security dynamics of the Transcaucasus.

Second, it seems unrealistic to expect quick solutions to the numerous problems bedevilling the Caucasus. There are too many of them, closely interlinked and often with roots in history and local traditions. Russian policy makers will therefore be well advised to aim at gradual transformation and slow readjustment in these territories. It can be argued that a stable security order in the Caucasus will necessitate an overall restructuring of the existing politico-administrative structures of several states—the federalization of Georgia, the creation of stable Lezgin and Talysh autonomous regions in Azerbaijan and the achievement of a compromise on the status of Nagorno-Karabakh.

Constructive engagement presupposes that Russia defends the principle of the inviolability of the existing interstate borders and simultaneously supports the rights of Russian and non-Russian minorities in the multi-ethnic states of the Transcaucasus. In the northern Caucasus the most important immediate task is to settle the conflict in Chechnya—by looking for an accommodation with the separatists, however difficult that might be, rather than by suppressing them by military means as seemed to be the preferred policy of Moscow. In the longer run, Russia should work out a *modus vivendi* with the CPC. It will be in Russia's greatest interest not to oppose the CPC but to contribute to its transformation into a non-territorial, non-military cultural–political umbrella organization. This organization will be necessary not only as a political vehicle expressing the growing solidarity of the mountain peoples: it could also be useful as a political forum for solving local border and ethnic disputes. Together with the Russian authorities, this forum could be in charge of conflict resolution in these territories and would allow Russia to distance itself from potential charges of neo-imperialist arbitrariness and prejudices. A non-military, non-territorial CPC would probably be a convenient political framework for bringing together the mountain peoples in the Russian and non-Russian Caucasus and relieving the separatist passions of the mountain peoples in Azerbaijan and Georgia. A loyal CPC would also be an additional guarantor of the continuity of political experience in the northern Caucasus, and could serve as an insurance against the rise of separatist or anti-Russian groups in individual north Caucasian republics.

Constructive engagement is based on pragmatic consideration of the costs and benefits of Russia's involvement in each particular conflict situation in the Caucasus. In other words, Russia would do better to adopt a selective approach, differentiating the degree and strength of Russian commitment, the political and military structures and forms of cooperation with other powers on the basis of its own pragmatic interests in crisis-hit areas.

Predictably, the Russian Federation's bilateral relations with the three Transcaucasian states are evolving towards greater diversity as opposed to uniformity. While all three will probably remain in the CIS, the levels of their individual dependence on Russia's security guarantees and their orientation towards a Russian-led alliance system will vary from a very strong link in the case of Armenia to a much weaker one in the case of Azerbaijan. In this situation, it is more beneficial for Russia to build the post-Soviet security order in the Caucasus on the basis of bilateral security relations. Bilateralization of relations will assure Russia greater influence on national security policy making, compensate for the weakness of CIS multilateral military structures and give Russia greater flexibility in dealing with the opposing sides in conflicts in the region.

Under the constructive-engagement scenario, Russia's strategic denial of excessive external influences will imply the rejection of any assertive military–political interventions in the region, but not of adjoining states' roles in developing the region's economies, trade and communication links. There will be no identity of interests between Russia and the West, but Russia will continue to press for implicit or explicit recognition of its special role in the military–strategic arrangements in the Caucasus region. It is also desirable to continue close cooperation with the efforts of international organizations (the UN and the Organization for Security and Co-operation in Europe, the OSCE) to try to resolve local disputes. Despite Russian–Western differences, a compromise formula for interaction between Russia and the Conference on Security and Co-operation in Europe (CSCE)[39] in conflict resolution in the former Soviet Union was found at the December 1994 CSCE summit meeting in Budapest in the shape of the agreement to send a 3000-strong multinational peacekeeping force to Nagorno-Karabakh. The agreement envisions Russian–OSCE cooperation as the central focus of the peace process in Nagorno-Karabakh and explicitly acknowledges Russia's special role by allowing it to contribute up to 50 per cent of the peacekeepers.[40]

The composition of the OSCE forces for Nagorno-Karabakh is still being debated. The Turkish Government's offer to supply one-third of the number of peacekeepers is unacceptable to Russia, since Turkey is not a disinterested player in Nagorno-Karabakh. While Russia itself, if judged in accordance with traditional UN peacekeeping standards, is far from being a neutral peacekeeper in the region, it is important to realize that for Moscow peacekeeping missions in the former Soviet republics are also an instrument of national security policy

[39] On 1 Jan. 1995 the CSCE became the OSCE.
[40] Rugman, J., 'Oil fuels enclaves peace initiative', *The Guardian*, 28 Dec. 1994, p. 11.

and of partial military disengagement from its former colonies. In the past, other European powers such as France and the UK argued for and received recognition of their special roles in former colonies during prolonged periods following the decolonization of their empires. There is a certain logic in the behaviour of great powers in their perceived spheres of influence, and it is unrealistic to expect Russia to renounce all its claims for a special role in the Transcaucasus or to allow Turkish military deployment there.

IV. Conclusions

At present, Russia's actual policy in the Caucasus contains elements of all the four policy scenarios analysed in this chapter. Russian strategy in this highly volatile and dynamic region is still partly in the process of formation. Difficulties, problems and contradictions are abundant and probably inevitable. The Chechnyan crisis shows how assertive and awkward Russian policy in the Caucasus could be. It would be a mistake, however, to conclude on the basis of the Chechnyan crisis that Russia is certain to embark on a course of neo-imperialist expansion in the Caucasus. Rather than demonstrating the strength of Russia's neo-imperialist thrust and resurgent Russian nationalism, the Chechnyan conflict shows the weakness of Russian nationalism as a force and ideology which can spearhead Russian expansion to the south. Vladimir Zhirinovsky's march to the Indian Ocean seems certain to end up in the Caucasian mountains. Ordinary Russians are tired of wars, revolutions and bloodshed and are increasingly aspiring to greater political stability, economic prosperity and peace on their borders. The media backlash against the military intervention in Chechnya and widespread public dissatisfaction with the way the war has been conducted show how far democratic instincts have taken root in Russia. The army has displayed little appetite for Chechnya-type military action. The Russian troops in Chechnya have shown themselves not as an aggressive or imperialist army but as one in urgent need of fundamental reforms, investment and a sense of purpose. The ability of such an army to fight 'neo-colonial' wars in the Transcaucasus or Central Asia is doubtful.

Despite the Chechnyan débâcle, therefore, there are grounds for cautious optimism and for believing that a more pragmatic, cost-effective and stability-oriented approach to the difficult problems of the region will steadily make headway in the intensive political and strategic debates going on within Russia. Much, of course, depends on the outcome of the political struggle for reform in Moscow. The best guarantee against the resurgence of Russian 'imperialism' is the continuation of Russia's advance towards democracy and a market economy.

The stakes are high both for the Russian Federation and for the region: if Russia learns to engage constructively in Caucasian affairs, it will have a good opportunity to reduce the instability of the Caucasus and to neutralize the most serious security risks for itself potentially emanating from the region. As

Russia's economy starts to recover, the Caucasus would then become an important economic, communications and trade bridge from Russia rather than emerging as a platform for threats and political pressures on the Federation. To win a new 'Great Game' in the Caucasus, Russia should emerge as a key provider of security and the main facilitator of economic development in the region. At the same time, it must be careful to achieve this goal by encouraging regional states' own voluntary movement towards closer association with Russia rather than imposing its will by force.

Part XI

Economic factors: implications for relations with Europe

Background chronology

1990

19 Oct.   Against a background of growing economic crisis, the Supreme Soviet of the RSFSR approves an outline programme to establish a market-oriented economy and abandon centralized state economic control

22 Nov.   The Supreme Soviet approves a law on agrarian reform which marks first step towards legalization of private (land) property

24–25 Dec.   The Supreme Soviet approves a law legalizing private property and a law on enterprises which establishes the legal framework for the operation of private, cooperative and state-owned enterprises

1991

4 July   The Supreme Soviet approves a law on foreign investment which permits foreigners to own enterprises for the first time since 1917

15 Nov.–30 Dec.   A package of presidential decrees, including liberalization of prices and external economic activities, aims at initiating the transition to a market economy

1992

2 Jan.   A presidential decree abolishing state controls on most retail and wholesale prices comes into force; considered the most important single step towards reform of the economy

29 Jan.   A presidential decree on the liberalization of commerce removes legal barriers to citizens engaging in market activities

27 Apr.   Russia is admitted to IMF and World Bank

11 June   The Supreme Soviet approves the first stage of the government privatization programme—privatization of large holdings of state-owned property by distributing vouchers to all citizens

7 July   Presidential decree on the transformation of state-owned enterprises into joint-stock companies and on commercialization of their activities

17 Sep.   Presidential decree allowing the price of oil exports to float freely; protests from neighbouring CIS member states dependent on Russian energy supplies

1993

24 July   The Russian Central Bank announces a currency reform measure: all roubles issued before 1993 are to be withdrawn from circulation and replaced by a new rouble, issued only by the Russian Central Bank—a step towards the separation of the other national monetary systems within the CIS from that of Russia, which was completed by end-1993

24 Sep.   Russia and 8 other former Soviet republics sign a treaty on economic union. It provides a framework for constructing a market-based common economic area with a view to strengthening economic and technological cooperation and the free movement of goods, services, labour and capital

1994

24 June   Russia–EU Partnership and Cooperation Agreement signed. It covers a wide range of trade, commercial and economic relations, instituting political dialogue at many levels, promoting cultural links, placing respect for human rights and the democratic process at the centre of the relationship and assuming Russia's inclusion in a wider area of cooperation in Europe, including the possibility of a free-trade zone between Russia and the EU

10 July   Yeltsin formally participates in political discussions at the G7 summit meeting

1995

14 June   Russian State Duma passes federal law on state support for small businesses

17 July   Negotiations on Russia's application (Dec. 1994) for membership of the World Trade Organization begin

25 Sep.	Russian Government launches second stage of its privatization programme—a 'shares for loans' scheme by which a large group of companies are to be privatized by transferring state share-holdings to a consortium of banks in return for loans: loans to be repaid after a fixed term
13 Oct.	Federal law on regulation of external economic activities
12 Dec.	Federal law establishes rules and mechanisms for the distribution of production and profit between domestic and foreign investors, the latter being given legal guarantees against the risks of investment
22 Dec.	The Russian Duma approves second part of the Civil Code. Together with the first part, passed in Oct. 1994, it establishes the legal basis for all kinds of economic activity in a market economy

1996

1 Feb.	Interim Agreement on Trade and Trade-related Matters between Russia and the EU called into operation; originally signed on 17 July 1995, it will operate until the Partnership and Cooperation Agreement comes into force
3 Mar.	Presidential decree on implementation of the constitutional right of citizens to own landed property, aimed to promote reform of Russian agriculture
26 Mar.	Following lengthy negotiations, IMF approves a 3-year credit to Russia worth *c*. $10 billion to support the medium-term macroeconomic programme
22 Apr.	Federal law establishes legal framework for securities markets
29 Apr.	Paris Club of creditor countries reaches agreement on a long-term rescheduling of *c*. $40 million of Russian debt; rescheduling agreement worked out and agreed in principle in Nov. 1995 with London Club of commercial creditors expected to be signed by end of 1996
16 May	Presidential decree on measures to provide for transition to full convertibility of the rouble
21 May	Russia applies for membership of the OECD

Key facts

Macroeconomic indicators of the Russian economy

	1991	1992	1993	1994	1995	1996[a]
GDP[b]	92.2	78.8	72.0	62.9	60.4	57.4
Industrial production[b]	91.9	75.4	64.8	51.2	49.7	47.7
Agricultural production[b]	92.1	83.8	80.4	70.8	65.1	60.5
Capital investment[b]	84.5	50.7	44.6	33.9	29.5	25.4
Trade[c]	96.8	93.9	95.8	95.9	89.2	87.4
Consumer price inflation[d]	8.3	31.2	20.6	10.0	7.2	2.4
Monthly salary[e]	100.0	67.0	67.3	61.9	45.8	49.9
Unemployment[f]	..	5.0	5.8	8.0	9.0	10.0
Official foreign currency reserves[g]	..	..	5.25	4.0	14.5	13.0

[a] First 6 months, annualized. [b] 1989 = 100. [c] 1990 = 100. [d] Monthly average, per cent. [e] Jan. 1991 = 100. [f] Percentage of total employment. [g] US$ billion. *Sources:* Russia, State Committee of Statistics, *Rossiya v Tsifrakh, 1996*, pp. 8, 12; *Byulleten Inostrannoy Kommercheskoy Informatsii*, no. 91 (8 Aug. 1996), p. 2; and *Finansovye Izvestiya*, 18 June 1996, p. 1.

Structure of GDP

	1991	1993	1994	1995
National production				
Goods	81.2	49.9	41.0	40.7
Services	14.9	43.0	50.5	51.5
Net taxes	3.9	7.1	8.5	7.8
Total	**100**	**100**	**100**	**100**
National expenditure				
Consumption: households	43.4	38.4	39.6	42.0
Consumption: state/non-commercial organizations	20.2	22.4	27.6	24.0
Gross national accumulation[a]	39.1	31.4	28.3	28.0
Net exports	– 2.7	7.8	4.5	6.0
Total	**100**	**100**	**100**	**100**

All figures are percentages of GDP. [a] Capital investment and household savings. *Sources: Sobranie Zakonodatelstva Rossiyskoy Federatsii*, no. 21 (22 May 1995), p. 3812; and 'Russia: foreign economic relations. Trends and prospects', *Quarterly Review* (Moscow), no. 1 (1996), p. 2.

Privatization in Russia

	1992	1993	1994	1995	1996[a]
Number of privatized enterprises (000s)	46.8	88.6	112.6	118.8	119.7
Percentage of all enterprises[b]	18.6	36.1	47.0	56.7	57.4
Percentage share of employment accounted for by the non-state sector	31.0	47.0	55.0	62.0	..
Percentage of GDP accounted for by the non-state sector	..	52.0	62.0	70.0	..

[a] As of 1 Mar. 1996. [b] Excludes small and medium-sized enterprises (SME). *Source: Byulleten Inostrannoy Kommercheskoy Informatsii*, no. 68 (13 June 1966), p. 2.

Number of small and medium-sized enterprises, Jan. 1996	877 300
Numbers employed in SME, Jan. 1996	8 944 800 (13.3% of labour force)

Source: Russia, State Committee of Statistics, *Rossiya v Tsifrakh, 1996*, pp. 36, 254, 257.

Distribution of Soviet/Russian external trade by region of the world
Figures are percentages.

	Excluding CIS countries			Including CIS countries		
	1988[a]	1992	1995	1993	1994	1995
Europe	71.5	69.2	66.5	48.1	53.7	52.3
EC/EU[b]	14.5	40.6	45.9	32.4	37.3	35.0
ECE[c]	50.1	18.3	14.3	12.7	11.8	13.3
Americas	10.1	8.4	11.3	6.7	7.1	8.5
USA	2.4	4.8	7.6	4.5	5.3	5.7
Cuba	5.5	1.1	0.4	0.6	0.3	0.3
Asia	16.1	20.7	21.0	18.2	14.5	15.6
former CMEA[d] and N. Korea	3.5	1.2	0.7	0.7	0.4	0.5
China	1.7	5.9	4.5	5.6	3.6	3.4
Japan	2.5	4.3	4.6	3.5	3.7	3.5
Sout-East Asia[e]	2.5	3.5	4.8	2.9	3.0	3.6
Africa	1.7	1.6	0.9	1.0	0.6	0.7
Australia–Pacific	0.5	0.1	0.3	0.2	0.3	0.2
CIS countries	..	..	..	25.8	23.9	22.7
in Europe	..	..	..	..	17.2	16.1
Ukraine	..	..	..	..	11.1	11.1
in Caucasus	..	..	..	..	0.6	0.4
in Asia	..	..	..	..	6.1	6.2
Kazakhstan	..	..	..	..	3.9	4.2
Total	**100.0**	**100.0**	**100.0**	**100.0**	**100.0**	**100.0**

[a] USSR. Inter-republican exchange of goods and services was not included in the external trade statistics of the USSR. According to official statistics, in 1989 the ratio of the RSFSR's exchange with the other Soviet republics to its other external trade was 58 : 42 by volume. *SSSR v Tsifrakh, 1989*, pp. 30–32. [b] Figures for 1994 include Austria, Finland and Sweden, which joined the EU in Jan. 1995. [c] East–Central Europe. In 1988 = the European member states of the CMEA (Bulgaria, Czechoslovakia, the German Democratic Republic, Hungary, Poland and Romania) and the former Yugoslavia; 1992–95 = Bulgaria, the Czech Republic, Hungary, Poland, Romania, Slovakia, the successor states of the former Yugoslavia, Estonia, Latvia and Lithuania. [d] Mongolia and Viet Nam. [e] Hong Kong, Indonesia, South Korea, Malaysia, the Philippines, Singapore, Taiwan and Thailand. *Sources: Narodnoe Khosyaystvo SSSR v 1989*, p. 634; USSR, Ministry of External Economic Relations and State Committee of Statistics, *Vneshnye Ekonomicheskie Svyazi SSSR v 1989 Godu: Statisticheskiy Sbornik*, pp. 10–16; Russia, State Committee of Statistics, *Rossiya v Tsifrakh, 1996*, pp. 141–44; and 'Russia: foreign economic relations. Trends and prospects', *Quarterly Review* (Moscow), no. 1 (1996), p. 65.

21. Russia and the political economy of the transformation period

Hans-Joachim Spanger

I. Introduction

Those concerned with hierarchies, order and power in the international system have discerned a new currency: economics. 'It is, indeed, probably the most important source of power, and in a world in which military conflict between major states is unlikely, economic power will be increasingly important in determining the primacy or subordination of states'. In other words, and even more succinctly, 'Economics is the continuation of war by other means'.[1] Is this so? Economists, at least those of neoclassical provenance who dominate contemporary economic thinking and debate, would hardly agree. In their view, economic competition does not mean political conflict but rather absolute gains for everyone. Yet barely four years after the alleged triumph of capitalism over 'real socialism' it is relative gains which are coming to the fore and even replacing military might as the main source of power.

This time it is not Russia which raises concern in this respect. The locus of conflict has moved upstream, as it were, to the triangle formed by the major economic powers, with Japan as the primary target of criticism for its failure to observe the new rules of the game—free trade—irrespective of the fact that its 'bubble economy' is having a hard time recovering breathing space. The Russian economy has not yet become part of this equation. Conceivably firmly locked at the low edge of competitiveness, it gives rise to strategic considerations only in so far as its potential for degenerating into chaos is concerned. It is therefore not accidental that the Russian economy has so far remained the exclusive domain of those concerned with the technicalities of transformation, be it Western economic theorists looking for a test site for their grand designs or the adherents of more earthly practicalities trying to exploit the unprecedented opportunities offered by a free-wheeling market.

The gradual re-emergence of Russia as a political player, however, and its renewed insistence upon 'national interests'—which, increasingly, are claimed to be located beyond its own borders—raise the question both of the economic foundation of those interests and of their implications for the transformation process. Is growing Russian assertiveness in the 'near abroad' and 'far abroad' merely a reflection of the need to provide relief along traditional political lines

---

[1] Huntington, S. P., 'Why international primacy matters', *International Security*, vol. 17, no. 4 (spring 1993), pp. 72, 81.

from an inferiority complex largely induced by a fledgling market economy with rather gloomy prospects? Or is it the first sign of recovery along the lines of a new economic rationale when, for instance, in the 'near abroad' Russia gives the impression of shifting from an attitude of malign neglect to one of benign hegemony?

The transformation process in Russia is set to strike a new balance between two contrasting principles of organizing human activities and social life: (a) the economic sphere—that is, the market, based on functional integration under the guise of relative prices and quantities, contractual relationships and expanding integration with a view to eliminating all obstacles to the operation of the price mechanism; and (b) the political sphere—that is, the state, based on territory, exclusivity, power entailing the functional equivalent of authority, and loyalty.[2] Neither principle exists in its pure form in the real world and it is the combination of the two which after all constitutes political economy. Nevertheless, the state-centred Soviet command economy clearly rested on the latter, because the allocation of economic resources was funnelled through nothing but the state apparatus.[3] Thus the introduction of market principles was bound to have deeply disruptive effects; and indeed the price mechanism, the adjustment between demand and supply via free pricing, introduced in January 1992 started to upset all established political and social relationships.

At the current stage of the nascent Russian transformation process it is still too early to predict where this might lead. Textbooks providing a sense of direction are yet to be written on the subject since the 'unscrambling of the egg' involved in Russia's shift to a market economy has proved to be an unprecedented experiment in economic history. (The reconversion of wartime command economies does not provide useful parallels here.) What can already be discerned, however, is the peculiar interaction between the two organizing principles which constitute the political economy of the Russian transformation process. This is already having important repercussions, which are examined in this chapter in three distinct areas: (a) the domestic level, where the building- and the stumbling-blocks of change are located in the first place; (b) the Commonwealth of Independent States (CIS), where Russia has detected its primary sphere of interest, with a view to enlarging its power base; and (c) the international division of labour, where the viability and future standing of Russia's economy will ultimately be put to the test.

---

[2] See, e.g., Gilpin, R., *The Political Economy of International Relations* (Princeton University Press: Princeton, N.J., 1987), pp. 10–11.

[3] The economic rationale has come to the fore only at the enterprise level in the shape of frequent efforts to evade state orders or when it proved necessary to bridge the gaps between bureaucratic *fiat* and lack of capabilities at the grass-roots level. This is why socialist economies attracted so little interest among economists in the West.

II. The Russian economy: coping with the inevitable

The resolute reforms introduced in January 1992 by what a vocal critic of shock therapy in the West once dubbed 'a group of theorists, who had a strong preference for rapid change and who were armed with some vague ideas about how to bring this about', unquestionably had a profound impact on the working of the Russian economy.[4] They released the price mechanism, which although imperfect may prove to be the most powerful source of change and which, for better or worse, prompted an equally powerful response within society and its economic agents. The result to date has been a peculiar mismatch, which has nevertheless sent Russia tumbling headlong towards a market economy.

To say this is not to join the ranks of either of the two contesting concepts of transformation: shock therapy and gradualism. Ultimately, they pursue the same objective—laying the foundations of a market economy along the familiar Western lines. They even share the same diagnosis, namely, that shock therapy was nothing but a brief interlude in a protracted reform process.[5] Adherents of the two opposing concepts are deeply divided, however, when it comes to explaining the disruptive effects on the Russian economy. Shock therapists tend to argue that they were due to a lack of determination and possibly sophistication on the part of the government, which furthermore too easily gave in to the expected resistance by forces holding on to the past. Gradualists come to exactly the opposite conclusion. In their view, there was too much determination, which led to political and social overload and gave rise to mounting and eventually irresistible opposition.

The two contrasting views of Russian shock therapy—that it did not work because it was not thoroughly employed and that it could not work because it was conceptually flawed—need to be looked at in the broader context of their underlying (political rather than economic) assumptions, which indeed have some relevance for understanding what is going on in Russia. For shock therapists speed and comprehensiveness are essential because there is only a small window of opportunity in the very early stages for creating the building-blocks of a functioning market economy and for overcoming vested interests;[6] societies facing hardship and disorientation are inherently alien to any such reforms, the shock therapists argue, and reforms therefore have to be imposed from the top down in order to create the necessary irresistible momentum. In the eyes of gradualists, overruling society in such a way is a recipe for disaster. In their view economies rest not only on formal institutions but also, and equally importantly, on informal structures and historically derived behaviour,

---

[4] Murrell, P., 'What is shock therapy? What did it do in Poland and Russia?' *Post-Soviet Affairs*, vol. 9, no. 2 (1993), p. 133.

[5] It lasted only 4–6 months. Indeed, initial liberalization in crucial areas such as foreign trade and energy prices was only partial and the aim of macroeconomic stabilization was given up barely 6 months after it had been declared a primary policy objective of the government.

[6] 'Greater speed implies less time for discussion.' Åslund, A., *Post-Communist Economic Revolutions: How Big a Bang?* Creating the Post-Communist Order series, vol. 14, no. 9 (Georgetown University, Center for Strategic and International Studies: Washington, DC, 1992), p. 32.

which change much more slowly than hastily implemented reform packages would require. Thus, it is argued, societies need to get deeply involved and become actively supportive of reforms because otherwise the necessary adaptation will be distorted.

Evidence suggests that this time, in the words of Karl Popper, 'piecemeal' change prevailed over 'utopian social engineering', which, considering the fate of Russia over the past 70 years, is not necessarily the worst of possible outcomes. The battle is largely over and its result inconclusive. Economically there was hardly an alternative to the jump-start in early 1992. Freeing the majority of prices was probably the only means of restoring money as the primary means of exchange, in view of the complete breakdown of supply in 1991. By and large, this proved successful. The attendant austerity measures, however, whose aim was to prevent inflation from spiralling, proved unsustainable, both economically and politically speaking. Placed under intense pressure, key economic agents, that is, business concerns and their directors,[7] used their considerable economic and political clout in a highly monopolistic environment and forced the government to compromise. Since then their position has been further consolidated.

At first glance, it may appear as if today 'the political forces representing the dominant economic interests of the old Soviet system were much stronger than they had been before those policies were introduced'.[8] It should not be forgotten, however, that the rules of the game have changed. The choice is no longer between reform and rollback, although this way of presenting it remains the best way of capturing newspaper headlines. There will be no forces behind a rollback once even those enterprise managers most resistant to market reforms have had a taste of the benefits of change (the more so since they can now reap where they have not sown), and it will be impossible to preserve the status quo in a volatile environment such as that now obtaining in the Russian economy.

At stake is something else. The middle course of the government of Prime Minister Viktor Chernomyrdin has not forfeited the essentials of a market economy, even though at the outset of his premiership in January 1993, with 'non-monetary' efforts to combat inflation and a number of public statements by the prime minister, there were hints that it might be prepared to do so. Nor has it shown any inclination to threaten vital corporate interests. It has thus portrayed itself as the only feasible alternative to the monetarist course pursued by its predecessor. Initially the government of Yegor Gaidar attempted to force the industrial sector into restructuring by cutting subsidies and imposing hard budget constraints, which in the absence of a supportive industrial policy would without doubt have led to an endless chain of bankruptcies.

The crucial question in the medium and longer term, therefore, is whether such a middle course of reconciling conflicting interests and needs, which is present government policy, is really conducive to injecting sufficient dynamism

---

[7] Consumers, squeezed between the desire for the goods of the consumer society and the increasing difficulties of getting hold of them, remained largely indifferent.

[8] Murrell (note 4), p. 137.

into a deteriorating economy, and whether it can generate the critical mass and the capacity necessary for modernization, structural change and adaptation to the needs of the market. Undoubtedly, as with any other transformation process, the reforms under way in Russia feature peculiarities which inevitably take time to correct, examples being the notorious knowledge gap,[9] the inadequacy of institutions and the unique combination of decrepit and infant industries, with the latter having to grow out of the former.[10] Furthermore, Russia is confronted with a task of unprecedented proportions in the scale of its obsolete capital stock, the weight of the military sector and the somewhat arbitrary (in terms of comparative advantages) spread of production facilities.

This quandary—which is not unfamiliar in economic history in a number of respects—is examined more closely in sections III and IV of this chapter in relation to its broader implications for the openness of the economy and Russia's relations with the outside world.

The standard advice of Western economists frequently applied in International Monetary Fund (IMF) structural adjustment programmes suggests that the rigidities and irrational elements of resource allocation in the domestic sphere are most effectively overcome by importing dynamism and rationality from the world market—that is, by applying liberal principles, opening up the economy to the outside world and embarking on export-led growth strategies. Russia is in fact set to opt for the opposite course, increasingly showing sympathies and preference for highly interventionist and protectionist approaches and for a corresponding path of economic development which relies on import substitution. The size of the domestic Russian market in tandem with its relatively high degree of self-sufficiency and abundance of revenue-earning raw materials may suffice to sustain an inward-looking strategy. An equally strong impetus, however, comes from the political and financial–industrial realignments which have emerged in response to the market reforms.

In this regard, it is illustrative to observe the ways in which, since early 1992, market incentives have operated against the background of established behavioural patterns and economic agents have reacted to the opportunities—and constraints—posed by the Gaidar Government's reform package. By and large business concerns behaved in a fairly rational manner. At the initial stage they did what every sound rent-seeking monopoly—privately- or state-owned—professes to do: they exploited the opportunities provided by price liberaliza-

---

[9] A case in point is Mikhail Malei's concept of 'economic conversion'. Until recently adviser to President Yeltsin on conversion of the defence sector, he suggested using the proceeds of arms exports (an expected $10 billion in 1992) to fund the scrapping of military production. These expectations never materialized: otherwise Malei would have had some difficulty implementing what upon closer scrutiny amounts to exactly the opposite of 'economic' conversion or of any reasonable approach to the issue in market conditions—replacing what has just proved its viability with something of which the competitiveness is yet to be put to a test. On concepts such as these, see Cooper, J., Royal Institute of International Affairs, *The Conversion of the Former Soviet Defence Industry* (RIIA: London, 1993).

[10] This makes it difficult to predict how enterprises will react to standard incentives. For instance, protection of infant industry may be necessary to facilitate its growth in the face of superior competitors, and it can safely be assumed that rising young companies generate enough dynamism on their own not to misuse such a privilege. This is by no means clear in an ageing industry which will have to convert and where protection may easily retard the required changes.

tion. Once confronted with the consequences of raising prices—a large drop in sales—and with the consequences of tough government-imposed budget constraints—a financial squeeze—they reacted equally vigorously: they stopped paying their suppliers and simultaneously granted large amounts of credit to their customers. For 'survival-oriented enterprises' beset with short-term difficulties in a highly unstable environment this was again quite rational,[11] but within a few months a chain of mutual indebtedness was created throughout the economy, the resolution of which became crucial to the fate of the reform process.[12]

In retrospect, the issue of inter-enterprise debt was crucial in the transformation process. Once the economic agents had demonstrated their strength—not particularly risky in an overall atmosphere in which even the state did not honour its obligations—the reform project was successfully undermined by its own logic and rapidly fell apart. This is not to say that the state subsequently resorted to old-style solutions: it did not. Instead of merely waiting for inflation to cancel existing debt, by mid-1992 it started a process of mutual clearing (with only the net balance to be settled by Central Bank credit) and introduced an obligatory and rigid system of prepayment for future deliveries. Both measures clearly demonstrated the willingness of the government to find a solution within the confines of market principles.

It did not work, and since then businesses have managed to squeeze ever new supplies of fresh credit out of the Central Bank and the government in order at least partially to satisfy their financial needs. Moreover, the combination of loose credit and obligatory prepayment has not prevented new debts from piling up. This is probably the best evidence available of the existence of more fundamental systemic problems and of the changed correlation of forces in the Russian political arena. The increasing amount of state subsidies indicates the growing political influence of the traditional industrial élite; the failure of prepayment regulations reflects the fact that the entropy of the state and administrative apparatus persists. Since the industrial élite and the state depend on and mutually reinforce each other, the state has become a source of plunder for particular corporate interests and the primary channel for advancing their demands.

This, too, can be seen as a direct result of the fact that the initial reform package was less than comprehensive and only affected some elements of the Soviet heritage. Although the introduction of the price mechanism effectively dissolved established lines of supply, giving rise to the rapid proliferation of commodity exchanges as a substitute, it did not dissolve the network of bureaucratic–corporate relations rooted in personal contacts. These did not remain wholly untouched: branch ministries, for instance, due to be dissolved

[11] Ickes, B. and Ryterman, R., 'Roadblock to economic reform: inter-enterprise debt and the transition to markets', *Post-Soviet Affairs*, vol. 9, no. 3 (1993), pp. 245–46.
[12] Russia was by no means unique in this regard but the size of the arrears was striking. By July 1992 arrears had risen to 3.2 trillion roubles, representing roughly 80% of the GDP of the first half of the year. Ickes and Ryterman (note 11), p. 232.

in the late days of Soviet President Mikhail Gorbachev's rule, rapidly converted into holding companies or merely into pressure groups of different branches of industry. More important, however, is the fact that the traditional pattern of relations between administrators and producers has been turned upside down. Whereas under Soviet conditions enterprises and their managements were subjected to command and control by the bureaucracy, they have now assumed a position of dominance and turned the bureaucracy into clients of their vested interests—a task made much easier in an overall atmosphere of pervasive corruption.

Although by no means the only factor, these peculiar realignments have in no small measure contributed to further undermining state authority and the state's ability to pursue rule-based, impartial and non-discretionary policies. These developments run exactly counter to what has been called the 'orthodox paradox' which says that 'for governments to reduce their role in the economy and expand the play of market forces, the state itself must be strengthened'.[13] What has appeared in Russia is therefore a kind of *laisser-faire* by default rather than the result of deliberate, properly implemented and supervised policy choices. Privatization, supposedly the greatest achievement to date in the transformation process, illuminates this point instructively.[14] Not only were company directors and their employees granted various privileges from the outset (such as closed subscriptions and majority shares at discount, not to mention the 'piratization' of assets by company managers at the initial stage of privatization), but in the vast majority of the public voucher auctions managers retained a decisive stake in their concerns. It is therefore highly uncertain whether this will contribute in any visible measure to proper market behaviour on their part. What has become clear, however, is that the bargaining position of enterprise directors *vis-à-vis* their counterparts in the state administration has been considerably strengthened.

The ashes of the old system proved fertile ground for the rapid evolution of a classical rent-seeking alliance between the semi-state, semi-private sector and the state bureaucracy. Not only have representatives of these economic agents been consolidating their position by making further inroads right up to the top echelons of political power in government and the parliament: even more striking is the gradual emergence of financial–industrial conglomerates which via share-holdings cut across various branches (predominantly vertically) and which have all acquired banking subsidiaries of their own. The virtually unrestricted mushrooming of (in most cases seriously under-capitalized) banks is particularly conspicuous. These are needed as a gateway to cheap Central Bank credit and promise unique returns on short-term lending, on currency trading and on all sorts of transactions in the prevailing high-inflation volatile

---

[13] Haggard, S. and Kaufman, R. (eds), *The Politics of Economic Adjustment: International Constraints, Distributive Conflicts and the State* (Princeton University Press: Princeton, N.J., 1992), p. 25.

[14] The Russian privatization programme is indicative of the nature of the reform process. Highly contested, it amounted to a classic compromise between the shock therapists, who insisted on speed and the creation of a critical mass, the corporate interests seeking to keep a say in their respective concerns, and the regional preoccupation with excluding outsiders. It is hard to say who in the end will be satisfied.

environment. To date, it is solely in this sphere that pockets of prosperity have emerged. The gains, however, have not found their way into productive investment.

Yet another striking feature is the efforts to turn what might easily be considered the Achilles' heel of innovative structural change within the Russian economy into a source of strength. With a strong bias towards the defence industry and its technological lead, a number of ministerial bodies have suggested creating between 30 and 100 financial–industrial groups or holdings involving leading research and manufacturing facilities together with commercial banks and even trading organizations. These proposals seem to have been inspired not just by the traditional Russian–Soviet preference for large-scale technocratic designs but by similar synergy-oriented strategic alliances in the West and, moreover, by East Asian experiences and models of fast-track catching up.[15] Their primary concern has been the—not entirely unfounded— assumption that in Russia as elsewhere technological capabilities can only be preserved and possibly enlarged by pooling activities vertically as well as horizontally.

The market potential of the overwhelmingly defence-related Russian technological innovations is questionable. It is also important not to confuse formal appearances with content in drawing supposed lessons from other countries. The (by no means uncontested) successes of Japanese *keiretsu* or South Korean *chaebols,* skilfully directed by the invisible hand of the state, are based on conditions which in Russia simply do not apply. To mention two such essential preconditions: for an interventionist state to be effective, it needs autonomy, that is, the insulation of decision makers from distributive claims, and it needs competence, that is, organizational and technical skills as well as institutional coherence. By contrast, developments in Russia seem much more inspired by self-preserving, rent-seeking alliances which not only rank consumption higher than saving and investment but also tend to expect the environment to adjust to them rather than the reverse and take this to be the *sine qua non* of market survival. Consequently, applying the promises of the East Asian model of authoritarian modernization in Russian conditions would entail a great risk of perpetuating stagnation along the lines of authoritarian Latin American regimes.

As a potential escape route, it has recently become the practice to bypass the central authorities in Moscow and target directly the regions of the Russian Federation. This approach among other things rests on the assumption that smaller territorial units are in a better position to steer the transformation process and that because of the size and diversity of the country at large regional élites are simply better acquainted with local conditions. None the less, in many respects the behaviour of regional authorities is merely a replica of that of the

---

[15] Given a background of rather different historical experiences and with a view to flexible detection and penetration of market niches in the export sector it is hardly accidental that the transforming economies of East–Central Europe have come up with the opposite set of preferences. In their view it is a sound middle class and small, 'smart' business which really matter.

centre. It is hardly incidental that among the most vocal proponents of sovereign rights being granted to the regions are resource-rich Tatarstan, Bashkortostan, Yakut-Sakha and the founding members of the Siberian Agreement.[16] Shielding their local economies against the adverse effects of reform and gaining a higher share of the revenues generated by their natural resources have been the primary motives behind this drive. This again resembles much classic rent-seeking and there are no indications as yet that the regions in question have made more productive use of the privileges they extracted from Moscow, such as export licences and higher quotas, exemption from mandatory currency exchange or retention of tariff earnings on exported commodities.

What the regional élites have managed to do fairly successfully has been to increase transaction costs in the federal division of labour, thereby multiplying the shock waves currently coursing through the Russian economy. Trade restrictions affecting up to 50 per cent of local products and justified on the grounds of securing supply, forced barter deals (raw materials in exchange for consumer goods) and the issuing of both coupons and book money (that is, credit for local companies) by the regional subsidiaries of the Russian Central Bank may reflect the legal and political disarray within the Federation. Economically, however, beggar-thy-neighbour policies have in the end almost always left every one worse off.

III. Reorganizing regional economic cooperation: coping with the undesirable

The bad habits coming to the fore in the constituent parts of the Russian Federation have plagued economic relations between the constituent republics of the former Soviet Union on an even greater scale. In the absence of any central authority and of enforceable rules there is no lever encouraging member states of the CIS to honour mutual commitments. Certainly forces of economic nationalism have been somewhat tempered by the division of labour elaborated within the CIS and by the experience of the damaging consequences of rapidly dismantling the Council for Mutual Economic Assistance (CMEA). Thus, immediately after the dissolution of the Soviet Union, numerous multilateral efforts were undertaken to preserve existing economic links. Attempts to forge a sound regulatory framework, however, only allowed for a broad consensus on principles and repeatedly failed to produce practical results when it came to negotiating concrete provisions. Bilateral agreements have been so poorly implemented that they could not prevent the steep fall in bilateral trade which has occurred since early 1992 and has seemingly still not bottomed out.

It would be inappropriate only to blame the intransigence of the political players for the twofold failure to negotiate and practise mutually beneficial

---

[16] The Siberian Agreement was established in Nov. 1990 by the chairmen of the soviets of the Kemerovo, Novosibirsk, Tomsk and Tyumen *oblasti* (regions) and the Altai and Krasnoyarsk *kraya* (territories). See the special issue of *International Affairs* (Moscow), no. 4 (Apr. 1993).

trade relations within the CIS. The upsetting effects of varying market reforms on fledgling economies in conjunction with the pervasive weakness of the states involved contributed strongly to the downward spiral. At the heart of the controversies, however, lies the classic problem of political sovereignty and its economic foundations, which in the light of the specific Soviet heritage has again taken on a peculiar nature. Because of the central position of Russia, this problem has evolved around it and has manifested itself partly in ways familiar from the Russian transformation process.

In parallel to domestic transformation, economic cooperation within the CIS unmasked the distortions generated by the Soviet planning system in relation to income distribution and investment policies. In several respects the impact of these distortions was strongly felt.

1. The emergence of 15 independent republics of which 12 have joined the CIS carved fairly incoherent economies out of the tightly interlinked division of labour within the former union, with only Russia displaying a reasonable degree of self-sufficiency.[17]

2. It became apparent that almost all republics are heavily dependent on Russian deliveries of raw materials and energy carriers.

3. Even more ironically in view of their drive for independence, it became obvious that all the republics relied heavily on subsidization by the Russian economy, as demonstrated by their rapidly deteriorating trade balances and increasing indebtedness.

4. In conjunction with shifting comparative advantages, a reversal of fortunes occurred which strongly favoured Russia and further compounded the difficulties encountered by the majority of the CIS member states. Whereas in the Soviet era predominantly defence-related heavy industry firmly occupied the privileged and subsidized commanding heights of the economy, the emerging market now tends to favour the primary sector. Thus the Soviet loser—that is, Russia because of its central position as supplier of natural resources—suddenly became the main winner within the CIS.

Politically as well as economically this situation has given rise to a host of interwoven and contradictory interests which have proved extremely difficult to reconcile. On a purely domestic level, it is feasible to employ redistributive mechanisms to offset relative gains and losses and implement coherent modernization strategies, although the growing resistance on the part of well-endowed regions of the Russian Federation indicates that this by no means goes uncontested. However, stretching beyond what have become borders in international law, relative gains and losses inevitably become an issue of national interests and, moreover, of national security. In this respect it was frustrating for the CIS member states to discover that the much-maligned Soviet income distribution

---

[17] If all foreign economic relations were to be cut off, only Russia would be able to maintain at least 65% of its present output. The ratio in the other cases ranges from close to zero (Belarus and Moldova) to a mere 27% (Kazakhstan). Bradshaw, M., Royal Institute of International Affairs, *The Economic Effects of Soviet Dissolution* (RIIA: London, 1993), p. 24.

was not only channelled via Moscow but also largely financed by Russia, since it demonstrated that their political aspirations were based on false economic assumptions. Russia, on the other hand, had to cope with the problem that at one and the same time it was least dependent on economic exchange with its partners and yet had most to lose from it.

Ironically enough, when it comes to meeting their own material needs those who could not resist the political drive away from Moscow now have hardly anything left at their disposal beyond begging Russia to pursue benevolent, inclusive policies at the expense of its own economic interests.[18] Even the partial relief which was temporarily afforded after the dissolution of the union by a common monetary space in the shape of the rouble zone is no longer available. Initially this was used to pile up inter-republican, inter-enterprise arrears in a manner akin to simultaneous developments within Russia. This indebtedness became part and parcel of the Russian debt crisis in mid-1992 and was subjected to the same procedure of mutual clearing and provisions such as 'correspondent accounts' for the respective state banks in the Russian Central Bank, with a view to preventing future misuse. As in the case of the domestic prepayment regulations, however, this procedure simply transferred financing responsibilities to the Central Bank, which subsequently felt obliged to grant 'technical credits' amounting to some 10 per cent of Russian gross domestic product (GDP). Well-endowed with 'book roubles' but constantly short of 'cash roubles' in this and other ways, many CIS member states also resorted to issuing money surrogates alongside the rouble, a development which in some measure contributed to inflationary pressure beyond Russia's immediate control. Viewed against this background the currency reform of July 1993 can be seen as an attempt to restore faith in Russia's macroeconomic policy by simply forcing other countries out of the rouble zone.[19]

Although the true impact of the CIS member states' behaviour in relation to rouble inflation remains open to closer scrutiny, up to the time of Russia's currency reform they clearly made use of the opportunities for free-riding. These were opened up by Russia's hegemonic role within the CIS—in which role it has, however, been far from perfect.[20] Although Russia clearly defined the rules for trade within the CIS by using its subsidized energy deliveries as a lever with which to force other member states to conclude a seemingly never-ending series of agreements, it managed neither to enforce these rules nor to set up a viable trading regime. Similarly, although Russia provides the biggest market for tradeable commodities within the CIS and has proved the only source of liquidity, here again severe limitations are obvious. Russia can neither

---

[18] Even political self-interest *vis-à-vis* the CIS does not seem entirely free of contradictions. In this regard it may be telling that it was the Russian defence sector which most vigorously pursued self-sufficiency, irrespective of the military's call for the extension of its presence well into the 'near abroad'.

[19] The new Russian rouble was to be transferred to other republics only if they agreed to submit their monetary and fiscal policies to strict Russian rules and supervision. With the sole exception of Tajikistan none accepted this. It resulted in a hasty introduction of national currencies.

[20] On the essential elements of economic hegemony, see Gilpin (note 2), pp. 75–80.

encourage the other member states to share costs, nor satisfy their financial needs in the longer run, nor afford the effects of their monetary free-riding.

In present circumstances, the asymmetrical relationship between Russia and the other CIS countries does not allow either for the maintenance of the traditional rouble zone or for a payments union void of financial backing from abroad. It remains to be seen whether pending projects for an alternative method of creating a unified monetary space with most responsibilities placed upon the Russian authorities ever materialize. From the point of view of the weaker CIS member states this means nothing less than forfeiting sovereignty in a crucial area of domestic politics. It is therefore hardly accidental that even the most advanced attempt to create a monetary union between Russia and Belarus (whose economy is controlled by Russia to a greater extent even than those of Yakut-Sakha or Tatarstan) failed in the summer of 1994, despite initial—politically rather than economically inspired—generous offers such as the exchange of rapidly depreciating Belarus coupons for roubles at a 1 : 1 rate. Russia also finds itself in an uncomfortable situation: in the same way that domestically it has to strike a balance between efforts at macroeconomic stabilization and the need to keep ailing Russian industries alive, it also operates on a knife-edge between its desire for appropriate earnings and the dangers inherent in the damage which pursuing this goal would inflict on its partners in the CIS. This creates the political paradox that Russia is on the one hand too strong to resist the temptation of exploiting present opportunities, but on the other hand too weak to employ instruments of control other than outright subordination under the guise of economic reintegration. For the time being, there is no relief from this tension in sight.

IV. Finding an appropriate place in the world: coping with great expectations

The economic and social upheavals generated by the post-Soviet unleashing of market forces once more revealed a fundamental lesson of political economy: ultimately it is welfare which secures democracy. The dictum 'Marshall Plan or martial law' captures well the essence and thrust of this concept. In the aftermath of World War II the USA vigorously followed this line of reasoning, irrespective of whether it was dealing with friend or foe. The lessons of the amazing (and possibly unique) success story of the Marshall Plan are still very much alive. This time, however, neither the USA nor the West at large is ready to deliver. There is a striking gap between the rhetoric concerning the urgent need to assist the Russian transformation process and the meagre practical results. The bigger Western aid packages grew at consecutive Group of Seven (G7) summit meetings in recent years, the less actually resulted from them.[21]

[21] This is not to say that no assistance at all was forthcoming. Of the impressive G7 figures, however, the bulk was either imposed on Western donors in terms of inescapable debt deferments (amounting to some $15 billion due in 1993) or happened to serve immediate donor interests at least as much as Russian needs, such as trade credits on commercial or at best marginally favourable terms (around $10 billion in

The failure to live up to the posture of generosity does not stem from a lack of willingness or determination on the part of the West. It is rather indicative of fairly limited capabilities. When in 1948 the USA decided to invigorate the ailing economies of (Western) Europe and (East) Asia, it did so on the basis of and equipped with the advantages of its position as uncontested dominant power in the world economic system. At that time no one could match the dynamics and resources of its economy; no one could challenge its lead in technological innovation and productive investment. The USA was thus in a position to provide a market of first resort, that is, to allow fairly unrestricted access to its domestic market, even while its trading partners fenced behind protective barriers. It could act as a lender of last resort who not only settled the chronic dollar shortage abroad by ensuring a steady flow of capital but also secured a stable international monetary system. Without such a favourable environment the Marshall Plan might easily have been a failure. In the circumstances of the time, it laid the foundations for the 'Golden Age' (the term of Ajit Singh) of absolute gains on a historically unprecedented scale.

Regrettably, the same no longer holds true today. The liberal *Pax Americana* carried the seeds of its own demise and within 25 years it had reached its nadir. The world of today looks fundamentally different: it is a world in which the absolute advantage of one economy has given way to intense competition for shifting relative advantages among various centres of growth, in which absolute gains have again given way to pressing concerns about relative gains. It is a world, too, which simply lacks the absorptive capacity to accommodate and rehabilitate an economy as big as Russia's. In contrast to the situation in the 1950s and 1960s, capital is again in short supply. Global financial flows have certainly expanded and accelerated on a previously unheard-of scale, with amounts in excess of a trillion dollars being shifted around every single day, but this happens according to a circular logic, fuelled by the search for lucrative short-term returns and the ever-increasing need of governments and banks to borrow, and has little relation to long-term productive investment. At the same time, deregulation of the global financial sphere has been accompanied by increasing efforts to regulate and control trade flows on the basis of the principle of reciprocity. In the hub of the industrialized world decrepit and infant industries alike have come under fierce competitive pressure, putting the liberal international trading regime of the past under severe stress. Furthermore, the multilateral management of the world economy supposed to fill the void left by the decline of the USA as the world's economic giant has clearly revealed its inherent limits in relation to stemming the protectionist tide and reconciling conflicting national interests.

1993). In fact fresh money remained scarce—from official sources in 1993, $1.5 billion, that is, half of the promised IMF ST (systemic transformation) facility. Thus only $350 million or roughly 10% of promised World Bank loans were disbursed. For a sceptical account reflecting Russian frustration, see *Whither Western Aid to Russia? A Russian View of Western Support*, Report directed by Sergei A. Karaganov (Bertelsmann Foundation: Gütersloh, 1994).

Essentially, developments in the world economy over the past 20 years may be considered typical side-effects of welfare economies which, driven by domestic inertia, tend to inflict the burden of economic adjustment on lenders abroad and merely provide the marginal degree of 'foreign social security' deemed necessary to shield the international order against outright political disruptions. This has created an unreceptive and unstable environment which is hardly friendly to late-comers. Russia, too, will have a hard time finding its place within it.

Recent experience has shown that it is only possible to overcome the obstacles created by fenced-off markets and scarce capital by pursuing aggressive export strategies using a low-wage, high-skill base, as in the case of the 'Asian dragons'. The crude call for markets to be opened up commonly heard from Russian decision makers travelling abroad may appeal most to those accustomed to blaming the environment for their own failures. Ultimately, competitiveness will be decided on the domestic front. The point to be made here, however, concerns the crucial link between domestic preparedness and foreign receptivity for successful penetration of international markets. Russia is increasingly disposed to rely on its own forces and turn away from the Organisation for Economic Co-operation and Development (OECD) countries. The question must be asked whether this tendency will be encouraged or countered from abroad—and here the answer seems obvious.

Opening up to the outside world has always been a sensitive issue in a country which was never an integral part of the international division of labour in the industrial age. Well-endowed with natural resources and lagging behind the front-runners of industrialization from the outset, Russia did not deem an open trade policy necessary or appealing. Even today, after it has become clear that the autarkic model of economic development did nothing but consign the Russian economy to inefficiency and backwardness, the lessons have not been generally absorbed. Undoubtedly, the Russia of today is more open than at any stage of its recent history. Yet again, however, this has happened largely by default. A combination of the inability of the Russian authorities to enforce their still fairly restrictive regulations and a host of legal loopholes provides the perfect conditions for innovative black marketeers, corrupt tax officers and 'businessmen' seeking a safe haven for their windfall profits. Influential interest groups can hardly be expected to proliferate from within these sections of society and actively promote an outward-looking economic policy. Much more influential have been the delaying tactics of those who oppose open-door policies on the simple grounds that this would spell the end of their ailing enterprises. Since business opportunities abroad are few and far between, their concerns have received an additional boost. Turning inwards, however, and resorting to an import-substitution strategy are not conducive to overcoming the country's endemic capital shortage. In this regard, Russia should have learned its lesson. Primary accumulation in the late tsarist period meant heavy levies on imported goods, premiums on domestic commodities and a surplus squeezed out of the peasantry and the urban workforce. The five-year plans of the 1930s aimed at much the same, and under Stalin opposition led straight to the Gulag.

The quarrels over energy prices show clearly that Russia currently finds itself in the midst of a similar problem, namely, changing the Soviet pattern of income distribution. For some time, the industrial lobby has managed to lock energy prices at their prevailing artificially low levels, thereby perpetuating their subsidization and the awkward system of export quotas and export duties. Only when Viktor Chernomyrdin and soon after him Yuriy Shafranik, both of whom were once prominent representatives of the Soviet energy sector, entered office in 1993 as prime minister and minister for the energy sector respectively did the balance of forces start to shift, resulting in energy prices gradually approaching world market levels. This episode may illustrate the fact that on balance different and possibly conflicting branches of the Russian economy might find it easier to strike a compromise than to be exposed to the harsh winds of international competition. They share the same legacy, and so far the Russian management of economic transformation has not yet created the impression that in the future they might develop in different ways. In this sense, the cartels gradually being formed and intimately linked to state bodies on various levels may be indicative of efforts to do away not only with threatening foreign competition but also with competitive pressure at home. Economic history, however, suggests that a Russian 'market economy' built along these lines will hardly develop the productive forces which once gave birth to the notion of protectionism.

V. Conclusions: the impact on Russia's relations with Europe

On both domestic and international counts the prevailing conditions favour a future Russian economy with a strong bias towards turning inwards, closing the doors and relying on its own forces. With hindsight, the liberal U-turn of early 1992 may prove to have been too short an episode to have a lasting effect or to sustain an economic policy line that drew on the substantive lessons from the utter failure of economic autarky. The international community, neglecting the lesson that good advice only matters if matched with deeds, proved supportive of Russia only on a fairly limited scale.

None the less, all that is discernible to date are contours and simple tendencies in policy which neither determine the eventual outcome in economic terms nor necessarily prescribe a given foreign policy course. This is particularly true with respect to Russia's relations with Europe, which, supposedly, offer the greatest potential. Europe or, more specifically, the European Union (EU) has a proven record as the biggest donor. Similarly, since the demise of the CMEA it has been unmatched as Russia's most important trading partner: more than

50 per cent of the country's officially recorded foreign trade is with the EU.[22] Furthermore, the EU and its member states have established the closest and most developed network of consultation and cooperation with the Russian Federation, the last milestone being the conclusion of the Partnership and Cooperation Agreement in June 1994.[23]

These features of bilateral relations may be indicative of a mutual desire to develop a stable partnership as a prerequisite for expanding the European division of labour in an easterly direction. Yet it took considerable time, persistent Russian pressure and many efforts on the part of various member states for the EU to make concessions of a more than merely symbolic nature. This has contributed to narrowing the gap between accommodating words and alienating deeds, but it is by no means closed yet. The European Union's aid programme, for instance, has been the subject of frequent criticism concerning its qualitative impact on the transformation process in Russia, and for good reason. This not only applies to the notorious export-promotion schemes of the EU member states but also to technical assistance, which has sacrificed much of its effectiveness to short-term self-interest.[24] The institutional arrangements were no less contentious. Originally conceived as only a modest departure from the European Community (EC) 1989 Trade and Co-operation Agreement with the Soviet Union, the more ambitious regulations insisted on by Russia took more than a year of controversial negotiations to be accepted by the EU. The 'four freedoms of movement'—of goods, persons, capital and services—however, may only be finalized within the framework of a free trade arrangement due to be considered in 1998. For the time being trade restrictions on 'sensitive' commodities as known from the association agreements with the former socialist countries will remain in place.

These quotas and tariffs on coal, steel, textiles and agricultural products are not yet seriously affecting Russian exports as much as they do the association partners of the EU in the former socialist countries. In the present circumstances, Russia, like the Soviet Union in the past, is a perfect complementary trading partner for the EU, providing scarce raw materials which account for roughly two-thirds of its overall exports to the western part of the continent. None the less, questions arise concerning the future of this relationship in market conditions. The present pattern is neither conducive to the transformation

---

[22] In 1993 Russian exports to the EU market, according to the Commission of the European Communities, were 30 times higher than to the USA and 10 times higher than to Japan. *Bulletin der Europäischen Union*, no. 1/2 (1994), p. 86.

[23] European Communities, Commission, Proposal for a Council and Commission decision on the conclusion of the Agreement on Partnership and Cooperation between the European Communities and their member states of the one part, and Russia, of the other part, COM(94)257 final, Brussels, 16 June 1994.

[24] Particularly explicit in its criticism has been the European Parliament, which repeatedly urged the Commission and individual member states to introduce changes in a number of programmes. The influence of and costs of Western experts who fly into Moscow for short-term consultancies, undue centralization, inadequate support for small business and neglect of environmental protection raised most concern during the parliamentary session held on 22 Apr. 1994.

process within Russia nor favourable to a mutually advantageous division of labour with the EU.

Domestically, Russia's resource richness has often proved a double-edged sword. On the one hand, resource-generated revenues constitute a stable source of income, alleviating the pervasive capital shortage. On the other, experience shows that constant and secured resource flows tend to preclude productive investment and capital formation, which in view of the emerging rent-seeking alliances in Russia may be a factor of particular relevance. An external impediment to international specialization beyond the exchange of traditional goods is posed by the EU's reluctance to open up its market to sensitive commodities, a fact which encourages neither Russian openness nor much-needed foreign investment in Russian manufacturing.[25] The current economic complementarity between Russia and the EU may therefore be considered a necessary but hardly sufficient condition for the development of mature economic integration which would lay the foundation for a stable and cooperative relationship between the two poles of gravity on the European continent.

In principle, functional economic integration and mutual dependence shape mind-sets in a way which tends to give criteria of economic efficiency and transnational non-discretionary rules higher status than purely national concerns about unilateral gains. This is true even if one does not share the high-flying and rather deterministic assumptions of liberal internationalism. Conversely, inward-looking strategies of economic nationalism proceed from the emphasis on unilateral vulnerability instead of the mutual gains to be derived from economic cooperation. In terms of foreign policy this is an important factor, although again it is important not to draw deterministic conclusions.

In the present circumstances, however, Russian economic neo-isolationism may prove a strong and attractive undercurrent for domestic forces in desperate search of a scapegoat. In the absence of moderating economic concerns this could easily translate into tit-for-tat aggressiveness. The best precaution, therefore, would be to see Russia becoming an integral part of the international (that is, in the first place, European) division of labour, and this is a task for both sides of the equation.

---

[25] In this regard it is not surprising that by far the biggest multi-billion dollar investment projects under negotiation are in the energy sector. These are awaiting legislation in Russia. By contrast foreign investment plans in the manufacturing sector have so far been negligible, a trend which can hardly be attributed to domestic instability alone.

22. Economic transformation in Russia and political partnership with Europe

Yuriy Borko

I. Introduction

The economic transformation in Russia has a direct impact on the climate of its political relations with Europe.[1] These relations are also affected by the state of the economic cooperation between Russia and Europe. This chapter analyses both these aspects.

The main questions to be examined are the following:

1. What are the prospects for economic transformation in Russia and in what way could they influence political relations with Europe, and with Western Europe in particular?

2. What are the prospects for economic cooperation between Russia and the European Union (EU) and what could be the political impact of this cooperation?

3. Could the development of economic cooperation between Russia and the former socialist countries[2] promote an improvement of their political relations with and the political climate in Europe as a whole?

4. In what way could economic integration in the Commonwealth of Independent States (CIS) under Russian leadership affect political relations in Europe?

5. What main conclusions can be drawn from this analysis as regards the correlation between economic transformation in Russia on the one hand and the political partnership between Russia and Europe on the other?

II. Economic reform in Russia and its relations with the West

The period since the beginning of economic reform in Russia is too short to answer the questions when a more or less stable economic system will be built and what kind of system it will be. It is clear that reform still needs a very long time. It is possible, however, to draw some conclusions as regards specific

---

[1] 'Europe' here means all the countries located to the west of the Commonwealth of Independent States (CIS) countries, including the Nordic and Baltic states. This interpretation is an operational one adopted for the purposes of examining Russia's position and implies nothing about the much-debated question where the economic and political borders of contemporary Europe run or its cultural identity stops.

[2] Defined here as the European members of the former Council for Mutual Economic Assistance (CMEA), but excluding the former German Democratic Republic (GDR) and including the former Yugoslavia and, since 1990, Estonia, Latvia and Lithuania. The CMEA when founded in 1949 consisted of Albania (withdrew in 1961) Bulgaria, Czechoslovakia, the GDR, Hungary, Poland, Romania, the USSR, Cuba, Mongolia and Viet Nam.

features of the processes of economic transformation in Russia and of the transitional period as a whole.

Some of these features are especially important for their influence on the network of economic and political relations between Russia and Europe.

1. Economic reform in Russia has tended to follow the same lines as in the Visegrad countries:[3] price liberalization, the legalization of private property, privatization in all economic sectors, the creation of a market economy infrastructure, the elaboration of a new pattern of macroeconomic policy aiming at low inflation and monetary stabilization, currency convertibility, the liberalization of external trade and economic links, and so on.

The most important result of these four years is that Russia has in fact passed from a totally state-owned and over-centralized planned economy to an economy in transition, with a dynamic private sector and with distinct features of the mixed economic system. There are many reasons to conclude that Russia has passed the stage where the economic changes are irreversible.

2. The process of economic transformation in Russia has been slower and more contradictory than it has in the Visegrad countries. Russia seems to be experiencing a specific type of post-communist evolution marked by such features as a long period of recession and general economic instability, very acute social problems and conflicts, a crisis of values and a decline of moral standards, lack of respect for the state and the law, an extensive shadow economy and very high levels of criminality. The positive processes (the formation of a new economic system, new political institutions, new values and national priorities, and so on) have not yet become more prominent than the negative aspects; at best a fragile balance has been achieved between the process of dismantling the old system and the resistance of its defenders. Society is split from top to bottom.

This is not only a result of political mistakes made by the new authorities, no matter how serious they seem to be. It is also the burdensome inheritance of the totalitarian system which lasted for more than 70 years. The extent of the economic, social and other distortions that system brought about has only now become clear. The country needs several decades to overcome them.

3. The state bureaucracy retains all the power. In Russia, unlike the Visegrad countries, the collapse of the communist regime did not result in victory for the democrats. Although they played a decisive role in the initial period after August 1991 when the putschists were defeated, on the whole they proved to be too weak not only to take power, but even to exert a strong and permanent influence on the course of events. The more flexible part of the former *nomenklatura*, which withdrew the communist ideology very quickly, and a younger generation of pragmatic professional administrators are at present trying to use the transition to the market economy and a pluralist society in their own interests and will continue to do so until the new-born democracy is able to defend

---

[3] The Czech Republic, Hungary, Poland and Slovakia.

its rights and interests more effectively. It is symptomatic that the developing economic and political system in Russia is defined more and more often as 'bureaucratic capitalism' or 'bureaucratic democracy'.

Four years' experience has shown that the bureaucracy tends to pursue a course of economic reform best described as 'forward-back-aside', and this kind of minuet is repeated again and again. Many actions of the government and local authorities correspond neither to the criteria of the market economy nor to the many social challenges of the transitional period. This makes it difficult to foresee either the social and political situation in the immediate future or the general prospects for economic transformation and development. The great weakness of the Russian bureaucracy, seen twice in this century, is its inability to achieve a flexible balance between its own corporate interests and the requirements of different social strata, particularly the lower classes. The question remains whether the Russian bureaucracy will be able to break with this tradition.

4. In the meantime, in the first half of 1996 the country approached macroeconomic stabilization. The rate of inflation fell to 1.2 per cent in June, 0.7 per cent in July and – 0.2 per cent in August. The fall in gross domestic product (GDP) and industrial output is now minimal; the standard of living is tending to stabilize. It is expected that the first signs of modest economic growth will appear as early as the second half of 1997. According to statements by Prime Minister Viktor Chernomyrdin, the new Vice-Prime Minister and Minister of Finance Alexandre Livshits, the Minister of Economics Evgeniy Yassin and other officials, the task of stimulating and promoting economic recovery, and investment in particular, will be the top government priority.[4]

The victory of Boris Yeltsin over his communist rival Gennadiy Zyuganov in the presidential election of June 1996 and the end of the war in Chechnya have contributed to political stabilization and favour further economic reform and revival. At the same time a new wave of sharp discussions as regards priorities and methods of economic policy is beginning. The government is criticized both by *dirigistes* and by liberals. The former continue to blame it for all the economic and social instability and to argue for the restoration of state control over the national economy.[5] The latter blame the government for incomplete or even frozen economic reforms and for excessive administrative measures to promote the development of the new-born market economy.[6]

---

[4] Livshits, A., 'Ekonomika Rossii v 1997 godu' [The Russian economy in 1997], *Izvestiya*, 27 Dec. 1995, p. 2; *Segodnya*, 6 June 1996, p. 2; 16 July 1996, p. 1; and 22 Aug. 1996, p. 3; and *Moscow News*, no. 33 (18–25 Aug. 1996), p. 13.

[5] [Lessons of liberalization in Russia], *Segodnya*, 30 Nov. 1993; and 'Ekonomika v lovushke liberalizma: gde vykhod?' [The economy in the trap of liberalism: Where is the way out?], *Segodnya*, 30 May 1996.

[6] Illarionov, A., 'Radikalnye reformy: zalog vozrozhdeniya ekonomiki' [Radical reforms are the pledge of economic revival], *Finansovye Izvestiya*, 14 May 1996, p. 7; and Vasilev, S., 'Problemy perekhoda k ekonomicheskomu rostu' [Problems of transition to economic growth], *Segodnya*, 14 Aug. 1996, p. 3. According to a Deputy Chairman of the Central Bank, Sergey Alexashenko, the country is at the crossroads and must choose either to intensify economic reform with a view to stimulating structural adjustment and growth or to return to the economic chaos of 1991–92 for some months or even for as long as

This collision of views reflects the real-life problem of finding a balance between the free play of market forces and institutional economic regulation. Government economic policy continues to oscillate between the two extremes. The long-term prospect has been defined by former Prime Minister Yegor Gaidar as a choice between the free market and the 'bureaucratic market'.[7] Given the current social and political situation and the weakness of democracy in particular, the second model seems to be more probable, for the next 10–15 years at least. It will be a scenario of transition to a mixed economy with a strong public sector and institutional regulation.

5. The correlation between state and market can change to and fro, but in any case the Russian economic system will continue to differ significantly from that of Western Europe and from that to be built in the former socialist countries. The turbulent political development of Russia is a dangerous source of economic and social disturbance. It is characterized by such features as an uncompromising struggle between different groups of the establishment, excessive personal ambitions, lack of competence and experience, nationalist trends, populism and, last but not least, political adventurism. The war in Chechnya has confirmed the worst fears. Besides the great suffering of the people, economic recovery may well be a victim of this military action.

These specific features, contradictions and uncertainties of the transitional period cannot but affect the overall political climate in which relations between Russia and the European countries are developing. It is important to stress that, apart from practical economic, political and cultural cooperation, a relation of partnership also requires a general context of favourable mutual perceptions, the replacing of old negative stereotypes and mutual confidence.

Over the past 10 years West European perceptions of the USSR and of Russia have changed twice, both times in a radical way. In 1985–90 they evolved from extreme scepticism about President Mikhail Gorbachev's *perestroika* to a short period of euphoria and 'Gorbymania'. The resolute abandonment of communist values proclaimed by the Russian leadership after the collapse of the Soviet Union continued this trend. Later the pendulum swung back and today perceptions are rather gloomy.

The new scepticism is not as monolithic and categorical as it was in the worst stages of the cold war. At present it is more an oscillating equilibrium of two opposite impressions caused both by the fundamental changes going on in Russia and by the current profound crisis and disorder. This ambivalent perception was reflected by the economic journal *Euromoney*: 'when trying to predict the future for Russia we step (as George Kennan would have had it) on "the unfirm substance of the imponderables". But one thing is for sure: the free-market genie is out of bottle and cannot be put back'.[8] In other words, the

---

5–6 years. 'Ekonomisty vpervye osmelilis podumat o dvukhtysyachnom gode' [For the first time economists dared to think about 2000], *Segodnya*, 19 Jan. 1996.

[7] Gaidar, Ye., 'Gosudarstvo i evolyutsiya' [The state and evolution], *Izvestiya*, 9 Nov. 1994.

[8] *Euromoney*, June 1994, p. 114.

collapse of the centrally planned economic system is a *fait accompli*, but no one knows how this mysterious genie will behave. Moscow's actions in Chechnya were considered by many as confirmation of this assessment, calling into question the very possibility of political partnership between Russia and the West. European perceptions of Russia will be of a grey colour for many years to come, and will have a cooling influence on the decision makers responsible for the course of foreign policy towards Russia.

Russian public opinion has also evolved. A new positive image of the West took shape in the second half of the 1980s. Besides a very high appreciation of Western society, its values and institutions, this perception was linked to two expectations—the expectation that Russia would be able to use Western experience and to pass the transitional period more or less quickly, and the expectation of significant economic assistance from the West, comparable, for example, with the Marshall Plan. The first hope proved to be illusory, and the second was without doubt excessive and naive. Now as a result the greater part of Russian society is suffering a sense of disappointment.

Does this mean that pro-Western attitudes and preferences are being replaced with anti-Western ones? There is no single, unequivocal answer. On the one hand, there is a tendency for traditional Russian suspicions of the rest of the world, and the West in particular, to revive. According to a poll carried out by the Russian Centre for Public Opinion Studies (VTsIOM) at the end of 1994, 81 per cent of respondents were afraid of foreign ownership of major plants and factories and 54 per cent were anxious about a threat of increasing dependence on the West.[9] In a May 1995 opinion poll, for instance, 26 per cent of respondents considered the Western countries as actual or potential allies.[10] The West is not perceived by Russians as a monolithic entity. In the same opinion poll, 26 per cent of respondents perceived the USA as an enemy, and only 8 per cent saw Western Europe in the same way.[11] A similar differentiation is made between NATO and the EU. The image of the former continues to be negative (not least because of the massive campaign against its enlargement), but regular polls by *Eurobarometer* in the European part of Russia bear witness to a consistently favourable attitude to the EU: in 1993, 38 per cent of respondents were positive, 33 per cent neutral and 9 per cent negative to the EU, and in 1995 the corresponding figures were 34, 23 and 7 per cent.[12]

It is not clear how far Russian public opinion about the West can evolve. It will depend on the course of events in the country. If the worst scenario comes to pass anti-Western perceptions will become dominant once again. If Russia experiences a more gradual transition, a more or less balanced attitude to the West and a preferential perception of Europe can be expected. Even so, and even taking into account all the advantages of cooperation, public opinion will give stronger support to those Russian politicians who have a cautious attitude

[9] *Mneniya*, no. 1 (1995), p. 9; and no. 2 (1995), p. 35.
[10] *Segodnya*, 9 June 1995, p. 9.
[11] *Segodnya*, 9 June 1995, p. 9.
[12] *Eurobarometer*, no. 6 (1995), p. 50.

to Western experience, Western models of society and close partnership with Western alliances. It would be very dubious indeed to interpret this kind of rank-and-file support as anti-Westernism. Moreover, anti-Western clichés played no visible role in the recent presidential election, even in the campaign of the national patriots such as Vladimir Zhirinovsky.

All things considered, it is likely that both Russia and Western Europe will take a very careful approach to any major political decisions that could involve long-term mutual obligations. Nevertheless, Russia is too important a partner to be neglected, both because of its potential for economic cooperation and because of its role in European security.

III. Russia and the EU

The idea of combining economic cooperation and political partnership[13] was one of the cornerstones of the Partnership and Cooperation Agreement signed by Russia and the EU in June 1994.[14] Ratification was significantly delayed by the war in Chechnya but the process resumed after a break in March–June 1995. In any event, most of the content of the Agreement is covered by the Interim Agreement on Trade and Trade-related Matters, which was signed on 17 July 1995, came into force on 1 February 1996 and will operate until the Partnership and Cooperation Agreement comes into force. In conceptual terms it opens a new perspective for cooperation between what were defined by Jacques Delors, former President of the Commission of the European Communities, as the two pillars of Europe—the EU and Russia.[15]

This cooperation is envisaged in a wide area, including political, economic and cultural aspects. In the economic sphere, which is by far the most important part of the Partnership and Cooperation Agreement, three points should be underlined: (*a*) the Partnership and Cooperation Agreement is the first bilateral document in which Western countries consider Russia as a partner with an 'economy in transition'; (*b*) it contains the first bilateral top-level conception of long-term economic relations with a view to Russia's future inclusion in a 'wider area of cooperation in Europe'; and (*c*) it is an unprecedentedly ambitious programme of economic cooperation.[16] It should be stressed that economic convergence achieved through this agreement will lead to more intensive political relations.

---

[13] 'Cooperation' is used here of the economic aspects of the relationship and of relationships based on mutual pragmatic interest; 'partnership' is used to indicate a political relationship and one based on at least some common values.

[14] European Communities, Commission, Delegation in Moscow, 'Agreement on Partnership and Cooperation: Full text signed in Corfu on 24 June 1994 by the European Union and the Russian Federation', 1994.

[15] The EU's strategy for a 'substantial partnership' was passed by the EU General Affairs Council in Nov. 1995 and approved by the Madrid summit meeting in Dec. 1995. *Bulletin of the European Union*, no. 11 (1995), pp. 134–35; and Agence internationale d'information pour la presse, *Europe Documents*, no. 1969 (10 Jan. 1996), pp. 1–4.

[16] Agreement on Partnership and Cooperation (note 14), Preamble, Articles 1 and 3, and Chapter VII.

Political dialogue

Special provisions of the Partnership and Cooperation Agreement (Title 2) focus on establishing a mechanism for regular political dialogue to promote: (*a*) a strengthening of the links between Russia and the EU; (*b*) an increasing *rapprochement* between their positions on international issues of mutual concern; and (*c*) their cooperation in the implementation and observance of the principles of democracy and human rights, on which the agreement is based. The latter, embodied in the Preamble and Article 2, does not, of course, guarantee a consistent and steady Russian advance towards democracy, but it gives the EU some modest opportunities to influence this process.

The brutal action of the Russian Government in Chechnya caused the first open crisis in EU–Russian relations after the Partnership and Cooperation Agreement was signed. The EU sought to influence Moscow's Chechnya policy by using postponement of ratification of the agreement as 'a message in advance' to warn of the danger to the very idea of partnership.[17] This crisis proved that the EU's opportunities to exercise leverage are modest, but cannot be ignored.[18] The most important aspect of the crisis may have been that the EU and Russia confirmed their willingness and ability to follow a course of cooperation in spite of deep disagreement in a sensitive area which is and will in the near future be much more vulnerable than trade and economic matters.

Trade and competition

The EU member countries are significant trading partners of Russia, accounting for over one-third of its total external trade. There are, however, several problems in the exchange. At present it is asymmetric in two senses. In 1995 Russia's share in the total trade of the EU was only 3.5 per cent while the EU's share in total Russian external trade (including trade with the CIS countries) was 35 per cent.[19] According to estimates 37.5 per cent of Russia's trade by volume is with the EU countries—over 50 per cent more than trade with its CIS

---

[17] The then French Foreign Minister, Alain Juppé, stressed during a visit to Moscow in Mar. 1995 that 'We do not want to isolate Russia; we do want to make it clear that Russia has to respect commitments entered into with the EU'. Open Media Research Institute (hereafter OMRI), *OMRI Daily Digest*, no. 47, part I (7 Mar. 1995), URL <http://www.omri.cz/Publications/Digests/DigestIndex.html> (hereafter, references to the *OMRI Daily Digest* refer to the Internet edition at this URL address). More specifically, the EU required progress on a political settlement in Chechnya, a stronger presence for the Organization for Security and Co-operation in Europe (OSCE), and better access for humanitarian aid.

[18] Another example of attempts to exercise leverage was the decision of the European Parliament in Oct. 1995 to hold up ratification of the agreement unless the influential Yabloko and Derzhava political groupings were registered for the forthcoming elections to the parliament. According to Hélène Carrère d'Encausse, a well-known analyst and member of the European Parliament, the delay was intended to send a message to Russia that 'there is a clause on democracy in the accord' between Russia and the EU. *OMRI Daily Digest*, no. 212, part I (31 Oct. 1995).

[19] European Communities, Statistical Office, *External Trade*, nos 7, 8, 9 (1996); and 'Russia: foreign economic relations. Trends and prospects', *Quarterly Review* (Moscow), no. 1 (1996), p. 65. The share of the EU is calculated by the author. The 3 new member states, Austria, Finland and Sweden, which joined the EU in Jan. 1995, are included in the EU figures for 1994.

partners.[20] The pattern of trade by product is also very asymmetric. Russia exports mainly fuel, raw materials and semi-manufactured goods. West European countries export mainly machines, transport equipment and manufactured goods.

In the long term the potential for trade exchange between Russia and Western Europe is very significant. According to estimates of EU experts, the volume of this trade could increase to near that of present trade between the EU and the USA.[21] However, neither the volume nor the structure of trade corresponds to the economic potential and needs of Russia. The approaches of the partners do not coincide. Russia is without any doubt interested in changing the pattern of trade to make it closer to that between developed countries, based on industrial specialization and the exchange of manufactured goods. Western Europe at present and at least for the immediate future is more interested in the existing pattern of trade, although in the long run the restructuring of imports from Russia could be the only way to ensure a stable growth of exports to Russia.

Second, a significant proportion of Russian businessmen, politicians and public opinion as a whole tends to interpret this ambiguity in the West European position as a deliberate policy to treat Russia as a permanent supplier of raw materials to the West. This point of view is a mixture of misunderstandings, old prejudices and the populist slogans of some politicians, but it has a real basis in a genuine divergence of economic interests and approaches. These misperceptions could weaken and disappear if and when an economic situation comes about in Russia which favours European investment in Russia and industrial cooperation with European companies. Meanwhile Russia and Western Europe seem to define their priorities in different ways.

A third problem in the trade exchange is competition. It was one of the most difficult topics during the negotiations between Russia and the EU. The regulation of international competition is a source of headaches for governments over all the contemporary world. EU–Russian trade relations are no exception, nor are they an unusual case. Fuel is the one class of goods where competition between Russia and West European countries is not significant, although there are exceptions (Norway and Russia compete as gas exporters and Russian Gazprom competes with German Ruhrgas). Where other kinds of goods are concerned, the problem of competition does exist.

Finally, in the spring of 1994, when the text of the Partnership and Cooperation Agreement was almost finalized, a very severe disagreement about the Russian export of nuclear materials put its signing into question. At the last moment a compromise was found, but the problem will remain at least until

---

[20] Calculated from *Finansovye Izvestiya*, 17 Aug. 1995. See also European Communities, Commission, Delegation in Moscow, 'EU–Russia Relations', Press Release, 8/95, p. 1.

[21] 'Russia in the framework of partnership and co-operation in Europe', A survey prepared by the Delegation of the Commission of the European Communities in Moscow for a symposium in Moscow, 23 Nov. 1994, p. 3. However, bearing in mind that the ratio between these volumes is at present 1 : 7, and assuming 10% annual growth in Russia–EU trade, it would take 20 years for Russia–EU trade to reach the present level of USA–EU trade.

1 January 1997, when, according to Article 22, a new agreement on this matter is to be signed and come into force.

The agreement changed both the character of the problems under consideration and the list of 'hard' questions. Russia is no longer considered as a 'state-trading country' and all the measures applied by the EU to this group of countries have to be lifted from Russia. The EU has no tariff protection for fuel, raw materials, minerals and metals (except for some goods covered by the 1952 treaty establishing the European Coal and Steel Community), and these constitute more than half of Russian exports in terms of value. Since January 1993 Russia has also been included in the EU Generalized Scheme of Preferences. According to official estimates of the Commission of the European Communities, in 1995 the average weighted tariff on imports from Russia was about 1 per cent.[22] These circumstances and the principle of mutual most-favoured-nation treatment have done away with many former sources of disputes between Russia and the EU.

In spite of these favourable changes, the problem of competition is still a source of potential disagreement and a topic of more or less regular discussion at the political level within the framework of the agreement. The EU has been accused many times of trying to build a protectionist 'fortress Europe', and with some justification, although the accusation is often made for polemical reasons. From the very beginning the European Communities were very sensitive to external competitors and the EU inherited this tradition. There are many signs that Russia will also be a very tough trade partner.

Russian competition on the EU markets applies with manufactured goods in particular. In 1994 Russia occupied 29th place as an exporter of machines and transport equipment to the EU (0.25 per cent of total EU imports of these goods), and 12th place as an exporter of other manufactured goods.[23] It is behind Norway, the Czech Republic, Thailand and Singapore as a supplier to EU countries. If Russia increased its exports of these goods to the EU by 12–14 per cent per year over the next 10 years it would only double these very low shares, and given the prospects for its economic development at least until the year 2005 this result could be considered a great success.

Future disputes could be connected first of all with a very limited group of 'vulnerable' goods, semi-manufactured and manufactured goods in particular, if a sharp increase in Russian exports were to threaten the balance on the global market of one particular kind of product—as happened in 1993–94 with aluminium. Other vulnerable goods include fissile materials, steel, fertilizers, and so on: the list could grow in future. As a competitor with Europe, however, Russia will remain far behind the USA, Japan and some other countries because it is uncompetitive on external markets and its internal market is far from saturated. The scale and extent of Russian competition on the EU markets should

---

[22] European Communities, Commission, 'The European Union and Russia: the future relationship', Commission communication to the Council, EU series no. 8 (May 1995), p. 4.

[23] Calculated from European Communities, Statistical Office, *External Trade*, nos 8–9 (1995), p. 25.

therefore not be exaggerated. There is also time for Russia to accommodate itself to the principles and standards of international trade cooperation.

A much more complicated situation will arise as regards competition on the Russian market. Liberalization of external trade and economic relations in the post-communist countries in transition is an ambivalent process. In some cases (Hungary and Poland) it has led to negative trade balances. The Partnership and Cooperation Agreement allows Russia some scope to protect infant industry and sectors that are undergoing reconstruction or facing serious social problems over a transitional five-year period (Articles 15 and 53, Annexes 2 and 90). The sales crisis in most branches of Russian manufacturing industry and agriculture has given rise to demands from the producers for protectionist tariffs on imports and has led to several government decisions to increase customs duties on many kinds of imported goods, including cars, foodstuffs and alcohol.[24]

For many years to come the Russian authorities will be engaged in searching for the 'golden mean' between on the one hand protection against foreign competitors to allow for the modernization of industry and agriculture and on the other hand integration in the world economy. In the immediate future the trend towards protectionism is very likely to prevail because of the poor competitiveness of the national economy and a political shift towards nationalism. The crucial point will be whether the government is able to carry out reasonable protectionist measures within the limits of its formal obligations under the Partnership and Cooperation Agreement and under future membership in the World Trade Organization, the successor to the General Agreement on Tariffs and Trade (GATT). West European countries are more experienced than Russia in both the interpretation and the practical implementation of the GATT principles and norms and will consider any infringements as being of a political character. The problem of competition on the Russian market will therefore be a likely source of political tension and a topic of sharp disagreement between the partners, in particular later, when all exceptions in favour of Russia are abolished. This may be the most sensitive issue of all for some years to come.

Energy

One of the politically important topics in the dialogue will be cooperation in the energy sector, because of its strategic character and its share in the trade exchange. In spite of the very concerned attitude of government and public opinion, oil and gas will be the main items of Russia's exports to Western Europe for the next 10–15 years at least. In 1992–94 about half of Russia's hard currency earnings came from energy exports. Russia provided about 10 per cent

---

[24] In 1994 the average tariff was raised from 5.6% to 7.5%. *Finansovye Izvestiya*, 12 Jan. 1995. After additional increases in 1995–96 it was raised to 13% and, according to the Minister of External Relations, Oleg Davydov, this average level will be more or less stable, even if tariffs on particular imports can be changed. *Byulleten Inostrannoy Kommercheskoy Informatsii*, no. 35 (30 Mar. 1996), p. 3.

of Western Europe's oil imports and 36 per cent of its gas imports.[25] It is likely that the Russian share of EU oil imports will fall because of the deep crisis in the national oil industry. Nevertheless, it will be an important source of diversification of the EU fuel supply. Opportunities in the gas industry are much broader because of Russia's enormous natural reserves. If the project for the Yamal–Germany pipeline (through Belarus and Poland) is carried out, Russian exports of gas to European countries could almost double.

In the Partnership and Cooperation Agreement, a special article, Article 65, defines the main lines of cooperation in this sector, including the coordination of energy policy, legislation, research and development (R&D), infrastructure, training, safety and environmental aspects. Many aspects of energy cooperation are covered by international organizations—the World Trade Organization, the International Monetary Fund (IMF), the World Bank, and the European Bank for Reconstruction and Development (EBRD)—especially in such matters as trade regimes and investment. Cooperation between these institutions and Russia is therefore an important item in the latter's political dialogue with Western countries.

As for priorities, West European consumers are interested first of all in the full liberalization of Russian fuel exports and in the security of supply. Russia is interested in large-scale investment in order to renew both equipment and technologies and to overcome the oil industry crisis. The interests of the partners do not coincide, but they are interconnected. They therefore need to be balanced on the basis of compromise.

One example of controversy was the problem of liberalizing Russian oil exports to Western Europe. This was resisted both by Russian consumers because it would inevitably have increased all production costs and by Russian oil companies with a monopoly on the exports. It was only after the World Bank's warning that new loans would not be made for the Russian oil industry if liberalization did not proceed that the Russian Government took the decision to abolish all licences and quotas for oil exports from January 1995.[26] It is doubtful whether this problem has been solved, however, and the compromise arrived at, which is of a political nature, will not be the last.

Another topic of political dialogue is the European Energy Charter signed in 1991. It embodies a comprehensive concept of international cooperation in Europe and beyond, aimed at efficient utilization of both natural energy resources, especially in Russia, and Western technology and investment. Russia was one of its initiators, but abstained until the last moment from signing the Energy Charter Implementing Treaty providing a legal framework for East–West energy investment, cooperation and trade. The compromise arrived at was to give Russia three years to adapt and complete its legislation in accordance

---

[25] European Communities, Statistical Office, *External Trade, 1994;* European Communities, Statistical Office, *Balance of Payments, 1994*; and *Moscow News*, no. 35 (28 Aug.–4 Sep. 1994), p. 27.
[26] *Izvestiya*, 15 Dec. 1994; and *Segodnya*, 6 Jan. 1995.

with the Charter and the Treaty. Russia finally signed this treaty in December 1994, together with 47 other states.[27]

To sum up, the energy sector is one of the most promising fields of economic cooperation between Russia and the EU, and the readiness of the partners to come to compromises certainly confirms its political importance.

Investment

The economic reasons for and stimuli to Western investment in Russia are well-known. Russia considers them a *sine qua non* of the modernization and reconstruction of its national economy, industry in particular, in the light of its domestic needs and the requirements of external trade. Western investors are interested in the vast new markets and in the expected great returns.

The potential scale and benefits make this form of cooperation a major political priority for both Russia and Western Europe. This was confirmed by the fact that several clauses (Chapter 2 and Articles 52, 57, 58 and 62) were included in the Partnership and Cooperation Agreement covering investment promotion and protection, liberalization of capital movement and payments, the conditions affecting the establishment and operation of companies, industrial cooperation and so on.

The approaches of the partners differ. For the Russian Government it is a high political priority and the real proof of the Western countries' readiness to help Russia in a time of transition. The Western countries, however, tend to perceive the problem of investment mainly as an economic and institutional issue and a question of the balance between incentives and risks.

The situation as regards Western investment in Russia is very far from being satisfactory. Different sources of information give contradictory data, but according to calculations of the Russian Ministry of Economics, which seem to be the most reliable, the aggregate foreign investment in the five-year period 1991–95 amounted to $6.8 billion—less than 2 per cent of total investment in the Russian economy.[28] Russia is among the third dozen on the world 'league table' and is lagging behind many Asian and Latin American countries.

Up to now the main donors to Russia have been the international institutions—the IMF, the World Bank and the EBRD. Their cooperation with the Russian authorities is evidence of the support rendered by the Group of Seven industrialized countries (G7) and other Western countries to promote economic reform in Russia. The activities of these institutions are, however, limited mainly to objectives of a 'pre-investment' nature—to support financial and economic stabilization, promote infrastructure development and create a more favourable climate for foreign direct investment in production. The latter depends on the Western private sector, and business there still prefers to maintain a 'wait-and-see' approach—in particular West European companies, which

---

[27] Agence internationale d'information pour la presse, *Europe Documents,* no. 1869 (20 Jan. 1994), pp. 1–7; and no. 6382 (19–20 Dec. 1994), p. 4.

[28] *Byulleten Inostrannoy Kommercheskoy Informatsii*, no. 88 (Aug. 1996), p. 2.

are now lagging behind more adventurous US investors. The reasons for this passivity are well-known—political instability, intensive national-patriotic propaganda against the 'enslavement of Russia by the West', unsatisfactory legislation as regards foreign investment, the inconsistent economic policy of the government, a very high level of criminality, and so on. In the *Euromoney* rating of country risk Russia occupied 136th place among 167 countries in September 1994—only one point higher than a year before[29]—142nd in September 1995 and 86th in September 1996. According to estimates made at the meeting of the Board of Directors of the EBRD in London in April 1995, all the risk factors affecting foreign investment in Russia continue to deteriorate.[30]

As far as the Russian Government is concerned, its aim is to promote foreign investment in national industry. In 1994–96 several new acts were passed and administrative decisions taken to stimulate this investment. These included some customs advantages for foreign exporters if they participate in a joint venture and make a direct investment, guarantees of property rights, freedom to repatriate profits, and so on. At the same time, the government is under increasing pressure from Russian business, which is afraid of competition from Western investors, in particular in the key sectors of the economy. An eloquent example of this is the fate of the legislation on shares of production which was to establish the rules and mechanisms of distribution of profit between national and foreign companies, the latter being given legal guarantees against investment risks. The first law on this matter was passed in December 1995, but pressure from the communist and national-patriotic opposition resulted in some clauses being included which do not correspond to international standards and undermine the effectiveness of the law. Opponents of this legislation are, moreover, resisting the adoption of another law to define a list of natural resources covered by the law on shares of production.

In this complex situation, the government can only try to manoeuvre between two imperatives—following its obligations under the Partnership and Cooperation Agreement and other international agreements, and satisfying the demands of domestic producers. However, the trend towards economic stabilization and the government measures mentioned above have resulted in a slow growth of foreign investment: $2.8 billion in 1995 (150 per cent more than in 1994) and, according to expert estimates, $3.5 billion in 1996.[31] Many projects frozen before the presidential election are now to be carried out. Some Russian and Western experts expect that foreign investment will increase to $10–15 billion annually for the next four or five years. There are also some other positive trends: increasing reinvestment by foreign companies in the rouble, the redistribution of new investment in favour of infrastructure (banking, communications networks and so on), manufacturing and R&D. The latest *Euromoney* rating, in

[29] *Euromoney*, no. 235 (1994), p. 379.
[30] *Finansovye Izvestiya*, 18 Apr. 1995.
[31] *Byulleten Inostrannoy Kommercheskoy Informatsii*, no. 88 (1 Aug. 1996), p. 2; and no. 89 (3 Aug. 1996), p. 2; and *Finansovye Izvestiya*, no. 34 (29 Mar. 1996), p. 5.

September 1996, placed Russia in 86th place.[32] It is a promising sign. The principal obstacles to foreign investment remain, however. These problems will be difficult items in the dialogue between Russia and Western Europe for several years to come at least. Massive Western investment in the Russian economy is a long-term prospect.

The same applies to Russian industrial cooperation. One of its most widespread forms has been the joint venture. As of January 1996, about 17 000 joint ventures and foreign enterprises had been established, but only one-third of them were operational, mainly small and medium-sized, and they were producing about 5 per cent of industrial output.[33] Industrial cooperation is included in the list of priorities for economic cooperation in the Partnership and Cooperation Agreement, and, if implemented on a large scale, could have a very positive impact on the political partnership. This, however, is also a matter for the long-term future.

Western assistance and Russian debts

Western assistance has been the source of the most acute disappointment for Russian democrats and for all adherents of reform, who had hoped for something like the Marshall Plan and did not get it.

At present the Russian political establishment and public opinion have lost their illusions and are tending to underestimate Western assistance. It is, however, important to make a distinction between the rather populist declarations addressed to the electorate and the businesslike approach of the Western and Russian authorities responsible for cooperation in this sphere. Western assistance will most probably be a topic of permanent public polemic between Russia and Western countries, as well as within Russia's political community. These discussions and divergences of opinions should not be exaggerated, however. In fact Russia and the West recognize both the usefulness and the political importance of the assistance.

Western Europe is most closely involved. The EU and its member states were the protagonists of assistance to the former Soviet Union, and they gave about 60 per cent of the total amount committed over the period September 1990–March 1994, including 46 per cent of humanitarian aid and 39 per cent of technical assistance.[34] However, there is a serious problem with the effectiveness of this assistance, with analysing previous experience, and with choosing the most promising fields and the most appropriate forms for assistance.[35]

---

[32] *Segodnya,* 22 Oct. 1996, p. 8.

[33] *Byulleten Inostrannoy Kommercheskoy Informatsii,* no. 84 (23 July 1996), p. 2; and no. 88 (1 Aug. 1996), p. 3.

[34] European Communities, Commission, 'World assistance to the new independent states', Working document for the Commission Seminar of 6 Apr. 1994, Brussels, 30 Mar. 1994, pp. 1, 10, 12, 14.

[35] Up to now the main instruments of EU assistance have been credits and credit guarantees—73% of the total amount as against 4% designated for technical assistance. Because of its debts, Russia is becoming less and less interested in credits and would like to get more assistance of a long-term nature—with education and training, infrastructure development and so on.

Finally, a matter of great political importance is Russian indebtedness, amounting by the beginning of 1996 to $120 billion, 75 per cent of which is owed to the EU and its member states. Negotiations on the restructuring of these debts, mainly inherited from the USSR, are held every year—with the Paris Club of creditor nations as regards state credits, and with the London Club of private lenders in relation to private credits. The most difficult question of these negotiations is the conditions of restructuring. Russia is interested in long-term postponement instead of rolling over its debts on an annual basis, as was arranged in 1992–94. In April 1996, agreement was reached with the Paris Club on debt rescheduling over a 25-year period. In November 1995 a similar arrangement was negotiated and agreed in principle with the London Club. It is expected to be signed by the end of 1996.[36]

Other fields of cooperation

The Partnership and Cooperation Agreement lists about 30 fields for economic cooperation. Apart from those mentioned above, it covers agriculture, construction, transport, postal services and telecommunications, informatics and information infrastructure, space, science and technology, education and training, the environment, small and medium-sized enterprises, standardization, regional development, social cooperation, tourism, statistical cooperation, and so on. It is neither possible nor necessary to consider these one by one, but several fields of cooperation should be mentioned because of their political importance.

The top priorities are: (a) R&D cooperation; (b) space; and (c) the safety of nuclear stations and control over nuclear materials. Besides its economic significance, the first is a very sensitive one for Russian public opinion, which is afraid of the 'brain drain' effect of opening borders to the West. Space is another field of great political importance in both scientific research and tough commercial competition: Russia has joined the 'club' of competitors, and compromises in this area are inevitable. The issue of nuclear safety is of special sensitivity to the West European countries.

IV. Russia and the former socialist countries[37]

It is known that in the initial post-cold war phase political relations between Russia and the former socialist countries have been far from idyllic.[38] Can economic cooperation between Russia and these countries counterbalance or soften the political complexities and promote the creation of a new political climate for relations between them?

After the collapse of the socialist system the trade patterns of the former socialist countries changed in a radical way. The Soviet Union was once by far

---

[36] Rutland, P., 'Russia concludes deal with Paris Club', *OMRI Daily Digest*, no. 84, part I (29 Apr. 1996); and *Finansovye Izvestiya*, no. 48 (7 May 1996), p. 3; and no. 79 (13 Aug. 1996), p. 1.

[37] See note 2.

[38] See chapter 17 in this volume.

their most important trading partner; in 1993 the ratio of their trade with the EU to their trade with Russia was 6 : 1.[39] This reorientation is a part of these countries' strategy of joining the EU. Russia, in its turn, has also reoriented its trade links to Western Europe. In 1994 the share of the European socialist countries in Russian external trade was 11.2 per cent—less than a quarter of the share of the EU as it then was plus the three countries which joined in January 1995.[40] In 1988 the respective shares had been 50.1 per cent and 14.5 per cent.

In the long-term perspective, economic cooperation with Russia will be of minor importance for these countries compared to their economic links with Western Europe. Nevertheless, it could create an additional opportunity to exploit the potential of the European division of labour, and in some respects is even more promising for these countries than economic cooperation with the EU, the sharp growth of their negative trade balances with the EU member states being taken into account.[41]

For these countries, trade with Western Europe and trade with Russia are complementary. Their exports to Western Europe consist mainly of food, textiles and steel products (40 per cent together) and machines, transport equipment and other manufactured goods (another 20 per cent). The first group is covered by the EU quota restrictions; the second meets the sharpest competition on saturated West European markets. On the other hand, their exports to Russia consist of machines, equipment and consumer goods (35–40 per cent) and food (35 per cent). Nor is there strong competition on their own markets between imported goods from the EU and from Russia. Seventy-five per cent of imported goods from the EU are machines and other manufactured products; 75 per cent of imports from Russia are energy and raw materials.[42] Moreover, in some other respects the Russian market is still more accessible for these countries than West European markets. Russia, in its turn, is interested in the diversification of external trade in order to export semi-manufactured and finished manufactured goods. The development of transport links connecting it with its main economic partner—Western Europe—is of great importance for Russia as well.

The mutual interest of the former socialist countries and Russia in restoring their trade was recognized very soon, but the negative trend was broken only in 1995 when the volume of this trade increased by 33 per cent, reaching a value of $12.6 billion.[43] The prospects for economic cooperation between them seem favourable, although rather modest because of the slowness of the Russian economic recovery, the redistribution of Russian oil and gas exports in favour

---

[39] Calculated from European Communities, Statistical Office, *External Trade,* no. 7 (1994); and *Finansovye Izvestiya,* 18–24 Aug. 1994, p. 2.

[40] *Vneshnyaya Torgovlya,* no. 5 (1995), p. 45; and *SSSR v Tsifrakh v 1989 godu* [The USSR is figures in 1989), p. 32. See also note 19.

[41] For the 4 Visegrad countries this increased from 0.3 billion ECU in 1989 to 4.5 billion ECU in 1993/94 or *c.* 25% of their exports to the EU countries. European Communities, Statistical Office, *External Trade,* no. 6 (1995).

[42] *External Trade* (note 39); and *Byulleten Inostrannoy Kommercheskoy Informatsii,* no. 89 (3 Aug. 1996), p. 2.

[43] *Byulleten Inostrannoy Kommercheskoy Informatsii,* no. 89 (3 Aug. 1996), p. 1.

of Western Europe and at the expense of the former socialist countries, and the growing competition on the markets of both Russia and its former partners.

Besides trade exchange, the intensification of economic links can be achieved by industrial cooperation, of which the partners have considerable and positive experience. The restoration of direct links between enterprises has begun, including industrial R&D cooperation, joint ventures, and so on. There are also various opportunities for extending exchange of services in transport, banking and information. On the whole, a gradual increase in reciprocal trade and a widening of the forms of economic cooperation can be expected. The most important political aspect of this turn to the restoration of economic links may well be that it is taking place in spite of these countries' applications for NATO membership. Economic cooperation between Russia and these countries there-fore follows its own logic of development and, if advanced more and more, can contribute to peace and security in Europe.

It is impossible as yet to evaluate what impact EU membership for the former socialist countries would have on economic cooperation between them and Russia. Russia will certainly see increasing obstacles to getting access to the area which until recently was a zone of its unquestionable predominance. On the whole, however, the Russian establishment and public opinion have de facto recognized that it is inevitable and acceptable if combined with Russia's gradual integration into the European economic area. As regards the conditions of competition, many things depend on whether the Partnership and Coopera-tion Agreement is put into operation effectively and Russia joins the World Trade Organization. Developing projects of common economic interest for Russia, the former socialist countries and the EU, such as transcontinental transport communications and pipelines and possibly some projects of multi-lateral industrial and R&D cooperation, would have a most positive political impact.

V. The European dimensions of CIS integration

Russian policy

Russian economic policy in the CIS pursues three main goals: (*a*) to reorganize and optimize economic links within the CIS; (*b*) to keep and strengthen its economic dominance in the CIS region, including by means of economic integ-ration; and (*c*) to use its dominant economic position for political purposes.

A very sharp increase in prices for oil and gas exported by Russia to the CIS countries, the transition to the usual system of commercial credits, the breaking up of the monetary systems and other actions of the Russian Government in 1993–95 testified that it had decided to change the principles of economic rela-tions with the 'near abroad' radically. It also aims to reduce its role as a donor, limiting it to emergency assistance.[44] This course has met with a negative response from the CIS countries, which have accused Russia of separatism and national selfishness on the one hand and of imperialist blackmail on the other. Irrespective of these critical arguments, some of which are well-founded, the reorganization of economic cooperation in the CIS was necessary both for the transition to a market economy and for participation in European and global economic cooperation.

The Russian policy for economic dominance in the CIS countries seems to be contradictory. On the one hand, Russia started to increase its trade with the EU, China, South Korea and other countries at the expense of the former Soviet republics. During 1991–94 their trade with Russia fell by two-thirds and in 1995 fell again to 21.1 per cent of total Russian external trade. In 1988 the ratio of the trade of the Russian Soviet Federative Socialist Republic (RSFSR) with the other Soviet republics to the RSFSR's trade with all other outside countries had been 58 : 42 by volume.[45]

On the other hand, Russia is nervous of Western interest in its CIS partners. They in their turn are trying to diversify their trade and reduce their dependence on Russia. Their trade potential is limited because of their poor competitiveness and the serious scarcity of hard currency but they do have some potential because of their natural resources, in particular Central Asia and the Caucasus, or their internal market capacity, most of all Ukraine. For the EU, they accounted for 0.5 per cent of its total external trade in 1995—less than Slovenia or Tunisia. Nevertheless, West and Central European countries play a visible role as trade partners of some CIS countries, in particular the European ones, and it is expected that the EU share in their trade will tend to increase. This is a source of anxiety for Russia. The broadening of the CIS countries' trading relations will mean that Russian equipment and consumer goods meet growing competition from West European goods. There is also clear evidence of a very jealous Russian response to the investment activity of Western companies within the CIS, especially as regards participation in exploiting oilfields and other natural resources (in Kazakhstan, Azerbaijan and elsewhere) or projects of industrial cooperation with Ukraine.

The trend towards integration

The trend towards integration seems to be growing at the same rate as the euphoria of the 'parade of sovereignties' is diminishing. In October 1993 the CIS member states signed a treaty establishing an economic union.[46] Many shortcomings apart, it is the first CIS document with the common conception of

---

[44] In 1992–94 Russia had a permanent positive trade balance with the CIS countries: its exports to them were one-third higher than its imports from them and its credits to them by mid-1995 were equivalent to $5.6 billion. *Finansovye Izvestiya*, 10 Aug. 1995, p. 1.

[45] *Finansovye Izvestiya*, 18 July 1995, p. 2; *Narodnoe Khozyaystvo SSSR v 1989 godu*, p. 634; and *Byulleten Inostrannoy Kommercheskoy Informatsii*, no. 12 (3 Feb. 1996), p. 3.

[46] 'Dogovor o sozdanii ekonomicheskogo soyuza' [Treaty establishing an economic union], *Diplomaticheskiy Vestnik*, no. 19–20 (Oct. 1993), pp. 36–41.

a gradual, stage-by-stage advance towards economic integration. In 1994–96 some other decisions were made, including agreements on establishing a free trade area, a payments union, an Interstate Economic Committee and a customs area between Russia, Belarus and Kazakhstan, among others.

When assessing the prospects for CIS integration, its inevitable slowness and the ambivalent position of Russia should also be taken into account. First, Russia will inevitably be a leader, and it has to take on the economic burden of leadership while suffering from enormous economic problems itself. How much will Russia have to pay for integration, and what will it get in return? Second, there is a contradiction between Russia's real 'input' into integration and the principle of equality of all participants. The core of this problem is finding a balance between national sovereignty and supranational institutions. The experience of European integration has shown the complexity of this problem; it is much more difficult for the CIS countries. These considerations explain to a great extent the hesitations of Russia as far as integration is concerned, and in particular its cold official response to the initiative of the President of Kazakhstan, Nursultan Nazarbaev, who put forward an idea for a Eurasian Union.[47]

In fact, most CIS members prefer to develop or, more precisely, to restore their economic links mainly in the framework of bilateral agreements.[48] Russia itself is at present tending to take cautious steps towards integration, in the strict sense of the term, on the basis of careful accounting for economic gains and losses at the same time as pursuing an active policy of bilateral cooperation.

Periodic attempts to build up a CIS protectionist customs union would probably have a boomerang effect, but cannot be excluded, and will be more likely if Russia turns towards anti-European political isolationism. The latter will be only reinforced if the economic divergences between the CIS countries continue and deepen and some of them, in particular Belarus, Kazakhstan and Ukraine, try to intensify separately their cooperation with European countries, Turkey or Iran.

Implications for Russia's relationship with Europe

In the long run, all European countries are interested in the steady and effective functioning of the system of economic cooperation within the CIS. Its vitality is important for consolidating European economic links; furthermore, it could prevent the inevitable economic and trade contradictions developing into sharp political conflicts.

---

[47] 'Proyekt formirovaniya Evroaziatskogo Soyuza' [The project to establish the Euro-Asian Union], *Nezavisimaya Gazeta*, 8 June 1994.

[48] It was due to these efforts, *inter alia*, that in 1996 the volume of trade between Russia and its CIS partners increased for the first time. In Jan.–Apr. 1996 it rose by 40% and the share of these countries reached 26% of Russia's total external trade. *Byulleten Inostrannoy Kommercheskoy Informatsii*, no. 73 (27 June 1996), p. 2.

The political consequences of trade and economic competition between Russia and the West in the CIS countries will depend on two factors. The first is the ability of competitors to follow the GATT/World Trade Organization principles. Russia, because it is economically weak, can try to use political pressure to keep its economic predominance in the CIS, and this kind of action could be a matter of political discussion and sometimes sharp disagreement.

The second factor is the ability of Russia and West European countries to cooperate within the post-Soviet region. In principle, the sphere of economic cooperation could be very broad. The most promising fields seem to be repairing the old transcontinental oil or gas pipelines and constructing new ones; constructing and reconstructing transport communications to bring them on to the European network; reconstructing nuclear power stations in the CIS countries and in particular ensuring their safety; cooperation on the environment; multilateral industrial and R&D cooperation; standardization and certification; and education and training. All these possibilities could be matters of trilateral or multilateral negotiations and agreements (Russia plus the EU or its member states plus one or more CIS countries) and the first steps towards cooperation in some of these fields have been taken.

The prospect of integration in the former Soviet space produces mixed responses in Europe. The source of anxiety is evident: will this integration prove to be nothing but a new edition of the Russian empire? The question is not without point in view of the growing nationalist trends in Russia. The Chechnyan tragedy has strengthened the new suspicions and fears in Europe, being interpreted as a sign of the Russian authorities' drift back to old-style power politics, although less ambitious and applying mainly to the ethnic minorities within the country and the CIS area. At the same time there is clear evidence that the West European countries take Russian predominance in the CIS for granted and recognize the potential paramount role of Russia in ensuring peace and stability in this vast region.[49] The main criterion for Europe therefore seems to be whether Russian integration policy as regards the CIS follows the principles of the Organization for Security and Co-operation in Europe (OCSE) and is compatible with all-European cooperation.

Russia is also suspicious about the Western approach to CIS integration. The idea of Zbigniew Brzezinski that the main goal of the West should be the support of 'geopolitical pluralism' in the area of the former USSR was perceived by most Russian politicians as an alarming omen. The growing attention paid by the EU and by the international financial organizations to the CIS countries other than Russia seems to be connected, *inter alia*, with Western disappointment about and fear of Russia in transition. From the Russian political point of view this can be interpreted in two ways—as a part of European economic cooperation compatible with CIS integration, or as a policy of preventing integ-

---

[49] The Partnership and Cooperation Agreement defined as a matter of priority the encouragement of regional cooperation between the countries of the former USSR 'in order to promote the prosperity and stability of the region' (Preamble). The agreement allows Russia for a transitional period of 5 years to give them better treatment than it accords to the EU (Article 5).

ration around Russia. Which interpretation wins acceptance will depend on the EU maintaining a carefully balanced policy towards Russia and the other CIS countries and on the further course of events in Russia. In either case, the situation in the CIS will be an important part of the political dialogue between Russia and Western Europe. Russia's future choice, to simplify, is between a balanced combination of CIS integration and cooperation with European countries on the one hand, and an exclusive focus on the CIS coupled with a kind of anti-Western isolationism on the other hand.

There are many obstacles which may hinder or delay EU–Russian cooperation in the CIS region. In the long run, however, it seems to be a realistic prospect. The crucial point is whether the Russian business and political establishment is ready to follow this way and its readiness is reciprocated by the West. It is impossible today to answer this question.

VI. Conclusions

Several conclusions seem to be relevant to the questions put at the beginning of this chapter.

1. It is now clear that Russia is moving towards a mixed economy and a new political system, both of which will be very different from those that were built up in Western Europe or are in the process of being built up in the former socialist countries, and that this way will be very long and dramatic. After the excessive expectations and hopes of the initial post-cold war period, it is becoming increasingly clear that the enormous gap between Russia and Europe will take several decades to be significantly reduced.

2. The international political impact of economic reforms in Russia and of its economic cooperation with Western Europe will be relatively limited until Russia achieves the stage of stable economic growth, which is expected to begin in the first decade of the next century at the earliest. Until then its impact will vary with periodic swings of government economic policy from pro-market measures to anti-market ones and back.

3. The economic incentives for political cooperation between Russia and Western Europe should not be underestimated. Furthermore, there are several important fields of economic cooperation to be intensified in the near future, first of all trade, energy, industrial cooperation, science and technology, space, transcontinental transport networks, telecommunications and informatics, the environment and nuclear safety, education and training. This will be the first significant experience of cooperation between the new-born Russian market economy and the most advanced European economic systems. There is also an unexploited economic potential for cooperation between Russia and the former socialist countries. The progress to be expected in each of these fields will most probably be modest, but could strengthen the economic base of political cooperation and of security.

4. Some of the economic contradictions between Russia and the West European countries could be sharp and cause political tension, in particular in such fields as trade competition, Western investment or Russian debt, but most of these could be seen as normal concomitants of developing trade and economic relations. They do not seem likely to be insurmountable obstacles to economic and political cooperation unless the extreme case comes to pass and the most radical nationalist groupings come to power in Russia.

5. The development of economic cooperation and integration in the CIS, in spite of some opinions to the contrary, is also not unfavourable to economic cooperation between Russia and the EU or Europe as a whole. These two areas of Russian external economic activity are complementary to a great extent. Moreover, there are some promising aspects of the triangle of economic cooperation between the European countries, Russia and Russia's CIS partners.

6. The correlation between two priorities of Russian foreign policy—cooperation with the EU and closer integration in the CIS—will depend mainly on the ideologies and political conceptions of the parties and individuals in power. CIS integration combined with aggressive nationalism of the kind of Vladimir Zhirinovsky could take on an anti-European character. If, however, integration within the CIS succeeds, future cooperation between the EU and the CIS might be possible and will probably require a specific institutional framework.

7. Some Russian politicians and high-ranking officials have advanced an idea of the country's joining the EU. It is doubtful whether this can be considered a realistic prospect, at least for the foreseeable future. Russia does not meet the requirements for EU membership or fit in to the very conception of European integration, nor is membership compatible with Russian national priorities, given its size and geopolitical position. Partnership seems to be the optimal concept and institutional framework for long-term cooperation between the two major actors in Europe.

In his famous declaration on 9 May 1950 the French Minister of Foreign Affairs, Robert Schuman, announced that 'L'Europe ne se fera pas d'un coup, ni dans une construction d'ensemble: elle se fera par des réalisations concrètes, créant d'abord une solidarité de fait'.[50] West European countries created their *solidarité de fait* over a period of more than 40 years, step by step. This strategy of advancement is relevant to economic and political cooperation between Russia and Europe as well. The way will be longer and more difficult. However, this is an argument for nothing so much as beginning the journey.

---

[50] European Communities, *Europe—a Fresh Start: The Schuman Declaration, 1950–1990* (Office for Official Publications of the European Communities: Luxembourg, 1990), p. 35.

Part XII

The emerging international order in Europe: what place for Russia?

Russia's relations with the principal multilateral institutions in Europe, Nov. 1996

Organization for Security and Co-operation in Europe (OSCE)[1]: 54 member states; Yugoslavia (Serbia and Montenegro) has been suspended since June 1992.

Russia has promoted the OSCE as the centrepiece of a pan-European security framework. It has proposed a number of institutional changes to enhance the effectiveness of the OSCE, including a proposal to establish an Executive Committee which would operate as a kind of Security Council for Europe.

The OSCE has contributed in various ways to conflict-settlement efforts on the territory of the former Soviet Union. Some of its activities, such as those in Nagorno-Karabakh, have been seen by Russia as competing with its own mediation and conflict-resolution efforts. In Apr. 1995 Russia agreed to the stationing of an OSCE Assistance Group in Chechnya, the first such mission permitted on the territory of the Russian Federation.

North Atlantic Treaty Organization (NATO): 16 member states

Russia is a member of the North Atlantic Cooperation Council (NACC), an institution established in 1991 for consultation and cooperation on political and security issues between NATO and the former WTO states and former Soviet republics; at the beginning of 1996, 38 states were members of NACC.

On 22 June 1994 Russia joined NATO's Partnership for Peace programme, established in Jan. 1994 to promote cooperation with other NACC and OSCE states in areas such as military planning, budgeting and training, under the authority of the North Atlantic Council.

Contacts between Russian and NATO military establishments have been institutionalized. In the former Yugoslavia Russian and NATO armed forces have cooperated under the auspices of IFOR implementing the Dayton peace accord; however, Russian units are not under NATO command.

Russia has strongly opposed NATO plans to enlarge the alliance to include new member states in East–Central Europe. In the near term, Hungary, Poland and the Czech Republic are the most likely new members.

European Union (EU): 15 member states

Russia has given high priority to developing economic cooperation and political dialogue with the EU. On 24 June 1994 Russia and the EU signed a Partnership and Cooperation Agreement which removed some tariff and other trade barriers between them and liberalized foreign investment and banking regulations in Russia; the issue of Russia's inclusion in a free-trade zone is deferred for later talks.

Western European Union (WEU): 10 member states, 3 associate members, 5 observers, 10 associate partners

Russia and the WEU have been engaged in a dialogue on maters of common concern at the parliamentary and intergovernmental levels. Russia has sought to intensify this dialogue and to institutionalize cooperation.

Council of Europe: 40 member states

Russia attached considerable political importance to joining the Council of Europe, with which it had established a regular pattern of cooperation and consultation. In Mar. 1993 it formally applied for membership in the body. In Feb. 1995 the Council of Europe suspended its consideration of Russia's application in the light of developments in Chechnya. Russia was finally admitted amid some controversy in Feb. 1996.

[1] Before 1 Jan. 1995 the CSCE.

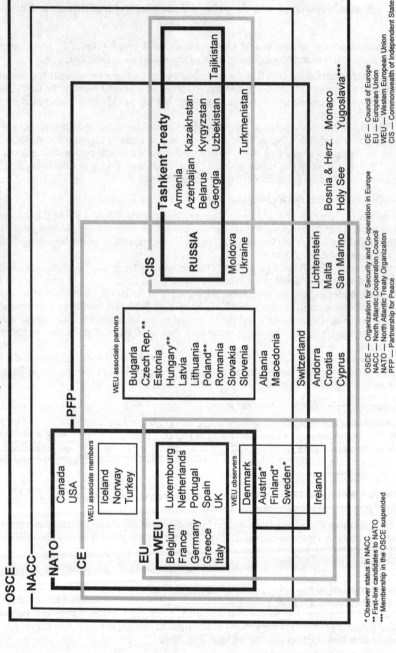

Russia in the European institutional architecture
(membership as of December 1996)

OSCE
NACC
NATO
CE
PFP
EU
WEU

Canada
USA

WEU associate members
Iceland
Norway
Turkey

WEU
Belgium
France
Germany
Greece
Italy

Luxembourg
Netherlands
Portugal
Spain
UK

WEU observers
Denmark

Austria*
Finland*
Sweden*

Ireland

WEU associate partners
Bulgaria
Czech Rep.**
Estonia
Hungary**
Latvia
Lithuania
Poland**
Romania
Slovakia
Slovenia

Albania
Macedonia

Switzerland

Andorra
Croatia
Cyprus

CIS

RUSSIA

Moldova
Ukraine

Tashkent Treaty

Armenia
Azerbaijan
Belarus
Georgia

Kazakhstan
Kyrgyzstan
Uzbekistan

Tajikistan

Turkmenistan

Lichtenstein
Malta
San Marino

Bosnia & Herz.
Holy See

Monaco
Yugoslavia***

* Observer status in NACC
** First-line candidates to NATO
*** Membership in the OSCE suspended

OSCE — Organization for Security and Co-operation in Europe
NACC — North Atlantic Cooperation Council
NATO — North Atlantic Treaty Organization
PFP — Partnership for Peace

CE — Council of Europe
EU — European Union
WEU — Western European Union
CIS — Commonwealth of Independent States

23. Redefining Russia's role in Europe

John Roper and Peter van Ham[*]

I. Introduction

This chapter analyses Russia's policy towards the West and towards Western Europe in particular. It examines first the main tenets of Russia's *Westpolitik*, starting with the Gorbachev era and ending in mid-1994, gives a concise overview of Russia's relationship with the major European actors, examines the main political forces and schools of thought within the Russian political élite concerning Russia's policy towards the West and the strength of these different political factions, and then analyses the implications for security and cooperation both in Europe and beyond. Finally it addresses the questions of what sort of role the West wants Russia to play in Europe and the former Soviet Union and whether, and if so how, the West can influence the shape and direction of Russia's future foreign policy. The chapter concludes with several suggestions as to how the West may affect the parameters for the Russian Federation's policy in the former Soviet Union as well as in Europe.

II. From a 'common European home' to *realpolitik*

The collapse of the Soviet Union's external and internal empire has significantly altered Russia's relations with the West. The Manichean cold war world is now a thing of the past and European politics have become much more complicated. The international system has been radically transformed and nearly all the conditions that defined Europe's security system since 1945 have been altered. In this new Europe, Russia is still a major—albeit a peripheral—power. It is clear that since 1989 Russia's influence in the economic and political development of Europe has diminished and its military power has also shrunk. None the less its sheer geopolitical weight inevitably gives it an important voice in the formation of Europe's security structure.

In the years that have passed since the fall of the Berlin Wall, Russia has had to reorient itself and to find a new position and role in European and world politics. Already in the second half of the 1980s the Soviet Union's approach towards Western Europe and the Western alliance had become more realistic, as well as more cooperative. Unrestrained East–West rivalry was no longer seen as opportune and economic cooperation with the West was considered

[*] John Roper was Director of the Institute for Security Studies of the Western European Union, Paris, from 1990 to 1995. Dr Peter van Ham was a Senior Research Fellow at the same institute from 1993 to 1996. The views expressed in this article are the authors' and do not necessarily reflect those of the WEU.

urgently necessary in order to sustain the Soviet model. Soviet President Mikhail Gorbachev's policy of establishing a 'common European home' was both an attempt to stimulate wider European economic cooperation and an echo of the traditional Soviet objective of excluding the United States and Canada from further pan-European economic, political and security ventures. Most West Europeans were wary about such a European home, mainly because 'in a common home stretching from the Atlantic to the Urals, the Soviet Union would simply occupy too high a proportion of the floor space for the psychological comfort of its fellow inhabitants'.[1] Gorbachev's policies associated with the vision of a common European home did, however, help to legitimize the Soviet Union as a major player on the European political stage. His statesman-like approach to the dismantling of the Iron Curtain and the unification of Germany did the rest to provide the Soviet Union with substantial goodwill within Western Europe's political élite and public opinion.

However, the 'return to Europe' of the former communist countries has not been without major difficulties. Reforming communist economic and political systems has proved to be a long-term and arduous process. On top of these changes, Moscow, as the capital of Russia, has also had to readjust itself economically, politically and psychologically to the disintegration of its 'internal empire', the Soviet Union. Its disintegration has been relatively peaceful, although it has resulted in several military clashes and conflicts in some southern republics of the former Soviet Union. Many aspects of the 'peaceful divorce' of Russia and the newly independent states still await settlement, and some aspects of Russia's policy towards what it calls the 'near abroad' have been criticized as a return to old-style Soviet or tsarist expansionism.

Until 1993 Russia's approach to the 'near abroad' and other regions was moderated by the Western orientation of its foreign policy. Both Soviet President Gorbachev and his successor in Russia Boris Yeltsin based much of their reformist policies on the active support of the West. Russia frequently made clear that Western backing was required to assist Russia's economic and political transformation. Although Western political support for Russia's democratic reformers has always been ample, most calls for a Western Marshall Plan of large-scale economic and financial assistance for the East have not led to an effective response. Like most other former communist countries, Russia has time and again complained about West European protectionism in sectors where Russia is competitive, such as non-ferrous metals. Although the continuing economic recession in Western Europe has made it difficult to open up its markets to these sensitive products, reluctance to do this has indicated a lack of political will on the side of the West to implement the slogan that trade, not aid is essential for successful economic transformations in the East.

After a short spell of euphoria after the end of the cold war, by late 1993 it became clear that the East–West honeymoon would soon be over; new patterns

---

[1] Malcolm, N., Royal Institute of International Affairs, *Soviet Policy Perspectives on Western Europe* (Routledge for the RIIA: London, 1989), p. 81.

of relationships between Russia and the West had to be based on national interests, preferably of the enlightened sort. After a relatively short period of confusion and indecision, Russia adopted a more assertive foreign policy which was based upon its aspirations to play a major role in Europe and Asia. Within a few years, Russia's policy has changed away from the equivocal concept of a common European home to a more explicit articulation of its strategic interests in Europe. In many respects this shift from a strong Western orientation to a rediscovery of Russia's distinct national interests was inevitable. In this light, Russia's objections to the accession of the former Warsaw Treaty Organization (WTO) countries to NATO cannot be surprising. On other fronts, Russian foreign policy has also become more assertive, as in the Caucasus, where it has tried to create its own sphere of influence through economic and military pressure and the deployment of peacekeeping troops. Russia still seems to be committed to multilateral cooperation, democratic values and international law, but its policy in the 'near abroad', for instance in Georgia and Moldova, at times fails to comply with internationally agreed standards of behaviour.

Russia's relations with Europe have always been complicated. Because of its geographical location and its sheer size, Russia has found itself both politically and culturally between Europe and Asia. Historically, Russia has expanded in search of defensible boundaries both towards the west and to its south-east.

In view of this imperialistic history, the East–Central European (ECE)[2] countries, and particularly Poland and Hungary, are wary of a renewed Russian *Drang nach Westen*. Poland, having been divided so many times in the course of its history, inevitably feels nervous, and the reversal of position over its membership in NATO by President Yeltsin in 1993[3] has certainly not reassured Poland. Other ECE countries have similar recent memories, but have tried to come to some sort of *modus vivendi* with their big neighbour in the East: Slovakia has come to a limited security arrangement with Russia,[4] and Hungary has acquired arms from Russia in part settlement of previous Soviet debts;[5] the Czech Republic does not have the same immediate geopolitical problems as the other Visegrad countries. ECE countries continue to press their security concerns over developments in Russia. Further south, Romanian–Russian relations have inevitably been affected by the continuing conflict between Moldova and Russia over the Trans-Dniester region.

The relations between Russia and the three Baltic states have been particularly complicated in view of the significant Russian populations there and the clear position of the three countries that their future is in an association with West European institutions and not the Commonwealth of Independent States (CIS). Western Europe and the USA put considerable pressure on Russia to

---

[2] The Czech Republic, Hungary, Poland and Slovakia, which are also the countries in the Visegrad Group.

[3] Rotfeld, A. D., 'Europe: towards a new regional security regime', *SIPRI Yearbook 1994* (Oxford University Press: Oxford, 1994), pp. 212–13.

[4] Larrabee, F. S., *East European Security after the Cold War* (RAND Corporation: Santa Monica, Calif., 1993), pp. 12, 45.

[5] *Military Technology*, no. 12 (1993), p. 57.

withdraw its forces from all three states, and their final withdrawal on 31 August 1994 was an important indication of Russia's continuing concern with its *Westpolitik*.

After 1989, relations between Russia and Germany quickly became close and friendly. This was all the more exceptional as Russia and Germany were respectively the main loser and the main winner of the post-cold war settlement. Russia, however, clearly realizes that after Germany's unification its economic and political weight has significantly increased. It is the largest provider of financial assistance to Russia, and policy makers in Bonn have been particularly responsive to political developments in ECE countries and Russia. Russia is also aware that in future the weight of Bonn in the development of Western policy towards the East will increase.

The UK and France have both had good relations with Russia at various stages in the past decade. Former British Prime Minister Margaret Thatcher, for instance, developed a useful relationship with President Gorbachev, although it is not clear that this has been maintained between their two successors. Similarly, in France the defeat of the Socialists in the 1993 parliamentary elections and the return to *cohabitation* made some difficulties for the extension of the relationship which President François Mitterrand had established. Both countries, as permanent members of the UN Security Council, have worked closely with Russia on a number of issues coming before the Council.

There are a number of Western and Atlantic security institutions in which Russia's relations with Western Europe are developing. The Soviet Union was and Russia since 1991 has of course been a full participant in the Conference on Security and Co-operation in Europe (CSCE, since 1 January 1995 the Organization for Security and Co-operation in Europe, or OSCE). In the past few years, CSCE missions have attempted to resolve problems in the southern republics of the CIS and in the Baltic states, with limited and varying success. The CSCE has therefore played a more active part in Russia's relations with the 'near abroad' than have most other multilateral security institutions. In December 1994 Russia suggested a major strengthening of the CSCE, calling for its transformation into an international organization in its own right, with its own Charter and an Executive Committee similar to the UN Security Council.[6] An important element of this proposal was that the CSCE would coordinate the security aspects of the work of organizations like NATO, the European Union (EU) and the CIS. These ideas were not welcomed by most Western governments, who suspect that Russia's proposals were aimed at gaining control over NATO.

Russia has also been actively involved in the North Atlantic Cooperation Council (NACC). In June 1994, after a heated domestic debate, Russia signed up for NATO's Partnership for Peace (PFP) programme, which will open the door for a constructive relationship between Russia and the alliance. In the same month it signed a Partnership and Cooperation Agreement with the EU,

---

[6] *Atlantic News*, 4/5 (July 1994).

which is intended to support a democratic and market-oriented Russia by encouraging foreign investment in Russia and by liberalizing trade.[7] The EU will, among other things, support Russia's accession to the new World Trade Organization and remove all quotas on Russian exports (except on certain sensitive products such as textiles and steel). The Partnership and Cooperation Agreement also deals with the removal of obstacles to the free flow of capital which includes direct investment and the repatriation of profits. It was hailed by President Yeltsin as 'the first step made by the European Community since the fall of the Iron Curtain towards the recognition of Russia as a fully fledged partner in the political and economic spheres'.[8] He also stated that the EU is 'the Russian Federation's most important partner in the world'.[9]

The last of the Western security institutions, the Western European Union (WEU), has for the time being no formal relationship with Russia. At its Ministerial Meeting of May 1994, the WEU introduced the status of associate partner for the six former members of the WTO and the three Baltic states. These countries are now closely involved in the workings of the WEU although they do not have a final say in the decision-making process. Initial reactions from Moscow were critical, and a spokesman of the Foreign Ministry stated: 'We regard this action as an attempt to find a new model for military and political cooperation', also noting that the WEU's closer ties with these countries were at variance with the need to build a truly pan-European system of security and stability under the aegis of the CSCE.[10]

At the same meeting in May, WEU member states also agreed to open a dialogue with Russia (as well as with Ukraine) and to develop cooperation on matters of common concern.

III. Policies towards the West: main political forces and the domestic balance of power

Russia is currently going through a period in which a new national identity is being shaped. Central to this process is the redefinition of Russia's national interest. This is all the more necessary since Russia has now not only changed its ideological and political spots but also found itself within new borders: of the old frontiers of the former Soviet Union, only the Nordic and Siberian ones remain frontiers of Russia today. In the light of these dramatic changes in Russia's geopolitical shape and role, it is not at all surprising that its foreign policy debate seems to have fallen back on several traditional political orientations.

---

[7] European Communities, Commission, Proposal for a Council and Commission decision on the conclusion of the Agreement on Partnership and Cooperation between the European Communities and their member states of the one part, and Russia, of the other part, COM(94)257 final, Brussels, 16 June 1994.

[8] *Summary of World Broadcasts—Former USSR* (hereafter SWB–SU), 25 June 1994.

[9] *Atlantic News*, 28 June 1994.

[10] SWB–SU, 16 May 1994.

The foreign policy mind-sets can be divided into three different groups: the 'Westernizers', the Russian nationalists and the 'Euro-Asianists'.[11] These groups are still fluid coalitions and to bring a complex debate down to three categories may risk oversimplification. The grouping does, however, provide a helpful framework for analysing Russia's domestic discourse on foreign policy. Among the major foreign policy questions are: What place and function should Russia have in European and international affairs? How close ties should Russia develop with the West, and Western Europe in particular? What kind of balance should be struck between Russia's ties with the West and with Asia?

The main supporters of close ties with the West also call for rapid economic and political reform within Russia. They follow the historical examples of Peter the Great and Catherine II by arguing that Russia finds its most natural allies and partners in the West and that only by rapid integration in the world economy can Russia fulfil its ambitions of becoming a respected great power. They realize that joining such forums as the Group of Seven industrialized countries (G7)[12] and the World Trade Organization and obtaining financial and economic assistance from the International Monetary Fund (IMF) and the World Bank are important steps in that direction.

The 'Westernizers' do not only choose the West for economic reasons. Their preference is also based on the idea that Russia can only become a viable democracy and a 'civilized' country when it adopts Western standards of economic and political behaviour. They consider Russia an integral part of the European Christian civilization and see the construction of Russian society on the West European values of democracy and the market economy as essential. The 'Europeanizing' of Russia is considered crucial to overcoming the economic, political and social obstacles to successful reform.

In concrete policy terms, this approach emphasises cooperation with the West on matters ranging from the former Yugoslavia or the Middle East to nonproliferation. It also encompasses deepening ties with Western security structures, such as NATO, the WEU and the OSCE. A closer relationship with the EU is envisaged, although few Westernizers go so far as to aim for fully-fledged membership of the EU. The Foreign Minister at the time, Andrey Kozyrev, summed up this approach in January 1992 when he argued that Russia is not surrounded by hostile powers but by 'a civilized international community, that has learned to value human interests above all else and that is open to mutual association and cooperation'.[13]

The reformist parties—Russia's Democratic Choice, the Yavlinskiy–Boldyrev–Lukin Bloc (Yabloko), and Sergey Shakhray's Party of Russian

---

[11] For a similar approach, see Alexandrova, O., 'Divergent Russian foreign policy concepts', *Aussenpolitik*, no. 4 (1993); MacFarlane, S. N., 'Russia, the West and European security', *Survival*, vol. 38, no. 3 (autumn 1993); and Zagorski, A., 'Russia and the CIS', ed. H. Miall, Royal Institute of International Affairs, *Redefining Europe: New Patterns of Conflict and Cooperation* (Pinter for the RIIA: London, 1994). A slightly different categorization is suggested by Alexei Arbatov in chapter 7 in this volume.

[12] Canada, France, Germany, Italy, Japan, the UK and the USA.

[13] Kozyrev, A., *Izvestiya*, 2 Jan. 1992, quoted in Porter, B. D., 'A country instead of a cause: Russian foreign policy in the post-Soviet era', *Washington Quarterly*, vol. 15, no. 3 (summer 1992), pp. 46–47.

Unity and Accord—were seen at the time of the 1993 election by outside observers as epitomizing the Westernizers' faction. President Yeltsin also initially held this point of view, but the Westernizers' perspective was subject to increasing criticism, and both Yeltsin and Kozyrev shifted their position and began increasingly to stress the pursuit of national power interests instead of integration in the international community. The failure of the reformists and the spectacular success of nationalists and traditionalists in the parliamentary elections of December 1993 appeared to give a signal that a policy of radical economic reform and close ties with the West was not supported by the majority of the Russian electorate (although this should not be interpreted as an anti-Western mood in public opinion at large).

The Russian nationalist faction is a very mixed group which comprises both radical nationalists with neo-fascist leanings (such as Vladimir Zhirinovsky) and more moderate elements such as the writer Alexander Solzhenitsyn, who returned to Russia after decades of exile in the spring of 1994. What brings them together is a dissatisfaction with Russia's current secondary status in world affairs and a desire to reconstruct the former glory of Russia beyond its present official borders. This is combined with the notions that Russia has a special role to play in European and world affairs and that the Western economic and political model is not applicable to Russia.

In their orientation, the nationalists have much in common with 19th-century Slavophilism: both stress the 'native' and 'essentially Russian' character of their country and are critical towards West European capitalist culture and politics. As in the 19th century, this faction encompasses two closely related elements: conservative reformism and pan-Slavism. Russian nationalists are generally calling for a slowing of the pace of reform and advocate a more independent Russian foreign policy based upon a rather narrow definition of their country's national interests. This is combined with a more assertive stance towards the 'near abroad', especially towards those countries of the former Soviet Union and the WTO where many million ethnic Russians and other 'fellow Slavs' are living.

Russian nationalists reject close relations with the West. They resent the West's imposition of monetary programmes (for instance, by the IMF) and accuse Westernizers of weakening Russia's economic and political power through a programme of shock therapy. This is seen as a Western scheme to keep Russia down; the USA is cast as the main villain. Russian nationalists accuse the Westernizers of blindly following the West's diplomatic initiatives (for instance in the UN Security Council and on matters like non-proliferation), and they argue that Russian foreign policy under Yeltsin and Kozyrev failed to defend Russia's interests in an adequate manner.

This perspective is, to a greater or lesser extent, shared by factions and political parties ranging from the far right to the far left. They include both Zhirinovsky's Liberal Democratic Party of Russia (LDPR), the Communist Party, the Agrarian Party and a fair proportion of independent delegates to Russia's State Duma (the lower house of the parliament). The degree of nationalism may range from the outrageous position of the LDPR to the more moderate variants in other parties. These parties find their power base among disgruntled sections of the electorate who hanker after the former great-power status of the Soviet Union and still to a great extent identify themselves with 'the Soviet people'. Support is also found with people working in state industries who are anxious about their future, fear unemployment and impoverishment, and worry about rising crime, disorder and 'weak government'.

The third category of perspectives on Russia's foreign policy, the Euro-Asianists, also has its origins in an historical stream of thought, mainly developed in the early 1920s. It is based upon the notion that Russia's geographical location, which makes it both a European and an Asian great power, provides it with an opportunity to play a crucial role in both continents. It stresses not so much the cultural uniqueness of Russia as its specific mixture of ethnic, cultural and religious roots in a country stretching from the Baltic Sea to the Bering Strait. The Euro-Asianists argue that Russia should not follow the West's economic and political advice and policies but find its own way by looking both to Europe and to Asia. From this perspective the 'loss of empire' is seen as a geopolitical catastrophe, and it is a central tenet in this approach that Russia should re-establish its influence in the 'near abroad' in a powerful manner.

The economic importance of the Asia–Pacific region is given as an additional reason to focus on Russia's eastern neighbours, and Russia's interests in the Central Asian region are considered substantial. Relations with China are deemed equally as important as its links with Western Europe and the USA, both for economic and for strategic reasons. Central Asia is looked upon with increasing concern, since the potential threat of assertive Islamic fundamentalism in this region might well spill over into the former Soviet Union and result in border conflicts, uncontrolled mass migration to Russia and secessionist movements within Russia itself.

The Euro-Asianist approach gives priority to consolidating the economic, political and security ties between the countries of the former Soviet Union, preferably within the context of the CIS. This faction tries to find the middle ground between the position of the Westernizers and the Russian nationalists. Euro-Asianists play down the cultural and ideological incompatibility of Russia and Western Europe and argue for ad hoc cooperation with the West on matters of common concern. This would be combined with efforts to confirm Russia's independence by strengthening ties with China and countries in the Middle East. Because of geographical factors, the Euro-Asianist voice is strongest in the eastern and southern parts of the Russian Federation, but representatives of this faction are not concentrated in one specific political party.

Although it is still too early to tell how strong these factions are in Russia's political arena, it is clear that a shift has already taken place from a westward-oriented foreign policy towards a preoccupation with domestic and regional matters and a more assertive nationalistic approach to the 'near abroad'.[14] The December 1993 elections struck a blow to the reformist camp of the Western-izers and boosted the prestige and political power of parties and groups of society (such as the military, the state bureaucracy and industry) who call for a slower pace of change and a return to a 'glorious' Russia. In itself, this shift should not have come as a surprise, nor should it be a reason for undue concern in the West, for, as one Russian commentator has argued, the Yeltsin–Gaidar policy 'was based on a simple negation of everything the Soviet Union did, despite the fact that some of that policy was dictated not so much by ideology as the logic of the international power game'.[15]

During the past three years, deputies who could be considered reformist in orientation have not constituted a majority in the Duma. It should, however, be stressed that the anti-reform group hardly forms a coherent whole and cannot be expected to constitute a solid coalition. The loyalties of a floating block of independents—who have been chosen in Russia's constituencies—often decide each issue on an ad hoc basis.

Under Russia's new constitution, which is based on a strong executive presi-dency, President Yeltsin and the government appointed by him determine the course of foreign policy. Under pressure of the success of the opposition, Yeltsin has found it opportune to make more assertive statements concerning Russia's interests in the 'near abroad' as well as towards the ECE. Russian officials have clearly stated their displeasure with the former WTO and the Baltic states' interest in joining NATO, arguing that NATO enlargement will isolate Russia and thus play into the hands of Russian nationalist forces. President Yeltsin has again, in sharp words, declared that Russia will defend the interests of ethnic Russians in the former Soviet Union, and that Russia therefore has a vital stake in political developments in its neighbouring countries. Thus, in his 1994 New Year address, Yeltsin declared: 'Dear com-patriots! You are inseparable from us and we are inseparable from you. We were and will be together. On the basis of law and solidarity, we defend and will defend your and our common interest'.[16]

At the present stage, the principal questions are how far Russia's foreign policy course is likely to shift from a Western orientation towards a preoccupa-tion with domestic and regional problems and what implications this will have for Russia's policy towards Western Europe.

Although Russia's economic reform programme has been moderately suc-cessful, the obstacles to creating a viable market economy remain daunting. Transforming Russia's state industries, bureaucracies and other vested interests requires a concerted political effort and will take considerable time. Since Russia's entrepreneurial class is still negligible, and no propertied middle class

---

[14] Crow, S., 'Russia asserts its strategic agenda', Radio Free Europe/Radio Liberty (hereafter RFE/RL), *RFE/RL Research Report*, vol. 2, no. 50 (17 Dec. 1993).

[15] Pushkov, A. K., 'Watch what Russia does not say', *Wall Street Journal*, 5 Apr. 1994.

[16] 'Yeltsin gives New Year address with pledge to stand by Russian citizens abroad', SWB–SU, 3 Jan. 1994.

has developed (which in the West has traditionally formed an important counterweight to authoritarianism), Russia's reform course will remain fragile and vulnerable. Since the economic reform programmes are by their very nature unlikely to yield fast and tangible positive results, anti-reformist sources may well gain political support and grow more powerful. Entrenched interests will continue to have an impact on Russia's domestic reform programme as well as on the direction of Russia's foreign policy.

On the political level, Russia is still far from having reached a level of civil society which imposes restrictions on the foreign policy behaviour of either the rulers in the Kremlin or the military. Russia's media have not yet achieved a practice of independence and scrutiny guaranteeing that they will monitor and disclose to the public any misdemeanours of the government and military. Politically, the state bureaucracy and the army are the most forceful opponents of change. Their loss of privilege and prestige has caused much resentment and explains their opposition to most policy proposals put forward by the Western-izers. It has been argued that President Yeltsin's remarkable volte-face concerning membership of NATO for the former WTO countries was pushed by the Russian military, possibly in exchange for its continued support for Yeltsin and his government. Although it is always difficult to substantiate these speculations, it is beyond doubt that Russia's shift towards a more assertive stance towards the 'near abroad' and the West has been coaxed and supported by the Russian military.

This has already resulted in a weakening of Russia's support for several Western policy priorities, for example in the area of non-proliferation. On several occasions, Russia has roused Western criticism by exporting arms to countries in the Middle East. In December 1993, Russian cargo planes flew special truck chassis to Syria which could be used for the mobile missile launchers which Damascus had bought from North Korea. Similar incidents occurred earlier with Russia's arms export policies towards India, Iran and Pakistan. Russia's suspected sale of submarines to North Korea in January 1994 and the sale of seven cryogenic rocket engines to India in July 1994 have only added to Western misgivings and distrust. Russia at present is still abiding by the rules and norms of most non-proliferation regimes (although there are suspicions that it is hiding work on poison gas, forbidden under the Biological Weapons Convention),[17] but these rules might be stretched in the future. Russian nationalists argue that by following these non-proliferation rules the country is losing its political influence in regions of vital interest, undermining its military–industrial and research and development (R&D) base, and losing out commercially to (allegedly Western) countries which may be less reluctant to supply. Politicians of a more moderate Euro-Asian orientation also argue that by joining Western non-proliferation mechanisms Russia is likely to lose its influence in Asia and the Middle East, which is considered a serious setback.

---

[17] Geissler, E., 'Biological weapons and arms control developments', *SIPRI Yearbook 1994* (Oxford University Press: Oxford, 1994), pp. 716–18.

A similar dichotomy in approaches can be discerned with several other questions facing Russian policy makers. Russia, for instance, has by and large been constructively abiding by the UN Security Council's resolutions concerning arms embargoes on countries such as Iraq, Yugoslavia (Serbia and Montenegro) and Libya. It has also been cooperating within other multilateral frameworks such as the OSCE and NACC. However, Russian cooperation and compliance are not always without direct economic and even political costs and disadvantages. The embargo on Serbia and Montenegro, for example, was criticized by Russian nationalists as a betrayal of a fellow Slav country, something which undermines Russia's influence in the former Yugoslavia at a high commercial cost. This was the main reason why from the second half of 1992 the position of the Russian Government on the civil war in the former Yugoslavia gradually shifted away from that of most Western countries. Russia was extremely reluctant to support NATO's threat to use air power in Bosnia and Herzegovina, and in January 1994 a motion opposing the use of NATO air power and calling for the lifting of sanctions against Serbia was carried by the State Duma (by 280 votes to 2).[18]

Similarly, opinions diverge on the wisdom of cooperation within Europe's security frameworks such as NACC and the PFP, which nationalists consider detrimental to Russia's national interests since it helps former WTO countries and those of the former Soviet Union to strengthen their institutional ties with Western powers.

On all these issues Russian policy makers have a choice between full compliance with the rules and norms set out by the Western countries and the international community on the one hand and a narrow interpretation of Russia's national interests on the other hand. Where President Yeltsin and the Russian Government position themselves on these matters almost certainly depends mainly on Russia's internal development, but this does not necessarily imply that the West is totally without instruments of statecraft.

For West European countries the key question for the coming years will be whether Russia will become a reliable partner or a factor of instability in European security.[19]

IV. Western influence over Russia's foreign and security policy

There is a general consensus that Western engagement in Russia's efforts to transform its economy and society is essential if Russia is to remain a partner in European security. Although such engagement cannot ensure that Russia maintains a Western orientation, it can lessen the danger of Russia once again becoming a security liability. US President Bill Clinton remarked: 'I believe if they [the Russians] continue as a democratic, market-oriented, reformist non-

---

[18] *International Herald Tribune*, 21 Jan. 1994.

[19] On this key question, see also Adomeit, H., International Institute for Strategic Studies, *Russia: Partner or Risk Factor in European Security*, Adelphi Paper no. 285 (Brassey's/IISS: London, 1994).

interventionist nation, they will become in a more traditional sense, a very great nation, not an empire . . . Their whole history and character and texture of Russia argues for that'.[20] Although Russian history can certainly be interpreted in a less optimistic manner, a modest hope is justified that building a web of economic, political and security links with the West may result in a fundamental change in the character of the Russian state.

Given the enormous importance of Russia's economic and political course to the future of European security, the West has for long found itself on the horns of a dilemma: Should it continue with its approach of strict conditionality in continuing assistance to Russian reform and continue to use Western norms of foreign policy behaviour to judge Russia's actions in the 'near abroad', or should it start to use 'political criteria' for aiding Russia and be prepared to accept Russia's assertive conduct in the former Soviet Union? The urgency of resolving this dilemma was increased by the strong showing of radical nationalist forces in parliamentary elections in Russia and the shift in Russia's foreign policy towards nationalism.

Directly after the December 1993 election, US Vice-President Albert Gore suggested that Western financial organizations should be prepared to provide more and speedier assistance to Russia to bolster the position of President Yeltsin and the reformists. Strobe Talbott, then US ambassador-at-large to the former Soviet Union, commented at the same time that Russia might now be helped by a policy of 'less shock, and more aid'. The IMF and the World Bank, however, have been reluctant to relax the criteria for providing loans and other support for Russia, and have argued that strict conditionality is an essential element in the successful economic transformation of the country. Nevertheless, it became clear that the IMF was prepared to be flexible when it agreed to provide the second part of its credit line to Russia, worth $1.5 billion, in late March 1994. It is indicative that this logic was also applied after the parliamentary election in November 1995: in March 1996 the IMF made an impressive $10 billion credit to Russia.

Although there are clear limits to what the West can do, Western efforts to help stabilize and reform Russia could nevertheless be significant. It should be clear that the Western instruments of statecraft are mainly economic in nature. Although there is much confusion as to how much economic assistance has actually been promised and delivered, figures in July 1994 indicated that, of the $43 billion promised to Russia, some $30 billion had already been approved by the G7 governments and the international financial institutions. The remaining $13 billion would be made available when Russia concluded a standby arrangement with the IMF; and another $6 billion in a currency stabilization fund would be forthcoming when Russia made the rouble fully convertible.[21] The EU Partnership and Cooperation Agreement was a further important step towards the economic involvement of Russia in Western Europe and another

---

[20] *International Herald Tribune*, 11 Jan. 1994.
[21] *Financial Times*, 4 July 1994.

significant element in strengthening the political relations between Russia and the West. The EU approach of avoiding multi-billion dollar macroeconomic stabilization packages à la IMF, but instead focusing on aid for training and other micro-economic measures aimed at encouraging private enterprise in Russia, is especially promising.

The finalizing and implementation of the Energy Charter between Russia and the West might be another element in opening Russia to Western firms and opening the West for Russian natural resources. The main goal of the Charter will be to provide a political and legal framework for Western companies, stimulating investment in the Russian energy sector in exchange for long-term export contracts. This is essential since many Western oil companies attempting to operate in Russia have become wary of high taxes, restrictive export quotas, bureaucratic delays and the infighting in and continuing hostility from Russian industrial associations. There are, of course, successes such as the agreement between Russia and the USA to develop oil and gas reserves on Russia's Sakhalin Island, signed in late June 1994.[22] The Energy Charter could provide a helpful framework to overcome many of difficulties which still remain. A draft treaty was presented to the 50 countries which had shown interest in the charter in late April 1994.[23]

As mentioned above, opening West European markets for Russian products may be the most important contribution the West can make to a successful economic transformation of Russia. This would, however, require a major rethinking of Western Europe's economic and political priorities. For the moment, West European policy makers are not prepared to slow down the process of economic, monetary and political unification among the member states of the EU and extend their integrative structures towards the East. This would require a significant restructuring of current EU economic arrangements. Although initial proposals were put forward by the Commission of the European Communities in July 1994 to review many of the protectionist elements in the EU's policy towards the East,[24] the lack of consensus among the present member states makes a bold change of policy rather unlikely.

In the political and strategic field, Western Europe may have little influence over the future course of Russia's foreign policy. The West may, nevertheless, consider two approaches to achieving an impact on Russia's external behaviour. They are not mutually exclusive and could well be conducted in parallel.

First, the West, operating directly through governments and indirectly through political and other foundations, could be effective through relatively low-key efforts, such as practical support and advice to the Russian media and support for those political parties that are oriented towards democracy and

---

[22] *Financial Times*, 24 June 1994; and *International Herald Tribune*, 30 June 1994.

[23] On the Energy Charter, see Fraser, P., 'Russia, the CIS and the European Community: building a relationship', ed. N. Malcolm, Royal Institute of International Affairs, *Russia and Europe: An End to Confrontation?* (Pinter for the RIIA: London, 1994), p. 219–20. See also 'Energieplan: Lubbers raakt in stroomversnelling' [Energy plan: Lubbers runs in to the rapids], *NRC Handelsblad*, 29 Apr. 1994; and chapter 22, section III, in this volume.

[24] *Financial Times*, 28 July 1994.

market economics. Both matters are of key importance, since only independent media will be able to check the autocratic tendencies of Russia's rulers (not only in Moscow, but throughout the whole country) and the construction of better organized and more influential political parties will be important to educate and inform voters and to channel public opinion through Moscow's policy-making élite. The West might also assist in improving civil–military relations in Russia, for example by intensifying educational projects for Russian military officers to visit Western civil and military establishments.

The West could also try to influence the course of Russia's foreign policy by a second approach, namely, by clarifying the parameters for Russia's conduct in the 'near abroad'. This is what Zbigniew Brzezinski has labelled a Western policy aimed at 'the consolidation of geopolitical pluralism within the former Soviet Union'.[25] Such a policy would imply that the best way to encourage the development of a democratic Russia is by strengthening Western ties with other Soviet successor states, especially with Ukraine. Brzezinski has correctly argued that a more balanced distribution of Western financial aid and political attention between Russia and the non-Russian states of the former Soviet Union would 'inhibit [Russia's] temptation to reinvent the empire, with its pernicious effects on prospects for democracy in Russia'.[26]

Although such a policy would affect Russia's options in shaping its relationships with its neighbours, it would do little to influence its domestic policy and would certainly not have prevented the civil war which broke out in December 1994 in Chechnya. However, it is important to indicate which of Russia's policies depart from its international obligations and the rules set out by the OSCE and the UN. Until now, the West has been rather reluctant to indicate publicly the boundaries of acceptable conduct in the former Soviet Union. For example, it has almost silently condoned the military activities of the Russian Army in Georgia, Moldova and Tajikistan even though they clearly go beyond the limits of traditional peacekeeping operations.[27] Western governments may well have commented upon these operations through diplomatic channels, but the absence of a public statement of disapproval of Russian military activities in the former Soviet Union may have had the undesirable effect of giving public opinion in both West and East the impression that a new Russian sphere of vital interests is being accepted by 'procedure of silence'.

Some Western leaders have aired some discomfort with Russia's sharper tone towards both its direct neighbours and the West, but it is not clear what impact these comments have on Russia's policy towards the 'near abroad'. German Chancellor Helmut Kohl, for example, argued in February 1994 that Germany expects Russia to continue its Western-oriented foreign policy marked by constructive participation in solving international problems. He added that 'Russia must foster trust particularly among its neighbours through its own actions.

[25] Brzezinski, Z., 'The premature partnership', *Foreign Affairs,* vol. 73, no. 2 (Mar./Apr. 1994), p. 79.
[26] Brzezinski (note 25), p. 79.
[27] Allison, R., Western European Union, Institute for Security Studies, *Peacekeeping in the Soviet Successor States,* Chaillot Paper no. 18 (ISS: Paris, Nov. 1994).

Thoughts of creating spheres of influence or interest would not be compatible with this'.[28] US Defense Secretary William Perry has also declared that: 'If Russian forces operate beyond Russia's borders, they must do so in accord with international law. Russia's legitimate concerns with stability on its borders must not be dealt with by relying on the old Soviet practices of intimidation and domination or by undermining the sovereignty and independence of Russia's neighbours'.[29]

Despite Russia's diplomatic offensive to obtain a UN or CSCE mandate for its peacekeeping activities, during the first half of 1994 it became clear that this had not provided the West with strong levers to limit Russia's actions. First of all, there is no agreement among governments in the West as to what is acceptable in peacekeeping operations and what is not. Established definitions have proved to be too rigid to provide a good guide for dealing with the challenges of the post-cold war era. It is therefore especially difficult to judge Russia's peacekeeping operations using what are perhaps anachronistic concepts. What is more, Russia seems to be resolute in continuing its peacekeeping operations anyway, even without an international mandate, and to consider the CIS umbrella quite sufficient sanction.[30]

Apart from these factors, both the USA and Western Europe are well aware that Russian cooperation in the UN Security Council and in other forums is a *sine qua non* for coming to terms with the challenges posed by countries like North Korea and Iraq, managing and ending the wars in the former Yugoslavia, and limiting nuclear and missile proliferation. Given the fact that Western governments are wary of risking Russian support in addressing these global and regional challenges, there seems to be a reluctance to upset Russia too much by criticizing its peacekeeping efforts. This is especially the case since a consensus seems now to have formed in Russia that Russia's vital interests lie at least as much in its relationships with the countries of the 'near abroad' as in good relationships with the USA and Western Europe.

Despite these problems in formulating a lucid policy to deal with Russia, there is growing agreement among Western leaders that Russia's assertive policy towards the 'near abroad' must be answered with a clear Western signal. Although publicly communicating Western concern about Russia's conduct in the 'near abroad' may antagonize many of Russia's political élite as well as parts of the Russian Army, the West seems to be increasingly aware that silent acceptance of these military activities may have even more negative consequences for the medium and long term. The main reason why the West cannot remain complacent about Russia's actions is the fact that Russia's 'near abroad' is, in many cases, also democratic Europe's 'near abroad': this applies not only to the obvious cases of the Baltic states, Belarus, Moldova and Ukraine, but also to a certain extent to Transcaucasian countries like Armenia and Georgia.

[28] *International Herald Tribune*, 7 Feb. 1994.

[29] *Financial Times*, 7 Feb. 1994.

[30] Raphael, T., Rosett, C. and Crow, S., 'An interview with Russian Foreign Minister Andrei Kozyrev', *RFL/RL Research Report*, vol. 3, no. 28 (15 July 1994), p. 40.

V. Conclusions

Russian foreign policy seems to be standing at a crossroads. Russia could choose between the continuation of a Western-oriented foreign policy and proceed with a cooperative approach towards Europe and the 'near abroad' or it could become more nationalistic and inward-looking and at the same time adopt a more outspoken and forceful policy towards its neighbours in the former USSR. In fact Russia's foreign policy has developed into a pragmatic mixture of both policy strands, whereby efforts to maintain close economic and political relations with the West are combined with a tougher, more assertive policy towards the West and towards the Soviet successor states.

Although there is general agreement that an internally stable and democratic Russia is in Western interests, there is no consensus on what to do if Russia's economic reform process comes to a standstill or if Russia adopts a more nationalistic and assertive, even neo-imperialist foreign policy. Given the limited influence the West has on the development of Russia's political course, the West will be tempted to adopt a wait-and-see approach, treating Russia in a circumspect manner, trying not to rock the boat even further. This may in many respects be a realistic policy, since it accepts that there are definite limits to the West's ability to influence Russia's domestic and foreign policies. In the end, Russia will be determining its own future, and bad economic and monetary policies will render useless all economic assistance the West may be prepared to give. Equally in the political and strategic field, Russia's stance towards the 'near abroad' and its attitude towards Europe will be primarily determined by Russia itself.

Russia is now engaged in the difficult process of redefining its place in Europe and its role as a great power on the world stage. This is a process which has already resulted in tension between Russia and the Soviet successor states, as well as between Russia and the West. Although the West should try to clarify the parameters for Russia's conduct abroad, it must acknowledge that it has relatively few powerful instruments to influence Russian behaviour.

24. Russia and European institutions

Andrei Zagorski

I. Introduction

Relations between Russia and European security institutions are the subject of diverging judgements. The optimistic view of a new Russia committed to democracy and economic freedom and to becoming a partner of the Western democracies has lost its gleam; the pessimistic view of a Russia which identifies itself as something distinct from the West, if not hostile to it, is gaining ground. Neither of those views reveals *the* truth. It would be idealistic to believe that immediately after the collapse of the communist system Russia could change instantly into a new society. However, it has entered a difficult period of transition, and there is no Fate that will determine the outcome.

It would be unwise to ignore either the profound changes that have already taken place or the strong autocratic, imperial and autarchic legacy which influences Russian politics. Both the continuity of traditions and a drive towards modernization are present in contemporary Russian politics. For some time to come, we will have to live with uncertainties, with the two views—the optimistic and the pessimistic—standing for two extreme options. Between those extremes there is a vast area of intermediate scenarios.

Whatever direction developments in Russia finally take, it will remain a major European nation. In the end, Russia could become a cooperative partner compatible with European civilization or it could re-emerge, after a period of introspection, as an uneasy European power or a European problem.[1] Even if the former scenario does not materialize fully, it is worth involving Russia in the network of European institutions, building upon the presumption that to grant it status in those institutions may not only be the result of Russia's satisfactory political development: it could be a means to encourage it.

Section II of this chapter sets out relevant factors affecting the relationship between Russia and European institutions. Section III discusses Russian interests and policy with respect to the Organization for Security and Co-operation in Europe (OSCE), the European Union (EU), the Western European Union (WEU), NATO, the Council of Europe and subregional organizations, and the final section summarizes the prospects for the further development of relations between Russia and the major European institutions.

---

[1] MacFarlane, S. N., 'Russia and European security', eds H.-G. Ehrhart, A. Kreikemayer and A. Zagorski, *The Former Soviet Union and European Security: Between Integration and Renationalisation* (Nomos: Baden-Baden, 1993), pp. 19–31.

II. Major factors

Among the factors that affect relations between Russia and European institutions, the following are relevant: (*a*) European developments which have placed Russia in a particular environment and reduced the number of options available to it; (*b*) domestic developments and debates in Russia; and (*c*) the competing priorities of Russian foreign policy.

European developments

After the end of the cold war, developments in Europe took a different course from that expected in 1990. It was the collapse of the Eastern bloc, and especially that of the Soviet Union, which hindered Europe from growing gradually together within a pan-European framework and the Conference on Security and Co-operation in Europe (CSCE, later the Organization for Security and Co-operation in Europe, the OSCE)[2] from becoming a major instrument for constructing a wider Europe. A new European unity is now emerging instead as a result of the prospective enlargement of Western institutions eastward. With all its uncertainties and limitations, this trend is gaining momentum. It is characterized by the gradual convergence of the former socialist countries with the EU, symbolized in the association agreements paving the way for enlargement of the Union. In May 1994 the East–Central European (ECE) countries,[3] Bulgaria, Romania and the three Baltic states were granted associate partnership in the WEU. The debate about NATO enlargement and the introduction of the Partnership for Peace (PFP) programme also fit into that trend. Last but not least, the Council of Europe's gradual extension to the East has pioneered this development from the early 1990s.

There has been a change in the broad direction of wider European politics, from building upon pan-European institutions to enlarging the Western ones. This does not imply a new division of Europe but rather another way of achieving European unity. Since 1991 the former socialist countries have preferred the latter course rather than building on the CSCE/OSCE. Their desire to be admitted to Western institutions has been one of the driving forces of that change.

This change matters to Russia more than to any other European nation. Being a member of the CSCE, Russia formerly could count on automatically becoming part of the European family and participating in designing the new European home without begging for admittance. The size and the broader interests of Russia, which extends far beyond the boundaries of Europe, call into question the feasibility and rationale of Russia becoming a member of major West European and/or Atlantic institutions. This implies that the current trend towards enlargement of Western institutions could develop without any

---

[2] On 1 Jan. 1995 the CSCE became the OSCE.
[3] The Czech Republic, Hungary, Poland and Slovakia.

major participation by Russia. EU enlargement and especially NATO enlargement are therefore largely viewed in Russia as trends which might result in its being isolated from European politics.

This explains the Russian emphasis on pan-European structures. The current conception for developing the European security architecture was elaborated in a series of official statements beginning with the autumn of 1993—after the introduction of the PFP—and was laid down in the programme for enhancing the effectiveness of the CSCE submitted for adoption at the CSCE Budapest summit meeting of December 1994.[4] The North Atlantic Cooperation Council (NACC) was proposed as the future pan-European framework for military–political cooperation, to be extended to neutral countries and to be provided with a permanent secretariat. It is also the coordinator of the implementation of the PFP.[5]

The development of other institutions and instruments of European security is not regarded as incompatible with constructing a pan-European collective security system. However, it will be accepted by Russia only so long as it does not, by extending Western security institutions, substitute for a collective security framework in which Russia plays a prominent role.

Domestic developments

Although Russian foreign policy has been taking shape over the past three years it has not yet reached a clear consensus. Consensus-building appears even more difficult since foreign policy is overshadowed by domestic politics, which remain at the top of the agenda. Foreign policy has in many instances become a function of domestic power struggles or political intrigues and is not guided by any clear foreign policy conception. This is why it often appears so puzzling, remains unstable and is affected by rather incidental and arbitrary factors which in many cases have displaced fundamental strategic considerations.

Diverging views have been put forward during the foreign policy debate—the 'Atlanticist', the 'Eurasianist' and the 'neo-anti-imperialist'.[6] The debate itself has revealed a trend away from the optimistic 'Atlanticist' perspective, which implied a Western orientation for Russian policy. The 'Eurasianist' perspective is clearly gaining ground, as became especially apparent after the 'romantic' period of Russo-Western relations had ended.[7] This does not represent a swing from one extreme to the other: the Atlanticist and the neo-anti-imperialist views are the two extremes while the Eurasianist perspective provides an eclectic ground for a centrist foreign policy which has been gradually taking shape

---

[4] See section III of this chapter.

[5] *Diplomaticheskiy Vestnik*, nos 17–18 (1994), p. 13.

[6] Zagorski, A. and Lucas, M., *Rossiya Pered Evropeyskim Vyzovom* [The European challenge for Russia] (Mezhdunarodnye Otnosheniya: Moscow, 1993), pp. 41–74.

[7] Kozyrev, A., 'Partnerstvo c zapadom: ispytanie na prochnost' [Partnership with the West: a test of strength], *Moskovskie Novosti*, 25 Oct. 1992.

since 1993,[8] is less oriented towards Russia's integration into the community of Western democracies and tends to define Russia instead as something distinct from Europe and European civilization. A Eurasianist perspective implies greater emphasis on Russia developing as an independent centre of power by asserting itself against other centres. The current revival of great-power rhetoric is only one example of this. However, because of the political and intellectual heterogeneity of the Eurasianist perspective, the particular shape of a centrist policy depends on the balance of power of major political groups and lobbies. It is precisely this which is not stable.

Competing priorities

While Europe remains in the focus of its foreign policy, Russia has broader interests and has to cope with challenges of non-European origin and nature. In contrast with the position of most other European nations, the European arena is not the only environment for Russia.

The Commonwealth of Independent States

According to the foreign policy guidelines of 1993,[9] preservation of the integrity of the former Soviet Union is Russia's major foreign policy objective. The post-Soviet space is perceived as an area of vital national interest, where the influence of third countries is not welcome. In 1992, largely because of centrifugal trends within the Commonwealth of Independent States (CIS), there was a movement to establish a Russo-Central Asian alliance[10] implying a stronger Asian orientation of Russian politics. Developments during 1993 and 1994, however, gave rise to expectations that, because of economic pressures, most of the newly independent states would come together within the CIS, and Russian policy began to be noticeably firm in promoting their reintegration.[11] Whatever trend prevails in the medium and long term, the concentration on the CIS absorbs much of the foreign policy activity of Russia and implies a kind of political disengagement from Europe.

Plans for reintegration in the area of the former Soviet Union encourage developments which in the medium term would make further improvement of Russian economic cooperation with Europe more difficult. The idea of a CIS economic union imposes limitations on Russia's objective of establishing a free trade area with the EU. In the Partnership and Cooperation Agreement with Russia of June 1994 the EU agreed to grant Russia a five-year transitional

[8] Zagorski, A., 'Russia and the CIS', ed. H. Miall, *Redefining Europe: New Patterns of Conflict and Cooperation* (Pinter: London and New York, 1994), pp. 69–72.

[9] The foreign policy guidelines were not published. For a survey, see Chernov, V., 'Natsionalnye interesi Rossii i ugrozy dlya yeyo bezopasnosti' [The national interests of Russia and threats to its security], *Nezavisimaya Gazeta*, 29 Apr. 1993, p. 1.

[10] *Commonwealth of Independent States: Developments and Prospects* (Moscow State Institute of International Relations: Moscow, 1992).

[11] Zagorski, A., 'Reintegration in the former USSR?', *Aussenpolitik*, vol. 45, no. 3 (1994), pp. 263–72.

period, thus allowing it to preserve the trading advantages it gives the former Soviet republics.[12] This provides a basis for the provisional operation of a special free trade area within the CIS. However, although this transitional period is extendable, it remains provisional, and in the long run any special regime within the CIS will have to be in accordance with the relevant General Agreement on Tariffs and Trade (GATT) provisions. This implies an obligation on Russia's part to abandon arrangements with the other CIS states unless special arrangements are agreed in the context of Russia's accession to the new World Trade Organization, the successor to GATT. If this does not take place, the maintenance of a CIS free trade area could hinder Russia's accession to the World Trade Organization and further improvement of its economic relations with the EU.

The Chinese factor

During the cold war, the 'Chinese factor' significantly affected Soviet policy towards Europe and increased the incentives for cooperation. Although it does not now preclude cooperation with the West, it imposes several restrictions, especially in the security field.

China is increasingly viewed as an emerging security challenge to Russia, possibly the most serious in the long run.[13] Recognition of this has given rise to controversy and debate and provided an argument for the opponents of a *rapprochement* with NATO. They have suggested that the development of closer security cooperation with the alliance could unnecessarily provoke China because it would imply that some kind of NATO security zone had been extended up to the Russian–Chinese border. Other experts have argued that it was precisely the challenge from China that made improved security cooperation with the West desirable for Russia.[14] However, it is generally recognized that China does not pose a common challenge for Russia and Europe. It thus does not provide a strong incentive for developing an alliance-like relationship between them.

In a longer-term perspective, the Russian desire to become part of the economic integration on the Pacific Rim may become another competing priority of its policy. However, it cannot yet be considered a relevant factor since the economic, and especially the infrastructural and demographic, potential of Russia in the Pacific is limited to say the least.

[12] Adopted on 23 June 1994. Commission of the European Communities, Proposal for a Council and Commission Decision on the conclusion of the Agreement on Partnership and Cooperation between the European Communities and their Member States of the one part, and Russia, of the other part, COM (94)257 final, Commission of the European Communities, Brussels, 15 June 1994. For the Russian text, see *Diplomaticheskiy Vestnik*, nos 15–16 (1994), p. 31.

[13] Chudakov, G. *et al.*, 'Russia's interests and approaches towards the system of interlocking European institutions', ed. von Plate, B., *Europa auf dem Wege zur Kollektiven Sicherheit?* (Nomos: Baden-Baden, 1994) (in English).

[14] Chudakov (note 13).

III. Institutionalizing relations with European structures

The 1993 foreign policy guidelines[15] specifically refer to the increasing importance of Russia's participation in European institutions in order to compensate at least partially for the obvious reduction of the policy resources available to it. This increasing interest in involvement in multilateral structures is a remarkable change when contrasted with the policies of the former Soviet Union. However, actual interaction with individual institutions has proved uneasy in recent years.

The OSCE

The OSCE was a privileged project both of Soviet and of Russian European policy. Its importance even increased with the end of the cold war when it remained the only European institution of which Russia was a full member, thus giving the Russian authorities the feeling of being an equal partner in designing a new Europe. The consensus rule also provides a guarantee that Russia can resist decisions which it considers are not in its interests.

Beginning in the summer of 1993, Russia submitted numerous proposals aimed at increasing the role of the CSCE in European politics. It actively participated in discussions on the eve of the Rome meeting of the CSCE Council in November–December 1993 in order to bring greater order into the system of CSCE institutions and to give greater regularity to political dialogue. It also pledged increased CSCE capability for conflict prevention and peacekeeping and sought a CSCE mandate for its own conflict-management initiatives in the area of the former Soviet Union. In 1994, while preparing for the CSCE's Budapest summit meeting of 5–6 December 1994, Russia submitted a comprehensive programme for enhancing the CSCE's effectiveness which provided for the adoption of a political declaration reserving for the CSCE the central role in ensuring peace and stability in the Euro-Atlantic region while at the same time transforming it into a capable regional organization with its own statute.[16] It was proposed that the CSCE should coordinate the activities of the CIS, NACC, the EU, the Council of Europe, NATO and the WEU in strengthening stability and security, peacekeeping and the protection of national minorities in Europe. The OSCE is expected to become the major partner of the UN in conflict management in its area. Most important, Russia suggested the establishment (while retaining the principle of consensus) of a CSCE Executive Committee consisting of no more than 10 members, both permanent and rotating ones, which would be authorized to make binding decisions on a unanimous vote. Russia suggested establishing open-ended groups of the most interested states on various crisis situations and regional round tables on security, stability and cooperation. It was also seeking to provide some form of representation for the CIS at the CSCE.

[15] See note 9.
[16] *Diplomaticheskiy Vestnik*, nos 15–16 (1994), p. 13.

The most intriguing issue is what the particular interest of Russia is in the OSCE. Russian experts specify several particular issues: (*a*) the provision of a political and legal basis for the inviolability of the Russian borders; (*b*) the protection of the rights of Russian minorities in the newly independent states; (*c*) the reform of domestic legislation; (*d*) the development of multilateral interaction with the ECE countries; (*e*) the promotion of institutionalized interaction with the West on the broad agenda of European problems; (*f*) the negotiation of new approaches to conventional arms control, implementation of the Treaty on Conventional Armed Forces in Europe (CFE Treaty) and other accords; (*g*) the provision of international support for and acceptance of Russia's efforts in maintaining security in the area of the former Soviet Union; and (*h*) the direct participation of Russia in discussion of all issues on the pan-European agenda.[17]

The view taken by this author is that, beyond retaining the institutional link with Europe, the particular Russian interests in the OSCE as they are currently seen by the political élite are rather narrow. They include the wish to use the OSCE for raising issues concerning Russian minorities in the former Soviet Union, although lately Russia appears to have relied more on bilateral or even unilateral actions. A unilateral (or bilateral) approach dominates Russian policy with respect to maintaining the inviolability of its borders. The OSCE, moreover, is not the only instrument for maintaining dialogue with Western institutions. Indeed, Russia has already started to institutionalize that dialogue on a bilateral basis.

Arms control issues are increasingly troublesome for Russia. Its unhappiness with the flank limitations under the CFE Treaty[18] and difficulties with the ratification of the Open Skies Treaty are examples. A long time has passed since Russia (or the Soviet Union) looked to the CSCE as a powerful tool to reform domestic legislation. The time has also passed when Russia looked to the CSCE to legitimize its peacekeeping activities in the area of the former Soviet Union; it now turns to the CIS for these purposes. Indeed, Russia now de facto objects to the development of the OSCE as a collective security body and is increasingly reluctant to see its military and political role in peacekeeping and conflict management in the former Soviet Union expand. The decision of the Budapest summit meeting to begin planning a peacekeeping operation in Nagorno-Karabakh once agreement was reached within the Minsk Group[19] was fairly exceptional and difficult for Russia, which up to that point had been hindering both the mounting of a CSCE operation there and access for the CSCE to negotiations in Nagorno-Karabakh and the Trans-Dniester region.[20] Further-

---

[17] Chudakov (note 13), pp. 275–76.

[18] See also chapter 8, section VII in this volume.

[19] The Minsk Group was set up in Mar. 1992 to monitor the situation in Nagorno-Karabakh. The original member countries were Belarus, Czechoslovakia, France, Germany, Italy, Russia, Sweden, Turkey and the USA. The membership is now Belarus, Finland, France, Germany, Hungary, Italy, Russia, Sweden, Turkey and the USA, plus Armenia and Azerbaijan.

[20] Zagorski, A., 'Russian peace support in the CIS: possibilities and limitations of its internationalization', ed. H.-G. Ehrhart, A. Kreikemeyer and A. Zagorski, *Crisis Management in the CIS: Whither Russia?* (Nomos: Baden-Baden, 1995), pp. 152–55.

more, discussions within the CSCE, initiated in 1993 by Russia itself and continued all through 1994, over a possible status for Russian peacekeepers as a 'third party' in conflicts in the area of the former Soviet Union were a bitter disappointment, with Russia increasingly reluctant to accept several provisions. In particular it refused to accept the procedures for observation of the peace-keepers' activities, the political role of the CSCE and the means of providing for a multinational composition for the peacekeeping forces. The issue completely reversed the Russian position in the CSCE, and largely contributed to the isolation of Russia during the Budapest review conference which started in October 1994. Russia found itself there not only confronted with strong opposition but abandoned by possible partners. In the end, Russia, which had initiated the discussion about 'third party status', was happy that no decision was reached at Budapest.

Recent developments, however, especially in Chechnya, have shown that there exist fairly strong groups among the Russian political élite which are ready to welcome a constructive conflict-management role for the OSCE, even on Russian soil. After an uneasy process of admitting the OSCE mission in Chechnya, the Russian Government came surprisingly quickly to rely on the good offices of the mission in assisting in negotiations with the rebel side, and it was prepared to accept the OSCE as one of the crucial monitoring institutions during implementation of the accords on cessation of military hostilities. Indeed, some senior Russian authorities admitted in 1995 that OSCE mediation would be most welcome in Chechnya and also in Baku, over the question of Nagorno-Karabakh. Interestingly, many of the Russian officials dealing in particular with the role of the OSCE in various conflicts in the former Soviet Union stress the positive nature of their experience of almost all the OSCE missions. This positive note has been reflected in the evaluation of Nikolay Afanasievskiy, Deputy Foreign Minister of the Russian Federation handling multilateral European institutions.[21]

Nevertheless, there are very general suspicions that behind the activities of international organizations in the 'backyard' of Russia there lies a wish on the part of the West and Turkey to diminish the role of Russia in the former Soviet Union and an attempt to interfere in the affairs of the newly independent states. For this reason, many in the Russian political élite, having admitted a greater role for the OSCE in Nagorno-Karabakh and Chechnya, would like either to reciprocate or to make further OSCE involvement in the former Soviet Union conditional on its being given a greater role in other areas such as Northern Ireland or the former Yugoslavia. The 'mainstream' understanding is that the OSCE's peacekeeping efforts should not be confined to the CIS only.

The reluctance of many OSCE participating states to accept the Russian idea of establishing an OSCE Executive Committee as an analogue to the UN Security Council has reduced Russia's prospects of raising its profile in the pan-European framework.

---

[21] *Diplomaticheskiy Vestnik*, no. 1 (1995), p. 32.

Since discussion of NATO enlargement started in 1993, the main rationale for the Russian CSCE-centred policy has boiled down to an attempt to cope with the prospective enlargement of Western institutions in Europe by seeking to fit this process into a broader pan-European framework (whether it was the CSCE or NACC) or even simply to keep this pan-European perspective on the agenda. One of the major fears on the Russian side now is that increasing scepticism about the OSCE, which is now widespread over Europe, could result in Russia's increasing marginalization. Hence the largely declaratory rhetoric about the necessity to strengthen the OSCE as a collective security framework. This also appears to be the reason for the close attention Russia has paid to developing the comprehensive security model for Europe which is at present under discussion.[22]

The European Union

Both economic cooperation and political dialogue with the EU are considered to be of the utmost importance to the economic security of Russia.[23] At the same time, full or even associate EU membership is not considered to be an objective. Although Russian officials sometimes admit that Russia might seek membership, so far it has limited itself to developing a kind of special relationship with the EU, including the establishment of a free trade area.

The attention which Russia has paid to the EU is not surprising. In 1995, Russian trade with West European (predominantly EU) countries was more than 50 per cent of its total foreign trade.[24] EU countries accounted for 60 per cent of the total economic assistance provided to Russia by the West in 1990–94.[25] The EU's prospective enlargement lends it additional importance: it and Russia, already immediate neighbours along the border with Finland, will have a common border 2000 km long.

The EU accepted Russia as the legal successor of the former Soviet Union and as a successor to the Trade and Cooperation Agreement concluded on 18 December 1989. While shaping its relations with the East, the EU decided to develop a special type of agreement with the former Soviet Union successor states, distinct from those endorsed with the ECE countries. The 'partnership and cooperation' agreements offered to the CIS states do not provide for association with the EU, nor do they include a membership option even in the

---

[22] Stockholm International Peace Research Institute, *A Future Security Agenda for Europe: Report of the Independent Working Group established by the Stockholm International Peace Research Institute* (SIPRI: Stockholm, Oct. 1996).

[23] Chudakov (note 13), p. 268.

[24] The next largest trading partners were the CIS states (*c.* one-third of the volume of trade with Western Europe in 1995), the European former CMEA countries, the USA, China and Japan in order of volume of trade. *Economic Union. Monthly Supplement to Rossiyskaya Gazeta*, 30 Mar. 1996, p. 8.

[25] 'Rossiya v ramkakh partnerstva i sotrudnichestva v Evrope' [Russia in the framework of partnership and cooperation in Europe], survey prepared by the mission of the Commission of the European Communities in Moscow for a symposium held on 23 Nov. 1994, pp. 3–4, 8.

course of intensified cooperation.[26] The nucleus of the concept of partnership agreements was the institutionalization of political dialogue.[27]

The EU is also pursuing a differentiated approach towards the newly independent states adopted by the General Affairs Council on 7 March 1994. It has already concluded partnership and cooperation agreements with Kazakhstan (24 May 1994), Kyrgyzstan (31 May 1994), Ukraine (18 June 1994), Moldova (July 1994) and Belarus (January 1995). The agreements with Belarus, Moldova and Ukraine provide for the possibility of transforming them into agreements on a free trade area. Since ratification procedures were expected to be lengthy, interim agreements were negotiated to enable partial implementation, beginning in early 1995.

From the beginning of negotiations on partnership agreements, the EU made the implementation of their provisions conditional on the partner countries' commitment to the principles of a liberal, democratic state with a market-based economic system.[28]

In October 1994, the EU decided to prepare for negotiations with the Transcaucasian states (Armenia, Azerbaijan and Georgia). Partnership and cooperation agreements with them were signed in April 1996.[29] It also decided to resume trade and economic relations with Turkmenistan and Uzbekistan; a partnership and cooperation agreement with the latter was signed in June 1996. Only with Tajikistan has no progress been feasible so far.[30]

The Partnership and Cooperation Agreement with Russia was concluded on 24 June 1994 after 18 months of negotiations and repeated confusions.[31] As with other partnership and cooperation agreements, an interim agreement has been negotiated to enable partial implementation before the agreement proper enters into force. However, in January 1995, as a reaction to the Russian military adventure in Chechnya started in December 1994, the EU suspended ratification of the agreement and conclusion of the interim agreement and made both conditional on the opening of negotiations between the Russian Government and the Chechen rebels for a peaceful resolution of the conflict. The interim agreement was finally signed in Brussels on 18 July 1995.

Access for Russian manufactured goods to EU markets has been the major problem. In the Russian view, the main purpose of the agreement was to define a new trade regime which would provide for non-discrimination against Russian goods. Although it was a compromise, the agreement finally included

[26] Lippert, B., 'Questions and scenarios on EC–CIS/republics relations: an outline of the political dimension', ed. Ehrhart (note 1), p. 134.

[27] Höhmann, H., Meier, C. and Timmermann, H., 'European Community and the post-Soviet states: the quest for new patterns of economic cooperation', ed. Ehrhart (note 1), p. 124.

[28] Höhman (note 27), p. 124.

[29] Fuller, E., 'Transcaucasus presidents sign accords with EU', *OMRI Daily Digest*, no. 80, part I (23 Apr. 1996).

[30] *Evropeiskiy Obzor* [European survey, a monthly information bulletin on EU and TACIS] (Brussels), Oct. 1994, pp. 2–4, 9, 15.

[31] See note 12. Initially the agreement was expected to be endorsed in June 1993 but was not because Russia was dissatisfied with its provisions. It failed again later in Dec. 1993 during a visit of President Yeltsin to Brussels and only a Political Declaration on Partnership and Cooperation was signed. For the text of the Declaration, see *Diplomaticheskiy Vestnik*, nos 1–2 (1994), pp. 15–16.

many of the Russian proposals. The following provisions are especially valued in Moscow: (a) regular political dialogue and consultations on political, economic and other issues will be developed; (b) the EU will regard Russia as an economy in transition and will remove the trade obstacles it applies to state economies; (c) in 1998, Russia and the EU will decide whether and when negotiations on including Russia in an extended free trade area can be opened; (d) the trade regime will largely be in conformity with the World Trade Organization rules (in particular, quantitative limitations on manufactured goods from Russia will be cancelled, with the exception of certain sectors); (e) trade in coal and steel, nuclear components and space services is partially liberalized; (f) further improvements may be negotiated before the agreement expires—after Russia joins the World Trade Organization but no later then three years after the agreement enters into force; and (g) during the transitional period Russia may make exceptions from the trade regime for the other CIS countries.

Russia also has particular interest in the clause enabling it to discuss special trade arrangements as EU enlargement proceeds. This is an important issue since, for instance, Russian steel exports to Finland have hitherto not been subject to the same restrictions as exports to the EU. Russia therefore seeks to ensure that trade conditions with the new EU members do not worsen. It is also worth noting that Russia has raised no objections to eventual EU enlargement eastwards.

Several important elements of the Russian position could not be introduced into the agreement. These would have committed the EU to liberalizing immigration rules; provided Russia with access to the European Investment Bank; developed a regime for road transport services; and specified full application of World Trade Organization rules in trade between Russia and the EU. Although a solution was found to the problem of Russian uranium exports, this issue remains a controversial one between France and Russia.

The institutionalization of political dialogue between Russia and the EU was one of the least controversial issues. The agreement provides for regular meetings of the Russian President, the President of the Council of the European Union and the President of the Commission of the European Communities twice a year. The dialogue at ministerial level will be maintained within the Cooperation Council assisted by the Cooperation Committee consisting of senior officials. A Committee on Parliamentary Cooperation will be set up, consisting of members of the Russian Parliament and the European Parliament.

The mechanism for political dialogue between Russia and the EU has been shaped like that provided for in the Transatlantic Declaration of November 1990 for developing dialogue between the EU and the USA. There is one major difference: the same level of commitment and habit of mutual adjustment of interests as obtains in the transatlantic frameworks should not be taken for granted from Russia. The political dialogue between Russia and the EU may also be subject to problems similar to those which arose in the transatlantic framework. Cooperation between the USA and the EU, although rather fruitful in some areas, has given rise to criticism on both sides of the Atlantic.[32] Among the problems which might be expected to characterize the dialogue with Russia are a tendency to overstretch it with frequent meetings at the political level without a proper underpinning at the working level and the reduction of the dialogue to exchange of information without breaking through to developing common or close approaches to the issues discussed or unity of action.

With the Partnership and Cooperation Agreement new opportunities are being opened in relations between Russia and the EU in both the economic and the political fields. However, it is still an open question to what extent the two sides are able and have the political will to increase cooperation.

The WEU

Russia inherited a relationship established by the former Soviet Union with the WEU, which was initiated by the first visit of a delegation of the Bureau of the WEU Assembly to Moscow in April 1987. Those contacts paved the way for the development of regular dialogue between the Assembly and the Supreme Soviet and for establishing contacts between the WEU ministerial organs and the Soviet Government. However, relations with the WEU were not a priority in Moscow's European policy and remained in the shadow of discussions about relations with the EU and especially with NATO. After the dissolution of the Soviet Union Russia did not show any greater interest in resuming regular parliamentary dialogue.

Beginning with 1994, the interest of the Russian authorities in intensifying dialogue with the WEU noticeably increased. This was certainly part of the overall policy of Russia to build up mechanisms for direct dialogue with West European institutions after it was confronted with the likelihood of their enlargement.

Russia's approach to the increasing convergence of ECE states with the WEU has not been clear-cut. When the WEU, in May 1994, granted the ECE countries, Bulgaria, Romania and the three Baltic countries a status of association, then Foreign Minister Kozyrev stated that Russia did not object to that development.[33] Intensive contacts between the WEU and Russia after May 1994 indicated that the latter was fairly well-prepared to accept it on condition that this was not a pretext for bringing the countries in question into NATO by the back door. At the same time, in a statement to the press on 12 May 1994, Kozyrev raised concerns as to the general trend towards the enlargement of Western institutions at the expense of the pan-European ones. He stated that attempts to find new forms of military and political cooperation within only a part of Europe ran counter to the need for a pan-European system of security and stability, and that it was wrong to bank on cooperation where there was no place

---

[32] Hellmann, G., 'EU und USA brauchen ein breiteres Fundament: Plädoyer für einen "Transatlantischen Vertrag"' [The EU and the USA need a broader base: plea for a transatlantic treaty], *Aussenpolitik*, vol. 45, no. 2 (1994), pp. 236–45.

[33] Kovalenko, Yu., [untitled report], *Izvestiya*, 11 May 1994.

for Russia. He therefore encouraged the WEU to become a prospective component of pan-European security structures under the auspices of the CSCE.[34]

At the same time Russia sought to intensify dialogue and institutionalize cooperation with the WEU, picking up an initiative of the WEU Council of Ministers which, on 9 May 1994, stated the importance of developing dialogue and exchanges of information on issues of common concern with Russia.[35] Possible forms and subjects of dialogue have been explored in a series of contacts between the WEU Secretary-General and the Russian Embassy in Brussels and in other contacts between the WEU and the Russian authorities. At the same time, beginning in October 1994, Russia resumed the regular parliamentary contacts established in 1987. It also clarified its views on the further development of relations with the WEU, which included the following suggestions: (a) the establishment of special partnership relations with the WEU in order to synchronize cooperation with the WEU and the EU in economic and political matters; (b) a more regular form for Russia's contacts with the WEU through meetings between the Russian foreign affairs and defence ministers, the secretariat-general and the ministers of the countries holding the presidency of the WEU; (c) the institutionalization of consultations with the WEU parallel to those between Russia and the EU. Such consultations would concern current problems relating to European and international security (i.e., peacekeeping, the crisis in former Yugoslavia and the Pact on Stability in Europe) and explore possibilities of cooperation on defence matters, particularly on tactical missile defence; and (d) the development of regular links between the Russian Parliament and the WEU Assembly.[36]

It is worth noting that there is an obvious convergence between the Russian concept of 'partnership' in relations with the WEU and the WEU's own. The WEU appears to be interested in setting up a regular political dialogue with Russia for the purpose of exchanging information in order to improve transparency and establish a climate of confidence. At the same time, it prefers a gradual approach and seeks first to establish a system of information exchange which, at a later stage, might develop into one of consultation and even move towards cooperation in certain specific areas to be determined.[37] At this stage, the WEU appears to prefer not to make the cooperative mechanism with Russia too formal in order to retain a certain freedom of action, while it admits the need to develop a degree of institutionalization of cooperation at both parliamentary and intergovernmental levels in order not to give Russia the impression that it is being held at a distance.

[34] Quoted from WEU, Fortieth Ordinary Session of the Assembly of the Western European Union, document 1440, 10 Nov. 1994, Report submitted on behalf of the Political Committee by Mr Baumel, Rapporteur, p. 24.
[35] WEU (note 34), p. 27.
[36] WEU (note 34), pp. 27–28.
[37] WEU (note 34), p. 28.

NATO

Relations with NATO have been one of the most controversial issues in Russian European policy. Discussions have concentrated on two major issues: possible early NATO enlargement and Russian participation in the PFP.

Discussion on NATO enlargement became surprisingly intense in the autumn of 1993 after a Russo-Polish declaration was endorsed on 25 August during the visit of President Boris Yeltsin to Warsaw. It stated that the wish of Poland to be admitted to NATO 'does not run contrary to the interests of other states including those of Russia'.[38] The declaration was largely misinterpreted as a sign that Russia had abandoned its previous objections to NATO enlargement. In fact it reopened the debate.

Arguments against NATO enlargement included reference to public opinion, which allegedly would oppose the approach of NATO closer to the Russian borders, to the nationalistic anti-Western opposition which could use this in the domestic power struggle[39] and to the threat that Russia would be isolated in the European security order.[40] An analysis of the impact of NATO enlargement on Russia was provided in a public report by the Russian Foreign Intelligence Service in November 1993.[41] It offered four conclusions. First, the absorption of the ECE countries by NATO could result in a strengthening of the 'hard-liners' in the alliance, which would make the transformation of NATO slower and more difficult. This could, in the view of the writers of the report, reduce the chances of overcoming the division of Europe and result in a relapse into bloc politics. Second, the idea of NATO's projecting security eastwards, allegedly including the newly independent states, through the enlargement of its membership or other forms of affiliation, was considered to be an attempt to make a CIS collective security system unnecessary. Third, although NATO enlargement was not considered a direct military threat to Russia, the move of a military alliance almost up to the Russian borders would overturn the balance established by the CFE Treaty and require a reconsideration of Russia's military posture, which would be costly. Finally, admitting the ECE states to NATO would establish a barrier between Russia and the rest of Europe.

Whatever the arguments and counter-arguments raised in that discussion, Russia proceeded on the assumption that the appearance of any military alliance close to its borders which did not include Russia itself, whether that alliance was or was not directed against Russia, was unacceptable. It tended to emphasize that it was not attempting to exercise a power of veto over NATO

---

[38] *Diplomaticheskiy Vestnik*, nos 17–18 (1993), p. 16.

[39] At least as of the autumn of 1993 this argument was far from being correct. The Russian élite, including its military establishment, at the time when debate over NATO enlargement was at its first peak, was rather indifferent to the issue. This was revealed in opinion polls conducted by the Moscow State Institute of International Relations (MGIMO) and the Vox Populi public opinion group.

[40] Karaganov, S., 'Rasshirenie NATO vedet k izolatsii Rossii' [Expansion of NATO leads to the isolation of Russia], *Moskovskie Novosti*, 19 Sep. 1993.

[41] *Perspectivy rasshireniya NATO i interesy Rossii* [The prospects for NATO expansion and the interests of Russia] (Foreign Intelligence Service: Moscow, 1993).

enlargement and was not in a position to stop the ECE countries from joining the alliance: those issues were to be solved between the alliance and the countries concerned.[42] At the same time, Russia clearly indicated that an enlargement of NATO would have consequences which would most probably imply reconsideration of Russia's commitments under the CFE Treaty or even withdrawal from it.[43]

Given Russian concerns about early NATO enlargement, it might have been expected that the approval of the PFP by the NATO Council in January 1994 would be welcomed by Moscow. Indeed, Russian officials regarded the PFP as a substitute for NATO enlargement, reacted positively initially and were expected to endorse the framework agreement fairly early.[44] However, a public debate produced an overwhelmingly negative approach to the PFP,[45] which became the subject of controversy in two hearings in the State Duma and between the Duma and the government. Arguments against Russian participation in the PFP included the following:

1. The idea of offering military cooperation to the 'partner countries' was not new. What was new was the statement that, theoretically, any of the partner countries could be admitted to NATO after they had met certain criteria. This implied that, formally, the door to NATO had been opened although certainly not all the partner countries would be able to pass through it. That message was largely interpreted among the Russian political élite as meaning that the PFP was designed to prepare the ECE countries to join NATO at a later stage rather than to be a substitute for NATO enlargement.

2. In 1993 few countries were considered as candidates for admission. The PFP extended, at least theoretically, the prospect of admission to all partner countries including the newly independent states. This encouraged suspicions in Moscow that NATO intended either in time to absorb the newly independent states or at the least to undermine Russia's role in the area of the former Soviet Union.

3. Russia was upset at being treated as equal to the smaller partners and therefore claimed a special relationship with NATO which would recognize its great-power status.

4. The PFP initiated a shift from NACC as a collective body to developing individual cooperation with partner countries. This not only enhanced the role of NATO but had the potential to diminish the roles of the CSCE and NACC.

---

[42] Kasantsev, B., 'Pervye shagi k partnerstvu Rossii s NATO' [First steps towards Russia's partnership with NATO], *Mezhdunarodnaya Zhizn,* no. 10 (1994), p. 25; and Pfeiler, W., 'Konflikte, Krisen, Kriege: Russlands Geopolitik und die künftige europäische Sicherheit' [Conflicts, crises, wars: Russia's geopoliics and the future security of Europe], *Aus Politik und Zeitgeschichte* (6 May 1994), B 18–19, p. 28.

[43] *Financial Times,* 17 Nov. 1994.

[44] A formal political decision on joining the PFP was taken in Moscow in Mar. 1994.

[45] Chernov, V., 'Moskva dolzhna khorosho podumat, prezhde chem otvechat na predlozhenie NATO' [Moscow should think properly before it responds to the NATO offer], *Nezavisimaya Gazeta,* 23 Feb. 1994; Migranyan, A., 'Zachem vstupat esli luchshe ne vstupat?' [Why join if it is better not to join?], *Nezavisimaya Gazeta,* 15 Mar. 1994; and an interview with Vladimir Lukin in *Moskovskie Novosti,* no. 16 (1994).

5. The orientation of the PFP towards 'standardization' of major weapon systems and interoperability of the armed forces was interpreted as a serious threat to the Russian arms markets in the ECE.

The arguments in favour of the PFP emphasized that the adoption of the programme was a compromise between those in favour of and those hesitant about NATO enlargement and in fact allowed that issue to be suspended.[46] Thus the introduction of the PFP was an important result of Russian policy. It was also argued that Russian non-participation would imply not isolation but self-isolation from Europe. Joining the partnership framework, on the other hand, would provide some possibility at least partly to influence the evolution of NATO and the development of the PFP itself; if it stayed outside, Russia would not have that possibility.[47] Furthermore, precisely because the PFP provided for the individualization of relations between NATO and partner countries and had the potential gradually to marginalize the collective framework of NACC, Russia should institutionalize direct individual political dialogue with NATO.[48]

Official policy, once again, evolved towards a compromise between the proponents and opponents of the PFP. In May 1994, the Russian authorities began linking accession to the PFP to the idea of developing a special relationship with NATO outside the PFP framework, including regular and ad hoc consultations. They also activated efforts to promote proposals to give the CSCE the possibility of coordinating the activities of other European security organizations. However, NATO rejected Russian proposals concerning a quasi-subordination of NATO to the CSCE and an independent role for NACC. It also held to its reservations about the idea of regular consultations between Russia and NATO, believing that Russia could misuse them to obtain a power of veto on important decisions of the alliance, including those over enlargement and activities outside the area of NATO's immediate responsibility—such as air strikes against the Bosnian Serbs.

At the North Atlantic Council meeting in Istanbul on 9 June 1994, NATO foreign ministers agreed to develop relations with Russia both within and outside the PFP framework, although the form and status of an 'additional protocol' that Russia requested still remained controversial.[49] On 22 June 1994 Russia finally acceded to the PFP, and at a press conference held on the same day a 'Summary of conclusions' of the discussions between Kozyrev and the Council was announced. The summary reflected the agreement to develop an Individual Partnership Programme (IPP) for cooperation within the PFP programme 'corresponding to Russia's size, importance and capabilities'. It also referred to the intention of both sides to develop far-reaching relations both

[46] *Nezavisimaya Gazeta*, 18 Mar. 1994.

[47] Kondrashov, S., 'Brussel, Korfu, Neapol i petushinye boi v Moskve' [Brussels, Corfu, Naples and cock-fights in Moscow], *Nezavisimaya Gazeta*, 2 July 1994.

[48] Zagorski, A, 'Kren ot SBSE k NATO?' [Tilting from the CSCE to NATO?], *Mezhdunarodnaya Zhizn*, no. 12 (1993), pp. 13–20.

[49] *Frankfurter Allgemeine Zeitung*, 10 June 1994.

within and outside the PFP framework.[50] On 5 July the presentational document describing Russia's view of the IPP was officially handed over in Brussels. The first part of the document—political partnership—merely reiterated Russian proposals for the development of a pan-European collective security system. It also suggested that consultations with NATO on problems of European and global security should be institutionalized. The document included proposals for developing cooperation with NATO in the military and other fields.

The uneasy debate over Russian participation in the PFP and, more generally, over its relations with NATO was now succeeded by the much less politicized task of drafting the basic documents reflecting the intentions of Russia and NATO to develop cooperation. Two documents had been drafted by December 1994 which were intended to provide a new framework for channelling, if not yet properly institutionalizing, the Russia–NATO dialogue: the IPP and a bilateral framework for enhanced dialogue cooperation between Russia and NATO outside the PFP. The second document provided for three areas of dialogue and cooperation beyond the PFP: (a) exchange of information on political–security matters of a European dimension; (b) political consultations on issues of common concern (proliferation of weapons of mass destruction, nuclear safety and specific crises in Europe); and (c) cooperation on a range of security-related matters, including peacekeeping. The main method of consultation and cooperation is ad hoc meetings in the 'NATO plus Russia' ('16 plus 1') format.[51]

The controversial discussions of 1993 and 1994 thus gave impetus to a gradual institutionalization of relations between Russia and NATO, although in a much more modest way than the former might have wished at the beginning. At the same time, relations between Russia and NATO appear to have suffered the least from the crisis in Chechnya. In December 1994 Foreign Minister Kozyrev suddenly refused to sign the two documents at NATO headquarters, and this was followed by a violent attack on the enlargement of NATO by President Yeltsin at the CSCE Budapest summit meeting. Nevertheless in May 1995 during a visit by US President Bill Clinton to Moscow, Yeltsin assured Clinton that Russia would endorse both documents without preconditions, and they were approved on 31 May 1995 by Kozyrev and the North Atlantic Council.

At the same time, Russia did not abandon its negative position on NATO enlargement.[52] The debate over enlargement, frozen from the autumn of 1995 until the Russian and US presidential elections were over, was aggravated again in the spring of 1996 on the occasion of the visits of NATO Secretary General Xavier Solana and US Secretary of State Warren Christopher. However, even

[50] 'Summary of conclusions of discussions between the North Atlantic Council and Foreign Minister of Russia Andrei Kozyrev, Brussels, 22 June 1994', *NATO Review*, no. 4 (1995), p. 35.

[51] See note 50.

[52] On the hardening of attitudes among Russia's political élite towards NATO expansion eastwards, see Council for Foreign and Defence Policy, 'Rossiya i NATO' [Russia and NATO], *Nezavisimaya Gazeta*, 21 June 1995. For an English translation, see Royen, C., *Russland und die NATO: Thesen des russischen Rats für Aussen- und Verteidigungspolitik* [Russia and NATO: theses of the Council on Foreign and Defence Policy] (Stiftung Wissenschaft und Politik: Ebenhausen, 1995), pp. 15–26.

before the Russian presidential and regional elections of June and July 1996, Moscow began to develop more flexible language on NATO. The new Foreign Minister, Yevgeniy Primakov, appointed in January 1996, has repeatedly confirmed Russia's negative position on enlargement but avoids saying that it is unacceptable; he has said that it is the extension of the NATO military infrastructure closer to Russia's borders which is unacceptable and pointed out that Russia is prepared to engage in dialogue on NATO enlargement. Commenting on the NATO Council meeting in Berlin in June 1996, Primakov emphasized: 'Russia, while retaining a negative attitude towards this process . . . has singled out the core which is absolutely unacceptable—the movement of NATO infrastructure towards our borders. On this basis, Russia offers a dialogue to NATO'.[53] The Russian Ambassador in Brussels, Vitaliy Churkin, is even more explicit: 'Recently, at a quite high level, we have let NATO people know that we are worried not so much by the simple fact of "extension" but only by the approach of the alliance's infrastructure towards Russian borders. This attitude opens up some space for a search for constructive solutions in the interest of pan-European security'.[54]

Since the summer of 1996, Russian government experts have been developing particular ideas especially on the further institutionalization of relations between Russia and NATO and on possible 'joint ventures' with the alliance which could follow up the IFOR (Implementation Force) operation in Bosnia and Herzegovina. One of these ideas was presented by Primakov in Berlin—joint efforts in developing tactical anti-ballistic [missile?] systems. However, even up to the autumn of 1996, Russian diplomacy was still not able to overcome the domestic problems concerning NATO enlargement, and the ideas being elaborated have not been represented as the official position of Russia, thus postponing substantial dialogue on the question.

The Council of Europe

During the mid-1980s, the Council of Europe was the first Western institution substantially to upgrade its relations and initiate increasing exchange with the former socialist countries. In 1989 it introduced a 'special guest' status for them and, beginning in 1990, started gradually to admit them as full members.

This process was paralleled by a mutual opening up between the Soviet Union and the Council of Europe which began in the spring of 1988. The Soviet Union was among the first countries to receive special guest status. A dense network of cooperation was developing with the Council of Europe, and as early as 1990 Russia began acceding to a number of Council of Europe conventions. The process was interrupted in January 1991 following the violent action of the Soviet Union in the Baltic states, and resumed after the failure of

---

[53] Izvestiya, 8 June 1996.
[54] Interview in Itogi, 9 July 1996, p. 43.

the coup in Moscow in August 1991.[55] As a successor state of the former Soviet Union, Russia assumed special guest status on 14 January 1992.

The special value of the Council of Europe for Russia lay in the fact that it is the only West European institution of which Russia could become and wished to become a full member. It indicated this interest in August 1992 and applied for membership formally in March 1993. A joint programme of action of the Council of Europe and Russia was elaborated by a contact group of the Council of Europe Secretariat and the Russian Foreign Ministry in order to promote cooperation in the areas covered by over 140 Council of Europe conventions.[56] Cooperation with the Council of Europe developed through regular parliamentary exchange, participation in the work of a number of committees of the Assembly and intensive exchange at government and expert level. After 1993, the issue of Russia's admission became the major one in all meetings with the Council of Europe.

However, this objective proved to be more difficult than generally expected in Moscow, and Russian interest in joining the Council of Europe seemed to have visibly declined, for various reasons. Some of the standard conditions for the admission of new members raised in discussions with Russia increased the scepticism of the leadership of the previous Supreme Soviet. These concerned mainly the requirement for a country to have held democratic multi-party elections and to prove the democratic nature of its constitution. Both issues were highly controversial in the domestic power struggle in Russia. In 1993, an even greater deterioration occurred in relations between the Supreme Soviet and the Council of Europe Parliamentary Assembly. During a visit to Strasbourg in August 1993 Ruslan Khasbulatov, then chairman of the Supreme Soviet, even declared that Russia should not be so eager to seek membership: rather the Council of Europe should solicit Russian membership.[57] The conditions for admission were largely seen as a conspiracy against the Supreme Soviet; at one stage the coordinator of the Communists of Russia parliamentary faction, Ivan Rybkin (during 1993–95 speaker of the State Duma) even suspected that the Russian Foreign Ministry was responsible for that conspiracy.[58] Later on, relations deteriorated further after Estonia and then Latvia were admitted in 1993 and 1995, respectively. Their early admission was largely interpreted in Russia as an example of double standards on the part of the Council of Europe and as a sign of its intention to keep Russia isolated.

From the political perspective, the Russian authorities, while recognizing the general importance of joining the Council of Europe, were aware that this was not a main priority in the context of ensuring Russia an adequate place in the new European architecture. However, with the parliamentary elections and the referendum on a new constitution of 12 December 1993, they sought to speed

[55] Lucas, M. R. and Kreikemeyer, A., 'Pan-European integration and European institutions: the new role of the Council of Europe', *Journal of European Integration*, vol. 16, no. 1 (1992), p. 101.

[56] Topornin, N., 'Mesto dlya Rossii' [A seat for Russia], *Nezavisimaya Gazeta*, 4 Aug. 1993.

[57] *Nezavisimaya Gazeta*, 16 July 1993.

[58] *Nezavisimaya Gazeta*, 19 May 1993.

up the process of admission, since two major conditions had apparently been fulfilled. At the same time, after the 1993 elections, hesitations within the Council of Europe as to whether Russia should be considered as a democratic state increased. Discussions on Russia's admission were suspended in January 1995 because of developments in Chechnya but resumed in the summer of 1995 with the beginning of negotiations there. In February 1996, Russia was officially admitted as a member of the Council of Europe.

Russia's participation in the Council of Europe will not be easy. While politically it is merely regarded in Moscow as a 'badge of respectability', confirming the progress of democracy in the country,[59] experts are well aware that legal and other (that is, environmental) standards in Russia are a long way from those required by the Council of Europe. Russia's admission therefore implies the need for a serious revision of legislation which is still inadequate. At the same time it provides Russian citizens with the right to call upon the European Court of Human Rights to defend their rights as they are enshrined in the European Convention and not in Russian legislation.

The impact of Russia's admission to the Council of Europe on domestic legislation could certainly be positive and help to accelerate implementation of Russia's international commitments related to human rights. However, it may also cause friction with the Council of Europe, given the inherited habit of the Russian authorities of explaining all deficiencies in the political, economic or legal system by the uniqueness of Russia among world civilizations.

Subregional organizations

After the demise of the Soviet Union, Russia revealed more enthusiasm for the idea of subregional cooperation than the former Soviet Union did. It has become a member of several such organizations, and participates in the 1990 Black Sea Economic Cooperation pact, the Council of Baltic Sea States and the Barents Euro-Arctic Council.[60] Subregional organizations involve several Russian interests such as the issue of minority rights or improvements in the links between the Russian transport infrastructure and Western and Eastern Europe, but they are regarded as being largely irrelevant as a tool for Russia's European policy, especially in the security field. Russia's approach to particular projects remains controversial and in some cases implicitly hostile.

Subregional organizations of which Russia is not a member, the Central European Initiative[61] and the Visegrad Group,[62] are generally viewed with

---

[59] *Rossiyskaya Gazeta,* 4 Aug. 1994.

[60] Zagorski and Lucas (note 6), pp. 102–105. On the Baltic and Barents areas, see also chapters 14 and 15 in this volume. For membership of the three organizations, see *SIPRI Yearbook 1996: Armaments, Disarmament and International Security* (Oxford University Press: Oxford, 1996), pp. xxxiv–xxxv.

[61] Astraldi, V., 'The Hexagonale initiative: a project to overcome 45 years of division in the Adriatic–Danube region', ed. NATO, *External Economic Relations of the Central and East European Countries, Colloquium 1992* (NATO: Brussels, 1992), pp. 95–109.

[62] Bielawski, J., 'Triangular cooperation in the period of transition: the case of Czechoslovakia, Hungary and Poland', ed. NATO (note 61), pp. 83–94; and Dunay, P., 'Security cooperation in the Vise-

greater mistrust, especially by the military establishment. This is especially true of initial measures taken within the Visegrad Group to promote military cooperation. Most of the reservations arise from allegations that subregional organizations of which Russia is not a member may tend to become hostile to it and, instead of linking Russia with Europe, to form a cordon sanitaire dividing it from Europe. Russia therefore prefers to be involved in most of the subregional groups emerging along its borders in order to be able to exercise influence on their development and to prevent them from becoming hostile. This is the major purpose of Russia's participation in at least some subregional organizations, especially with respect to Black Sea cooperation, which is largely regarded in Moscow as an attempt by Turkey to extend its influence to the Caucasus.

Approaches towards subregional organization may thus be only one example of the stereotyped, almost paranoid Russian geopolitical thinking which is obsessed with the idea of hostile encirclement by any coalitions of which Russia is not a member.

IV. Conclusions

This survey clearly reveals that there is no one European institution with which Russia maintains easy relations. Even the OSCE, which remains the favourite project of Russia, is no exception. Furthermore, the implicit logic of Russian arguments in the institutional bargaining over the forthcoming European security architecture suggests a rather pessimistic conclusion.

Russia objects to the establishment of a cordon sanitaire separating it from Europe. However, this already exists in the form of a 'security vacuum' in the ECE area. The removal of that cordon sanitaire therefore implies that those countries should become members of some security-oriented alliance—either of the Western one or of one under Russian leadership. Since Russia objects to the enlargement of NATO eastwards, it would be logical to assume that it has not yet given up the idea of regaining its influence in the ECE area. In its present situation of relative weakness, however, the best strategy Russia can adopt is that of avoiding *faits accomplis*.

This conclusion is not just speculation. Discussions in Moscow about the ECE states clearly reveal that the Russian élite has not yet psychologically adjusted to the fact that they have quitted its sphere of influence and looks for means of restoring that influence.[63] These trends in Russian policy give rise to legitimate concern in the ECE and provide ground for the rather pessimistic expectation that Russia is likely to re-emerge as an uneasy European power.

This point can be made but should not become a self-fulfilling prophecy. It should not be forgotten that the views of the broader Russian élite may differ

grad quadrangle: present and future', ed. A. Williams, *Reorganizing Eastern Europe: European Institutions and the Refashioning of Europe's Security Architecture* (Aldershot: Dartmouth, 1994), pp. 121–44.

[63] 'Vostochnaya Evropa i Rossiya' [Eastern Europe and Russia], *Mezhdunarodnaya Zhizn*, no. 1 (1994), pp. 15–27; and Portnikov, V., 'Rossiya vozvrashtchaetsa v Evropu' [Russia returns to Europe], *Nezavisimaya Gazeta*, 1 Dec. 1993.

from those of the politically active groups which now formulate Russian policy. There is space for change which hopefully will expand with progress in economic reforms, and the change in the paradigm of building a wider Europe, although it does matter to Russia, is not disastrous. Russia can easily cope with it in a cooperative manner provided real partnership is developed with West European and Atlantic institutions.

A number of developments facilitate the recognition of this fact or even make it unavoidable. First, general European trends rather preclude a new division of Europe, and in that respect the association of ECE states with the EU and the prospective enlargement of the latter eastwards appear even more relevant than NATO enlargement. This clearly manifests that the ECE already belongs to a wider Europe and that there will be no return to the Russian 'sphere of influence'. Second, whether deliberately or not, Russia has already started to adjust to the recent changes in its European environment. While retaining the declaratory pan-European rhetoric, it has started the process of institutionalizing its relations with major Western institutions. The process has been developing at different speeds with different institutions—most effectively with the EU. Hesitations on the part of Western institutions about going ahead quickly may be understandable, but it is essential that the process is facilitated in order to strengthen the socializing effect it may have on Russia and to avoid Russia's feeling isolated in a new Europe.

These are only the very first steps towards institutionalizing dialogue between Russia and Western institutions. They provide for regular or ad hoc consultations which, so far, are in most cases limited to the exchange of information. There is a long way to go yet before they are given real substance and the chance of achieving convergence of policies or even unity of action. However, this should be the objective if both Russia and the West really mean partnership when they use the word.

It is important also to be aware of obstacles which are mainly related to competing priorities in Russian foreign policy. Some of them are mentioned above, in particular the diverging views among the Russian élite about the relative importance of relations with the EU and with the CIS. Growing protectionism in Russia should be mentioned in this context as well. However, it seems important at this stage of developments to admit that Europe is only at the beginning of the transition to a new system and that it may take a shape other than that expected immediately after the end of the cold war.

Russia's war in Chechnya suspended the process of institutionalization of the political dialogue between Russia and most of the West European institutions for half a year. However, so far the West appears not to have given up the idea of developing a mode for the integration of Russia into a European security system on the basis of partnership. The chances to institutionalize the political dialogue are still there.

Part XIII
Conclusion

25. Assessing Russia's interaction with Europe

Vladimir Baranovsky

1. Russia's relations with, and its place in, Europe are fundamentally affected by the fact that the country is in a state of profound transition: the highly centralized economy based on the overwhelming predominance of state ownership is giving way to a market economy; the totalitarian political system is being transformed into a democracy; and what used to be a single country—the USSR—has been replaced by 15 new independent states, with the patterns of relations among them still to be crystallized.

None of these processes is complete or has produced any relatively stable pattern. This in itself creates a highly volatile situation. Previous values, beliefs, structures, institutions, links, economic mechanisms and behavioural patterns have been either destroyed or discredited, while new ones are either non-existent or just beginning to emerge. In these circumstances, uncertainty and inconsistency in external policy are inevitable and open up the way for different scenarios of relations between Russia and the outside world, many of which are fraught with unpredictable consequences for international stability.

2. In the most general sense, the changes in Russia are basically irreversible. The country has already passed the point of no return in terms of re-establishing the economic and political system which existed in Soviet times. Even if the backward-looking political forces gain the upper hand domestically, it is certain that they will be unable, and most probable that they will be unwilling to try, to restore the 'old order'. The traditional attributes of the old order in the field of foreign and security policy—overwhelming ideologically motivated hostility towards the West, obsession with an unlimited military build-up, challenging involvement in regional conflicts all over the world, and so on—could not be expected to reappear.

3. However, the impact of domestic developments on Russia's evolving foreign and security policy agenda is of paramount importance. There are numerous distortions in the process of creating a market economy, developing a civil society and establishing democracy. The fact that these distortions are becoming a rule rather than an exception seems to be affecting the character of the emerging regime in the most fundamental way.

Thus, although the model of 'pure restoration' seems unrealistic, the future organization of society in Russia remains in many respects unclear and continues to give cause for serious concern. So do Russia's future external interactions—even if the country proclaims the abandonment of, or even actually abandons, the 'old' foreign and security policy patterns.

4. The profound dislocations and turmoil accompanying Russia's painful transition to a new political system have dramatically undermined the coherence of its foreign and security policy, not to mention its manageability. The main domestic factors affecting the formulation and implementation of Russia's foreign and security policy are the following:

– the disruptive side-effects of economic transformations, including (a) the collapse of industrial and agricultural production, (b) the broadening criminalization of the society, and (c) the threat of social explosions;
– the unrestrained partisan competition between new political forces operating in the absence of established rules of intra-societal dialogue;
– the overall weakness of the state and the predominance of an ungoverned bureaucracy;
– ethno-territorial conflicts within the country, compounded by mass movements of refugees and migrants; and
– disintegrative trends within the Russian Federation.

Containing these trends and establishing a viable political system are the *sine qua non* of Russia's being able to pursue any coherent foreign and security policy. Otherwise, whatever substitutes for a foreign and security policy will in all likelihood be unpredictable and tend towards an erratic (at best) and hostile (at worst) relationship with the external world.

5. At the same time, the very fact that state-building is by far the main domestic priority may have disturbing consequences for Russia's foreign and security policy making:

– the logic of 'external threat' (or, in a milder form, of an 'unfriendly environment') may re-emerge as an easily available means of domestic consolidation;
– the trends towards authoritarianism may endanger democratic control over foreign and security policy, as well as damaging Russia's image internationally; and
– violent means of containing domestic conflicts may spill over the borders of Russia, threatening relations with its neighbours.

Thus, domestic stability is by no means a panacea against instabilities in Russia's relations with the external world. It is a necessary but not sufficient condition of stable external relations.

6. The political role of the senior military establishment represents one of the key domestic factors which may greatly influence Russia's relations with the outside world. Although the poor state of the national economy will most probably prevent a significant military build-up in the foreseeable future, the impact of the military on foreign and security policy assessments is becoming more salient because of a number of factors:

– in both the major crises in Moscow in recent years (in August 1991 and October 1993), the ultimate arguments in the power struggle were provided by the military;

– the military is considered to be the only organized force which would be able to operate in the event of major riots or criminal explosions;

– the armed forces may be viewed as indispensable for preserving the territorial integrity of Russia (as was clearly demonstrated in Chechnya);

– Russia's armed forces provide it with an important lever of influence over a number of post-Soviet states; and

– military power, however diminished and disorganized after the collapse of the Soviet Union, is still regarded as one of the essential components of Russia's international role.

It would be premature to conclude that the military has become an independent and all-powerful political actor in Russia, but the failures both to reform the armed forces and to establish viable civil control over them are spectacular. Some aspects of Russia's interaction with the outside world—specifically, in the field of the arms control and with respect to NATO eastward enlargement—seem to have been strongly affected by the military establishment.

7. The status of Russia within the international system, if compared with that of the former Soviet Union, is also characterized by a remarkable transition:

– from confrontational towards cooperative relations with the West (since ideological, political and military antagonism has lost its *raison d'être* as the basic element of foreign and security policy);

– from the pattern of behaviour of a bloc leader to that of a single player deprived of allies and clients;

– from the unquestioned superpower status of the former USSR to a much more modest ability to influence the world's development; and

– from a situation of relatively secure relations with its neighbourhood to one in which there are numerous risks in the immediate environment.

Assessing the new reality has been a painful process both for the political élites and for public opinion in general. Adapting to its new status and developing adequate patterns of behaviour remain formidable challenges for Russia.

8. The emergence of independent public opinion and the fact that the mass media are addressing the fundamental issues of foreign and security policy are among the most significant achievements in Russia's move towards democracy. The 'great debate' over Russia's relations with the outside world has, however, revealed a number of basic incoherences which will be of great relevance to the country's interaction with Europe:

– the very notion of 'national interest' in the international arena often becomes a matter of political gamesmanship and a stake in the power struggle between new political groups;

– old-style political traditionalism has only been replaced by a superficial, pseudo-democratic 'credo' which has failed to create an adequate conceptual basis upon which to build an effective foreign and security policy; and

– initial post-imperial frustration coexists, paradoxically, with a residual (or, rather, re-emerging) superpower syndrome.

Thus, Russian foreign and security policy thinking remains in many respects chaotic and conceptually erratic. It is worth noting, however, that debates in Russia have drawn a fundamental division between two broad approaches:

– one which starts with the assumption that Russia's surest path to security and sound relations with its neighbours is through reassurance—that is, by consciously attempting to alter and eventually to remove the 'enemy image' associated by outsiders with Russia; and

– the other which is more focused on Russia's use of power to influence its neighbours, either crudely and aggressively or in more subtle and refined ways.

The latter approach is considerably more widespread, testifying to a growing assertiveness within the country's foreign policy community.

9. This trend is also reflected by the extensive reference to the 'great-power' predicament of Russia. In a broad sense, the argument points to Russia's cultural heritage, gigantic territory, enormous potentials of wealth, considerable military might and unique geopolitical location; consequently Russia has the legitimate right to prominent international status and should aim to be recognized in this capacity. Indeed, consolidating (or re-establishing) its great-power status has become a central theme of Russia's foreign policy debates and, to a significant extent, a constant motif in its actual international behaviour— particularly with respect to Europe.

At the same time, what is striking in these debates is how imprecise and apparently confused most participants are about what is meant by the very notion of an 'influential actor' and about what the role of a great power entails—apart from being treated with respect and having a dominant voice in the immediate vicinity. There is remarkably little discussion of what the country should look for in the wider world and what responsibility it should assume—which would proceed from the understanding that there is a basic difference between the status of a great power (accorded by others to Russia) and the role of a great power (which must be defined by Russians themselves).

10. Russia's role in the post-Soviet geopolitical space is undoubtedly one of the most important and controversial issues in the foreign and security policy agenda of the country. Russia has faced a number of serious disputes with its immediate neighbours springing from their common Soviet heritage over frontiers, the disruption of economic linkages, the inheritance of military forces and the status of national minorities:

– the deep (almost all-embracing) interdependence of the post-Soviet states is coupled with the overwhelming economic, demographic and territorial predominance of Russia in the area;

– Russia has become directly or indirectly involved in practically all the armed conflicts within the former Soviet Union; and

– the overall model of Russia's relations with the countries of the Commonwealth of Independent States (CIS) still embodies the most serious contradictions and is by far the most crucial issue for the political future of what used to be the Soviet Union.

Russia's political mentality has developed from the initial 'divorce and forget' approach to a much more assertive one, stipulating that the whole territory of the former Soviet Union should be considered as a zone of Russia's special interests.

11. Moscow's policy in the 'near abroad' cannot but greatly affect Russia's relations with Europe, albeit in quite a controversial way.

On the one hand, a number of considerations make the Western countries receptive to Moscow's arguments:

– Russia's unique stakes in the post-Soviet space cannot be overlooked;

– Russia has the military and political potential to reduce the scope of conflicts in this area or at least to minimize their spillover effects;

– furthermore, Russia is expected to act as an external stabilizer of domestic turbulence in some CIS countries; and

– finally, Russia's role in counterbalancing the possible role of the Islamic and, to a lesser degree, the Chinese factors could also be considered as a stabilizing factor.

On the other hand, the self-imposed imperative of Russia's policy within the former Soviet Union is not only becoming more assertive but also taking on an exclusionary character. There are serious signs that it aims to create (or re-create) a sphere of influence to which other international actors will be denied access, or their access at least significantly limited. In this respect the debate on the relevance of what is alleged to be a new Monroe Doctrine for the post-Soviet pattern seems highly indicative. Significantly, any suspicion that the Western countries—operating either individually or through their multilateral security structures, such as NATO, the Western European Union (WEU) or the European Union (EU)—seek to challenge Russia's influence within the CIS zone elicits increasing nervousness in Moscow.

12. Russia, however, seems excessively optimistic in the wake of its perceived recent policy successes within the post-Soviet area:

– operating as the Eurasian pacifier would entail much more than mandating its military capabilities;

– even these capabilities are limited in view of the formidable task of conflict management in the numerous areas of instability;

– still more challenging are the economic costs of leadership in relations with the CIS partners; and

– the overall international image of a 'new Russia' will be significantly dependent on its behaviour in the 'near abroad'.

In all these respects, Russia's specific interests in the post-Soviet space might be better served by a broader Euro-Atlantic cooperative pattern of relations than by its absence—not to mention confrontation, which is the alternative. However, such an approach would require much deeper 'liberal internationalist' thinking than currently exists in Russia. Nor are domestic instabilities conducive to a proper assessment of long-term foreign policy interests; increasing activism in the 'near abroad' becomes a substitute for the spectacular failures within the country and gives the ruling élites an impressive argument against both allegations of weakness and accusations of submission to the West.

13. Russia's relations with Belarus and Ukraine will have a crucial impact on the future development of the CIS and on the role of Russia both within the post-Soviet space and in Europe. In this respect, however, Russia does not seem to have articulated a serious strategy. Its thinking about its two Slav neighbours is a curious mixture of a conviction of their profound dependence on itself, fear of their possible estrangement, desire for 'soft' political control and reluctance to pay for it.

Relations between Russia and Ukraine have been considerably damaged by the excessive post-independence euphoria in Kiev and by the initial post-imperial frustration in Moscow. Both sides, however, are interested in avoiding any major crisis, although elements of low-key confrontation may persist. Ukraine's ability to succeed economically and in its state building and Russia's acceptance of it as an independent entity will be crucial for preventing destabilization and ensuring a certain *modus vivendi* between the two countries.

Belarus is the most 'pro-Russian' of the post-Soviet states; public opinion there favours reintegration, whereas the local political élites seem ready to exchange independence for a more secure (albeit lower) political status and economic assets. In fact, Russia is in a position to decide what pattern of relationship to choose and whether absorption is a more advantageous model than a protectorate-type association with a junior partner.

In any case, Russia's concerns about the future of the two states have been significantly alleviated. Both seem to have accepted (Ukraine reluctantly, Belarus enthusiastically) that they are in the sphere of Russian influence. Russia will certainly aim to preserve this pattern and to prevent any attempts to undermine it. Whether the three Slav states could constitute a 'core area' of a Russia-led alliance as a power pole in the eastern part of Europe remains an open question, although by no means an implausible proposition.

14. In the north-western neighbourhood of Russia, the Baltic/Nordic region, Russia's geo-strategic position has changed radically with the independence of the Baltic states, the emergence of new state borders and the withdrawal of

Russian troops from the area. Russia has actually accepted a reduced position and can hardly aim to re-establish the status quo ante, whatever changes occur on the domestic scene.

However, there are certain enduring factors in Russian policy:

– the strategic importance of the Baltic Sea area and of the Barents region will continue to be considerable in the light of Russia's renewed emphasis on its great-power status;

– the security role of the Barents region will be crucial because of Russia's reliance on the strategic nuclear weapons based there and its interest in a 'blue-water' navy for the future;

– the Kaliningrad Region is viewed as an important military exclave providing access to the Baltic Sea and mitigating the strategic losses in the area; and

– no Russian government will be able to shirk responsibility for protecting the interests of the Russian populations in the Baltic states.

The increasing overall assertiveness of Russia has also manifested itself with respect to the Baltic states, although here it has an almost exclusively declaratory character. However, there are risks of a return to a strategy of pressure. Russia's relations with the Nordic countries—which have considerably improved during recent years—may worsen as a result of the more active involvement of these countries in the future of the Baltic states. Furthermore, Russia may be extremely sensitive to anything it could consider to be an unfavourable alteration of the geopolitical balance in the area, such as the Baltic states joining NATO.

15. After the collapse of the Yalta system and the dissolution of the Soviet Union, East–Central Europe (ECE) ceased to be a matter of immediate security concern for Moscow. The prospect of NATO's enlargement eastwards has restored this problem to importance in Russia's perception.

Russia's nervous reaction reveals its intrinsic assumption that the ECE region is a kind of 'no-man's zone', where the possible emergence of a hostile coalition should be forestalled by all possible means. However, political considerations seem to be much more salient than those related to security; Russia fears being relegated to the sidelines of European developments more than unspecified security risks.

In fact, the whole problem has become a hostage of Russia's painful search for a new international role and its attempts to secure a worthy place in the emerging European system. For Russia, this goal—which is undoubtedly of paramount importance—has completely overshadowed the task of building a friendly environment in the ECE *per se*, thereby inflicting considerable damage on Russia's future relations with the countries of the region, whatever the outcome of the debate on their joining NATO.

16. Russia's broad objectives in the Balkans may be summarized as follows:

– to ensure that it remains a major player in Europe;
– to demonstrate its abilities both to other international actors and to domestic critics (in particular, in order to defuse and deflect pressures from the nationalists); and
– to gain actual or potential allies in the area and to provide a counterweight to the growing influence of other states in the region.

Compared with those in the post-Soviet space or in direct relations with the West, Russia's stakes in the Balkans are of secondary importance and are insufficient to turn the region into a main foreign policy priority. However, Russia does have some levers in the Balkans. Its mediation efforts there have contributed to Russia's self-confidence and to the realization of its declared goal of being treated as a great power. Russian involvement in peace settlement efforts in the former Yugoslavia, however limited, may affect the emerging geopolitical configuration of the Balkans.

17. The Caucasus has become the most turbulent and unstable region of the former Soviet Union, one that is marked by political turmoil and economic collapse as well as by inter-ethnic conflicts that challenge the existing frontiers, the territorial integrity and the domestic arrangements of all the states of the area, including Russia itself. Against this background, Russia faces numerous and often conflicting security interests:

– to contain secessionist trends and territorial and inter-ethnic disputes in the northern Caucasus;
– to prevent a spillover of conflicts in the Transcaucasus into Russian territory and to minimize their consequences, especially in the adjacent southern regions of the Russian Federation (refugees, additional ethnic tensions, growing Cossack radicalism, and so on);
– to combine a partial disengagement from the Transcaucasus with establishing itself as the guarantor of regional stability;
– to ensure that the ongoing transformation of the political and economic landscape in the three Transcaucasian states does not result in their overall reorientation away from Russia;
– to consolidate its current and future economic assets (especially with respect to the Caspian Sea shelf and oil and gas pipelines); and
– to prevent other international actors from achieving a deeper penetration and involvement in the Caucasus.

Moscow has been more successful in re-establishing a dominant position with respect to the three Transcaucasian states than in managing the problem of Chechnya's secession within the Russian Federation. The latter case represents a major failure of Russian policy, leaving its overall prospects in the region highly volatile and uncertain. Furthermore, although the peripheral status of the Caucasus with respect to Europe facilitates Russia's goal of 'strategic denial' to third countries, its assertive military engagement and taking sides in local conflicts may provide an opening for competing influences from adjacent Middle Eastern countries and politico-religious groups.

18. Russia's relations with Western Europe (and with the West in general) are promoted by several fundamental factors:

– the ideological parameters of the classic cold-war pattern have become a thing of the past and are unlikely to re-emerge;
– traditional military-related considerations, based on the assumption of a major conflict with the West in Europe, are no longer relevant;
– Russia's interest in economic links with the West has considerably increased, due both to the imperatives of domestic reforms and to a desire to obtain better positions in the world market; and
– political interaction with the West is essential to respectable international status for Russia.

However, in Russia's perceptions of—and its attitude towards—the West, a competitive pattern certainly prevails over a cooperative one:

– ideologically, this is manifested by Moscow's deepening suspicion that, behind the encouraging and supportive rhetoric of the West, there is a strong pragmatic desire to downgrade Russia to or to keep it at the position of a second-rank power;
– the existing incentives for Russian economic neo-isolationism seem to have growing implications for Russia's foreign policy; and
– in contrast to the initial post-Soviet period, Russia's relations with the West are no longer regarded as a value *per se*; instead, the possible scope, forms and concrete parameters of these relations are assessed as a function of other goals and policy aims considered to have a higher priority for the country.

As a result, in developing and even highlighting pragmatic relations with the West Moscow seems increasingly to proceed from the assumption that it would be in Russia's best interests to operate as a leader of an alternative power pole in Europe.

19. This trend has clearly affected Russia's policy line with respect to the multilateral security institutions operating in Europe.

Russia's nervous reaction to the prospect of NATO's enlargement eastward has clearly revealed that the alliance is still perceived as a challenge to Russia's security interests, all the rhetoric about an emerging strategic partnership with the West notwithstanding. Another and even more significant rationale is to prevent the central security role in Europe being played by a structure to which Russia will not have direct access. Different NATO-centred patterns (the North Atlantic Cooperation Council (NACC), the Partnership for Peace, and even the '16 plus 1' formula) are often suspected of being aimed at downgrading or marginalizing Russia, or else at disengaging it from potential allies in the post-Soviet space. However, some kind of 'special relationship' with NATO may be considered as a more practical strategy than promoting the re-emergence of the confrontational model—while not closing off the latter option.

The EU is regarded as being the most powerful economic partner and important political actor in Europe, whereas its security role is assessed as marginal and as not (yet) threatening Russia's interests. However, EU enlargement and expansion of its security dimension, especially if accompanied by a merger with the WEU, may exacerbate Russia's concerns about its own role on the continent and provoke a stronger reaction from Moscow unless mitigated by significantly stronger incentives for further *rapprochement* with the EU.

Ambivalent feelings characterize Russia's current attitude towards the Council of Europe. On the one hand, accession to this structure is viewed as an important political gain which attests to the quality of the changes in Russia. On the other hand, it is feared that failure to satisfy the Council's high standards regarding human rights and democracy would leave Russia vulnerable to severe criticism that might seriously damage its prestige and push it to reconsider the very idea of becoming internationally accountable.

The Organization for Security and Co-operation in Europe (OSCE) is by far the most attractive multilateral institution for Russia. It corresponds to many of Russia's concerns regarding Europe and merits its preferential treatment. However, Russia's attempts to increase the role of the OSCE are mostly motivated by the intention to oppose it to NATO—an effort which cannot but discredit any pro-OSCE design. Furthermore, Russia seems to fear that the OSCE might limit its freedom of action within the post-Soviet space, particularly with respect to peacekeeping. Thus, while having a clear interest in upgrading the OSCE, Russia remains one of its most 'difficult' participants.

The CIS, all its shortcomings and lack of viability notwithstanding, is of key importance for Russia as the structure where it plays an undoubted primary role. Although by no means substituting for bilateral relations in the 'near abroad', it certainly provides a means to institutionalize Russia's sphere of influence within the post-Soviet space and responds to Russia's understanding of great-power status. In seeking to give a prominent international position to the Moscow-led CIS and to place it on an equal footing with Western institutions, Russia presumably aims to consolidate its leadership in the shape of the recognized ability to operate on behalf of its clients.

20. Against this background, Russia's basic options with respect to Europe are:

– unilateralism (with an emphasis on power politics in promoting Russia's 'special interests' and reluctance to accommodate itself to other international actors' interests);

– a balance-of-power strategy (requiring both cautious selective alliance-building and the skilled application of restraint); and

– cooperative multilateralism (highlighting the necessity to strengthen multilateral institutions and to promote great-power cooperation in consolidating
stability at all levels of the international system).

In practical terms, Moscow's policy represents a combination of all three
elements, with a gradual shift towards the first, considerable complexities in
practising the second and increasing volatility in the third.

21. Similarly, Europe's options with respect to Russia could be formulated as
follows:

– to continue on an ad hoc basis (with limited and largely symbolic steps to
ease the hardships of post-Soviet development, a hope that Moscow will be
successful in containing domestic tensions and restrain itself externally, de
facto acceptance of a Russian sphere of influence and reluctance to get engaged
in it);
– to choose a neo-containment strategy (preventively, in order to divert
Russia from excessive assertiveness, or as a reaction to Russia's intensified
unilateralism); and
– to aim to link and weave together the security agendas of Europe and
Russia (with the increasing involvement of Russia in a broader international
setting, an adequate adaptation of multilateral institutions operating in Europe,
and careful political engagement by the West in post-Soviet arrangements—on
the assumption that promoting Russia's natural central role in the region should
be coupled with cooperative efforts by the other great powers).

Europe remains predominantly attached to the first of these three options—
constrained by institutional and policy-thinking inertia, by lack of resources and
by the number of other domestic and external challenges. Such a policy line is
not sustainable as a longer-term strategy.

22. The integrating of Russian and post-Soviet security with European
security is of crucial importance for stability in the post-cold war setting.
Regrettably, trends in both Europe and Russia have been gradually sliding in
opposite direction—which can, in the long run, significantly damage the
security interests of both and put at risk broader international prospects.

Indeed, the most serious threat to the emerging international system on the
continent is that Russia will proceed—either deliberately or under perceived
domestic and external constraints—from a narrow-minded and self-centred
approach to its national security interests without considering those of other
states. In turn, these other states might find it quite legitimate to take appropriate countermeasures. As a result, a new cycle of confrontational developments
could start. The rest of Europe, however, will not be innocent if this happens.
The chances of this scenario coming about are proportional to the degree of
Europe's indifference to or neglect of the concerns which are pushing Moscow
to operate on its own.

The alternative is to develop more active and cooperative relations between Russia and Europe on two tracks—by promoting Europe's involvement within the post-Soviet area, on the one hand, and by Russia participating in managing European affairs, on the other hand. On both tracks, Europe's algorithm should be operating together with, and not without, Russia (let alone against it). On both tracks, Russia's rationale should consist in taking great-power responsibility, rather than just searching for token status in the international arena. Thus a strong and unambiguous commitment to engage Russia in a broader pan-European security pattern is essential both for Russia and for Europe.

About the authors

Nadia Alexandrova-Arbatova (Russia) is Section Head in the Institute of World Economy and International Relations (IMEMO), Moscow. Her recent articles include 'Uroki Yugoslavii dlya Rossii i Zapadom' [The lessons of Yugoslavia for Russia and the West] in *Mirovaya Ekonomika i Mezhdunarodnye Otnosheniya'* (1995); 'Spies, aid and intervention: the uncomfortable new state of US–Russian relations', *Perspectives on Change*, 1994; 'The Balkans test for Russia', *Perspectives on Change,* 1993; and articles in *Nezavisimaya Gazeta. Russia in the Black Sea–Balkan Region: Facing the Challenge of the New Cold War* (with A. Arbatov) and *Russian Perceptions and Misperceptions of Western Expansionism in Eastern Europe* are forthcoming.

Roy Allison (UK) is the Head of the Russian and Eurasia Programme at the Royal Institute of International Affairs (RIIA), London. His recent publications include *Internal Factors in Russian Foreign Policy* (with N. Malcolm, A. Pravda and M. Light, 1996); *Challenges for the Former Soviet South* (1996); *Peacekeeping in the Soviet Successor States* (1994); *Military Forces in the Soviet Successor States* (1993); and *Radical Reform in Soviet Defence Policy* (1992).

Alexei Arbatov (Russia) is a member of the State Duma of the Russian Federation and Vice-Chairman of the Committee on Defence. He is also Director of the Center for Geopolitical and Military Forecasts in Moscow and part-time Head of the Department for Disarmament Studies of IMEMO. His most recent book is *Rossiya: v Poiskakh Strategii Bezopasnosti* [Russia: searching for a security strategy] (1996) and he has edited and contributed to *Russia in the World Community: The Problems of Stability, Disarmament and Foreign Policy* (1995) and written widely on arms control and Russian foreign policy topics.

Vladimir Baranovsky (Russia) is Leader of the SIPRI Project on Russia's Security Agenda. His recent publications include 'Security in Europe: Russia's approach', ed. G. Herolf, *Europe: Creating Security through International Organizations* (1996); 'Conflicts in and around Russia', *SIPRI Yearbook 1996*; 'Russia', ed. A. Krohn, *The Baltic Sea Region: National and International Security Perspectives* (1996); and 'A Russian perspective on future European security arrangements', eds G. Bonvicini *et al., A Renewed Partnership for Europe* (1995); and among many journal articles [A micromodel of European security?], *Mirovaya Ekonomika i Mezhdunarodnye Otnosheniya*, no. 6 (1996); 'Rusija i evropska bezbednost' [Russia and European security], *Medunarodni Problemi/International Problems* (Belgrade), vol. 47, no. 3 (1995); 'Russian foreign policy priorities and Euroatlantic multilateral institutions', *International Spectator* (Rome), 1995; and 'La Russie et la sécurité européenne' [Russia and European security], *Politique étrangère*, no. 1 (1995).

Yuriy Borko (Russia) is Deputy Director of the Institute of Europe, Moscow, and President of the Association of European Studies in Russia. His recent publications include 'Integratsionnye ekonomicheskie protsessy v zapadnoy Evrope' [Economic integration processes in Western Europe] in *Evropa i Rossiya: Opyt ekonomicheskikh preobrazovanii* [Europe and Russia: comparative analysis of economic reforms] (1996); 'Rossiya i Evropa: stoitsa li partnerstvo?' [Russia and Europe: will the partnership take place?], *Svobodnaya Mysl*, no. 3 (1996); 'Russland und die Europäissche Union: Perspektiven des Partnership' [Russia and the European Union: perspectives on the partnership], *Berichte des Bundesinstituts für ostwissenschaftliche und internationale Studien*, no. 36 (1996); and 'Evropeyskaya tsivilizatsiya i Evropeyskaya ideya' [European civilization and the European idea] in *Obshcheevropeyskiy protsess i gumanitarnaya Evropa: Rol' universitetov* [The all-Europe process and humanitarian Europe: the role of universities] (1995).

Yuriy Davydov (Russia) has been Head of the Center for European Studies in the Institute of USA and Canada Studies in Moscow since 1991 and is Professor in the Theory of International Relations at Moscow State Institute of International Relations (MGIMO) and Moscow State Linguistic University. He is the author or editor of seven monographs on US policy towards Western and Eastern Europe including *The Slavic Factor in the Mid-90s* (1995); and *Russian–American Relations: Test by Choice* (1995); and *Liberal Nationalism in Russia's Foreign Policy* (1994); and of numerous journal and newspaper articles. His most recent work is 'Russia: policy analysis and options', ed. R. Smoke, *Perceptions of Security* (1996).

Peter van Ham (Netherlands) is a Professor at the College of Strategic Studies and Defence Economics at the George C. Marshall European Center for Security Studies in Garmisch-Partenkirchen, Germany. From 1993 to 1996 he was a Senior Research Fellow at the Institute for Security Studies of the Western European Union in Paris. He has published widely on European defence and security issues—most recently *The Baltic States: Security and Defence After Independence* (1995); *Ukraine, Russia and European Security* (1994); and *The EC, Eastern Europe and European Unity* (1993).

Pierre Hassner is Research Director at the Centre d'Études et de Recherches Internationales, Paris and Professor of Political Science at the Institut d'Études Politiques, and has worked in France and the USA. He has recently published *La Violence et la Paix* (1995); 'Beyond the three traditions: the philosophy of war and peace in historical perspective', *International Affairs*, Oct. 1994; and 'Beyond nationalism and internationalism: ethnicity and world order', ed. M. Brown, *Ethnic Conflict and International Security* (1993). His *Violence and Peace: From Nuclear Deterrence to Ethnic Cleansing* is forthcoming.

Lena Jonson (Sweden) has been a Senior Research Fellow at the Swedish Institute of International Affairs since 1988, before which she was a lecturer and Research Fellow in the Department of Political Science at the University of Gothenburg. Her recent publications include *Peacekeeping and the Role of Russia in Eurasia* (co-edited with C. Archer, 1996); and 'Russia and European security: new wine in old bottles?', eds R. Lindahl and G. Sjöstedt, *New Thinking in International Relations: Swedish Perspectives: Yearbook of the Swedish Institute of International Affairs* (1995).

Sergei Karaganov (Russia) is Deputy Director of the Institute of Europe in Moscow and was previously at the Institute of USA and Canada Studies, also in Moscow, specializing in economic aspects of foreign policy, US–Soviet relations, US military strategy, arms control and European security. He is the author or editor of 14 books and brochures and 130 articles. Some of his recent publications are *The Russian Economic Role in Europe* (co-authored with O. Lambsdorf, 1995); *Damage Limitation or Crisis? Russia and the Outside World* (co-edited with R. Blackwill, 1994); and *Where is Russia going? Foreign and Defence Policies in a New Era* (1994).

Alexander A. Konovalov (Russia) worked at the Institute of USA and Canada Studies in Moscow from 1981 to 1996, most recently as Director of the Centre for Military Policy and System Analysis. Since spring 1996 he has been President of the Institute for Strategic Assessments, an independent research and expert organization, and a member of the special analytical group of the Secretary of the Defence Council of the Russian Federation. His current research is on Russian–US relations in the military–political field, problems of civil–military relations in Russia and the CIS states and the demilitarization of the Russian economy. Recent publications include 'International institutions and European security: the Russian debate', ed. M. Carnovale, *European Security and International Institutions after the Cold War* (1995) and various newspaper and journal articles.

Vasily Kremen (Ukraine) is presently head of the Humanitarian Policy Department at the Administration of the President of Ukraine and Head of the Policy-Making Methodology Department at the National Institute for Strategic Studies in Kiev. He worked previously as researcher and Deputy Director at the Institute of Social and Political Studies in the Russian Academy of Sciences. His recent publications include 'Political strategy of Ukraine: a comparative analysis', *Viche*, no. 10 (1995) and forthcoming publications are 'Ukraine and Russia: on the road to mutually advantageous cooperation' in *Viche* and *The Path for Ukraine: External and Internal Problems in the Formation and Genesis of the Ukrainian State*.

Victor Kremeniuk (Russia), whose training was in international relations, is Deputy Director of the Institute for USA and Canada Studies in Moscow. He has been Professor of Political Science since 1990 and a researcher at the International Institute for Applied Systems Analysis (IIASA) in Vienna since 1988. Recent publications include 'The Soviet Union and Europe in historical perspective', ed. K. Gottstein, *Tomorrow's Europe* (1995); *Conflicts In and Around Russia* (1994); and 'Russia's role in peacemaking and confidence-building in the Middle East', eds G. Bender and D. Dewitt, *Confidence-Building Measures in the Middle East* (1994).

Wojtek Lamentowicz (Poland) is a Member of Parliament, Under-Secretary of State and Foreign Policy Adviser to the President of Poland and a member of the Political Science Committee of the Polish Academy of Sciences. His recent publications include 'Nongovernmental think tanks in Poland', eds C. D. Goodwin and M. Nacht, *Beyond Government: Extending Public Policy Debate in Emerging Democracies* (1995); 'Poland: towards a modern concept of sovereignty in an integrated Europe', eds B. Lippert and H. Schneider, *Monitoring Association and Beyond: The European Union and the Visegrad States* (1995); and 'Politische instabilität in Ost- und Mitteleuropa: innenpolitische Gafährdungen der europäischen Sicherheit und Integration' [Political instability in Eastern and Central Europe: domestic policies jeopardizing European security and integration], ed. W. Weidenfeld, *Demokratie und Marktwirtschaft in Osteuropa* [Democracy and market economy in Eastern Europe] (1995).

F. Stephen Larrabee (USA) is a senior staff member in the International Policy Department at the RAND Corporation in Santa Monica, California. Before joining RAND he served as Vice-President and Director of Studies of the Institute of East–West Security Studies in New York and on the US National Security Council staff as a specialist on Soviet–East European affairs and East–West political–military relations. He is the author of *East European Security after the Cold War* (1994), editor of *The Volatile Powderkeg: Balkan Security After the Cold War* (1994) and *The Two German States and European Security* (1989), and co-editor with Robert D. Blackwill of *Conventional Arms Control and East–West Security* (1989).

Robert Legvold (USA) is at present Professor of Political Science at Columbia University where from 1984 to 1992 he was Director of the Harriman Institute. Formerly Director of Soviet Studies at the US Council on Foreign Relations, he specializes in the international relations of the post-Soviet states. Recent publications include 'The challenge of the post-Soviet states for Europe and Asia', *Business and the Contemporary World*, Sep. 1996; and 'Russia and the strategic quadrangle', ed. M. Mandelbaum, *The Strategic Quadrangle in East Asia* (1995).

Marie Mendras (France) is Professor at the Institut des Sciences Politiques in Paris and a researcher at the Centre d'Études et de Relations Internationales. Her latest publications deal with Russian political developments and the questions of state-building and local government and include 'Yeltsin and the great divide in Russian society', *East European Constitutional Review*, spring–summer 1996; 'Tchétchénie, la guerre du Kremlin', *Esprit*, no. 210 (Mar.–Apr. 1995); *Un État pour la Russie* [A state for Russia] (1993); and 'Les trois Russies: analyse du référendum du 25 avril 1993' [The three Russias: analysis of the referendum of 25 April 1993], *Revue Française de Science Politique*, vol. 43, no. 6 (Dec. 1993). 'Rule by bureaucracy in Russia', eds Y. Mény and D. della Porta, *Democracy and Corruption in Europe* is forthcoming (1997).

John Roper (UK) was from 1990 to 1995 the founding Director of the Institute for Security Studies of the Western European Union and is now a Research Associate at the RIIA in London. His most recent publications include *Towards a Common Defence Policy* (co-edited with L. Martin, 1995) and *Towards a New Transatlantic Partnership* (co-edited with N. Gantz, 1993).

Adam Daniel Rotfeld (Poland) is Director of SIPRI and Leader of the SIPRI Project on Building a Cooperative Security System in and for Europe. In his capacity as Director of SIPRI he was appointed Personal Representative of the CSCE Chairman-in-Office to examine the settlement of the conflict in the Trans-Dniester region (1992–93). He is the author or editor of over 20 books and more than 200 articles on the legal and political aspects of European security, was co-editor of the SIPRI volume *Germany and Europe in Transition* (1991) and of *Europejski System bezpieczenstwa* in statu nascendi [European security system *in statu nascendi*] (1990, in Polish) and has written for the *SIPRI Yearbook* since 1991.

Christoph Royen (Germany) is Senior Researcher on Russian and East–Central European international relations at the Stiftung Wissenschaft und Politik, Ebenhausen, where he has worked since 1970. His recent publications include 'Russia and the future of the transatlantic alliance', ed. C. Barry, *Reforging the Transatlantic Relationship* (1996); 'Pochemu Rossiya ne soglasna s rasshireniem NATO na Vostok?' [Why is Russia opposing NATO's enlargement to the East?], *Novoe Vremya*, Mar. 1996; 'Russia and NATO: theses of the Russian Council on Foreign and Defence Policy. Comments and text', *Nação e Defesa* (Oct.–Dec. 1995); and 'Die Visegrad-Staatengruppe: Zu früh für einen Nachruf' [The Visegrad Group: too early for an obituary], *Europa–Archiv* (Nov. 1994).

Lothar Rühl (Germany) is Professor at the Forschungsinstitut für Politische Wissenschaft in Cologne and a member of the SIPRI Governing Board and was State Secretary at the German Federal Ministry of Defence from 1982 to 1989. He has written and published extensively, among his recent books being *Deutschland als europäische Macht: nationale Interessen und internationale Verantwortung* [Germany as a European power: national interests and international responsibility] (1996); *Aufstieg und Niedergang des Russischen Reiches: der Weg eines tausendjährigen Staates* [The rise and fall of the Russian Empire: the path of a thousand-year state] (1992) and (co-edited with A. Clesse), *Beyond East-West confrontation: Searching for a New Security Structure in Europe* (1990). Recent journal articles include: 'Russland und seine neue militärdoktrin: Zwischen NATO und Kaukasus' [Russia and its new military doctrine: between NATO and the Caucasus], *Europäische Sicherheit*, 1994; 'Jenseits der "Partnerschaft für den Frieden": eine neue Demarkationslinie durch Europa?' [On the other side of the Partnership for Peace: a new demarcation line through Europe], *Europa Archiv*, 1994; and 'European security and NATO's eastward expansion', *Aussenpolitik*, 1994.

Aleksei M. Salmin (Russia) is President of the Russian Public Policy Centre, Member of the Presidential Advisory Council of the Russian Federation, Chairman of the Scientific Council of the Foundation for the Development of Parliamentarianism, Chairman of the Russian Section of the International Human Rights Society and member of the Academic Councils of the Comparative Political Science Institute and the Institute of Europe in Moscow. He has published approximately 200 articles and several books analyzing political systems, political cultures and inter-ethnic relations as well as *Modern Democracy: Genesis, Structure, Cultural Conflicts* (1992).

Alexander A. Sergounin (Russia) is Professor of Political Science and Chairman of the Department of Political Science at the University of Nizhniy Novgorod, having been Associate Professor of World History there from 1990 to 1994. He has been visiting scholar at numerous European and US research centres and universities. His recent publications include *Regional Security System in Russia: Challenges and Opportunities* (1996); and *The Russian Dimension of Nordic Security* (1993). *Postmodernism and Western Political Science* (co-authored with A. Makarychev) is forthcoming.

Maxim Shashenkov (Russia) is a graduate of the Institute of Asian and African Studies of Moscow State University. In 1995 he joined Merrill Lynch as a Russian analyst on the European and Mediterranean Emerging Markets team. His publications include 'Russia in Central Asia: emerging security links', ed. A. Ehteshami, *From Gulf to Central Asia: Players in the New Great Games* (1994); and *Security Issues of Post-Soviet Central Asia* (1992).

Hans-Joachim Spanger (Germany) is Senior Researcher at the Peace Research Institute in Frankfurt. From 1987 to 1988 he was Research Associate at the International Institute for Strategic Studies (IISS) in London, and in 1991 held a teaching assignment at the Centre for Foreign Relations in Dar es Salaam. Publications since 1992 include *Bridges to the Future: Prospects for Peace and Security in Southern Africa* (co-edited with P. Vale, 1995); *Brücken, Achsen—und neue Gräben: Die deutsch-russischen Beziehungen im multilateralen Spannungsfeld* [Bridges, arches and new gulfs: German–Russian relations in the multilateral field of tension] (co-authored with A. Kokeev, 1995); and *In From the Cold: Germany, Russia and the Future of Europe* (co-edited with V. Baranovsky, 1992).

Andrei Zagorski (Russia) is Vice-Rector at MGIMO, where he has worked since 1981, engaged in negotiation and European studies. In the late 1980s and early 1990s he was adviser to the Soviet delegations at numerous CSCE meetings and he is known for his recent studies on the CIS. He is the co-editor with A. Lopukhin and S. Rossi of *From Reform to Stability: Russian Foreign, Military and Economic Policy (Analysis and Forecasts) 1993–1995* (1995); and with H.-G. Ehrhart and A. Kreikemeyer of *Crisis Management in the CIS: Whither Russia?*; and author of numerous other works. He also edits the MGIMO series of reports and studies on Russian foreign policy.

Index